THE MERLEAU-PONTY READER

Northwestern University
Studies in Phenomenology
and
Existential Philosophy

Founding Editor †James M. Edie

General Editor Anthony J. Steinbock

Associate Editor John McCumber

THE MERLEAU-PONTY READER

Edited by Ted Toadvine
and Leonard Lawlor

Northwestern University Press
Evanston, Illinois

Northwestern University Press
www.nupress.northwestern.edu

Copyright © 2007 by Northwestern University Press. Published 2007. All rights
reserved.

Printed in the United States of America

10 9 8 7 6 5 4 3 2 1

Library of Congress Cataloging-in-Publication Data

Merleau-Ponty, Maurice, 1908–1961.
    The Merleau-Ponty reader / edited by Ted Toadvine and Leonard Lawlor.
        p. cm. — (Northwestern university studies in phenomenology and
    existential philosophy)
    Includes bibliographical references and index.
    ISBN-13: 978-0-8101-1950-5 (cloth : alk. paper)
    ISBN-10: 0-8101-1950-1 (cloth : alk. paper)
    ISBN-13: 978-0-8101-2043-3 (pbk. : alk. paper)
    ISBN-10: 0-8101-2043-7 (pbk. : alk. paper)
    1. Philosophy, Modern—20th century. I. Toadvine, Ted, 1968– II. Lawlor,
Leonard, 1954– III. Title. IV. Series: Northwestern University studies in
phenomenology & existential philosophy
B804.M383 2007
194—dc22

                                                                    2007023571

⊗ The paper used in this publication meets the minimum requirements of
the American National Standard for Information Sciences—Permanence
of Paper for Printed Library Materials, ANSI Z39.48-1992.

We dedicate this volume to the memory of
Martin C. "Mike" Dillon.

Contents

Acknowledgments

We would like to thank Sue Betz, former editor at Northwestern University Press, and Anthony Steinbock, general editor of Northwestern University Press's Studies in Phenomenology and Existential Philosophy series, for their continuous support of our project. We received a lot of support from our respective philosophy departments (at the University of Oregon, Emporia State University, and the University of Memphis). Students in our seminars and conversations with our colleagues frequently oriented us in the selection of texts and the organization of the volume. In particular, we would like to thank Jacque Fehr at Emporia State University, who spent many hours typing the original transcriptions for us. At the University of Memphis, Cathy Wilhelm helped with scanning and text preparation. We would like to thank Paul Mendelson, who copyedited the volume; Bryan Bannon (at the University of Memphis), who proofread the book; and Elizabeth Caldwell (at the University of Oregon), who wrote the index. Paul, Bryan, and Elizabeth did an outstanding job. Finally, we wish to thank Madame Merleau-Ponty for her support of the project and Renaud Barbaras, who brought to our attention the dossier of unpublished working notes for *The Visible and the Invisible* housed at the old Bibliothèque Nationale in Paris.

Editors' Introduction

In the nearly fifty years since his premature death in 1961 at the age of fifty-three, Merleau-Ponty's work has continued to attract the interest of new generations of scholars and students of philosophy. In fact, the last decade of Merleau-Ponty studies has witnessed something of a renaissance, spurred on by the publication and translation of the lecture courses from his last years, the formation of the first journal devoted to his thought,[1] and the application of his thinking to new philosophical areas of research, including feminism, environmental philosophy, and neuroscience.[2] Merleau-Ponty's work emerges from a very specific moment in twentieth-century philosophy and history, but his writings continue to speak to us today and to repay our study with fresh insights for our own time, justifying the status of Merleau-Ponty's oeuvre as a classic.

Our volume, responding to this growing interest in Merleau-Ponty's work, offers a comprehensive introduction to his thought for the general reader, as well as making available new resources for scholars concerned with his work. The texts are arranged chronologically into three periods in order to indicate the evolution of Merleau-Ponty's thinking. Within each of these three periods, we have included selections from Merleau-Ponty's major theoretical works addressing the body, perception, and ontology, his most significant writings on the arts, and essays and interviews representing the evolution of his political thinking. We have also aimed to include a mix of extracts from book-length works, freestanding essays, interviews, and discussions. As the bibliography of Merleau-Ponty's works later in this book demonstrates, the wide range and extent of his writings have made the exclusion of many important texts unavoidable. However, our hope is that this selection will offer the reader a glimpse of the power and range of Merleau-Ponty's thought that may serve as an invitation to further exploration of his work.

From Merleau-Ponty's first period, prior to his appointment at the Sorbonne in 1949, we have included selections from both of his theses: the final chapter of *The Structure of Behavior*, completed in 1938 and published in 1942, which applies the insights of Gestalt psychology and phenomenology to the problem of the relation between soul and body; and the preface to *Phenomenology of Perception* (1945), in which Merleau-Ponty develops his own original appropriation of the phenomenological method. The themes of *Phenomenology of Perception* are further developed in "The Primacy of Perception and Its Philosophical Consequences" (1947), Merleau-Ponty's presentation of this work to the Société Française de Philosophie. In "The War Has Taken Place" (1945), an editorial from the very first issue of *Les Temps Modernes,* Merleau-Ponty reflects on his generation's turbulent lesson in the realities of politics and history. Concerning art, this period of writings includes "Cézanne's Doubt" (1945), a study of artistic expression that is contemporaneous with the publication of *Phenomenology of Perception;* and "Reality and Its Shadow" (1948), Merleau-Ponty's editorial introduction to Emmanuel Levinas's essay on the relationship between art, expression, and truth.[3] This brief note, in which Merleau-Ponty contrasts Sartre's and Levinas's approaches to the status of art, offers us a rare glimpse of Merleau-Ponty's reaction to Levinas's work. We have also included in this first section a brief interview with Merleau-Ponty for a popular audience, "The Contemporary Philosophical Movement" (1946), in which he summarizes the aims of *Phenomenology of Perception* and discusses his relationship with Sartre.

The second section of our volume includes writings from the period of Merleau-Ponty's appointment at the Sorbonne, between 1949 and 1952. A selection from Merleau-Ponty's lecture course on "The Child's Relations with Others" (1951) is representative of his teaching during this period. Several short texts demonstrate the development of his political thinking, including "A Note on Machiavelli" (1949) and "The Adversary Is Complicit" (1950). In the first, Merleau-Ponty rediscovers a certain "humanism" in Machiavelli that clarifies the problem of political power confronting contemporary Marxism. The second selection offers Merleau-Ponty's response to a critic of *Les Temps Modernes* on the question of the Soviet forced-labor camps, indicating his "wait and see" relation to Communism and to the Soviet Union prior to his rupture with Jean-Paul Sartre in 1952. Merleau-Ponty's editorial introduction to an essay by Michel Crozier, "Human Engineering: The New 'Human' Techniques of American Big Business" (1951), concerns the new social psychology of propaganda at work in the formation of "public opinion" in the United States. In "Man and Adversity" (1951), his presentation at the Rencontres Internationales in Geneva, Merleau-Ponty demonstrates how the essential contingency and ambiguity of the human condition are revealed by recent studies of the body, literature, and contemporary politics. The wide-ranging discussion following this presentation, offered here in English for the first time, clarifies Merleau-Ponty's position on philosophical method, ambiguity, literature, politics, and religion. "Indirect Language and the Voices of Silence" (1952), the most significant writing on painting and language from this period, develops Merleau-Ponty's theory of expression in response to the writings of André Malraux and Sartre. Lastly, we have included here the prospectus that Merleau-Ponty submitted for his candidacy to the Collège de France, which offers the philosopher's own account of his achievements to date and the aims of his future work.

Our third section concerns Merleau-Ponty's years at the Collège de France, from 1952 to 1961, and begins with the epilogue from his second major political work, *Adventures of the Dialectic* (1955), a critique of contemporary Marxism that Merleau-Ponty aims primarily at Sartre. Here Merleau-Ponty rejects the notion of a pure proletarian revolution and calls for a "new liberalism" of the non-Communist left. Merleau-Ponty's view of the relationship between the political and philosophical lives is developed in two later texts: his 1958 interview with Madeleine Chapsal, "Merleau-Ponty in Person," and the preface to *Signs* (1960), both of which set these political concerns against the backdrop of Merleau-Ponty's later ontological investigations. "Eye and Mind" (1961), presented here in a virtually new English translation, was Merleau-Ponty's last published essay. We would like to point the reader to this text in particular since it is *not* posthumous. It indicates, as perhaps no other text published during Merleau-Ponty's lifetime, the condition of his thinking at the moment of his death. It combines his reflections on politics, art, and ontology. Even more importantly, it seems to us, "Eye and Mind" shows us Merleau-Ponty's perennial concern with Descartes and, more generally, with the classical movement of rationalism. Unless one recognizes Merleau-Ponty's continuing engagement with rationalism (and in particular with its idea of a positive infinite), it is probable that one cannot understand Merleau-Ponty's work overall. "Eye and Mind" shows us clearly—though one could see this point as early as *The Structure of Behavior*—that Merleau-Ponty's final idea of the flesh, which is a mixture of finitude and infinity, comes from Descartes' descriptions of the union of the mind and body in the "Sixth Meditation." Of course, we are including the famous culminating chapter of *The Visible and the Invisible* (drafted during 1960 and 1961) precisely because it presents the flesh as "The Intertwining—The Chiasm." Finally and most significantly for the scholar, we present here previously unpublished working notes from the period of *The Visible and the Invisible* in both French and English. We selected these notes on the basis of two criteria. On the one hand, we selected notes that are relatively readable and therefore relatively easy to understand due to their completeness. On the other hand, we selected notes according to content, that is, ones that elaborate on ideas found in Merleau-Ponty's other last writings, including "Eye and Mind" and *The Visible and the Invisible*.

By contextualizing Merleau-Ponty's writings on the philosophy of art and politics within the overall development of his thought, our volume allows the reader to see both the breadth of Merleau-Ponty's contribution to twentieth-century philosophy and the convergence of the various strands of his reflections. We hope, furthermore, that this variety of texts conveys something of the flavor of Merleau-Ponty's manner of engagement and philosophical style. The volume serves, then, as a comprehensive introduction to Merleau-Ponty's thought, suitable for the student or the general reader. The volume also provides new resources for the scholar. In the first place, all of the existing English translations have been revised. In this process, we have aimed to make the texts terminologically consistent. Additionally, five of the selections appear here in English translation for the first time. Most importantly, the previously unpublished working notes from Merleau-Ponty's final period bring into relief new relationships and developments in his last reflections. Therefore, the volume you are about to read presents not only a comprehensive view of Merleau-Ponty's thinking, but also, we hope, a new view on his thinking.

THE MERLEAU-PONTY READER

The Pre-Sorbonne Period (Preceding 1949)

The Relations of the Soul and the Body and the Problem of Perceptual Consciousness

Part 1. The Classical Solutions

1. Naive Consciousness and Its Empirical Realism

That naive consciousness is realistic has been affirmed too much. Or at least a distinction should be made in this regard between the opinions of common sense, the manner in which it verbally accounts for perception,[1] and the perceptual experiences themselves; verbalized perception should be distinguished from lived perception. If we return to objects as they appear to us when we live in them without speech and without reflection and if we try to describe their mode of existence faithfully, they do not evoke any realistic metaphor. If I adhere to what immediate consciousness tells me, the desk which I see in front of me and on which I am writing, the room in which I am and whose walls enclose me beyond the sensible field, the garden, the street, the city and, finally, the whole of my spatial horizon do not appear to me to be causes of the perception which I have of them, causes which would impress their mark on me and produce an image of themselves by a transitive action. It seems to me rather that my perception is like a beam of light which reveals the objects there where they are and manifests their presence, latent until then. Whether I myself perceive or consider another subject perceiving, it seems to me that the gaze "is posed" on objects and reaches them from a distance—as is well expressed by the use of the Latin *lumina* for designating the gaze. Doubtless I know that my present experience of this desk is not complete, that it shows me only some of its aspects: be it the color, the form, or the size, I know very well that they would vary under another lighting, from another point of view and standing in another place; I know that "the desk" is not reducible to the determinations with which it is presently clothed. But in immediate consciousness this perspectival character of my knowledge is not conceived as an accident in regard to it, as an imperfection relative to the existence of my body and its proper point of view; and knowledge by "profiles"[2] is not treated as the degradation of a true knowledge which would grasp the totality of the possible aspects of the object all at once. Perspective does not appear to me to be a subjective deformation of things but, on the contrary, to be one of their properties, perhaps their essential property. It is precisely because of it that the perceived possesses in itself a hidden and inexhaustible richness, that it is a "thing." In other words, when one speaks of the perspectivism of knowledge, the expression is equivocal. It can mean that only the perspectival projection of objects would be given to primitive knowledge; and in this sense the expression is inexact, since the first reactions of an infant are adapted, for example, to the distance of objects[3]—a fact which excludes the idea of a phenomenal world originally without depth. From the beginning perspectivism is known as such and not something to which we are subject. Far from introducing a coefficient of subjectivity into perception, it provides it on the contrary with the assurance of communicating with a world which is richer than what we know of it, that is, of communicating with a real world. The profiles of my desk are not given to direct knowledge as appearances without value, but as "manifestations" of the desk. Although naive consciousness never confuses the thing with the manner which it has of appearing to us, and precisely because it does not make this confusion, it is the thing itself which naive consciousness thinks it is reaching, and not some inner double, some subjective reproduction. It does not imagine that the body or that mental "representations" function as a screen between itself and reality. The perceived is grasped in an indivisible manner as "in-itself," that is, as gifted with an interior which I will never have finished exploring; and as "for-me," that is, as given "in person" through its momentary aspects. Neither this metallic spot which moves while I turn my gaze toward it, nor even the geometric and shiny mass which emerges from it when I look at it, nor finally, the set of perspectival images which I have been able to have of it *are* the ashtray; they do not exhaust the sense of the "this" by which I designate it; and, nevertheless, it is the ashtray which appears in all of them. This is not the place to analyze further the paradoxical relation of the "aspects" to the thing, of the "manifestations"[4] to that which is manifested by them and beyond them. But what we have said is sufficient to show that this relation is original and founds a consciousness of reality in a specific manner. The perspectival aspect of the ashtray is not to the "ashtray itself" what one event is to another event which it indicates, or what a sign is to that which it signifies. Neither the sequence of "states of consciousness" nor the logical organization of thought accounts for perception: the first, because it is an external relation while the perspectival appearances of the ashtray are representative of each other; the second, because it presupposes a mind in possession of its object while my will is without direct action on the unfolding of the perceived perspectives and because their concordant multiplicity is organized of itself. A "cube" is not what I see of it, since I see only three sides at a time; but no more is it a judgment by which I link together the successive appearances. A judgment, that is, a coordination conscious of itself, would be necessary only if the isolated appearances were given beforehand, which is counter to the hypothesis of intellectualism. Something of the empiricism which it surmounts always remains in intellectualism—something like a repressed empiricism. Thus, to do justice to our direct experience of things it would be necessary to maintain at the same time, against empiricism, that they are beyond their sensible manifestations, and, against intellectualism, that they are not unities in the order of judgment, that they are incarnated in their apparitions. The "things" in naive experience are evident as *perspectival beings:* it is essential to them both to offer themselves without interposed milieu and to reveal themselves only gradually and never completely; they are mediated by their perspectival appearances; but it is not a question of a logical mediation, since it introduces us to their carnal reality; I grasp *in* a perspectival appearance, which I know is only one of its possible aspects, the thing itself which transcends it. A transcendence which is nevertheless open to my knowledge—this is the very definition of a thing as it is intended by naive consciousness. Whatever difficulty one may find in conceptualizing perception described in this way, it is for us to accommodate ourselves to it; this is the way that we perceive and that consciousness lives in things. Nothing is more foreign to perception, therefore, than the idea of a universe which would produce in us representations which are distinct from it by means of a causal action. To speak Kantian language, the realism of naive consciousness is an empirical realism—the assurance of an external experience in which there is no doubt about escaping "states of consciousness" and acceding to solid objects—and not a transcendental realism which, as a philosophical thesis, would posit these objects as the ungraspable causes of "representations" which alone are given.

The bodily mediation most frequently escapes me: when I witness events that interest me, I am scarcely aware of the perpetual breaks which the blinking of the eyelids imposes on the spectacle, and they do not figure in my memory. But after all, I know very well that I am able to interrupt the spectacle by closing my eyes, that I see by the intermediary of my eyes. This knowledge does not prevent my believing that I see the things themselves when my gaze is posed upon them. This is because the body proper and its organs remain the bases or vehicles of my intentions and are not yet grasped as "physiological realities." The body is *present* to the soul as external things are present; in neither case is it a question of a causal relation between the two terms. The unity of the human has not yet been broken; the body has not been stripped of human predicates; it has not yet become a machine; and the soul has not yet been defined as existence for-itself. Naive consciousness does not see in the soul the *cause* of the movements of the body, nor does it put the soul in the body as the pilot in his ship. This way of thinking belongs to philosophy; it is not implied in immediate experience. Since the body itself is not grasped as a material and inert mass or as an external instrument but as the living envelope of our actions, the principle of these actions has no need of being a quasi-physical force. Our intentions find their natural clothing or their embodiment in movements and are expressed in them as the thing is expressed in its perspectival aspects. Thus, thinking can be "in the throat," as the children questioned by Piaget say it is,[5] without any contradiction or confusion of the extended and the non-extended, because the throat is not yet an ensemble of vibrating cords capable of producing the sonorous phenomena of language, because it remains that privileged region of a qualitative space where my signifying intentions are unfolded in words. Since the soul remains coextensive with nature, since the perceiving subject does not grasp himself as a microcosm into which messages of external events would make their way mediately and since his gaze extends over the things themselves, to act upon them is not for him to get outside the self and provoke a local movement in a fragment of extension; it is to make an intention explode in the phenomenal field in a cycle of significative gestures, or to join to the things in which he lives the action which they solicit by an attraction comparable to that of the first unmoved mover. One can say, if you like, that the relation of the thing perceived to perception, or of the intention to the gestures which realize it, is a magical relation in naive consciousness; but it would still be necessary to understand magical consciousness as it understands itself and not to reconstruct it from subsequent categories. The subject does not live in a world of states of consciousness or representations from which he would believe himself able to act on and know external things by a sort of miracle. He lives in a universe of experience, in a milieu which is neutral with regard to the substantial distinctions between the organism, thought, and extension; he lives in a direct commerce with beings, things, and his own body. The ego as a center from which his intentions radiate, the body which carries them, and the beings and things to which they are addressed are not confused: but they are only three sectors of a unique field. Things are things, that is, transcendent with respect to all that I know of them and accessible to other perceiving subjects, but intended precisely as things; as such they are the indispensable moment of the lived dialectic which embraces them.

2. The Philosophical Realism of the Sensible

But on the other hand consciousness discovers, particularly in illness, a resistance of the body proper. Since an injury to the eyes is sufficient to eliminate vision, we must then see through the body. Since an illness is sufficient to modify the phenomenal world, it must be then that the body forms a screen between us and things. In order to understand this strange power of the body to upset the entire spectacle of the world, we are obliged to renounce the image of it which direct experience gives us. The phenomenal body, with the human determinations which permitted consciousness not to be distinguished from it, is going to take on the status of appearance; the "real body" will be the one which we know through anatomy or, more generally, through the isolating methods of analysis: an ensemble of organs of which we have no notion in immediate experience and which interpose their mechanisms, their unknown powers, between ourselves and things. One could still conserve the favorite metaphor of naive consciousness and admit that the subject perceives *according to* his body—as a colored glass modifies what the beam illuminates—without denying him access to the things themselves or putting them outside him. But the body appears capable of manufacturing a pseudo-perception. Thus certain phenomena of which it is the seat must be the necessary and sufficient condition for perception; the body must be the necessary intermediary between the real world and perception, which are henceforth disassociated from each other. Perception can no longer be a taking-possession of things which finds them in their proper place; it must be an event internal to the body and one which results from their action on it. The world divides in two. There will be the real world as it is outside my body and the world as it is for me, numerically distinct from the first; the external cause of perception and the internal object which it contemplates will have to be separated. The body proper has become a material mass and, correlatively, the subject withdraws from it to contemplate its representations within himself. Instead of the three inseparable terms bound together in the living unity of an experience which a pure *description* reveals, one finds oneself in the presence of three orders of events which are external to each other: the events of nature, the organic events, and those of thought, which will explain each other. Perception will result from an action of the thing on the body and of the body on the soul. First it is the sensible, the perceived itself, to which the functions of extramental things are attributed; then the problem is to understand how a duplicate or an imitation of the real is aroused in the body, then in thought. Since a picture makes us think of what it represents, it will be supposed—based on the privileged case of the visual apparatus—that the senses receive "little pictures" of real things which excite the soul to perceive them.[6] The Epicurean "simulacra" or the "intentional forms," "all those little images fluttering through the air"[7] which bring the sensible aspect of things into the body, only transpose the ideal presence of the thing to the perceiving subject into terms of causal explanation and real operations. It is the former, as we have seen, which is an evidence for naive consciousness. In default of a numerical identity the philosopher seeks to maintain a specific identity between the perceived and the real, to have the distinctive characteristic of the perceived come from the things themselves; this is why perception is understood as an imitation or a duplication in us of sensible things, or as the actualization in the soul of something which was potentially in an external sensible thing.

The difficulties which this explanatory mythology encounters would not have to be mentioned if they issued only from the realism of the sensible which has been abandoned since Descartes. In fact they are the permanent difficulties of any causal explanation applied to perception. The Descartes of the *Optics* rejects the transitive action by means of which sensible things, identical with perceived objects, would impress their image in the body, where the soul would find it. Since light is only a movement, there is no need to suppose any resemblance between the things external to the body, the physiological phenomena, and what the soul perceives. And, moreover, even if the perceived object resembled the bodily phenomena which condition perception or their external causes, perception would still not have been explained. "Now, when this picture thus passes to the inside of our head, it still bears some resemblance to the objects from which it proceeds. . . . [H]owever, we must not think that it is by means of this resemblance that the picture causes our sensory perception of these objects—as if there were yet other eyes within our brain with which we could perceive it. Instead, we must hold that it is the movements composing this picture which, acting directly upon our soul insofar as it is united to our body, are ordained by nature to make it have such sensations."[8] The external thing and the bodily impression do not act therefore as exemplar causes; they are the occasional causes[9] of the feelings of the soul. But all the difficulties are not removed; if the cerebral impressions are only the occasional causes of perception, there must still be a regulated correspondence between certain cerebral impressions and certain perceptions. One has indeed gotten rid of the myths which made the idea of a real transference of sensible things into the mind inevitable; but one is obliged to construct physiological schemata which make comprehensible how sensory impressions are prepared in the brain to become the adequate occasions of our perceptions. Since we perceive only one object in spite of the two images which it forms on our retinas, only one space in

which the givens of the different senses are distributed, it will be necessary
to imagine a bodily operation which combines these multiple elements
and provides the soul with the occasion of forming a single perception.[10]
Thus the substitution of occasional causes for exemplar causes does not
eliminate the necessity of placing some physiological representation of
the perceived object in the brain. This necessity is inherent in the realist
attitude in general.

3. The Pseudo-Cartesianism of Science

It is found again in the pseudo-Cartesianism of scientists and psychologists. Both consider perception and its proper objects as "internal" or
"mental phenomena," as functions of certain physiological and mental
variables. If by "nature" one means a group of events bound by laws, perception would be a part of nature, the perceived world a function of the
real world of primary qualities. Then the problem is to designate in the
body the adequate conditions of perception. Just as Descartes is obliged
to reserve the mediation of the body and perception to the pineal gland[11]
as the seat of common sense, so physiologists have had to give up designating fixed spatial and chromatic values in the periphery of the nervous
system and to make those which in perception are distributed over the different points of the visual field depend on the assimilation of the corresponding excitations into variable associative circuits. Descartes' pineal
gland plays the role of the association zone of modern physiologists. As
soon as one accepts as given, as realism wants it, that the soul "does not see
directly, but only by means of the brain,"[12] this mediation, even if it is not
a transitive action, necessitates looking in the body for a physiological
equivalent of the perceived. But the nerve functioning which distributes
their spatial or chromatic values to the different points of the sensory
field, and which in normal cases, for example, renders diplopia impossible, is not itself conceivable without reference to the phenomenal field
and its laws of internal equilibrium; it is a process of form, the notion of
which is borrowed in the final analysis from the perceived world. "It is the
soul which sees, and not the eye," Descartes said[13] in order to get rid of the
"little images fluttering through the air." The evolution of modern physiology shows that this expression must be taken literally and turned back
against Descartes himself. It is the soul which sees and not the brain; it is
by means of the perceived world and its proper structures that one can
explain the spatial value assigned to a point of the visual field in each particular case. The coordinate axes of the phenomenal field, the direction
which at each moment receives the value of "vertical" or "horizontal"
and "frontal" or "lateral," the ensembles to which are assigned the index

"immobile" and with respect to which the remainder of the field appears "in movement," the colored stimuli which are seen as "neutral" and determine the distribution of the apparent colors in the rest of the field, and the contexts of our spatial and chromatic perception—none of these result as effects from an intersection of mechanical actions; they are not a function of certain physical variables. Gestalt theory believed that a causal explanation, and even a physical one, remained possible on the condition that one recognized processes of structuration in physics in addition to mechanical actions. But, as we have seen, physical laws do not furnish an explanation *of* the structures, they represent an explanation *within* the structures. They express the least integrated structures, those in which the simple relations of function to variable can be established. They are already becoming inadequate in the "acausal" domain of modern physics. In the functioning of the organism, the structuration is constituted according to new dimensions—the typical activity of the species or the individual—and the preferred forms of action and perception can be treated even less as the summative effect of partial interactions. Thus the properties of the phenomenal field are not expressible in a language which would owe nothing to them. The structure of the "thing perceived" now offers a new support to this conclusion. The relation of the perspectival aspects to the thing which they present to us is not reducible to any of the relations which exist within nature. As we have seen, it is neither the relation of effect to cause, nor that of function to corresponding variable. All the difficulties of realism arise precisely from having tried to convert this original relation into a causal action and to integrate perception into nature. As soon as the presence or the presentation of a "thing" to consciousness—instead of remaining an ideal relation, as in naive experiences—is interpreted as a real operation of the thing on the body and on the perceiving subject, it becomes impossible to reconstitute the descriptive content of perception, the actual spectacle of the world, as an effect. This difficulty was evident in the theory of "simulacra" or in that of "intentional forms" since, as copies of the thing itself, these "little pictures" which were transported into the body could not assume the variable perspectival aspects through which we nevertheless perceive things. Perspectival variation becomes understandable, on the contrary, once optics and the theory of light have excluded the idea of a resemblance between the real thing and the perceived. But, inversely, it is the constancy of perceived things under their variable perspectival aspect which is going to become a problem. How are retinal images—so different depending on the points of view—going "to provide the soul with a means" of perceiving the same thing under several profiles? It would be necessary to suppose some association of present cerebral impressions with traces left by

past impressions. But modern physiology has precisely given up the supposition of stores of cerebral traces, of "image centers" distinct from "perception centers"; and the physiological substrate of our perception is conceived as an indecomposable coordinating process in which the influence
of prior excitations is not separately assignable. Most often one tries to
"explain" the constancy of the phenomenal thing by a psychological process, by some "projection"[14] of memories which will complete or correct
the present lacunary givens. To the extent that this "psychological explanation" is only a new kind of causal thinking, we can reject it as we can
every "explanation." Whether it is a question of memories or of cerebral
traces, only a real transformation of sensible givens can be obtained by the
real operations of a psychological or physiological causality: it will be
shown how the "mental image" of an object does not follow exactly the
perspectival variations of its "retinal image," how its phenomenal size when
it is at some distance represents a mean between the size of the retinal
image for a short distance and the size of the retinal image for a long one.
But even if it could be established (which is false) that the mental image
remains constant for variable distances, one would still not have explained the presentation of an identical thing under variable aspects,
since one would have purely and simply eliminated the perspectival variation by replacing it with the inertia of a constant "conscious content,"
with an immutable "mental image." The spectacle of a thing seen through
its "profiles," this original structure, is nothing which can be "explained"
by some real physiological or psychological process. When I see an object
at a distance I do not contemplate a *mental image of a determinate size,* as a
sensitive plate can receive a physical image. I grasp in and by the perspectival aspect a constant thing which it mediates. The phenomenal object is not spread out on a plane, as it were; it involves two layers: the layer
of perspectival aspects and that of the thing which they present. This ideal
reference, this ambiguous mode of organization, can be described or understood, but not explained—with the help of a psycho-physiological law,
for example—as if the "mental image" were another retinal image the size
of which could be measured and related to certain variables.

4. The Cartesian Analysis of Perceptual Consciousness

But until now we have spoken only of a pseudo-Cartesianism. The *Optics,*
the *Treatise of Man,* and the *Passions of the Soul* are situated in a ready-
made world in which they delineate the human body and into which the
soul is finally introduced. This is evidently not the principal undertaking
of Cartesianism. Descartes' first step was to abandon the extra-mental
things which philosophical realism had introduced in order to return to

an inventory, to a description, of human experience without presupposing anything at first which explains it from the outside. With regard to perception, the radical originality of Cartesianism is to situate itself within perception itself, not to analyze vision and touch as functions of our body, but "solely the thought of seeing and touching."[15] Beyond causal explanations which constitute the appearance of perception as an effect of nature, Descartes, in search of the internal structure, makes its meaning explicit and disengages the grounds which assure naive consciousness that it is acceding to "things"; that, beyond the transitory appearances, it is grasping a solid being in a piece of wax, for example. If, as is always said, methodic doubt concerning sensible things is distinguished from skeptical doubt—the one finding in itself that which brings it to an end, the other being a state of uncertitude which does not admit of a solution—this difference in the results should stem from a difference in the operations which lead to them. Skeptical doubt is insurmountable because it is not radical; it presupposes extra-mental things as the ideal term of knowledge, and it is in relation to this inaccessible reality that dreams and perception take on the character of equivalent appearances. The Cartesian doubt necessarily carries its solution within itself precisely because it presupposes nothing—no realist idea of knowledge—and because—bringing attention back in this way from the vision or touch which lives in things to the "thought of seeing and touching" and laying bare the internal sense of perception and of acts of knowledge in general—it reveals to thought the indubitable domain of meanings. Even if I see and touch nothing which exists outside my thought, it is still a fact that I think I am seeing and touching something and that certain judgments are possible concerning the sense of this thought considered as such. The cogito not only discloses to me the certitude of my existence, but more generally it provides me with access to a whole field of knowledges by giving me a general method: the method of searching, by reflection, for the pure thought in each domain which defines it; with regard to perception, for example, of analyzing the thought of perceiving and the sense of the perceived which are immanent in the sight of a piece of wax, which animate it and sustain it internally. One can say that here Descartes was very close to the modern notion of consciousness understood as the center in which all the objects about which man can speak and all the mental acts which intend them take on an indubitable clarity. With the help of this notion, Kant was able to go definitively beyond skepticism and realism by recognizing the descriptive and irreducible characteristics of external and internal experience as the sufficient foundation of the world. From this point of view perception could no longer appear to be the effect in us of the action of an external thing, nor the body as the intermediary of this causal action; the external thing and the body, defined as the "thought of" the thing

and the "thought of" the body, as the "meaning thing" and the "meaning
body," became indubitable as they present themselves to us in a lucid experience at the same time that they lost the occult powers that philosophical realism had given them. But Descartes does not follow this path to the
end. The analysis of the piece of wax gives us only the essence of the thing,
only the intelligible structure of dream objects or of perceived objects.[16]
The imagination already contains something which this analysis does not
take into account: it gives us the pentagon as "present."[17] In perception,
the object "presents" itself without having been willed.[18] There is an existential index which distinguishes the perceived or imaginary object from
the idea and which manifests "something" in them "which differs from my
mind,"[19] whatever this "other" may be in other respects.[20] Thus the experience of a sensible presence is explained by a real presence; the soul,
when it perceives, is "excited" to think such and such an existing object by
means of a bodily event to which it "applies itself" and which "represents"
to it an event from the real extension.[21] The body ceases to be what it was
vis-à-vis the understanding—a fragment of extension in which there are
no real parts and in which the soul could not have a special seat[22]—to become, like the cubic foot of which Malebranche will speak,[23] a real individual. As such, it could be the occasional cause of perceptions and it
could even be so in only one of its parts to which the soul is immediately
connected.[24] The experience of my body as "mine"[25]—which discredits
the Aristotelian metaphor of the soul as a pilot of his ship[26]—is explained
in turn by a real "mixture" of "the mind with the body." Thus the universe
of consciousness revealed by the cogito and in the unity of which even
perception itself seemed to be necessarily enclosed was only a universe of
thought in the restricted sense. It accounts for the thought of seeing, but
the fact of vision and all the things that we know existentially remain outside of it. The intellection which the cogito had found in the heart of perception does not exhaust its content; to the extent that perception opens
out on an "other," to the extent that it is the experience of an existence, it
arises from a primary and original notion which "can be understood only
through itself,"[27] from an order of "life" in which the distinctions of the
understanding are purely and simply annulled.[28] Thus Descartes did not
attempt to integrate the knowledge of truth and the experience of reality,
intellection, and sensation.[29] It is not in the soul, it is in God that they are
linked with each other. But after Descartes this integration was to appear
to be the solution of the problems posed by philosophical realism. It
would permit abandoning the action of the body or of things on the mind
and allow them to be defined as the indubitable objects of a consciousness; it would permit surpassing the alternatives of realism and skepticism
by associating, following Kant's terms, a transcendental idealism and an
empirical realism.

5. The Critical Idea. The Problems of the Relations of the Soul and Body Resolved by an Intellectualist Theory of Perception

The conception of sensible knowledge which was taught by Descartes is taken up again by a philosophy in the critical tradition. To know something is not only to find oneself in the presence of a compact set of givens and to live in it as it were; this "conascence" [*co-naissance*],[30] this blind contact with a singular object and this participation in its existence would be as nothing in the history of a mind and would leave no more acquisitions and available memories in the mind than would a physical pain or a fainting spell if the contrary movement by which I detach myself from the thing in order to apprehend the meaning were not already contained in them. Red, as sensation, and red, as *quale,* must be distinguished; the quality already includes two moments: the pure impression of red and its function, which for example is to cover a certain extension of space and of time.[31] To know therefore is always to grasp a given in a certain function, in a certain relation, "as" it signifies to me or presents to me such or such a structure. Psychologists often speak as if the whole question were to know where the signification of the perceived *comes from;* they treat it as an aggregate of additional givens and explain it by means of a projection of images over the brute givens of the senses. They do not see that the same problem poses itself with respect to the images introduced. If they are the simple copy of old perceptions, "little pictures" which are less clear, the becoming aware of these new "things" will still have to be analyzed once they have been brought back under the gaze of the mind by some psychological or physiological mechanism. And even if a "dynamic schema" presides over the evocation of memories, it remains an operation in the third person as long as *I* do not recognize an illustration of the schema in the memory evoked. One does not construct perception as one does a house: by assembling the material gotten from the senses and the material gotten from memory; one does not explain it as an event of nature by situating it at the confluence of several causal series—sensory mechanisms and mnemonic mechanisms. Even if the search for physiological and psychological determinants were to make possible the establishment of a relation of function to variable between them and the view perceived—we have seen that this is not at all the case—this explanation would give us only the conditions of existence of the view; since it connects the view with bodily and mental events situated in space and time, this explanation would make it a mental event also. But there is something else. If I look steadily at an object in front of me, the psychologist will say that—external conditions remaining the same—the mental image of the object has remained the same. But it would still be necessary to analyze the act by which at each instant I recognize this image as identical in its meaning to that of the preceding instant. The mental image of the psychologist is one thing; what the consciousness of that thing is must still be understood. The act of knowing is not of the order of events; it is a taking-possession of events, even internal ones, which is not mingled with them; it is always an internal "re-creation" of the mental image and, as Kant and Plato have said, a recognizance, a recognition. It is not the eye, not the brain, but no more is it the "psychism" of the psychologist which can accomplish the act of vision. It is a question of an inspection of the mind in which events are known in their sense at the same time as they are lived in their reality. No matter how evident the determination of the perceived contents by natural conditions may be in each particular case, perception, by its general structure at least, eludes natural explanation and admits of only an internal analysis. It follows from this that the moments of knowledge in which I grasp myself as determined to perceive a thing by that thing itself should be considered as derived modes of consciousness, founded in the final analysis on a more originary mode of consciousness. Since the grounds for our affirmations can only be sought within their own sense, the experience of a real thing cannot be explained by the action of that thing on my mind: the only way for a thing to act on a mind is to offer it a sense, to manifest itself to it, to *constitute* itself in front of the mind in its intelligible articulations. The analysis of the act of knowing leads to the idea of a constituting or naturizing thought which internally subtends the characteristic structure of objects. In order to indicate both the intimacy of objects to the subject and the presence in them of solid structures which distinguish them from appearances, they will be called "phenomena"; and philosophy, to the extent that it adheres to this theme, becomes a phenomenology, that is, an inventory of consciousness as milieu of the universe.

Thus philosophy returns to the evidences of naive consciousness. Transcendental idealism, by making the subject and the object inseparable correlatives, guarantees the validity of perceptual experience in which the world appears in person and nonetheless as distinct from the subject. If knowledge, instead of being the presentation to the subject of an inert picture, is the apprehension of the sense of this picture, the distinction of the objective world and subjective appearances is no longer that of two sorts of beings, but of two meanings; as such, it is unchallengeable. It is the thing itself which I reach in perception, since everything of which one can think is a "meaning of thing" and since the act in which this meaning is revealed to me is precisely called perception. One must go back, not to Bergson, but to Kant for this idea that the perception of point "0" is at point "0."[32] It follows immediately from a notion of consciousness as universal life in which every affirmation of object finds its grounds.

The body becomes one of the objects which is constituted vis-à-vis consciousness. It is integrated into the objective world; and since any nature is conceivable only as the correlate of a naturizing knowledge, there is no longer any question of treating knowledge as a fact of nature. No doubt consciousness itself recognizes that natural laws determine the order of its perceptual events in terms of the position of the body and of bodily phenomena. In this sense it manifests itself as a part of the world, since it can be integrated into the relations which constitute it. It seems to include two aspects: on the one hand it is milieu of the universe, presupposed by every affirmation of a world; on the other hand it is conditioned by it. Thus, the first moment of critical philosophy will be to distinguish, on the one hand, a general form of consciousness which cannot be derived from any bodily or psychological event, in order to do justice to its analysis of knowledge; and, on the other, the empirical contents whose actual existence could be related to such and such external events or to this or that particularity of our psycho-physical constitution, in order to account for the external conditions which govern perception as well as the passivity which we grasp in it. Such is approximately the meaning of the "Transcendental Aesthetic."[33] But this attitude can only be provisional, as is shown by the second edition of the *Critique of Pure Reason*. How, as a matter of fact, are we to conceive the relations of the "given" and "thought," the operation of consciousness on inert "things" which pure sensations would be, the connection of "affection" and knowledge and the connection of sensible and intellectual consciousness? In the final analysis, then, there will be no sensible consciousness, no hiatus between the aesthetic and the analytic, and no naturized consciousness.[34] An analysis which would try to isolate the perceived content would find nothing; for all consciousness of something, as soon as this thing ceases to be an indeterminate existence, as soon as it is identifiable and recognizable, for example, *as* "a color" or even as "this unique red," presupposes the apprehension of a sense through the lived impression which is not *contained* in consciousness and is not a real part of it. The matter of knowledge becomes a limit-notion posited by consciousness in its reflection upon itself, and not a component of the act of knowing. But from then on perception is a variety of intellection and, in all of its positive aspects, a judgment. Critical philosophy would resolve the problems posed by the relations of form and matter, given and thought, and soul and body by terminating in an intellectualist theory of perception.[35] If as a matter of fact an incipient science, a first organization of experience which is completed only by scientific coordination, could be shown in perception, the alleged sensible consciousness would no longer pose any problem, since the "original" characteristics of perceptual experience would be nothing but privation and

negation: "The universe of immediate experience contains, not *more* than
what is required by science, but *less;* for it is a superficial and mutilated
world; it is, as Spinoza says, the world of *conclusions without premises.*"[36] The
problem of the relations of the soul and the body would be posed only
at the level of a confused thought which adheres to the products of consciousness instead of rediscovering in them the intellectual activity which
produces them. Put back into the intellectual context which alone gives it
a sense, "sensible consciousness" is eliminated as a problem. The body rejoins the extension whose action it undergoes and of which it is only a
part; perception rejoins judgment, which subtends it. Every form of consciousness presupposes its completed form: the dialectic of the epistemological subject and the scientific object.

Part 2. Is There Not a Truth of Naturalism?

1. In What Sense the Preceding Chapters Lead to the Transcendental Attitude. Matter, Life, Mind Defined as Three Orders of Meaning

Are we compelled in this direction by the preceding analyses? At least they
lead to the transcendental attitude, that is, to a philosophy which treats all
conceivable reality as an object of consciousness. It has seemed to us that
matter, life, and mind could not be defined as three orders of reality or
three sorts of beings, but as three planes of meaning or three forms of
unity. In particular, life would not be a force which is added to physico-
chemical processes; its originality would be that of modes of connection
without equivalent in the physical domain, that of phenomena gifted with
a proper structure and which bind each other together according to a
special dialectic. In a living being, bodily movements and moments of behavior can be described and understood only in a specially tailored language and in accordance with the categories of an original experience.
And it is in this same sense that we have recognized a psychological order
and a mental order. But these distinctions, then, are those of different regions of experience. We have been moved from the idea of a *nature* as *om-
nitudo realitatis* to the wide idea of objects which could not be conceived
in-themselves [*en soi*], *partes extra partes,* and which are defined only by an
idea in which they participate, by a meaning which is realized in them.
Since the relations of the physical system and the forces which act upon
it and those of the living being and its milieu are not the external and
blind relations of juxtaposed realities, but dialectical relations in which

the effect of each partial action is determined by its meaning for the whole, the human order of consciousness does not appear as a third order superimposed on the two others, but as their condition of possibility and their foundation.

The problem of the relations of the soul and the body seems to disappear from the point of view of this absolute consciousness, milieu of the universe, as it did from the critical point of view. There can be no question of a causal operation between three planes of meaning. One says that the soul "acts" on the body when it happens that our conduct has a rational signification, that is, when it cannot be understood by any play of physical forces or by any of the attitudes which are characteristic of the vital dialectic. In reality the expression is improper: we have seen that the body is not a self-enclosed mechanism on which the soul could act from the outside. It is defined only by its functioning, which can present all degrees of integration. To say that the soul acts on the body is wrongly to suppose a univocal notion of the body and to add to it a second force which accounts for the rational meaning of certain conducts. In this case it would be better to say that bodily functioning is integrated with a level which is higher than that of life and that the body has truly become a human body. Inversely, one will say that the body has acted on the soul if the behavior can be understood without residue in terms of the vital dialectic or by known psychological mechanisms. Here again one does not, properly speaking, have the right to imagine a transitive action from substance to substance, as if the soul were a constantly present force whose activity would be held in check by a more powerful force. It would be more exact to say that the behavior had become disorganized, leaving room for less integrated structures. In brief, the alleged reciprocal action is reducible to an alternation or a substitution of dialectics. Since the physical, the vital, and the mental individual are distinguished only as different degrees of integration, to the extent that man is completely identified with the third dialectic, that is, to the extent that he no longer allows systems of isolated conduct to function in him, his soul and his body are no longer distinguished. If one supposes an anomaly of vision in El Greco, as has sometimes been done, it does not follow that the form of the body in his paintings, and consequently the style of the attitudes, admit of a "physiological explanation." When irremedial bodily peculiarities are integrated with the whole of our experience, they cease to have the dignity of a cause in us. A visual anomaly can receive a universal meaning by the mediation of the artist and become for him the occasion of perceiving one of the "profiles" of human existence. The accidents of our bodily constitution can always play this revealing role on the condition that they become a means of extending our knowledge by the consciousness which we have

of them, instead of being submitted to as pure facts which dominate us.
Ultimately, El Greco's supposed visual disorder was conquered by him and
so profoundly integrated into his manner of thinking and being that it
appears finally as the necessary expression of his being much more than
as a peculiarity imposed from the outside. It is no longer a paradox to say
that "El Greco was astigmatic because he produced elongated bodies."[37]
Everything which was accidental in the individual, that is, everything
which revealed partial and independent dialectics without relationship to
the total meaning of his life, has been assimilated and centered in his
deeper life. Bodily events have ceased to constitute autonomous cycles, to
follow the abstract patterns of biology and psychology, and have received
a new sense. It is nevertheless the body, it will be said, which in the final
analysis explains El Greco's vision; his freedom consisted only in justifying
this accident of nature by infusing it with a metaphysical sense. Unity does
not furnish an adequate criterion of the sense which has been won, since
a man dominated by a complex, for example, and subject to the same psychological mechanism in all his undertakings, realizes unity in slavery. But
here it is only a question of an apparent unity, of a stereotyped unity,
which will not withstand an unexpected experience. It can be maintained
only in a chosen milieu which the sick person has constructed for himself
precisely by avoiding all situations in which the apparent coherence of his
conduct would be disorganized. True unity, on the contrary, is recognized
from the fact that it is not obtained by a restriction of the milieu. The same
sensory or constitutional infirmity can be a cause of slavery if it imposes
on man a type of vision and monotonous action from which he can no
longer escape, or the occasion of a greater freedom if he makes use of it
as an instrument. This supposes that he knows it instead of obeys it. For
a being who lives at the simply biological level, it is a fatality. For a being
who has acquired the consciousness of self and his body, who has reached
the dialectic of subject and object, the body is no longer the cause of the
structure of consciousness; it has become the object of consciousness.
Then one can no longer speak of a psycho-physiological parallelism: only
a disintegrated consciousness can be paralleled with physiological processes, that is, with a partial functioning of the organism. By acceding to
true knowledge, by going beyond the dialectic of the living or the social
being and its circumscribed milieu, by becoming the pure subject who
knows the world objectively, man ultimately realizes that absolute consciousness with respect to which the body and individual existence are no
longer anything but objects; death is deprived of sense. Reduced to the
status of object of consciousness, the body could not be conceived as an
intermediary between "things" and the consciousness which knows them;
and since consciousness, having left the obscurity of instinct, no longer

expresses the vital properties of objects but their *true* properties, the parallelism here is between consciousness and the true world which it knows directly. All the problems seem to be eliminated: the relations of the soul and the body—obscure as long as the body is treated in abstraction as a fragment of matter—are clarified when one sees in the body the bearer of a dialectic. Since the physical world and the organism can be conceptualized only as objects of consciousness or as meanings, the problem of the relations of consciousness and its physical or organic "conditions" would exist only at the level of a confused thought which adheres to abstractions; it would disappear in the domain of truth in which the relation of the epistemological subject and its object alone subsists as original. This would constitute the only legitimate theme of philosophical reflection.

Let us consider a subject who turns his eyes toward a sensible object placed in front of him. Our preceding remarks permit us to say that the consecutive modification of his perceptual field is not an "effect" of the physical phenomenon of excitation or of the corresponding physiological phenomenon. We have shown that the most remarkable characteristics of the perceived object—its distance, its size, its apparent color—cannot be deduced from the physiological antecedents of perception. The modern theory of nerve functioning relates them to "transverse phenomena" of which there is neither a physical nor a physiological definition and which are conceived precisely by borrowing from the perceived world and the image of its descriptive properties. It becomes impossible to assign a *somatic* substrate of perception. The elaboration of stimuli and the distribution of motor influxes are accomplished according to articulations proper to the phenomenal field; what is introduced under the name of "transverse phenomena" is in reality the perceived field itself. For us this means that the living body and the nervous system, instead of being like annexes of the physical world in which the occasional causes of perception would be prepared, are "phenomena" emerging from among those which consciousness knows. Perceptual behavior, as science studies it, is not defined in terms of nerve cells and synapses; it is not in the brain or even in the body; science has not been able to construct the "central sectors" of behavior from the outside like something which is enclosed within a cranial box; it can understand it only as a dialectic, the moments of which are not stimuli and movements but phenomenal objects and actions. The illusion of a transitive operation of stimuli on the sensory apparatus and of the latter "against" consciousness comes from the fact that we actualize separately the physical body, the body of the anatomists or even the organism of the physiologists, all of which are abstractions, snapshots taken from the functional body.

When its existence is accepted, the hallucinatory image is no longer

treated in recent works as an isolated phenomenon which could be explained by some irritation of centers: it is connected with the whole of
organic-vegetative functioning;[38] which is to say that, rather than a perception without object, hallucination is a global conduct related to a global
alteration of nerve functioning. It supposes a complete structure the description of which, like that of normal functioning, cannot be given in
somatic terms. The somatic events do not act directly. The division of the
optic nerve can be called the cause of blindness only in the sense in which
Beethoven's deafness "explains" his last works. It provokes a change of
the phenomenal field only by rendering impossible the functioning of the
whole of the cortex under the action of luminous excitants. Is it this functioning itself which can be considered as a cause? No, if it is understood
as the sum of the nerve events which are produced in each point of the
cortex. This whole can be only the *condition of existence* of such and such
a sensible spectacle; it accounts for the *fact that* I perceive but not for *that
which* I perceive,[39] not for the spectacle as such, since this latter is presupposed in a complete definition of the nerve process. Everything takes
place as if my perception opened out on a network of original meanings.
The passage of nerve influx in such and such conductors does not produce the visible spectacle; it does not even determine its structure in a univocal manner, since it is organized according to laws of equilibrium which
are neither those of a physical system nor those of the body considered as
such. The somatic substrate is the passage point, the base of a dialectic. In
the same way, nobody thinks of explaining the content of a delirium by its
physiological conditions, even though this form of consciousness presupposes *in existendo* some alteration of the brain.

Speaking generally, it seems that we are rejoining the critical idea.
Whatever the external conditions may be—bodily, psychological, social—
upon which the development of consciousness depends and even if it is
only gradually constituted in history, the history itself out of which it
comes is only a view which consciousness gives itself with regard to the acquired consciousness of self. A reversal of perspective is produced vis-à-vis
adult consciousness: the historical becoming which prepared it was not
before it, it is only *for* it; the time during which it progresses is no longer
the time *of* its constitution, but a time which it constitutes; and the series
of events is subordinated to its eternity. Such is the perpetual reply of critical thought to psychologism, sociologism, and historicism.

2. But Our Conclusion Is Not Inspired by Critical Philosophy

This discussion of causal thinking has seemed valid to us and we have
pursued it at all levels of behavior. It leads, as we have just said, to the tran-

scendental attitude.[40] This is the first conclusion which we have to draw from the preceding chapters. It is not the only one, and it would even be necessary to say that this first conclusion stands in a relation of simple homonymy with a philosophy inspired by critical philosophy.[41] What is profound in the notion of "gestalt" from which we started is not the idea of signification but that of *structure,* the joining of an idea and an existence which are indiscernible, the contingent arrangement by which materials begin to have a sense in our presence, intelligibility in the nascent state. The study of the reflex has shown us that the nervous system is the place in which an order without anatomical guarantee is realized by means of a continuing organization. It already permitted us to establish a rigorously reciprocal relation between function and substrate; there was not an area which was not linked in its functioning to the global activity of the nervous system, but also not a function which was not profoundly altered by the subtraction of a single one of these areas; and function was nothing outside the process which is delineated at each instant and which, based on the nerve mass, organizes itself.[42] The study of the "central sector" of behavior confirmed this ambiguity of bodily nature. On the one hand, it appeared that absolutely no function could be localized, since each region plays a role only in the context of a global activity and since the diverse movements which it governs correspond to several modes of qualitatively distinct functioning rather than to several locally differentiated devices. On the other hand, it was equally clear that certain parts of the nerve substance are indispensable for the reception of certain stimuli, that the execution of certain movements is assigned to certain receptive regions or to some muscular ensemble, and that, even when nerve substance is not the depository of any special power of this kind, there can be no substitution for the nerve substance in each place. Thus, we were dealing less with two types of localization than with an inextricable intersecting of "horizontal" and "vertical" localizations—without the body being anywhere pure thing, *but also without it being anywhere pure idea.*[43] It is not possible to designate separate contributions of the visual and auditory regions of the brain; both function only with the center, and integral thinking transfigures the hypothetical "visual contents" and "auditory contents" to the point of rendering them unrecognizable; but also the alteration of one of these regions is manifested in thought by a determinate deficit: it is the intuition of simultaneous wholes or that of successive wholes which becomes impossible.[44] Thus the integration of the optic or auditory regions in a functional whole, although it infuses the corresponding "contents" with a new meaning, does not annul their specificity; it uses and sublimates it.

For life, as for the mind, there is no past which is absolutely past; "the moments which the mind seems to have behind it are also borne in its present depths."[45] Higher behavior retains the subordinated dialectics in the present depths of its existence, from that of the physical system and its topographical conditions to that of the organism and its "milieu." They are not recognizable in the whole when it functions correctly, but the disintegration in case of partial lesion attests to their imminence. There is no essence of thinking which would receive the particular forms of "visual thought" and "auditory thought" by a contingency of our nerve organization and as a condition of existence. The alleged conditions of existence are indiscernible in the whole with which they collaborate, *and reciprocally the essence of the whole cannot be concretely conceptualized without them and without its constitutive history.* Consequently, the relations of matter and form in the object-organism and the relations of the soul and body were found to be conceived differently than in critical thought. While critical philosophy, having step-by-step repressed quality and existence—residues of its ideal analysis—to place them finally in a matter about which nothing can be thought and which is for us therefore as if it were not, deploys a homogeneous activity of the understanding from one end of knowledge to the other; each formation appears to us on the contrary to be an event in the world of ideas, the institution of a new dialectic, the opening of a new region of phenomena, and the establishment of a new constitutive layer which eliminates the preceding one as isolated moment, but conserves and integrates it. While critical thought pushed the problem of the relations of the soul and body back step-by-step by showing that we never deal with a body in-itself but with a body for-a-consciousness and that thus we never have to put consciousness in contact with an opaque and foreign reality, for us consciousness experiences its inherence in an organism at each moment; for it is not a question of an inherence in material apparatuses, which as a matter of fact can be only *objects* for consciousness, but of a presence to consciousness of its own history and of the dialectical stages which it has traversed. Therefore, we could not accept any of the materialistic models to represent the relations of the soul and body—but neither could we accept the mentalistic models, for example, the Cartesian metaphor of the artisan and his tool.[46] An organ cannot be compared to an instrument, as if it existed and could be conceived apart from integral functioning, nor the mind to an artisan who uses it: this would be to return to a wholly external relation like that of the pilot and his ship which was rightly rejected by Descartes. The mind does not use the body, but realizes itself through it while at the same time transferring the body outside of the physical space. When we were describing the structures of behavior,[47] it was indeed to show that they are irreducible to the dialectic of physical stimulus and muscular contraction and that in this sense behavior, far from being a thing which exists in-itself, is a whole significative for a consciousness which considers it, but it was at the same time and reciprocally to make manifest in "expressive conduct" the *view of a consciousness* under our eyes, to show a mind which *comes into the world.* Doubtless it is understood why we cannot even accept without reservations a relation of expression between the soul and the body comparable to that of the concept and the word, nor define the soul as the "sense of the body," the body as the "manifestation of the soul."[48] These formulae have the inconvenience of evoking two terms, solidary perhaps, but external to each other and the relation of which would be invariable. But sometimes our body manifests externally an intention arising from a dialectic which is higher than biology; sometimes, by a play of mechanisms which its past life has built up, it limits itself to mimicking intentions which it *does not have* any longer, as do the movements of a dying person, for example;[49] from one case to the other the relation of the soul and the body and even the terms themselves are modified depending on whether the "formation" succeeds or fails and whether the inertia of the subordinated dialectics allows itself to be surmounted or not. Our body does not always make sense, and our thoughts, on the other hand—in timidity, for example—do not always find in it the plentitude of their vital expression. In these cases of disintegration, the soul and the body are apparently distinct; and this is the truth of dualism. But the soul, if it possesses no means of expression—one should say rather, no means of actualizing itself—soon ceases to be *anything whatsoever* and in particular ceases to be the soul, as the thought of the aphasic weakens and becomes dissolved; the body which loses its sense soon ceases to be a living body and falls back into the state of a physicochemical mass; it arrives at non-sense only by dying. The two terms can never be distinguished absolutely without ceasing to be; thus their empirical connection is based on the originary operation which establishes a sense in a fragment of matter and makes it live, appear, and be in it. In returning to this *structure* as the fundamental reality, we are rendering comprehensible both the distinction and the union of the soul and the body. There is always a duality which reappears on one level or another: hunger or thirst prevents thought or feelings; the properly sexual dialectic ordinarily reveals itself through a passion; integration is never absolute and it always fails—at a higher level in the writer, at a lower level in the aphasic. There always comes a moment when we divest ourselves of a passion because of fatigue or self-respect. This duality is not a simple fact; it is founded in principle—all integration presupposing the normal functioning of subordinated formations, which always demand their own due. But it is not a duality of substances; or in other words, the notions of soul and body must be relativized: there is the body as mass of chemical com-

ponents in interaction, the body as dialectic of living being and its biological milieu, and the body as dialectic of social subject and his group;
even all our habits are an impalpable body for the ego of each moment.
Each of these degrees is soul with respect to the preceding one, body with
respect to the following one. The body in general is a set of paths already
traced, of powers already constituted; the body is the acquired dialectical
soil upon which a higher "formation" is accomplished, and the soul is the
sense which is then established.[50] The relations of the soul and the body
can indeed be compared to those of concept and word, but on the condition of perceiving, beneath the separated products, the constituting
operation which joins them and of rediscovering, beneath the empirical
languages—the external accompaniment or contingent clothing of
thought—the living *word* which is its unique actualization, in which the
sense is formulated for the first time and thus establishes itself as sense
and becomes available for later operations. In this way our analyses have
indeed led us to the ideality of the body, but it was a question of an idea
which proffers itself and even constitutes itself in the contingency of existence. By a natural development the notion of "gestalt" led us back to its
Hegelian meaning, that is, to the concept before it has become self-
consciousness. Nature, we said, is the exterior of a concept.[51] But precisely
the concept as concept has no exterior, and the gestalt still had to be conceptualized as unity of the interior and exterior, of nature and idea.[52] Correlatively, the consciousness *for* which the gestalt exists was not intellectual
consciousness but perceptual experience.[53] Thus, it is perceptual consciousness which must be interrogated in order to find in it a definitive
clarification. Let us limit ourselves here to indicating how the status of the
object, the relations of form and matter, those of soul and body, and the
individuality and plurality of consciousnesses are founded in it.

3. It Is Necessary to Distinguish Between Consciousness as the Place of Meanings and Consciousness as the Flux of Lived Experiences

A. External Perception. The Phenomenon of the Thing. The Phenomenon of the Body Proper. Return to the Perceptual Field as to an Originary Experience. Realism as a Well-Founded Error

I cannot simply identify what I perceive and the thing itself. The real color
of the object which I look at is and will always remain known to myself
alone. I have no means whatsoever of knowing if the colored impression
which it gives to others is identical to my own. Our intersubjective confrontations bear only upon the intelligible structure of the perceived
world: I can assure myself that another viewer employs the same word as

I to designate the color of this object and the same word, on the other hand, to qualify a series of other objects which I also call red objects. But, the relationships being conserved, it could happen that the scale of colors which he sees is completely different from mine. However, it is when objects give me the unique impression of the "sensed," when they have that direct manner of taking hold of me, that I say they are existing. It follows from this that perception, as knowledge of existing things, is an individual consciousness and not the consciousness in general of which we were speaking above. This sensible mass in which I live when I gaze at a sector of the field without trying to recognize it, the "this" which my consciousness wordlessly intends, is not a meaning or an idea, although subsequently it can serve as base for acts of logical explicitation and verbal expression. Already when I name the perceived or when I recognize it *as* a chair or tree, I substitute the subsumption under a concept for the experience of a fleeting reality; even when I pronounce the word "this," I already relate a singular and lived existence to the essence of lived existence. But these acts of expression or reflection intend an originary text which cannot be deprived of sense. The meaning which I find in a sensible whole was already adherent in it. When I "see" a triangle, my experience would be very poorly described by saying that I conceive or comprehend the triangle with respect to certain sensible givens. The meaning is embodied. It is here and now that I perceive this triangle as such, while conception gives it to me as an eternal being whose sense and properties, as Descartes said, owe nothing to the fact that I perceive it. It is not only the matter of perception which comes off the thing as it were and becomes a content of my individual consciousness. In a certain manner, the form also makes up a part of the psychological individual, or rather is related to it; and *this reference is included in its very sense,* since it is the form *of* this or that thing which presents itself to me here and now and since this encounter, which is revealed to me by perception, does not in the least concern the proper nature of the thing and is, on the contrary, an episode of my life. If two subjects placed near each other look at a wooden cube, the total structure of the cube is the same for both; it has the value of intersubjective truth, and this is what they both express in saying that there is a cube there. But it is not the same sides of the cube which, in each of them, are strictly seen and sensed. And we have said that this "perspectivism" of perception is not an indifferent fact, since without it the two subjects would not be aware of perceiving an existent cube subsisting beyond the sensible contents. If all the sides of the cube could be known at once, I would no longer be dealing with a thing which offers itself for inspection little by little, but with an idea which my mind would truly possess. This is what happens when I think of objects which I hold to be existent without actually perceiving them. In affirming that they continue to exist, I mean that a properly placed psycho-physical subject would see this or that sensible sight, articulated in this or that way, and connected with the view which I perceive here and now by such and such objective transitions. But this *knowing about* the world must not be confused with my *perception of* this or that segment of the world and its immediate horizon. The objects which do not belong to the circle of the perceived exist in the sense in which truths do not cease to be true when I am not thinking about them: their mode of being is one of logical necessity and not of "reality." For I certainly suppose a "perspectivism" in them also, and it is essential to them to present themselves to a viewer through a multiplicity of "profiles." But since I do not perceive them, it is a question of a perspectivism in idea and of an essence of the viewer; the relation of the one to the other is itself a relation of meanings. These objects belong therefore to the order of meanings and not to that of existences.[54] A perception which would be coextensive with sensible things is inconceivable; and it is not physically but logically that it is impossible. For there to be perception, that is, apprehension of an existence, it is absolutely necessary that the object not be completely given to the gaze which rests on it, that aspects intended but not possessed in the present perception be kept in reserve. A seeing which would not take place from a certain point of view and which would give us, for example, all the sides of a cube at once is a pure contradiction in terms; for, in order to be visible all together, the sides of a wooden cube would have to be transparent, that is, would cease to be the sides of a wooden cube. And if each of the six sides of a transparent cube were visible as square, it is not a cube which we would be seeing. Thus the Bergsonian idea of a "pure perception," that is, adequate to the object or identical with it, is inconsistent. It is the cube as meaning or geometrical idea which is made of six equal sides. The relation—unique and characteristic of existing things—of the "aspects" to the total object is not a logical relation like that of sign to a signification: the sides of the chair are not its "signs," but precisely the sides.

In the same way, the phenomena of my body should be distinguished from purely logical meanings. What differentiates it from external things even as they are presented in lived perception is the fact that it is not, like them, accessible to an unlimited inspection. When it is a question of an external thing, I know that by changing places I could see the sides which are hidden from me; by occupying the position which was that of my neighbor a moment ago, I could obtain a new perspectival view and give a verbal account which would concur with the description of the object which my neighbor gave a moment ago. I do not have the same freedom with my body. I know very well that I will never see my eyes directly and that, even in a mirror, I cannot grasp their movement and their living expression. For me, my retinas are an absolute unknowable. This is, after all, only a particular case of the perspectival character of perception. To say that I have a body is simply another way of saying that my knowledge is an individual dialectic in which intersubjective objects appear, that these objects, when they are given to knowledge in the mode of actual existence, present themselves to it by successive aspects which cannot coexist, and that, finally, it is a way of saying that one of them offers itself obstinately "from the same side" without my being able to go around it. Reservation made for its image which mirrors give me (but *this image moves* as soon as I try to see it from different points of view, by leaning the head to the right and left; it is not a true "thing"), my body as given to me by sight is broken at the height of the shoulders and terminates in a tactile-muscular object. I am told that an object is visible for others in this lacuna in which my head is located; science teaches that organs, a brain, and—each time I perceive an external thing—"nerve influxes" in this visible object would be found by means of analyses. I will never see anything of all that. I could never make an actually present experience of my body adequately correspond to the meaning, "human body," as it is given to me by science and witnesses. There are entities which will always remain pure meanings for me under some of their aspects and which will never be offered to other than lacunary perception. In itself, this structure is not much more mysterious than that of external objects with which, moreover, it is one: how could I receive an object "in a certain direction" if I, the perceiving subject, were not in some way hidden in one of my phenomena, one which envelops me since I cannot go around it? Two points are necessary for determining a direction. We have not completely described the structure of the body proper, which also includes an affective perspective, the importance of which is obvious. But the preceding is sufficient to show that there is no enigma of "my body," nothing inexpressible in its relation to myself. It is true that, by describing it, we are transforming into meaning the lived perspective which by definition is not one. But this alogical essence of perceived beings can be clearly designated: one will say, for example, that to offer themselves through profiles which I do not possess as I possess an idea is included in the idea of perceived being and of the body. Reduced to its positive sense, the connection of the soul and body means nothing other than the *ecceitas* of knowledge by profiles; it appears to be a marvel only if, by a dogmatic prejudice, it is posited that all entities which we experience should be given to us "completely," as meanings claim to be. Thus the obscure causality of the body is reducible to the original structure of a phenomenon; and we do not dream of explaining perception as an event of an individual consciousness "by means of the body" and in terms of causal thinking. But if it is still not a question of externally connecting my consciousness to a body whose point of view it would adopt in an inexplicable manner, and if, in order to remain faithful to this phenomenon, it all comes back in brief to accepting the fact that some *humans see things which I do not see,* the zone of individual perspectives and that of intersubjective meanings must be distinguished in my knowledge. This is not the classical distinction between sensibility and intelligence, since the horizon of the perceived extends beyond the perimeter of vision and encloses, in addition to the objects which make an impression on my retina, the walls of the room which are behind me, the house, and perhaps the town in which I am, arranged perspectively around the "sensible" nucleus. Nor are we returning to the distinction of matter and form since, on the one hand, the very form of perception participates in the *ecceitas* and since, inversely, I can bring acts of recognition and denomination to bear on the sensible content which will convert it into a meaning. The distinction which we are introducing is rather that of the lived and the known. The problem of the relations of the soul and body is thus transformed instead of disappearing: now it will be the problem of the relations of consciousness as flux of individual events, of concrete and resistant structures, and that of consciousness as tissue of ideal meanings. The idea of a transcendental philosophy, that is, the idea of consciousness as constituting the universe before it and grasping the objects themselves in an indubitable external experience, seems to us to be a definitive acquisition as the first phase of reflection. But is one not obliged to reestablish a duality within consciousness which is no longer accepted between it and external realities? The objects as ideal unities and as meanings are grasped through individual perspectives. When I gaze at a book placed in front of me, its rectangular form is a concrete and embodied structure. What is the relation between this rectangular "physiognomy" and the meaning, "rectangle," which I can make explicit by a logical act?

Every theory of perception tries to surmount a well-known contradiction: on the one hand, consciousness is a function of the body—thus it is an "internal" event dependent upon certain external events; on the other hand, these external events themselves are known only by consciousness. In other language, consciousness appears on one hand to be part of the world and on the other to be coextensive with the world. In the development of methodical knowledge, of science, that is, the first observation seems initially to be confirmed: the subjectivity of the secondary qualities seems to have as a counterpart the reality of the primary qualities. But a deeper reflection on the objects of science and on physical causality finds relations in them which cannot be posited in-themselves and which make sense only before the inspection of mind. The antinomy of which we are speaking disappears along with its realistic thesis at the level of reflective thought; it is in perceptual knowledge that it has its proper location. Until now critical thought seemed to us to be incontestable. It shows marvelously that the problem of perception does not exist for a consciousness which adheres to objects of reflective thought, that is, to meanings. It is subsequently that it seems necessary to leave it. Having in this way referred the antinomy of perception to the order of life, as Descartes says, or to the order of confused thought, one claims to show that it has no consistency there: if perception conceptualizes itself ever so little and knows what it is saying, it reveals that the experience of passivity is also a construction of the mind. Realism is not even based on a coherent appearance, it is an *error.* One wonders then what can provide consciousness with the very notion of passivity and why this notion is confused with its body if these natural errors rest on no authentic experience and *process strictly no sense whatsoever.* We have tried to show that, as a matter of fact, to the extent that the scientific knowledge of the organism becomes more precise, it becomes impossible to give a coherent sense to the alleged action of the world on the body and of the body on the soul. The body and the soul are meanings and make sense, then, only with regard to a consciousness.

From our point of view also, the realistic thesis of common sense disappears at the level of reflective thought, which encounters only meanings in front of it. The experience of passivity *is not explained* by an actual passivity. But it should have a sense and be able *to be understood.* As philosophy, realism is an error because it transposes into a dogmatic thesis an experience which it deforms or renders impossible by that very fact. But it is a motivated error; it rests on an authentic phenomenon which philosophy has the function of making explicit. The proper structure of perceptual experience, the reference of partial "profiles" to the total meaning which they "present," would be this phenomenon. Indeed, the alleged bodily conditioning of perception, taken in its actual sense, requires nothing more—and nothing less—than this phenomenon in order to be understood. We have seen that excitations and nerve influxes are abstractions and that science links them to a total functioning of the nervous system in the definition of which the phenomenal is implied. The perceived is not an effect of cerebral functioning; it is its meaning. All the consciousnesses which we know present themselves in this way through a body which is their perspectival aspect. But, after all, each individual dialectic has cerebral stages, as it were, of which it itself knows nothing; the meaning of nerve functioning has organic bases which do not figure in it. Philosophically, this fact admits of the following translation: each time that certain sensible phenomena are actualized in my field of consciousness, a properly placed observer would see certain other phenomena in my brain which cannot be given to me myself in the mode of actuality. In order to understand these phenomena, he would be led to grant them (as we did in chapter 2 [of *The Structure of Behavior*]) a meaning which would concur with the content of my perception. Inversely, I can represent for myself in the virtual mode, that is, as pure meanings, certain retinal and cerebral phenomena which I localize in a virtual image of my body on the basis of the actual spectacle which is given to me. The fact that the spectator and myself are both bound to our bodies comes down in sum to this: that that which can be given to me in the mode of actuality, as a concrete perspective, is given to him only in the mode of virtuality, as a meaning, and conversely. In sum, my total psycho-physical being (that is, the experience which I have of myself, that which others have of me, and the scientific knowledge which they and I apply to the knowledge of myself) is an interlacing of meanings such that, when certain among them are perceived and pass into actuality, the others are only virtually intended. But this structure of experience is similar to that of external objects. Even more, they mutually presuppose each other. If there are things for me, that is, perspectival beings, reference to a point from which I see them is included in their perspectival aspect itself. But to be situated within a certain point of view necessarily involves not seeing that point of view itself, not possessing it as a visual object except in a virtual meaning. Therefore, the existence of an external perception, that of my body and, "in" this body, the existence of phenomena which are imperceptible for me are rigorously synonymous. There is no relation of causality between them. They are *concordant phenomena*. One often speaks as if the perspectivism of perception were explained by the projection of objects on my retina: I see only three sides of a cube *because* I see with my eyes, where a projection of only these three sides is possible; I do not see objects which are behind me *because* *they* are not projected on my retina. But the converse could be said just as well. Indeed, what are "my eyes," "my retina," "the external cube" in itself, and "the objects I do not see"? They are logical meanings which are bound up with my actual perception by means of valid "motivations,"[55] and which make its sense explicit, but which get *the index of real existence from it*. These meanings do not have in themselves therefore the means to explain the actual existence of my perception. The language which one habitually uses is nevertheless understandable: my perception of the cube presents it to me as a complete and real cube; my perception of space, as a space which is complete and real beyond the aspects which are given to me. Thus it is natural that I have a tendency to detach the space and the cube from the concrete perspectives and to posit them in-themselves. The same operation takes place with respect to the body. And as a consequence, I am naturally inclined to engender perception by an operation of the cube or of objective space on my objective body. This attempt is natural, but its failure is no less inevitable: as we have seen, one cannot reconstitute the structure of perceptual experience by combining ideal meanings (stimuli, receptors, associative circuits). But if physiology does not explain perception, optics and geometry do not explain it either. To imagine that I see my image in the mirror *because* the light waves form a certain angle in reaching my eyes and because I situate their origin at their point of coincidence is to make the use of mirrors during so many centuries when optics was not yet invented mysterious indeed. The truth is that humans first see their image "through" the mirror, without the word yet having the meaning which it will take on vis-à-vis the geometrical mind. Then he constructs a geometrical representation of this phenomenon which is *founded* on the concrete articulations of the perceived field, which makes them explicit and accounts for them—without the representation ever being able to be the cause of the concrete articulations, as realism wants to do, and without our being able to substitute it for them, as critical idealism does. Access to the proper domain of perception has been rendered difficult for all philosophies which, because of a retrospective illusion, actualized a "natural geometry" in perception on the pretext that it has been possible to construct a geometry of perceived objects. The perception of a distance or a size is not the same as the quantitative estimations by which science makes distance and size precise. All the sciences situate themselves in a "complete" and real world without realizing that perceptual experience is constituting with respect to this world. Thus we find ourselves in the presence of a field of lived perception which is prior to number, measure, space, and causality and which is nonetheless given only as a perspectival view of objects gifted with stable properties, a perspectival view of an objective world and an objective state. The problem of perception consists in trying to discover how the intersubjective world, the determinations of which science is gradually making precise, is grasped through this field. The antinomy of which we spoke above is based upon this ambiguous structure of perceptual experience. The thesis and the antithesis express the two aspects of it: it is true to say that my perception is always a flux of individual events and that what is radically contingent in the lived perspectivism of perception accounts for the realistic appearance. But it is also true to say that my perception accedes to things themselves, for these perspectives are articulated in a way which makes access to interindividual meanings possible; they "present" a world. Thus there are things *exactly in the sense in which I see them,* in my history and outside it and inseparable from this double relation. I perceive things directly without my body forming a screen between them and me; it is a phenomenon just as they are, a phenomenon (gifted, it is true, with an original structure) which precisely presents the body to me as an intermediary between the world and myself although it *is not* as a matter of fact. I see with my eyes, which are not a set of transparent or opaque tissues and organs, but the instruments of my gaze. The retinal image, to the extent that I know it, is not yet produced by the light waves issuing from the object; but these two phenomena resemble and correspond to each other in a magical way across an interval which is not yet space. We are returning to the givens of naive consciousness which we were analyzing at the beginning of this chapter. The philosophy of perception is not ready-made in life: we have just seen that it is natural for consciousness to misunderstand itself precisely because it is consciousness of things. The classical discussions centering around perception are a sufficient testimony to this natural error. The constituted world is confronted with the perceptual experience of the world and one either tries to engender perception from the world, as realism does, or else to see in it only a commencement of the science of the world, as critical thought does. To return to perception as to a type of originary experience in which the real world is constituted in its specificity is to impose upon oneself an inversion of the natural movement of consciousness;[56] on the other hand, every question has not been eliminated: it is a question of understanding, without confusing it with a logical relation, the lived relation of the "profiles" to the "things" which they present, of the perspectives to the ideal meanings which are intended through them.[57] The problem which Malebranche tried to resolve by occasionalism or Leibniz by preestablished harmony is carried over into human consciousness.

B. Error; The Psychical and Social Structures

Yet until now we have considered only the perspectivism of true perception. Instances in which lived experience appears clothed with a signification which breaks apart, so to speak, in the course of subsequent experience and is not verified by concordant syntheses would still have to be analyzed. We have not accepted the causal explanation which naturalism provides in order to account for this subjectivity in the second degree. What is called bodily, psychological, or social determinism in hallucination and error has appeared to us to be reducible to the emergence of imperfect dialectics, of partial structures. But why, *in existendo*, does such a dialectic at the organic-vegetative level break up a more integrated dialectic, as happens in hallucination? Consciousness is not only and not always consciousness of truth; how are we to understand the inertia and the resistance of the inferior dialectics which stand in the way of the advent of the pure relations of impersonal subject and true object and which affect my knowledge with a coefficient of subjectivity? How are we to understand the adherence of a fallacious meaning to lived experience, which is constitutive of illusion? We have rejected Freud's causal categories and replaced his energic metaphors with structural metaphors. But although the complex is not a thing outside of consciousness which would produce its effects in it, although it is only a structure of consciousness, at least this structure tends as it were to conserve itself. It has been said that what is called the unconscious[58] is only an inapperceived meaning. It may happen that we ourselves do not grasp the true sense of our life, not because an unconscious personality is deep within us and governs our actions, but because we understand our lived states only through an idea which is not adequate for them. But, even unknown to us, the efficacious law of our life is constituted by its true meaning. Everything happens as if this meaning directed the flux of mental events. Thus will it be necessary to distinguish their ideal meaning, which can be true or false, and their immanent meaning, or—to employ a clearer language which we will use from now on—their ideal *meaning* and their actual *structure*. Correlatively, it will be necessary to distinguish in the development an ideal liberation, on the one hand, which does not transform us in our being and changes only the consciousness which we have of ourselves, and, on the other, a real liberation which is the *Umgestaltung* of which we spoke, along with Goldstein. We are not reducible to the ideal consciousness which we have of ourselves any more than the existent thing is reducible to the meaning by which we express it.

It is easy to argue in the same way, in opposition to the sociologist, that the structures of consciousness which he relates to a certain economic structure are in reality the consciousness of certain structures. This argument hints at a freedom very close to spirit, capable by reflection of grasping itself as spontaneous source, and naturizing from below the contingent forms with which it has clothed itself in a certain milieu. Like Freud's complex, the economic structure is only one of the objects of a transcendental consciousness. But "transcendental consciousness," the full consciousness of self, is not ready-made; it is to be achieved, that is, realized in existence. In opposition to Durkheim's "collective consciousness" and his attempts at a sociological explanation of knowledge, it is rightly argued that consciousness cannot be treated as an effect since it is that which constitutes the relation of cause and effect. But beyond a causal thinking which can be all too easily challenged, there is a truth of sociologism. Collective consciousness does not produce categories, but neither can one say that collective representations are only the objects of a consciousness which is always free in their regard, only the consciousness in a "we" of an object of consciousness in an "I." The mental, we have said,[59] is reducible to the structure of behavior. Since this structure is visible from the outside and for the spectator at the same time as from within and for the actor, another person is in principle accessible to me as I am to myself, and we are both objects laid out before an impersonal consciousness.[60] But just as I can be mistaken concerning myself and grasp only the apparent or ideal meaning of my conduct, so can I be mistaken concerning another and know only the envelope of his behavior. The perception which I have of him is never, in the case of suffering or mourning, for example, the equivalent of the perception which he has of himself unless I am sufficiently close to him that our feelings constitute together a single "form" and our lives cease to flow separately. It is by this rare and difficult consent that I can be truly united with him, just as I can grasp my natural movements and know myself sincerely only by the decision to belong to myself. Thus I do not know myself because of my special position, but neither do I have the innate power of truly knowing another. I communicate with him by the meaning of his conduct; but it is a question of attaining its structure, that is, of attaining, beyond his words or even his actions, the region where they are prepared. As we have seen,[61] the behavior of another expresses a certain manner of existing before signifying a certain manner of thinking. And when this behavior is addressed to me, as may happen in dialogue, and seizes upon my thoughts in order to respond to them—or more simply, when the "cultural objects" which fall under my regard suddenly adapt themselves to my powers, awaken my intentions, and make themselves "understood" by me—I am then drawn into a *coexistence* of which I am not the unique constituent and which founds the phenomenon of social nature as a perceptual experience founds that of physical nature. Consciousness can *live* in existing things without reflection, can abandon itself to their concrete structure, which has not yet been converted into expressible meaning. Certain episodes of its life, before having been reduced to the condition of available memories and inoffensive objects, can imprison its freedom by their proper inertia, shrink its perception of the world, and impose stereotypes on behavior; likewise, before having conceptualized our class or our milieu, we *are* that class or that milieu.

Thus, the "I think" can be as if hallucinated by its objects. It will be replied (which is true) that it "should be able" to accompany all our representations and that it is presupposed by them, if not as a term of an act of actual consciousness, then at least as a possibility in principle. But this response of critical philosophy poses a problem. The conversion of seeing which transforms the life of consciousness into a pure dialectic of subject and object, which reduces the thing in its sensible density to a bundle of meanings, the traumatic reminiscence into an indifferent memory, and which submits the class structure of my consciousness to examination—does this conversion make explicit an eternal "condition of possibility" or does it bring about the appearance of a new structure of consciousness? It is a problem to know what happens, for example, when consciousness disassociates itself from time, from this uninterrupted gushing forth at the center of itself, in order to apprehend it as an intellectual and manipulable signification. Docs it lay bare only what was implicit? Or, on the contrary, does it not enter as into a lucid dream in which indeed it encounters no opaqueness, not because it has clarified the existence of things and its own existence, but because it lives at the surface of itself and on the envelope of things? Is the reflective passage to intellectual consciousness an adequation of our knowing to our being or only a way for consciousness to create for itself a separated existence—a quietism? These questions express no empiricist demand, no complaisance for "experiences" which would not have to account for themselves. On the contrary, we want to make consciousness equal with the whole of experience, to gather into consciousness for-itself all the life of consciousness in-itself. A philosophy inspired by critical philosophy founds moral theory on the reflection which discovers the thinking subject in its freedom behind all objects. If, however, one acknowledges—be it in the status of phenomenon—an existence of consciousness and of its resistant structures, our knowledge depends upon what we are; moral theory begins with a psychological and sociological critique of oneself; man is not assured ahead of time of possessing a source of morality; self-consciousness is not given in man by right; it is acquired only by the elucidation of his concrete being and is verified only by the active integration of isolated dialectics—body and soul—between which it is initially broken up. And finally, death is not *deprived of sense*, since the contingency of the lived is a perpetual menace for the eternal meanings in which it is believed to be completely expressed. It will be necessary to assure oneself that the experience of eternity is not the unconsciousness of death, that it is not on this side but beyond; similarly, moreover, it will be necessary to distinguish the love of life from the attachment to biological existence. The sacrifice of life will be philosophically impossible; it will be a question only of "staking" one's life, which is a deeper way of living.

4. Structure and Meaning: The Problem of Perceptual Consciousness

If one understands by perception the act which makes us know existences, all the problems which we have just touched on are reducible to the problem of perception. It resides in the duality of the notions of structure and meaning. A "form," such as the structure of "figure and ground," for example, is a whole which has a sense and which provides therefore a base for intellectual analysis. But at the same time it is not an idea: it constitutes, alters, and reorganizes itself before us like a spectacle. The alleged bodily, social, and psychological "causalities" are reducible to this contingency of lived perspectives which limit our access to eternal meanings. The "horizontal localizations" of cerebral functioning, the adhesive structures of animal behavior and those of pathological behavior are only particularly striking examples of this. "Structure" is the philosophical truth of naturalism and realism. What are the relations of this naturized consciousness and the pure consciousness of self? Can one conceptualize perceptual consciousness without eliminating it as an original mode; can one maintain its specificity without rendering inconceivable its relation to intellectual consciousness? If the essence of the critical solution consists in driving existence back to the limits of knowledge and of discovering intellectual meaning in concrete structure, and if, as has been said, the fate of critical thought is bound up with this intellectualist theory of perception, in the event that this was not acceptable, it would be necessary to define transcendental philosophy anew in such a way as to integrate with it the very phenomenon of the real. The natural "thing," the organism, the behavior of others and my own behavior exist only by their sense, but the sense which springs forth in them is not yet a Kantian object; the intentional life which constitutes them is not yet a representation; and the "understanding" which gives access to them is not yet an intellection.

2

The War Has Taken Place

Events kept making it less and less probable that peace could be maintained. How could we have waited so long to decide to go to war? It is no longer comprehensible that certain of us accepted Munich as a chance to test German good will. The reason was that we were not guided by the facts. We had secretly resolved to know nothing of violence and unhappiness as elements of history because we were living in a country too happy and too weak to envisage them. Distrusting the facts had even become a duty for us. We had been taught that wars grow out of misunderstandings which can be cleared up and accidents which can be averted through patience and courage. We were attending an old school in which generations of socialist professors had been trained. They had experienced World War I, and their names were inscribed by entire classes on the memorials to the dead. But we had learned that memorials to the dead are impious because they make heroes out of victims. We were encouraged to suspend the history which had already been made, to recapture the moment when the Trojan War might still not have taken place and a free act might still, in a single stroke, have exploded all the exterior fatalities. This optimistic philosophy, which reduced human society to a sum of consciousnesses always ready for peace and happiness, was in fact the philosophy of a barely victorious nation, an imagined compensation for the memories of 1914. We knew that concentration camps existed, that the Jews were being persecuted, but these certainties belonged to the world of thought. We were not as yet living face-to-face with cruelty and death: we had not as yet been given the choice of submitting to them or confronting them. Outside the peaceful garden of our school where the fountain immemorially and everlastingly murmured, there awaited us for our vacation of '39 that other garden which was France, the France of walking trips and youth hostels, which was as self-evident as the earth itself—or so we thought. We lived in a certain area of peace, experience, and freedom, formed by a combination of exceptional circumstances. We did not know that this was a soil to be defended but thought it the natural lot of men. Even those of us who, better informed by their travels or made sensitive to Nazism by their birth or already equipped with a more accurate philosophy, no longer separated their personal fate from European history, even they did not know how right they were. Debating with them as we came back together, we justified the objections: the die has not yet been cast; history has not yet been written. And they answered us in conversational tones. From our birth we had been used to handling freedom and to living an individual life. How then could we have known that these were hard to come by? How could we have learned to commit our freedom in order to preserve it? We were consciousnesses naked before the world. How could we have known that this individualism and this universalism had their place on the map? What makes our landscape of 1939 inconceivable to us and puts it once and for all beyond our grasp is precisely the fact that we were not conscious of it as a landscape. In the world in which we lived, Plato was as close to us as Heidegger, the Chinese as close as the French—and in reality one was as far away as the other. We did not know that this was what it was to live in peace, in France, and in a certain world situation.

Whether by chance or by design, the representatives whom Germany sent among us were ambiguous. Bremer, a lecturer at the University of Paris, revered the values of war, consorted with Montherlant, and was to make some of the ties he had formed before the war useful to his government when he came back here in 1940 as cultural attaché. But in 1938 he was fond of saying he was an "old radical." By talking loud enough, one could get him to back down on the principal articles of Nazism. He showed surprise and injured feelings one day when, as he was speaking of the Spanish government officials and insistently calling them "Reds," we asked him to take his propaganda elsewhere. I witnessed his dismay when, in 1938, he had to leave France to put in a period of military service in Germany. He believed—as much as a man of his sort can believe in anything—Germany's "European" propaganda; or at least he wanted to believe in it, since it allowed him to reconcile his pleasure at living in France with his loyalty to the government of his country. One morning in March 1939, I entered the room of another Parisian German to tell him of the occupation of Prague. He leaped up, ran to the map of Europe (which he did have on the wall), and said, with every intonation of sincerity, "But that is mad! That is impossible!" Naivete? Hypocrisy? Probably neither. These fellows said what they thought, but they didn't think anything very clearly, and they kept themselves in the dark to avoid a choice between their humanism and their government, a choice by which they would have lost their respect either for themselves or for their country. There was only one solution to their inner debate: a German victory. When they came back to Paris in 1940, squared away with their country now that they had followed it into war, they were of course prepared to "collaborate" with France (within the limits imposed upon them by the German high command and Nazi policies) and to forget the military interlude. Before 1939 their slackness led them to choose to represent Germany in Paris; this

played a part in the propaganda, and their irresolution sustained our un-
awareness. After 1940 their good feelings were supposed to serve the same
ends, and they lent themselves half-consciously to this game until the day
total mobilization caught them up, hurling Bremer to the Russian front
where he met his death and the other to the African front where, it is said,
he was severely burned. So it is that history attracts and seduces individuals. Thus when we look closely at things, we find culprits nowhere but accomplices everywhere; so it is that we all played a part in the events of
1939. The only difference between our Germans and ourselves was that
they had had Nazism right under their noses, and as yet we had not. They
could not have been unaware of how they were being used; we had not yet
learned that game.

* * *

Our being in uniform did not essentially change our way of thinking during the winter of 1939–40. We still had the leisure to think of others as
separate lives, of the war as a personal adventure; and that strange army
considered itself a sum of individuals. Even when we worked with a will
at the job of war, we did not feel involved, and all our standards were still
those of peacetime. Our colonel had a 155 fired to disperse a German pa-
trol near our position, and a captain was detailed to recover the shoulder
straps and papers of two dead Germans: we were as bemused over those
stretchers as we would have been over a deathbed. We lingered over that
German lieutenant who had lain dying in the barbed wire, a bullet in his
stomach, and had cried out, "French soldiers, come get a dying man" (it
was night, our position was isolated, and we had been ordered not to go
out before daybreak). We looked long and compassionately at the narrow
chest which the uniform barely covered in that near-zero cold, at the ash-
blond hair, the delicate hands, as his mother or wife might have done.

After June of 1940, however, we really entered the war, for from then
on we were no longer permitted to treat the Germans we met in the street,
subway, or movies as human beings. If we had done so, if we had wanted
to distinguish Nazis from Germans, to look for the student beneath the
lieutenant, the peasant or working man beneath the soldier, they would
have had only contempt for us and would have considered it a recognition
of their government and their victory, and then they would have felt like
victors. Magnanimity is a rich man's virtue: it is not hard to be generous
with the prisoners one has at one's mercy. But we were the prisoners. We
had to relearn all the childish behavior which our education had rid us
of; we had to judge men by the clothes they wore, reply rudely to their
well-mannered commands, live side by side with them for four years with-

out living with them for one minute, feel ourselves become not men but "Frenchmen" beneath their glance. From then on our universe of individuals contained that compact gray or green mass. Had we looked more sharply, we could already have found masters and slaves in peacetime society, and we could have learned how each consciousness, no matter how free, sovereign, and irreplaceable it may feel, will become immobile and generalized, a "worker" or a "Frenchman," beneath the gaze of a stranger. But no enslavement is more apparent than that of an occupied country. Even those of us who were not disturbed and continued to paint, write, or compose poetry, sensed—when they went back to work—that their former freedom had been sustained by the freedom of others and that one is not free alone. If they had once felt cheerfully in control of their lives, that, too, had been a mode of coexistence, possible only in a certain atmosphere; and they became aware of that general milieu—unmentioned in their past philosophy—where each consciousness communicates with every other.

German anti-Semitism not only horrified but mystified us. With our background we had to ask ourselves every day for four years: how is anti-Semitism possible? There was of course a way to avoid the question, by denying that anyone really lived anti-Semitism. Even the Nazis pardoned certain Jews whom they found serviceable, and a chance connection allowed a Jewish actor to appear on the Paris stage for four years. Maybe there was not a single anti-Semite after all? Maybe anti-Semitism was wholly a propaganda device? Maybe the soldiers, the SS, the newspapermen were only obeying orders in which they did not believe, and maybe the very authors of this propaganda did not believe in it any more than they did? Launched by calculating agitators and borne along by confused elemental forces, anti-Semitism would have been a sinister mystification. So we thought up to 1939: now that we have seen those busloads of children on the Place de la Contrescarpe, we can no longer think so. Anti-Semitism is not a war machine set up by a few Machiavellis and serviced by the obedience of others. It is not the creation of a few people any more than language is, or music. It was conceived in the depths of history. In the last analysis, that cops and con men conception of history which emphasizes agitators and elemental forces, cynicism and stupidity, is naive: it attributes too much awareness to the leaders and too little to the masses. It does not see any middle ground between the voluntary action of the former and the passive obedience of the latter, between history's subject and object. The Germans made us understand, on the contrary, that leaders are mystified by their own myths and that the troops are their half-knowing accomplices, that no one commands or obeys absolutely. An anti-Semite could not stand to see Jews tortured if he really saw them, if he perceived that suffering and agony in an individual life—but this is just the point: he does not see Jews suffering; he is blinded by the myth of *the* Jew. He tortures and murders the Jew through these concrete beings; he struggles with dream figures, and his blows strike living faces. Anti-Semitic passion is not triggered by, nor does it aim at, individuals.

Thus we encountered the Marxist formula, which at any rate has the merit of placing us in a social context: "Anti-Semitism is the socialism of imbeciles." A convulsed society with a foreboding and dread of revolution will transfer the anguish it feels about itself to the Jews and in this way appease it. This might explain the hypocritical anti-Semitism of the Maurrasians, which is always accompanied by reservations or exceptions and which retreats before particular cases. But what about the racism of the SS, what about Drancy, what about the children taken from their mothers? Like all explanations based on a transferred emotion, this too collapses before passion. Transference of passion is not a final explanation, since the question is, precisely, what motivates it and why the anguish and sadism of a decadent society focus on the Jews. Here, as with all passion, we run into an element of chance and pure irrationality without which passion would be grounded in something and would no longer be passion. A certain man loves a certain woman today because his past history has prepared him to love that particular personality and face, but also because he *met* her, and this meeting awakens possibilities in his life which would have remained dormant without her. This love seems like fate once it has become established, but on the day of the first meeting it is absolutely contingent. An obsession may indeed be motivated by an individual's past, but it yields more than it promises: it has, when actualized, its own weight, which is the brute force of the present and of what exists. It is likewise impossible to explain all the whys and wherefores of anti-Semitism. One may point out its motivations, such as the social problem and the role the Jews once played in the development of a certain form of capitalism, but such motivations only sketch the outline of a possible history. The most that rational explanation can do is to say that the anguish in Germany around 1930 went back into the past and chose to find relief in anti-Semitism. Since anguish always turns away from the future, such explanation can go no further. Passion creates itself apart from its motivations and cannot be understood in a universe of consciousnesses. German anti-Semitism makes us face a truth we did not know in 1939. We did not think there were Jews or Germans but only men, or even consciousnesses. It seemed to us that at every moment each of us chose to be and to do what he wished with an ever-new freedom. We had not understood that, just as an actor slips into a role which envelops him and which alters the meaning of all his gestures, just as he carries this great phantom with him, animating it and yet controlled by it, so, in coexistence, each of us is presented to others against a historical background which we did not choose; and our behavior toward others is dictated by our role as "Aryan," Jewish, French, or German. We had not understood that consciousnesses have the strange power to alienate each other and to withdraw from themselves; that they are outwardly threatened and inwardly tempted by absurd hatreds, inconceivable with respect to individuals; and that if men are one day to be human to one another and the relations between consciousnesses are to become transparent, if universality is to become a fact, this will be in a society in which past traumas have been wiped out and the conditions of an effective liberty have from the first been realized. Until that time, the life of society will remain a dialogue and a battle between phantoms—in which real tears and real blood suddenly start to flow.

* * *

We were no longer permitted to be neutral in this combat. For the first time we were led not only to awareness but to acceptance of the life of society. Before '39 we were not interested in the police: they existed, but we would never have dreamed of joining them. Who among us would have helped arrest a thief, who would have been willing to be a judge, to pass sentence? For our part we did not want to be criminals or thieves, because this is what we had decided. But what right did our freedom have to annul that of another person, even if the murderer had himself decided the outcome of another man's life? We found it intolerable that sanction should wish to parade a moral character, and we reduced it to one of the necessities of police order, which we carefully distinguished from moral rules. It was base work to which we did not want to consent even if we were involved in it. I remember my bewilderment when I learned that, as a second lieutenant in the reserves, I could be required by the police to aid in an arrest and that I was even supposed to offer my services. We certainly had to revise our thinking on this subject, and we saw that it was indeed up to us to judge. If the arrest and conviction of an informer had depended on us, we could not have left this task to others. Before the war, politics seemed unthinkable to us because it treats men as statistics, and we saw no sense in treating these unique beings, each of whom is a world unto himself, according to a set of general rules and as a collection of interchangeable objects. Politics is impossible from the perspective of consciousness. But the moment came when our innermost being felt the impact of these external absurdities.

We have been led to take upon ourselves and consider as our own not only our intentions—what our actions mean for us—but also the external consequences of these actions, what they mean in a historical context. Twenty years ago a historian denounced the Allies' share of responsibility for World War I. During the Occupation we were stupefied that this same historian should publish—with the permission of the censors—a pamphlet denouncing England's role in starting World War II. He did not understand that to implicate England with the Germans occupying Paris was to accept responsibility for propaganda no pacifist had the right to further, since it was the instrument of a martial regime. In the spring of 1944 all professors were asked to sign a petition entreating Marshal Pétain to intervene and stop the war. It would be overly simple to assume that the men who composed and signed this petition were agents of the Germans trying to end the war before the German defeat. Treason is rarely committed with such clarity, at least among professors, and they are the type of men who are never swayed by self-interest alone, but also by ideas. Let us then try to imagine one of the authors of this petition. For him, the passions of war *do not exist:* they gain their apparent strength from the consent of men who are *equally free at every moment.* Therefore there is no world at war, with democracies on one side and Fascist states on the other, or with the established empires lined up against the latecomer nations eager to found empires for themselves (the former accidentally allied to a "proletarian" state). There are no empires, no nations, no classes. On every side there are only men who are always ready for freedom and happiness, always able to attain them under any regime, provided they take hold of themselves and recover the only freedom that exists: their free judgment. There is only one evil, war itself, and one duty, refusing to believe in victories of right and civilization and putting an end to war. So this solitary Cartesian thinks—but he does not see his shadow behind him projected onto history as onto a wall, this sense, this figure that his actions assume on the outside, this Objective Spirit that is himself.

The Cartesian would doubtless reply that if we hold ourselves responsible for the most distant consequences of our thoughts and actions, the only thing left for us to do is refuse all compromise as does the hero. And, he would add, how many heroes are there among the men who today take pride in their having resisted? Some were civil servants and continued to draw their salary, swearing in writing—since they had to—that they were neither Jews nor Masons. Others of them agreed to seek authorization of what they wrote or staged from a censorship which let nothing pass which did not serve its purpose. Each in his own way marked out the frontier of the permissible. "Don't publish anything," said one. "Don't publish anything in the newspapers or magazines," said another. "Just publish your books." And a third said, "I will let this theater have my play if the director is a good man, but if he is a servant of the government, I will withdraw it."

The truth is that each of them settled with outward necessity, all except a few who gave their lives. One could either stop living, refusing that corrupted air, that poisoned bread, or one could continue, which meant contriving a little hideout of private freedom in the midst of the common misery; and this is what most of them did, putting their consciences to rest by means of some carefully weighed sacrifices. Our compromise does not acquit the traitors who called this regime down upon us, aided it more than what was absolutely necessary, and were the self-appointed keepers of the new law. It does, however, prohibit us from judging them in the name of a morality which no one followed to the letter and from basing a new philosophy on the experience of those four years, since we lived according to the old one. Only the heroes really were outwardly what they inwardly wished to be; only they became one with history at the moment when it claimed their lives. Those who survived, even at the greatest risk, did not consummate this cruel marriage, and no one can speak of this silence or recommend it to others. Heroism is a thing not of words but of deeds, and any preaching would be presumptuous here, since the man who is still able to speak does not know what he is speaking of.

This line of reasoning is hard, but it leads in the direction we want to go. It is true that we are not innocent and that the situation in which we found ourselves admitted of no irreproachable conduct. By staying here we all became accomplices to some extent, and we must say of the Resistance what the combatants said about the war: no one comes back except the man who at some moment or another reduced the risks he was running, who, in that sense, elected to save his life. Nor can those who left France to pursue the war elsewhere with arms or propaganda lay any more claim to purity, for they escaped a direct compromise only by yielding the ground for a while, and in this sense they too had a part in the ravages of the Occupation. Several of our comrades asked themselves the question and made the best choice, but nothing can turn their decision into a true solution. One compromised oneself whether one stayed or left; no one's hands are clean (which is perhaps why the Germans found the corpses of Martel and several others at Paris). We have unlearned "pure morality" and learned a kind of vulgar immoralism, which is healthy. The moral man does not want to dirty his hands. It is because he usually has enough time, talent, or money to stand back from enterprises of which he disapproves and to prepare a good conscience for himself. The common people do not have that freedom: the garage mechanic had to repair German cars if he wanted to live. One of our comrades used to go to the Rive Gauche Bookstore for the German philosophy books he needed. When the day came, he took part in the uprising and was shot by the Germans. We are in the world, mingled with it, compromised with it. This is no reason to surrender all that is exterior and to confine ourselves to our thoughts, which are always free, even in the mind of a slave. This division of interior and exterior is abstract. We give the world both too little and too much credit. Too much because we bring weight to it when the time comes, and the state, as was evident with the Vichy State, is nothing without our consent. Too little because it arouses our *interest,* because we exist in it, and the wish to be free on the fringe of the world will end in our not being free at all. A judgment without words is incomplete; a word to which there can be no reply is nonsense; my freedom is interwoven with that of others by way of the world. Of course, those of us who were neither Jews nor declared Communists could manage to meditate during those four years: we were not denied Plato or Descartes or rehearsals at the Conservatory on Saturday mornings. We could begin our adolescence all over again, return to our gods and our great writers as if they were vices. This did not bring us any nearer to ourselves or to the spirit of the times. Yet for all that, we did not get out of history. Our finest thoughts, seen from London, New York, or Moscow, had a place in the world, and they had a name—the reveries of captives—and even their value as thoughts was altered as a result. One cannot get beyond history and time; all one can do is manufacture a private eternity in their midst, as artificial as the eternity of the madman who believes he is God. There is no vital spirit in gloomy isolated dreams; spirit only appears in the full light of dialogue. We were no more free, as we meditated on our great men, and no more pure consciousnesses, than the Jew or the deportee who became pure suffering, unable to see and unable to choose. No effective freedom exists without some power. Freedom exists in contact with the world, not outside it.

* * *

In this we rediscovered one of the truths of Marxism. But even Marxism had to be taken up anew, for it threatened to confirm our prewar prejudices. Under the pretext that history is the history of class struggle and that ideological conflicts are only its superstructure, a certain kind of Marxism detaches us from all situations in which the fate of the classes is not immediately at stake. Marxists of this type classed the Second World War as imperialistic, at least until the intervention of the U.S.S.R., and were not interested in it. True history would recommence for them on the day when the social struggle could again manifest itself. Since Fascism was, after all, nothing but a poor relative of capitalism, the Marxist didn't have to take sides in this family quarrel, and whichever faction won made little difference to him. Certain of us thought that capitalism could not allow itself to be liberal in a crisis, that it would become rigid in all things, and that the same necessities which gave birth to Fascism would stifle freedom in the pretended democracies. The worldwide war was just an appearance; what remained real beneath that appearance was the common fate of the proletariats of all nations and the profound solidarity of all forms of capitalism through the internal contradictions of the regime. Thus there could be no question of the national proletarians in any way assuming responsibility for the events in which they found themselves involved: no proletarian in uniform can feel *anything but* proletarian. Thus certain among us frowned on their own delight at the news of some German defeat and pretended not to share the general satisfaction. When we presented the situation of an occupied country to them as the prototype of an inhuman situation, they did their best to dissolve this phenomenon in the more general one of capitalistic exploitation and oppression. Entrusted from the start with the secret of history, they understood patriotic rebellion better than it understood itself and absolved it in the name of the class struggle. And yet when the liberation came they called it by name, just like everyone else.

They didn't have to give up Marxism in order to do so. The experience of those four years had, in fact, brought a better understanding of the concrete relationship of the class struggle to Marxist ideology. The class struggle is not *more real* than ideological conflicts; they cannot be reduced to it, as appearances to reality. Marx himself pointed out that, once they become established, ideologies have a weight of their own and set history in motion in the same way that the flywheel drives the motor. There must be more, consequently, to a Marxist analysis of Hitlerism than summarily classifying it as "a capitalistic episode." Such an analysis undoubtedly lays bare the combination of economic events without which it would not have existed, but this situation is unique, and to define it fully, to bring it back into contact with actual history, we must take local particularities into account and consider Nazism's human function as well as its economic one. The Marxist must not simply keep applying the capital-work formula in some mechanical way, but must think each new event through afresh to determine in each case the serpentine route of the proletarian future. He is not obliged to consider oppression in an occupied country as a surface phenomenon, beneath which the truth of history is to be sought. There are not two histories, one true and the other empirical; there is only one, in which everything that happens plays a part, if one only knows how to interpret it. For a Marxist in a French environment, the German Occupation was not a historical accident but an event of the first magnitude. The German and Anglo-Saxon victories are not equivalent from the point of view of the class struggle. No matter how reactionary the Anglo-Saxon govern-

ments are and wish to be, they are curbed in their own countries by their
liberal ideology, and the social struggle's imminent reemergence into the
spotlight gains in interest for men who do not have a hundred years to live
and who would have had to spend perhaps fifty years under Fascist oppression. Marxism does not suppress history's subjective factors in favor of
objective ones; it binds the two together. The ideology of nationalism cannot be classed once and for all as bourgeois: its function in shaping the historical conjunction must be newly appreciated at every moment, and this
function may at times be progressive and at other times reactionary. Na-
tionalistic feeling (which is not to say chauvinism) is revolutionary in the
France of today and was so in 1940. This does not merely mean that national feeling is in fact opposed to the immediate interest of French capitalism and that, by a pious trick, the Marxists can make it serve their own
struggle. It means that the historical conjuncture frees the national reality
from the reactionary mortgages which encumbered it and authorizes the
proletarian consciousness to integrate it. One might try to argue that in
Marxist political thinking the nation can only be a means, never an end,
that Marxist patriotism can only be tactical, and that for the Marxist a pur-
gation of morals, for example, serves the ends of revolution, whereas the
primary concern of the patriot is, on the contrary, the integration of the
movement of the masses into the nation. But even this kind of language
is not Marxist. It is the particular attribute of Marxism not to distinguish
the means from the end, and, in principle, no system of political thought
is less hypocritical and less Machiavellian. It is not a question of abusing
the patriots' good faith and leading them where they do not wish to go.
Not the Marxist but history transforms nationalist feeling into the will to
revolution. It is a question of making the patriots see (and events as well as
Marxists undertake to do this) that in a weakened country like France,
which the movement of history has reduced to a second-rate power, a certain political and economic independence is possible only through a dangerous oscillation or within the framework of a Socialist Confederation of
States which has no chance of becoming a reality except through revolution. To be a Marxist is not to renounce all differences, to give up one's
identity as a Frenchman, a native of Tours or Paris, or to forego individuality in order to blend into the world proletariat. It is indeed to become
part of the universal, but without ceasing to be what we are. Even in a
Marxist perspective the world proletariat is not a revolutionary factor so
long as it only exists objectively, in economic analysis. It will become such
a factor when it realizes that it is a world proletariat, and this will only
happen through the concerted pressure or a meeting at the crossroads of
actual proletarians, such as they exist in the different countries, and not

through an ascetic internationalism wherein each of them loses his most compelling reasons for being a Marxist.

* * *

To sum it all up, we have learned history, and we claim that it must not be forgotten. But are we not here the dupes of our emotions? If, ten years hence, we reread these pages and so many others, what will we think of them? We do not want this year of 1945 to become just another year among many. A man who has lost a son or a woman he loved does not want to live beyond that loss. He leaves the house in the state it was in. The familiar objects upon the table, the clothes in the closet mark an empty place in the world. He converses with the absent person, he changes nothing in his life, and every day his actions, like an incantation, bring this ever more evanescent shadow back to life. The day will come, however, when the meaning of these books and these clothes will change: once the books were new, and now they are yellow with age; once the clothes were wearable, and now they are out of style and shabby. To keep them any longer would not be to make the dead person live on; quite the opposite, they date his death all the *more* cruelly. In the same way there will come a moment when what we wish to preserve of the friends who were tortured and shot is not our last image of them, what they were in those four years and in that feverish summer, but a timeless memory in which the things they did mingle with what they might have done, given the direction of their lives. We have not of course gotten to this point, but since what concerns us here is writing, not recounting our griefs, should we not go beyond our feelings to find what they may contain of durable truth?

The war was not over before everything had already begun to change—not only because of man's inconstancy but also because of an inner necessity. Unity had been easy during the Resistance, because relationships were almost always man-to-man. Over against the German army or the Vichy government, where social generality ruled, as it does in all machines of state, the Resistance offered the rare phenomenon of historical action which remained personal. The psychological and moral elements of political action were almost the only ones to appear here, which is why intellectuals least inclined to politics were to be seen in the Resistance. The Resistance was a unique experience for them, and they wanted to preserve its spirit in the new French politics because this experience broke away from the famous dilemma of being and doing, which confronts all intellectuals in the face of action. This was the source of that *happiness* through danger which we observed in some of our comrades, usually so tormented. It is only too obvious that this balance between action

and personal life was intimately bound up with the conditions of clandestine actions and could not survive it. And in this sense it must be said that
the Resistance experience, by making us believe that politics is a relationship between man and man or between consciousnesses, fostered our illusions of 1939 and masked the truth of the incredible power of history
which the Occupation taught us in another connection. We have returned
to the time of *institutions*. The distance between the laws and those to whom
they apply is once more apparent; once again one legislates for X; and
once again the good will of some resumes its class features which make it
unrecognizable to others. We must again worry about the consequences
of what we say, weighing the objective meaning of every word, with no
hope of convincing by the sheer force of truth. This is what we did during
the Occupation when we had to avoid any public gesture which might
have "played into the hands of the occupying forces." But among friends
at that time we had a freedom to criticize, which we have already lost. Are
we now going to subject our words and gestures to that completely exterior rule—which so aroused Péguy's indignation—which enjoins us not
to "play into the hands" of the reactionaries, the Communists, or the government? For four years we witnessed the abrogation of personal life.
There is nothing more to *learn* from that, and if politics is definitely hell,
we have no choice but to give it up. Indeed, this is why, on the eve of another war, the founders of the N.R.F invited authors and public to abandon the values and the attitudes of the war. They wanted to demobilize
consciousness, to return to purely aesthetic problems, to disengage themselves from history. . . .

Assuredly—and this is the point we want to make—those five years
have not taught us to think ill of what we once judged to be good, and in
the eyes of conscience it is still absurd to hide a truth because it harms
one's country, to kill a man because he lives on the other side of the river,
to treat another person as a means rather than an end. We were not wrong,
in 1939, to want liberty, truth, happiness, and transparent relations among
men, and we are not now abandoning humanism. The war and the Occupation only taught us that values remain nominal and indeed have no
value without an economic and political infrastructure to make them
participate in existence. What is more, in actual history values are only
another way of designating human relationships, as these become established according to a man's mode of work, the nature of his loves, and the
shape of his hopes; in brief, according to the way he lives with others. It is
a question not of giving up our values of 1939 but of realizing them. Imitating the tyrants is not the question, and, insofar as such imitation was
necessary, it is precisely for having forced us to it that we cannot forgive
them. It is doubtful whether tyranny can ever be eliminated from political

life, whether the State could wither away and men's political or social relations could ever be reintegrated into their human relationships. But even if we have no guarantee that these goals will ever be realized, we can at least see very clearly the absurdity of an anachronistic tyranny like anti-Semitism and of a reactionary expedient like Fascism. And this is enough to make us want to destroy them roots and branch and to push things forward in the direction of effective liberty. This political task is not incompatible with any cultural value or literary task, if literature and culture are defined as the progressive awareness of our multiple relationships with other people and the world, rather than as extramundane techniques. *If all truths are told, none will have to be hidden.* In man's coexistence with man, of which these years have made us aware, morals, doctrines, thoughts and customs, laws, works, and words all express each other; everything signifies everything. And outside this unique fulguration of existence there is nothing.

June 1945

3

What Is Phenomenology?

What is phenomenology? It may seem strange that this question has still to be asked half a century after the first works of Husserl. The fact remains that it has by no means been answered. Phenomenology is the study of essences; and according to it, all problems amount to finding definitions of essences: the essence of perception, or the essence of consciousness, for example. But phenomenology is also a philosophy which puts essences back into existence, and does not expect to arrive at an understanding of man and the world from any starting point other than that of their "facticity." It is a transcendental philosophy which puts the assertions arising out of the natural attitude in suspense, the better to understand them; but it is also a philosophy for which the world is always "already there" before reflection begins—as an inalienable presence; and all its efforts are concentrated upon rediscovering this naive contact with the world, and endowing that contact with a philosophical status. It is the search for a philosophy which shall be a "rigorous science," but it also offers an account of "lived" space, "lived" time, and the "lived" world. It tries to give a direct description of our experience as it is, without taking account of its psychological genesis and the causal explanations which the scientist, the historian, or the sociologist may be able to provide. And yet Husserl in his last works mentions a "genetic phenomenology,"[1] and even a "constructive phenomenology."[2] Will we do away with these contradictions by making a distinction between Husserl's and Heidegger's phenomenologies? But the whole of *Being and Time* springs from an indication given by Husserl and amounts to no more than an explicit account of the "natürlicher Weltbegriff" or the "Lebenswelt" which Husserl, toward the end of his life, identified as the primary theme of phenomenology, with the result that the contradiction reappears in Husserl's own philosophy. The reader pressed for time will be inclined to give up the idea of covering a doctrine which has said everything, and will wonder whether a philosophy which cannot define its scope deserves all the discussion which has gone on around it, and whether he is not faced rather by a myth or a fashion.

Even if this were the case, there would still be a need to understand the prestige of the myth and the origin of the fashion, and philosophical seriousness will translate this situation by saying that *phenomenology can be practiced and identified as a manner or style of thinking, that it existed as a move-*

ment before arriving at complete consciousness of itself as a philosophy. It has been long on the way, and its disciples find it everywhere, certainly in Hegel and Kierkegaard, but equally in Marx, Nietzsche, and Freud. A philological commentary on the texts would yield nothing; we find in texts only what we put into them, and if ever any kind of history has called forth our interpretation, it is the history of philosophy. It is in ourselves that we shall find the unity of phenomenology and its true sense. It is less a question of counting up quotations than of determining and objectifying this *phenomenology for ourselves* which has given a number of our contemporaries, while reading Husserl or Heidegger, the feeling less of encountering a new philosophy than of recognizing what they were waiting for. Phenomenology is accessible only through a phenomenological method. Let us, therefore, try systematically to tie together the celebrated phenomenological themes as they have tied themselves together spontaneously in life. Perhaps we shall then understand why phenomenology has for so long remained in a state of being at the beginning, in the state of being a problem and a vow.

* * *

What is at issue is to describe and not to explain or analyze. This first directive that Husserl gave to phenomenology, in its state of being at the beginning—to be a "descriptive psychology" or to return to the "things themselves"—is from the start a disavowal of science. I am not the result or the intersection of numerous causal agencies which determine my bodily or psychological makeup. I cannot conceive myself as a part of the world, as the simple object of biology, psychology, and sociology, nor shut myself up within the universe of science. All of what I know of the world, even through science, I know on the basis of a view, which is mine, or on the basis of an experience of the world without which the symbols of science would be meaningless. The whole universe of science is constructed upon the lived world, and if we want to conceive science itself with rigor, to appreciate exactly its sense and scope, we must reawaken first this experience of the world of which science is the second-order expression. Science has not and never will have the same ontological sense as the perceived world, for the simple reason that it is a determination or an explanation of that world. I am not a "living being" or even a "human," or even "a consciousness," with all the characteristics which zoology, social anatomy, or inductive psychology recognize in these products of nature or history—I am the absolute source, my existence does not come from my antecedents, from my physical and social environment; it goes toward them and sustains them. It is me who makes exist for myself (and therefore exist in the sole sense that the word can have for me) the tradition that I choose to take up or this horizon whose distance from me would collapse—since the distance does not belong to the horizon as one of its properties—if I were not there to traverse it with my gaze. Scientific views, according to which I am a moment of the world, are always naive and hypocritical, because they take for granted, without mentioning it, this other view, that of consciousness, through which first a world forms itself round me and begins to exist for me. To return to the things themselves is to return to that world which precedes knowledge, of which knowledge always *speaks,* and in relation to which scientific determination is abstract, significative, and dependent, as is geography in relation to the countryside in which we have learnt first what a forest, a prairie, or a river is.

This movement is absolutely distinct from the idealist return to consciousness, and the demand for a pure description excludes the procedure of reflective analysis as well as that of scientific explanation. Descartes and particularly Kant *detached* the subject, or consciousness, by showing that I could not possibly apprehend anything as existing unless I first experienced myself as existing in the act of apprehending it. They presented consciousness, the absolute certainty of my existence for myself, as the condition without which there would be nothing at all and the act of relating as the foundation of relatedness. Undoubtedly, the act of relating is nothing without the spectacle of the world that it relates. The unity of consciousness in Kant is precisely contemporaneous with the unity of the world, and in Descartes methodical doubt makes us lose nothing, since the whole world, at least insofar as we experience it, is reintegrated into the cogito, certain with it, and merely affected with the index of "thought of. . . ." But the relations between subject and world are not rigorously bilateral: if they were, the certainty of the world would be immediately, in Descartes, given with that of the cogito, and Kant would not have talked about his "Copernican revolution." Starting from our experience of the world, reflective analysis goes back to the subject as to a condition of possibility distinct from the experience, and makes the universal synthesis be seen as that without which there would be no world. To this extent it ceases to adhere to our experience, it substitutes a reconstruction for an account. Thereby we understand why Husserl had been able to scold Kant for adopting a "psychologism of the faculties of the soul,"[3] and had been able to oppose, to a noetic analysis which makes the world rest on the synthesizing activity of the subject, his "*noematic reflection*" which remains within the object and explicates the primordial unity of the object instead of engendering it.

The world is there before any analysis that I can make of it, and it would be artificial to make it derive from a series of syntheses which relate the sensations, then the perspectival aspects of the object, while both are precisely products of analysis and must not have been realized before the analysis. Reflective analysis believes that it can follow, in the reverse direction, the path of a prior constitution and join back up with, in the "inner man," to use Saint Augustine's expression, a constituting power which has always been that inner man. Thus reflection is carried off by itself and places itself back in an impregnable subjectivity, this side of being and time. But here we have a naivete, or, if you prefer, an incomplete reflection which loses sight of its own beginning. When I begin to reflect, my reflection is a reflection upon an unreflected; my reflection cannot be unaware of itself as an event, and so it appears to itself as a genuine creation, as a structural change of consciousness, and yet it has to recognize, this side of its own operations, the world which is given to the subject because the subject is given to itself. The real is to be described, not constructed or constituted. That means that I cannot assimilate perception to the syntheses which belong to the order of judgment, of acts, or of predication. At each moment, my perceptual field is filled with reflections, noises, and fleeting tactile impressions which I cannot relate precisely to the perceived context, and yet which I "place" immediately in the world, without ever confusing them with my daydreams. At each instant also I dream around things. I imagine objects or people whose presence here is not incompatible with the context, and yet they are not mixed in with the world: they are ahead of the world, upon the stage of the imaginary. If the reality of my perception were founded only on the intrinsic coherence of "representations," it should always be hesitant and, delivered over to my conjectures on probabilities, I should at each moment undo illusory syntheses and reintegrate into the real the aberrant phenomena which I had excluded in the first place. But this does not happen. The real is a closely woven fabric. It does not await our judgment before incorporating the most surprising phenomena, or before rejecting the most plausible figments of our imagination. Perception is not a science of the world, it is not even an act, a deliberate taking up of a position; it is the background from which all acts stand out and it is presupposed by them. The world is not an object such that I have in my possession its law of constitution; it is the natural milieu and the field of all my thoughts and all my explicit perceptions. Truth does not "inhabit" merely "the inner man,"[4] or rather, there is no inner man; man is in the world, and it is in the world that he knows himself. When I return to myself starting from the dogmatism of common sense or from the dogmatism of science, I find, not a focal point of intrinsic truth, but a subject vowed to the world.

* * *

Thereby we see the true sense of the famous phenomenological reduction. Undoubtedly, there is no question which Husserl himself has spent more time trying to make understood—also no question to which he has more often returned, since the "problematic of reduction" occupies an important place in his unpublished texts. For a long time, and even in recent texts, the reduction is presented as the return to a transcendental consciousness before which the world is spread out in an absolute transparency, animated through and through by a series of apperceptions which it is the philosopher's task to reconstitute on the basis of their result. Thus my sensation of redness is *apperceived as* the manifestation of a certain sensed redness, this as the manifestation of a red surface, which is the manifestation of a piece of red cardboard, and this finally is the manifestation or profile of a red thing, of this book. This would be therefore the apprehension of a certain *hylē* as signifying a phenomenon of a higher degree, the *Sinn-gebung*, the active operation of meaning which would define consciousness, and the world would be nothing but the "world-meaning," the phenomenological reduction would be idealistic, in the sense of a transcendental idealism. This transcendental idealism treats the world as a unity of validity that is indivisible between Peter and Paul, a unity of validity in which their perspectives intersect, and which makes "Peter's consciousness" and "Paul's consciousness" communicate, because the perception of the world "by Peter" is not Peter's doing any more than its perception "by Paul" is Paul's doing, but in each of them it is the doing of pre-personal consciousnesses, whose communication raises no problem, since it is demanded by the very definition of consciousness, of sense, of truth. Insofar as I am a consciousness, that is, insofar as something makes sense for me, I am neither here nor there, neither Peter nor Paul; I am in no way distinguishable from an "other" consciousness, since we are all immediate presences to the world and since the world is, by definition, unique, being the system of truths. A logically consistent transcendental idealism rids the world of its opacity and its transcendence. The world is precisely that thing of which we form a representation, not as humans or as empirical subjects, but insofar as we are all one sole light and insofar as we participate in the One without dividing it. Reflexive analysis knows nothing of the problem of the other, just as it knows nothing of the problem of the world, because it makes appear in me, with the first glimmer of consciousness, the power to go to an in principle universal truth, and because the other, being equally without hecceity, without place and without body, the Alter and the Ego are one and the same in the true world which is the relation of minds. There is no difficulty in understanding how I can conceive the Other, because the I and consequently the Other are not taken into the tissue of phenomena and deserve not to exist. There is nothing hidden behind these faces or these gestures, no countryside to which I have no access, just a little shadow which exists only by means of the light. For Husserl, on the contrary, we know that there is a problem of others and the alter ego is a paradox. If the other is truly for itself, beyond his being for me, and if we are for each other and not both for God, it is necessary that we appear to one another. He must and I must have an exterior, and there must be, besides the perspective of the For Itself—my view of myself and the view of the other on himself—a perspective of the For Others—my view of Others and the view of the Others of me. Of course, these two perspectives, in each one of us, cannot be simply juxtaposed, *for in that case it is not I that the other would see, nor he that I would see.* I must be my exterior, and the body of the other must be himself. This paradox and this dialectic of the Ego and the Alter are possible only if the Ego and the Alter Ego are defined by their situation and are not freed from all inherence; that is, if philosophy does not culminate in a return to the self, and that I discover by reflection not only my presence to myself, but also the possibility of an "alien spectator"; that is, again, if, at the very moment when I experience my existence, and up as far as this extreme point of the reflection, I still lack this absolute destiny which makes me exist outside of time, and I discover within myself a kind of internal weakness which stops me from being absolutely individualized and exposes me to the gaze of others as one human among humans or at least as one consciousness among consciousnesses. Hitherto the cogito depreciated the perception of others, teaching me that the I is accessible only to itself, since it defined *me* by the thought which I have of myself, and which clearly I am alone in having, at least in this ultimate sense. For the "other" to be more than an empty word, it is necessary that my existence is never reduced to the consciousness that I have of existing. It is necessary that it envelop also the consciousness that *one* can have of it and therefore my incarnation in some nature and the possibility, at least, of a historical situation. The cogito must discover me in a situation, and it is on this condition alone that transcendental subjectivity will be able, as Husserl says,[5] *to be* an intersubjectivity. As a meditating Ego, I can clearly distinguish from myself the world and things, since I certainly do not exist in the way in which things exist. I must even set aside from myself my body understood as a thing among things, as a collection of physico-chemical processes. But even if the *cogitatio*, which I thus discover, is without location in objective time and space, it is not without place in the phenomenological world. The world, which I distinguished from myself as the collection of things or of processes linked by causal relationships, I rediscover "in me" as the permanent horizon of all my *cogitationes* and as a dimension in re-

(SEE BUTLER, "GIVING AN ACCOUNT OF ONESELF" AS A MORAL PHILOSOPHY BASED ON THIS SUPPOSITION / CONCESSION)

lation to which I am constantly situating myself. The genuine cogito does not define the existence of the subject by the thought he has of existing, and does not convert the certainty of the world into the certainty of the thought about the world, and finally it does not replace the world itself by the meaning world. On the contrary, it recognizes my thought itself as an inalienable fact, and it eliminates any kind of idealism by discovering me as "being-in-the-world."

It is because we are through and through relation to the world that, for us, the only way to notice this fact is to suspend this movement, to refuse it our complicity (to gaze at it *ohne mitzumachen,* as Husserl often says), or yet again, to put it "out of play." Not because we reject the certainties of common sense and the natural attitude—they are, on the contrary, the constant theme of philosophy—but because, precisely as the presupposed basis of all thought, they are "obvious," and go unnoticed, and because, in order to arouse them and to make them appear, we have to abstain from them for a moment. The best formulation of the reduction is probably that given by Eugen Fink, Husserl's assistant, when he spoke of "wonder" in the face of the world.[6] Reflection does not withdraw from the world toward the unity of consciousness as the foundation of the world; it steps back to see the transcendencies spring forth; it slackens the intentional threads which attach us to the world in order to make them appear; it alone is consciousness of the world because it reveals that world as strange and paradoxical. Husserl's transcendental is not Kant's and Husserl objects to Kant's philosophy as being "worldly," because it *makes use* of our relation to the world, which is the motive force of the transcendental deduction, and makes the world immanent to the subject, instead of *being filled with wonder* at it and conceiving the subject as transcendence toward the world. All the misunderstandings with his interpreters, with the existentialist "dissidents" and finally with himself, have arisen from the fact that in order to see the world and grasp it as paradoxical, we must break with our familiarity with it and that from this break we can learn nothing but the unmotivated springing forth of the world. The most important lesson which the reduction teaches us is the impossibility of a complete reduction. This is why Husserl always questions himself again and again concerning the possibility of the reduction. If we were absolute mind, the reduction would not be problematic. But since, on the contrary, we are in the world, since even our reflections are carried out in the temporal flux on to which we are trying to seize (since they *sich einströmen,* as Husserl says), there is no thought which embraces all our thought. The philosopher, as the unpublished works declare, is a perpetual beginner. That means that the philosopher holds nothing as an acquisition that humans or scientists believe they know. It means also that philosophy itself must not hold itself as an acquisition within what it has been able to say as true. It means that philosophy is an ever-renewed experience of its own beginning, that it consists wholly in the description of this beginning, and finally that radical reflection amounts to a consciousness of its own dependence on an unreflective life which is its initial, constant, and final situation. Far from being, as has been thought, the formula of an idealistic philosophy, the phenomenological reduction is the formula of an existential philosophy: Heidegger's "being-in-the-world" appears only against the background of the phenomenological reduction.

* * *

A misunderstanding of a similar kind confuses the notion of "essences" in Husserl. Every reduction, says Husserl, as well as being transcendental is necessarily eidetic. This means that we cannot subject our perception of the world to the philosophical gaze without ceasing to be identified with this thesis of the world, with this interest in it which defines us, without stepping back from our engagement in order to make it itself appear as a spectacle, without passing from the *fact* of our existence to the *nature* of our existence, from the *Dasein* to the *Wesen*. But it is clear that the essence is here not the end, but a means, that our actual engagement in the world is precisely that which it is necessary to understand and to lead to the concept and polarize all our conceptual determinations. The necessity of passing by way of essences does not mean that philosophy takes them as its objective, but, on the contrary, that our existence is too tightly held in the world in order to know itself as such at the moment of its being thrown into the world, and that it needs the field of ideality in order to know and to conquer its facticity. The Vienna Circle, as it is well known, lays it down once and for all that we have relations only with meanings. For example, "consciousness" is not for the Vienna Circle identifiable with what we are. It is a complex meaning which has developed late in time, which we should use only with circumspection and only after having explicated the many meanings which have contributed to determine it over the course of the word's semantic evolution. Logical positivism of this kind is the antithesis of Husserl's thought. Whatever the shifts of sense may be which have ultimately brought us, as a linguistic acquisition, the word and the concept of consciousness, we have a direct means of access to what it designates. For we have the experience of ourselves, of that consciousness which we are, and it is on the basis of this experience that all meanings of language are to be measured, and precisely through it that language means something for us. "It is that as yet mute experience . . . which we are concerned to lead to the pure expression of its own sense."[7] Husserl's

essences must bring back with them all the living relationships of experience, as the fisherman's net draws up from the depths of the ocean quiv-
ering fish and seaweed. One must not say therefore with Jean Wahl that
"Husserl separates essences from existence."[8] The separated essences are
those of language. It is the function of language to make essences exist in
a state of separation which is, truly, only apparent, since through language
they still rest upon the pre-predicative life of consciousness. In the silence
of originary consciousness, we see appearing not only what words mean,
but also what the things mean, the kernel of primary meaning round
which the acts of naming and expression are organized.

Seeking the essence of consciousness will therefore not consist in developing the *Wortbedeutung* of consciousness and escaping from existence
into the universe of things said; it will consist in rediscovering this actual
presence of me to myself, the fact of my consciousness which is what the
word and the concept of consciousness finally mean. Seeking the world's
essence is not to seek what it is as an idea once we have reduced it to a
theme of discourse; it is to seek what it is in fact for us before all themati-
zation. Sensationalism "reduces" the world by noting that after all we never
experience anything but states of ourselves. Transcendental idealism too
"reduces" the world since, if it renders the world certain, it does so by
regarding it as thought or consciousness of the world, and as the mere correlative of our knowledge, with the result that it becomes immanent to
consciousness and the aseity of things is thereby suppressed. The eidetic
reduction is, on the contrary, the resolution to make the world appear as
it is before any turning back on ourselves, it is the ambition to make reflection measure up to the unreflective life of consciousness. I aim at and
I perceive a world. If I said, with sensationalism, that there are only "states
of consciousness," and if I sought to distinguish my perceptions from my
dreams by means of "criteria," I would miss the phenomenon of the world.
For if I am able to talk about "dreams" and "reality," to question myself
about the distinction between imaginary and real, and cast doubt upon
the "real," this is because this distinction is already made by me before any
analysis. It is because I have an experience of the real as of the imaginary,
and the problem is then not of investigating how critical thought can provide for itself secondary equivalents of this distinction, but of making explicit our primordial knowledge of the "real," of describing the perception of the world as that which founds forever our idea of truth. We must
not, therefore, wonder whether we perceive a world truly, we must instead
say: the world is what we perceive. In more general terms, we must not wonder whether our self-evident truths are really truths, or whether, through
some perversity of our minds, that which is self-evident for us would not
be illusory in relation to some truth in itself. For if we speak of illusion, it

is because we have recognized illusions, and we have been able to do that only in the name of some perception which, in the same moment, gave assurance of its own truth. It follows that doubt, or the fear of being mistaken, asserts at the same time our power of unmasking error and could never finally uproot us from truth. We are in the truth and evidence is "the experience of truth."[9] To seek the essence of perception is to declare that perception is not presumed true, but defined for us as access to truth. So, if I now wanted, with idealism, to found this factual evidence, this irresistible belief, upon an absolute evidence, that is, upon the absolute clarity of my thoughts for me; if I wanted to rediscover in myself a naturizing thought which makes the inner framework of the world or illuminate it through and through, I would be once more unfaithful to my experience of the world, and I would be seeking what makes the experience possible instead of seeking what it is.[10] The evidence of perception is not adequate thought or apodeictic evidence.[11] The world is not what I think, but what I live. I am open to the world, I communicate indubitably with it, but I do not possess it; it is inexhaustible. "There is a world," or rather "There is the world"; I can never completely account for this constant thesis of my life. This facticity of the world is what makes the *Weltlichkeit der Welt*, which makes it that the world is world, just as the facticity of the cogito is not an imperfection in itself, but on the contrary what makes me certain of my existence. The eidetic method is the method of a phenomenological positivism which founds the possible on the real.

(see p. 57)

* * *

We can now come to its notion of intentionality, too often cited as the main discovery of phenomenology, whereas it is understandable only through the reduction. "All consciousness is consciousness of something"; there is nothing new in that. Kant showed, in the *Refutation of Idealism,* that inner perception is impossible without outer perception, that the world, as the connection of phenomena, is anticipated in the consciousness of my unity, and is the means whereby I realize myself as consciousness. What distinguishes intentionality from the Kantian relation to a possible object is that the unity of the world, before being posited by knowledge in a deliberate act of identification, is "lived" as ready-made or already there. Kant himself shows in the *Critique of Judgment* that there exists a unity of the imagination and the understanding and a unity of subjects *before the object,* and that, in experiencing the beautiful, for example, I am aware of a harmony between sensation and concept, between myself and others, which is itself without any concept. Here the subject is no longer the universal thinker of a system of objects rigorously interrelated, the positing power who subjects the manifold to the law of the understanding; if he must be able to form a world, he discovers and appreciates himself as a nature spontaneously in harmony with the law of the understanding. But, if there is a nature of the subject, then the hidden art of the imagination must condition the categorical activity. It is no longer merely the aesthetic judgment, but knowledge too which rests upon this art, an art which forms the basis of the unity of consciousness and of consciousnesses. Husserl takes up the *Critique of Judgment* when he talks about a teleology of consciousness. It is not a matter of duplicating human consciousness with some absolute thought which, from outside, would assign to it its ends. It is a question of recognizing consciousness itself as a project of the world, destined for a world which it neither embraces nor possesses, but toward which it is perpetually directed—and the world as this pre-objective individual whose imperious unity prescribes to knowledge its goal. This is why Husserl distinguishes between act-intentionality, which is that of our judgments and of our voluntarily taking up positions—the only intentionality discussed in the *Critique of Pure Reason*—and operative intentionality (*fungierende Intentionalität*), that which produces the natural and pre-predicative unity of the world and of our life, which appears in our desires, our evaluations, and in the landscape more clearly than in objective knowledge, and which furnishes the text which our knowledge seeks to translate into exact language. Our relationship to the world, as it is untiringly enunciated within us, is not a thing which can be any further clarified by analysis; philosophy can only place it once more before our gaze and offer it to our observation.

Through this broadened notion of intentionality, phenomenological "understanding" is distinguished from classical "intellection," which is limited to "true and immutable natures," and so phenomenology can become a phenomenology of genesis. Whether we are concerned with a thing perceived, a historical event, or a doctrine, to "understand" is to take in the total intention—not only what these things are for representation, the "properties" of the thing perceived, the mass of "historical facts," the "ideas" introduced by the doctrine—but the unique way of existing which is expressed in the properties of the pebble, the glass, or the piece of wax, in all the facts of a revolution, in all the thoughts of a philosopher. It is a matter, in the case of each civilization, of finding the Idea in the Hegelian sense, that is, not a law of the physico-mathematical type, discoverable by objective thought, but that formula which sums up some unique manner of behavior toward others, toward Nature, time, and death: a certain way of putting the world into a form which the historian must be capable of seizing upon and making his own. These are the *dimensions* of history. In relation to them, there is not a human word, not a gesture, even habitual or distracted, which does not have a meaning. I believe that tiredness is making me be quiet, some minister thought he said only what the circumstances called for, and then my silence or his words become meaningful, because my tiredness or his falling back upon a ready-made formula are not accidental, for they express a certain lack of interest, and still therefore a certain position-taking in relation to the situation. When an event is considered at close quarters, at the moment when it is lived through, everything seems subject to chance: one man's ambition, some lucky encounter, some local circumstance or other appears to have been decisive. But chance happenings offset each other, and then this dust of facts coalesces, outlines a certain way of taking a position in relation to the human situation, an *event* whose contours are defined and about which we can speak. Should the starting point for the understanding of history be ideology, or politics, or religion, or economics? Should we try to understand a doctrine from its manifest content, or from the psychology of the author and from the events of his life? We must seek an understanding from all these angles simultaneously, everything has a sense, and we rediscover this same ontological structure under all relationships. All these views are true on the condition that we do not isolate them, that we delve deeply into history and reach the unique kernel of existential meaning which makes itself explicit in each perspective. It is true, as Marx says, that history does not walk on its head, but it is also true that it does not think with its feet. Or rather, we have to concern ourselves neither with its "head" nor with its "feet," but with its body. All economic and psychological explanations of a doctrine are true, since the thinker never thinks from any starting point but the one that he is. The very reflection on a doctrine will be complete only if it succeeds in linking up with the doctrine's history and the external explanations of it, and in putting back the causes and the sense of the doctrine in an existential structure. There is, as Husserl says, a "genesis of meaning" (*Sinngenesis*)[12] which alone, in the last analysis, teaches us what the doctrine "means." Like understanding, critique will have to be pursued at all levels, and naturally, we will not be able to content ourselves, for the refutation of a doctrine, with reconnecting it to some accidental event in the author's life: it means beyond that, and there is no pure accident in existence or in coexistence, since both assimilate random events and make them rational. Finally, as it is indivisible in the present, history is indivisible in its sequences. In regard to its fundamental dimensions, all the historical periods appear as manifestations of a single existence or as episodes in a single drama—without our knowing whether it has an ending. Because we are in the world, we are *condemned to the sense,* and we cannot do or say anything without its acquiring a name in history.

* * *

Undoubtedly, the most important acquisition of phenomenology is to have united extreme subjectivism and extreme objectivism in its notion of the world or of rationality. Rationality is precisely proportioned to the experiences in which it is disclosed. There is rationality, that is: perspectives intersect, perceptions confirm each other, a sense appears. But it must not be posited apart, transformed into absolute Spirit, or into a world in the realist sense. The phenomenological world is not pure being, but the sense which shows through at the intersection of my experiences, and at the intersection of my experiences and those of others, by their engaging each other like gears—this world is therefore inseparable from the subjectivity and from the intersubjectivity which find their unity through the taking up of my past experiences in my present experiences, the taking up of the other's experience in my own. For the first time, the philosopher's meditation is conscious enough in order not to realize its own results, and prior to the meditation, in the world. The philosopher tries to conceive the world, others, and himself and to conceive their relations. But the meditating Ego, the "impartial spectator" (*uninteressierter Zuschauer*) [13] does not rediscover an already given rationality, they "establish themselves," [14] and establish it by an act of initiative which has no guarantee in being and whose right rests entirely on the actual power which it gives us of taking up our own history. The phenomenological world is not the bringing to explicit expression of a prior being, but the foundation of being. Philosophy is not the reflection of a prior truth, but, like art, the realization of a truth. One may well ask how this realization is *possible*, and if it does not join up with, in things, a preexisting Reason. But the sole Logos that preexists is the world itself, and the philosophy which brings it into manifest existence does not begin by being *possible;* it is actual or real like the world of which it is a part, and no explanatory hypothesis is clearer than the act whereby we take up this unfinished world in an effort to totalize it and conceive it. Rationality is not a *problem.* There is behind it no unknown that we have to determine deductively or prove inductively on the basis of it. We are present in each instant at this prodigy of the connection of experiences, and no one knows better than we do how it is made, since we are this knot of relations. The world and reason are not problematical. Let us say, if we wish, that they are mysterious, but this mystery defines them: there can be no question of dispelling it by some "solution," it is on the hither side of all solutions. True philosophy consists in relearning to see the world, and in this sense a historical account can signify the world with as much "depth" as a philosophical treatise. We take our fate in our hands, we become responsible for our history through reflection, but equally by a decision on which we stake our life, and in both cases what is involved is a violent act which verifies itself by being performed.

Phenomenology, as a disclosure of the world, rests on itself, or rather founds itself.[15] All branches of knowledge are sustained by a "soil" of postulates and finally by our communication with the world as the primary establishment of rationality. Philosophy, as radical reflection, deprives itself, in principle, of this resource. As, however, it too is in history, it too exploits the world and constituted reason. It will therefore be necessary that it address to itself this interrogation that it addresses to all branches of knowledge. It will therefore do itself over indefinitely; it will be, as Husserl says, a dialogue or an infinite mediation, and, insofar as it remains faithful to its intention, it will never know where it is going. The unfinished nature of phenomenology and the inchoative allure which has surrounded it are not to be taken as a sign of failure; they were inevitable because phenomenology's task was to reveal the mystery of the world and of reason.[16] If phenomenology was a movement before becoming a doctrine or a philosophical system, this was attributable neither to accident nor to fraud. It is as painstaking as the works of Balzac, Proust, Valéry, or Cézanne—by reason of the same kind of attentiveness and wonder, the same demand for awareness, the same will to seize the sense of the world or of history in the nascent state. In this way it merges into the effort of modern thought.

4

Cézanne's Doubt

It took him one hundred working sessions for a still life, one hundred fifty sittings for a portrait. What we call his work was, for him, only the attempt and the approach of his painting. In September of 1906, at the age of sixty-seven—one month before his death—he wrote: "I was in such a state of mental agitation, in such great confusion that for a time I feared my weak reason would not survive. . . . Now it seems I am better and that I see more clearly the direction my studies are taking. Will I ever arrive at the goal, so intensely sought and so long pursued? I am still working from nature, and it seems to me I am making slow progress." Painting was his world and his mode of existence. He worked alone, without students, without admiration from his family, without encouragement from the critics. He painted on the afternoon of the day his mother died. In 1870 he was painting at L'Estaque while the police were after him for dodging the draft. And still he had moments of doubt about this vocation. As he grew old, he wondered whether the novelty of his painting might not come from trouble with his eyes, whether his whole life had not been based upon an accident of his body. The hesitation or muddle-headedness of his contemporaries equaled this strain and self-doubt. "The painting of a drunken privy cleaner," said a critic in 1905. Even today, C. Mauclair finds Cézanne's admissions of powerlessness an argument against him. Meanwhile, Cézanne's paintings have spread throughout the world. Why so much uncertainty, so much labor, so many failures, and, suddenly, the greatest success?

Zola, Cézanne's friend from childhood, was the first to find genius in him and the first to speak of him as a "genius gone wrong." An observer of Cézanne's life such as Zola was, more concerned with his character than with the sense of his painting, might well consider it a manifestation of ill health.

For as far back as 1852, upon entering the Collège Bourbon at Aix, Cézanne worried his friends with his fits of temper and depression. Seven years later, having decided to become an artist, he doubted his talent and did not dare to ask his father—a hatter and later a banker—to send him to Paris. Zola's letters reproach him for his instability, his weakness, and his indecision. When finally he came to Paris, he wrote: "The only thing I have changed is my location: my ennui has followed me." He could not tolerate discussions, because they wore him out and he could never give his reasoning. His nature was basically anxious. Thinking that he would die young, he made his will at the age of forty-two; at forty-six he was for six months the victim of a violent, tormented, overwhelming passion of which no one knows the outcome and to which he would never refer. At fifty-one he withdrew to Aix, in order to find the nature best suited to his genius but where also he returned to the milieu of his childhood, his mother and his sister. After the death of his mother, Cézanne turned to his son for support. "Life is terrifying," he would often say. Religion, which he then set about practicing for the first time, began for him in the fear of life and the fear of death. "It is fear," he explained to a friend; "I feel I will be on earth for another four days—what then? I believe in life after death, and I don't want to risk roasting *in aeternum*." Although his religion later deepened, its original motivation was the need to put his life in order and be relieved of it. He became more and more timid, mistrustful, and sensitive. Occasionally he would visit Paris, but when he ran into friends he would motion to them from a distance not to approach him. In 1903, after his pictures had begun to sell in Paris at twice the price of Monet's and when young men like Joachim Gasquet and Émile Bernard came to see him and ask him questions, he relaxed a little. But his fits of anger continued. In Aix a child once hit him as he passed by; after that he could not bear any contact. One day when Cézanne was quite old, Émile Bernard steadied him as he stumbled. Cézanne flew into a rage. He could be heard striding around his studio and shouting that he wouldn't let anybody "get his hooks into me." Because of these "hooks" he pushed women who could have modeled for him out of his studio, priests, whom he called "pests," out of his life, and Émile Bernard's theories out of his mind, when they became too insistent.

This loss of flexible human contact; this inability to master new situations; this flight into established habits, in a milieu which presented no problems; this rigid opposition between theory and practice, between the "hook" and the freedom of a recluse—all these symptoms permit one to speak of a morbid constitution and more precisely, as, for example, in the case of El Greco, of schizothymia. The notion of painting "from nature" could be said to arise from the same weakness. His extremely close attention to nature and to color, the inhuman character of his paintings (he said that a face should be painted as an object), his devotion to the visible world: all of these would then only represent a flight from the human world, the alienation of his humanity.

These conjectures nevertheless do not give any idea of the positive sense of his work; one cannot thereby conclude that his painting is a phenomenon of decadence and of what Nietzsche called "impoverished" life or that it has nothing to say to the educated person. Zola's and Émile

Bernard's belief in Cézanne's failure probably arise from their having put too much emphasis on psychology and their personal knowledge of Cézanne. It is nonetheless possible that Cézanne conceived a form of art which, while occasioned by his nervous condition, is valid for everyone. Left to himself, he was able to look at nature as only a human being knows how to do it. The sense of his work cannot be determined from his life.

This sense will not become any clearer in the light of art history—that is, by considering influences (the Italian school and Tintoretto, Delacroix, Courbet, and the impressionists), Cézanne's technique, or even his own pronouncements on his work.

His first pictures—up to about 1870—are painted fantasies: a rape, a murder. They are therefore almost always executed in broad strokes and present the moral physiognomy of the actions rather than their visible aspect. It is thanks to the impressionists, and particularly to Pissarro, that Cézanne later conceived painting not as the incarnation of imagined scenes, the projection of dreams outward, but as the exact study of appearances: less a work of the studio than a working from nature. Thanks to the impressionists, he abandoned the baroque technique, which seeks *first* to capture movement, for small dabs placed close together and for patient hatchings.

He quickly parted ways with the impressionists, however. Impressionism was trying to capture, in the painting, the very way in which objects strike our eyes and attack our senses. Impressionism represented them in the atmosphere through which instantaneous perception gives them to us, without absolute contours, bound together by light and air. To capture this envelope of light, one had to exclude siennas, ochres, and black and use only the seven colors of the spectrum. In order to represent the color of objects, it was not enough to put their local tone on the canvas, that is, the color they take on isolated from their surroundings; one also had to pay attention to the phenomena of contrast which modify local colors in nature. Furthermore, by a sort of reversal, every color we see in nature elicits the vision of its complement; and these complementaries heighten one another. To achieve sunlit colors in a picture which will be seen in the dim light of apartments, not only must there be a green—if you are painting grass—but also the complementary red which will make it vibrate. Finally, the impressionists break down the local tone itself. One can generally obtain any color by juxtaposing rather than mixing the colors which make it up, thereby achieving a more vibrant tone. The result of these procedures was that the canvas—which no longer corresponded point by point to nature—restored a general truth of the impression through the action of the separate parts upon one another. But at the same time, depicting the atmosphere and breaking up the tones submerged the object and caused it to lose its proper weight. The composition of Cézanne's palette leads one to suppose that he had another aim. Instead of the seven colors of the spectrum, one finds eighteen colors—six reds, five yellows, three blues, three greens, and one black. The use of warm colors and black shows that Cézanne wants to represent the object, to find it again behind the atmosphere. Likewise, he does not break up the tone; rather, he replaces this technique with graduated mixtures, with a progression of chromatic nuances across the object, with a modulation of colors which stays close to the object's form and to the light it receives. The suppression of exact contours in certain cases and giving color priority over the outline obviously do not have the same sense in Cézanne and in impressionism. The object is no longer covered by reflections and lost in its relationships to the air and to other objects: it seems subtly illuminated from within, light emanates from it, and the result is an impression of solidity and material substance. Moreover, Cézanne does not give up making the warm colors vibrate, but achieves this chromatic sensation through the use of blue.

One must therefore say that Cézanne wished to return to the object without abandoning the impressionist aesthetic which takes nature as its model. Émile Bernard reminded him that, for the classical artists, painting demanded outline, composition, and distribution of light. Cézanne replied: "They created pictures; we are attempting a piece of nature." He said of the old masters that they "replaced reality with imagination and by the abstraction which accompanies it." Of nature, he said, "the artist must conform to this perfect work of art. Everything comes to us from nature; we exist through it; let us forget everything else." He stated that he wanted to turn impressionism into "something solid, like the art in the museums." His painting would be a paradox: investigate reality without departing from sensations, with no other guide than the immediate impression of nature, without following the contours, with no outline to enclose the color, with no perspectival or pictorial composition. This is what Bernard called Cézanne's suicide: aiming for reality while denying himself the means to attain it. This is the reason for his difficulties and for the distortions one finds in his pictures between 1870 and 1890. Cups and saucers on a table seen from the side should be elliptical, but Cézanne paints the two ends of the ellipse swollen and expanded. The work table in his portrait of Gustave Geffroy stretches, contrary to the laws of perspective, into the lower part of the picture. By departing from the outline, Cézanne would be handing himself over to the chaos of the sensations. Now, the sensations would capsize the objects and constantly suggest illusions—for example, the illusion we have when we move our heads that objects themselves are moving—if our judgment did not constantly set these appearances straight. According to Bernard, Cézanne engulfed "the painting in ignorance and his mind in shadows."

In fact, one can judge his painting in this way only by letting half of what he said drop away and only by closing one's eyes to what he painted.

It is clear from his conversations with Émile Bernard that Cézanne was always seeking to avoid the ready-made alternatives suggested to him: the senses versus intelligence; the painter who sees versus the painter who thinks; nature versus composition; primitivism versus tradition. "We have to develop an optics," Cézanne said, "by which I mean a logical vision— that is, one with nothing absurd." "Are you speaking of our nature?" asked Bernard. Cézanne: "It has to do with both." "But aren't nature and art different?" "I want to unite them. Art is a personal apperception. I place this apperception in the sensations and I ask intelligence to organize them into a work."[1] But even these formulas put too much emphasis on the ordinary notions of "sensibility" or "sensations" and "intelligence"—which is why Cézanne could not persuade and this is why he liked to paint better. Rather than apply to his work dichotomies, which moreover belong more to the scholarly traditions than to the founders—philosophers or painters—of these traditions, we would do better to let ourselves be persuaded to the proper sense of his painting, which is to challenge those dichotomies. Cézanne did not think he had to choose between sensation and thought, as if he were deciding between chaos and order. He did not want to separate the stable things which appear before our gaze and their fleeting way of appearing. He wanted to paint matter as it takes on form, the birth of order through spontaneous organization. He makes a basic distinction not between "the senses" and "intelligence" but rather between the spontaneous order of perceived things and the human order of ideas and sciences. We perceive things; we agree about them; we are anchored in them; and it is with "nature" as our base that we construct the sciences. Cézanne wanted to paint this primordial world, and this is why his pictures give us the impression of nature at its origin, while photographs of the same landscapes suggest man's works, conveniences, and imminent presence. Cézanne never wished to "paint like a savage." He wanted to put intelligence, ideas, sciences, perspective, and tradition back in touch with the world of nature which they were intended to comprehend. He wished, as he said, to confront the sciences with the nature "from which they came."

By remaining faithful to the phenomena in his investigations of perspective, Cézanne discovered what recent psychologists have come to formulate: the lived perspective, that of our perception, is not a geometric or photographic one. In perception, the objects that are near appear smaller, those far away larger, than they do in a photograph, as we see in the cinema when an approaching train gets bigger much faster than a real train would under the same circumstances. To say that a circle seen obliquely is seen as an ellipse is to substitute for our actual perception the schema of what we would have to see if we were cameras. In fact, we see a form which oscillates around the ellipse without *being* an ellipse. In a portrait of Mme Cézanne, the border of the wallpaper on one side of her body does not form a straight line with that on the other: and indeed it is known that if a line passes beneath a wide strip of paper, the two visible segments appear dislocated. Gustave Geffroy's table stretches into the bottom of the picture, and indeed, when our eye runs over a large surface, the images it successively receives are taken from different points of view, and the whole surface is warped. It is true that I freeze these distortions in repainting them on the canvas; I stop the spontaneous movement in which they pile up in perception and tend toward the geometric perspective. This is also what happens with colors. Pink upon gray paper colors the background green. Academic painting shows the background as gray, assuming that the picture will produce the same effect of contrast as the real object. Impressionist painting uses green in the background in order to achieve a contrast as brilliant as that of objects in nature. Doesn't this falsify the color relationship? It would if it stopped there, but the painter's task is to modify all the other colors in the picture so that they take away from the green background its characteristics of a real color. Similarly, it is Cézanne's genius that when the overall composition of the picture is seen globally, perspectival distortions are no longer visible in their own right but rather contribute, as they do in natural vision, to the impression of an emerging order, an object in the act of appearing, organizing itself before our eyes. In the same way, the contour of objects, conceived as a line encircling the objects, belongs not to the visible world, but to geometry. If one outlines the contour of an apple with a continuous line, one turns the contour into a thing, whereas the contour is rather the ideal limit toward which the sides of the apple recede in depth. To outline no contour would be to deprive the objects of their identity. To outline just one contour sacrifices depth—that is, the dimensions which give us the thing, not as spread out before us, but as full of reserves and as an inexhaustible reality. That is why Cézanne follows the swelling of the object in a colored modulation, and outlines *several* contours in blue lines. Referred from one to the other, the gaze captures a contour that emerges from among them all, just as it does in perception. Nothing could be less arbitrary than these famous distortions which, moreover, Cézanne abandoned in his last period, after 1890, when he no longer filled his canvases with colors and when he gave up the closely woven texture of his still lifes.

The drawing must therefore result from the colors, if one wants the world to be rendered in its thickness. For the world is a mass without gaps, an organism of colors across which the receding perspective, the contours, the angles, and the curves are set up as lines of force; the spatial frame is constituted by vibrating. "The drawing and the color are no longer distinct. Gradually as you paint, you draw; the more the colors harmonize, the more the drawing becomes precise. . . . When the color is at its richest, the form is at its fullest." Cézanne does not try to use color to *suggest* the tactile sensations which would give form and depth. These distinctions between touch and sight are unknown in primordial perception. It is only as a result of a science of the human body that we finally learn to distinguish between our senses. The lived object is not rediscovered or constructed on the basis of the data of the senses; rather, it presents itself to us from the start as the center from which the data radiate. We *see* the depth, the smoothness, the softness, the hardness of objects; Cézanne even claimed that we see their odor. If the painter wants to express the world, the arrangement of his colors must bear within this arrangement this indivisible Whole, or else his painting will only be an allusion to the things and will not give them in the imperious unity, the presence, the insurpassable fullness which is for us the definition of the real. That is why each brushstroke must satisfy an infinite number of conditions; that is why Cézanne sometimes meditated for an hour before putting down a certain stroke, for, as Bernard said, each stroke must "contain the air, the light, the object, the composition, the character, the drawing, and the style." Expressing what *exists* is an endless task.

Nor did Cézanne neglect the physiognomy of objects and faces: he simply wanted to capture it emerging from the color. Painting a face "as an object" is not to strip it of its "thought." "I agree that the painter must interpret it," said Cézanne, "the painter is not an imbecile." But this interpretation must not be a thought separated from vision. "If I paint all the little blues and all the little browns, I make it gaze as he gazes. Who gives a damn if they have any idea how one can sadden a mouth or make a cheek smile by wedding a shaded green to a red." The mind is seen and read in the gazes, which are, however, only colored wholes. Other minds are given to us only as incarnate, as belonging to faces and gestures. It serves no purpose to oppose here the distinctions between the soul and the body, thought and vision, since Cézanne returns to just that primordial experience out of which these notions are pulled and which gives them to us as inseparable. The painter who thinks and seeks the expression first misses the mystery—renewed every time we gaze at someone—of a person's appearing in nature. In *The Wild Ass's Skin* Balzac describes a "tablecloth white as a layer of fresh-fallen snow, upon which the place settings rose symmetrically, crowned with blond rolls." "All through my youth," said

Cézanne, "I wanted to paint that, that tablecloth of fresh-fallen snow. . . . Now I know that one must only *want* to paint 'rose, symmetrically, the place settings' and 'blond rolls.' If I painted 'crowned' I'm done for, you understand? But if I really balance and shade my place settings and rolls as they are in nature, you can be sure the crowns, the snow and the whole shebang will be there."

We live in the midst of man-made objects, among tools, in houses, streets, cities, and most of the time we see them only through the human actions which put them to use. We become used to thinking that all of this exists necessarily and unshakably. Cézanne's painting suspends these habits and reveals the base of inhuman nature upon which man has installed himself. This is why Cézanne's people are strange, as if viewed by a creature of another species. Nature itself is stripped of the attributes which make it ready for animistic communions: there is no wind in the landscape, no movement on the Lac d'Annecy, the frozen objects hesitate as at the beginning of the world. It is an unfamiliar world in which one is uncomfortable and which forbids all human effusiveness. If one looks at the work of other painters after seeing Cézanne's paintings, one feels somehow relaxed, just as conversations resumed after a period of mourning mask the absolute change and restore to the survivors their solidity. But indeed only a human being is capable of such a vision, which penetrates right to the root of things beneath constituted humanity. All indications are that animals cannot *gaze at* [*regarder*] things, cannot penetrate them in expectation of nothing but the truth. Émile Bernard's statement that a realistic painter is only an ape is therefore precisely the opposite of the truth, and one sees how Cézanne was able to revive the classical definition of art: man added to nature.

Cézanne's painting denies neither science nor tradition. He went to the Louvre every day when he was in Paris. He believed that one must learn how to paint and that the geometric study of planes and forms is necessary. He inquired about the geological structure of his landscapes. These abstract relationships must be operative in the act of painting, but ruled over by the visible world. Anatomy and design are present in each stroke of his brush just as the rules of the game underlie each stroke of a tennis match. What motivates the painter's movement can never be perspective alone or geometry alone or the laws governing the breakdown of colors, or, for that matter, any particular knowledge. Motivating all the movements from which a picture gradually emerges there can be only one motif: the landscape in its totality and in its absolute fullness, precisely what Cézanne called a "motif." He would start by discovering the geological foundation of the landscape; then, according to Mme Cézanne, he would halt and gaze, eyes dilated; he "germinated" with the countryside.

What was at issue, all science forgotten, was to recapture, *through* these sciences, the constitution of the landscape as an emerging organism. All the partial views that the gaze catches sight of must be welded together; all that the eye's versatility disperses must be reunited; one must, as Gasquet put it, "join the wandering hands of nature." "A minute of the world is going by which must be painted in its full reality." The meditation was suddenly complete: "I have a hold on my *motif*," Cézanne would say, and he explained that the landscape had to be tackled neither too high nor too low, caught alive in a net which would let nothing escape. Then he attacked his picture from all sides at once, using patches of color to surround his original charcoal sketch of the geological skeleton. The image saturated itself, composed itself, drew itself, became balanced; it came to maturity all at once. "The landscape thinks itself in me," he said, "and I am its consciousness." Nothing could be farther from naturalism than this intuitive science. Art is not imitation, nor is it something manufactured according to the wishes of instinct or good taste. It is a process of expression. Just as words name—that is, grasp in its nature and place before us as a recognizable object what appears in a confused way—the painter, said Gasquet, "objectifies," "projects," and "fixes." Just as words do not *resemble* what they designate, a picture is not a trompe l'oeil. Cézanne, in his own words, "writes in painting what is not yet painted, and turns it into painting absolutely." We forget the viscous, equivocal appearances, and by means of them we go straight to the things they present. The painter recaptures and converts into visible objects what would, without him, remain closed up in the separate life of each consciousness: the vibration of appearances which is the cradle of things. Only one emotion is possible for this painter—the feeling of strangeness—and only one lyricism—that of the continual rebirth of existence.

Leonardo da Vinci's motto was persistent rigor, and all the classical statements concerning how to make poetry tell us that the work [*l'oeuvre*] is difficult. Cézanne's difficulties—like those of Balzac or Mallarmé—are not of the same nature. Balzac—probably based on Delacroix's comments—imagined a painter who wants to express life itself through the use of color alone and who keeps his masterpiece hidden. When Frenhofer dies, his friends find nothing but a chaos of colors and elusive lines, a wall of painting. Cézanne was moved to tears when he read *The Unknown Masterpiece* and declared that he himself was Frenhofer. The quest of Balzac, himself obsessed with "realization," sheds light on Cézanne's. In *The Wild Ass's Skin* Balzac speaks of "a thought to be expressed," "a system to be built," "a science to be explained." He makes Louis Lambert, one of the abortive geniuses of the Comédie Humaine, say: "I am heading toward certain discoveries . . . , but how shall I describe the power which binds my hands, stops my mouth, and drags me in the opposite direction from my vocation?" To say that Balzac set himself to understand the society of his time is not sufficient. It is no superhuman task to describe the typical traveling salesman, to "dissect the teaching profession," or even to lay the foundations of a sociology. Once he had named the visible forces such as money and passion, once he had described the manifest workings of things, Balzac wondered where it all led, what the impetus behind it was, what the *meaning* was of, for example, a Europe "whose efforts tend toward some unknown mystery of civilization." In short, he wanted to understand what inner force holds the world together and causes the proliferation of visible forms. Frenhofer had the same idea about the meaning of painting: "A hand is not simply part of the body, but the expression and continuation of a thought which must be captured and conveyed. . . . That is the real struggle! Many painters triumph instinctively, unaware of this theme of art. You draw a woman, but you do not see her." The artist is the one who fixes the spectacle in which most men take part without really seeing it and who makes it visible to the most "human" among them.

There is thus no art for pleasure's sake alone. One can manufacture objects that are pleasurable by linking ready-made ideas in a different way and by presenting forms that have been seen before. This second painting or speaking is what is generally meant by culture. Cézanne's or Balzac's artist is not satisfied to be a cultured animal but takes up culture from its inception and founds it anew: he speaks as the first human spoke and paints as if no one had ever painted before. Expression cannot, therefore, be the translation of a thought that is already clear, since clear thoughts are those that have already been said within ourselves or by others. "Conception" cannot precede "execution." Before expression, there is nothing but a vague fever, and only the work itself, completed and understood, will prove that there was *something* rather than *nothing* to be found there. Because he has returned to the source of silent and solitary experience on which culture and the exchange of ideas have been built in order to take cognizance of it, the artist launches his work just as a human once launched the first word, not knowing whether it will be anything more than a shout, whether it can detach itself from the flow of individual life in which it was born and give the independent existence of an identifiable *sense* to the future of that same individual life, or to the monads coexisting with it, or the open community of future monads. The sense of what the artist is going to say *does not exist* anywhere—not in the things, which as yet have no sense, nor in the artist himself, in his unformulated life. It calls one away from the already constituted reason in which "cultured men" are content to shut themselves, toward a reason which would embrace its origins. To Bernard's attempt to bring him back to human intelligence, Cézanne replied: "I am oriented toward the intelligence of the

Pater Omnipotens." He was, in any case, oriented toward the idea or project of an infinite Logos. Cézanne's uncertainty and loneliness are not essentially explained by his nervous temperament but by the intention of his work. Heredity may well have given him rich sensations, strong emotions, and a vague feeling of anguish or mystery which upset the life he might have wished for himself and which cut him off from humanity; but these gifts produce a work of art only by the expressive act, and they have no bearing on the difficulties or the virtues of that act. Cézanne's difficulties are those of the first word. He thought himself powerless because he was not omnipotent, because he was not God and wanted nevertheless to paint the world, to change it completely into a spectacle, to make *visible* how the world *touches* us. A new theory of physics can be proven because the idea or sense is connected, through calculations, to the standards of measurement which belong to a domain that is already common to all human beings. A painter like Cézanne, an artist, or a philosopher, must not only create and express an idea, but must also awaken the experiences which will make the idea take root in the consciousness of others. If a work is successful, it has the strange power of being self-teaching. By following the clues of the picture or of the book, by establishing intersections, by being jostled from side to side, guided by the confused clarity of a style, the reader or the spectator will in the end find what was intended to be communicated. The painter can do more than construct an image. It is necessary to wait for this image to come to life for others. Then, the work of art will have joined together these separate lives; it will no longer exist in only one of them like a stubborn dream or a persistent delirium, nor will it exist only in space as a colored piece of canvas. It will dwell undivided in several minds, presumably in every possible mind, as an acquisition for always.

Thus, the "hereditary traits," the "influences"—the accidents in Cézanne's life—are the text which nature and history gave him to decipher. They give only the literal sense of his work. But an artist's creations, like a person's free decisions, impose on this given a figurative sense which did not exist before them. If Cézanne's life seems to us to carry the seeds of his work within it, it is because we know his work first and see the circumstances of his life through it, charging them with a sense borrowed from the work. If the givens for Cézanne which we have been enumerating, and which we spoke of as pressing conditions, were to figure in the web of projects which he was, they could have done so only by proposing themselves to him as what he had to live, and by leaving the way of living it indeterminate. An imposed theme at the start, they become, when placed back in the existence which embraces them, only the monogram and the emblem of a life which freely interprets itself.

But let us really understand this freedom. Let us not imagine some abstract force which would superimpose its effects on life's "givens" or would insert breaches in life's development. It is certain that life does not *explain* the work; but it is equally certain that they communicate. The truth is that *that work to be done required that life*. From the very start, Cézanne's life found balance only by applying itself to the work that was still in the future. His life was the project of his future work, and the work was announced in the life through warning signs that we would be mistaken to take for causes, although these signs turn the life and the work into one single adventure. Here there are no longer causes or effects; they are gathered together in the simultaneity of an eternal Cézanne who is the formula at once of what he wanted to be and what he wanted to do. There is a relationship between Cézanne's schizoid temperament and his work because the work reveals a metaphysical sense of the illness (schizothymia as the reduction of the world to the totality of frozen appearances and the suspension of expressive values). The illness then stops being an absurd fact and destiny in order to become a general possibility of human existence when the illness confronts consistently one of its paradoxes—the phenomenon of expression—and finally, in this sense, to be schizoid and to be Cézanne are one and the same thing. It would therefore be impossible to separate creative freedom from the lowest-level deliberate behaviors which were already indicated in Cézanne's first gestures as a child and in the way in which things struck him. The sense that Cézanne will give to objects and faces in his paintings proposed itself to him in the very world which appeared to him. Cézanne simply released that sense: it was the things themselves and the faces themselves as he saw them that demanded to be painted in this way, and Cézanne simply said what they *wanted* to say. But, then, where is the freedom? True, conditions of existence can determine a consciousness only through the detour of reasons to be and justifications that a consciousness gives to itself. We can see only before us and under the lens of ends what it is that we are—so that our life always has the form of the project or the choice, and thus it seems to us spontaneous. But to say that we are from the start the intention of a future is also to say that our project has already stopped with our first ways of being, that the choice is already made with our first breath. If nothing constrains us from the outside, it is because we are our whole exterior. This eternal Cézanne whom we see springing forth from the start and who then brought upon the human Cézanne the events and influences that we believe to be exterior to him, and who sketched all that happened to him—this attitude toward humanity and toward the world which was not chosen through deliberation—may be free from external causes, but is it free in respect to itself? Is the choice not pushed back beyond life, and can a choice exist where there is as yet no clearly articulated field of possibilities, only one probability and, as it were, only one temptation? If I am a certain project from birth, it is impossible to distinguish in me the given and the created, and it is therefore impossible to designate a single gesture which is merely hereditary or innate and a single gesture which is not spontaneous—but also a single gesture which is absolutely new in regard to this way of being in the world which, from the very beginning, is me. There is no difference between saying that our life is completely constructed or that it is completely given. If there is a true freedom, it can come about only in the course of our life, by going beyond our original situation and yet not ceasing to be the same. Such is the problem. Two things are certain about freedom: that we are never determined and yet that we never change, that, retrospectively, we can always find in our past the anticipation of what we have become. It is up to us to understand both these things simultaneously and how freedom dawns in us without breaking our bonds with the world.

There are always bonds, even and above all when we refuse to admit they exist. Inspired by the paintings of da Vinci, Valéry described a monster of pure freedom, without mistresses, without creditors, without anecdotes, and without adventures. No dream masks for him the things themselves; nothing taken for granted supports his certainties; and he does not read his fate in any favorite image, such as Pascal's abyss. Instead of struggling against the monsters he has understood what makes them tick, has disarmed them by his attention, and has reduced them to the state of known things. "Nothing could be more free, that is, less human, than his judgments on love and death. He hints at them in a few fragments from his notebooks: 'In the full force of its passion,' he says more or less explicitly, 'love is something so ugly that the human race would die out (la natura si perderebbe) if lovers could see what they were doing.' This contempt is brought out in various sketches, since the leisurely examination of certain things is, after all, the height of scorn. Thus, he now and again draws anatomical unions, frightful cross-sections of love's very act."[2] He has complete mastery of his means, he does what he wants, going at will from knowledge to life with a superior elegance. Everything he did was done knowingly, and the artistic process, like the act of breathing or living, is not beyond his knowledge. He has discovered the "central attitude," on the basis of which it is equally possible to know, to act, and to create because action and life, when turned into exercises, are not contrary to the detachment of knowledge. He is an "intellectual power"; he is a "man of the mind."

Let us look more closely. For Leonardo there was no revelation; as Valéry said, no abyss yawned at his right hand. Undoubtedly true. But in Saint Anne, Virgin, and Child the Virgin's cloak suggests a vulture where it touches the face of the Child. There is that fragment on the flight of birds where da Vinci suddenly interrupts himself to pursue a childhood memory: "I seem to have been destined to be especially concerned with the vulture, for one of the first things I remember about my childhood is how a vulture came to me when I was still in the cradle, forced open my mouth with its tail, and struck me several times between the lips with it."[3] So even this transparent consciousness has its enigma, whether truly a child's memory or a fantasy of the grown man. It did not come out of nowhere, nor did it sustain itself alone. We are caught in a secret history and in a forest of symbols. One would surely protest if Freud were to decipher the enigma from what we know about the meaning of the flight of birds and about fellatio fantasies and their relation to the period of nursing. But it is still a fact that to the ancient Egyptians the vulture was a symbol of maternity because they believed all vultures were female and that they were impregnated by the wind. It is also a fact that the Church Fathers used this legend to refute, on the grounds of natural history, those who were unwilling to believe in a virgin birth, and it is probable that Leonardo came across the legend in the course of his endless reading. He found in it the symbol of his own fate: he was the illegitimate son of a rich notary who married the noble Donna Albiera the very year Leonardo was born. Having no children by her, he took Leonardo into his home when the boy was five. Thus Leonardo spent the first four years of his life with his mother, the deserted peasant girl; he was a child without a father, and he got to know the world in the sole company of that unhappy mother who seemed to have miraculously created him. If we now recall that he was never known to have a mistress or even to have felt anything like passion; that he was accused— but acquitted—of sodomy; that his diary, which tells us nothing about many other, larger expenses, notes with meticulous detail the costs of his mother's burial, as well as the cost of linen and clothing for two of his students—it is no great leap to conclude that Leonardo loved only one woman, his mother, and that this love left no room for anything but platonic tenderness he felt for the young boys surrounding him. In the four decisive years of his childhood he had formed a fundamental attachment, which he had to give up when he was recalled to his father's home, and into which he had poured all his resources of love and all his power of abandon. As for his thirst for life, he had no other choice but to use it in the investigation and knowledge of the world, and, since he himself had been *detached,* he had to become this intellectual power, this man who was all mind, this stranger among men. Indifferent, incapable of any strong indignation, love or hate, he left his paintings unfinished to devote his time to bizarre experiments; he became a person in whom his contemporaries sensed a mystery. It was as if Leonardo had never quite grown up, as if all the places in his heart had already been spoken for, as if the spirit of investigation was a way for him to escape from life, as if he had invested all his power of assent in the first years of his life and had remained true to his childhood right to the end. His games were those of a child. Vasari tells how "he made up a wax paste and, during his walks, he would model from it very delicate animals, hollow and filled with air; when he breathed into them, they would fly; when the air had escaped, they would fall to the ground. When the wine-grower from Belvedere found a very unusual lizard, Leonardo made wings for it out of skin of other lizards and filled these wings with mercury so that they waved and quivered whenever the lizard moved; he likewise made eyes, a beard, and horns for it in the same way, tamed it, put it in a box, and used the lizard to terrify his friends."[4] He left his work unfinished, just as his father had abandoned him. He paid no heed to authority and trusted only nature and his own judgment in matters of knowledge, as is often the case with people who have not been raised in the shadow of a father's intimidating and protective power. Thus even that pure power of examination, that solitude, that curiosity—which are the essence of mind—only developed in da Vinci in relation to his personal history. At the height of freedom he was, *in that very freedom,* the child he had been; he is detached on one side only because he is attached on the other. Becoming a pure consciousness is still a way of taking a position in relation to the world and other people. Leonardo had learned this way by taking up the situation into which his birth and childhood had put him. There can be no consciousness that is not sustained by its primordial involvement in life and by the mode of this involvement.

Whatever is arbitrary in Freud's *explanations* cannot in this context discredit the *psychoanalytic intuition.* The reader is stopped more than once by the lack of evidence. Why this and not something else? The question seems all the more pressing since Freud often offers several interpretations, each symptom being "overdetermined" according to him. Finally, it is obvious that a doctrine which brings in sexuality everywhere cannot, by the rules of inductive logic, establish its effectiveness anywhere, since, excluding all differential cases beforehand, it deprives itself of any counterevidence. This is how one triumphs over psychoanalysis, but only on paper. For if the suggestions of the analyst can never be proven, neither can they be eliminated: How would it be possible to credit chance with the complex correspondences which the psychoanalyst discovers between the child and the adult? How can we deny that psychoanalysis has taught us to perceive echoes, allusions, repetitions from one moment of life to another—a concatenation we would not dream of doubting if Freud had stated that theory correctly? Unlike the natural sciences, psychoanalysis was not meant to give us necessary relations of cause and effect but to point to motivational relationships which are in principle simply possible. We should not take Leonardo's fantasy of the vulture, or the infantile past which it masks, for a force which determined his future. Rather, it is like the words of the oracle, an ambiguous symbol which applies in advance to several possible chains of events. To be more precise: in every life, one's birth and one's past define categories or fundamental dimensions which do not impose any particular act but which can be found in all. Whether Leonardo yielded to his childhood or whether he wished to flee from it, he could never have been other than he was. The very decisions which transform us are always made in reference to a factual situation; such a situation can of course be accepted or refused, but it cannot fail to give us our impetus or to be for us, as a situation "to be accepted" or "to be refused," the incarnation of the value we give to it. If it is the aim of psychoanalysis to describe this exchange between future and past and to show how each life muses over enigmas whose final sense is nowhere written down, then we have no right to demand inductive rigor from it. The psychoanalyst's hermeneutic musing, which multiplies the communications between us and ourselves, which takes sexuality as the symbol of existence and existence as the symbol of sexuality, and which looks in the past for the sense of the future and in the future for the sense of the past, is better suited than rigorous induction to the circular movement of our lives, where the future rests on the past, the past on the future, and where everything symbolizes everything else. Psychoanalysis does not make freedom impossible; it teaches us to conceive this freedom concretely, as a creative revival of ourselves, which is after the fact always faithful to ourselves.

Thus it is true both that the life of an author can teach us nothing and that—if we know how to read it—we can find everything in it, since it opens onto the artwork. Just as we may observe the movements of an unknown animal without understanding the law that inhabits and controls it, so Cézanne's observers did not divine the transmutations he imposed on events and experiences; they were blind to *his* meaning, to that glow from out of nowhere which surrounded him from time to time. But he himself was never at the center of himself: nine days out of ten all he saw around him was the wretchedness of his empirical life and of his unsuccessful attempts, the debris of an unknown celebration.[5] It is still in the world, upon a canvas, with colors, that he has to realize his freedom. It was from the approval of others that he had to await the proof of his worth. That is why he questioned the picture emerging beneath his hand, why he hung on the gazes other people directed toward his canvas. That is why he never finished working. We never get away from our life. We never see ideas or freedom face to face.

5

The Contemporary
Philosophical Movement

[Interview conducted by Maurice Fleurent, from *Carrefour,* no. 92 (May 23, 1946): 6.]

Sign of the times: an interview with a philosopher does not necessarily lead the jour-
nalist to a study full of large tomes, walls covered with austere bindings, before a
scholar of respectable age. . .[1]
    The author of Phenomenology of Perception *is a big young man, simple*
and pleasant: our encounter takes place at the Café Flore. *Contrary to the opin-*
ion of those naysayers who too often tend to liken existentialism to "café philosophy,"
Maurice Merleau-Ponty shows proof, despite his youth, of a solid philosophical
background. A graduate, in the same class as J.-P. Sartre, of the École Normale
Supérieure, agrégé at the university, professor at the University of Lyon, he agreed
to discuss with us his remarkable doctoral thesis.

FLEURENT: Could you summarize—to the extent that one can do so in
matters of philosophy—the essential features of your work?
    MERLEAU-PONTY: The *Phenomenology of Perception* attempts to answer
a question I asked myself ten years ago and which, I think, all philosophers
of my generation have asked themselves: how to escape idealism without
falling back into the naivete of realism? The work of Léon Brunschvicg
taught us once and for all that science, the construction of an intelligence
coming to terms with the concrete, remains open and could not be interpreted in a dogmatic sense. But the philosophy proper to Brunschvicg did
not seek to explore this concrete world that remains at the margins of
science. Perception, art, religion were for him mere sketches of scientific
knowledge and philosophy remained, for him, the simple knowledge of
the spiritual activity at work in science. Now, there is the scientific representation of the world and there is the lived and perceived world that must
be described for itself and cannot be considered as less real. If one rediscovers it, one notices the distinction between consciousness and object,
and the very notion of consciousness becomes obscured. For instance, my

body is not an object: it is the medium of all my relations with the world. Insofar as I have a body, I am not a pure consciousness, but am engaged in the world through this body with the aid of which I perceive. I do not merely know the world; as Heidegger says, I am in the world. The role of philosophy is to make us rediscover this bond with the world that precedes thought itself.

On another level, you see the consequences: if man is not only a thinking subject but a situated subject, our relations with others cannot, from the beginning, be the relation of a pure thought with a pure thought. They are dominated by differences of situation; classical liberal politics appear abstract. Generally speaking, philosophy rediscovers a "thickness" and a relation with concrete problems it had lost when it became pure reflection on science.

FLEURENT: What are, according to you, the essential contributions made to contemporary philosophy by German and American philosophers?

MERLEAU-PONTY: What seemed important to me in American thought is the idea of behavior.[2] What the Americans mean by this is the whole of our concrete relations with the world, which are far from reducible, as classical psychology believed, to relations of knowledge. For them, man has a "current of activity" in relation to his surroundings: he is enrooted in nature and in history.

With respect to the German philosophers, Husserl and Heidegger give us precisely what we were looking for: a broadened philosophy, an analysis of phenomena, which is to say of the environment in which our concrete life unwinds, devoid of prejudices. Husserl contends that Western philosophy has for centuries been founded on a rationalist dogma whose origin is theological: the world is entirely rational. The nineteenth century understood this for the first time, even though we cannot affirm it a priori, which does not authorize us to abandon reason but obligates us to redefine the human situation in order to see reason's tasks more clearly. There is reason and logic in the course of things, but only de facto, not de jure, and we have to describe the human conditions with this mixture of chance and reason that defines it. Existentialism is, for me, above all the sharp consciousness of this equivocation. Hegel had already described the human situation in these terms. Those who mistake existential philosophy for a fad or an invention of the "Nazi" Heidegger or for a new disguise of idealism don't know what they're talking about. Existential philosophy is the formulation of the problem that has been posed ever since reason simultaneously recognized its power and its limits; it has been the order of the day for more than a century.

FLEURENT: You accept and defend the philosophy laid out by Sartre in *Being and Nothingness*. Nevertheless, I believe your thought differs from his on several points: could you point them out for me?

MERLEAU-PONTY: I have known Sartre for twenty years. I have had countless conversations with him, and it would be difficult for me to measure how much I owe him. I am in complete agreement with him when it comes to defining the human through a certain number of contradictions such as those of consciousness and object, in-itself and for-itself, or that of the for-itself and the for-others. My thinking would differ from his to the extent that he describes these fundamental antitheses as insurmountable. On the contrary, it seems to me that they are overcome in the very fact that we live, that we perceive things, that we perceive others. In this sense, the synthesis is given along with the antithesis. This is particularly important in the domain of philosophy, history, and politics.

Sartre seems to have thought for a long time that there was no middle ground between a dogmatic philosophy of history, a fatalism, and the philosophy of freedom according to which history has no sense other than that which we decide to give it. In my opinion, there is, on the contrary, a science of history that takes shape in the facts and that we have only to complete, this human intervention being, moreover, a decisive one.

But these are questions to be examined. On this topic, Sartre has not yet expressed himself fully, and one has never demanded of a philosopher that he say, at the age of forty, his last word on all of the nuances of his thought.

With a modesty that honors him, Maurice Merleau-Ponty ends the interview speaking about the author of Nausea, *his friend, "a young man who is not at all the philosopher of despair," but rather whose life and work are devoted entirely to the quest for truth.*

6

The Primacy of Perception and Its Philosophical Consequences

Preliminary Summary of the Argument

1. Perception as an Original Modality of Consciousness

The study of perception, pursued without prejudice by psychologists, ends up by revealing that the perceived world is not a collection of objects in the sense in which the sciences use this word, that our relation to the world is not that of a thinker to an object of thought, and that finally the unity of the perceived thing, about which several consciousnesses agree, cannot be assimilated to the unity of a theorem that several thinkers recognize, nor can perceived existence be assimilated to ideal existence.[1]

As a result, we cannot apply the classical distinction of form and matter to perception, nor can we conceive the perceiving subject as a consciousness which "interprets," "deciphers," or "orders" a sensible matter whose ideal law it would possess. Matter is "pregnant" with its form, which is to say that in the final analysis every perception takes place within a certain horizon and ultimately in the "world," that both are present to us practically rather than being explicitly known or posited by us, and that finally the relation, which is somehow organic, of the perceiving subject and world involves, in principle, the contradiction of immanence and transcendence.

2. The Generalization of These Results

Do these results have any value beyond that of psychological description? This would be the case, if we could superimpose a world of ideas on the perceived world. But in reality the ideas to which we give our assent are valuable only for a period of our lives or for a period in the history of culture. Evidence is never apodictic, nor is thought timeless, though there is some progress in objectification and thought is always valid for more than an instant. The certainty of ideas is not the foundation of the certainty of perception but is, rather, based on it—in that it is perceptual experience which gives us the passage from one moment to the next and thus realizes the unity of time. In this sense all consciousness is perceptual, even the consciousness of ourselves.

3. Conclusions

The perceived world is the foundation that is always presupposed by all rationality, all value, and all existence. This kind of conception destroys neither rationality nor the absolute. It only tries to bring them down to earth.

Report of the Session

MERLEAU-PONTY: The point of departure for these remarks is that the perceived world involves relations and, in a general way, a type of organization which has not been recognized by classical psychology and philosophy.

If we consider one of the objects which we perceive and in this object one of the sides that we do not see, or if we consider the objects which are not within our visual field at this moment, what is happening behind our back or what is happening in America or at the South Pole—how should we describe the existence of these absent objects or the nonvisible fragments of the objects that are present?

Should we say, as psychologists have often done, that I *represent* to myself the sides of this lamp which are not seen? If I say these unseen sides are represented, I imply that they are not grasped as actually existing; because what is represented is not here before us, I do not actually perceive it. It is only a possible. Now, since the sides of this lamp are not imaginary, but are situated behind what I see (in order to see them I just have to move a little bit), I cannot say that they are represented.

Should I say that the unseen sides are somehow anticipated by me, as perceptions which would be produced necessarily if I moved, given the law of the object? If, for example, I look at a cube, knowing the structure of the cube as it is defined in geometry, I can anticipate the perceptions which this cube will give me while I would move around it. Under this hypothesis I would know the non-seen side as the necessary consequence of a certain law of development of my perception. But, if I turn to perception itself, I cannot interpret it in this way because this analysis can be formulated as follows: it is *true* that the lamp has a back, that the cube has another side. But this formula, "It is true," does not correspond to what is given to me in perception. Perception does not give me truths like geometry but presences.

I grasp the unseen side as present, and I do not affirm that the back of the lamp exists in the same sense that I say the solution of a problem exists. The hidden side is present in its own way. It is in my vicinity.

Thus I should not say that the unseen sides of objects are simply possible perceptions, nor that they are the necessary conclusions of a kind of analysis or geometrical reasoning. It is not through an intellectual synthesis which would freely posit the total object that I am led from what is given to what is not actually given; that I am given, together with the visible sides of the object, the nonvisible sides as well. It is, rather, a kind of practical synthesis: I can touch the lamp, and not only the side turned toward me but also the other side; I have only to extend my hand to hold it.

The classical analysis of perception reduces all our experience to the single level of what, for good reasons, is judged to be true. But when, on the contrary, I consider the whole setting of my perception, it reveals to me another modality which is neither the ideal and necessary being of geometry nor the simple sensory event, the *percipi*, and this is precisely what remains to be studied now.

But these remarks on the setting of what is perceived enable us better to see the perceived itself. I perceive before me a road or a house, and I perceive them as having a certain dimension: the road may be a country road or a national highway; the house may be a shanty or a manor. These identifications presuppose that I recognize the true size of the object, quite different from that which appears to me from the point at which I am standing. It is frequently said that I restore the true size on the basis of the apparent size by analysis and conjecture. This is inexact for the very convincing reason that the apparent size of which we are speaking is not given to me. It is a remarkable fact that the uninstructed have no awareness of perspective and that it took a long time and much reflection so that humans became aware of a perspectival deformation of objects. Thus there is no deciphering, no mediate inference from the sign to the signified, because the alleged signs are not given to me separately from what they signify.

In the same way, it is not true that I deduce the true color of an object on the basis of the color of the setting or of the lighting, which most of the time is not given to me. At this hour, since daylight is still coming through the windows, we perceive the yellowness of the artificial light, and it alters the color of objects. But when daylight disappears, this yellowish color will no longer be perceived, and we will see the objects more or less in their true colors. The true color thus is not deduced, taking account of the lighting, because it appears precisely when daylight disappears.

If these remarks are true, what is the result? And how should we understand this "I perceive" which we are attempting to grasp?

We observe at once that it is impossible, as has often been said, to decompose a perception, to make it into a collection of sensations, because in it the whole is prior to the parts—and this whole is not an ideal whole. The meaning which I ultimately discover is not of the conceptual order. If it came about from the concept, the question would be how I can recognize it in the sense data, and it would be necessary for me to interpose between the concept and the sense data certain intermediaries, and then other intermediaries between these intermediaries, and so on. It is necessary that the meaning and the signs, the form and matter of perception, be related from the beginning, and that, as we say, the matter of perception be "pregnant with its form."

In other words, the synthesis which constitutes the unity of the perceived objects and which gives a sense to the perceptual data is not an intellectual synthesis. Let us say with Husserl that it is a "synthesis of transition"—I anticipate the unseen side of the lamp because I can touch it—or a "horizon synthesis"—the unseen side is given to me as "visible from another standpoint," at once given but only imminently.[2] What prohibits me from treating my perception as an intellectual act is that an intellectual act would grasp the object either as possible or as necessary. But in perception it is "real"; it is given as the infinite sum of an indefinite series of perspectival views in each of which the object is given but in none of which it is given exhaustively. It is not accidental for the object to be given to me in a "deformed" way, from the place which I occupy. That is the price of its being "real." The perceptual synthesis thus must be accomplished by the one who can at once delimit certain perspectival aspects in the object, the only ones actually given, and at the same time go beyond them. This subject, which takes up a point of view, is my body insofar as it is a perceptual and practical field, insofar as my gestures have a certain scope and circumscribe as my domain the whole group of objects familiar to me. Perception is here understood as a reference to a whole which can be grasped, in principle, only through certain of its parts and aspects. The perceived thing is not an ideal unity in the possession of the intellect, like a geometrical notion, for example; it is rather a totality open to the horizon of an indefinite number of perspectival views which blend with one another according to a certain style, a style which defines the object in question.

Perception is thus a paradox, and the perceived thing itself is paradoxical. The perceived thing exists only insofar as someone can perceive it. I cannot even for an instant imagine an object in itself. As Berkeley said, if I attempt to imagine some place in the world which has never been seen, the very fact that I imagine it makes me present at that place. I thus cannot conceive a perceptible place in which I am not myself present. But the very places in which I find myself are never completely given to me; the things which I see are things for me only under the condition that they always recede beyond their immediately given aspects. Thus there is a paradox of immanence and transcendence in perception. Immanence, because the perceived object would not be able to be foreign to the one who perceives; transcendence, because it always involves a beyond of what is actually given. And these two elements of perception are not, properly speaking, contradictory. For if we reflect on this notion of perspective, if we reproduce the perceptual experience in our thought, we see that the kind of evidence proper to the perceived, the appearance of "something," requires both this presence and this absence.

Finally, the world itself, which (to give a first, rough definition) is the totality of perceptible things and the thing of all things, must be understood not as an object in the sense the mathematician or the physicist could give to this word—that is, a kind of unified law which would cover all the partial phenomena or as a fundamental relation verifiable in all— but as the universal style of all possible perceptions. We must make this notion of the world, which guides the whole transcendental deduction of Kant, though Kant does not tell us its origin, more explicit. "If a world is to be possible," he says sometimes, as if he were thinking before the origin of the world, as if he were present at its genesis and could posit its a priori conditions. In fact, as Kant himself said profoundly, we can only think the world because we have already experienced it; it is through this experience that we have the idea of being, and it is through this experience that the words "rational" and "real" receive a sense simultaneously.

If I now consider not the problem of knowing how it is that there are things for me or how it is that I have a unified, unique, and developing perceptual experience of them, but rather the problem of knowing how my experience is related to the experience which others have of the same objects, perception will again appear as the paradoxical phenomenon which renders being accessible to us.

If I consider my perceptions as simple sensations, they are private: they are mine alone. If I treat them as acts of the intellect, if perception is an inspection of the mind, and the perceived object an idea, then you and I are talking about the same world, and the communication is in principle between us because the world has become an ideal existence and is the same for all of us—just like the Pythagorean theorem. But neither of these two formulas accounts for our experience. If a friend and I are standing before a landscape, and if I attempt to show my friend something which I see and which he does not yet see, we cannot account for the situation by saying that I see something in my own world and that I attempt, by sending verbal messages, to give rise to an analogous perception of the world of my friend. There are not two numerically distinct worlds plus a mediating language which alone would bring us together. There is—and I really sense it if I become impatient—a kind of demand that what is seen by me be seen by him also. And at the same time this communication is required by the thing itself that I see, by the reflections of sunlight upon it, by its color, by its sensible evidence. The thing imposes itself not as true for every intellect, but as real for every subject who shares my situation.

I would never know how you see red, and you will never know how I see it; but this separation of consciousnesses is recognized only after a failure of communication, and our first movement is to believe in an undivided being between us. There is no reason to treat this primordial communication as an illusion, as the sensationalists do, because even then it would become inexplicable. And there is no reason to base it on our common participation in the same intellectual consciousness because this would suppress the undeniable plurality of consciousnesses. It is thus necessary that, in the perception of another, I find myself in relation with another "myself" who is, in principle, open to the same truths as I am, in relation to the same being that I am. And this perception is realized. From the depths of my subjectivity I see another subjectivity appear invested with the same rights, because the behavior of the other takes shape within my perceptual field. I understand this behavior, the words of another; I espouse his thought because this other, born in the midst of my phenomena, appropriates them and treats them in accord with typical behaviors which I myself have experienced. Just as my body, as the system of all my holds on the world, founds the unity of the objects which I perceive, in the same way the body of the other—as the bearer of symbolic behaviors and of the behavior of true reality—tears itself away from being one of my phenomena, offers me the task of a true communication, and confers on my objects the new dimension of intersubjective being or of objectivity. Such are, in a quick résumé, the elements of a description of the perceived world.

Some of our colleagues who were so kind as to send me their observations in writing grant me that all this is valid as a psychological inventory. But, they add, there remains the world of which we say "It is true"—that is to say, the world of knowledge, the verified world, the world of science. Psychological description concerns only a small section of our experience, and there is no reason, according to them, to give such descriptions a general scope. They do not touch being itself but only the psychological peculiarities of perception. These descriptions, they add, are all the less admissible as being in any way definitive because they find contradictions in the perceived world. How can we admit contradictions as ultimate? Perceptual experience is contradictory because it is confused. It is necessary to think it. When we think it, its contradictions disappear under the light of the intellect. Finally, one correspondent tells me that we are invited to return to the perceived world as we live it. That is to say that there is no need to reflect or to think and that perception knows better than we what it is doing. How could this disavowal of reflection be philosophy?

It is true that we arrive at contradictions when we describe the perceived world. And it is also true that if there were such a thing as a non-contradictory thought, it would exclude the world of perception as a simple appearance. But the question is precisely to know whether there is such a thing as logically coherent thought or a thought of pure being. This is the question Kant asked himself, and the objection which I have just sketched is a pre-Kantian objection. One of Kant's discoveries, whose consequences we have not yet fully grasped, is that all our experience of the world is throughout a tissue of concepts which lead to irreducible contradictions if we attempt to take them in an absolute sense or transfer them into pure being, and that they nevertheless found the structure of all our phenomena, of everything which *is* for us. It would take too long to show (and besides it is well known) that Kantian philosophy itself failed to utilize this principle fully and that both its investigation of experience and its critique of dogmatism remained incomplete. I wish only to point out that the accusation of contradiction is not decisive, *if the acknowledged contradiction appears as the very condition of consciousness.* It is in this sense that Plato and Kant, to mention only them, have taken up the contradiction that Zeno or Hume did not want to take up. There is a vain contradiction which consists in affirming two theses which exclude one another at the same time and under the same aspect. And there are philosophies which show the contradictions present at the very heart of time and of all relationships. There is the sterile noncontradiction of formal logic and the justified contradictions of transcendental logic. The objection with which we are concerned would be admissible only if we could put a system of eternal truths in the place of the perceived world, freed from its contradictions.

We willingly admit that we cannot rest satisfied with the description of the perceived world as we have sketched it up to now and that it appears as a psychological curiosity if we leave aside the idea of the true world, the world as thought by the understanding. This leads us, therefore, to the second point which I propose to examine: what is the relation between intellectual consciousness and perceptual consciousness?

Before taking this up, let us say a word about the other objection which was addressed to us: you go back to the unreflected; therefore you renounce reflection. It is true that we discover the unreflected. But the unreflected we go back to is not that which is prior to philosophy or prior to reflection. It is the unreflected which is understood and conquered by reflection. Left to itself, perception forgets itself and is ignorant of its own accomplishments. Far from thinking that philosophy is a useless repetition of life, philosophy is, on the contrary for us, the agency without which life would probably dissipate itself in ignorance of itself or in chaos. But this does not mean that reflection should be carried away with itself or pretend to be ignorant of its origins. By fleeing difficulties it would only fail in its task.

Should we now generalize and say that what is true of perception is also true in the order of the intellect and that in a general way all our experience, all our knowledge, has the same fundamental structures, the same synthesis of transition, the same kinds of horizons which we have found in perceptual experience?

No doubt some would oppose the absolute truth or evidence of scientific knowledge to this idea. But it seems to me that the acquisitions of the philosophy of the sciences confirm the primacy of perception. Does not the work of the French school at the beginning of this century, and the work of Brunschvicg, show that scientific knowledge cannot be closed in on itself, that it is always an approximate knowledge, and that it consists in clarifying a prescientific world the analysis of which will never be finished? Physico-mathematical relations take on a physical sense only to the extent that we at the same time represent to ourselves the sensible things to which these relations ultimately apply. Brunschvicg reproached positivism for its dogmatic illusion that the law is truer than the fact. The law, he adds, is conceived exclusively to make the fact intelligible. The perceived event can never be reabsorbed in the complex of transparent relations which the intellect constructs because of the event. But if this is the case, philosophy is not only consciousness of these relations; it is also consciousness of the obscure element and of the "non-relational foundation" on which these relations are based. Otherwise it fails at its task of universal clarification. When I think the Pythagorean theorem and recognize it as true, it is clear that this truth is not for this moment only. Nevertheless, later progress in knowledge will show that it is not yet a final, unconditioned evidence and that, if the Pythagorean theorem and the Euclidean system once appeared as final, unconditioned evidences, that is itself the mark of a certain cultural epoch. Later developments would not annul the Pythagorean theorem but would put it back in its place as a partial, and also as an abstract, truth. Thus, here also we do not have a timeless truth but rather the recovery of one time by another, just as, on the level of perception, our certainty about perceiving a given thing does not guarantee that our experience will not be contradicted, or dispense us from a fuller experience of that thing. Naturally it is necessary to establish here a difference between ideal truth and perceived truth. I do not propose to undertake this immense task just now. I am only trying to show the, so to speak, organic connection between perception and intellection. Now it is incontestable that I dominate the stream of my conscious states and even that I am unaware of their temporal succession. At the moment when I am thinking or considering an idea, I am not divided into the instants of my life. But it is also incontestable that this domination of time, which is the work of thought, is always somewhat deceiving. Can I seriously say that I will always hold the ideas I do at present—and mean it? Do I not know that in six months, in a year, even if I use more or less the same formulas to express my thoughts, they will have changed their sense slightly? Do I not know that there is a life of ideas, as there is a sense of everything I experience, and that every one of my most convincing thoughts will need additions and then will be, not destroyed, but at least integrated into another whole? This is the only conception of knowledge that is scientific and not mythological.

Thus perception and thought have this much in common—that both of them have a future horizon and a past horizon and that they appear to themselves as temporal, even though they do not move at the same speed or in the same time. We must say that at each moment our ideas express not only the truth but also our capacity to attain it at that given moment. Skepticism begins if we conclude from this that our ideas are always false. But this can only happen with reference to some idol of absolute knowledge. We must say, on the contrary, that our ideas, however limited they may be at a given moment—since they always express our contact with being and with culture—are capable of being true provided we keep them open to the field of nature and culture which they must express. Now this possibility is always open to us, just because we are temporal. The idea of going straight to the essence of things is an inconsistent idea if one thinks about it. What is given is a path, an experience which gradually clarifies itself, which gradually rectifies itself and proceeds by dialogue with itself and with others. Thus what we tear away from the dispersion of instants is not an already-made reason; it is, as has always been said, a natural light, our openness to *something*. What saves us is the possibility of a new development, and our power of making even what is false, true—by thinking through our errors and replacing them within the domain of truth.

But finally, it will be objected that I grasp myself in pure reflection, completely outside perception, and that I grasp myself not now as a perceiving subject, tied by its body to a system of things, but as a thinking subject, radically free with respect to things and with respect to the body. How is such an experience of self, of the cogito, possible in our perspective, and what sense does it have?

There is a first way of understanding the cogito: it consists in saying that when I grasp myself I am limited to noting, so to speak, a psychic fact, "I think." This is an instantaneous observation, and under the condition that the experience has no duration I adhere immediately to what I think and consequently cannot doubt it. This is the cogito of the psychologists. It is of this instantaneous cogito that Descartes was thinking when he said that I am certain that I exist during the whole time that I am thinking of it. Such certitude is limited to my existence and to my pure and completely naked thought. As soon as I make it specific with any particular thought, I fail, because, as Descartes explains, every particular thought uses premises not actually given. Thus the first truth, understood in this way, is the only truth. Or rather it cannot even be formulated as truth; it is experienced in the instant and in silence. The cogito understood in this way—in the skeptical way—does not account for our idea of truth.

There is a second way of understanding the cogito: as the grasping not only of the fact that I think but also of the objects which this thought intends, and as evidence not only of a private existence but also of the things which it thinks, at least as it thinks them. In this perspective the cogito is neither more certain than the *cogitatum,* nor does it have a different kind of certainty. Both are possessed of ideal evidence. Descartes sometimes presented the cogito in this way—as, for example, in the *Regulae* when he placed one's own existence (*se esse*) among the most simple evidences. This supposes that the subject is perfectly transparent for itself, like an essence, and is incompatible with the idea of the hyperbolic doubt which even reaches to essences.

But there is a third meaning of the cogito, the only solid one: the act of doubting in which I put in question all possible objects of my experience. This act grasps itself at work, and thus cannot put itself in doubt. The very fact of doubting obturates doubt. The certitude I have of myself is here a genuine perception: I grasp myself, not as a constituting subject which is transparent to itself, and which constitutes the totality of every possible object of thought and experience, but as a particular thought, as a thought engaged with certain objects, as a thought in act; and it is in this sense that I am certain of myself. Thought is given to itself; I somehow find myself thinking and I become aware of it. In this sense I am certain that I am thinking this or that as well as being certain that I am simply thinking. Thus I can get outside the psychological cogito—without, however, taking myself to be a universal thinker. I am not simply a constituted happening; I am not a universal *naturans.* I am a thought which recaptures itself as already possessing an ideal of truth (which it cannot at each moment wholly account for) and which is the horizon of its operations. This thought, which touches itself rather than sees itself, which searches after clarity rather than possesses it, and which creates truth rather than finds it, is described in a formerly celebrated text of Lagneau. Should we submit to life or create it, he asked. And he answered: "Once again this question does not pertain to the domain of the intellect; we are free and, in this sense, skepticism is true. But to answer negatively is to make the world and the self unintelligible; it is to decree chaos and above all to establish it in the self. But chaos is nothing. To be or not to be, the self and everything else, we must choose" (*Treatise on the Existence of God*). I find here, in an author who spent his whole life reflecting on Descartes, Spinoza, and Kant, the idea—sometimes considered barbarous—of a thought which remembers that it was born and then takes itself up sovereignly and in which fact, reason, and freedom coincide.

Finally, let us ask what happens, from such a point of view, to rationality and practice, whether there can be any absolute affirmation already implied in practice.

The fact that my experiences agree with each other and that I experience the agreement of my own experiences with those of others is in no way compromised by what we have just said. On the contrary, this fact is put in relief, against skepticism. Something appears to me, as to anyone else, and these phenomena, which set the boundaries of everything thinkable or conceivable for us, are as such certain. There is sense. But rationality is guaranteed neither as total nor as immediate. It is somehow open, which is to say that it is menaced.

Doubtless, a conception like this one would run up against a double critique, one from the side of psychology and the other from the side of philosophy.

The very psychologists who have described the perceived world as I did above, the Gestalt psychologists, have never drawn the philosophical conclusions of their description. In that respect they remain within the classical framework. Ultimately they consider the structures of the perceived world as the simple result of certain physical and physiological processes which take place in the nervous system and completely determine the *Gestalten* and the experience of the *Gestalten*. The organism and consciousness itself are functions of external physical variables. Ultimately the real world is the physical world as science conceives it, and it engenders our consciousness itself.

But the question is whether Gestalt theory, after the work it has done in calling attention to the phenomena of the perceived world, can fall back on the classical notion of reality and objectivity and incorporate the world of the forms within a being in the classical sense of the word. Without doubt one of the most important acquisitions of this theory has been its overcoming of the classical alternatives between objective psychology and introspective psychology. Gestalt psychology went beyond this alternative by showing that the object of psychology is the structure of behavior, accessible both from within and from without. In his book on the chimpanzees, Köhler applied this idea and showed that in order to describe the behavior of a chimpanzee it is necessary, in characterizing this behavior, to bring in notions such as the "melodic line" of behavior. These are anthropomorphic notions, but they can be utilized objectively because it is possible to agree on interpreting "melodic" and "non-melodic" behaviors in terms of "good solutions" and "bad solutions." The science of psychology thus is not something constructed outside the human world; it is, in fact, a property of the human world to make the distinction between the true and the false, the objective and the fictional. When, later on, Gestalt psychology tried to explain itself—in spite of its own discoveries— in terms of a scientistic or positivistic ontology, it was at the price of an internal contradiction which we have to reject. By returning to the perceived world as we have described it above, and basing our conception of being on the phenomena, we do not in any way sacrifice objectivity to the interior life, as Bergson has been accused of doing. As Gestalt psychology has shown, structure, gestalt, meaning are no less visible in objectively observable behavior than in the experience of ourselves—provided, of course, that objectivity is not confused with what is measurable. Is one truly objective with respect to the human when we think we can consider him as an object which can be explained as an intersection of processes and causalities? Is it not more objective to attempt to constitute a true science of human life based on the description of typical behaviors? Is it objective to apply tests to man which deal only with abstract aptitudes, or to attempt to grasp the situation of the human as it is present to the world and to others by means of still more tests?

Psychology as a science has nothing to fear from a return to the perceived world, or from a philosophy which draws out the consequences of this return. Far from hurting psychology, this attitude, on the contrary, clarifies the philosophical meaning of its discoveries. For there are not two truths; there is not an inductive psychology and an intuitive philosophy. Psychological induction is never more than the methodological means of bringing to light a certain typical behavior, and if induction includes intuition, conversely intuition does not occur in empty space. It exercises itself on the facts, on the material, on the phenomena brought to light by scientific research. There are not two kinds of knowledge, but two different degrees of clarification of the same knowledge. Psychology and philosophy are nourished by the same phenomena; it is only that the problems become more formalized at the philosophical level.

But the philosophers might say here that we are giving psychology too big a place, that we are compromising rationality by founding it on the agreement of experiences, as it is manifested in perceptual experience. But either the demand for an absolute rationality is only a wish, a personal preference which should not be confused with philosophy, or this point of view, to the extent that it is well-founded, satisfies it as well as, or even better than, any other. When philosophers wish to place reason above the vicissitudes of history they cannot purely and simply forget what psychology, sociology, ethnography, history, and psychiatry have taught us about the conditioning of human behavior. It would be a very romantic way of showing one's love for reason to base its reign on the disavowal of acquired knowledge. What can be validly demanded is that the human never be submitted to the fate of an external nature or of an external history and stripped of his consciousness. Now, in this regard, a perspective such as mine satisfies this demand. By speaking of the primacy of perception, I have never, of course, meant to say (this would amount to being the theses of empiricism) that science, reflection, and philosophy are only transformed sensations or that values are deferred and calculated pleasures. By these words, the "primacy of perception," we mean that the experience of perception is our presence at the moment when things, truths, values are constituted for us; that perception is a nascent Logos; that it teaches us, outside all dogmatism, the true conditions of objectivity itself; that it summons us to the tasks of knowledge and action. It is not a question of reducing human knowledge to sensation, but of being present at the birth of this knowledge, to make it as sensible as the sensible, to recover the consciousness of rationality. This experience of rationality is lost when we take it for granted as self-evident, but is, on the contrary, rediscovered when it is made to appear against the background of nonhuman nature. The work [*Phenomenology of Perception*] which was the occasion for this paper is still, in this respect, only a preliminary study, since it hardly speaks of culture or of history. On the basis of perception—taken as a privileged realm of experience, since the perceived object is by definition present and living—this book attempts to define a method for getting closer to present and living being, and which must then be applied to the relation of humans to humans in language, in knowledge, in society and religion, as it was applied in this work to humans' relation to perceptible reality and with respect to humans' relation to others on the level of perceptual experience. We call this level of experience "primordial"—not to assert that everything else derives from it by transformations and evolution (we have expressly said that humans perceive in a way different from any animal), but rather that it reveals to us the permanent data of the problem which culture attempts to resolve. If we have not tied the subject to the determinism of an external nature and have only placed it back in the bed of the perceptible, which it transforms without ever quitting it, much less will we submit the subject to some history that is in itself. History is others; it is the interrelationships we establish with them, outside of which the realm of the ideal appears as an alibi.

This leads us . . . to draw certain conclusions from what has preceded as concerns the realm of the practical. If we admit that our life is inherent to the perceived world and to the human world, even while it re-creates it and contributes to its making, then morality cannot consist in the private adherence to certain values. Principles are mystifications un-less they are put into practice; it is necessary that they animate our rela-tions with others. Thus we cannot remain indifferent to the figure that our acts take in the perspective of others, and the question is posed whether intention is sufficient justification. It is clear that the approval of such or such a group proves nothing, since, in looking for it, we choose our own judges—which comes down to saying that we are not yet thinking for our-selves. It is the very demand of rationality which imposes on us the need to act in such a way that our action cannot be considered by others as an act of aggression but, on the contrary, as generously meeting the other in the very particularity of a given situation. Now, from the very moment when we start bringing the consequences of our actions for others into morality (and how can we avoid doing so if the universality of the act is to be anything more than a word?), it appears possible that our relations with others are involved in immorality, if perchance our perspectives are irreconcilable—if, for instance, the legitimate interests of one nation are incompatible with those of another. Nothing guarantees us that morality is possible, as Kant said in a passage whose sense has not yet been ex-hausted. But even less is there any fatal assurance that morality is impos-sible. We observe it in an experience which is the perception of others, and, by having evoked the threat that the plurality of consciousnesses makes weigh upon morality, we are more aware of what there is in moral-ity that is hopeless, difficult, and valuable. Just as the perception of a thing opens me up to being, by realizing the paradoxical synthesis of an infinity of perceptual aspects, in the same way the perception of others founds morality by realizing the paradox of an alter ego, of a common situation, by placing me myself, my perspectives and my incommunicable solitude, back in the visual field of another and of all the others. Here as every-where else the primacy of perception—the recognition, at the very heart of our most personal experience, of a fecund contradiction which submits this experience to the gaze of others—is the remedy to skepticism and pessimism. If we admit that sensibility is enclosed within itself, and if we do seek communication with the truth and with others only on the level of a fleshless reason, then there is not much to hope for. Nothing is more pessimistic or skeptical than the famous text in which Pascal, asking him-self what it is to love, remarks that one does not love a woman for her beauty, which is perishable, or for her mind, which she can lose, and then suddenly concludes: "One never loves anybody; one loves only qualities." Pascal is proceeding like the skeptic who asks *if* the work exists, remarks

that the table is only a sum of sensations, the chair another sum of sensations, and finally concludes: one never sees anything; one sees only sensations. If, on the contrary, as the primacy of perception requires, we call
what we perceive "the world," and what we love "the person," there is a type
of doubt concerning the human, and a type of spite, which become impossible. Certainly, the world which we thus find is not absolutely reassur-
ing. We measure the boldness of the love which promises beyond what it
knows, which claims to be eternal when a sickness, perhaps an accident,
will destroy it . . . But it is *true,* at the moment of this promise, that our love
extends beyond *qualities,* beyond the body, beyond time, even though we
could not love without qualities, without bodies, and without time. In
order to rediscover the unity beyond, Pascal breaks human life into fragments at will and reduces the person to a discontinuous series of states.
The absolute which he looks for beyond our experience is implied in it.
Just as I grasp time through my present and by being present, I perceive
others through my singular life, in the tension of an experience which
goes beyond it.

There is thus no destruction of the absolute or of rationality here,
only of the absolute and the rationality separated from experience. To tell
the truth, Christianity consists in replacing the separated absolute by the
absolute in men. Nietzsche's idea that God is dead is already contained in
the Christian idea of the death of God. God ceases to be an external object
in order to mingle in human life, and this life is not simply a return to a
nontemporal solution. God needs human history. As Malebranche said,
the world is unfinished. My viewpoint differs from the Christian viewpoint
to the extent that the Christian believes in another side of things where the
"renversement du pour au contre" takes place. In my view this "reversal"
takes place before our eyes. And perhaps some Christians would agree that
the other side of things must already be visible in the environment in which
we live. By advancing this thesis of the primacy of perception, I have less
the feeling that I am proposing something completely new than the feeling of drawing out the conclusions of the work of my predecessors.

* * *

Discussion

BRÉHIER:[3] Your paper contains not only the exposition of your ideas but
also a discussion of them. You have spoken on two different points: a
theory of perception and a certain philosophy. . . . I will speak to the second point, which I find the more interesting.

On the first point you have made a number of remarks of great interest. You have shown that the problem of perception should not be posed in the manner in which it is usually posed, by first presupposing objects, then a human who enters into the middle of these objects from without, and then the relations between this human and these objects. Merleau-Ponty recognizes neither these objects nor this human, and he retains only the perception. And I believe he has said some very interesting things on this point, with which I am in full agreement.

But there is in Merleau-Ponty a philosopher, and with this philosopher we can certainly find many points of disagreement. Merleau-Ponty changes and inverts the ordinary sense of what we call philosophy.

Philosophy was born of the difficulties encountered in ordinary perception. It was from ordinary perception and by getting away from it that we have first philosophized. The first among philosophers, Plato, our common ancestor, philosophized in this way. Far from wanting to return to an immediate perception, to a lived perception, he took his point of departure in the insufficiencies of this lived perception in order to arrive at a conception of the intelligible world which was coherent, which satisfied reason, which supposed another faculty of knowledge other than perception itself.

You take up this Platonic idealism and follow the reverse path precisely. You attempt to reintegrate it in perception, and I believe that all your difficulties lie here, strictly speaking. These are difficulties which you yourself have indicated.

The first is a relativism which you attempt not to excuse but to explain in a manner which would satisfy the demands of our scientific and intellectual life. But I believe your explanation is insufficient, and the question I would pose is this: is not your relativism purely and simply a Protagorism? When you speak of the perception of the other, this very other exists, according to you, only in relation to us and in his relations with us. This is not the other as I perceive him immediately; it certainly is not an ethical other; it is not this person who suffices to himself. It is someone I posit outside myself at the same time I posit objects. Now this is very serious; the other is posited by us in the world just like other things.

But even this is not the principal difficulty. It is a question of whether philosophy consists in engaging oneself in the world, in engaging oneself in things—not to the point of identifying oneself with them, but to the point of following all their sinuosities—or of whether philosophy does not consist precisely in following a route directly contrary to this engagement.

In my view philosophy always supposes an inversion of this kind. Suppose philosophers had been phenomenologists from antiquity. I ask you this question: Would our science exist now? Could you have constructed your science if Anaximenes and Anaximander had not said: this perception, we do not believe in it; the true reality is air, or fire, or (as the Pythagoreans said) number. If instead of positing these realities they had already been phenomenologists, do you think they could have created a philosophy?

MERLEAU-PONTY: This hypothesis is itself impossible. Phenomenology could never have come about before all the other philosophical efforts of the rationalist tradition, or prior to the construction of science. It measures the divergence between our experience and this science. How could it ignore it? How could it precede it? Second, there have not always been phenomenologists, but there have always been skeptics who have always been accorded a place in the history of philosophy. If there had been only the Greek skeptics, or only Montaigne, or only Hume, could science have progressed? It seems to me that your objection is even more valid with respect to them.

BRÉHIER: I do not think so. Montaigne criticized reason in a manner which helped science progress.

MERLEAU-PONTY: The will to apply reason to what is taken as irrational is a progress for reason.

BRÉHIER: You do not have the right to incorporate Montaigne and Hume into your viewpoint. They followed a route completely different from yours.

MERLEAU-PONTY: Hume is one of the authors Husserl read the most. For my part, I read Montaigne and Hume very sympathetically, though I find them too timid in the return to the positive after their skeptical criticisms. The whole question is to know whether by recognizing the difficulties in the exercise of reason one is working for or against reason. You have said that Plato tried to quit perception for ideas. One could also say that he placed the movement and life in the ideas, as they are in the world— and he did it by breaking through the logic of identity, by showing that ideas transform themselves into their contraries.

BRÉHIER: To combat the rationalists you have to attribute to them a notion of reason which they do not hold.

MERLEAU-PONTY: Then I am in agreement with them.

BRÉHIER: Then your position in fact forces you to agree with them.

I would say that in the very formulation of your doctrine you destroy it. If I am exaggerating a little, I beg your pardon. In order to formulate your doctrine of perception you are obliged to say that humans perceive objects, and consequently you are obliged to posit humans and objects separately in the way you speak. There results a fatal contradiction, which you indicate under the name of the contradiction of immanence and transcendence. But this contradiction comes from the fact that, once you formulate your doctrine, you necessarily posit an object exterior to man.

Thus your doctrine, in order not to be contradictory, must remain unformulated, only lived. But is a doctrine which is only lived still a philosophical doctrine?

MERLEAU-PONTY: Assuredly a life is not a philosophy. I thought I had indicated in passing that description is not the return to immediate experience; one never returns to immediate experience. It is a question simply of knowing whether we propose to understand it. I believe that to attempt to express immediate experience is not to betray reason but, on the contrary, to work toward its aggrandizement.

BRÉHIER: It is to betray the immediate.

MERLEAU-PONTY: It is to begin the struggle of expression and the expressed; it is to accept the condition of a reflection that is at the stage of beginning. What is encouraging in this effort is that there is no pure and absolutely unexpressed life in the human; the unreflected comes into existence for us only through reflection. To enter into these contradictions, as you have just said, seems to me to be a part of the critical inventory of our lives which is philosophy.

BRÉHIER: I see your ideas as being better expressed in literature and in painting than in philosophy. Your philosophy results in a novel. This is not a defect, but I truly believe that it results in that immediate suggestion of realities which we associate with the writings of novelists. . . .

MERLEAU-PONTY: I would like to answer briefly one of Bréhier's earlier remarks—namely, that it is "serious" to posit the other in his relations with us and to posit him in the world. I think that you mean to say "ethically serious." It was never my intention to posit the other except as an ethical subject, and I am sure I have not excluded the other as an ethical subject.

BRÉHIER: It is a consequence.

MERLEAU-PONTY: It is a consequence which you draw.

BRÉHIER: Yes.

MERLEAU-PONTY: From the simple fact that I turn morality into a problem, you conclude that I deny it. But the question is posed for all of us. How do we know there is someone there before us unless we gaze in front of ourselves? What do we see, first of all, but corporeal appearances? How do these automata "who move by springs" become human for me? It is not the phenomenological method which creates this problem—though it does, in my view, allow us better to solve it. When Brunschvicg said that the "I" is achieved by reciprocity and it is necessary that I become able to think the other as reciprocable with me, he meant that morality is not something given but something to be made. I do not see how anyone could posit the other without the self; it is an impossibility for my experience.

BRÉHIER: The other is "reciprocable to me" by reason of a universal norm. Where is your norm?

MERLEAU-PONTY: If it is permissible to answer one question by another, I would ask: where is yours? All of us are in an experience of the self and of others which we attempt to dominate by thinking of it, but without ever being able to flatter ourselves that we have completely achieved this. Even when I believe I am thinking universally, if the other refuses to agree with me, I experience this universality as only a private universality (as I am verifying once more at this moment). Apart from a pure heteronomy accepted by both sides (but I do not think you meant "norm" in the sense of "heteronomy"), there is no given universality; there is only a presumptive universality. We are back at the classical problem: how do we reach the universal? It is a problem which has always existed in philosophy, though it has never been posed in such a radical manner as it is today because two centuries after Descartes philosophers, in spite of their professions of atheism, are still thinking on the basis of Cartesian theology. Thus these problems seem to me more or less traditional. If I have given a different impression to those who have heard this paper, it is only a question of terminology.

LENOIR: By reversing the order you have followed, and by moving from the philosophical consequences to the very details of what constituted your subject matter, Bréhier and Parodi have made us lose sight of this subject matter, which is the problem of perception.

I was struck by the resolutely realistic attitude which you adopted. I find no fault with this. The aftermaths of all the great social upheavals have presented a similar phenomenon. Already in 1920 we saw the very important Anglo-American movement of neorealism; a plethora of different philosophical systems arose in the same year in the United States. There was a similar development in an even more troubled epoch, at the time Victor Cousin dictated the laws of traditional philosophy and when he attempted to lay down the fundamental attitudes of mind which determine the main lines of the various philosophical systems: materialism, idealism, skepticism, mysticism. And here you give us, with your realism, a kind of materialism in reverse. But if you apply it to the problems of perception, it is vitiated, and I agree with Bréhier. Your analysis is somehow paralyzed by terminological difficulties. We live, in the realm of psychology, based on a set of word associations that do not go together, that do not correspond to one another. Somehow, alongside the real problems which are suggested by this terminology there arise false problems or deviations from the true problems. But I think that the French tradition has attempted to overcome this danger of terminology. Auguste Comte himself indicated the way out. He attempted to get away from the tendency common to ideologists, "psychologists," and phrenologists. For this psychological orientation he substituted a fundamental notion of contemporary physics—energy. The notion of energy was his starting point. He showed how all the encyclopedic divisions which attempt to classify the human attitudes called behavior should be abandoned. He returned to the classical attitude, that of Descartes, who distinguished reflection, meditation, and contemplation. Comte appealed only to secondary aspects. But he insisted on *synergie*, on the contrast between impression and impulsion—that is to say, between the aspects which come from without and those which come from within. You also have alluded to this.

The difficulties that arose for philosophy after Comte, which accepted the data of voluntarism and those of Renouvier, came from an attempt to effect an exchange analogous to the exchange in physics between the notion of matter and the notion of energy. Perception is dematerialized into true hallucinations in Taine, into the immediate data of consciousness in Bergson, into mystical experience in Lévy-Bruhl. However, William James attempted to materialize sensation by turning to the work of the artist. Perception, which has been so impoverished that it is now reduced to nothing but a motor schema in present life, would be able to recover its fullness and its sense in aesthetic activity.

MERLEAU-PONTY: I deliberately avoided the use of the word "realism," since this would involve us in all sorts of historical explanations of the kind you have gone into, and I see no advantage in using this term. It only prolongs the discussion without clarifying it. For my part, I would prefer to answer a concrete question rather than a question bearing on the interrelations of historical doctrines.

LUPASCO: What I have to say concerns mathematical experience. Euclidean geometry, which is the geometry of the perceived world, has been shown to be only an ideal geometry, and the physical universe, whose geometry is Riemannian, and whose internal structure is of a more and more abstract mathematical complexity, escapes more and more from the psychology of perception.

MERLEAU-PONTY: There is a misunderstanding, doubtless through my fault. I did not mean to say that mathematical thought was a reflection, or a double, of perceptual experience. I meant to say that mathematical thought has the same fundamental structures; it is not absolute. Even when we believe we are dealing with eternal truths, mathematical thought is still tied to history.

LUPASCO: It is conceived independently; it has its own history. It is, rather, mathematics which commands and modifies perception, to the extent that it commands and modifies the physical world and even history.

Generally speaking, I do not see what would become of the mathematical world in a universe in which everything is perception.

BAUER: Perhaps my language will appear naive, but it seems to me impossible to base a theory of knowledge on perception. Perception is almost as far removed from the primitive data of our senses as science itself. It seems to me that there is a discontinuity between perception and scientific knowledge; the first is an instinctive and rudimentary scientific knowledge. When we perceive a table, or a lamp on this table, we already interpret our visual sensations to a large extent. We associate them with other possible sensations, tactile or visual—for example, of the underside of the table, its solidity, or of the other side of the lamp. We thus make a synthesis; we enunciate an invariable connection between certain actual sensations and other virtual sensations. Science does nothing more than extend and make this process of synthesis more and more precise.

From this point of view we can say that the most abstract sciences, geometry, and even arithmetic or algebra, are colored by sensations. It seems to me at any rate that when I affirm, as a physicist, that "the sky is blue because there are molecules of air which diffuse the light of the sun," the workings of my mind are about the same as when I say "I perceive a lamp" at the moment when I see a green shade covering a brightly lighted spot. However, in this latter case, the sense of my affirmation is more easily understood and its experimental verification more immediate.

MERLEAU-PONTY: This answers Lupasco's question. I would only add that it is necessary to distinguish perception from the construction of a mathematical theory; it is necessary to create a theory of language and of presumptively "exact" science.

I did not mean to say that culture consists in perceiving. There is a whole cultural world which constitutes a second level above perceptual experience. Perception is rather the primary soil beyond which we cannot go.

SALZI: I would like to indicate that what I am going to say has a triple intention, since the primacy of perception can have three senses, and I think Merleau-Ponty moves from one sense to the other.

The first would be that of the primacy of psychology. The primacy of perception would follow necessarily from the notion of consciousness in which it is comprised. Concerning this first point, I believe that this is already a psychological error. When a small baby is hungry, the consciousness of its hunger is the consciousness of a lack. At the beginning, in the psychology of the infant, there is no distinction between the consciousness of a lack and the consciousness of an object or of a subject. There is no duality; there is consciousness of a lack without there being either object or subject. This is one objection to this conception of the primacy of perception.

The second sense of "the primacy of perception" could be that of perception, as intuition or the basic contact with the real, as the exclusive source of truth. But it seems to me that, no matter how brilliant present-day science may be, we cannot erase metaphysical intuition any more than we can do away with mystical intuition or, perhaps even less, psychological intuition.

The third sense would involve saying that this is not a question of fact but of principle, that, whatever the development of the human intellect through history may have been, we know henceforth, through the triumphs of contemporary science—and Merleau-Ponty seems to incline in this direction—that all our hypotheses must be supported by contact with perceptual experience.

And here I would be opposed to this primacy. For contemporary science has little by little extracted its postulates and its implications from perception. It denounces the postulates and implications derived from perception as inexact and says they must be replaced by other postulates which have nothing to do with perception—thus, the discontinuity of the quantum of energy. We could evoke the recent analysis of subatomic particles, this species of perception in which time and space—which, it seems, since the time of Kant have served as the basis of perception—disappear, and consequently in which we no longer have anything to do with perception. Thus the world of the scientists escapes the fetters of perception to a greater and greater degree. . . .

MERLEAU-PONTY: I have never claimed that perception (for example, the vision of colors or forms), insofar as it gives us access to the most immediate properties of objects, has a monopoly on truth. What I meant to say is that we find in perception a mode of access to the object which is rediscovered at every level, and in speaking of the perception of the other I insisted that the word "perception" includes the whole experience which gives the thing itself. Consequently I do not detract anything from the most complex forms of knowledge; I only show how they refer to this fundamental experience as the basic experience which they must render more determinate and explicit. Thus it has never entered my mind to do away with science, as you say. It is rather a question of understanding the scope and the meaning of science. It is the problem of Poincaré in his book *The Value of Science;* when he put this title on his work no one thought that he was denying science. To be more specific, do you think that natural science gives you a total explanation of the human—I say "total"—or do you not think there is something more?

SALZI: Without any doubt. I have, therefore, misunderstood the sense of the "primacy of perception."

MERLEAU-PONTY: If we reflect on our objects of thought and science, they ultimately refer us to the perceived world, which is the terrain of their final application. However, I did not mean to say that the perceived world, in the sense of the world of colors and forms, is the totality of our universe. There is the ideal or cultural world. I have not diminished its original character; I have only tried to say that it is somehow created on the face of the earth.

It seems to me that these objections could be made to any author who recognizes that philosophy has an original role distinct from that of science. The scientists have often said to philosophers, "Your work is otiose; you reflect on science but you do not understand it at all. This disqualifies you." And it is certain that by asserting that there is a philosophy we thereby take something away from the scientist; we take away his monopoly on the true. But this is the only way in which I limit the role of science.

As to mystical experience, I do not do away with that either. It is only a question of knowing just what it proves. Is it the effective passage to the absolute, or is it only an illusion? I recall a course by Brunschvicg which was entitled *Les techniques du passage à l'absolu* (Techniques for the transition to the absolute). Brunschvicg studied the various methods, all of which he considered fallacious, by which humans attempt to reach the absolute. When I ask myself whether mystical experience means exactly what it thinks it means, I am posing a question to myself which everyone should pose. If, in order to be fair with respect to the fact of mystical experience, it is necessary to grant in advance that it is what it claims to be, if every question is an offense, then we must give up the quest for truth altogether.

I have expressed myself poorly if I have given the impression that I meant to do away with everything. On the contrary, I find everything interesting and, in a certain way, *true*—on the sole condition that we take things as they are presented in our fully elucidated experience. Bréhier asked me just now, "Do you posit the other as an absolute value?" I answered, "Yes, insofar as a human can do so." But when I was in the army, I had to call for an artillery barrage or an air attack, and at that moment I was not recognizing an absolute value in the enemy soldiers who were the objects of these attacks. I can in such a case promise to hold generous feelings toward the enemy; I cannot promise not to harm him. When I say I love someone at this moment, can I be sure that in this love I have reached the substance of the person, a substance which will absolutely never change? Can I guarantee that what I know of this person and what makes me love her will be verified throughout her whole life? Perception anticipates, goes ahead of itself. I would ask nothing better than to see more clearly, but it seems to me that no one sees more clearly. I can promise here and now to adopt a certain mode of behavior; I cannot promise my future feelings. Thus it is necessary to confide in the generosity of life—which enabled Montaigne to write in the last book of his *Essays:* "J'ai plus tenu que promis ni dû" [I did more than I promised or owed].

ROIRE: Is there a scale of values in all these experiences, and what is it? For example, are mystical experiences or the mathematical sciences at the top? Is there a scale of values with respect to the primacy of perception? How are the other forms to be situated?

MERLEAU-PONTY: Assuredly for me there is a scale. This does not mean, however, that what is at the bottom is to be suppressed. It seems to me, for instance, that if we make it our goal to reach the concrete, then in certain respects we must put art above sciences because it achieves an expression of the concrete human which science does not attempt. But the hierarchies of which you are speaking suppose a point of view; from one point of view you get one hierarchy and from another point of view you get another hierarchy. Our research must be concentric rather than hierarchized.

PRENANT: . . . First of all, in this scale of values which has just been mentioned, does Merleau-Ponty place a higher value on the sun of the astronomer or on the sun of the peasant? . . . Does he consider the scientific theory as absolutely opposed to perception? And yet does not what he has said of the asymptotic character of scientific truth in Brunschvicg establish a certain continuity between ordinary perception and scientific perception? Are these diverse theories of perception opposed to one another, and should not Bauer's question be repeated?

My second question is related to the first: . . . Do I not possess a way of thinking which shows me that the sun of the astronomer is superior to the sun of the peasant?

MERLEAU-PONTY: I am in complete agreement with this and for two reasons. Recall the famous phrase from Hegel: "The earth is not the physical center of the world, but it is the metaphysical center." The originality of the human in the world is so much more visible as we acquire a more exact knowledge of the universe of science. It is strictly necessary that we teach everybody about the world and the sun of the astronomer. There is no question of discrediting science. Philosophical awareness is possible only on the basis of science. It is only when one has conceived the world of the natural sciences in all their rigor that one can see appear, by contrast, the human in his or her freedom. What is more, having passed a certain point in its development, science itself ceases to hypostatize itself; it leads us back to the structures of the perceived world and somehow recovers them. For example, the convergence between the phenomenological notion of space and the notion of space in the theory of relativity has been pointed out. Philosophy has nothing to fear from a mature science, nor has science anything to fear from philosophy.

PRENANT: By the same token, history is a concrete study.

MERLEAU-PONTY: Certainly. For my part, I would not separate history from philosophy. That is what I meant to say when I said that we could not imagine philosophers being phenomenologists from the beginning.

PRENANT: One could say that geodesy is also a science of the concrete.

MERLEAU-PONTY: Why not? But human geography much more so. As to the asymptotic character of scientific truths, what I meant to say was that, for a long time and in some respects, science seems to have tried to give us an image of the universe as immobile. It seemed to lack any orientation toward processes. To that extent, we can consider it to have been incomplete and partial.

PRENANT: I believe that it makes up for that.

MERLEAU-PONTY: That makes me happy.

CÉSARI: I only wish to ask Merleau-Ponty for a simple clarification. He seems to affirm that there is a certain continuity between science and perception. We can admit this point of view, which is that of Brunschvicg and which could be that of Bachelard, to the extent that new experiences can bring about an evolution within the frameworks of reason. But Merleau-Ponty has insisted in an exaggerated fashion on the instability of the frameworks of reason. But that is a question of degree; what confuses me is something else. I do not see how the phenomenological study of perception can serve the evolution of science in any way. It seems to me that there is a solution of continuity between perception as you describe it—that is, lived perception—and the perception on which the scientist bases himself in order to construct certain theories. It seems to me that there is a contradiction in your arguments. You say, "The study of perception, carried out by psychologists without presuppositions, reveals that the perceived world is not a sum of objects in the sense in which the sciences understand this word." Perfect. We are in complete agreement. It is a fact that perception at the level of lived experience does not describe objects in the way science does. But this being the case, what purpose does it serve for us to appeal to this purely lived experience to constitute scientific experience, which, as Bachelard has said, must distance itself from the immediate? Science will not be constituted unless we abandon the sensations and perceptions of ordinary experience, unless we define facts as technical effects—like the Compton effect, for example.

Under these conditions, I do not see how phenomenology can be of any use to science.

MERLEAU-PONTY: The first thing to be said is that I do not know whether the phenomenological attitude is of any use to the other sciences, but it certainly is of use to psychology.

CÉSARI: I agree as to psychology, but to evaluate the role of reason in science itself is another matter. You have compared phenomenological experience with that of Brunschvicg, who speaks of a highly elaborated experience which has nothing to do with lived experience.

MERLEAU-PONTY: Lived experience is of immediate interest only to those who are interested in the human. I have never hoped that my work would be of much interest to the physicist as physicist. But your complaint could as well be addressed to all works of philosophy.

CÉSARI: I am not making a complaint. I consider your point of view very interesting as it concerns the psychology of perception, but in its relation to scientific thought, I do not see its relevance except, once again, for psychology.

There is a second question which I would like to pose. You said at one point in your paper that "matter is pregnant with its form," and at that point you follow Gestalt theory. And in this theory there is an explanation of the genesis of perception (isomorphism). You have, on the contrary, compared your point of view to that of Bergson as it is given at the beginning of *Matter and Memory*. But I have been unable to understand whether, according to you, the problem of the relation of the stimulus to perception really poses itself, since it is a question which interests knowledge, while the existential viewpoint obliges you to consider the human-world complex as indissoluble, as giving perception immediately. I separate myself from the world when I ask about the relation between sensation and perception.

Since in your paper you uphold the view that there is no discontinuity between the existentialist viewpoint and that of knowledge, at some point the question of the relation between the stimulus and perception will perhaps pose itself, no doubt in a paradoxical manner. Exactly what solution do you give for this problem? For Bergson it was a question of possible reactions of the body to the world.

MERLEAU-PONTY: I have said that the point of view of the scientist with respect to perception—a stimulus in itself which produces a perception—is, like all forms of naive realism, absolutely insufficient. Philosophically I do not believe that this image of perception is ultimately defensible. But it seems to me indispensable for science to continue its own study of perception. For the time comes when, precisely because we attempt to apply the procedures of scientific thought to perception, we see clearly why perception is not a phenomenon of the order of physical causality. We observe a response of the organism which "interprets" the stimuli and gives them a certain configuration. To me it seems impossible to hold that this configuration is produced by the stimuli. It comes from the organism and from the behavior of the organism in their presence.

It seems to me valuable, even for psychology and philosophy, that science attempt to apply its usual procedure even if, and precisely if, this attempt ends in failure.

CÉSARI: Doubtless these explanations are satisfactory. The only question which remains is that of the relation between the motivating rationalism of science and the phenomenology of perception.

MERLEAU-PONTY: I refuse to recognize a dilemma here.

HYPPOLITE:[4] I would say simply that I do not see the necessary connection between the two parts of your paper—between the description of perception, which presupposes no ontology, and the philosophical conclusions which you draw, which do presuppose an ontology, namely, an ontology of sense. In the first part of your paper you show that perception has a sense, and in the second part you arrive at the being of the same sense, which the unity of the human constitutes. And the two parts do not seem to me to be absolutely coherent. Your description of perception does not necessarily entail the philosophical conclusions of the second part of your paper. Would you accept such a de-coherence?

MERLEAU-PONTY: Obviously not. If I have spoken of two things it is because they have some relation to one another.

HYPPOLITE: Does the description of perception entail the philosophical conclusion on "the being of sense" which you have developed after it?

MERLEAU-PONTY: Yes. Only I have not, of course, said everything which it would be necessary to say on this subject. For example, I have not spoken of time or its role as foundation and basis.

HYPPOLITE: This problem of "the being of sense," with the implied unity of the relative and absolute, which is the purposiveness—this rediscovered unity leads me to a question which is perhaps more specific: it does not seem to me that you have explicated the drama which reflection brings about in unreflective life—that is, the new form of life which the projection of an eternal norm by means of reflection brings about. The fact of reflection, adding itself to unreflective life, results in a going-beyond, in a transcendence—formal perhaps, illusory perhaps, but without which reflection could not occur.

PRENANT: The Drama of the evil genius.

HYPPOLITE: Perhaps. Do you agree that this reflection launches us into a new sense of transcendence?

MERLEAU-PONTY: Certainly there is much to be added to what I have said. On the basis of what I have said, one might think that I hold that humans live only in the real. But we also live in the imaginary, also in the ideal. Thus it is necessary to develop a theory of imaginary existence and of ideal existence. I have already indicated in the course of this discussion that by placing perception at the center of consciousness I do not claim that consciousness is enclosed in the observation of a natural datum. I meant to say that even when we transform our lives in the creation of a culture—and reflection is an acquisition of culture—we do not suppress our ties to time and space; in fact, we utilize them. Reciprocally, one could say that in a completely explicated human perception we would find all the originalities of human life. Human perception is directed to the world; animal perception is directed to an environment, as Scheler said. The same creative capacity which is at work in imagination and in ideation is present, in germ, in the first human perception (and I have obviously been incomplete on this point). But the essential difference between my point of view and that of a philosophy of the understanding is that, in my view, even though consciousness is able to detach itself from things in order to see itself, human consciousness never possesses itself without something left over and does not recover itself at the level of culture except by recapitulating the expressive, discrete, and contingent operations by means of which philosophical interrogation itself has become possible.

HYPPOLITE: My question does not only concern the incomplete character of your exposition. It concerns knowing whether human reflection, contrary to every other form of life, does not pose problems not only of this or that sense but of sense in general, and whether this introduction of a reflection on "the very being of all sense" does not imply a new problem and a new form of life.

MERLEAU-PONTY: I am in complete agreement with that.

HYPPOLITE: Still, it does not seem to me that the solution you give is a satisfying one, because the human is led to posit to itself the problem of a "being of all sense," the problem of an "absolute being of all sense."

In other words, there is in human reflection a kind of total reflection.

MERLEAU-PONTY: Taking up something Rimbaud said, I have already said, in my thesis, that there is a center of consciousness by which "we are not in the world." But this absolute emptiness is observable only at the moment when it is filled by experience. We do not ever see it, so to speak, except marginally. It is perceptible only on the ground of the world. In short, you are simply saying that I have no religious philosophy. I think it is proper to the human to think God, which is not the same thing as to say that God exists.

HYPPOLITE: You said that God was dead.

MERLEAU-PONTY: I said that to say God is dead, as the Nietzscheans do, or to speak of the death of God, like the Christians do, is to tie God to the human, and that in this sense the Christians themselves are obliged to tie eternity to time.

HYPPOLITE: You attempted to do a kind of ontology of the problem, which I have the right to call ambiguous, when you spoke of the death of God.

MERLEAU-PONTY: One is always ambiguous when one tries to understand others. What is ambiguous is the human condition. But this discussion is going too fast; it is necessary to go back over all of this.

HYPPOLITE: Therefore you are not engaged by your description of perception, and you acknowledge it!

MERLEAU-PONTY: I do not acknowledge it at all. In a sense, perception is everything because there is not one of our ideas or one of our reflections which does not carry a date, whose objective reality exhausts its formal reality, or which carries itself outside of time.

BEAUFRET:[5] What I have to say will not add much to what Hyppolite has already said. I wish only to emphasize that many of the objections which have been addressed to Merleau-Ponty seem to me unjust. I believe that they come down simply to objecting to his perspective itself, which is that of phenomenology. To say that Merleau-Ponty stops at a phenomenology without any means of going beyond it is to fail to understand that the overcoming of the empirical belongs to the phenomenon itself, in the phenomenological sense of the term. The phenomenon in this sense is not empirical but rather that which manifests itself really, that which we can truly experience, in opposition to what would be only the construction of concepts. Phenomenology is not a falling back into phenomenalism but the maintenance of contact with "the thing itself." If phenomenology rejects "intellectualist" explanations of perception, it is not to open the door to the irrational but to close it to verbalism. Nothing appears to me less pernicious than the *Phenomenology of Perception*. The only reproach I would make to the author is not that he has gone "too far," but rather that he has not been sufficiently radical. The phenomenological descriptions which he uses in fact maintain the vocabulary of idealism. In this they are in accord with Husserlian descriptions. But the whole problem is precisely to know whether phenomenology, fully developed, does not require the abandonment of subjectivity and the vocabulary of subjective idealism as, beginning with Husserl, Heidegger has done.

PARODI: We may have to leave one another without treating the principal question—namely, to come to a precise understanding of your theory of perception. In general, what do you think of the classical doctrine of perception which you seem to reject? I would like to see the positive part of your thesis recalled before we end this session. If perception is only a construction composed of materials borrowed from memory and based on immediate sensations, how do you explain the process?

MERLEAU-PONTY: Naturally there is a development of perception; naturally it is not achieved all at once. What I have attempted to say here presupposes (perhaps too much) the reading of the thesis which I devoted to this question. On the other hand, it seemed neither possible nor desirable for me to repeat it here.

PARODI: Could you tell us what is your most important contribution on this factual question? You began with very clear examples: we think we perceive things which we really only see in part, or more or less. What, according to you, is the essential element in this operation?

MERLEAU-PONTY: To perceive is to render oneself present to something through the body. All the while the thing keeps its place within the horizon of the world, and the structurization consists in putting each detail in the perceptual horizons which belong to it. But such formulas are just so many enigmas unless we relate them to the concrete developments which they summarize.

PARODI: I would be tempted to say that the body is much more essential for sensation than it is for perception.

MERLEAU-PONTY: Can they be distinguished?

7

Reality and Its Shadow

[This is a presentation by Merleau-Ponty, signed T.M. (for *Les Temps Modernes*), of Emmanuel Levinas's article "La Réalité et son ombre," in *Les Temps Modernes*, no. 38 (November 1948): 769–70.][1]

The study one is going to read gives a striking description of the prehuman environment, prior to time and life, which is that of art and literature. If the author disconnects them from the concern of expressing the human experience, it is because art, according to him, places itself prior to the true world, and the artist as artist is not yet a human. Even if he respects the indifference of the artistic consciousness, he does not consent to calling it generosity, and there is disdain in this respect. He reserves truth for philosophy and action.

It must be admitted that there is here a problem for everyone. Even if one reintegrates literature into human signifying activity, even if one takes it entirely as speech and as a question of the author to his audience, there is in reality a solitude on the part of the writer; there is, in literary and artistic expression, a putting into question of oneself, a pensive mood that make of the writer a bad advocate, and frequently a human without character, as they say.

In this regard, Sartre's ideas on the engagement of literature have only cursorily been examined. No one has done more to call attention to the difficulties of literary communication, which threaten at every instant to send the writer back to his solitude. *The Psychology of Imagination* already described the image as a magical conduct.[2] Consciousness seeks to fascinate itself, to call up the thing, which is irreparably absent, through its physiognomy, its style, its cloak. It was to define art as the strange attempt to obtain a pseudo-presence of the world without the means of objective knowledge and through the sole force of metaphor. More recently, Sartre indicated here that a painting does not signify in the same way as prose and that it unites minds without going through the concept. The poet, he remarked elsewhere, seeks in words the "signifying humus" they still bear, under the concept they commonly serve to designate. And since, finally, the "driest prose always contains a little poetry," since "no writer of prose, even the most lucid, understands completely what he means," the entire enterprise of human expression finds itself in a precarious position. It is an act of signification, to be sure, since what is at issue is for one human to communicate with other humans, for one freedom to call out to other freedoms, but one that deposits, in order to be accomplished, no ready-made Intelligible World, one that associates freedoms, each of which is in a singular situation, one that has to create its means of communication from all the fragments and bring out meanings from the very clay of the world.

But then, no matter the difficulties of literary expression, they never allow the writer to mask a failure as a victory, to seek refuge, as M. Blanchot said, in the "small hell of literary eternity," to turn away from an experience that is his contact with the world, the avowed or secret theme of everything he says. Emmanuel Levinas leaves to a philosophical critique the task of reclaiming art for truth, of retying the bonds between "disengaged" thought and the other, between the play of art and the seriousness of life. Sartre, who is more optimistic, thinks that art and literature can save themselves if they recognize themselves as living speech or meaning, and that the freedom of art has an accomplice in every man. Or, if one prefers, more pessimistically, he does not believe that the difficulties of action or of philosophical expression are less than those of literature and art, nor of another order. For one as for the other, the artistic consciousness has to be saved from itself, and we hope that Emmanuel Levinas will here contribute to reawakening it respectfully.

The Sorbonne Period
(1949–1952)

8

A Note on Machiavelli

How could he have been understood? He writes against good feelings in politics, but he is also against violence. Since he has the nerve to speak of *virtue* at the very moment he is sorely wounding ordinary morality, he disconcerts the believers in Law as he does those who believe that the State is the Law. For he describes that knot of collective life in which pure morality can be cruel and pure politics requires something like a morality. We would put up with a cynic who denies values or an innocent who sacrifices action. We do not like this difficult thinker without idols.

He was certainly tempted by cynicism: he had, he says, "much difficulty in shielding himself" from the opinion of those who believe the world is "ruled by chance."[1] Now if humanity is an accident, it is not immediately evident what would uphold collective life if it were not the sheer coercion of political power. Thus the entire role of a government is to hold its subjects in check.[2] The whole art of governing is reduced to the art of war,[3] and "good troops make good laws."[4] Between those in power and their subjects, between the self and the other person, there is no area where rivalry ceases. We must either undergo or exercise coercion. At each instant Machiavelli speaks of oppression and aggression. Collective life is hell.

But what is original about Machiavelli is that, having laid down the source of struggle, he goes beyond it without ever forgetting it. He finds something other than antagonism in struggle itself. "While men are trying not to be afraid, they begin to make themselves feared by others; and they transfer to others the aggression that they push back from themselves, as if it were absolutely necessary to offend or be offended." It is in the same moment that I am about to be afraid that I make others afraid; it is the same aggression that I repel and send back upon others; it is the same terror which threatens me that I spread abroad—I live my fear in the fear I inspire. But by a counter-shock, the suffering that I cause rends me along with my victim; and so cruelty is no solution but must always be begun again. There is a circuit between the self and others, a Communion of Black Saints. The evil that I do I do to myself, and in struggling against others I struggle equally against myself. After all, a face is only shadows, lights, and colors; yet suddenly the executioner, because this face has grimaced in a certain way, mysteriously experiences a slackening—another *anguish* has relayed his own. A sentence is never anything but a statement, a collection of significations which as a matter of principle could not possibly be equivalent to the unique savor that each person has for himself. And yet when the victim admits defeat, the cruel man perceives another life beating through those words; he finds himself before *another himself.* We are far from the relationships of sheer force that hold between objects. To use Machiavelli's words, we have gone from "beasts" to "man."[5]

More exactly, we have gone from one way of fighting to another, from "fighting with force" to "fighting with laws."[6] Human combat is different from animal combat, but it is a fight. Power is not naked force, but neither is it the honest delegation of individual wills, as if the latter were able to set aside their differences. Whether new or hereditary, power is always described in *The Prince* as questionable and threatened. One of the duties of the prince is to settle questions before they have *become insoluble* as a result of the subjects' emotion.[7] It would seem to be a matter of keeping the citizens from becoming aroused. There is no power which has an absolute basis. There is only a crystallization of opinion, which tolerates power, accepting it as acquired. The problem is to avoid the dissolution of this consensus, which can occur in no time at all, no matter what the means of coercion, once a certain point of crisis has been passed. Power is of the order of the tacit. Men let themselves live within the horizon of the State and the Law as long as injustice does not make them conscious of what is unjustifiable in the two. The power which is called legitimate is that which succeeds in avoiding *contempt* and *hatred.*[8] "The prince must make himself feared in such a way that, if he is not loved, he is at least not hated."[9] It makes little difference that the power is blamed in a particular instance; it is established in the interval which separates criticism from repudiation, discussion from disrepute. Relationships between the subject and those in power, like those between the self and others, are tied together at a level deeper than judgment. As long as it is not a matter of contempt's radical challenge, they survive challenge.

Neither pure fact nor absolute right, power does not coerce or persuade; it thwarts—and we are better able to thwart by appealing to freedom than by terrorizing. Machiavelli formulates with precision that alternation of tension and relaxation, of repression and legality, whose secret is held by authoritarian regimes, but which, in a sugarcoated form, constitutes the essence of all diplomacy. We sometimes *prize* more highly those to whom we give credit: "A new prince has never disarmed his subjects; far from it, he hastens to arm them if he finds them without arms; and nothing is shrewder, for henceforth the arms are his. . . . But a prince who disarms his subjects offends them by leading them to believe that he mistrusts them, and nothing is more likely to arouse their hatred."[10] "A city accustomed to freedom is more easily preserved by being governed through its own citizens."[11] In a society in which each man mysteriously resembles every other, mistrusting if he is mistrustful and trusting if he is trustful, there is no pure coercion. Despotism calls forth contempt; oppression would call forth rebellion. The best upholders of authority are not even those who created it; they believe they have a right to it, or at least feel secure in their power. A new power will make an appeal to its adversaries, provided that they rally around it.[12] If they are not retrievable, then authority will lose half its force: "Men must either be won over or gotten rid of; they can avenge themselves for slight offenses, but not for serious ones."[13] Thus the conqueror may hesitate between seducing and annihilating the vanquished, and sometimes Machiavelli is cruel: "The only way to preserve is to lay waste. Whoever becomes master of a town which has begun to enjoy freedom and does not destroy it should expect to be destroyed by it."[14] Yet pure violence can only be episodic. It could not possibly procure the deep-seated agreement which constitutes power, and it does not replace it. "If [the prince] finds it necessary to punish by death, he should make his motives clear."[15] This comes down to saying that there is no absolute power.

Thus he was the first to form the theory of "collaboration" and rallying the opposition (as he was the first, moreover, to form that of the "fifth column"), which are to political terror what the Cold War is to war. But where, it will be asked, is the profit for humanism? It lies first of all in the fact that Machiavelli introduces us to the milieu proper to politics and allows us to estimate the task we are faced with if we want to bring some truth to it. It also lies in the fact that we are shown a beginning of humanity emerging from collective life as if those in power were unaware of it, and by the sole fact that they seek to seduce consciousnesses. The trap of collective life springs in both directions: liberal regimes are always a little less so than is believed; others are a little more so. So Machiavelli's pessimism is not *closed*. He has even indicated the conditions for a politics which is not unjust: it will be the one which satisfies the people. Not that the people know everything, but because if anyone is innocent they are. "The people can be satisfied without injustice, not the mighty: these seek to practice tyranny; the people seek only to avoid it. . . . The people ask nothing except not to be oppressed."[16]

In *The Prince*, Machiavelli says no more than this about the relationships between those in power and the people. But we know that in the *Discourses on Titus Livy* he is a republican. So perhaps we may extend to the relationships between those in power and the people what he says about the relationships between the prince and his advisors. He describes, then, under the name of *virtue*, a means of living with others. The prince should not decide according to others; he would be despised. Nor should he govern in isolation, for isolation is not authority. But there is a possible way of behaving which lies between these two failures. "The priest Luke said of the emperor Maximilian, his master, who was reigning at the time, that he took counsel from no one and yet never acted according to his own opinions. In this respect he follows a course diametrically opposed to the one I have just sketched out. For since this prince does not reveal his projects to any of his ministers, observations come at the very moment these projects must be carried out, so that, pressed for time and overcome by conflicts which he had not foreseen, he gives way to the *opinions* others give him."[17] There is a way of affirming oneself which aims to suppress the other person—and which makes him a slave. And there is a relationship of consultation and exchange with others which is not the death but the very act of the self. The originary struggle always threatens to reappear: it must be the prince who asks the questions; and he must not, under pain of being despised, grant anyone a permanent authorization to speak frankly. But at least during the moments when he is deliberating, he communicates with others; and others can rally around the decision he makes, because it is in some respects their decision. The ferocity of origins is dissipated when the bond of common works and destiny is established between the prince and his ministers. Then the individual grows through the very gifts he makes to those in power; there is exchange between them. When the enemy ravages their territory, and the subjects, sheltered with the prince inside the town, see their possessions lost and pillaged, it is then that they devote themselves unreservedly to him: "for who does not know that men are attached as much by the good they do as by that which they receive?"[18] What difference does it make, it will be said, if it is still only a matter of deception, if the chief ruse of those in power is to persuade men that they are winning when they lose? But Machiavelli nowhere says that the subjects are being deceived. He describes the birth of a common life which does not know the barriers of self-love. Speaking to the Medici, he proves to them that power cannot be maintained without an appeal to freedom. In this reversal, it is perhaps the prince who is deceived. Machiavelli was a republican because he had found a principle of communion. By putting conflict and struggle at the origins of social power, he did not mean to say that agreement was impossible; he meant to underline the condition for a power which does not mystify, that is, participation in a common situation.

Machiavelli's "immoralism" thereby takes on its true meaning. We are always quoting maxims from him which restrict honesty to private life and make the interest of those in power the only rule in politics. But let us see his reason for withdrawing politics from purely moral judgment; he gives two of them. The first is that "a man who wants to be perfectly honest among dishonest people can not fail to perish sooner or later."[19] A weak argument, since it could be applied equally well to private life, where Machiavelli nevertheless remains "moral." The second reason goes much further: it is that in historical action, goodness is sometimes catastrophic and cruelty less cruel than the easygoing mood.

> Cesare Borgia was considered cruel; but it was to his cruelty he owed the advantage of reuniting Romagna and its States, and reestablishing in this province the peace and tranquillity it had so long been deprived of. And all things considered, it will be admitted that this prince was more humane than the people of Florence who, to avoid seeming cruel, let Pistoia be destroyed.[20] When it is a question of holding one's subjects to their duty, one should never be worried about being reproached for cruelty, especially since in the end the Prince will be found to have been more humane in making a small number of necessary examples than those who, through too much indulgence, encourage disorders and finally provoke murder and brigandage. For these tumults overturn the State, whereas the punishments inflicted by the Prince bear on only a few private individuals.[21]

What sometimes transforms softness into cruelty and harshness into value, and overturns the precepts of private life, is that acts of authority intervene in a certain state of opinion which changes their meaning. They awake an echo which is at times immeasurable. They open or close hidden fissures in the block of general consent, and trigger a molecular process which may modify the whole course of events. Or as mirrors set around in a circle transform a slender flame into a fairyland, acts of authority reflected in the constellation of consciousnesses are transfigured, and the reflections of these reflections create an appearance which is the proper place—the truth, in short—of historical action. Power bears a halo about it, and its curse (like that of the people, by the way, who have no better understanding of themselves) is to fail to see the image of itself it shows to others.[22] So it is a fundamental condition of politics to unfold in the realm of appearance:

> Men in general judge more by their eyes than their hands. Every man can see, but very few know how to touch. Each man easily sees what he seems to be, but almost no one identifies what he is; and this small number of perceptive spirits does not dare contradict the multitude, which has the majesty of the State to shield it. Now when it is a matter of judging the inner nature of men, above all of princes, since we cannot have recourse to courts we must stick only to consequences. The main thing is to keep oneself in power; the means, whatever they may be, will always seem honorable, and will be praised by everyone.[23]

This does not mean that it is necessary or even preferable to deceive. It means that at the distance and the degree of generality at which political relations are established, a legendary character composed of a few words and gestures is sketched out; and that men honor or detest blindly. The prince is not an impostor. Machiavelli writes expressly: "A prince should try to fashion for himself a reputation for goodness, clemency, piety, loyalty, and justice; *furthermore, he should have all these good qualities.* . . ."[24] What he means is that even if the leader's qualities are true ones, they are always prey to legend, because they are not *touched* but seen—because they are not known in the movement of the life which bears them, but frozen into historical attitudes. So the prince must have a feeling for these echoes that his words and deeds arouse. He must keep in touch with these witnesses from whom all his power is derived. He must not govern as a visionary. He must remain free even in respect to his virtues. Machiavelli says the prince should have the qualities he seems to have but, he concludes, "remain sufficiently master of himself to show their contraries when it is expedient to do so."[25] A political precept, but one which could well be the rule for a true morality as well. For public judgment in terms of the appearance, which converts the prince's goodness into weakness, is perhaps not so false. What is a goodness incapable of harshness? What is a goodness which wants to be goodness? A meek way of ignoring others and ultimately despising them.

Machiavelli does not ask that one govern through vices—lies, terror, trickery; he tries to define a political *virtue,* which for the prince is to speak to these mute spectators gathered around him and caught up in the dizziness of communal life. This is real spiritual strength, since it is a question of steering a way between the will to please and defiance, between self-satisfied goodness and cruelty, and conceiving of a historical undertaking all may adhere to. This virtue is not exposed to the reversals known to moralizing politics, because from the start it establishes a relationship to others which is unknown to the latter. It is this virtue and not success which Machiavelli takes as a sign of political worth, since he holds up Cesare Borgia (who did not succeed but had *virtù*) as an example and ranks Francesco Sforza (who succeeded, but by good fortune) far behind him.[26] As sometimes happens, tough politics loves men and freedom more truly than the professed humanist: it is Machiavelli who praises Brutus, and Dante who damns him. Through mastery of his relationships with others, the man in power clears away obstacles between man and man and puts a little daylight in our relationships—as if men could be close to one another only at a sort of distance.

The reason why Machiavelli is not understood is that he combines the most acute feeling for the contingency or irrationality in the world with a taste for the consciousness or freedom in man. Considering this history in which there are so many disorders, so many oppressions, so many unexpected things and turnings-back, he sees nothing which predestines it for a final harmony. He evokes the idea of a fundamental element of chance in history, an adversity which hides it from the grasp of the strongest and the most intelligent of men. And if he finally exorcises this evil spirit, it is through no transcendent principle but simply through recourse to the givens of our condition. With the same gesture he brushes aside hope and despair. If there is an adversity, it is nameless, unintentional. Nowhere can we find an obstacle we have not helped create through our errors or our faults. Nowhere can we set a limit to our power. No matter what surprises the event may bring, we can no more rid ourselves of expectations and of consciousness than we can of our body. "As we have a free will, it seems to me that we must recognize that chance rules half, or a little more than half, our actions, and that we govern the rest."[27] Even if we come to assume a hostile element in things, it is as nothing for us since we do not know its plans: "Men ought never give way to despair; since they do not know their end and it comes through indirect and unknown ways, they always have reason to hope, and hoping, ought never give way to despair, no matter what bad luck and danger they are in."[28] Chance takes shape only when we give up understanding and willing. Fortune "exercises her power when no barriers are erected against her; she brings her efforts to bear upon the ill-defended points."[29] If there seems to be an inflexible course of events, it is only in past events. If fortune seems now favorable, now unfavorable, it is because man sometimes understands and sometimes misunderstands his age; and according to the case, his success or ruin is created by the same qualities, but not by chance.[30] Machiavelli defines a virtue in our relationships with fortune which (like the virtue in our relationships with others) is equally remote from solitude and docility. He points out as our sole recourse that presence to others and our times which makes us find others at the moment we give up oppressing them—that is, find success at the moment we give up chance, escape destiny at the moment we understand our times. Even adversity takes on a human form for us: fortune is a woman. "I think it is better to be too bold than too circumspect, because fortune is a woman; she gives in only to violence and boldness; experience shows she gives herself to fierce men rather than to cold ones."[31] For a man it matters absolutely not who is wholly against humanity, for humanity is alone in its order. The idea of a fortuitous humanity which has no cause already won is what gives absolute value to our *virtue*. When we have understood what is humanly valuable within the possibilities of the moment, signs and portents never lack. "Must heaven speak? It has already manifested its will by striking signs.

Men have seen the sea half open up its depths, a cloud mark out the path to follow, water spring forth from the rock, and manna fall from heaven. It is up to us to do the rest; since God, by doing everything without us, would strip us of the action of our free will, and at the same time of that portion of choice reserved for us."[32] What humanism is more radical than this one? Machiavelli was not unaware of values. He saw them living, humming like a shipyard, bound to certain historical actions—barbarians to be booted out, an Italy to create. For the man who carries out such undertakings, his terrestrial religion finds the words of that other religion: "Esurientes implevit bonis, et divites dimisit inanes."[33] As Renaudet puts it:

> This student of Rome's prudent boldness never intended to deny the role played in universal history by inspiration, genius, and that action of some unknown daemon which Plato and Goethe discerned. . . . But in order for passion, aided by force, to have the property of renewing a world, it must be nourished just as much by dialectical certainty as by feeling. If Machiavelli does not set poetry and intuition apart from the practical realm, it is because this poetry is truth, this intuition is made of theory and calculation.[34]

* * *

What he is reproached for is the idea that history is a struggle and politics a relationship to men rather than principles. Yet is anything more certain? Has not history shown even more clearly after Machiavelli than before him that principles commit us to nothing, and that they may be adapted to any end? Let us leave contemporary history aside. The progressive abolition of slavery had been proposed by Abbé Gregory in 1789. It is passed by the Convention in 1794, at the moment when, in the words of a colonist, "domestic servants, peasants, workers, and day laborers are manifesting against the appointive aristocracy,"[35] and the provincial bourgeoisie, which drew its revenues from San Domingo, is no longer in power. Liberals know the art of holding up principles on the slope of inopportune consequences. Furthermore, principles applied in a suitable situation are instruments of oppression. Pitt discovers that 50 percent of the slaves brought into the British islands are being resold to French colonies. English Negroes are creating San Domingo's prosperity and giving France the European market. So he takes a stand against slavery. "He asked Wilberforce," James writes, "to join the campaign. Wilberforce represented the influential Yorkshire region. He was a man of great reputation. Expressions such as humanity, justice, national shame, etc., pealed from his mouth. . . . Clarkson came to Paris to stir the torpid energies [of the Société des Amis des Noirs], to subsidize them, and to inundate France with British propaganda."[36] There can be no illusions about the fate this propaganda had in store for the slaves of San Domingo. At war with France a few years later, Pitt signs an agreement with four French colonists which places the colony under English protection until peacetime, and reestablishes slavery and discrimination against mulattoes. Clearly, it is important to know not only *what principles* we are choosing but also what forces, which men, are going to apply them. There is something still more clear: the same principles can be used by two adversaries. When Bonaparte sent troops against San Domingo who were to perish there,

> many officers and all the men believed they were fighting for the Revolution; they saw in Toussaint a traitor sold to the priests, the émigrés, and the English . . . the men still thought they belonged to a revolutionary army. Yet certain nights they heard the Blacks within the fortress sing *La Marseillaise,* the *Ça ira,* and other revolutionary songs. Lacroix tells how the deluded soldiers, hearing these songs, raised up and looked at their officers as if to say: "Could justice be on the side of our barbaric enemies? Are we no longer soldiers of republican France? Could it be that we have become vulgar political tools?"[37]

But how could this be? France was the fatherland of the revolution. Bonaparte, who had consecrated a few of its acquisitions, was marching against Toussaint-L'Ouverture. So it was evident that Toussaint was a counterrevolutionary in the service of the enemy. Here, as is often the case, everyone is fighting in the name of the same values—freedom and justice. What distinguishes them is the kind of men for whom liberty or justice is demanded, and with whom society is to be made—slaves or masters. Machiavelli was right: values are necessary but not sufficient; and it is even dangerous to stop with values, for as long as we have not chosen those whose mission it is to uphold these values in the historical struggle, we have done nothing. Now it is not just in the past we see republics refuse citizenship to their colonies, kill in the name of freedom, and take the offensive in the name of law. Of course, Machiavelli's tough-minded wisdom will not reproach them for it. History is a struggle, and if republics did not struggle they would disappear. We should at least realize that the means remain bloody, merciless, and sordid. The supreme deception of the Crusades is not to admit it. The circle should be broken.

It is evidently on these grounds that a criticism of Machiavelli is possible and necessary. He was not wrong to insist upon the problem of power. But he was satisfied with briefly evoking a power which would not be unjust; he did not seek very energetically to define it. What discourages him from doing so is that he believes men are immutable, and that regimes follow one another in cycles.[38] There will always be two kinds of men, those who live through history and those who make it. There are the miller, the baker, and the innkeeper with whom the exiled Machiavelli spends his day, chatters, and plays backgammon. ("Then," he says, "disputes, vexatious words, insults arise; they argue at the drop of a hat and utter cries that carry all the way to San Casciano. Closed up in this lousy hole, I drain the cup of my malignant destiny down to the lees.") And there are the great men whom he reads history with and questions in the evening, clothed in court dress, and who always *answer him.* ("And during four long hours," he says, "I no longer feel any boredom; I forget all misery; I no longer fear poverty; death no longer terrifies me. I pass completely into them.")[39] No doubt he never resigned himself to parting company with spontaneous men. He would not spend days contemplating them if they were not like a mystery for him. Is it true that these *men could* love and understand the same things he understands and loves? Seeing so much blindness on one side, and such a natural art of commanding on the other, he is tempted to think that there is not one mankind, but historic men and enduring men—and to range himself on the side of the former. It is then that, no longer having any reason to prefer one "armed prophet" to another, he no longer acts except at random. He bases rash hopes upon Lorenzo di Medici's son; and the Medici, following their own rules, compromise him without employing him. A republican, he repudiates in the preface to the *History of Florence* the judgment the republicans had brought against the Medici; and the republicans, who do not forgive him for it, will not employ him either. Machiavelli's conduct accentuates what was lacking in his politics: a guideline allowing him to recognize among different powers the one from which something good could be hoped for, and to elevate *virtue* above opportunism in a decisive way.

To be just, we must also add that the task was a difficult one. For Machiavelli's contemporaries the political problem was first of all one of knowing if Italians would long be prevented from farming and living by French and Spanish incursions, when they were not those of the papacy. What could he reasonably hope for, if not for an Italian nation and soldiers to create it? It was necessary to begin by creating this bit of human life in order to create the human community. Where in the discordancy of a Europe unaware of itself, of a world which had not taken stock of itself and in which the eyes of scattered lands and men had not yet met, was the universal people which could be made the accomplice of an Italian city-state? How could the peoples of all lands have recognized, acted in concert with, and rejoined each other? There is no serious humanism except the one which looks for man's effective recognition by his fellow man throughout the world. Consequently, it could not possibly precede the moment when humanity gives itself its means of communication and communion.

Today these means exist, and the problem of a real humanism that Machiavelli set was taken up again by Marx a hundred years ago. Can we say the problem is solved? What Marx intended to do to create a human community was precisely to find a different base than the always equivocal one of principles. In the situation and vital movement of the most exploited, oppressed, and powerless of men he sought the basis for a revolutionary power, that is, a power capable of suppressing exploitation and oppression. But it became apparent that the whole problem was to constitute a power of the powerless. For those in power either had to follow the fluctuations of mass consciousness in order to remain a proletarian power, and then they would be brought down swiftly; or, if they wanted to avoid this consequence, they had to make themselves the judge of proletarian interests, and then they were setting themselves up in power in the traditional sense—they were the outline of a new ruling class. The solution could be found only in an absolutely new relationship between those in power and those subject to it. It was necessary to invent political forms capable of holding power in check without annulling it. It was necessary to have leaders capable of explaining the reasons for their politics to those subject to power, and to obtain from themselves, if necessary, the sacrifices power ordinarily imposes upon subjects. These political forms were roughed out and these leaders appeared in the Revolution of 1917; but from the time of the Commune of Kronstadt on, the revolutionary power lost contact with a fraction of the proletariat (which was nevertheless tried and true), and in order to conceal the conflict, it begins to lie. It proclaims that the insurgents' headquarters is in the hands of the White Guards, as Bonaparte's troops treat Toussaint-L'Ouverture as a foreign agent. Already difference of opinion is faked up as sabotage, opposition as espionage. We see reappearing within the revolution the very struggles it was supposed to move beyond. And as if to prove Machiavelli right, while the revolutionary government resorts to the classic tricks of power, the opposition does not even lack sympathizers among the enemies of the revolution. Does all power tend to "autonomize" itself, and is this tendency an inevitable destiny in all human society? Or is it a matter of a contingent development which was tied to the particular conditions of the Russian Revolution (the clandestine nature of the revolutionary movement prior to 1917, the weakness of the Russian proletariat) and which would not have occurred in a Western revolution? This is clearly the essential problem. In any case, now that the expedient of Kronstadt has become a system and the revolutionary power has definitely been substituted for the proletariat as the ruling class, with the attributes of power of an unchecked elite, we can conclude that, one hundred years after Marx, the problem of a real humanism remains intact—and so we can show indulgence toward Machiavelli, who could only glimpse the problem.

If by humanism we mean a philosophy of the inner man which finds no difficulty in principle in his relationships with others, no opacity whatsoever in the functioning of society, and which replaces political cultivation by moral exhortation, Machiavelli is not a humanist. But if by humanism we mean a philosophy which confronts the relationship of man to man and the constitution of a common situation and a common history between men as a problem, then we have to say that Machiavelli formulated some of the conditions of any serious humanism. And in this perspective the repudiation of Machiavelli which is so common today takes on a disturbing sense: it is the decision not to know the tasks of a true humanism. There is a way of repudiating Machiavelli which is Machiavellian; it is the pious ruse of those who turn their eyes and ours toward the heaven of principles in order to turn them away from what they are doing. And there is a way of praising Machiavelli which is just the opposite of Machiavellianism, since it honors in his works a contribution to political clarity.

9

The Adversary Is Complicit

[This is Merleau-Ponty's response in *Les Temps Modernes* to a critic of that magazine on the question of the Soviet forced-labor camps. The article appeared in *Les Temps Moderne,* no. 57 (July 1950): 1–11.]

Following our January issue, we received, along with many other letters, a text by J.-D. Martinet that appears in the May issue of *Révolution Prolétarienne.* We carefully examined all of this mail; we did not believe it necessary to publish it, because it was not possible to do so without responding to it, and the response would have been the simple repetition of what the editorials of *Les Temps Modernes* have attempted to express countless times.

Today, it would be improper to leave the readers who follow us ignorant of the public interpellation that is addressed to us. Here, then, is J.-D. Martinet's text, followed by the response we offer him willingly and without much hope.

As a simple subscriber to *Les Temps Modernes,* I take the liberty of asking J.-P. Sartre and M. Merleau-Ponty the following questions:

1. Does not a difference *in nature* exist between the Russian camps, the centerpiece of a planned economy (this subject is addressed in all of its scope in the last translated work of Dallin,[1] and more succinctly in the second issue of the *Bulletin des Groupes de Liaison Internationale*), and the other concentration camps of which we currently know, in Spain, in Greece, and in the colonies?

    The latter have as their goal repression and extermination, but in no way constitute a coherent system of economic exploitation: they are not integrated into a conception of state capitalism that supports slavery, and thus remain a rather ancient and, dare I say, "classical" aspect of social iniquity.
2. If it is likely that the Soviet camps cannot be considered extermination camps and are therefore opposed to the Nazi camps, doesn't this fact take on in your eyes some rather disturbing aspects?

    Indeed, the Soviet system of concentration is economically viable and is an integral part of the "socialist" conception of the current leaders of the U.S.S.R.: Molotov admitted as much prior even to the war.

This is what sets Russian "planism," with all of its consequences (in an isolated and backward country), apart from the perversions of Hitler, and from those of his Greek and Spanish emulators: Nazism was a monstrosity of decadent capitalism. And we know that in every area (economic or biological), monsters have but an ephemeral existence.

Any impartial mind must recognize that it is thanks to the servile labor force that Russian state capitalism was able to complete a considerable part of its immense and nonprofitable construction projects. In particular, the construction of strategic canals and railroads, prospecting for gold in northern Siberia, the installation of great industrial combines where the ore is extracted several thousands of kilometers away from the coalfield of which it is a tributary. Such achievements perhaps demand great sacrifices and were required in order to address urgent questions of national security, but bear no relation, either closely or from afar, to scientific socialism, other than as special manifestations of primitive accumulation in a time when liberal capitalism is outdated; such record production would be unthinkable if not for the enslavement of several million men. It is a coherent system of exploitation, a far cry from the Nazi absurdity, and there is no reason for it to collapse because of its own contradictions. One can accept or reject it, but to call it socialism is to be in bad faith.

3. You remark, and rightly so, that the *Code of Corrective Labor of the U.S.S.R.*[2] is not a revelation of David Rousset's, but was edited in London as early as 1936. Why did you, too, wait until 1950 to become officially interested in this problem?

The story of the Russian camps, as you say, is not a new one. I remember, for instance, having seen as early as 1934 the projection (at the Bellevilloise, in a private showing) of a Soviet propaganda film concerning the construction of the famous canal that runs from the Baltic to the White Sea, with suggestive images of the conditions of life of the "socialist" convicts: French subtitles left no doubt as to the size of the workforce used, since we were told that more than 70,000 people were released for their good conduct.

It is also around 1936 that conversations with survivors of the U.S.S.R revealed to us the extent of the Siberian camps.

And it is doubtless the knowledge of these facts, the implications we deduced from them, that pushed a certain number of us to silence and to impotent inaction in the face of the Nazi occupier. The choice the Internationalists then had to make was either to help a German victory or a Stalinist victory. Faced with this dreadful dilemma, there were some of us who (rightly or wrongly) preferred to abstain, having a taste neither for treason nor for a sacred union. Since no one thought of socialism any longer, we had to content ourselves with a negative attitude. To be sure, we helped members of the Resistance on occasion, in the same way we would like to help whoever is today hunted down by an omnipotent police, whether in Russia or elsewhere. But we seek to draw no glory from an attitude that is perfectly natural. I call attention to these facts only because we have too often forgotten the problems of conscience of the unaffiliated militants. And had the U.S.S.R. not been the paradise of the wardens, our position would have been simpler and more dignified.

4. What, in practice, does your current political position of a balance between the two imperialist blocs (American and Soviet) mean?

In no way, it goes without saying, is it a matter of excusing the flaws of the one with the iniquities of the other. We know that all manner of monstrous abuses exist, in metropolitan France, in our colonies, in Europe, and on the American continent.

But let us classify the problems fairly and, if one calls oneself socialist (Marxist or not), let us speak without doctrinal artifice: let us say *what is* [*ce qui est*] before speaking of *what could happen.*

Let us say that in the U.S.S.R., aside from a handful of new privileged persons (whose origin is amongst the workers, it is true), the condition of the manual laborer is tied to bureaucratic arbitrariness or comes close to simple slavery. To be sure, all of this could change with the years, but *this currently is the case.*

On the American side, inversely, social injustices are innumerable. The society is imperfect, unstable, contradictory; the development of the country is uncertain. But a free man can still survive there, work there, read his favorite authors, go on strike if need be, have a home that an edict of the masters could hardly break up. Perhaps one day soon life in the U.S.A. will be worse than in Russia, but *in the present, it is false to speak of American fascism and totalitarianism,* in the senses we attribute to these terms in the West.

Your ambiguous position, made all the more regrettable by the fact that your publication has a useful and considerable influence on the youth in other areas, allows for all sorts of ruses and renunciations; it reduces to very little a whole collection of good will and good intentions.

J.-D. Martinet

P.S.—*Les Temps Modernes* did not publish this letter.

* * *

That the Russian camps are an essential part of the Soviet system of production is a point on which we insisted in the editorial that prompted J.-D. Martinet's letter. We also said that the population of these camps is probably large enough for us to speak of a servile class and that we must, as a result, contest the socialist character of the U.S.S.R., and it is not on these points that there is contention between him and us.

Why, then, does he think it necessary to write to us? It is undoubtedly that we did not say it *with the proper tone*. We will see later which tone that is.

We find it rash to affirm that the Nazi system, an economic monster, was condemned to die young. In the organization of the German camps, Nazi sadism was combined (not without conflict) with a very meticulous technique of recuperation of riches and exploitation of the workforce. The "absurdity" was fairly carefully organized. The going is tough for "decadent capitalism." To present the Nazi universe as an episode that *could only be* ephemeral is to underestimate the effort that was required to destroy it, to overestimate the logic of history and leave it to solve the problems that bother us.

"Why did you wait until 1950 to become officially interested in the *Code of Corrective Labor of the U.S.S.R.?*" asks J.-D. Martinet. Because, in truth, we became aware of it only at that time. Granted, we knew before 1950 that there existed camps in Russia. We were not aware of their scope, their role in Soviet production, nor the extent to which they denatured the state socialism of the U.S.S.R. It is assuredly cruel to tolerate the camps as long as they are *not overpopulated*. But nevertheless, all the regimes history has shown us or shows us tolerate or presuppose certain horrors. As long as one could think that the violence of Russian Communism was exerted only on a political elite, as long as one did not know that it maintains at the heart of Russian production a servile workforce whose importance in the economic output of the system is considerable, one could allow that the existence of the camps did not put the nature of the Soviet state in question. A workers' state that had degenerated, but a workers' state nonetheless. This was Trotsky's position until his death. It would have been easy to convince him of the inhumanity of the camps by reminding him of the survivors of Siberia. Though he knew them better than anyone, he did not think himself obligated to abandon his theses on the defense of the U.S.S.R.—because he knew, having governed and having participated in the 1917 Revolution, that revolution brings with it certain horrors, that political judgment is a statistical judgment, finally, that the political question is to know which, of horror and the valuable, tends to predominate in a system, and what the *sense* of the system is. We waited to become "officially interested" in the Russian camps to know that they were altering the sense of the Russian system.

J.-D. Martinet tells us that we could have known earlier, as early as 1934 or 1936. The argument would be more fairly addressed to Malraux or Gide, who, at that same date, placed themselves, all things considered, on the side of the U.S.S.R.—or even to Trotsky, who persisted in thinking that the Soviet system was ambiguous. We were never Trotskyites, nor Communists, and the question of the exertion of violence is precisely one of the questions that dissuaded us. Having never adhered either to Bolshevism or Stalinism, we were, far more than its adherents or declared sympathizers, dispensed from having to explain ourselves on the Soviet camps, and free to abstain on the problem of the nature of the system, as long as facts of sociological import were not produced.

In particular, we were free to welcome fondly the Communist politics of 1944 to 1946 in Central Europe and in France. From the beginning, Martinet, you've *known* that this "liberal" politics could not last and that the nature of the Soviet system would exclude it before long. But you always know everything: you were sure that Nazism would be ephemeral, that the Communists would keep the popular democracies in line. Perhaps it is we who understand too late. Perhaps too were you right *too soon, before the right time*. It perhaps was not inevitable that the U.S.S.R had to keep popular democracies in line, if the American position had been different. It was not inevitable that Nazi Germany disappeared soon—especially if the Allies had adopted with regard to the U.S.S.R. and Nazism an attitude like yours.

You justify an attitude of abstention during the war with the alternatives with which you found yourself, of helping a German victory or a Stalinist victory. The alternatives of which you speak existed for the Balts, the Hungarians, the Poles; they did not exist for Western Europe, as the course of events later showed, and even less so for the entire world, with the result that it is improper to speak of a "Stalinist victory." In the Baltic, the Russian occupation created about as many victims as the German occupation. They would have been justified in thinking that one amounted to the other. This was not the question for us. To the extent of our courage, our task was to work against the Nazi victory, with the Communists, while maintaining our freedom in relation to them, by initiating with them a discussion that could have been carried on after the war and could have promoted, within the French Party, a tendency toward "Western Communism." If you reasoned in the way the Balts could legitimately have done, it is that *against the Stalinists and with the Stalinists, you acquired the habit of treating every political question under the angle of the strengthening of the U.S.S.R.*—it is that, like them, you practice a *political nominalism* that makes you tolerate just about everything that is anti-Soviet, in the same way that it makes them tolerate that which can advance the affairs of the U.S.S.R., and which is the very negation of a healthy political life and culture.[3]

During the war, you could not associate yourself with those who wanted Hitler's defeat because it was also Stalin's victory. Today, you feel obligated to express a preference between America and the U.S.S.R. Today, like yesterday, you think in terms of blocs, to the point of denaturing our position because you see it through your own categories.

We do not hold, as you say, a balance "between the two imperialist blocs (American and Soviet)." For this first reason that we do not dream of identifying Soviet expansion with classical forms of imperialism. There is a Trotskyist thesis of "*bureaucratic* imperialism." Let us assume it to be established. It contains a serious analysis of Soviet society; it differentiates it from known forms of capitalist expansion, even if, in perspective, it admits to a sort of convergence between the two systems. These nuances are in our opinion essential; by failing to call attention to them, one misrepresents political consciousness, since one risks including imperialist exploitation and any attempt at planning in one vague objection.

Where American expansion is concerned, we have indicated that there might be reason to revise our classical conception of imperialism, which does not suffice to define the Marshall Plan, at least at its inception. For two reasons, therefore, we refuse to place the U.S.S.R. and the U.S.A. on the common denominator of imperialism.

Similarly, we never established any parallel between the political forms of the U.S.S.R. and those of the U.S.A. We carefully called attention to that which, within American society, indicates certain aggressive passions, and can one day transform its regime in an openly authoritarian way. A collaborator, in a rather long and very explicit text, might have used another language in passing. If each had to account to every one for every word he writes, no magazine could ever be published. At least, never have the editorials of this one spoken of an American fascism. We explained that it was more pleasant to live in the U.S.A. than in the U.S.S.R., adding only that if the Soviet system was truly turning to socialism, this was not enough to condemn the U.S.S.R. We precisely contested the type of parallel between the two regimes that you seem to ascribe to us and that presupposes the "bloc" ideology, since it conflates within the U.S.S.R. the effects of planning and those of the bureaucracy, and within the American system the pleasures of freedom and the principle of "free enterprise."

In truth, we do not really know what *America* is. We know Americans with whom we do not have a single idea, a single reflex, in common. We have American friends—Meyer Shapiro, Harold Rosenberg, Bernard Wolfe, as well as others—with whom we had the pleasure of getting along from the start, as though we had always known each other. They write in this magazine, or will, we hope. We also know French "separatists" who more or less think what we think, but we know they cannot be counted on to write it, even if they say it, nor to bring about an action within the Communist Party; they are paralyzed by a false idea of what discipline can demand, by their loyalty to an adherence they do not wish to question right now, and finally, by the need to believe. To be sure, if the war starts tomorrow or in two years, all of these friends and our efforts will not be worth much. But if, as is possible, the Cold War lasts twenty years, intersected by pauses and *détentes,* we will have, to the extent we could, maintained and cultivated the instruments of political discussion in a time that knows less and less how to use them because it is haunted by blocs, and can think only in terms of geography when it should be thinking in terms of society. We are not hesitating between two blocs; we think that blocs have only a diplomatic and military existence. This "ambiguous position" of which you speak, that would allow for all manner of ruses and renunciations, is ambiguous only in the eyes of the generals and the ambassadors. Maybe a day will come when only they will be able to speak. In our opinion, this will be an unfortunate day, since the winner, whoever it may be, will everywhere bring along *his* evil with *his* good. It will be enough, if the event occurs, for us to be subjected to this confusion. We should not anticipate it. We must do everything to avoid it.

"Let us classify the problems . . . ," you say. Why, like Rousset, do you wish to classify them geographically? And why, if you please, wait until the end of the Soviet camps to talk of colonial exploitation, when, regardless of the differences between the two systems, the same complaint condemns them? But you are so immersed in the bloc ideology that any critique of colonialization or of the condition of blacks in the U.S.A. is in your eyes a point scored by the U.S.S.R. That would be true only if the war were here, and the war is but a possibility. And you were not, you say, in favor of a sacred union with the possible invader?

We have explained in this magazine why, unless one believes in miracles, it seemed to us impossible to be Communist today. Whenever we will have the opportunity to provide information seriously on the social relations in the U.S.S.R., we will do so. Anything more would be propaganda, and our readers can find it in their usual newspaper. With regard to the youth of whom you're thinking, and of whom we're thinking as well, believe me, they will not be saved by moving from Communist reticence to anti-Communist reticence, from one tortured passion to another. They will be saved when, trained in social critique and involved in a free, popular movement, they will be in a position to do something they like without restriction. You say that unhappy consciousnesses find in our position pretexts under which to use trickery on themselves and on the facts. They can do so only by forgetting a large part of what we write here. An attitude such as yours confirms the crypto-Communists' position by allowing them to believe that one cannot leave Communism without placing oneself on the side of its adversaries, and thus without renouncing the values that inspired it. In ill-stated problems, the adversary is complicit. But this, too, we have already said.

The Child's Relations with Others

Part 1. The Problem of the Child's Perception of Others

1. The Theoretical Problem

Before studying the different relations established between the child and his parents, his peers, other children, brothers, sisters, or strangers, before undertaking a description and analysis of these different relations, a question of principle arises: How and under what conditions does the child come into contact with others? What is the nature of the child's relations with others? How are such relations possible from the day of birth on?

Classical psychology approached this problem only with great difficulty. One might say that it was among the stumbling blocks of classical psychology because it is admittedly incapable of being solved if one confines oneself to the theoretical ideas that were elaborated by academic psychology.

How does such a problem arise for classical psychology? Given the presuppositions with which that psychology works, given the prejudices it adopted from the start without any kind of criticism, the relation with others becomes incomprehensible for it. What, in fact, is the psyche—mine or the other's—for classical psychology? All psychologists of the classical period are in tacit agreement on this point: the psyche, or the psychic, is *what is given to only one person.* It seems, in effect, that one might admit without further examination or discussion that what constitutes the psyche in me or in others is something incommunicable. I alone am able to grasp my psyche—for example, my sensations of green or of red. You will never know them as I know them; you will never experience them in my place. A consequence of this idea is that the psyche of another appears to me as radically inaccessible, at least in its very existence. I cannot reach other lives, other thought processes, since by hypothesis they are open only to inspection by a single individual: the one who owns them.

Since I cannot have direct access to the psyche of another, for the reasons just given, I must grant that I seize the other's psyche only indirectly, mediated by its bodily appearances. I see you in flesh and bone; you are there. I cannot know what you are thinking, but I can suppose it, guess at it from your facial expressions, your gestures, and your words—in short, from a series of bodily appearances which I witness.

The question thus becomes this: How does it happen that, in the presence of this mannequin that resembles a human, in the presence of this body that gesticulates in a characteristic way, I come to believe that it is inhabited by a psyche? (I am using this vague word, "psyche," on purpose in order not to imply, by using a more precise word, some particular theory of consciousness.) How am I led to consider that this body before me encloses a psyche? How can I perceive across this body, so to speak, another's psyche? Classical psychology's conceptions of the body and the consciousness we have of it are here a second obstacle in the way of a solution of the problem. Here one wants to speak of the notion of *cenesthesia,* meaning a mass of sensations that would express to the subject the state of his different organs and different bodily functions. Thus my body for me, and your body for you, could be reached, and be knowable, by means of a cenesthesic sense.

A mass of sensations, by hypothesis, is as *individual* as the psyche itself. That is, if in fact my body is knowable by me only through the mass of sensations it gives me (a mass of sensations to which you obviously have no access and of which we have no concrete experience), then the consciousness I have of my body is impenetrable by you. You cannot represent to yourself how I feel my own body, and it is impossible for me to represent to myself how you feel your body. How, then, can I suppose that, in back of this appearance before me, there is someone who experiences his body as I experience mine?

Only one recourse is left for classical psychology—that of supposing that, as a spectator of the gestures and utterances of the other's body before me, I consider the set of signs thus given, the set of facial expressions this body presents to me, as the occasion for a kind of decoding. Behind the body whose gestures and characteristic utterances I witness, I project, so to speak, what I myself feel of my own body. No matter whether it is a question of an actual association of ideas or, instead, a judgment whereby I interpret the appearances, I transfer to the other the intimate experience I have of my own body.

The problem of the experience of others poses itself, as it were, in a system of four terms: (1) myself, my "psyche"; (2) the image I have of my body by means of the sense of touch or of cenesthesia, which, to be brief, we shall call the "introceptive image" of my own body; (3) the body of the other as seen by me, which we shall call the "visual body"; and (4) a fourth (hypothetical) term which I must reconstitute and guess at—the "psyche" of the other, the other's feeling of his own existence—to the extent that I can imagine or suppose it across the appearances of the other through his visual body.

Posed thus, the problem raises all kinds of difficulties.

First, there is the difficulty of relating my knowledge or experience of the other to an association, to a judgment by which I would project into him the data of my intimate experience. The perception of others comes relatively early in life. Naturally we do not at an early age come to know the exact *meaning* of each of the emotional expressions presented to us by others. The exact knowledge is, if you like, late in coming; what is much earlier is the very fact that I perceive an expression, even if I may be wrong about what it means exactly. At a very early age children are sensitive to facial expressions, e.g., the smile. How could that be possible if, in order to arrive at an understanding of the global sense of the smile and to learn that the smile is a fair indication of a benevolent feeling, the child had to perform the complicated task I have just mentioned? How could it be possible if, beginning with the visual perception of another's smile, he had to compare that visual perception of the smile with the movement that he himself makes when he is happy or when he feels benevolent—projecting to the other a benevolence of which he would have had intimate experience but which could not be grasped directly in the other? This complicated process would seem to be incompatible with the relative precociousness of the perception of others.

Again, in order for projection to be possible and to take place, it would be necessary for me to begin from the analogy between the facial expressions offered me by others and the different facial gestures I execute myself. In the case of the smile, for me to interpret the visible smile of the other requires that there be a way of comparing the visible smile of the other with what we may call the "motor smile"—the smile as felt, in the case of the child, by the child himself. But in fact do we have the means of making this comparison between the body of the other, as it appears in visual perception, and our own body, as we feel it by means of introception and of cenesthesia? Have we the means of systematically comparing the body of the other as seen by me with my body as sensed by me? In order for this to be possible there would have to be a fairly regular correspondence between the two experiences. The child's visual experience of his own body is altogether insignificant in relation to the kinesthetic, cenesthesic, or tactile feeling he can have of it. There are numerous regions of his body that he does not see and some that he will never see or know except by means of the mirror (of which we will speak shortly). There is no point-for-point correspondence between the two images of the body. To understand how the child arrives at assimilating the one to the other, we must, rather, suppose that he has other reasons for doing it than reasons of simple detail. If he comes to identify as bodies, and as animated ones, the bodies of himself and the other, this can only be because he globally identifies them and not because he constructs a point-for-point correspondence between the visual image of the other and the introceptive image of his own body.

These two difficulties are particularly apparent when it comes to accounting for the phenomenon of imitation. To imitate is to perform a gesture in the image of another's gesture—like the child, for example, who smiles because someone smiles at him. According to the principles we have been entertaining, it would be necessary for me to translate my visual image of the other's smile into a motor language. The child would have to set his facial muscles in motion in such a way as to reproduce the visible expression that is called "the smile" in another. But how could he do it? Naturally he does not have the other's internal motor feeling of his face; as far as he is concerned, he does not even have an image of himself smiling. The result is that if we want to solve the problem of the transfer of the other's conduct to me, we can in no way rest on the supposed analogy between the other's face and that of the child.

On the contrary, the problem comes close to being solved only on condition that certain classical prejudices are renounced. We must abandon the fundamental prejudice according to which the psyche is that which is accessible only to myself and cannot see itself from the outside. My "psyche" is not a series of "states of consciousness" that are rigorously closed in on themselves and inaccessible to anyone but me. My consciousness is turned first toward the world, turned toward things; it is above all a relation to the world. The other's consciousness as well is chiefly a certain way of behaving toward the world. Thus it is in his conduct, in the manner in which the other deals with the world, that I will be able to discover his consciousness.

If I am a consciousness turned toward things, I can meet in things the actions of another and find in these actions a sense, because they are themes of possible activity for my own body. Guillaume, in his book *Imitation in the Infant*,[1] says that we do not at first imitate others but rather the actions of others, and that we find others at the point of origin of these actions. At first the child imitates not someone but conducts. And the problem of knowing how conduct can be transferred from another to me is infinitely less difficult to solve than the problem of knowing how I can represent to myself a psyche that is radically foreign to me. If, for example, I see another draw a figure, I can understand the drawing as an action because it speaks directly to my own unique motility. Of course, the other qua author of a drawing is not yet a whole person, and there are more re-vealing actions than drawing—for example, using language. What is essential, however, is to see that a perspective on the other is opened to me from the moment I define him and myself as "conducts" at work in the world, as ways of "grasping" the natural and cultural world surrounding us.

But this presupposes a reform not only of the notion of the "psyche" (which we will replace henceforth by that of "conduct") but also of the idea we have of our own body. If my body is to appropriate the conducts given to me as a spectacle and make them its own, it must itself be given to me not as a mass of utterly private sensations but instead by what has been called a "postural schema" or "corporeal schema." This notion, introduced long ago by Henry Head, has been taken over and enriched by Wallon, by certain German psychologists, and has finally been the subject of a study in its own right by Professor Lhermitte in *The Image of Our Body.*[2]

For these authors, my body is no agglomeration of sensations (visual, tactile, "cenesthesic"). It is first and foremost a *system* whose different introceptive and extroceptive aspects express each other reciprocally, including even the roughest of relations with surrounding space and its principal directions. The consciousness I have of my body is not the consciousness of an isolated mass; it is a *postural schema.* It is the perception of my body's position in relation to the vertical, the horizontal, and certain other axes of important coordinates of the milieu in which it finds itself.

In addition, the different sensory domains (sight, touch, and the sense of movement in the joints) which are involved in the perception of my body do not present themselves to me as so many absolutely distinct regions. Even if, in the child's first and second years, the translation of one into the language of others is imprecise and incomplete, they all have in common a *certain style* of action, a certain *gestural* meaning that makes of the collection an already organized totality. Understood in this way, the experience I have of my own body could be transferred to another much more easily than the cenesthesia of classical psychology, giving rise to what Wallon calls a "postural impregnation" of my own body by the conducts I witness.

I can perceive, across the visual image of the other, that the other is an organism, that that organism is inhabited by a "psyche," because the visual image of the other is interpreted by the notion I myself have of my own body and thus appears as the visible envelopment of another "corporeal schema." My perception of my body would, so to speak, be swallowed up in a cenesthesia if that cenesthesia were strictly individual. On the contrary, however, if we are dealing with a schema, or a system, such a system would be relatively transferable from one sensory domain to the other in the case of my own body, just as it could be transferred to the domain of the other.

Thus in today's psychology we have one system with two terms (my behavior and the other's behavior) which functions as a whole. To the extent that I can elaborate and extend my corporeal schema, to the extent that I acquire a better-organized experience of my own body, to that very extent will my consciousness of my own body cease being a chaos in which I am submerged and lend itself to a transfer to others. And since at the same time the other who is to be perceived is himself not a "psyche" closed in on himself but rather a conduct, a behavior in a relation with the world, he offers himself to the grasp of my motor intentions and to that "intentional transgression" (Husserl) by which I animate him and transport myself into him. Husserl said that the perception of others is like a "phenomenon of coupling." The term is anything but a metaphor. In perceiving the other, my body and the other's body are coupled, resulting in a sort of action which pairs them. This conduct which I am able only to see, I live somehow from a distance. I make it mine; I take it up or understand it. Reciprocally, I know that the gestures I make myself can be the objects of another's intention. It is this transference of my intentions to the other's body and of his intentions to my own, my alienation of the other and his alienation of me, that makes possible the perception of others.

All these analyses presuppose that the perception of others cannot be accounted for if one begins by supposing an ego and another that are *absolutely* conscious of themselves, each of which lays claim, as a result, to an absolute originality in relation to the other that confronts it. On the contrary, the perception of others is made comprehensible if one supposes that psychogenesis begins in a state where the child is unaware of himself and the other as different. We cannot say that in such a state the child has a genuine communication with others. In order that there be communication, there must be a sharp distinction between the one who communicates and the one with whom he communicates. But there is initially a state of *pre-communication* (Max Scheler), wherein the other's intentions somehow play across my body while my intentions play across his.

How is this distinction made? I gradually become aware of my body, of what radically distinguishes it from the other's body, at the same time that I begin to live my intentions in the facial expressions of the other and likewise begin to live the other's volitions in my own gestures. The progress of the child's experience results in his seeing that his body is, after all, closed in on itself. In particular, the visual image he acquires of his own body (especially from the mirror) reveals to him a hitherto unsuspected isolation of two subjects who are facing each other. The objectification of his own body discloses to the child his difference, his "insularity," and, correlatively, that of others.

Thus the development has somewhat the following character: there is a first phase, which we call *pre-communication,* in which there is not one individual over against another but rather an anonymous collectivity, an undifferentiated group life. Next, on the basis of this initial community, both by the objectification of one's own body and the constitution of the other in his difference, there occurs a segregation, a distinction of individuals—a process which, moreover, as we shall see, is never completely finished.

This kind of conception is common to many trends in contemporary psychology. One finds it in Guillaume and Wallon; it occurs in Gestalt theorists, phenomenologists, and psychoanalysts alike.

Guillaume shows that we must neither treat the origin of consciousness as though it were conscious, in an explicit way, of itself nor treat it as though it were completely closed in on itself. The first *me* is, as he says, virtual or latent, i.e., unaware of itself in its absolute difference. Consciousness of oneself as a unique individual, whose place can be taken by no one else, comes later and is not primitive. Since the primordial *me* is virtual or latent, egocentrism is not at all the attitude of a *me* that expressly grasps itself (as the term "egocentrism" might lead us to believe). Rather, it is the attitude of a *me* which is unaware of itself and lives as easily in others as it does in itself—but which, being unaware of others in their own separateness as well, in truth is no more conscious of them than of itself.

Wallon introduces an analogous notion with what he calls "syncretic sociability." Syncretism here is the indistinction between me and the other, a confusion at the core of a situation that is common to us both. After that the objectification of the body intervenes to establish a sort of wall between me and the other: a partition. Henceforth it will prevent me from confusing myself with what the other thinks, and especially with what he thinks of me; just as I will no longer confuse him with my thoughts, and especially my thoughts about him. There is thus a constitution, a correlation of me and the other as two human beings among all others.

While the first *me* is both at once unaware of itself and at the same time all the more demanding for being unaware of its own limits, the adult *me,* on the contrary, is a *me* that knows its own limits yet possesses the power to go out from them by a genuine sympathy that is at least *relatively* distinct from the initial form of sympathy. The initial sympathy rests on the ignorance of oneself rather than on the perception of others, while adult sympathy occurs between the "other" and "other"; it does not assume that the differences between myself and the other are abolished.

2. The Placement of the Corporeal Schema and the First
Phases of a Perception of Others (from Birth to Six Months)

What has been gained from these introductory remarks has been the correlation between consciousness of one's own body and the perception of
the other. To be aware that one has a body and that the other's body is animated by another psyche are two operations that are not simply logically
symmetrical but form a real system. In both cases it is a question of becoming conscious of what might be called "incarnation." To notice, on the
one hand, that I have a body which can be seen from outside and that for
others I am nothing but a mannequin, gesticulating at a point in space
and, on the other hand, to notice that the other has a psyche—i.e., that
this body I see before me like a mannequin gesticulating at a point in
space is animated by another psyche—are two moments of a single totality. This does not mean that the experience of this total phenomenon in
the child cannot privilege first one of these aspects; rather, any progress
realized on one side unbalances the whole and is the dialectical ferment
that results in subsequent progress in the system. There are complementary operations, and the experience of my body and the body of the other
form a totality and constitute a "form." In saying this, naturally I do not
mean that the perception of others and the perception of one's own body
always go hand in hand or that they develop at the same rhythm. On the
contrary, we shall see that the perception of one's own body is ahead of the
recognition of the other, and consequently if the two form a system, it is a
system that becomes articulated in time. To say that a phenomenon is one
of "form" (*Gestalt*) is in no way to say that it is innate in its different aspects
or even in regard to a single one of its aspects. Rather, it is to say that it develops according to a law of *internal* equilibrium, as if by *auto-organization*.
Gestalt theorists have by no means limited the use of the notion of "form"
to the instant or to the present. They have, on the contrary, insisted on the
phenomenon of form in time (melody). I said that the perception of one's
own body comes earlier than perception of the other. The child takes notice of his own body sooner than he does of the physiognomic expressions
of the other. That does not prevent the two phenomena from being internally linked. The perception of one's own body creates an imbalance as it
develops: through its echo in the image of the other, it awakens an appeal
to the forthcoming development of the perception of others. It echoes in
another phase, in which the perception of others appears predominant,
and so on throughout the development. The two phenomena can easily
form a system, although they are emphasized only successively. Each of
the phases of this development contains the germs which prepare the way
for its being surpassed. And to say that the phenomenon is a formal one

is by no means to say that it is, in each of its stages, completely at rest. Any form (e.g., those we perceive in space—colored forms) is actually subject to a play of forces from different directions. The imbalance can be infinitesimal at first and give rise to no appreciable change. Then, when it passes a certain threshold, a change occurs. In the same way there may well be something at the core of each phase of development which anticipates the next phase and which will animate a series of restructurations. The notion of form is essentially dynamic.

Let us now consider the state of the perception of one's own body and the state of the perception of others, each in its turn.

1. One's Own Body from Birth to Six Months

The body, as Henri Wallon suggests in his excellent analysis in *The Origins of Character in the Infant*,[3] begins by being introceptive. At the beginning of the child's life there emerges an entire phase in which extroceptivity (i.e., vision, hearing, and all other perceptions relating to the external world), even if it begins to operate, cannot in any case do so in collaboration with introceptivity. At this age the latter is the best-organized means for bringing us into relation with things. In the beginning of the child's life, external perception is impossible for very simple reasons: visual accommodation and muscular control of the eyes are insufficient.

As has been often said, the body is at first "buccal" in nature. Stern has even spoken of a "buccal space" at the beginning of the child's life, meaning by this that the limit of the world for the child is the space that can be contained in, or explored by, his mouth. One could say more generally, as Wallon does, that the body is already a respiratory body. Not only the mouth but the whole respiratory apparatus gives the child a kind of experience of space. After that, other regions of the body intervene and come into prominence. All the regions linked to the functions of expression, for example, acquire an extreme importance in the months that follow. While waiting for the union that will arise between the data of external perception and those of introceptivity, the introceptive body functions as extroceptive. In another context, this is what psychoanalysts say about the origin of the child's experiences when they show, for example, that the child's relations to the mother's breast are the child's first relations with the world.

It is only between the third and sixth month that a union occurs between the introceptive and the extroceptive domains. The different neural paths are not yet ready to function at birth. Myelinization, which makes their functioning possible, is late in taking place; this is particularly true of the connective fibers we are speaking of right now. It occurs between the third and sixth month, connecting the mechanisms which furnish the various sensory data as well as those which correspond respectively to extroceptivity and introceptivity.

Up to that moment perception is impossible for yet another reason: it presupposes a minimum of equilibration. The functioning of a postural schema—that is, a global consciousness of my body's position in space, with the corrective reflexes that impose themselves at each moment, the global consciousness of the spatiality of my body—all this is necessary for perception (Wallon). In fact, the effort at equilibration continually accompanies all our perceptions except when we are lying on our back. But also, observes Wallon, it is above all in this position that the child's thinking and perception fade away; it is sleep. This link between motility and perception shows at what point it is true to say that the two functions are only two aspects of a single totality and that the perception of entering and of the world and that of one's own body form a system.

When the necessary neural paths have been acquired, there remains a considerable gap between the precision of the consciousness of the body in certain domains and in others. You know, for example, that myelinization occurs much later in the nerve fibers corresponding to the activity of the feet than it does in those which correspond to the activity of the hands. The delay is about three weeks long. All the same, in the case of the hands there is a slight lag of about twenty-six days in the myelinization of the left hand as compared with the right. Consequently there is a phase in which the child calls up the physiological conditions for a precise perception of the right hand's movements but not yet those for a precise perception of the movements of the left hand.

It is not surprising, therefore, that the child does not really interest himself in his body or in its parts until relatively late. It is only on the 115th day of his life, or around the fourth month, that one notices the child actually paying attention to his right hand. Only in the twenty-third week of life, or around the sixth month, does one find the child systematically making the experiment of exploring one hand with the other. At that moment—having clasped his right hand with his left hand, for example—he interrupts his movement and gazes attentively at his hands. At the twenty-fourth week, or at the end of the sixth month, the child is perplexed at the sight of a glove placed next to his hand. He is seen comparing the glove and his hand, gazing attentively at the moving hand. All these experiments are aimed at familiarizing the child with the correspondence between the hand which touches and the hand which is touched, between the body as visible and the body as felt by introceptivity.

The consciousness of one's own body is thus fragmentary at first and gradually becomes integrated; the corporeal schema becomes precise, restructured, and mature little by little.

2. The Other from Birth to Six Months

This entire putting of the corporeal schema in place is at the same time a putting of the perception of others in place. Reactions to others, according to Guillaume in *Imitation in the Infant,* are extremely precocious. To tell the truth, it seems that the first forms of reaction to others described by Guillaume are not connected with a visual perception of others; they correspond, rather, to the data of introceptivity. Guillaume says that between the ninth and the eleventh day, he noticed an astonished and attentive expression in the child, directed toward faces and fleeting smiles. At sixteen days he found differences in the attitude of the child according to whether he was in the arms of his mother, his wet nurse, or his father.

In Wallon's view, it is not a question, in these different attitudes, of a genuine extroceptive perception of the mother, the father, and the nurse. Instead, it is a question of differences felt by the child in the state of his body—differences in his well-being according to whether the nurse's breast is present or absent and also according to the way in which the child is held in the arms of each of the persons involved.

Up to the age of three months, according to Wallon, there is no external perception of others by the child, and what ought to be concluded when, for example, the child is seen to cry because someone goes away is that he has an "impression of incompleteness." Rather than truly perceiving those who are there, he feels incomplete when someone goes away. This negative experience does not mean that there is a precise perception of the other qua other in the preceding moment. The first external contact with others can be truly given only through extroceptivity. Insofar as others are felt only as a kind of state of well-being in the baby's organism because he is held more firmly or more tenderly in their arms, we cannot say that they are actually perceived.

The first active extroceptive stimulus would be the voice. With it begin the reactions that can be called without any possible doubt reactions *in regard to others.* At first the human voice as heard by the child provokes only cries when the child is afraid; then, at two months, it provokes smiles. At two or three months one observes that deliberately gazing at the child makes him smile. At that moment there will be in the child at least one perception of a gaze as of something that makes him complete. At the same age the child responds to the cries of other children by calling out himself; there is a kind of contagion of cries that disappears later as the visual perception of others develops. Around that same age, too, the child cries when anyone at all leaves the room and not, as in the beginning, only at the departure of the wet nurse or the person who is feeding him.

At two months and five days one observes, says Wallon, an unmistakably visual experience of another—a recognition of the father at a distance of two yards. This assumes that the father presents himself in his habitual environment; in an unfamiliar setting, he would not be recognized. At three months the child cries out at all persons who come into his room, even when they are not persons from whom he can expect care.

Concerning relations with other children, here is roughly what happens: I said that at two to three months there is a contagion of cries among babies and that afterward this contagion disappears, to the extent that visual perception of the other develops. Consequently, for a child older than three months the contagion of cries is much rarer than before, and a baby of this age can gaze with cool detachment at another baby who is crying.

The first beginnings of an observation of others consist in fixations on *the parts of the body*. The child gazes at the feet, the mouth, the hands; he does not gaze at the person. The difference is intuitively quite noticeable between a mere scrutiny of the parts of the body and a gaze oriented toward the other's gaze, which seeks to grasp the other as such. The scrutiny of the parts of the other's body considerably enriches the perception that the child can have of his own body. We see him systematically relating to himself, after six months, the different things he has learned about the other's body from looking at him. Still, at five months there is no fraternization with children of the same age. At six months, at last, the child gazes upon the other child in the face, and one has the impression that here, for the first time, he is perceiving another.

3. After Six Months: Consciousness of One's Own Body and the Specular Image

It is now up to us to describe the phase intervening after six months, which will be characterized by a sharp opposition to the first phase. It involves the development of the perception of one's own body—a step which is considerably aided by the child's becoming acquainted with the image of his body in the mirror. This is a phenomenon of great importance, since the mirror furnishes the child with a perception of his own body that he could never have gotten by himself. On the other hand, there is an extraordinarily rapid development of contacts with others—so rapid, in fact, that Wallon was led to speak of and characterize the period between six months and one year as one of "incontinent sociability."

1. The Syncretic System "Me-and-Other" (After Six Months)

At this point we propose to examine simultaneously the development of the experience of one's own body (in its introceptive aspect and in the specular image) and that of the consciousness of the other, beginning at six months.

a. *The specular image.* The major fact that concerns the development of consciousness of one's own body is the acquisition of a representation or a visual image of the body itself, in particular by means of the mirror. We are going to concern ourselves first with the study of this specular image, the recognition of this image and the different stages it passes through.

On this point there is a contrast between the behavior of animals and of children. We cannot say that animals pay no attention to their images in the mirror or that they show no reaction to their specular images. But the conduct of animals is very different from that of children. The first information on the subject was given by Preyer in his now outdated book. The story concerns a duck who, deprived of his mate's company by her death, developed the habit of sitting in front of a windowpane in which his body was reflected. This behavior, according to Wallon (*The Origins of Character in the Infant*), would not be comparable to what one finds in the child. The animal, "made incomplete" by his mate's death, completes himself with his image in the windowpane. He does not take it to be an image of himself, since it is capable of taking the place of another living being; it is like a second animal facing him. Again, inversely, one could say that if in truth the reflected image represents for the animal what was formerly represented by the presence of his mate, the mate was, while he was perceiving her, only a kind of mirror image of himself. In both cases the conduct characteristic of the child (which we shall define shortly) does not yet appear.

Wallon describes the reactions of two dogs to their images in the mirror. One of the dogs displays reactions of fear and avoidance; when he sees his image in the mirror he turns and runs. The other dog, caressed by his master while looking at his image in the mirror, calmly stands still and at the same time turns his head toward his master, who caresses him. The image he sees in the mirror is not, for him, another dog, but neither is it *his own* visual image. The visual image is a kind of complement for him, and as soon as his master's caress recalls him to his body as given in introceptivity, he neglects the mirror image and turns toward the master.

Here again, in other words, the animal does not display conduct that is characteristic of the symbol, of the external image as such. In the presence of the mirror he is disoriented, confused, and turns away hastily in order to return to the objects that for him are fundamental—that is, to return to introceptive experience.

The behavior of chimpanzees toward the mirror was studied by Köhler in his fine book, *The Mentality of Apes.*[4] There the author shows that when the chimpanzee is placed in front of a mirror and finds an image in it, he passes his hand behind it and shows signs of dissatisfaction at finding nothing behind the image. From then on he stubbornly refuses to interest himself in the mirror. Wallon interprets this as follows. At the moment when—through the manual exploration that could convince him that there was really only a simple image instead of another body—the chimpanzee was about to reach consciousness of the image or treat what is in the mirror as a simple reflection or symbol of his real body, he recoils from the object and treats it as foreign. Consciousness of the image qua image scarcely appears, and is only roughly outlined in him.

Köhler, however, indicates that the chimpanzee seems to recognize himself in a portrait of himself when presented to him. A repeated experimental study of this phenomenon might well be made in order to see whether in fact chimpanzees are conscious of their portraits and, if so, why they do not achieve a full consciousness of the specular image.

These conducts, we have said, must be contrasted with those of the child.

Let us begin by considering not the child's image of his own body in the mirror but instead the image he has of others' bodies. One notices, in effect, that he acquires the latter much more rapidly, that he distinguishes much more quickly between the other's specular image and the reality of the other's body than he does in the case of his own body. Thus it is possible that the experience he has of the other's specular image helps him arrive at an understanding of his own specular image.

According to Guillaume (*Imitation in the Infant*), the consciousness of the other's image in the mirror comes at an early age. Guillaume observes grimaces before a mirror in the first weeks of life. Wallon thinks, however, that clear reactions to the specular image are not noticeable before the end of the third month.

At first there is a reaction of simple fixation on the specular image (around four or five months). This is followed by reactions of interest in the same image. At the same moment, one notices reactions in the child, e.g., to a portrait by Frans Hals. Finally, after six months, reactions other than the mimic or affective are seen to appear. These are genuine conducts. After five or six months, for example, there occurs the following.

A child smiles in a mirror at the image of his father. At this moment his father speaks to him. The child appears surprised and turns toward the father. As a result it seems that at this moment he *learns* something. What exactly does he learn? He is surprised, because at the moment before his father spoke, he did not have a precise awareness of the relation of image to model. He is surprised that the voice comes from another direction than that of the visible image in the mirror. The attention he gives to the phenomenon shows, in effect, that he is in the process of understanding something, that it is not a question of simple training. One might be tempted to say that we are here present at the formation of a conditioned reflex and that the mirror image becomes "compre-hensible" by becoming the conditioned stimulus of responses that were formerly evoked by the father. In Wallon's eyes there can be no ques-tion either of a blind training or of an intellectual mastery of the image. Certainly one cannot say that the child comes into possession of a per-fectly clear relation between the image and the model or that he learns to consider the mirror image as a spatial projection of the visible aspect of his father. The experience of which we are speaking occurs at about five or six months and does not give the child possession of a stable con-duct. Just as the child studied by Wallon turned away from the specular image toward his father after a week, so several weeks later he still tried to grasp the image in the mirror with his hand; this means that he had not yet identified this image as a "simple image" that was nothing other than visible.

We should say that in this first phase of his apprenticeship, the child gives the image and the model an existence relatively independent of each other. There is the model, which is the father's body, the real father; there is in the mirror a sort of double or phantom of the father, having a "sec-ondary existence" without the image being reduced to the simple state of a reflection of light and color in external space. When the child turns away from the mirror toward his father, we may indeed say that he recog-nizes his father in the image but in an altogether practical way. He turns toward his father because that is where the voice is coming from; but it cannot be said that at this point he has divested the specular image of its quasi-reality, the phantom existence it first had for him, which we can try to render with the aid of certain analogies borrowed from primitive thought. The image thus has an existence inferior to that of the father's real body—but it does have a sort of marginal existence.

Let us now consider the acquisition of the specular image of one's own body. It is around the age of eight months—hence later than in the case of the specular image of the other—that one clearly finds a reaction of surprise when the child sees his own image in the mirror. At thirty-five weeks the child still extends his hand toward his image in the mirror and appears surprised when his hand encounters the surface of the glass. At the same age he happens to look at his image in the glass when he is called. The illusion of reality, the quasi-reality he lends to the image, still remains, just as after several weeks the child still turns away from the specular image and toward his father. This confirms the fact that, if the child has an adaptive reaction, this does not entail that he has acquired a symbolic consciousness of the image.

Why does the specular image of one's own body develop later than that of the other's body? According to Wallon (whose analysis we are following here), it is because the problem to be solved is much more difficult in the case of one's own body. The child is dealing with two visual experiences of his father: the experience he has from looking at him and that which comes from the mirror. Of his own body, on the other hand, the mirror image is his only complete visual evidence. He can easily look at his feet and his hands but not at his body as a whole. Thus for him it is a problem first of understanding that the visual image of his body which he sees over there in the mirror is not himself, since he is not in the mirror but here, where he feels himself; and second, he must understand that, not being located there, in the mirror, but rather where he feels himself introceptively, he can nonetheless be seen by an external witness *at the very place at which he feels himself to be* and with the same visual appearance that he has from the mirror. In short, he must displace the mirror image, bringing it from the apparent or virtual place it occupies in the depth of the mirror back to himself, whom he identifies at a distance with his introceptive body.

Consequently, in the case of the image of his own body, we must admit, says Wallon, that the child begins by seeing the specular image as a sort of double of the real body—much more so indeed than in the case of the image of the other's body.

Many pathological facts bear witness to this kind of external perception of the self, this "autoscopy." First, it is found in many dreams, in which the subject figures as a quasi-visible character. There would also be phenomena of this kind in dying people, in certain hypnotic states, and in drowning people. What reappears in these pathological cases is comparable to the child's original consciousness of his own visible body in the mirror. "Primitive" people are capable of believing that the same person is in several places at the same time. This possibility of *ubiquity*, difficult for us to understand, can be illuminated by the initial forms of the specular image. The child knows well that he is there where his introceptive body is, and yet in the depth of the mirror he sees the same being present, in a bizarre way, in a visible appearance. There is a mode of spatiality in the specular image that is altogether distinct from adult spatiality. There is here, says Wallon, a kind of space clinging to the image. All images tend to present themselves in space, including the image of the mirror as well. According to Wallon, this spatiality of adherence will be reduced by intellectual development. We will learn gradually to return the specular image to the introceptive body and, reciprocally, to treat the quasi-locatedness and pre-spatiality of the image as an appearance that counts for nothing against the unique space of real things. Our intelligence would, so to speak, redistribute the spatial values, and we would learn to consider as relevant to the same place appearances which, on first sight, present themselves in different places. Thus an ideal space would be substituted for the space clinging to the images. It is necessary, in effect, that the new space be ideal, since for the child it is a question of understanding that what seems to be in different places is in fact in the same place. This can occur only in passing to a higher level of spatiality that is no longer the intuitive space in which the images occupy their own place.

This constitution of an ideal space would include all kinds of degrees. First, there would be, as we have just mentioned, the reduction of the image to a simple appearance lacking its own spatiality. This reduction occurs fairly early, at around one year. Guillaume describes an observation made on his own daughter, who steps before a mirror with a straw hat which she has been wearing since morning. She puts her hand not to the image of the hat in the mirror but to the hat on her head; the image in the mirror suffices to call forth and regulate a movement adapted to the object itself. In this case one can say that the reduction has been accomplished, that the mirror image is no longer anything but a symbol, and that it returns the child's consciousness to the reflected objects in their proper places.

A counterproof: each time there occur troubles with the symbolic consciousness—as, for example, in cases of aphasia or apraxia—one also finds troubles with spatiality. Apraxic subjects are known in particular for their difficulty in ordering movements adapted to objects by means of a mirror (or in imitating a subject who is facing them). For them the relation of the image to the model is disturbed and confused.

At one year, according to Wallon, one could say that this development is essentially complete. But this does not mean that the system of correspondence between the image of the body and the body itself is complete or that it is precise. This is shown by a whole series of events, certain of which come fairly late. For example, from twelve to fifteen months of age, the child is seen practicing a series of exercises that prepare for the habit of performing movements in front of the mirror. He is trying out the kind of movements that the apraxic is asked to perform. And this occurs after the first year, at between twelve and fifteen months; that is, the system at this moment is still quite fragmentary and the child needs to confirm it by repeated experiments. At sixty weeks (i.e., at more than a year), when the mother is sitting beside the child with a mirror in front of them and the child is asked to point to his mother, the child points to her in the mirror *while laughing* and turns back to her. The specular image has become the subject of a game, an amusement. But the very fact that the child thinks of using his specular image to play with shows that he is not so far removed from the experiments that first introduced him to the specular image. The apprenticeship is not yet very stable. At fifty-seven weeks (thus at more than a year) Preyer's son looked at himself in the mirror, passed his hand behind the mirror, brought his hand back, and contemplated it. This, as we have seen, is exactly what chimpanzees do. The next day he turned away from the mirror, just like the chimpanzees. All the same, this fact would appear a bit difficult to admit if, as Guillaume thinks, the consciousness of the specular image has already been acquired at the age of one year. How could one revert after that age to the conduct of chimpanzees, which, as we have seen, is inferior to the level of consciousness of the image? Wallon proposes an explanation: in the case we are considering, he says, it is not so much a misunderstanding of the specular image; it is on the mirror, not on the image, that the inquiry bears. The child would have discovered once for all that what is portrayed over there on the mirror is only an appearance, a reflection, but it remains for him to understand *how* an object (the mirror) is capable of obtaining a duplicate of the surrounding objects. Wallon's interpretation is not entirely convincing. In order for there to be an exact consciousness of the image in its relation to the model, it seems necessary for there to be some understanding of the role of the mirror. Insofar as the mirror is not at all understood, to the extent that the child expects to find in back of it something like the objects which outline themselves on its surface, he has not yet fully understood the existence of the reflection; he has not yet fully understood the image. If his consciousness of the image were entirely perfect, the child would no longer search behind the mirror for real objects similar to the ones reflected in it. The constitution of a specular image that would be in the fullest sense a *reflection* of the real object presupposes the gradual constitution of an entire naive physics, into which would enter the causal relations that are designed to explain how the phenomenon of the reflection is possible. The facts set forth by Preyer thus would seem to show that at fifty-seven weeks there is still no full understanding of the specular image. Hence we will not be astonished that even at sixty-one weeks Preyer's son still touched, licked, struck, and played with his image. Like the game of the child who laughed at his mother's image, this game seems to show that the child is not far from the time when the image was still a double, a phantom of the object. Wallon says that a child of twenty months kisses his image very ceremoniously before going to bed and even at thirty-one months is seen to play with his own image.

We have seen that Wallon considers that these games played by the child with his own image represent a phase beyond the simple consciousness of his specular image. If the child plays with his own image in the mirror, says Wallon, it is because he is amusing himself by finding in the mirror a reflection which has all the appearances of an animated being and yet is not one. Here it would be a question of "animistic games," an activity which proclaims that animistic *beliefs* have been suppressed. But why should it be so amusing somehow to verify the animistic appearance if there remained in the subject no traces of this amazing phenomenon which on first encounter so fascinated the child—namely, the presence of a quasi-intention in a reflection? The child happily makes a sort of fairy dance before it and clings to it, although it is not "for real."

This leads us to make a remark which perhaps will have to be recalled in concluding. For adults like ourselves, the mirror image has really become what Wallon would like it to be in an adult mind: a simple reflection. Nonetheless, there are two ways in which we can consider the image—one, a reflective, analytic way according to which the image is nothing but an appearance in a visible world and has nothing to do with me; the other, a global and direct one, of the kind which we use in immediate life when we do not reflect and which gives us the image as something which *solicits* our belief. Let us compare the mirror image to a picture. When I see a picture of Charles XII of Sweden, with his elongated face and that head which, according to his contemporaries, only one idea could enter at a time, I know very well that Charles XII has been dead for a long time and that what I am looking at is no more than a picture. Nonetheless there is a *quasi-person* who is smiling; that line joining nose and lips, that flashing in the eyes are not simply things. This congealed movement is, all the same, a *smile*. In the same way the image in the mirror, even for the adult, when considered in direct unreflective experience, is not simply a physical phenomenon: it is mysteriously inhabited by me; it is something of me.

This experience allows us to understand the significance attached to images. In certain civilizations, one is forbidden to make images of humans because this is similar to deliberately creating other human beings—and this is not what humans are supposed to do. This group of beliefs related to images can be understood only if images are more than black-and-white sketches or simple signs of a person who remains absolutely distinct from them. In a singular way the image incarnates and makes appear the person represented in it, as spirits are made to appear at a séance. Even an adult will hesitate to step on an image or photograph; if he does, it will be with aggressive intent. Thus not only is the consciousness of the image slow in developing and subject to relapses, but even for the adult the image is never a simple reflection of the model; it is, rather, its "quasi-presence" (Sartre).

This also explains why the work of "reduction," even when done by the child in respect to the image in the mirror, never ends with a *general* result, such as a concept. The child must do the work all over again in respect to other analogous phenomena—shadows, for example. Wallon remarks that Preyer's son, at the age of four years, noticed for the first time that he cast a shadow and noticed it with fright. A little girl, four and a half years old, observed by Wallon, pretended that when she stepped on Wallon's shadow she was stepping on Wallon himself. The participationist beliefs with which, as we have said, the specular image is at first endowed have not been reduced by an intellectual critique that would apply indifferently to all phenomena of the same order. The progress consists in a restructuration of the specular image. The child puts this image at a distance, but this distance is not that of the concept.

Wallon would like to say that in the case of the shadow it is a matter of beginning the same development that has already been acquired in the case of the specular image. But this would be to say that the progressive reduction of the specular image is not, properly speaking, an intellectual phenomenon. A genuine intellectual event would obey the "all or nothing" law: either one knows or one does not know. One cannot "slightly know" the sum of two and three. The intellectual phenomenon is not susceptible to that series of gradations that one observes in the development of the specular image.

This leads us to ask whether, in the light of several other facts, there is room to reattempt to interpret the development of the specular image and relate it to phenomena other than those of knowledge.

Wallon's book also contains indications along these lines. Wallon himself, in certain passages in *The Origins of Character in the Infant*, suggests that the progress in experiencing one's own body is a "moment" in a global development that also involves the perception of others.

At the end of his analysis Wallon sharply criticizes the notion of cenesthesia, considered as a series of images given directly and immediately by my organs and bodily functions and representing these organs and functions to me. According to Wallon, this cenesthesia, when it exists, is the result of a very long development; it is a fact of adult psychology and altogether fails to express the relation between the child and his body. The child distinguishes at first absolutely between what is furnished by introception and what comes from external perception. There is no distinction between the data of what the learned adult calls introceptivity and the data of sight. The specular image, given visually, participates globally in the existence of the body itself and leads a "phantom" life in the mirror, which "participates" in the life of the child himself. What is true of his own body, for the child is also true of the other's body. The child himself feels that he is in the other's body, just as he feels himself to be in his visual image. It is this that Wallon suggests in showing by the examination of pathological cases: *that disorders in "cenesthesia" are closely linked with troubles in my relations with others.*

Sick people feel a voice speaking in the region of the epigastrium, in the throat, the chest, or the head. Classical psychiatrists thought that this must be a question of hallucinations involving different regions of the body. They translated and "put into images" the complaints of the sick, taking quite literally what the patients said.

Modern psychiatry shows, however, that what is essential and primary about the phenomena in question is not the location of voices in the subject's body, but rather a sort of "syncretism" that intervenes in his relations with others and causes alien voices to inhabit his own body. If the patient hears voices in his head, this is because he does not absolutely distinguish himself from others and because, for example, when he speaks, he can just as well believe that someone else is speaking. The patient, says Wallon, has the impression of being "without boundaries" in relation to the other, and this is what makes his acts, his speech, and his thoughts appear to him to belong to others or to be imposed by others.

This interpretation of the so-called cenesthesic disorders is closely connected with the analyses of Daniel Lagache in *Verbal Hallucinations and Speech*.[5] Lagache thinks that the question, "How can we understand a subject who believes that he is hearing when it is he who is speaking?" can be answered only if one conceives language to be a kind of "pair-operation." There is a sort of indistinction between the act of speaking and the act of hearing. The word is not understood or even heard unless the subject is ready to pronounce it himself, and, inversely, every subject who speaks carries himself toward the one who is listening. In a dialogue, the participants occupy both poles at once, and it is this that explains why the phenomenon of "speaking" can pass into that of "hearing." It is this primordial unity that reappears in pathological cases.

What this observation reveals when we rid ourselves of sensationalist prejudices, says Wallon, is the "inability to distinguish the active from the passive," myself from the other. Here we come very close to what the psychoanalysts call "projection" and "introjection," since these mechanisms consist, for the subject, in assuming as his own the conduct of another or in attributing to the other a conduct that is really his own.

There is thus a system (my visual body, my introceptive body, the other) which establishes itself in the child, never so completely as in the animal but imperfectly, with gaps. It is founded on the indistinction of the several elements that enter into it, rather than on an ordered relation and a two-way correspondence of its different elements. One may presume that, just as there is a global identification of the child with his visual image in the mirror, so also will there be a global identification of the child with others. If the child under six months of age does not yet have a visual notion of his own body (that is, a notion that locates his body at a certain point in visible space), that is all the more reason why, during this same period, he will not know enough to limit his own life to himself. To the extent that he lacks this visual consciousness of his body, he cannot separate what *he* lives from what *others* live as well as what he sees them living. Thence comes the phenomenon of "transitivism," i.e., the absence of a division between me and others that is the foundation of syncretic sociability.

These remarks made by Wallon at the end of his book go much further than does his analysis of the specular image, and allow us to correct and complete the latter.

Wallon's study of the specular image scarcely characterizes it in a positive way. It shows us how the child learns to consider the mirror image as unreal, to reduce it; hence the disillusionment with which the child deprives the specular image of the quasi-reality he gave it at first. But we must also ask why the specular image interests him and what it is for the child to know that *he has a visible image.* Wallon himself says that the child "amuses himself" with his image "to the point of excess."[6] But why is the image so *amusing?*

It is this that the psychoanalysts have tried to understand. Dr. Lacan begins by observing exactly what Wallon noticed: the child's extreme amusement in the presence of his image, his "jubilation" at seeing himself moving in the mirror. The child is not yet walking; he stands sometimes with difficulty. All traces of prenatal life have not yet been effaced in him; all neural connections have not yet matured. He is still far from being adapted to the physical world around him. Is it not surprising, under these conditions, that he takes such a lively, universal, and constant interest in the phenomenon of the mirror? Dr. Lacan's answer is that, when the child looks at himself in the mirror and recognizes his own image there, it is a matter of *identification* (in the psychoanalytic sense of the word)— that is, of "the transformation occasioned in the subject when he assumes."[7] For the child, understanding the specular image consists in *recognizing as his own* this visual appearance in the mirror. Until the moment when the specular image arises, the child's body is a strongly felt but confused reality. To recognize his image in the mirror is for him to learn that *he can have in it a spectacle of himself.* Hitherto he has *never seen himself,* or he has only caught a glimpse of himself in looking out of the corner of his eye at the parts of his body he can see. By means of the image in the mirror he becomes capable of being a *spectator of himself.* Through the acquisition of the specular image the child notices that he is *visible,* for himself and for others. The passage from the introceptive *me* to the visual *me,* from the introceptive *me* to the "specular *I*" (as Lacan still says), is the passage from one form or state of personality to another. The personality before the advent of the specular image is what psychoanalysts call, in the adult, the "ego" [soi], i.e., the collection of confusedly felt impulses. The mirror image itself makes possible a contemplation of self. With the specular image appears the possibility of an ideal image of oneself—in psychoanalytic terms, the possibility of a superego. And this image would henceforth be either explicitly posited or simply implied by everything I see at each minute. Thus one sees that the phenomenon of the specular image is given by psychoanalysts the importance it really has in the life of the child. It is the acquisition not only of a new content but of a new function as well: the narcissistic function. Narcissus was the mythical being who, after looking at his image in the water, was drawn as if by vertigo to rejoin his image in the mirror of water. At the same time that the image of oneself makes possible the knowledge of oneself, it makes possible a sort of alienation. I am no longer what I felt myself, immediately, to be; I am that image of myself that is offered by the mirror. To use Dr. Lacan's terms, I am "captured, caught up" by my spatial image. Thereupon I leave the reality of my lived *me* in order to refer myself constantly to the ideal, fictitious, or imaginary *me*, of which the specular image is the first outline. In this sense I am torn from myself, and the image in the mirror prepares me for another still more serious alienation, which will be the alienation by others. For others have only an exterior image of me, which is analogous to the one seen in the mirror. Consequently, others will tear me away from my immediate inwardness much more surely than will the mirror. The specular image is the "symbolic matrix," says Lacan, "where the I springs up in a primordial form before objectifying itself in the dialectic of identification with the other."

The general function of the specular image would be to tear us away from our immediate reality; it would be a "de-realizing" function. The author insists that it is astonishing that such a phenomenon appears in a subject of whom we have said earlier that he is very far from maturity in the biological and motor spheres. The human child is that being who is capable of sensitivity to others and of considering himself one among other similar men long before the true state of physiological maturity. "Prematuration" and anticipation are essential phenomena for childhood; childhood makes possible both a development unknown to animality and an insecurity that is proper to the human child. For inevitably there is conflict between the *me* as I feel myself and the *me* as I see myself or as others see me. The specular image will be, among other things, the first occasion for aggressiveness toward others to manifest itself. That is why it will be assumed by the child both in jubilation and in suffering. The acquisition of a specular image, therefore, interests not only our *relations of knowledge* but also our *relations of being*, with the world and with others.

Thus in this phenomenon of the specular image, so simple at first glance, will be revealed to the child for the first time the possibility of an attitude of self-observation that will develop subsequently in the form of narcissism. For the first time the *me* ceases to confuse itself with what it experiences or desires at each moment. On this immediately lived *me* there is superimposed a constructed *me*, a *me* that is visible at a distance, an imaginary *me*, which the psychoanalysts call the superego. Henceforth the child's attention is captured by this "*me* before the *me*." From this moment on, the child also is drawn from his immediate reality; the specular image has a de-realizing function in the sense that it turns the child away from what he actually is, in order to orient him toward what he sees and imagines himself to be. Finally, this alienation of the immediate *me*, its "confiscation" for the benefit of the *me* that is visible in the mirror, already outlines what will be the "confiscation" of the subject by the others who look at him.

An analysis of this kind extends what we have found in Wallon, while at the same time it is different. It is different mainly because it emphasizes the affective significance of the phenomenon. In reading Wallon one often has the feeling that in acquiring the specular image it is a question of a labor of knowledge, of a synthesis of certain visual perceptions with certain introceptive perceptions. For psychoanalysts the visual is not simply one type of sensibility among others; it has an altogether different type of significance for the subject's life from those of other modes of sensibility. The view is the sense of spectacle, it is also the sense of the imaginary. Our images are predominantly visual, and this is no accident; it is by means of vision that one can sufficiently dominate and control objects. With the visual experience of the self, there is thus the advent of a new mode of relatedness to self. The visual makes possible a kind of schism between the immediate *me* and the *me* that can be seen in the mirror. The sensory functions themselves are thus redefined in proportion to the contribution they can make to the existence of the subject and the structures they can offer for the development of that existence.

In addition, the study of the phenomenon made by the psychoanalysts stresses both the anticipations and the regressions contained in its development.

"Pre-maturation," the anticipation by the child of adult forms of life, is for the psychoanalysts almost the definition of childhood. It is an advance made by the subject beyond his present means. The child always lives "beyond his means"; birth itself is "premature," since the child comes into the world in a state in which independent life in his new environment is impossible for him. The first Oedipal impulse is a "psychological puberty," in contrast to the organic puberty of the individual, and is awakened by his relations with the adult world. The child lives in relations that belong to his future and are not actually realizable by him.

But while the child may anticipate, the adult may regress. Child-hood is never radically liquidated; we never completely eliminate the cor-poreal condition that gives us, in the presence of a mirror, the impression of finding in it something of ourselves. This magical belief, which at first gives the specular image the value not of a simple reflection, of an "image" in the proper sense, but rather of a "double" of oneself—this belief never totally disappears. It re-forms itself in the emotional makeup of the adult. For this reduction to be possible, the "reduction" of the image must be not so much an irreversible progression of the understanding as a re-structuration of our entire manner of being continually exposed to the ac-cidents of emotional experience.

If the understanding of the specular image were solely a matter of cognition, then once the phenomenon was understood its past would be completely reabsorbed. Once the purely physical character of the reflec-tion or of the phenomenon of the image was understood, there would re-main nothing of the "presence" of the person reflected in his image. Since this is not the case, since the image-reflection is unstable, the operations that constitute it involve not only the intelligence proper but, rather, all the individual's relations with others.

Moreover, what distinguishes the psychoanalysts' remarks concern-ing the specular image is that they relate the specular image to identifica-tion with others. I understand all the more easily that what is in the mir-ror is my image for being able to represent to myself the other's viewpoint on me; and, inversely, I understand all the more the experience the other can have of me for seeing myself in the mirror in the aspect I offer him.

Wallon, we have said, accounts for the reduction of the specular image in terms of an intellectual operation. I first see in the mirror a double of myself; then an act of intellectual consciousness of my own ex-perience makes me withdraw existence from this image and treat it as simple symbol, reflection, or expression of the same body that is given in introceptivity. Intellectual activity operates at every moment of these re-ductions and integrations, and detaches the specular image from its spa-tial roots, transferring this visual appearance and introceptive experience to an ideal place in a space that is not the spatiality adhering to the sensed but the spatiality constructed out of the intelligence.

It is altogether undeniable that such a reduction occurs. But the question is one of knowing whether the intellectual operation in which it culminates can offer a *psychological explanation* for what takes place. The emergence of an ideal space, the redistribution, by the intelligence, of the spatial values that makes me withdraw from the image its own location in order to treat it as a simple modality of a unique placement of my body—is all this the *cause* or the *result* of the development?

Wallon remarks incidentally that we should not suppose that the child *begins by locating his own body in two places* or that there is a certain place where the tactile, introceptive body is situated and another place for the aspect, or visual appearance, of the body. If this were done, one would be realizing twice over in the child a rigorous form of spatiality that in fact belongs only to the adult. The child at first sees the image "over there" and feels his body "here." This does not mean that when he visually perceives the image and tactually perceives his body, he actually places each one at a distinct point in space in the same sense in which the adult, for example, perceives this microphone and that lamp *as being in two distinct places*. The two "spaces," says Wallon, are not immediately comparable, and any precise intuition of their mutual exteriority would require a sort of common denominator between them which is not immediately given by sense experience. In the case of the specular image, instead of a second body which the child would have and which would be located elsewhere than in his tactile body, there is a kind of *identity at a distance,* a *ubiquity* of the body; the body is at once present in the mirror and present at the point where I feel it tactually. But if this is the case, the two aspects that are to be coordinated are not really separated in the child and are in no way separated in the sense in which all objects in space are separated in adult perception. Wallon's analysis then is to be taken up, since it rests on the idea that what is at issue is a *re*distribution of spatial values, the substitution of an ideal space for a perceived space, and that, as we catch sight of it now, an absolute duality of visual image and sensed body does not have to be surmounted. The reduction to unity is not a dramatic surprise, if it is true that there is no genuine duplicity or duality between the visual body and the introceptive body despite the phenomenon of distance that separates the image in the mirror from the felt body.

If the presence of others were allowed a role in the phenomenon of the specular image, one would have a better idea of the difficulty the child has to surmount. The child's problem is not so much one of understanding that the visual image and the tactile image of the body—both located at two points in space—in reality comprise only one, as it is of understanding that the image in the mirror is *his* image, that it is what others see of him, the appearance he presents to other subjects; and the synthesis is less a synthesis of intellection than it is a synthesis of coexistence with others.

In looking at the matters more closely, moreover, we see that the two interpretations are not mutually exclusive. For we must consider the relation with others *not only as one of the contents of our experience but as a genuine structure.* We can admit that what we call "intelligence" is only another name for designating an original type of relation with others (the relation of "reciprocity") and that, from the start to the finish of the development, the living relation with others is the support, the vehicle, or the stimulus for what we abstractly call the "intelligence."

Thus understood, the phenomenon will necessarily be fragile and variable, as are our affective relations with others and with the world. The anticipations as well as the regressions are more easily conceivable. Lacking this kind of concrete and effective interpretation, we should then have to suppose an intellectual control of our experience that never ceases— an activity which, as Wallon holds, operates at every moment to produce the reductions and the integrations. But in no way are we conscious of such an activity; while gazing at the image in the mirror we are not conscious of judging, of doing intellectual work. We must thus suppose that there is an unperceived activity in us that would constantly reduce the perceptual space or the space of the image, and would succeed in redistributing spatial values. On the contrary, if we suppose that the conquest of the image is only one aspect in the total continuum in which all of our lived relations with others and the world participate, it becomes easier to understand at once how this continuum, once realized, functions as though all by itself and how, participating in all the contingencies of our relations with others, it is susceptible to degradations and regressions.

In our hypothesis it is a question of the acquisition of a certain *state of equilibrium* in our perception which, like any privileged state of equilibrium, tends to maintain itself unsheltered from the intervention of experience. Our interpretation would permit us to understand how the adult state can be distinct from the state of childhood without being sheltered from relapses into childhood.

b. *Syncretic sociability.* Between the ages of six and twelve months, says Wallon, there occurs an outburst of sociability. Wallon speaks of an "incontinent sociability." From the sixth to the seventh month the child, one notices, abandons the behavior of fixation—without gestures—on others. While this attitude formerly represented a good half of the child's conduct toward others, its frequency now falls to one quarter. Gestures toward his partners (other children) multiply, as do gestures oriented toward his own body. Movements aimed at the other are now four times as frequent as in the first six months of life. In the same period (between seven and twelve months), there are one third more movements directed toward others than there will be during the entire second year. Thus there is an abrupt forward thrust in relations with others, a sharp increase in the quantity and quality of these relations. The very nature of the child's conduct is modified. For example, it is at about seven months that the child begins to smile when he is looked at (and not merely when he is spoken to). Rarely at this time does the child smile at an animal or when alone.

Social sensibility develops in an extraordinary manner, and it is remarkably more advanced than relations with the physical world, which at this time are still quite inadequate.

The general character of these relations with others has been competently described by Charlotte Bühler in her 1927 book, *Sociological and Psychological Studies of the First Year*.[8] Ms. Bühler observed children who found themselves together in the waiting room of a consultation clinic. She first remarks that before the age of three years, it is extremely rare that children are very interested in other children much younger than themselves, probably because until the age of three the child does not emerge from his own situation or at least not enough to interest himself in subjects who are in an altogether different situation. This is why relations will be established only among children of relatively close ages, as elsewhere the most ordinary observation shows. Among other children of similar ages a frequent relation is that of the child who shows off before another child who gazes at him. Often one sees pairs of children, one of whom exhibits himself in his most remarkable activities (playing with this or that latest toy, talking, holding forth) while the other gazes at him. This relation is often at the same time a relation of despot and slave. In general this despotism requires a gap of at least three months between the children's ages, with the biggest child usually the master. This is not, however, an absolute rule. There are also cases of active despotism on the part of the smallest. This occurs often when the smallest has been brought up with special attention. When, for example, his approval is always sought, he becomes condescending and immediately adopts an attitude which is complementary to the one taken toward him. As Wallon remarks, there is an automatic logic of affective situations; any attitude taken toward the child immediately provokes in him the complementary attitude. Like all weak persons, he takes the signs of excessive interest to be a mark of weakness. What characterizes the relation between the child who shows off and the child who gazes at him, says Wallon, is that the two children find themselves founded in the situation. The child who contemplates is truly identified with the one he contemplates; he no longer exists except through his favorite comrade. As for the despot, his despotism is naturally founded on the weakness of the slave, but also and above all it is founded on the feeling that the slave has to be a slave. As Wallon observes, what really counts, in order for a despotic relation to be established, is not that one party be stronger or more clever than the other; it is that the other recognize that he is weaker, less clever. What the despot seeks, following Hegel's famous description of the relation between master and slave, is recognition (*Anerkennung*) by the slave, the consent of the slave to be a slave. The despot is nothing without the humiliation of the slave; he would not feel alive without this abasement of the other. The relation in question, says Wallon, would include a confusion of self with another in the same situation of sentiments. The despot exists through the recognition of his mastery by the slave, and the slave himself has no other function than to be there to admire and identify with the master. We have here a state of "combination with the other," as Wallon says, which defines childish affective situations.

Under these conditions, we understand the importance of the relation of jealousy for the child. In jealousy the couple constituted by the child creating a spectacle and the child admiring him is of concern to the latter: the jealous child would like to be the one that he contemplates. Wallon takes as an example the jealousy of dogs. If one is caressed, the other jumps forward to take his place. The desire to be caressed is not so much a positive desire as the feeling of being *deprived of the caresses* given the other. What is essential to jealousy is this feeling of privation, frustration, or exclusion. This jealousy appears at seven months, according to Guillaume, at nine months, according to Wallon. In any case, it appears around the critical period we are speaking of. It is later that this jealousy is expressed in sulking. Sulking is the attitude of the child who renounces what it wanted to be and who consequently accepts the anxiety of a repressed action.

One might say that the jealous person sees his existence invaded by the success of the other and feels himself dispossessed by him, and that in this sense jealousy is essentially a confusion between the self and the other. It is the attitude of the one who sees no life for himself other than that of achieving what the other has achieved, who does not define himself by himself but in relation to what others have. According to Wallon, all jealousy, even in the adult, represents a nondifferentiation of that kind between oneself and the other, a positive inexistence of the individual that gets confused with the contrast that exists between others and himself. Thus, says Wallon, we must consider adult jealousy as a regression to the mode of childish affectivity.

In relations of jealousy we often find phenomena of cruelty. The child tries to make the other suffer precisely because he is jealous of him, because everything the other has is stolen from him. In fact, however, cruelty is even more complex. I would not covet, in right and principle, what others have if I did not sympathize with them, if I did not consider others as "other myselves." Cruelty must, then, be understood as a "suffering sympathy" (Wallon). When I hurt the other, therefore, I am hurting myself. Consequently to like to hurt the other is to like to hurt oneself also. Here Wallon reaches the psychoanalytic idea of sadomasochism. "If sadism is a pursuit of the other's suffering, it is, however, a suffering felt to the point of pleasure as well as pain by the person who inflicts it."

It is thus with the jealous person. He likes to make himself suffer. He multiplies his investigations, he seeks information, he forms hypotheses that are always designed to stimulate his anguish or uneasiness. Wallon even indicates that in jealousy there is a sort of complacency that has as its end a heightening of the intensity of sexual passion. Wallon points out that the psychological explanation of certain ménage à trois is to be found here. The trio would have no other meaning than to organize permanently an experience of jealousy that is sought by its initiators as an increase of anxiety and because it intensifies the reactions of aggressiveness and sexuality.

For the child, jealousy represents a stage wherein he participates in a total affective situation and senses the complementary life of his own without yet knowing how to isolate or affirm his own. He thus allows himself to be inwardly dominated by the one who plunders him. Having, all told, nothing of his own, he defines himself entirely in relation to others and by the lack of what the others have. Here again we converge with psychoanalytic thought and its definition of jealousy.

Freud admits that a jealousy which seems to be directed toward one person is in reality directed toward another. A man's jealousy of his wife is the rivalry between that man and that woman in the presence of a third person who is the occasion of the jealousy. This leads us to say that in all jealous conduct there is an element of homosexuality. Wallon takes this kind of view when he admits that the jealous man is the one who lives, as his own, not only his own experiences but those of others as well, when he assumes the attitudes of the other (and, for example, the attitudes toward a third). Our relation with another is also always a relation with the other persons whom that other knows; our feelings toward another are interdependent with his feelings toward a third, and blend with them. Relations between two people are in reality more extensive relations, since they extend across the second person to those with whom the second person is vitally related. Likewise, when Wallon writes of jealousy, "This feeling is the feeling of a rivalry in a person who does not know how to react except as a spectator possessed by the action of the rival," he is very close to the psychoanalytic considerations of the attitude of the "voyeur" (of which the voyeur, in the current sense of the term, is merely an extreme case). The jealous person allows himself to be trapped or captured by the other, and inversely, moreover, he would like to trap or capture the other in his turn. In his mind he plays all the roles of the situation he finds himself in and not only his own role, of which he has no separate notion.

These analyses also remind us of Proust. As a child, Proust begins to love Gilberte one day when he has been taken out to play in the Champs-Elysées and sees before him the group of children to which Gilberte, but not himself, belongs. His feeling of love is at first the feeling of being excluded. It is not so much that he finds Gilberte lovable as it is that he feels himself outside the group of children.

One is also reminded of the famous analysis of the narrator's jealousy toward Albertine. He cannot tolerate the fact that something of Albertine escapes him completely—for example, her past before he met her. The sole fact that she has a past suffices to make him suffer, and this suffering almost confuses itself with his love. When she is not there he no longer feels anything for Albertine and even believes that he no longer loves her; he can only love her without suffering when she is inanimate in sleep (or, later, when she has disappeared in death). But even at this moment his love consists in *contemplating* her in sleep; that is, it remains under the law of jealousy, which is identification of oneself with a seen spectacle.

The negative attitudes of jealousy and cruelty are not the child's only attitudes, although they are quite frequent. There are also attitudes of sympathy. Sympathy must, in Wallon's eyes, be understood as a primordial and irreducible phenomenon. It appears in the child on a foundation of mimesis, at the moment when, all the same, consciousness of self and consciousness of others begin to be distinguished from one another. Mimesis is the ensnaring of me by the other, the invasion of me by the other; it is that attitude whereby I assume the gestures, the conducts, the favorite words, the ways of doing things of those whom I confront. Wallon shows great insight in relating mimesis to the postural function that allows me to govern my body. It is a manifestation of a unique system which unites my body, the other's body, and the other himself. Mimesis, or mimicry, is the power of assuming conducts or facial expressions on my own; this power is given to me with the power I have over my own body. It is the "postural function appropriate to the needs of expression" (Wallon). The constant regulation of bodily equilibrium, without which no function (and in particular no perceptual function) would be possible in the child, is not merely the capacity to reunite the minimal conditions for balancing the body but is more generally the power I have to realize with my body gestures that are analogous to those I see. Wallon speaks of a kind of "postural impregnation" that is resolved into gestures of imitation. He cites the example of a child who is observed watching a chirping bird for a long time and who, after this "postural impregnation," sets himself to reproducing the bird's sounds as well as something of the bird's bearing. Not only the perception of another child but even that of an animal quite different from the child himself shows up, thanks to the postural function, in attitudes which resemble those of the other and have their same expressive value. In sum, our perceptions arouse in us a reorganization of motor conduct, without our already having learned the gestures in question. We know the famous example of the spectators at a football game who make the proper gesture at the moment when the player would make it. Authors like Guillaume have tried to explain this phenomenon in terms of the awakening of the memory of gestures already made. On such accounts we would substitute ourselves for the other in thought; we would perform, on our own, acts we already knew how to perform. In fact, however, we observe phenomena of this kind even when what is at issue are acts that have never been executed—as, for example, in the case of the child just mentioned who imitates a bird. In Wallon's eyes there is, as a result, a necessity for acknowledging that the body has a capacity for "collection," for the "inward formulation" of gestures. I see unfolding the different phases of the process, and this perception is of such a nature as to arouse in me the preparation of a motor activity related to it. It is this fundamental correspondence between perception and motility—the power of perception to organize a motor conduct that Gestalt theorists have insisted on—that allows the perception of fear to translate itself into an original motor organization. This is what would be the function of mimesis, or mimicry, in its most fundamental and irreducible form.

Sympathy would emerge from this. Sympathy does not presuppose a genuine distinction between self-consciousness and consciousness of the other, but rather the absence of a distinction between the self and the other. It is the simple fact that I live in the facial expressions of the other, as I feel him living in mine. It is a manifestation of what we have called, in other terms, the system "me-and-other."

Before passing to the crisis at three years, let us try to shed light from another viewpoint on what we were able to say about the period from six months to three years, by insisting on two points: first, on the conception of the personality that seems to be immanent in this phase of childhood development; and finally on the expression which the phenomenon of pre-communication finds in the language of the child.

In the period of pre-communication, of which we spoke earlier, the personality is somehow immersed in the situation and is a function of the child himself or the other beings with whom he lives. A frequent example is that of children who fully recognize their father only on condition that he is found in his customary setting. A child said, for example, that his real father was in Vienna and that the father on vacation with him in the country was not his real father.

But the child confuses himself with his situation. One recalls the example of a child who had a glass in his hand (against his father's wishes), put it down and, on hearing the sound of breaking glass five minutes later, started and became just as agitated as if he still had the glass in his hand. He created a sort of magic link between the forbidden thing he had done several minutes earlier and the breaking of the glass, far away from him.

In a case like this one, there is in the child no distinct conception of moments of time, nor is there any distinct conception of causal relations. The child confuses himself with his situation. He is someone who has been holding a glass in his hand, someone who has had a relation with the glass, so that the subsequent breaking of the glass concerns him.

Elsa Köhler, in her book on the personality of the three-year-old, tells the story of a child who had eaten her brother's candy while her brother and parents were away.[9] The moment the father returned, the little girl ran up to him, telling him enthusiastically how much fun she had had eating her brother's candy and trying to make him share her pleasure. The father reprimanded her; the little girl cried and appeared convinced that she had done something wrong. A short time later the mother appeared, and *the same scene was repeated.* How are we to explain this? At bottom it is the problem of children who, as their parents say, "go right back and do it again." In order to understand why—immediately following a scene of repentance, tears, and good resolutions—the child repeats exactly the same offense, it is necessary to think that she establishes no connection between the arrival of her mother and that of her father; the two events must be absolutely distinct in her eyes. The child *is,* in fact, the situation and has no distance from it. The situation is taken in its most immediate meaning, and all that happened before is nothing, canceled from the time when a new situation—the mother's return—arises. This incapacity to distinguish between different situations, to adopt a conduct that is autonomous in its relation to the situations and constant in relation to the variable conditions, is what makes the child's attitude understandable. The child is really not the same even when she underwent her father's reproaches, deferred to them, and made good resolutions as when her mother returned several minutes later.

William Stern tells of how his son, at the birth of a younger sister, suddenly identified himself with his elder sister, pretended to have her name, and gave her another name. This seems to show that the child identifies himself absolutely with his family situation; and from the birth of the new child, which makes the youngest into a relatively older child, he takes over absolutely the role of the eldest, even to the point of usurping the place of the rightful eldest.

Hence, perhaps, the possibility of understanding how the child can feel himself to be several persons and can simultaneously play several roles—resembling the ill in this respect. Wallon mentions the case of a patient of Janet who declared that she was at the same time both the daughter of the Virgin and the Virgin herself and who showed this, in effect, by all her mimicry, playing the roles of both the expectant mother and the child.

Hence also the real meaning of the child's dialogues with himself.

When the child chats with himself (a familiar occurrence to anyone who has raised children), there is an actual plurality of roles; one role converses with another.

Finally, we have the possibility of understanding the frequent phenomena of what is called "transitivism" in the sick and also in the child. Transitivism consists in attributing to others what belongs to the subject himself. For example, a patient will pity another patient for having had a crisis which, in fact, he himself underwent during the night—as though it were the other who had suffered the crisis. Transitivism is also the attitude of hypochondriacs who look for signs of ill health in the faces of others. All that we are, all that happens to us can furnish us with explanatory categories and in every case plays the role of exploratory tools for knowing the other. Everything that happens to us makes us sensitive to a certain aspect of the other and makes us seek in the other the equivalent of, or something that corresponds to, what has happened to us. This is why Goethe was right in saying that for each of us our circle of friends is what we ourselves are. Our *Umwelt* is what we are, because what happens to us does not happen only to us but to our entire vision of the world. Transitivism is, in other words, the same notion that psychoanalysts are using when they speak of *projection,* just as mimesis is the equivalent of *introjection.*

There are striking examples of transitivism in children, too. Wallon mentions one of them, borrowed from the work of Charlotte Bühler. It is the case of a little girl who, when seated beside her maid and another little girl, seemed uneasy and unexpectedly slapped her companion. When asked why, she answered that it was her companion who was naughty and who hit her. The child's air of sincerity ruled out any deliberate ruse. We have here a manifestly aggressive child who gives an unprovoked slap and explains herself right afterward by saying that it is the other child who slapped her. Psychoanalysts have stressed the childlike attitude that consists in imputing the wrong to the other ("You're the one who's lying!"). The child who seemed uneasy was passing through a phase of anxiety, and this anxiety impregnated her entire view of things and people around her—in particular her view of the little girl sitting beside her. This little girl appeared to her to be surrounded by the same anguishing aura. The child was living her anxiety, and the gestures appropriate to lessening it, not as interior events but as qualities of things in the world and of others. In the absence of a reduction of the anxiety to its subjective source and a concentration of the anxiety within the child in whom it was actually located, the anxiety was lived as something that has an external origin as well as an internal origin. Slapping her companion was the little girl's response to the aggression of the anxiety that came from outside. The child's own personality is at the same time the personality of the other, that indistinction of the two personalities that makes transitivism possible; this presupposes an entire structure in the child's consciousness. The guilty act of taking the glass, that has just occurred, and the breaking of the glass are now joined in a quasi-magical way. Similarly there is a sort of spatial syncretism—i.e., a presence of the same psychic being in several spatial points, a presence of me in the other and the other in me. In a general way, there is an inability to conceive space and time as environments that contain a series of perspectives which are absolutely distinct from one another. The child switches from perspective to perspective, erasing them in the identity of the thing, unaware even of the different profiles or different perspectives in which space can present itself. It is an aspect of the same structure of consciousness that expresses itself in certain childish persons we studied last year (sudden change of direction [*rabattement*]). The reduction of external perception to what is visible from a single point of view—in short, the perspective given—is possible only much later. There is also an indistinction between the symbol and what it symbolizes. Words and things are not absolutely distinguished; of this we have already had more than one reminder.

The absence of what we call in the adult the symbolic consciousness, the fusion of the sign and the signified, the different moments of time and of space in the thing are so many evidences of the same fact.

The syncretic relations with others that show up in the child's conception of personality also show up clearly in the child's use of language. The child's first words, considered by the psychologists and the linguists as standing for sentences (word-sentences), can be the equivalent of entire sentences only through the effects of syncretism. The first word-sentences, as we have already seen, aim just as much at the actions of others as at one's own actions or conducts. When the child (even the very young child) says "hand" (hand-hand), this means his father's hand as well as the hand represented by a photograph or his own hand. This seems to presuppose a kind of abstraction, a recognition of the same object in a plurality of cases. And in fact the object identified is greatly different (for example, there is not a great resemblance between a child's hand and the photograph of an adult's hand). In reality, however, there is no abstraction here. There is simply no radical distinction in the child between his own hand and that of another. The child's extraordinary facility in recognizing the parts of the body in a drawing or an even rougher sketch, the promptness and skill with which he identifies parts of his own body in the bodies of animals that scarcely resemble the human body or familiar domestic animals, the plasticity of vision that allows him to recognize homologous structures of the body in quite different organisms—all this can be explained by the state of neutrality in which he lives, in regard to the distinction between the self and others. The child's own body is for him a way of understanding other bodies through "postural impregnation" (Wallon). The child's person, says Wallon, is in a way scattered through all the images his action gives rise to, and it is because of this that he is apt to recognize himself in everything.

This explains the relative ease with which children understand the modern way of painting and drawing. It is altogether startling to see certain children much more apt to understand this drawing or that painting by Picasso than the adults around them. The adult hesitates before this kind of drawing because his cultural formation has trained him to take as canonical the perspective inherited from the Italian Renaissance, a perspective that works by projection of different external data on a single plane. To the extent that the child is a stranger to this cultural tradition and has not yet received the training that will integrate him within it, he recognizes with great freedom in a number of traits what the painter meant to show. If you like, childhood thought is general from the start and at the same time is very individual. It is a physiognomic thought that gets to the essentials by means of a corporeal taking up of objects and given conducts.

This allows us to understand why the use of the word *I* comes relatively late to the child. He will use it when he has become conscious of his own proper perspective, distinct from those of others, and when he has distinguished all of the perspectives from the external object. In the initial state of perception there is consciousness not of being enclosed in a perspective and of guessing—picking out across it a thing which would be beyond—but of communicating directly with things across a personal-universal vision. The *I* arises when the child understands that every *you* that is addressed to him is for him an *I;* that is, that there must be a consciousness of the reciprocity of points of view in order that the word *I* be used.

Guillaume points out that in the early months of the second year the child is first seen to acquire a large number of names of persons. Finally, around the sixteenth month, he acquires his own name, which at first he uses only in very limited cases, i.e., in answering questions like "What is your name?" or to designate the situations in which he is placed along with other children—for example, in the distribution of gifts. In this case the child can employ his own name because of the collective operation in which he is involved just like one of the others. The use of his own name in these circumstances does not indicate that he is conscious of his privileged perspective, which seems to escape him completely at sixteen months or thereabouts. For example, when he wants to say "I want to write," he uses the infinitive, without a subject. Guillaume's son said "write" for

"I want to write," but he said "Papa write"; that is, he used the subject only when the subject was another person. When it was he himself who was involved, he never expressed the subject at all. And the "Paul writes" that he finally came to say grew somehow within the formula "Papa writes." The use of his own name was learned from the use of other people's names.

Use of the pronoun *I* comes still later than use of the proper name, at least as it is understood in its full meaning, i.e., in its relative meaning. The pronoun *I* has its full meaning only when the child uses it not as an individual sign to designate his own person—a sign that would be assigned once for all to himself and to nobody else—but when he understands that each person he sees can in turn say *I* and that each person is an *I* for himself and a *you* for others. It is when he understands that even though others call him *you* he can nonetheless say *I*, that the pronoun *I* is acquired in all its significance. Thus it is not because a child of around nineteen months finds he has used the sound "I" that we say that he has acquired the use of the pronoun. In order for it to have been a real acquisition, he must have grasped the relations between the different pronouns and the passage from one of the meanings to the others. In other cases the sound "I" is used mechanically, as its materiality [*physique*], but it is not used in its fullest linguistic and grammatical meaning. Only at nineteen months did Guillaume's son use *me* or *I* in their fullest senses. At nineteen months he used *mine* and *yours* in a systematic way; at twenty months he used *mine, yours, his, everybody's*. At this moment the operation of distribution is conceived in the same way whether it is addressed to the child or to others. The use of *I* takes the place of the child's first name and occurs regularly only at the end of the second year. While the name is an attribute of the person alone, the pronoun designates either the speaker or the person he is speaking to. The same pronoun can serve to designate different persons, while each person has only one proper name.

2. The "Crisis at Three Years"
This crisis has been well described by Elsa Köhler in her book on the personality of the three-year-old, as well as by Wallon in *The Origins of Character in the Infant.*

At around three years the child stops lending his body and even his thoughts to others, as we have seen happen in the phase of syncretic sociability. He stops confusing himself with the situation or the role in which he may find himself engaged. He adopts a proper perspective or viewpoint of his own—or rather he understands that whatever the diversity of situations or roles, he is *someone* above and beyond these different situations and roles.

The acquisition of perspective in drawing (which will occur later) can serve us here as a symbol; it will be possible only for a subject to whom the notion of an individual *perspective* is a familiar one. The child cannot understand what it is to portray the things before him as one sees them from a single viewpoint, unless he has come to the idea that he sees them from a single point instead of living in them. There must thus be a kind of duplication of the immediately given sensory spectacle in which the child was at first engulfed and of a subject who is henceforth capable of re-ordering and redistributing his experience in accordance with the directions chosen by thought. Wallon indicates a certain number of typical attitudes by which one can disclose the advent of this distance between the child on the one hand and the spectacle of others and the world on the other. It is at around the age of three years that one sees in the child the deliberate decision to do everything all alone. Wallon also shows the change in the child's reactions to the look of the other. Up to the age of three years, in general, except in pathological cases, the other's look encourages the child or helps him. Beginning at three years a whole quite different set of reactions is seen to arise; they bring to mind certain pathological reactions. The other's gaze becomes an annoyance for the child, and everything happens as though, when he is gazed at, his attention is displaced from the task he is carrying out to a representation of himself in the process of carrying it out.

This is related to certain pathological phenomena.[10] Wallon mentions the case of a hemiplegic described by Davidson, in whom a convulsive laugh broke out, shaking him all over, whenever he was gazed at. Wallon also mentions the case of a subject whose job was testing automobiles. When alone the subject drove skillfully at ninety miles an hour, but when he had a passenger he was tormented by irrepressible tics. This extreme sensitivity to the other's gaze had shown up very early in this subject— after convulsions at the age of two and a half years. Wallon again recalls the case of general paralytics who, when gazed at, show questioning, approving, or satisfied expressions, as though it were absolutely necessary that their faces show something, as though the other's gaze demanded these expressions of them.

Some subjects who are perfectly normal are afraid of seeming insignificant when being photographed. We can also mention idiots who howl when anyone gazes at them. If the three-year-old child is inhibited by the other's gaze, it is because from this point on he is not simply what he is in his own eyes; he feels himself also to be that which others see him to be. The phenomenon of the specular image, mentioned earlier, becomes generalized. The specular image teaches the child that he is not only what he believed he was by inner experience but that he is in addition that figure he sees in the mirror. The other's gaze tells me, as does the image in the mirror, that I am *also* that being who is limited to a point in space, that I am that visible "stand-in" [*doublure*] in whom I would recognize only with difficulty the lived *me*. To be sure, as we have seen, this *me* scarcely distinguishes itself from the other before the age of three years. But for this very reason there was never any question of being controlled or inhibited by others; and when this phenomenon appears, it is because the indistinction of myself and the other is at an end.

The *ego*, the *I*, cannot truly emerge at the age of three years without doubling itself with an *ego in the eyes of the other*. In the case of this phenomenon it is not a question of shame, in the sense in which it exists later on as the shame of being naked (which appears only around the age of five or six), any more than it is the fear of being reprimanded. It is simply a question of the fear experienced by the child when he is gazed at.

At the same age the child wants attention and will go to the point of misbehaving in order to get it. Conducts of duplicity that until now were absent are seen to emerge at this time. The child interferes with the play of others for the sake of his own pleasure. He also changes his attitude toward giving. When he gives an object away, he often does it while saying that he does not like the object anymore. The thoughtless gift of the previous stage disappears. The child takes things away from others solely for the fun of it; as soon as he has taken them he abandons them. The gift is transformed into transaction.

In sum, the child constantly calls into play the relation of "me-and-other," which therefore stops being indivision, indifferentiation, as it is in the preceding phase.

These remarks lead us to ask ourselves to what extent the crisis at three years brings about a transformation and a total restructuration in the child and whether the state of indivision, of pre-communication, of which we have been speaking until now, is visibly abolished. Wallon himself writes that the already surpassed forms of activity are not abolished. Syncretic sociability is perhaps not liquidated in the third-year crisis. The state of indivision from others, this mutual encroachment of the other and myself within situations in which we are confused, this presence of the same subject in several roles—all are met with again in adult life. The crisis at three years pushes syncretism farther away rather than suppressing it altogether. Certainly after three years, a neutral or objective ground is set up between me and the other: a "lived distance" divides us, as Minkowski says. There is no longer that dizzying proximity of others which made possible certain disorders, certain hallucinations, as well as transitivism.

The child understands, for example, that there is a way of accusing the other that amounts to a confession. Unlike the child, an adult will no longer say, "*You're* the one who's lying." The adult understands that certain resentments disclose in the person expressing them precisely the faults for which he reproaches another. He must be capable of certain meannesses in order to suspect others of them. The adult is conscious of transitivism and the projections whereby we lend others our own ways of being. But if transitivism is thus pushed out of a whole sector of his life, does this mean that it has completely disappeared? The indistinction between me and the other does not inevitably reappear except in certain situations that for the adult are limiting situations but are quite important in his life.

Could one conceive of a love that would not be an encroachment on the freedom of the other? If a person wanted in no way to exert an influence on the person he loved and consequently refrained from choosing on her behalf or advising her or influencing her in any way, he would act on her precisely by that abstention, and would incline her all the more strongly toward choosing in such a way as to please him. This apparent detachment, this will to remain without responsibility arouses in the other an even more lively desire to come closer. There is a paradox in accepting love from a person without wanting to have any influence on her freedom. If one loves, one finds one's freedom precisely in the act of loving, and not in a vain autonomy. To consent to love or to be loved is to consent also to influence someone else to decide to a certain extent on behalf of the other. To love is inevitably to enter into an undivided situation with another.

From the moment when one is joined with someone else, one suffers from her suffering. If physical pain is involved, in which one can participate only metaphorically, one strongly feels his inadequacy. One is not what he would be without that love; the perspectives remain separate— and yet they overlap. One can no longer say, "This is mine, this is yours"; the roles cannot be absolutely separated. And to be joined with someone else is, in the end, to live her life, at least in intention. To the very extent that it is convincing and genuine, the experience of the other is necessarily an alienating one, in the sense that it tears me away from my lone self and creates instead a mixture of myself and the other.

As Alain has said, to love someone is to swear and affirm more than one knows about what the other will be. In a certain measure, it is to relinquish one's freedom of judgment. The experience of the other does not leave us at rest within ourselves, and this is why it can always be the occasion for doubt. If I like, I can always be strict and put in doubt the reality of the other's feelings toward me; this is because such feelings are never *absolutely* proved. This person who professes to love does not give every instant of her life to her beloved, and her love may even die out if it is constrained. Certain subjects react to this evidence as though it were a refutation of love and refuse to be trusting and believe in an unlimited affirmation on the basis of an always finite number of professions. The en-snaring love of the child is the love that never has enough proofs, and ends by imprisoning and trapping the other in its immanence.

The normal, non-pathological attitude consists in having confi-dence above and beyond what can be proved, in resolutely skirting these doubts that can be raised about the reality of the other's sentiments, by means of the generosity of the praxis, by means of an action that proves it-self in being carried out.

But if these matters are as we have depicted them, all relations with others, if deep enough, bring about a state of insecurity, since the doubt we mentioned always remains possible and since love itself creates its own proper truth and reality. The state of union with another, the disposses-sion of me by the other, are thus not suppressed by the child's arrival at the age of three years. They remain in other zones of adult life. This is a par-ticular case of what Piaget has called *displacement* [*décalage*]. The same con-duct, acquired at a certain level, is not yet (and perhaps never will be) ac-quired at a higher level. Transitivism, which has been surpassed in the realm of immediate daily life, is never surpassed in the realm of feelings. That is why, as the psychoanalysts have shown, syncretic sociability can be found in the sick to the extent to which they regress in the direction of the conduct of children and show themselves incapable of making the transi-tion to praxis, to the selfless, outgoing attitude of the adult.

We might ask what kind of relationship must be established between the crisis at three years mentioned by Wallon and the Oedipal phase of de-velopment which certain psychoanalysts locate at the same moment and which accompanies the emergence of the superego, the true "objective" relation, and the surpassing of narcissism.

11

Human Engineering

The New "Human" Techniques of American Big Business

[This is a presentation by Merleau-Ponty, signed T.M. (for *Les Temps Modernes*), of Michel Crozier's article in *Les Temps Modernes*, no. 69 (July 1951): 44–48.]

"Culturalism" and certain investigations in American social psychology, to whose introduction in France *Les Temps Modernes* has contributed and will continue to contribute, are an important acquisition to the extent that they attempt to reveal the tacit words, unofficial, yet lived between men, beyond the ideas or official mottos that mask them at least as much as they express them. They give access to what Politzer called the interhuman "drama" amidst the living history where we find meeting up all causalities, all determinants whose objective workings economics, demographics, law, and the history of ideas study. They take on the task of applying the incontestable principle that the truth of a social system lies in the type of human relations it makes possible. Marxist sociology had already noted the correlation within a single human life of moral, juridical, and religious conceptions with the techniques, the labor, and the forces of production. But many authors seem to ground it on a mystical causality of the economy, when the notion of *culture* as a totality that has its laws of balance, its molecular changes, its crises, its restructurations—and that of a *structure of a basic personality,* sometimes stereotyped, sometimes wrought by a principle of change in every human group—comes to clarify the connection between "ideas" and "economic facts." These investigations are a new invitation to pursue the inventory of everyday conflicts and of this latent history that silently animates the official history as it waits to manifest itself in the explosion of events.

If "culturalism" and certain investigations in social psychology are in fact such in the writings of the best American authors, they can become something else entirely in others, and in the use the economic apparatus, the press, the radio, and common sense make of them. The article by Crozier that one is about to read admirably shows how, as an inquiry into the living dynamic that bears (and judges) official relations, social psychology can degenerate into a means of governing and an apparatus of conservation as soon as it posits as *natural* existing social relations, as *normal* the integration of the individual into these relations, and explains the difficulties it encounters through the failings of a private order. It is at that point no longer a psychology *of social life,* that is, an inquiry into the lived aspect of the social; it is psychology put in place of social life. The investigation into opinions, which ought to be a consciousness that has become aware of all conflicts, can change into a new means of masking them, if only, rather than going all the way to the real opinions men manifest in matters of business and where their lives are concerned, we merely test a certain decorum of the opinion and remain loyal to the idols of the right way. Crozier shows how the same worker, in his factory and in those work conflicts in which he is vitally invested, is an intransient syndicalist, but he is favorable to the Taft-Hartley law if he is consulted by his newspaper or Gallup, because it is then the "American" in him who is being asked, the adherent to the ideology of the "American way of life," who is formed precisely by other Gallup polls, by the radio, and by the press. And if the workers do in fact refuse to forget their own struggle in favor of received ideas, they will be overwhelmed by the weight of the "public at large," who suffer because of a public transportation strike, but not because of the low wages paid by the corporations in charge of public transportation. The need to "communicate"—to put it another way, the will to be "recognized"—which is a motive for social creation, becomes a factor of stagnation if the worker learns to communicate with the prejudices of those who employ him rather than with the universal history of the workers' movement, if he learns to take them into account, and allows himself to be convinced by the slogans of national society qua closed society. At that point the very honesty of an employer who decides to "hide nothing" serves only to disarm his opponents, and we see the appearance of a new form of propaganda, a "propaganda through truth." Objectivity becomes the most profound of ruses. A false democracy begins to emerge, a "statistical democracy," which is to say the seductive dictatorship of the "normal," the superficial, and the conventional.

All of these analyses, which show the ambiguity of the new techniques, are in our eyes remarkable. All that remains is to draw conclusions with respect to the methods of research they utilize. In this case, too, we are in full agreement with the conclusions toward which Crozier gestures rather than develops, and which we would like to emphasize. *Mystification does not arise from the very principle of a social psychology; it arises from the fix-*

ated and optimistic postulate we add to it: if the situation of the employee, the worker, or the peasant in the face of the employer, the owner, or the trust, such as it results from American history, is founded on a divine decree, then the conflicts it occasions are nothing more than misunderstandings, and the only task left for social psychology is to accommodate man to it, since it is inevitable, and also good, like God himself. It is then that all revolt is neurosis and that the social engineers work to make the subjugated accept their condition, to transform, in the service of the "normal," the energies freed by social disintegration into a force of conservatism. But no sooner have we set aside metaphysical and religious prejudices, or, more precisely, incorporated them into the social dynamic, than the study of the relations of consciousness in conflictual situations—masculinity and femininity, adult and child, employer and subjugated, white and non-white—reveals these conflicts in all of their depth, because it can—and only it can—reveal the supreme victory of the oppressor, which is, as Nietzsche said, that of giving the oppressed a bad conscience by imposing one's own norms on them. Only a social psychology can show that the oppressor assures for himself a certain complicity on the part of the oppressed by making them accept, as Bernard Wolfe showed here, writing of American blacks, an image of themselves that, even if it is flattering, maintains them in their difference.

The truth can become propaganda only if it is a half-truth. Objectivity can become a ruse only if it is a false objectivity (by its true name: resignation). We can move from a "truth" ruse only to true truth, from a "statistical democracy" only to a more real democracy, and from a neutered psychology only to a whole, social psychology. The way to remedy superficial opinion polls is not to eliminate polls, but to extend them to vital and latent opinions. Social consciousness does not demand that we eliminate psychology, but that we go further than it, in the direction that should be its own. If Americans seek in psychoanalysis the means to satisfy a fascination with the "normal," that is not the fault of psychoanalysis, which has done more than any other research to go beyond the notion of a statistical norm. Against a superficial psychoanalysis—an abridged analysis, a narcoanalysis—that substitutes mechanical procedures for the investigation of the interpersonal dynamic, we can have recourse only to true psychoanalysis. Humanity cannot give up on nuclear energy for the sole reason that it has up to now been used only to manufacture means of destruction. Tomorrow, perhaps, it will be used to build and produce. Similarly (on a lesser scale), one cannot give up on the knowledge of the energies that are employed in human intersubjectivity for the sole reason that these energies are, here and there, captured on behalf of an established order. Crozier indicates in passing that most of those who work on human engineering believe in it and that, except for a few cynics, the system is accepted as true. *This means that human engineering is a ruse of big capital, but also that, past a certain point in social history, the powers and interests cannot maintain themselves without seeking to found themselves as truth,* and therefore that certain truths are going to pass through these avenues of research. When the powers, after having avoided the social question for so long, come to pose it on the terrain of truth, there is nothing left to do but take them at their word. Granted, only in a society without private interests could objectivity be without hesitations and truth be without postulates, and we would be more at ease if this return to truth were proposed by a socialist society. That is not the case. But one cannot, without obscurantism, evacuate the terrain of truth. Even socialist forms of property would not dispense us from having a social psychology, which would measure or verify the realization of socialism in human relations. A true socialism will be realized only when it will dare to give a voice to those who have always remained quiet, and will reveal to the light of recognized knowledge human relations about which only literature and testimonials had up to now informed us.

12

Man and Adversity

It is clearly impossible to tick off in one hour the advances made in the philosophical investigation of man during the past fifty years. Even if we could assume that this infinite ability existed in one single brain, we would be brought up short before the discord among the authors who must be taken into account. The impossibility of ever progressing in any other than an oblique fashion operates like a cultural law, each new idea becoming, after the one which instituted it, different than it was for this instituting idea. A man cannot receive a heritage of ideas without transforming it by the very fact that he comes to know it, without injecting his own and always different way of being into it. In proportion as ideas arise, a tireless volubility sets them stirring; just as a never-satisfied "need for expressiveness," the linguists say, transforms languages at the very moment one would think that, having succeeded in ensuring an apparently unequivocal communication among speaking subjects, they were reaching their goal. How would we dare enumerate *acquired ideas,* since even when they have gotten themselves almost universally accepted, they have always done so by also becoming different from themselves?

Furthermore, a catalog of acquired knowledge would not suffice. Even if we were to lay the "truths" of this half century end to end, in order to restore their hidden affinity, we would still have to revive the personal and inter-individual experience they are a *response* to, and the logic of situations in reference to which they were defined. The great or valuable work is never an effect of life, but it is always a *response* to life's very particular events or most general structures. Although the writer is free to say yes or no to such circumstances, and to justify and limit his refusal or assent in different ways, he never can arrange things so that he does not have to choose his life in a certain historical landscape or state of problems which excludes certain solutions even if it imposes none, and which give Gide, Proust, and Valéry (no matter how different they may be) the undeniable quality of contemporaries. The movement of ideas comes to discover truths only by responding to some pulsation of interpersonal life, and every change in our understanding of man is related to a new way he has of carrying on his existence. If man is the being who is not content to coincide with himself like a thing but represents himself to himself, sees himself, imagines himself, and gives himself rigorous or fanciful symbols of himself, it is quite clear that in return every change in our representation of man translates a change in man himself. Thus it is the whole history of this half century, with its projects, disappointments, wars, revolutions, audacities, panics, inventions, and failures, that we would have to evoke here. We can only refuse this unlimited task.

Yet this transformation of the knowledge of man, which we cannot hope to determine by a rigorous method on the basis of works, ideas, and history, is sedimented in us. It is our substance; we have a lively, total feeling for it when we look back to the writings or the facts of the beginning of the century. What we can try to do is to mark within ourselves, according to two or three selected relationships, the modifications in the human situation. We would have to present infinite explanations and commentaries, clear up a thousand misunderstandings, and translate quite different systems of concepts into one another in order to establish an objective relationship between, for example, Husserl's philosophy and Faulkner's works. And yet within us readers they communicate. The very men who (like Ingres and Delacroix) think themselves adversaries are reconciled in the eyes of a third person who witnesses them, because they are responding to a single cultural situation. We men who have lived as our problem the development of Communism and the war, and who have read Gide and Valéry and Proust and Husserl and Heidegger and Freud, are the same. Whatever our responses have been, there should be a way to circumscribe perceptible zones of our experience and formulate, if not ideas about man that we hold in common, at least a new experience of our condition.

With these reservations, we propose to acknowledge that our century is distinguished by a completely new association of "materialism" and "idealism," of pessimism and optimism, or rather by the overcoming of these antitheses. Our contemporaries have no difficulty thinking both that human life is the demand for an original order and that this order could not possibly endure or even truly exist except under certain very precise and very concrete conditions which can fail to materialize, no natural arrangement of things and the world predestining them to make a human life possible. There were philosophers and scientists in 1900 who set certain biological and material conditions for human existence. But they were ordinarily "materialists" in the sense the term had at the end of the last century. They made humanity an episode of evolution, civilizations a particular case of adaptation, and even resolved life into its physical and chemical components. For them the properly human perspective on the world was a superfluous phenomenon; and those who saw the contingency of humanity ordinarily treated values, institutions, works of art, and words as a system of signs referring in the last analysis to the elementary needs and desires of all organisms. On the other hand, there were "spiritualist" authors who assumed other motive forces than these in humanity; but when they did not derive them from some supernatural source, they related them to a human nature which guaranteed their unconditional efficacy. *Human nature* had truth and justice for attributes, as other species have fins or wings. The epoch was full of these absolutes and these notions that are separated from one another. There was the absolute of the State pervading all events; and a State which did not reimburse its lenders was considered dishonest, even if it was in the midst of a revolution. The value of money was an absolute, and men scarcely dreamed of treating it as simply an aid to economic and social functioning. There was also a moral gold standard: family and marriage were the good, even if they secreted hatred and rebellion. "Things of the spirit" were intrinsically noble, even if books (like so many works in 1900) translated only morose reveries. There were values and, on the other hand, realities; there was mind and, on the other hand, body; there was the interior and, on the other hand, the exterior. But what if it were precisely the case that the order of facts invaded that of values, if it were recognized that dichotomies are tenable only this side of a certain point of misery and danger? Even those among us today who are taking up the word "humanism" again no longer maintain the *shameless humanism* of our elders. What defines our time is perhaps to dissociate humanism from the idea of a humanity fully guaranteed by natural law, and not only reconcile the consciousness of human values and the consciousness of the infrastructures which keep them in existence, but insist upon their inseparability.

* * *

Our century has erased the dividing line between "body" and "mind," and sees human life as through and through mental and corporeal, always based upon the body and always (even in its most carnal modes) interested in relationships between persons. For many thinkers at the close of the nineteenth century, the body was a bit of matter, a network of mechanisms. The twentieth century has restored and deepened the notion of flesh, that is, of animate body.

In psychoanalysis, for example, it would be interesting to follow the development from a conception of the body which for Freud was initially that of nineteenth-century doctors to the modern notion of the lived body. Did not psychoanalysis originally take up the tradition of mechanistic philosophies of the body—and is it not still frequently understood in this same way today? Does not the Freudian system explain the most complex and elaborate behavior of adults in terms of instinct and especially sexual instincts, that is to say physiologically, in terms of a composition of forces beyond the grasp of our consciousness or even realized once and for all in childhood prior to the age of rational control and properly human relationships to culture and to others? Perhaps things seemed this way in Freud's first works, and for a hurried reader; but as his own and his successors' psychoanalysis rectifies these initial ideas in contact with clinical experience, we see the emergence of a new idea of the body which was called for by the initial ideas.

It is not false to say that Freud wanted to base the whole of human development upon the development of instincts; but we would get further if we said that from the start his works overturn the concept of instinct and break down the criteria by which men had previously thought they could circumscribe it. If the term "instinct" means anything, it means a mechanism within the organism which with a minimum of use ensures certain responses adapted to certain characteristic situations of the species. Now what defines Freudianism is surely to show that in this sense man has no sexual instincts, that the "polymorphously perverse" child establishes a so-called normal sexual activity (when he does so) only at the end of a difficult individual history. Unsure about its instruments as it is about its goals, the power to love wends its way through a series of investments which approach the canonical form of love, anticipates and regresses, and repeats and goes beyond itself without our ever being able to claim that what is called normal sexual love is nothing but that. The child's attachment to his parents, so powerful at the beginning as to retard that history, is not itself of the instinctual order. For Freud it is a mental attachment. It is not because the child has the same blood as his parents that he loves them; it is because he knows he is their issue or because he sees them turned toward him, and thus identifies himself with them, conceives of himself in their image, and conceives of them in his image. For Freud the ultimate psychological reality is the system of attractions and tensions which attaches the child to parental images, and then through these to all the other persons, a system within which he tries out different *positions* in turn, the last of which will be his adult attitude.

It is not simply the love object which escapes every definition in terms of instinct, but the very way of loving itself. As we know, adult love, sustained by a trusting tenderness which does not constantly insist upon new proofs of absolute attachment but takes the other person as he is, at his distance and in his autonomy, is for psychoanalysis won from an infantile "erotic attachment" ["*aimance*"] which demands everything at all times and is responsible for whatever devouring, impossible aspects may remain in any love. And though development to the genital stage is a necessary condition of this transformation to adult love, it is never sufficient to guarantee it. Freud himself described an infantile relationship to others which is established through the intermediary of those regions and functions of the child's body which are least capable of discrimination and articulated action: the mouth, which does not know whether to suck or bite—the sphincteral apparatus, which can only hold in or let go. Now these primordial modes of relationship to others may remain predominant even in the genital life of the adult. In this case the relation to others remains trapped in the impasses of absolute immediacy, oscillating between an inhuman demand, an absolute egotism, and a voracious devotion which destroys the subject himself. Thus sexuality and, more generally, corporeality, which Freud considers the soil of our existence, is a power of investment which is at first absolute and universal. This power is *sexual* only in the sense that it reacts immediately to the visible differences of the body and the maternal and paternal roles. Instinct and the physiological are enveloped in a central demand for absolute possession which could not possibly be the act of a bit of matter but is of the order of what is ordinarily called consciousness.

And yet it is a mistake to speak of consciousness here, since to do so is to reintroduce the dichotomy of soul and body at the moment Freudianism is in the process of contesting it, and thus to change our idea of the body as well as our idea of the mind. "Psychical facts have a meaning," Freud wrote in one of his earliest works. This meant that no human behavior is simply the result of some bodily mechanism, that in behavior there is not a mental center and a periphery of automatism, and that all our gestures in their fashion participate in that single activity of explication and signification which is ourselves. At least as much as he tries to reduce superstructures to instinctive infrastructures, Freud tries to show that in human life there is no "inferior" or "lower part." Thus we could not be further from an explanation in "terms of the lower part." At least as much as he explains adult behavior by a fate inherited from childhood, Freud shows a *premature* adult life in childhood, and in the child's sphincteral behavior, for example, a first choice of his relationships of generosity or avarice to others. At least as much as he explains the psychological by the body, he shows the psychological meaning of the body, its hidden or latent logic. Thus we can no longer speak of the sexual organ taken as a localizable mechanism, or of the body taken as a mass of matter, as an ultimate cause. Neither cause nor simply instrument or means, it is the vehicle, the fulcrum, and the steadying factor of our life. None of the notions philosophy had elaborated upon—cause, effect, means, end, matter, form—suffices for thinking about the body's relationships to life as a whole, about the way it meshes into personal life or the way personal life meshes into it. The body is enigmatic: a part of the world certainly, but offered in a bizarre way, as its dwelling, to an absolute desire to draw near the other person and meet him in his body too, animated and animating, the natural face of the mind. With psychoanalysis mind passes into body as, inversely, body passes into mind.

Along with our idea of the body, these investigations cannot fail to disrupt the idea we form of its partner, the mind. It must be admitted that in this respect much remains to be done to draw from psychoanalytic experience all that it contains, and that psychoanalysts, beginning with Freud himself, have been satisfied with a structure of hardly satisfactory ideas. In order to account for that osmosis between the body's anonymous life and the person's official life which is Freud's great discovery, it was necessary to introduce something *between* the organism and our selves considered as a sequence of deliberate acts and explicit understandings. This was Freud's *unconscious*. We have only to follow the transformations of this Protean idea in Freud's works, the diverse ways in which it is used, and the contradictions it involves to be convinced that it is not a fully developed idea, and that, as Freud himself implies in his *Essais de psych-analyse*,[1] we still have to find the right formulation for what he intended by this provisional designation. At first glance "the unconscious" evokes the realm of a dynamics of impulses whose results alone would presumably be given to us. And yet the unconscious cannot be a process "in third person," since it is the unconscious which chooses what aspect of us will be admitted to official existence, which avoids the thoughts or situation we are resisting, and which is therefore not an *un-knowledge* but rather a non-recognized and unformulated knowledge that we do not want to take up. In an approximative language, Freud is on the point of discovering what other thinkers have more appropriately named *ambiguous perception*. It is by working in this direction that we shall find a civil status for this consciousness which brushes its objects (eluding them at the moment it is going to designate them, and taking account of them as the blind man takes account of obstacles rather than recognizing them), which does not want to know about them (which does not know about them to the extent that it knows about them, and knows about them to the extent that it does not know about them), and which subtends our explicit acts and understandings.

Whatever their philosophical formulations may be, there is no denying that Freud had an increasingly clear view of the body's mental function and the mind's incarnation. In his mature works he speaks of the "sexual-aggressive" relationship to others as the fundamental datum of our life. As aggression does not aim at a thing but a person, the intertwining of the sexual and the aggressive means that sexuality has, so to speak, an interior (that it is lined throughout with a person-to-person relationship), and that the sexual is our way (since we are flesh, our carnal way) of living our relationships with others. Since sexuality is relationship to other persons, and not just to another body, it is going to weave the circular system of projections and introjections between other persons and myself, illuminating the unlimited series of reflecting reflections and reflected reflections which are the reasons why I am the other person and he is myself.

Such is this idea of the individual incarnate and (through incarnation) given to himself but also to others—incomparable yet stripped of his congenital secret and faced with his *fellows*—that Freudianism ends up offering us. At the very moment Freud was forming it, and without there being ordinarily any *influence,* writers were expressing the same experience in their own way.

It is in this way, to begin with, that the *eroticism* of writers during this half century must be understood. When in this respect we compare Proust's or Gide's works with the particular works of the preceding literary generation, the contrast is striking. Passing over the generation of writers of the 1890s, Proust and Gide pick up from the start the Sadian and Stendhalian tradition of a direct expression of the body. With Proust, with Gide, an unwearying report on the body begins. It is confirmed, consulted, listened to like a person. The intermittencies of its desire and (as they put it) its fervor are spied on. With Proust it becomes the keeper of the past; and it is the body which, in spite of the deteriorations which render it almost unrecognizable itself, maintains from one time to another a substantial relationship between us and our past. In the two inverse cases of death and awakening, Proust describes the meeting point of mind and body, showing how, in the dispersion of the sleeping body, our gestures at awakening renew a meaning from beyond the grave; and how on the contrary meaning is undone in the tics of the death agony. He analyzes Elstir's paintings and the milk seller glimpsed in a country station with the same emotion; because in both instances there is the same strange experience, the experience of *expression,* the moment when color and flesh begin to speak to the eyes or the body. Gide, enumerating a few months before his death what he had loved in his life, calmly named pleasure and the Bible side by side.

As an inevitable consequence, obsession with other persons appears in their works too. When man takes an oath to exist universally, concern for himself and concern for others become indistinguishable for him; he is a person among persons, and the others are other himselves. But if on the contrary he recognizes what is unique in incarnation lived from within, the other person necessarily appears to him in the form of torment, envy, or at least uneasiness. Cited by his incarnation to appear beneath an alien gaze and justify himself before it, yet riveted to his own situation by the same incarnation; capable of feeling the lack of and need for others, but incapable of finding his resting place in others; he is enmeshed in the to-and-fro of being for self and being for others that produces the tragic element of love in Proust's works and what is perhaps the most striking element in Gide's *Journal.*

We find admirable formulations of the same paradoxes in the writer who is perhaps least capable of being satisfied with the approximations of Freudian expression, that is, in Valéry. The reason is that for him the taste for rigor and the keen awareness of the fortuitous are two sides of the same coin. Otherwise he would not have spoken so well of the body as a double-edged being, responsible for many absurdities but also for our most certain accomplishments. "The artist brings along his body, withdraws, puts down and takes away something, behaves with his whole being as his eye and completely becomes an organ which makes itself at home, changes its shape, and seeks the point, the sole point, which belongs virtually to the profoundly sought oeuvre—which is not always the one we are seeking."[2] And for Valéry, too, consciousness of the body is inevitably obsession with others.

> No one could think freely if his eyes could not take leave of different eyes which followed them. As soon as gazes meet, we are no longer wholly two, and it is hard to remain alone. This exchange (the term is exact) realizes in a very short time a transposition or metathesis—a chiasma of two "destinies," two points of view. Thereby a sort of simultaneous reciprocal limitation occurs. You capture my image, my appearance; I capture yours. You are not *me,* since you see me and I do not see myself. What I lack is this me that you see. And what you lack is the you I see. And no matter how far we advance in our mutual understanding, as much as we reflect, so much will we be different. . . .[3]

As we approach mid-century, it becomes increasingly evident that incarnation and the other person are the labyrinth of reflection and feeling—of a sort of feeling reflection—in contemporary works. Including this famous passage in which a character in *Man's Fate* in turn poses the question: if it is true that I am welded to myself, and that for me there is still an absolute difference between other persons (whom I hear with my ears) and myself, the "incomparable monster" (who hears me with my throat), then which one of us will ever be able to be accepted by others as he accepts himself, beyond things said or done, praise or blame, even beyond crimes? But Malraux, like Sartre, has read Freud; and whatever they may think of him in the last analysis, it is with his help that they have learned to know themselves. And that is why, seeking as we are to establish certain traits of our times, it has seemed more significant to us to disclose an earlier experience of the body which is their starting point because their elders had prepared it for them.

* * *

Another characteristic of this half century's investigations is the recognition of a strange relationship between consciousness and its language, as between consciousness and its body. Ordinary language thinks that it can establish, as the correlate of each word or sign, a thing or signification which can exist and be conceived of without any sign. But literature has long taken exception to ordinary language. As different as the ventures of Rimbaud and Mallarmé may well have been, they had this much in common: they freed language from the control of "obvious facts" and trusted it to invent and win new relationships of meaning. Thus language ceased to be (if it ever had been) simply a tool or means the writer uses to communicate intentions given independently of language. In our day, language is of a piece with the writer; it is the writer himself. It is no longer the servant of significations but the act of signifying itself, and the writer or man speaking no longer has to control it voluntarily any more than living man has to premeditate the means or details of his gestures. From now on there is no other way to comprehend language than to dwell in it and use it. As a professional of language, the writer is a professional of insecurity. His expressive operation is renewed from oeuvre to oeuvre. Each work, as it has been said of the painter, is a step constructed by the writer himself upon which he installs himself in order to construct (with the same risk) another step and what is called the oeuvre—the sequence of these attempts—which is always broken off, whether it be by the end of life or through the exhaustion of his speaking power. The writer endlessly attempts to cope with language of which he is not the master, and which is nevertheless incapable of anything without him, a language that has its own caprices and its graces, but always won through the writer's labor. Distinctions of figure and ground, sound and meaning, conception and execution are now blurred, as the limits of body and mind were previously. In going from "signifying" language to pure language, literature freed itself at the same time painting did from resemblance to things, and from the idea of a *finished* work of art. As Baudelaire already said, there are finished works which we cannot say have ever been *completed,* and unfinished works which say what they meant. What defines expression is to never be more than approximate.

In our century this *pathos of language* is common to writers who mutually detest one another but whose kinship is from this moment on confirmed by it. In its first stages, surrealism certainly had the air of an insurrection against language, against all meaning, and against literature itself. The fact is that Breton, after a few hesitant formulations which he quickly corrected, proposed not to destroy language to the profit of nonsense but to restore a certain profound and radical usage of speech which he realized all the writings called "automatic" were far from giving an adequate example of.[4] As Maurice Blanchot recalls, Breton already replies to the celebrated investigation *Pourquoi Écrivez-Vous?*[5] by describing a task or vocation of speech which has always been expressed in the writer and which bids him enunciate and endow with a name what has never been named. To write in this sense, Breton concludes[6]—that is, in the sense of revealing or making manifest—has never been a vain or frivolous occupation. The polemic against the critical faculties or conscious controls was not carried on in order to deliver speech up to chance or chaos; it sought to recall language and literature to the whole extent of their task by freeing them from the literary world's petty formulas and fabrications of talent. It was necessary to go back to that point of innocence, youth, and unity at which speaking man is not yet man of letters, political man, or moral man—to that "sublime point" Breton speaks about elsewhere, at which literature, life, morality, and politics are equivalent and substituted for one another, because in fact each of us is the same man who loves or hates, who reads or writes, who accepts or refuses political destiny. Now that surrealism, in slipping into the past, has rid itself of its narrowness—at the same time it has rid itself of its fine virulence—we can no longer define it in terms of what it originally rejected. For us it is one of those recalls to *spontaneous speech* which from decade to decade our century issues.

At the same time, surrealism has intermingled with these other recalls in our memory, and with them constitutes one of the constants of our time. Valéry, who was at first greatly admired and subsequently rejected by the surrealists, remains beneath his academic image very close to their experience of language. For it has not been sufficiently noticed that what he contrasts to *signifying* literature is not, as might be thought at a hasty reading, simply a literature of exercises based upon linguistic and prosodic conventions which are more efficacious to the extent they are more complicated and, in short, more absurd. What constitutes the essence of poetic language for him (he sometimes goes so far as to say the essence of all literary language) is that it does not die out in the face of what it communicates to us. It is that in poetic language meaning calls again for the very words which have served to communicate it, and no others. It is that a work cannot be summed up but must be reread to be regained. It is that in poetic language the idea is not produced by the words as a result of the lexical significations assigned to them in the common language but as a result of more carnal relationships of meaning, the halos of signification words owe to their history and uses—as a result, in short, of the life that words lead within us, a life which from time to time ends up in those meaning-laden accidents, the great books. In his own way, Valéry calls again for the same adequation of language to its total meaning that motivates the surrealistic uses of language.

Both Valéry and the surrealists have in view what Francis Ponge was to call the "semantic thickness" and Sartre the "signifying humus" of language, that is, the characteristic power that language as gesture, accent, voice, and modulation of existence has to signify in excess of what it signifies part by part according to existing conventions. It is not very far from here to what Claudel calls the word's "intelligible mouthful." And the same feeling for language is found even in contemporary definitions of prose. For Malraux too, to learn to write is "to learn to speak with one's own voice."[7] And in the works of Stendhal, who believed he was writing "like the civil laws," Jean Prévost detects a *style* in the strong sense of the term. That is, a new and very personal ordering of the words, forms, and elements of the narrative; a new order of correspondence between signs; an imperceptible yet characteristically Stendhalian warping of the whole language system—a system which has been constituted by years of usage and of life, which (having become Stendhal himself) finally allow him to improvise, and which should not be called a system of thought (since Stendhal was so little aware of it) but rather a system of speech.

Thus language is that singular apparatus which, like our body, gives us more than we have put into it, either because we ourselves learn our thought by speaking, or because we listen to others. For when I read or listen, words do not always happen to hit upon meanings already present in me. They have the extraordinary power to draw me out of my thoughts; they cut out fissures in my private universe through which *other thoughts* irrupt. "At least in that moment, I have been you," Jean Paulhan rightly says. As my body (which nevertheless is only a bit of matter) is gathered up into gestures which aim beyond it, so the words of language (which considered singly are only inert signs that only a vague or banal idea corresponds to) suddenly swell with a meaning which overflows into the other person when the act of speaking binds them up into a single whole. Mind is no longer set apart but springs up beside gestures and words as if by spontaneous generation.

* * *

These changes in our conception of man would not echo so deeply within us if they did not converge in a remarkable way with an experience which all of us, scholars or non-scholars, have been participating in, and which has therefore contributed more than any other to shaping us: I mean the experience of political relationships and history.

It seems to us that for at least thirty years our contemporaries have in this respect been living through an adventure that is much more dangerous than, but analogous to, that which we have thought to meet in the anodyne order of our relationships to literature or to our body. The same ambiguity that, upon analysis, leads the idea of mind into the idea of body or language has visibly invaded our political life. And in both cases it is more and more difficult to distinguish what is violence and what is idea, what is power and what is value, with the aggravating circumstance that in political life the mixture risks ending up in convulsion and chaos.

We grew up in a time when, *officially*, world politics were juridical. What definitively discredited juridical politics was seeing the victors of 1918 concede (and then some) to a Germany which had become powerful again what they had previously refused Weimar Germany. But six months later this new Germany took Prague as well. Thus the demonstration was complete: the victors' juridical politics was the mask for their preponderance, the vanquished's claim to "equality of rights" was the mask for a coming German preponderance. We were still faced with power relationships and death struggles; each concession was a weakness and each gain a step toward further gains. But what is important is that the decline of juridical politics has in no way involved a pure and simple return among our contemporaries to a power politics or politics of efficacity. It is a remarkable fact that political cynicism and even political hypocrisy are discredited too, that public opinion remains astonishingly sensitive about this point, that until these last months governments took care not to collide with it, and that even now there is not one of them which openly declares that it is relying on naked force, or which is effectively doing so.

The truth is that during the period immediately following the war it could almost be said that there was no world politics. Forces did not confront one another. Many questions had been left open, but just for that reason there were "no-man's-lands," neutral zones, provisional or transitional regimes. Europe, totally disarmed, lived through years without invasion. We know that for some years now the aspect of things has changed. From one end of the world to the other, zones which were neutral for the two rival powers no longer are; armies have appeared in a "no-man's-land"; economic aid has turned into military aid. Yet to us it seems remarkable that this return to power politics is nowhere lacking in reticence. Perhaps it will be said that it has always been easy to hide violence with declarations of peace, and that this is propaganda. But seeing the powers' behavior, we have come to wonder if it is only a matter of pretexts.

It is possible that all the governments believe their propaganda; that in the confusion of our present they no longer know themselves what is true and what is false, because in a sense everything they say conjointly is true. It is possible that each policy is really and simultaneously peaceful and warlike.

There would be room here to analyze a whole series of curious practices which clearly seem to be becoming general in contemporary politics. For example, the twin practices of *purging* and crypto-politics, or the politics of the fifth columns. Machiavelli has pointed out the recipe for it, but in passing; and it is today that these practices are tending on all sides to become institutional. Now if we really think about it, this presupposes that a government always expects to find accomplices on the side of its adversary and traitors in its own house. It is thus an admission that all causes are ambiguous. It seems to us that today's policies are distinguished from former ones by this doubt which is extended even to their own cause, coupled with expeditious measures to suppress the doubt.

The same fundamental uncertainty is expressed in the ease with which the heads of state turn aside or turn back from their policies, without of course ever recognizing that these oscillations are oscillations. After all, history has seldom seen a head of state discharge an illustrious and long-unchallenged commander in chief, and grant his successor more or less what he refused him a few months earlier. We have seldom seen a great power refuse to intervene in order to restrain one of its satellites in the process of invading a neighbor—and after one year of war, propose a return to the status quo. These oscillations are understandable only if, in a world whose peoples are against war, governments cannot look it in the face and yet do not dare to make peace, which would mean admitting their weakness. Sheer power relationships are altered at each instant; governments *also* want opinion to be in their favor. Each troop movement becomes a political operation *as well.* Governments act less to obtain a certain factual result than to put their adversary in a certain moral predicament. Thus we have the strange idea of a *peace offensive;* to propose peace is to disarm the adversary, to win over opinion, and thus almost to win the war. But at the same time governments are well aware that they must not lose face, that by speaking too much of peace they would encourage their adversary. This is so true that on all sides governments alternate or, better yet, associate peaceful speeches and forceful measures, verbal threats and actual concessions. Peace overtures are made in a discouraging tone and are accompanied by new preparations for war. No one wants to reach an agreement and no one wants to break off negotiations. So we have actual armistices that are observed by everyone for weeks or months on end and that no one wants to legalize, as among irritated people who put up with one another but no longer speak. We ask a former ally to sign a treaty he disapproves of with a former enemy. But we fully expect him to refuse. If he accepts, it is a felony. This is how we have a peace that is not a peace. And also a war that—except for the combatants and the inhabitants—is not completely a war. We let our friends fight because by providing them with arms which would decide the battle we would really risk war. We withdraw before the enemy and seek to suck him into the trap of an offensive that would put him in the wrong. In addition to its manifest meaning, each political act bears a contrary and latent meaning. It seems to us that governments get lost there and, in the extraordinary subtlety of means-ends relationships, are no longer able to know themselves what they are actually doing. The dialectic invades our newspapers, but a fear-crazed dialectic which turns on itself and solves no problems. In all this we see less duplicity than confusion, and less wickedness than perplexity.

We are not saying that this situation itself is without risk: it is possible that we could go to war obliquely, and it could suddenly loom up before us at one of the detours of some main political highway which seemed no more likely than another to set it going. We are only saying that these characteristics of our politics prove (all things considered) that there is no profound basis for war today. Even if it comes out of all this, no one will be entitled to say that it was ineluctable. For the contemporary world's true problems are due less to the antagonism of two ideologies than to their common disarray before certain major facts that neither one controls. If war comes, it will come as a diversion or as bad luck.

The two great powers in their rivalry have accused and are accusing one another concerning Asia. Now it is not the satanism of one government or another which has caused countries like India and China (where for centuries men have died of hunger) to come to refuse famine, debility, disorder, or corruption. It is the development of radio, a minimum of instruction, newspapers, communications with the outside, and the population increase which have suddenly made an age-old situation intolerable. It would be shameful to allow our obsessions as Europeans to hide the real problem posed there, the drama of countries to be equipped that no humanism can ignore. With the awakening of these countries, the world is closing on itself. Perhaps for the first time, the developed countries are being faced with their responsibilities toward a human community which cannot be reduced to two continents.

This fact in itself is not a sad one. If we were not so obsessed by our own concerns, we would not find it without grandeur. But what is serious is that *all* Western doctrines are too narrow to face up to the problem of developing Asia. The classical means of the liberal economy or even those of American capitalism are not, it seems, up to operating even India's equipment. As for Marxism, it has been conceived of to assure the passage of a developed economic apparatus from the hands of a bourgeoisie which has become parasitical to those of an old and highly conscious and cultivated proletariat. It is a wholly different matter to bring an underdeveloped country up to modern forms of production, and the problem posed for Russia is posed in a far more extreme way for Asia. It is not surprising that Marxism, confronted with this task, has been profoundly modified, that it has in fact abandoned its conception of a revolution rooted in the history of the working class, substituting transferals of property managed from the top for revolutionary contagion, and putting the theory of the withering away of the State and that of the proletariat as the universal class in cold storage. But this also means that the Chinese revolution (which the U.S.S.R. has not especially encouraged) to a large extent escapes the previsions of Marxist politics. So just when Asia is intervening as an active factor in world politics, none of the conceptions Europe has invented enables us to think about its problems. Here political thought is mired down in historical and local circumstances; it gets lost in these voluminous societies. This is undoubtedly what makes the antagonists circumspect; it is our chance for peace. It is also possible that they will be tempted to go to war, which will not solve any problems but which would allow them to put them off. So it is at the same time our risk of war. World politics is confused because the ideas it appeals to are too narrow to cover its field of action.

* * *

If we were asked in concluding to give our remarks a philosophical formulation, we would say that our times have experienced and are experiencing, more perhaps than any other, contingency. The contingency of evil to begin with: there is not a force at the beginning of human life which guides it toward its ruin or toward chaos. On the contrary, each gesture of our body or our language, each act of political life, as we have seen, spontaneously takes account of the other person and goes beyond itself in its singular aspects toward a universal meaning. When our initiatives get bogged down in the paste of the body, of language, or of that world beyond measure which is given to us to finish, it is not that a *malin génie* sets his will against us; it is only a matter of a sort of inertia, a passive resistance, a dying fall of meaning—an anonymous *adversity*. But good is contingent too. We do not guide the body by repressing it, nor language by putting it in thought, nor history by dint of value judgments; we must always espouse each one of these situations, and when they go beyond themselves they do so spontaneously. Progress is not necessary with a metaphysical necessity; we can only say that experience will very likely end up by eliminating false solutions and working its way out of impasses. But at what price, by how many detours? We cannot even exclude in principle the possibility that humanity, like a sentence which does not succeed in drawing to a close, will suffer shipwreck on its way.

It is true that the set of beings known by the name of men and defined by the commonly known physical characteristics also have in common a natural light or opening to being which makes cultural acquisitions communicable to all men and to them alone. But this lightning flash we find in every gaze called human is just as visible in the most cruel forms of sadism as it is in Italian painting. It is precisely this flash which makes everything possible on man's part, and right up to the end. Man is absolutely distinct from animal species, but precisely in the respect that he has no original equipment and is the place of contingency, which sometimes takes the form of a kind of miracle (in the sense in which men have spoken of the *miracle of Greece*), and sometimes the form of an unintentional adversity. Our age is as far from explaining man by the lower as it is by the higher, and for the same reasons. To explain the *Mona Lisa* by the sexual history of Leonardo da Vinci or to explain it by some divine motion Leonardo da Vinci was the instrument of or by some human nature capable of beauty still involves giving way to the retrospective illusion, realizing the valuable in advance—misunderstanding the human moment par excellence in which a life woven out of chance events turns back upon, regrasps, and expresses itself. If there is a humanism today, it rids itself of the illusion Valéry designated so well in speaking of "that little man within man whom we always presuppose." Philosophers have at times thought to account for our vision by the image or reflection things form upon our retina. This was because they presupposed a second man behind the retinal image who had different eyes and a different retinal image responsible for seeing the first. But with this man within man the problem remains untouched, and we must still come to understand how a body becomes animate and how these blind organs end up bearing a perception. The "little man within man" is only the phantom of our successful expressive operations; and the admirable man is not this phantom but the man who—installed in his fragile body, in a language which has already done so much speaking, and in a reeling history—gathers himself together and begins to see, to understand, and to signify. There is no longer anything decorous or decorative about today's humanism. It no longer loves man in opposition to his body, mind in opposition to its language, values in opposition to facts. It no longer speaks of man and mind except in a sober way, with modesty: mind and man never *are:* they show through in the movement by which the body becomes gesture, language an oeuvre, and coexistence truth.

Between this humanism and classical doctrines there is almost a homonymous relationship. In one way or another the latter affirmed a man of divine right (for the humanism of necessary progress is a secularized theology). When the great rationalist philosophies joined battle with revealed religion, what they put in competition with divine creation was some metaphysical mechanism which evaded the idea of a fortuitous world just as much as it had. Today a humanism does not oppose religion with an explanation of the world. It begins by becoming aware of contingency. It is the continued confirmation of an astonishing junction between fact and meaning, between my body and my self, my self and others, my thought and my speech, violence and truth. It is the methodical refusal of explanations, because they destroy the mixture we are made of and make us incomprehensible to ourselves. Valéry profoundly says: "One does not see what a god could think about"—a god and, moreover (he explains in another connection), a demon as well. The Mephistopheles of *My Faust* quite rightly says:

> I am the fleshless being who neither sleeps nor thinks. As soon as these poor fools draw away from instinct, I lose my way in caprice, in the uselessness or depth of these irritations of their brains they call "ideas" . . . I lose myself in this Faust who seems to me sometimes to understand me in a wholly different fashion than he should, as if there were another world than the other world! . . . It is here that he shuts himself in and amuses himself with what there is in the brain, and brews and ruminates that mixture of what he knows and does not know, which they call Thought . . . I do not know how to think and I have no soul.[8]

Thinking is a man's business, if thinking always means coming back to ourselves and inserting between two distractions the thin empty space by which we see something.

A stern and (if you will excuse the word) almost vertiginous idea. We have to conceive of a labyrinth of spontaneous steps which revive one another, sometimes cut across one another, and sometimes confirm one another—but across how many detours, and what tides of disorder!—and conceive of the whole undertaking as resting upon itself. It is understandable that our contemporaries, faced with this idea (which they glimpse as well as we do), retreat and turn aside toward some idol. With all reservations made concerning other modes of approaching the problem, Fascism is a society's retreat in the face of a situation in which the contingency of moral and social structures is clear. It is the fear of the new which galvanizes and reaffirms precisely the very ideas that historical experience had worn out. A phenomenon which our times are far from having gone beyond. The favor an *occult* literature meets with in France today is somewhat analogous. Under the pretext that our economic, moral, or political ideas are in a state of crisis, occult thought would like to establish institutions, customs, and types of civilizations which answer our problems much less well, but which are supposed to contain a *secret* we hope to *decipher* by dreaming around the documents left for us. Whereas it is the role of art, literature, and perhaps even philosophy to create sacred things, occultism seeks them ready-made (in sun cults or the religion of American Indians, for example), forgetting that ethnology shows us better each day what terrors, what dilapidation, what impotence archaic paradise is often made of. In short, fear of contingency is everywhere, even in the doctrines which helped reveal it. Whereas Marxism is based entirely upon going beyond nature through human praxis, today's Marxists veil the risk that such a transformation of the world implies. Whereas Catholicism, particularly in France, is being crossed by a vigorous movement of inquiry next to which the modernism of the beginning of the century seems sentimental and vague, the hierarchy reaffirms the most worn-out forms of theological explanation with the Syllabus. Its position is understandable: it is indeed true that a man cannot seriously think about the contingency of existence and hold to the Syllabus. It is even true that religion is bound up with a minimum of explanatory thought. In a recent article, François Mauriac implied that atheism could receive an honorable meaning if it took issue only with the God of philosophers and scientists, God in idea. But without God in idea, without the infinite thought which created the world, Christ is a man and his birth and Passion cease to be acts of God and become symbols of the human condition. It would not be reasonable to expect a religion to conceive of humanity, according to Giraudoux's beautiful phrase, as the "caryatid of the void." But the return to an explanatory theology and the compulsive reaffirmation of the *Ens realissimum* drag back all the consequences of a massive transcendence that religious reflection was trying to escape. Once again the church, its sacred depository, its unverifiable secret beyond the visible, separates itself from actual society. Once more the heaven of principles and the earth of existence are disjointed. Once more philosophic doubt is only a formality. Once more adversity is called Satan and the war against it is already won. Occult thought scores a point.

Once again, between Christians and non-Christians, as between Marxists and non-Marxists, conversation is becoming difficult. How could there possibly be any real exchange between the man who knows and the man who does not know? What can a man say if he sees no relationship, not even a dialectical one, between state Communism and the withering away of the State, when another man says that he does? If a man sees no relationship between the Gospels and the clergy's role in Spain, when another says they are not irreconcilable? Sometimes one starts to dream about what culture, literary life, and teaching could be if all those who participate, having for once rejected idols, would give themselves up to the happiness of reflecting together. But this dream is not reasonable. The discussions of our time are so convulsive only because it is resisting a truth which is very close, and because it is closer perhaps than any other in recognizing—without any intervening veil—the menace of adversity and the metamorphoses of Fortune.

Discussion

Man and Adversity

"Knowledge of Man in the Twentieth Century," Rencontres Internationales of Geneva, September 8–14, 1951. Merleau-Ponty presented "Man and Adversity" on September 10, 1951. The second closed discussion, on September 12, 1951, concerned this presentation. Jeanne Hersch, who chaired, opened the session by recalling that Merleau-Ponty's presentation concerned "the ambiguity that was set up between consciousness and the body, and in language, the ambiguity between its sense and its form. It unconcealed the ambiguity that rules in the political situation, where, for instance, the will for war and the will for peace mingle inextricably." Hersch designated these three kinds of ambiguity "points" to be discussed in the session, while "keeping our eyes fixed on two essential problems: the consequences of this ambiguous situation for truth, on the one hand, and for action—morality—on the other." Jean Wahl posed the first question.[9]

JEAN WAHL: Merleau-Ponty has spoken of Valéry and Gide, but one could just as well have evoked earlier philosophers, such as Feuerbach or Nietzsche—who speaks of the "great body" in contrast with the body as we normally imagine it. I would even mention Maine de Biran and Descartes, Merleau-Ponty's great precursor—and there is no irony in my words.

I find myself saying that perhaps Merleau-Ponty has taken what was necessary for him in certain philosophers, and I could have proceeded this way as well in expressing my thought. Perhaps, in contemporary thought, one could choose other examples than Valéry and Gide. But it is in them that Merleau-Ponty has found what is important for him and what will develop in the future.

MERLEAU-PONTY: I agree that the union of the soul and the body has been raised before, before Valéry and Gide. Even so, there may be differences. In Descartes, the union of the soul and the body is something that we live, but something about which we say little. When he wants to reflect, to expound, he goes to clear ideas, as everyone knows. So there is a difference between this idea that Descartes acknowledged in the end, this residue that he pointed out very honestly, and making this union the central phenomenon in relation to which we try to think bare matter or pure mind. By always making minor modifications and emphasizing what has come before, our contemporaries are therefore quite different from Descartes.

WAHL: I want to respond to what you are saying about Descartes. He does indeed speak of this idea in the end, but it's not a residue; it's a third substance that is very important. He has not developed this point but has left it for the future. I don't believe that the word "residue" would be appropriate.

MERLEAU-PONTY: It is a substantial union of two substances which, even so, is difficult to think.

WAHL: This is also ambiguous.

MERLEAU-PONTY: I have never claimed to be clear and distinct.

CHAIR: You have been, however.

RENÉ LALOU: It is progress over Descartes!

MERLEAU-PONTY: Let's not be provocative. Each of us, when he reflects, always believes himself to think more truly than his predecessors. Otherwise, he wouldn't reflect. This is presumptuous in the case of Descartes, but it doesn't keep us from recognizing that Descartes was someone far more significant than any of us.

WAHL: My remark has tended to cut off the discussion.

FATHER DUBARLE: I would like to pose a question to Merleau-Ponty: what does this ambiguity consist of exactly? On the question of the soul and the body, one could go back to philosophical theories a lot older than that of Descartes. All through the first part of M. Merleau-Ponty's lecture, I heard in my memory, not so much Aristotle's sentence that the soul forms the body—I don't know if he said that—but a phrase that he used very distinctly in his treatise on the soul: "The soul is the actuality of the organized physical body." Here he is truly thinking of an actuality penetrated by all corporeal flesh "through and through," as Merleau-Ponty put it. However, I don't think that the Aristotelian philosophy would be a philosophy of ambiguity. Where exactly does the ambiguity stand in this con-

nection and interpenetration of the actuality of the soul with the matter
of the body?

MERLEAU-PONTY: I'm not a great Aristotelian; consequently, I will
answer, but with reservations.

FATHER DUBARLE: The ambiguity is an issue for Merleau-Ponty much
more than for Aristotle.

MERLEAU-PONTY: There are great differences between these ideas of
ambiguity and the Aristotelian conceptions. I mentioned this dichotomy
of matter and form in my lecture in order to say that it does not appear
sufficient to me for thinking the phenomenon in question. The difference, it seems to me, would be that no matter how I understand the two
notions of matter and form. . . .

FATHER MAYDIEU: It is actuality that Father Dubarle mentioned.

MERLEAU-PONTY: Let's say potentiality and actuality. . . .

FATHER DUBARLE: The actuality of the organized physical body.

MERLEAU-PONTY: Take the notions of potentiality and actuality. Aristotle holds, it seems to me, that one could think the lower stage that constitutes matter. . . .

WAHL: The philosophy of Aristotle is not a philosophy of ambiguity;
allow me to say, though, that it is slightly ambiguous on certain points.

CHAIR: All philosophy is ambiguous.

MERLEAU-PONTY: Some are ambiguous knowingly and others without
intending it. It seems to me that Aristotle would be ambiguous without
intending it.

FATHER DUBARLE: Nevertheless, in Aristotle's idea of the soul and
the body, there is a usage of the notions that remains clear. It follows that
one could perhaps weigh things slyly and find ambiguity, but it would be
good to explain oneself on this point. I think the idea of ambiguity represents a certain reaction against the too-clear and too-distinct concepts of
Descartes. But Aristotle never claimed that concepts should be put under
glass and contemplated like objects in a museum. For the most part, they
are there to be used mixed together.

MERLEAU-PONTY: Would Aristotle admit that when we reflect on a
concept, it is transformed into something other than itself?

FATHER DUBARLE: Aristotle would accept that, on reflection, there is
what you would call a sort of passage from the body into the soul and from
the soul into the body. This is precisely what he wants to express with the
concept of *actuality*, in the sense of the actuality of the organized physical
body, which has substance only to the extent that there is an underlying
body and which, however, gives the body the very actuality of existing.

MERLEAU-PONTY: I have no reason to reject this famous patronage,
if Aristotle thinks what you have said.

FATHER DUBARLE: It is not at all my intention to offer you the patronage of the venerable father of scholasticism, but rather to see what this ambiguity that you discuss consists of substantially. There are, in fact, great differences between your position and that of Aristotle. I do not at all wish to return you to that category, but rather to see in this light where exactly the ambiguity stands in the relation between consciousness and the body, between the soul and the body, between this actuality and the organized physical body.

MERLEAU-PONTY: I have chosen Freudianism as an example, and in my mind, it was a clear one. In Freudianism, there is a double relation between the higher and the lower. The higher, adult life, the higher forms of action, etc., are all connected with the past of the infant. Consequently, the higher is connected to the lower. But in another sense, the life of the child is treated entirely like *premature* adult life. The notion of prematuration, if common among psychoanalysts, changes the relation; here, we can no longer explain the lower by the higher. The alleged lower, namely, the infant, is regarded as wanting immediately to be adult. This is the source of its drama. It is this circular relation that I call ambiguity.

FATHER DUBARLE: Is it the things thought about that are ambiguous, or is it rather that the ideas for thinking them admit a sort of essential ambiguity?

MERLEAU-PONTY: I know the things only by my ideas. If the ideas of things are ambiguous, then I am obliged to say that the things are ambiguous.

FATHER DUBARLE: It is the link between the ideas of things and the ideas by which you make use of them that does not seem very good.

CHAIR: To return to the problem of the soul and the body, or of consciousness and the body, the fact of becoming more clearly conscious of the intimate link between consciousness and the body is not ambiguous. To become conscious of two things intimately linked is not ambiguous. What is it that you are calling ambiguity?

MERLEAU-PONTY: It seems that, by definition, there could be no consciousness of ambiguity without ambiguity of consciousness. This is not a play on words. At the moment when you admit that consciousness of ambiguity is perfectly clear, then the ambiguity is there like this notebook with consciousness in front of it, the consciousness perfectly clear and the ambiguity perfectly ambiguous—then, there is no consciousness of ambiguity. You see the ambiguity as an omnipotent thought would see it. To you, it is no longer ambiguity.

FATHER DUBARLE: What you say is extremely illuminating; the question that remains to be asked is that of knowing how consciousness goes from the unconsciousness of ambiguity to the consciousness of ambiguity.

UMBERTO CAMPAGNOLO: We have come back again to the positions of traditional skepticism: is there a genuine difference between a philosophy of ambiguity and a skeptical philosophy?

MERLEAU-PONTY: Skepticism is ambiguity undergone, while the philosophy of ambiguity is ambiguity understood or taken up.

CAMPAGNOLO: No, skepticism is conscious: it becomes aware of the necessity of not surpassing skepticism. Naturally, it falls prey to the critique with which you are familiar. I wonder if it isn't necessary to return the philosophy of ambiguity to the traditional position of skepticism. Is there something new here?

MERLEAU-PONTY: I have been given a series of patrons: Aristotle, Descartes. . . . I accept them all, naturally, but they are only half-praises. This is very dangerous. If I say: yes, there is a skepticism that I accept as true—which I may be inclined to say privately, but perhaps not in a public conversation, even a closed one—someone will draw from this affirmation certain conclusions. Someone will say: he is Cartesian, he is Aristotelian, he is a skeptic.

LALOU: I could add for you a half-patronage: there is a great book of American literature called *Pierre, or The Ambiguities*.[10] In the plural, I understand. I address myself to the philosopher, and I ask how you pass from the idea of different ambiguities, which to us was clear and common to all, to a sort of generalized ambiguity?

MERLEAU-PONTY: I do not hold so much to the singular. We say: ambiguity, as we say: the body, as we say: matter; even though, evidently, there are only matters, in the plural, and bodies, in the plural.

LALOU: You do not attribute to it a metaphysical value?

MERLEAU-PONTY: Yes, but I don't make it into an entity.

CAMPAGNOLO: Is there an idea of ambiguity that is not ambiguous?

MERLEAU-PONTY: I have said that it would no longer be ambiguity if one could conceive of it with total clarity. Consequently, you are right.

CAMPAGNOLO: This is the tragic aspect of philosophy.

JEAN STAROBINSKI: Once this ambiguity is noted, won't we be forced to return to dichotomy as a method? To take account of certain phenomena, it is necessary to isolate them; and to isolate them is to treat them, for example, in the objective system of space and time, of energies, as does so-called objective science and as did so-called objective physiology. Is it that, when all is said and done, this noting of the ambiguity of the body and of consciousness is not something fundamental to begin with, but something from which dichotomies and separations will burst forth all the same, if we want to continue to transform man and the world? The question here concerns the powers that emerge from a consciousness of ambiguity. Can we found something other than a behavior or a science on this consciousness of ambiguity?

MERLEAU-PONTY: I want to emphasize that I did not put the word "ambiguity" in the title of my lecture. I used the word as an adjective, and more in the plural; but I have never said: I will make a philosophy of ambiguity.

These difficulties that you raise with this idea of ambiguity taken as a central idea find their equivalent in all the philosophies that I know. The start of this discussion recalled for me the problem of the circle within which every philosophical reflection that begins finds itself. Husserl, who was not an "existentialist," recognized this difficulty. He explained it very well in the *Ideas*[11] by saying: in a sense, every reflection is incapable of grasping the unreflected, since it is no longer the unreflected. He gave an answer to this difficulty: the fact of the initial philosophical situation is that I reflect on something that is prior to reflection, but I have an idea of this unreflected only by means of the movement by which I try to take it up and reflect on it.

To wish to separate the two, like you do, and to send me back to the silence of the skeptics, this I find to be impossible. The actual situation of the man who begins to philosophize is that he reflects, and that he will never attain the pure unreflected, because he would not be a philosopher if he attained it.

The initial situation is already dialectical. I want to say that there is a double polarity. We start to reflect on something that is prior to reflection and of which we have the idea only through this reflection.

FATHER DUBARLE: You are absolutely right to bring us back to this circle of reflection. Each philosopher has his own manner of entering into it. It came to you to enter it precisely by discovering ambiguity, which could be linked, consecutively, not only to the situation, but also to the reflexive gesture.

An interesting question to pose would be the following: How is it that you would be let into this philosophical circle by experiencing this ambiguity so strongly and from the situation and the individual who reflects on it? Is there something to be controlled even behind this position? You did not give a lecture on ambiguity but one entitled "Man and Adversity." Is there a link between this idea of ambiguity—which reappeared many times—and this feeling of adversity?

MERLEAU-PONTY: Adversity is the dead weight that we feel behind ourselves when we reflect.

FATHER DUBARLE: Would ambiguity be ambiguity without this consciousness of adversity?

MERLEAU-PONTY: Certainly not.

FATHER DUBARLE: This is what I'm getting at. And in order to take up again the illustrious patronage of Aristotle, perhaps the idea of ambiguity was not posed for him in such a closed fashion because for him, perhaps, reflection did not encounter the adversity of thought in the same way.

MERLEAU-PONTY: Certainly.

CAMPAGNOLO: This question is very important, since it is truly the starting point. You say that one starts from the unreflective, that is, the immediate. But this is precisely in order to break the circle. The case of ambiguity or skepticism follows from being condemned to the circle.

Campagnolo notes that every philosopher wants precisely to "break the circle."

MERLEAU-PONTY: The circle isn't genuine if we are certain ahead of time that we will break it.

CAMPAGNOLO: We are not certain ahead of time, yet it is necessary to break it all the same. This is the philosophical moment of thought. Science is not concerned with this, but philosophy needs this beginning.

MERLEAU-PONTY: Philosophy is the tension between this circle where one is caught and the will to think, which is consequently the will to overcome the circle.

ERNST VON SCHENCK [*summary of the German*]: We seem to have arrived at an essential point of misunderstanding. If this discussion truly concerns the first part of M. Merleau-Ponty's lecture, then I haven't understood it, because it did not seem to me that M. Merleau-Ponty made ambiguity into the starting point of a system; it is only a fact that he recognized in passing. In surrendering to the operation of thinking, he came up against this ambiguity, but this is not at all the starting point for a system.

I would like to raise a question and to know if I was right to be particularly struck in this first part by the following point: between the soul and the body, M. Merleau-Ponty emphasized that there seemed to be something that, by contrast, broke the ambiguity and did not establish it. The body seemed to be a means of communication, like an intermediary toward others [*autrui*]. More than a means. . . .

MERLEAU-PONTY: I am in complete agreement with what M. von Schenck has said, and I am pleased at having had my intentions so well understood.

FATHER DANIÉLOU: I do not at all agree with M. von Schenck's comments. M. Merleau-Ponty's lecture not only noted a fact but also offered an interpretation of this fact. This seems to bring us to a fundamental point: M. Merleau-Ponty puts the emphasis very strongly on a certain reciprocal causality of the soul and the body. It is on this point that Father Dubarle and myself would be in complete agreement with him. But the expression that puts everything into question is the one that Merleau-Ponty himself repeated a few minutes ago when he said that they become each other. That is the crux of the whole question, because it is a refusal to admit that the soul and the body are distinct entities. It is not a question only of the fact that they would be united, but rather of the fact that they become each other, that we cannot distinguish here between two formally distinct concepts of a distinct nature.

This is connected at the same time to the foundation of M. Merleau-Ponty's thought, to the extent that he would see in my idea of nature something that seems like a determination prior to ambiguity, and that consequently would oblige him to put forward a certain permanent order of value concepts—which would lead us back to a metaphysical position that he does not accept.

Campagnolo shares Father Daniélou's point of view and notes that it is not a factual question since, as Merleau-Ponty himself declared, "ambiguity is in the idea and in the matter of knowledge."

MERLEAU-PONTY: It is a question of a philosophical fact in the sense that the Cartesian cogito is a fact.

CAMPAGNOLO: You encounter it at the beginning and not among the phenomena of nature. It's your very starting point. It is not arbitrary that you have begun by examining this point that is the logical starting point.

MERLEAU-PONTY: There is some contingency in things. It is not a reason because you have started like this, so that the truth starts like this. You think it through your ideas.

CAMPAGNOLO: It's very possible and even natural, but it was not superfluous to know that you think the ambiguity is in the idea.

MERLEAU-PONTY: Father Daniélou has entirely confirmed my brief remarks on Aristotle, since what he accepts would be, to him, Aristotelian. . . .

FATHER MAYDIEU: I don't think so.

MERLEAU-PONTY: . . . and what I myself say would not be Aristotelian. When I said that, in reflection, a thing becomes something other than itself, I do not start from prior concepts that would allow us to say this, but by reflecting on what the body is as the body—in every sense that the term can have—in everyday experience or in the organized everyday experience that is called science. When we consider the brain and try to analyze its functioning, we see the brain in order to get rid of it, so to speak. At the beginning, we believe we know what we're talking about, namely, nerve cells, bits of matter, etc. Then when we see what the brain is in its functioning, according to the modern theories of localization, for example, we realize that all the boundaries collapse, that, for example, in modern nerve physiology, it is no longer possible to consider the brain part by part, and that there is a whole expanse of cerebral regions in which this type of organization is impossible. When I say that one thing becomes something else, I am translating into conceptual terms the phenomenon to which we are present in the development of scientific knowledge or in that of our experience.

I don't know how you understand philosophy; for my part, I always go from particular things to more essential things. The idea of ambiguity did not come to me from out of nowhere but in connection with things I thought about.

FATHER DANIÉLOU: I think that ambiguity expresses very accurately the "given" such as we attain it immediately, but philosophy consists precisely in detecting the ambiguities within this "given" and determining different orders. In this sense, there is a difference of order between what we call body and what we call soul, so that we could never say that the soul becomes the body or the body becomes the soul. That would lead to a kind of confusion and identification of the process of thought with the immediate sensible experience.

MERLEAU-PONTY: No, not at all. I certainly acknowledge that we drive back ambiguity by thinking, that we form clear concepts, and this is already an advance. In other words, I don't wish that Descartes had not existed.

Father Dubarle wishes to raise the following question: "How does this awakening to ambiguity take place from within consciousness? How does the encounter happen, to use Kantian language?"

CAMPAGNOLO: M. Merleau-Ponty answered with an example when he spoke of the brain.

MERLEAU-PONTY: What I call ambiguity is the fact that when we reflect on what the brain is, we end up finding something that is no longer the initial mass of matter, even though the brain continues to be the initial mass of matter nonetheless.

CAMPAGNOLO: This is a rather unusual notion of ambiguity.

Lionel Abel thinks of poetry—that of Rimbaud, Mallarmé, Valéry—"poets cut off from others" and for whom "speech arrived at an ambiguity that was sought after and intentional." The question that he then poses to Merleau-Ponty is of knowing whether or not speech is the essence of language. "It seems to me," he adds, "that it is not enough to say, in speaking of poetry, that it is a kind of ambiguous speech;

it is a sort of speech where ambiguity becomes value, *whereas in ordinary language, much to the contrary, ambiguity is not valorized."*

MERLEAU-PONTY: I prepared a much longer section on language for this lecture. But the day before my lecture—luckily for all of you—I cut a large part of what I had written. And in the very part that I removed, I tried to explain that all valid prose—by this I mean all writing that expresses something that has never before been expressed—is essentially poetry. This means that what we generally call prose is the genre of speech or discourse in which our words, our signs, come to awaken in the minds of others thoughts or ideas which are already there. In these conditions, in fact, language is not difficult. For example, if I say: "There is a notebook on this table," we have all of the precise correspondences between the words I use and certain ideas, but no one is mistaken. There is no ambiguity, in fact. But this is not interesting language. This language is useful, indispensable, but it is dependent on another, much more difficult language that consists in saying what has never been said. When a child begins to speak, his language is much more interesting and significant than when we speak with an already established system of words and of ideas.

It seems to me that even the analysis of prose, if pursued along these lines, reveals that each prose writer reinvents language or reintroduces what Malraux calls a "coherent deformation"; Malraux applied this expression to painting, but one could also apply it to language. From this section of my lecture, there remains only a short passage on Stendhal as treated by Jean Prévost.[12] In principle, I strongly acknowledge this idea that all language is poetry, on the condition that this language seeks to express something new.

ABEL: Do you believe, on these terms, that our current manner of speaking is a degradation of language?

MERLEAU-PONTY: When I say "The notebook is on the table," this is not a degradation, it's an instituted language, already established, which requires no effort from either of us. I have nothing against this language, and I use it constantly; even when I give a lecture, there are a certain number of expressions that belong to this language.

ABEL: It is language in this latter sense that is our relation with others [*autrui*].

MERLEAU-PONTY: Not on your life. When we speak like we are doing, do you believe that each of my words touches ideas in your mind that are already there? This is what happens when we don't understand each other. Each stays in his hole and does a monologue. But when there is truly dialogue, even at the most concrete level, as long as it's not a question of a simple "matter of fact"[13] but of something more, then one passes to a language that surpasses given signification. This is done even with gestures. When I see you speaking, I understand not only with the help of the words that you say, but also with the help of your physiognomy, of your expression and gestures. That is all a deciphering on the same order as poetic decipherings.

CHAIR: I ask: when do we use an ambiguous language?

MERLEAU-PONTY: When I said "ambiguity," I did not mean that we always remained at the same point, that there wasn't any more or less or any development. I meant that even when we speak in a way that succeeds, even when we make ourselves understood by another, this isn't founded on the other's prior possession of the ideas that we are expressing, because then the expression would be useless. But this comprehension always happens with a risk of error to which each of our conversations bears witness.

FATHER MAYDIEU: Couldn't we say that we understand each other when we both know that we are using an ambiguous language, when we become conscious of this ambiguity?

MERLEAU-PONTY: The word "ambiguity" is misunderstood. Melanie Klein, Freud's student, distinguished ambiguity from ambivalence. She said that ambivalence is the far inferior situation of a thought in which the same object, or the same being, is qualified in two irreconcilable ways, for example, the "good mother" and the "bad mother." A child has two points of view of his mother: the helpful mother, on the one hand, and the angry mother, on the other.

Melanie Klein shows that the ambiguity which can be found in adult thought, and which perhaps even characterizes it, is not at all ambivalence. It does not consist in having two alternative images of the same object, but in firmly and truly thinking that the *same* object is good and bad.

When I speak of ambiguity, this does not mean a wavering thought which passes from white to black, affirming first the black and then the white. I want to speak of a thought that discerns different relations between things, the interior movement that makes them participate in their contraries.

By taking up the example of Stendhal, I have not chosen the example of a hesitant thought but, on the contrary, the example of a bold thought, one that takes risks and makes itself understood only in a risky fashion. The proof of this is that he needed a hundred years before being understood. I also take the example of Rimbaud and that of Mallarmé. "Poets cut off from others," you say. I don't know if they wanted to be cut off from others, for one writes in order to be read, and if they had truly been loners as you say, they would never have spoken. Rimbaud would have begun by staying quiet, though he only ended by staying quiet, after having written some little things that we still talk about.

LALOU [*agrees entirely with Merleau-Ponty; he would make only one criticism*]: This would be having chosen the privileged case of poetry and having limited all examples to French poetry. I believe that most of what he has said about French poetry could be applied to an English poet like T. S. Eliot.

MERLEAU-PONTY: I haven't studied poetry in all languages, especially since I can only speak one fluently—French. It is impossible, then, for me to respond to this remark or to say whether all existing poets conform to the canon of poetry defined by Mallarmé and the others.

There is one more thing that I have cut from my lecture and that I would like to say now. These conceptions of language are not only based on Jean Paulhan, Mallarmé, Rimbaud, and the others. In Saussure's theory of language, for example, which is not restricted to poetic language, we find some ideas that go exactly in this direction. In his *Course in General Linguistics,*[14] Saussure explains that there is not, in a language, a signification answering to each word, each form, or each sign, but only *differences of signification*. This idea seems extraordinarily fruitful. You cannot take the verbal chain, cut it into pieces, and make an idea or a thing correspond to each of its elements. This is not how things happen when we speak or write. When speaking or writing, each of the elements of discourse must be considered to have meaning only by its difference from another element of discourse which, itself, only has meaning by a difference from a third. And Saussure creates tables of words showing that they do not each have a meaning. For example, the words "lead" [*conduire*] and "bring up" [*éduquer*], "link" [*lier*] and "chain" [*enchaîner*]. There is no lexical signification for these words. They are not signs corresponding to clear significations but differentiations within a whole—speech or language used in the considered context.

If we pushed further in this direction, we would converge on the idea that the most prosaic language, of which I spoke a few minutes ago, is a limit case. In fact, we never reach it. This inert language teaches us nothing. The view I propose is not only based on poetic examples; it is a conception that could be generalized and applied to all language.

The Chair notes that becoming conscious of ambiguity is often accompanied by a certain complacency or lyricism, rather than arousing an effort to overcome it.

MERLEAU-PONTY [*Returns to the example of Valéry: "No one had the horror of the confused and ambiguous more than he did, and no one has spoken of it better than he did." He continues.*]: There is no complacency. I don't know what we should think of the attitude of the existentialist public, if there is one; I think it is in complacency with ambiguity, but I can't do anything about that. I have never done anything to encourage it. When faced with ambiguity, there are two attitudes: either wallowing in it or not wanting to hear a word about it. These are roughly the same, and neither approach is more genuine than the other. I would add a third attitude that consists in reflecting on the ambiguity and never taking a place either within it or outside of it. I like Valéry because of this. He was an extremely rigorous man, he applied his rigor appropriately to ambiguous experiences, and he described the body better than anyone.

The Chair returns to her idea that one must go in the opposite direction from becoming conscious of ambiguity.

MERLEAU-PONTY: To go in the opposite direction is to repress.

CHAIR: Valéry goes in the opposite direction; to illuminate ambiguity is to go in the opposite direction.

MERLEAU-PONTY: Everyone speaks as if there were *one* plane of ambiguity. But at the very moment when we clarify and have made the ambiguity cease on one point, when we have fixed and objectified it, it reappears a little further on.

CAMPAGNOLO: There is the contradiction.

VON SCHENCK [*summary of the German*]: Man today no longer believes in language, neither the scholar, nor the ordinary man, nor the poet; no poets or scholars presently succeed in restoring for men the univocity of language. This leads to a sort of loss of language as the means of ordinary communication with others. The simplest relations between a subject, verb, and complement, as in the form "I love you," is a form in which we no longer have confidence, in which we no longer believe. It has no meaning that can be fixed or determined in itself. This meaning can be found only through existence, always needing to be verified by existence and life. Whatever is not verified by existence and life we don't believe in. Language no longer supports itself.

PIERRE DE BOISDEFFRE [*Recalls Merleau-Ponty's "condemnation of occultism" at the end of his lecture. But hasn't occultism inspired great works of literature? Isn't it precisely "a search for and an elucidation of a language that has brought us some essential texts, such as the Bible?" he asks.*]: Why do you condemn a form of reflection that, while it has perhaps not yet achieved the dignity of scientific reflection, is perhaps in the process of enlightening us on the human condition in general and on the interpretation of history?

LALOU: Occultism as a source is so little exhausted that, even outside of sacred texts, it has given us poetical works such as that of Gérard de Nerval.

MERLEAU-PONTY: Because it is Nerval who makes use of it! I have certainly spoken of an expanded language, and I have rightly tried to show, even with respect to surrealism, that there was an attempt to expand language beyond already established and received significations. I have not limited all language to the prosaic, to things already said. What seems to me characteristic of the attitude that I have called "occultism" is that it does not genuinely seek to *bring about* a communication between men, to say things that others succeed in understanding without these having already been said. Rather, occultism seeks to avoid this work, it seeks everywhere—preferably in the less perceptible and accessible places—a sacred that it would rightly be the role of literature and poetry to create.

What I call occultism is this permission that we give ourselves precisely to talk nonsense, the more bizarre the more interesting, under the pretext that language should not restrict itself to significations that are already evident, acquired, and expressed.

DE BOISDEFFRE: I don't believe this would be nonsense. One could say, on the contrary, that a prophetic mind is doing this, and your condemnation of occultism would apply equally to any prophetic mind in general.

MERLEAU-PONTY: That is possible.

FATHER MAYDIEU: There is a great danger in including the Bible within occultism, which I protest emphatically. This goes against what M. Merleau-Ponty has said.

FATHER DANIÉLOU: M. Merleau-Ponty used the expression "inert weight of words" as a contrast with the fact that the essential object of language is to express what has not been said. There is something completely inaccurate about this with regard to what is at stake in language. The mark of the ambiguity of words is fundamentally much smaller than you seem to say. I am something of a linguist, and one of the things that strikes me the most regarding linguistics is the extraordinary resistance of words. There is a kind of permanence of language here.

And even an astonishing permanence: consider certain Indo-European roots that come up again for "thousands of centuries."

MERLEAU-PONTY: You speak of linguistics, but who opposes etymology, and in particular this type of Indo-European etymology? The linguists do. It is the same with Saussure, who has shown that all etymologies are constructions after the fact and that the meaning of the word is determined by its usage within a living linguistic community.

FATHER DANIÉLOU: This is entirely different than the words being always relative in relation to each other. In fact, these systems of relations are permanent systems. It is not a question of making the word into an in-itself; the word is not a substance but is essentially something relative. But the word maintains constant relations with other complementary words, and basically we can trigger these relations, but always within a system. One of the essential functions of language, just the same, is to preserve what has been said.

MERLEAU-PONTY: No, it is to say.

FATHER DANIÉLOU: The fact that things have been said once and for all in a sacred text seems more essential.

MERLEAU-PONTY: One must truly speak in order to begin; one must create in order to able to preserve.

FATHER DANIÉLOU: The role of creation exists and has its value, but the value of preserving language is perhaps something still more fundamental. You put the emphasis too exclusively on this aspect of the initiative of current freedom and not enough on the total historical given.

MERLEAU-PONTY: A language that exists is in fact a tradition, but a tradition is a call to renew expression, to recommence the initial creative work.

FATHER DANIÉLOU: Not only that.

MERLEAU-PONTY: Without this present work, the language [*la langue*] itself will have nothing to say.

FATHER MAYDIEU: I am sorry, but my experience has been contrary to that of Father Daniélou. I have seen the opposite in my life. Having studied philosophy, coming from Aristotelianism and—I will not surprise anyone—from Saint Thomas, nineteen years ago, I bumped into a certain number of modern philosophers, and I experienced much embarrassment. Not only did the words have another meaning, but they had a different meaning in relation to each other: "substance," "causality," "intellect," "agent." When I used these words, people understood the opposite from what I had intended. It was necessary—and this is what seems interesting in the thought of M. Merleau-Ponty—on the contrary to put oneself into the totality, to become aware of this ambiguity from the beginning. I have been happy to hear it said that it was necessary to make an effort of conquest, precision, and distinctness. Once that is done, we truly grasp, on the one hand, that we find ourselves bound to an ambiguity from the beginning, and then, that we will still find other ambiguities there.

André Chamson first denounces the passionate element underlying the discussion of ambiguity.

CHAMSON: We will be completely in agreement, I think, to note that ambiguity is a reality that preexists in the universe, just like nuclear energy.

Nuclear fission is not an invention of our scientists, but a thing that exists in the order of the universe and that man is succeeding in taking hold of. All irony aside, it seems that we are faced with a problem very similar to that of nuclear energy: something that exists in the world and that enters, so to speak, into our handling.

But one says to Merleau-Ponty: "Be careful with the handling of this ambiguity, for it seems that we have arrived here at a certain number of confusions." And M. Merleau-Ponty has responded something like this: "What would you like me to do about this, what the military does with nuclear energy? I am a laboratory scientist; if the military blows up the globe, that's another problem. I am not complicit with my students when they are moved, propelled by this notion of ambiguity, and fall into a certain number of confusions."

For his part, Chamson would be inclined to say "complexity of things" rather than "ambiguity." But in short, he wants to come to a notion of responsibility.

CHAMSON: I will also pose the following question: to the extent that you direct the mind of men, of young men in particular, toward an ambiguous awareness of the reality that surrounds them and of themselves, how will you allow them to overcome the kind of shock that they receive? Because it truly seems that the history of our predecessors has consisted, in great measure, in always overcoming the ambiguities before which they were placed.

MERLEAU-PONTY: I have never said that I take no interest in what students could make of these philosophical ideas. I spend my time explaining that they are mistaken when they take them in the way that I have indicated. I would like to say that I am not teaching this in courses or lectures, and that I have never taught it, which is very different.

On the other hand, the situation being ambiguous as you say, there are two attitudes: the first is saying nothing about it, but I don't at all think that one does the students a service in making them believe that there is an absolute system of references for thinking about the body, language, or politics. They are not more stupid than us, as you well know, and they will realize one day or the other that this isn't true. Then they will break down. Given the existence of ambiguity, there is a politics of the ostrich that consists in refusing to see it, and then an attitude that I find more philosophical, more serious, and more effective, which consists in saying that it exists and showing where it exists.

WAHL: It seems to me that the word "ambiguity" is ambiguous, and I notice that M. Merleau-Ponty has used this word very little in this part of the lecture. He has explained that language, like our body, gives us more than what we have put there. I see that we are talking about ambiguity even though he has not said much about it here. We have given the title of ambiguity to a book, but this is not the central question with respect to language. This richness of language in relation to ourselves—analogous, in a sense, to the body's richness in relation to ourselves, which is what connects the two things—has been noticed, for example, in other countries. Before being noticed in France or England, allusion to it was made even more in Germany; it is Hölderlin's conception of poetry.

MERLEAU-PONTY: I can only be delighted at this.

FATHER DUBARLE: Pardon me for returning to a point that we passed over quickly a moment ago. We noted man's lack of confidence regarding all language, having in view ordinary language, philosophical language, and scientific language. I would like to raise this question again from the point of view of scientific language in order to shed some light on the debate. It is certain that the situation of man with respect to scientific language—up to and including the most abstract: mathematical language— is no longer entirely the same as it was fifty years ago. This situation is not simply an event of life, not simply a phenomenon that happens just like that without our knowing why. The internal shake-up of scientific language is of a very particular sort, in the sense that it is the action of a thought that knows how to manage a whole of quite complex demonstrative rays, and that quite recently has precisely won over the possibility of managing them, in such a way that this thought discovers the limitations of its parts. When we posit a mathematical theory like that of wholes, this theory gives us methods of proof such that, when we apply them to the notions or conceptions of this theory, it manifests a certain "shift" in the initial position, something that we do not come to stabilize in a complete way. In this sense, the proof is well and good, because if the complete stabilization existed, it would be contradictory and destroy the system. It is then, if you like, an attitude of reflection on language that we are given.

In this sense, the modes of man's non-confidence in scientific language are very particular, because these modes are reflexive and essentially indicated by proofs, while on the contrary the modes of man's non-confidence in ordinary language are simply indicated by disagreeable experiences, and such disagreeable experience is not clarified.

Would one of the endeavors of philosophy at the present time not be to do, with respect to its own language, what science has been capable of doing? Would the growing poetic awareness concerning language then not be preliminary to what must be pursued in the case of properly philosophical thought?

MERLEAU-PONTY: I feel entirely in agreement with Father Dubarle, and what I try to do in philosophy is a work of this type. I believe moreover that every writer who begins to write is in exactly the same situation. I have never said that the writer was condemned to silence. I have never said that one could not speak because of the ambiguity of language. What is marvelous in language is precisely that it is ambiguous and nevertheless we speak, we understand more or less well, but we understand. There is no place for underestimating the experience of writers, as it is parallel. It consists in conquering what has never been said.

FATHER DUBARLE: If the writer conquers what has never been said, the mathematician conquers the limits of the possibilities of his diction.

CHAIR: And the philosopher also.

FATHER DUBARLE: This is the duty of the philosopher: to put forward the act of philosophical reflection proportionally in the same way that the mathematician puts forward the act of proof and discovers that the act of proof is not as categorical as has traditionally been thought.

The mathematician has discovered that the system was not categorical, that it allows for an infinity of alternatives, and the day when he would like to reunite these alternatives by saying "we will make an encompassing synthesis," he will come to a contradiction that will destroy the synthesis.

SAMUEL BAUD-BOVY: I am embarrassed to take part in this debate, since it goes beyond me on so many levels. Perhaps I can follow along the same lines with some of M. Merleau-Ponty's points simply by speaking of music. The problem of the educator raised by M. Chamson seems to me serious enough that we might dwell on it for a moment.

If, in music, I think of the permanent element that is the succession of notes of the *do* scale, this element could be considered as permanent, traditional, and hereditary. However, in every epoch, these notes of the scale, even in their regular order, have taken a different meaning. If you encounter a *do* scale in Stravinsky, it does not play the same role as a *do* scale in Bach, or as the succession *do, re, mi, fa, sol, la, ti, do* in a plainsong.

Different attitudes are therefore possible. The question is whether we want to claim that there is only *one* scale of *do* that should be considered under only one aspect, and whether this is what we should teach students; or if, on the contrary, we should explain to them that this scale of *do* itself has an ambiguity—since this is the word that we have used—and that we must examine it according to the lived experience of each of those who have made use of it.

I think this question is not asked of any epoch other than our own, in music, simply because there was no historical music in any other epoch than our own. One made the music of his time and was not occupied with the music of other times. Even from the point of view of teaching music, we are obliged today to become aware of this diversity of signification of a phenomenon as simple as the *do* scale.

As for knowing *why* we are placed in this ambiguity, we generally evade this question, and I think this is a phenomenon of taking the easy way out. I think that in music, redoing the work of the creators who have given a different meaning to the *do* scale demands a considerable activity, an activity, besides, that most human beings do not carry any further, so that it becomes a matter for philosophers or writers.

MERLEAU-PONTY: Your comments are very interesting and in agreement, it seems to me, with what Father Dubarle has said. We attend to the same type of work in music as that pursued in the history of mathematics. We still speak today of whole numbers, but the meaning that we give to the word, with the generalized notion of number that we have at our disposal, is much wider than the initial meaning, which is now treated as a particular case. I certainly acknowledge this work of sedimentation that makes us reorganize and restructure the initial givens in subsuming them under a new and broader signification. Ambiguity consists simply in the fact that any manner of thinking the whole number, in any given epoch, is only a provisional crystallization. We know that there is still more to say about the whole number, since today's arithmeticians continue to speak of it.

FATHER DUBARLE: It is not just due to a kind of powerlessness that we wallow in ambiguity, but due to a kind of necessity of lucid consciousness itself. And one of the difficulties of our problem is this link between the action of lucid consciousness and the presence of ambiguity. This is what happens in mathematics. The day when mathematics abandons definite proof of its principles, it will disfigure itself and probably waste away. We feel very strongly, as mathematicians, that there is no unfortunate event for thought here, but that it does not reach its categoricity, and that there is probably the indication and the reminder of the fact that mathematical thought is still infinitely limited and awaits new creations. If in this sense we hold to ambiguity at the mathematical level, this is not simply because we are powerless to go beyond it and make a system that would restore us to the lost paradise of truly coherent axiomatics. Rather, it is because we await from man something inventive from which, for the time being, the first pioneers make what they can. A Gödel discovers a certain number of essential or continuous problems, while some other axiomaticians discover an unsuspected mathematical field. One fine day we will discover, in relation to present mathematics, something as original as Descartes was in relation to the mathematics of the Greeks. It is in this sense that we turn to ambiguity as mathematicians have demonstrated it, and not to passively experienced ambiguity as, for example, in the teaching of geometry to students who do not understand it.

STAROBINSKI: It is not a matter of an ambiguity without exit, of an ambiguity that would be the final completion of a thought, but of an ambiguity that helps to free us from ambiguous situations by re-creating ambiguous situations anew.

FATHER DUBARLE: Be careful. The ambiguity will always remain in a certain fashion, since it is linked to the steps of the proof, and one cannot abandon it without abandoning the steps of the proof itself. The paradox of the situation is that the proof reveals the action necessary for arriving at something else. And this action carries along the givens that can no longer be reconsidered, at least without abandoning the debates themselves.

MERLEAU-PONTY: This is what I wanted to say in indicating that rigorous consciousness is the taste for rigor and, at the same time, for what is obscure and not rigorous in the given. It is the same philosophers in general who have a strong rationalist will and an extreme sensibility to the irrational.

GEORGE POULET: This question of overcoming ambiguity is extremely important, and this is exactly what I want to speak about in relation to poetic language. I would like to ask M. Merleau-Ponty if, for him, poetic language is essentially ambiguous; if, on the other hand, poetry is ambiguous; or if it is the poem that is ambiguous?

We should say without hesitation that the language of Rimbaud or Mallarmé is ambiguous. But should we also say without hesitation that, in a certain sense, a poem of Rimbaud or of Mallarmé, when these are truly poems and are fully successful, are beyond this initial ambiguity? Perhaps the goal of all poetry is to escape this ambiguity, to leave ambiguity behind as a type of engagement.

MERLEAU-PONTY: You use the word "ambiguity" in a way that I myself have not used it. Once again, I have not spoken much about it. You call ambiguity the *failure* of expression. I wanted to say that there are successes of expression—in this sense, we leave behind bad ambiguity—but these successes of expression result from linguistic, artistic, or scientific creations, creations in the strong sense. They are not guaranteed by a collection of prior ideas that would supply this language with the security of a kind of safety net—the net that we spread under acrobats in case they fall. This is all that I wanted to say. Ambiguity, then, is not a failure.

POULET: I believe I understand you on this point. But it seems to me necessary simultaneously to consider a poem as something nearly impure and at the same time as something absolutely pure. So I ask myself how your notion of ambiguity can consider this purity.

MERLEAU-PONTY: This is exactly the ambiguity, the fact that the pure would be impure and the impure would be pure.

* * *

Campagnolo observes that "the word ambiguity resists every attempt to reduce it to the signification that one wants to give it. Striking example of the resistance of words."

CHAIR: I propose that we now pass to the third point of M. Merleau-Ponty's lecture: ambiguity in history. I give the floor to Jean Wahl who has wished to begin the discussion.

WAHL: I find that there are different uses, not of the word "ambiguity" at this point, but of the word "confusion," because there is a good and a bad confusion. Naturally, it would be very difficult to define good and bad and to justify these values.

The first kind of confusion, as we see it in the first two parts of your lecture, is rather good in itself: the confusion of soul and body, which is more than confusion or confusion in a very strong sense of the term, and equally the confusion of language and thought, which is a very strong unity. The other confusion, which we catch a glimpse of in the last part of your lecture, I don't know if it is good or bad. You will tell me that I am entirely wrong to ask this question, that it is the question that is bad. At one point you spoke of a "fear-crazed dialectic," so this confusion is bad.[15]

Here I glimpse a difference between the first confusion, which dominates the first two parts, and the second. Besides, if the first is true, there will always be—and not only in 1951, as if this were another epoch—the third confusion, since it is inherent in the human race, if we can use that term.

Consequently, the third part, just like the other two, should characterize—I think this is what you say—the awareness of confusion. In the end, then, it will be the lucidity with which we see confusion that you will be led to clarify. At least this is what I understood.

MERLEAU-PONTY: In answer to your second point, I do not believe that just because the confusion is raised—and consequently is a good confusion—in the case of the body and of language, that this should necessarily lead to its being raised in the collective life of humanity. The fact is that men do speak and are understood on a minimum of points; the fact is that they come to terms with their bodies and make them into something more than corporeal, and this does not prevent the world from being divided. This means that our speech is not perfect.

WAHL: This would lead to an opposition. There is a very strong opposition with the third part, which engages values more strongly.

MERLEAU-PONTY: This leads me to the first question: I do not believe we could say that the confusion is always good in the case of the relations of consciousness with the body or with language. There are also cases of failure here. In the case of neurosis, for example, or of aphasia, the confusion is not overcome. The ambiguity remains bad ambiguity, meaning that the unity of the instincts, the entire infrastructure, is not restructured by the total individual. Consequently, there is failure. Therefore, already in the first two orders of facts, confusion is bad sometimes and also good sometimes. In any case, a brain is needed to make a writer, and a brain is needed to make a neurotic. Confusion is good or bad depending on whether or not adversity succeeds in being transformed into fortune. The case of language is the same. There are people who would like to write but never end up writing, painters who would like to paint but never end up doing so.

As a parallel in the order of politics, it seems to me that the epoch in which we live is characterized by bad confusion—which does not mean that this bad confusion would be an absolute destiny. The solidarity of values and facts, of power and ideology, is a truth. But it could be translated in two ways: either by a perpetual zigzag between the two, which is the fear-crazed dialectic: we no longer dare to use pure force, we no longer dare to place ourselves on the terrain of pure ideology. This is a true confusion. It is founded on the fact that the two orders cannot be separated from each other, but this doesn't mean that we would always be stuck in such a confusion.

WAHL: The emphasis will instead be on lucidity. It is interesting that, in the end, we realize that what you put at the first level is, in a sense, lucidity.

MERLEAU-PONTY: Of course, as long as it is understood that lucidity does not consist in thinking politics under the sole light of values or ideas. It consists in truly thinking the total state of the world at the time that we are concretely in.

WAHL: Is there more confusion in our epoch than others? The question of petroleum, for example, throws a brighter light on certain motives in the international situation. Perhaps we have more light and see with less confusion than in other epochs.

MERLEAU-PONTY: It is a question of evaluating the facts of present history, and I am presenting my contribution only as a conjecture. I have repeatedly said "perhaps," "it may be. . . ."

FATHER NIEL: Do you accept that our task is to clarify the confusion?

MERLEAU-PONTY: Yes.

FATHER NIEL: Do you accept that because one confusion is clarified, every confusion is not automatically good?

MERLEAU-PONTY: I don't see what you mean. Give me an example.

FATHER NIEL: For example, do you hold that overcoming a contradiction means automatically that this surpassing is good?

MERLEAU-PONTY: What do you have in mind?

FATHER NIEL: Is it that, because it is clarified, every confusion is good, or instead that every clarified confusion may be good or bad?

MERLEAU-PONTY: If it is truly clarified. . . .

FATHER NIEL: Consequently, there is a clarification that is genuine, and a clarification that is not.

MERLEAU-PONTY: Of course.

FATHER NIEL: How do you distinguish the genuine clarification from the one that is not?

CHAIR: When would a political situation be cleared up?

MERLEAU-PONTY: I could find a purely verbal solution to the contradictions of the present by the following means. I would say that all men are born free and equal by right; consequently all pending problems have only to be resolved on this basis. I call this clarifying the confusion in a verbal fashion, and in reality not clarifying it at all. In fact, the world we are in at this moment already has a certain historical realization. There are countries in which this notion of men being free and equal by right has no historical root—and I'm thinking not only of the U.S.S.R., but also of Asia and Africa, and when we look closely, of four-fifths of the world. I do not know what we will achieve by applying it massively in these countries. Consequently, I have not truly clarified the contradiction, I have passed to the universal, but it is a purely verbal universal.

FATHER NIEL: For the unification to be a good one, would you say that it must include all parts of the problem?

MERLEAU-PONTY: Yes.

FATHER NIEL: Would you see the need for any other condition?

MERLEAU-PONTY: You put me in an awkward situation. This is like a police interrogation—I don't know where you want to lead me. What is your other condition, since you surely have one in mind?

FATHER NIEL: I don't see any others.

MERLEAU-PONTY: Then we are in agreement.

FATHER NIEL: How do we evaluate the difference between this ideal integration of all the conditions and the concrete solution? How do you conceive this ideal, perhaps slightly mythical state where all the conditions would be integrated?

MERLEAU-PONTY: I do not *conceive* it. Just as I cannot think the idea starting from words, I cannot think this before it exists. But by the same development of reflective consciousness, I am oriented from this side; this is a condition for hoping that there would be a humanity.

FATHER NIEL: I would agree with you perhaps for saying that you do not accept that the idea of completely unifying preexists the work of unification?

MERLEAU-PONTY: No, absolutely not. But what exists is that I speak to you, and universality commences from this, it spreads out from us.

FATHER NIEL: Do you accept that this possibility of unification comes from the fact that we are always, under a certain aspect, beyond our present situation? We are not bound together in speech. You make an effort and I make an effort to go beyond what I tell you.

MERLEAU-PONTY: This is exactly what I think, as far as I follow you. I think that now I understand you correctly, and I share your opinion entirely.

G. A. RAADI: I would like to ask for certain clarifications from you. On your view, the politicians are now overwhelmed by what is unfolding in Asia. You have indicated that the political conceptions of the two antagonists are no longer capable of resolving the Asian problems. You have begun by noting a fact, but I wonder if you stop there or instead recommend a position, and if so, precisely what this position would be?

I would also like to know what, in your opinion, is the nature of this confusion in the case of Asia?

MERLEAU-PONTY: I have a negative position at least. There are some things that I do not want. What looks to me like a false solution to the political problems of the world is to simply say, as do all of the ideas of economic and political liberalism: "It is very simple, there are Chinese and Hindus, and these people have the same rights as we do, so we will adopt all of the methods used by the civilization of economic liberalism to resolve their problems." This does not seem genuine. I have had the occasion to speak with a functionary, whose nationality I will not mention, who was especially responsible for studying the possibilities for supplying India, and I was struck by what he said to me: "In the present state of economic and financial resources, even of the United States, taking military budgets into consideration, it is absolutely impossible to keep people from dying of hunger within a century." He could be mistaken; we are more than ever in the order of contingency. But if he is right, we cannot hope to resolve the problem of Asia using the methods that have made possible the development of Europe and the United States, along with all of the ideas that these methods imply.

I see, on the other hand, another universalist ideology, Marxism, which declares: social problems will be resolved and unity will be established when a universal class comes to power, namely, the proletariat, the same in all countries, all of whom will be concretely in agreement.

The events since 1917 show that, whatever the value of this conception might be from the ethical point of view, it does not seem to be inscribed in the facts, because the Russian Revolution has not become a universal revolution; it does not at all appear to be on the path of becoming in the classical Marxist sense. The American proletariat does not seem to be much in sympathy with the Russian proletariat. In my opinion, this is due to the circumstances of the Russian Revolution in particular. So, we can no longer count on this universalist ideology to shed light on the Asian problem.

In the countries where Russian influence has been established, this influence does not proceed according to Marx's conceptions, which would have meant giving power to the proletarian class. It carries out transfers of property, as in the countries of Central Europe, that actually strip the former owners but do not give real power to the proletariat. It establishes states, while the initial ideology of Marxism entailed what was called the "withering away of the State." The facts certainly seem to indicate that the ideas of classical Marxism cannot be considered sufficient for understanding the situation such as it is.

We encounter another contingency here, namely, the fact that the historical structures of China or India do not allow for an analysis of the situation using Marxist thought (unless it is completely transformed). I note this double resistance of facts to ideas, and I would call abstract any unity that we claimed to establish by returning to the ideology of liberalism or heavily to the ideology of Marxism.

This does not amount to a positive position, but it is a call for intervention. I have never occupied myself with political debates, and the debates of the Rencontres are not of this sort. I am not a political engineer. All I can do in this case is to note the clash of a group of universalist ideologies with the subject matter to be understood. What I call the subject matter in this instance is existing humanity, with its historical and geographical variety. I said all of this in my lecture. There is a journalist from Geneva who said that, in my lecture, one saw the "ear of the partisan" coming through. He has good eyes. . . . This negative position is obviously the weakness of the third perspective, but it would be necessary to write a political treatise in this case, and that is not what I have wanted to do. It seemed to me that the philosophical structure of the problem was the same as that of the problems to which we have just been devoting our efforts.

CHAIR: Are you certain that the political powerlessness of which you spoke in your lecture stems from the confusion in which governments are immersed? Wouldn't it stem precisely from the negative and powerless clarity in which you yourself are immersed?

MERLEAU-PONTY: Yes, I am certain. They are up to their necks in ambiguity. I don't think they know any longer what they are doing. The proof of this is that they make opposite decisions at three-week intervals. They are shooting wildly.

FATHER MAYDIEU: Haven't you wanted to ask them precisely to become aware of this ambiguity?

MERLEAU-PONTY: This is what I have tried to do, for my modest part.

RAADI: If you became a head of state and we asked you to act, how do you predict that you would act?

MERLEAU-PONTY: You surely recognize that one could write a clinical description of paranoia without yet having the means to cure it. I find that all of our politics is paranoid. I call a paranoiac one who cannot say one thing without thinking of what will deduce the opposite from it, one who cannot hear a word without interpreting it as having a clearly defined opposite intention. For now, I have given a brief description of this paranoia, and I have tried to point out some facts in a philosophical language. I have not claimed to do anything else.

DE BOISDEFFRE: Doesn't it seem to you, on the contrary, that this ambiguity manifests itself through hesitations of moral character, and that we are in the process of seeing governments abandon these hesitations and commit themselves to the path of a relentless logic? Doesn't this logic risk being much more relentless—since it would be a logic of force—than these hesitations that you have described and where we have struggled until now?

MERLEAU-PONTY: When I compare what is taking place now with the situation before 1939, I find hesitations in today's politics that I have not seen in German politics, for example. It is very new, this back and forth from week to week, these decisions that apparently contradict each other (according to our logic, evidently superficial). German politics before the war were different. They were hypocritical, meaning that Hitler declared: "This is my last demand," and three months later there was another. I don't have the impression that the governments that we are talking about would be very clear about things. Now, Hitler was very clear; he had a perfectly clear thought.

FATHER DUBARLE: Did Neville Chamberlain have a perfectly clear thought in going to Munich?

MERLEAU-PONTY: We would have to read his memoirs. What strikes me is that the two antagonists seem to me so hesitant, while in 1938 Neville Chamberlain was certainly not as decided as Hitler. Then there was at least one who was decided, while now no one is decided.

RAADI: Still considering Asia, do these hesitations originate in the development taking place in Asia, or does the development of Asia result from a change of political conceptions?

MERLEAU-PONTY: We don't know what is going on between the U.S.S.R. and China, but what we can affirm, I believe, is that things are not always that easy, that there must be problems. As for America, I have the impression that if America's Asian politics are so hesitant—and not only since the Korean War—this is because the United States says to itself: "What do we do with these millions of people? We invested plenty of money during the earlier period; this money has disappeared and the arms have passed to others. Will we start over?" They don't know what to do. This plays an enormous role in all of the debates about the Korean War, in all of American foreign politics, and much more than we believe.

CALEB GATTEGNO: I do not want to intervene as a philosopher, but the moment seems right to intervene as a man of action. If you are particularly hesitant, this is because, despite everything, you have affective attachments to something, either your homeland or your party. . . .

MERLEAU-PONTY: When we have no party! . . .

GATTEGNO: There seems to be a new phenomenon that we have not yet seen closely enough, namely, the existence of a very great number of stateless persons, of which I am one, who have a particular task today. These are persons who do not want to belong to a culture, who do not want to belong to a country or to some group or another, who are in the process of working because they are men of action, and who want to act through education on the problems that we are currently considering. The uneasiness that has appeared seems to me to be the result of the fact that we cannot abandon something already acquired, each holds on to what he has, while those who are stateless, who are legion and who will not be absorbed—because we cannot easily absorb them, or, better, because we don't want to—are in the process of providing a remedy. I will tell you what this remedy is.

To begin with, this remedy consists in looking reality in the face. This reality is very complex, and it is necessary to analyze it. We will not be able to offer a solution to the global situation by a theoretical decision. We must know people as they are. This knowledge is not yet at our disposal. Ethnologists and anthropologists have given us information. There is urgent work to be done, which consists of knowing the modes of thought of different people. You have spoken in a very knowledgeable way about language, but aren't there modes of thought that raise barriers between people? But it is late, and I will not dwell on this any longer.

Father Daniélou wants to pose two questions to Merleau-Ponty concerning the problem of religion:

1. *What exactly does Merleau-Ponty understand by speaking of Incarnation? What interpretation does he give of God making himself man? That God ceases to be God in a sense by becoming man, or that he becomes perfectly both man and God, Man-God?*

* * *

FATHER DANIÉLOU: This has importance for the interpretation that Merleau-Ponty has given of the current situation. He indicated that there was presently in the church a crisis that appeared to him to be infinitely more explosive than that of modernism. I wonder if the opposition of the two currents—the first a reactionary current maintaining the former categories, taking the side of being and transcendence, and the other taking the side of progress, invention, and the human—does not consist in reducing the theological opposition of the divine and the human, two things which should always coexist and cannot be separated, to a humanization of transcendence. This would follow along the same lines as a general humanism, but it would represent a genuine renunciation of a coherent theological understanding from this point on.

2. *Is a Christian existentialism possible?*

FATHER DANIÉLOU: The importance of this question is that it would allow us to discern in existentialism a certain method and a certain system.

MERLEAU-PONTY: There is evidently no system. What do you mean by a system?

FATHER DANIÉLOU: You assign certain values to certain categories of *being*. To the extent that you disvalue the category of being in favor of the category of becoming, to the extent that you disvalue God in favor of man. . . .

MERLEAU-PONTY: According to you, as soon as we are against systems, we create a system against systems.

FATHER DANIÉLOU: You have the right to take sides. I say that you are taking a side and, in this sense, you are going beyond phenomenological description.

MERLEAU-PONTY: It is the word "system" that does not seem suitable. I have never thought that phenomenology was only an introduction to philosophy; I believe that it is philosophy.

FATHER DANIÉLOU: If you would like, I will replace the word "system" with another that is frequently used, the word "explanation." Since you are a philosopher, you consequently give a certain explanation.

MERLEAU-PONTY: There is a misunderstanding. I used the word "explanation" in its current sense in German philosophical language, which opposes *erklären* and *verstehen*.

FATHER DANIÉLOU: In fact, you give an explanation to the extent that you offer certain interpretations of reality.

MERLEAU-PONTY: An interpretation is not the same thing.

FATHER DANIÉLOU: I am not attaching any importance to the word "explanation."

MERLEAU-PONTY: I have not understood your first question very well, but what I would like to say, speaking for myself, is that the pope is right to condemn existentialism. There are a great many Christians who are interested in existentialism as a method, as an entrance, as a vestibule. But insofar as they are Catholic, this can be no more than a vestibule or an entrance, and afterward they must come back to ontology in the classical sense of the word. For me, this is the negation of phenomenology, of philosophy. I find that the pope is absolutely right to condemn existentialism. But it is necessary to see what is going to happen. I think that those who take a deep interest in phenomenology or existentialism while being Catholic are inconsistent.

FATHER DANIÉLOU: The pope condemned what he called atheist existentialism, on the one hand, and on the other hand, the existentialism that claims that it is impossible to reach any absolute affirmation. He did not condemn existentialism as such. One could call Kierkegaard an existentialist.

MERLEAU-PONTY: As far as I know, Kierkegaard was not a Christian in the sense of the Syllabus. He refused to say "I am a Christian."

FATHER DANIÉLOU: Kierkegaard believed in God and in Christ. Pastor Westphal is Christian like me.

MERLEAU-PONTY: Since you are trying to provoke me, I will tell you what I think: we absolutely cannot speak of a theistic existentialism. I think this does exist, in fact, and that Gabriel Marcel is an example. But these are individual inconsistencies. I do not like to talk much about all of this, because I know that things are less straightforward than this as far as individuals are concerned. This is why we can speak; we can speak even to those people who, in the end, rally to a different ontology, in the classical sense of the word.

FATHER DANIÉLOU: I don't agree with you on this point. For my part, I believe that it is possible for a Catholic to be an existentialist.

CHARLES WESTPHAL: I am happy that this question has been raised, because I also had the intention of raising it. Naturally, I have a different position than that of Father Daniélou. For me, there is neither pope nor Syllabus, so we have greater freedom. But there are many of us Protestants who find in existentialism a system of thought that does not seem to us to be incompatible with the facts of faith, as long as existentialism is treated as only a philosophy. Jaspers acknowledges that there are limits. There is a modesty of philosophy that recognizes the limits of its knowledge and for which something unknowable remains. I would like to ask M. Merleau-Ponty: Would you go further? Does your philosophy, your phenomenology, or your existentialism allow you to reach "total" conclusions? Like Father Daniélou, I was a little astounded to hear you say, at the end of your lecture, that there is a rejection of all explanations. Is this truly a philosophical attitude?

MERLEAU-PONTY: It is the philosophical attitude, in my opinion. Philosophy is *thaumazein,* the consciousness of strangeness. It does away with "philosophical" explanations by systems.

WESTPHAL: You do not accept that there could be other explanations beyond philosophy? I have never liked the word "explanation," because for me faith is not an explanation. It is a revealed fact, and it is very difficult to fit into an intellectual formula. But in saying that you refuse all explanation, in compelling man to remain in this ambiguity, don't you offer him only the call to invention? You leave him in a situation that you yourself call vertiginous, but can we live in a vertiginous situation?

MERLEAU-PONTY: Philosophy is not a hospital. If people are vertiginous and want to take medication against it, I don't stop them, but I say: this is medication.

WESTPHAL: We have situated the debate on the political terrain, but this question is also raised concerning the bodily and linguistic. I was perfectly charmed by the demonstration of each of the parts of your lecture, but at the end of each paragraph I said to myself, "What does this mean in practical terms?" For me, the most precise example is that of language. You have given an admirable definition: "Language is the activity of what signifies." How can we utter such speech unless we put a moral content there, in one fashion or another, unless this engages a manner of being [*un comportement de l'être*]?

MERLEAU-PONTY: I remove absolutely nothing from what is, nor from the makeup of our experience. If you have an experience of the unknowable—and I do not deny that you have such an experience—I have one, otherwise I would not be an "existentialist," as you say. You must know that something else is necessary in order to go from this to what we call religion, and this is what I tried to explain in my lecture. It is here that I find the pope to be right. He is right from the point of view of the pope. Of course, I am not the pope, and consequently I do not share his opinion.

WESTPHAL: In that case, what allows you to say—and I find this monstrous—that Kierkegaard is not a Christian?

MERLEAU-PONTY: I never said that Kierkegaard was not a Christian, but there is a text by Kierkegaard where he says something like this: "The true Christian is a man who will not even say: I am Christian." I am saying that, having reached this point, it is no longer a question of *faith* but rather of *silence.* I find the pope to be correct in saying that this does not make one a Catholic. I would even say that this does not make one a Protestant, at least a religious Protestant. It makes a man who is quite a lot like me. After all, this is not so bad. . . .

WESTPHAL: You yourself say that the true Christian is the one who does not say "I am Christian." In refusing to say this, however, he bears witness to the reality of his faith.

It remains the case that Kierkegaard's work implies a Christian testimony, one of the most powerful that has been given through all of the centuries. When you, philosophers, deny Kierkegaard to us, I say: We cannot accept that.

MERLEAU-PONTY: I have never said this.

WAHL: In Kierkegaard's thought, this means: "The Christian determination is too high for me."

MERLEAU-PONTY: It means something more: it would be practically to deny that Christianity could be called Christian.

FATHER MAYDIEU: . . . When you say that dialogue with Christians has become impossible, I am completely in agreement with Father Daniélou for saying that the current crisis is very different from that of modernism. I am not a historian, not even a historian of the church, and I have not thoroughly studied modernism. It was characterized by the fact that the problems posed were able to lead the modernists to wonder about faith in Christ, dead and risen, and Son of God. By contrast, the effort of current Catholic thought is characterized by such a great certainty in the faith in Christ dead and risen that the rest seems relatively much less important. Also, when you say that dialogue with Catholics has become impossible. . . .

MERLEAU-PONTY: I said "difficult."

FATHER MAYDIEU: . . . This has to do with you. We have seen this morning that dialogue was possible, that it could exist; demonstrating this does not require a great deal of insistence from me. If you take Catholics as a whole and the church, with its central affirmation, summed up in the idea that Christ the Son of God died and arose, this is not a dialogue. Barth spoke about this two years ago and said: "I can't help it, I am the bearer of a message, I am the bearer of a letter, I repeat it." I do not participate in a dialogue with the church or with the pope. There have been times when I have said that I had a dialogue with God: this is true in a sense, but in another sense, there is no dialogue with God.

On the other hand, if dialogue with Christians is difficult, the reason why it seems difficult to you is because you say: "These are men who already know." Now, the Christian does not know. He believes, which is not the same thing. He puts forward an affirmation, but precisely when he wants to penetrate this affirmation, the dialogue that he carries on with anyone is a help, an assistance, a progress.

MERLEAU-PONTY: Here is what I mean by knowing and not knowing: a true *exchange* assumes that each person is disposed to receive from the other what can appear true to him in what the other says. It seems to me that we can use this attitude with Christians superficially but not fundamentally, when we are in disagreement on an essential point, like the existence of infinite thought. That is what I believe.

FATHER MAYDIEU: This is the opposite of what I think. This is why I disagreed with introducing the problem of contingency, that of universality or truth, or even of the existence of infinite thought. Our starting point is Christ dead and risen. On this point, I maintain that I have received something from you.

MERLEAU-PONTY: Do you refuse, on this point that concerns us, to follow all the way through to the conclusions?

FATHER MAYDIEU: I am waiting to see your book, because I have not seen the conclusions very clearly, either in your lecture or in your writings.

MERLEAU-PONTY: I don't spend my time saying that I'm an atheist, because that is not a concern, and because doing so would transform an entirely positive philosophical consciousness into a negation. But if, at the end of the story, someone asks me about it, I say "yes."

FATHER MAYDIEU: I am not asking you not to be an atheist, I am asking you if an atheist and a man who is not can have a profound conversation nonetheless.

MERLEAU-PONTY: Thanks to God, men are inconsistent. My believer is at the same time a man. I have memories of the religion in which I was raised and that I even continued to practice beyond childhood. This allows us to exchange words that are not devoid of meaning. I say frankly that when I am conversing productively about a moral question, for example, it is with someone who is an atheist like me.

FATHER MAYDIEU: This is the case for you, but it is not universal. If, in order to carry on a dialogue with someone, it is necessary to be entirely in agreement with his conclusions, this seems to me a little contrary to your philosophy, I will not say of ambiguity, but based on ambiguity. How far will this lead us?

MERLEAU-PONTY: You ask where this leads? Philosophy consists in not wondering where this leads.

FATHER MAYDIEU: It is you who has just said: "You do not wish to follow me to the point where this leads. You refuse to follow all the way through to the conclusions."

CHAIR: You reason as if the word "atheist" had a single fixed meaning, outside of all context, which is entirely contrary to what you have said about language. I am convinced that the word "atheist" and the term "atheism" depend just as much on the context as on a profession of faith.

MERLEAU-PONTY: I use it only when provoked.

FATHER MAYDIEU: I do not wish to provoke you but only to say the same thing as Hersch.

MERLEAU-PONTY: I have never written in black and white: "I am an atheist." But times are such that one is considered to be a believer until proven otherwise. Today it is necessary to declare that one is not a believer or else people will say, "He seems to be this way . . . , but you'll see."

FATHER MAYDIEU: This is not the meaning of my comment. I agree with Hersch. I add, moreover, that the pope was undoubtedly correct to have condemned existentialism.

MERLEAU-PONTY: The notion of being an atheist brings with it many historical connotations, which is why I do not talk about it. But all the same, it must be said that philosophy, in my sense, can breathe only when it rejects the infinitely infinite thought in order to see the *world* in its strangeness.

CHAIR: In particular, we do not know what we are denying.

MERLEAU-PONTY: We no longer know what we are affirming.

CHAIR: We know neither what we affirm nor what we deny. The term "atheist" implies God, so look to see what we are designating with this name. This is why there is something falsely clear-cut in the opposition that you offered sincerely to Father Maydieu.

MERLEAU-PONTY: Even so, it is necessary to know where we are on this, otherwise we are in the dark. If I am a theist without knowing it, of course. . . .

PIERRE THÉVANEZ: Isn't it necessary to take this question the other way around? You say that you are not so far from a Kierkegaard deep down. One might wonder if your attitude is not a secularized theology, or a secularized Christian existentialism. Can we speak of ambiguity or contingency otherwise than in the plenary and deep sense that is at the origin of a Christian conception?

MERLEAU-PONTY: To me, this is the height of confusion. You speak of ambiguity? This means that you are Christian! But no, it means that you think there is ambiguity.

FATHER MAYDIEU: I did not say this.

VON SCHENCK [*summary of the German*]: Is it possible to deal with the problems within a philosophy without bringing in the term "God"?

MERLEAU-PONTY: If there is a philosophy, it would be just that.

CHAIR: Then it is possible to do it with others without bringing in the term "God." Is it possible to discuss other problems with other men, believers or not?

MERLEAU-PONTY: For me, philosophy consists in giving another name to what has long been crystallized under the name of God.

VON SCHENCK: This is the problem.

Jeanne Hersch closes the session.

13

Indirect Language and the Voices of Silence

to Jean-Paul Sartre

What we have learned from Saussure is that, taken singly, signs do not signify anything, and that each one of them does not so much express a sense as mark a divergence of sense between itself and other signs. Since the same can be said for all other signs, we may conclude that language is made of differences without terms; or more exactly, that the terms of language are engendered only by the differences which appear among them. This is a difficult idea, because common sense tells us that if term *A* and term *B* do not have any meaning at all, it is hard to see how there could be a difference of sense between them; and that if communication really did go from the whole of the speaker's language to the whole of the hearer's language, one would have to know the language in order to learn it. But the objection is of the same kind as Zeno's paradoxes; and as they are overcome by the act of movement, it is overcome by the use of speech. And this sort of circle, according to which language, in the presence of those who are learning it, precedes itself, teaches itself, and suggests its own deciphering, is perhaps the marvel which defines language.

Language is learned, and in this sense one is certainly obliged to go from the parts to the whole. The whole which is first in Saussure cannot be the explicit and articulated whole of the complete language as it is recorded in grammars and dictionaries. Nor does he have in mind a logical totality like that of a philosophical system, all of whose elements can (in principle) be deduced from a single idea. Since what he is doing is rejecting any other than a "diacritical" sense of signs, he cannot found language upon a system of positive ideas. The unity he is talking about is a unity of coexistence, like that of the sections of an arch which shoulder one another. In a whole of this kind, the learned parts of a language have an immediate value as a whole, and progress is made less by addition and juxtaposition than by the internal articulation of a function which is in its own way already complete. It has long been known that for a child the word first functions as a sentence, and perhaps even certain phonemes as words. But contemporary linguistics conceives of the unity of language in an even more precise way by isolating, at the origin of words—perhaps even at the origin of form and style—"oppositive" and "relative" principles to which the Saussurean definition of the sign applies even more rigorously than to words, since it is a question here of components of language which do not for their part have any assignable sense and whose sole function is to make possible the discrimination of signs in the strict sense. Now these first phonemic oppositions may well have gaps and be enriched subsequently by new dimensions, and the verbal chain may well find other means of self-differentiation. The important point is that the phonemes are from the beginning variations of a unique speech apparatus, and that with them the child seems to have "caught" the principle of a mutual differentiation of signs and at the same time to have acquired *the sense of the sign*. For the phonemic oppositions—contemporaneous with the first attempts at communication—appear and are developed without any relation to the child's babbling. His babbling is often repressed by the oppositions, and in any case retains only a marginal existence without its materials being integrated to the new system of true speech. This lack of relation between babbling and phonemic oppositions seems to indicate that possessing a sound as an element of babbling which is addressed only to itself is not the same as possessing a sound as a stage in the effort to communicate. It can be said that beginning with the first phonemic oppositions the child *speaks,* and that thereafter he will only learn to apply the principle of speech in diverse ways. Saussure's insight becomes more precise: with the first phonemic oppositions the child is initiated to the lateral liaison of sign to sign as the foundation of an ultimate relation of sign to sense—in the special form it has received in the language in question. Phonologists have succeeded in extending their analysis beyond words to forms, to syntax, and even to stylistic differences because the language in its entirety as a style of expression and a unique manner of handling words is anticipated by the child in the first phonemic oppositions. The whole of the spoken language surrounding the child snaps him up like a whirlwind, tempts him by its internal articulations and brings him *almost* up to the moment when all this noise begins to mean something. The untiring way in which the train of words crosses and recrosses itself, and the emergence one unimpeachable day of a certain phonemic scale according to which discourse is visibly composed, finally sways the child over to the side of those who speak. Only the language as a whole enables one to understand how language draws the child to itself and how he or she comes to enter that domain whose doors, one might think, open only from within. It is because the sign is diacritical from the outset, because it is composed and organized in terms of itself, that it has an interior and ends up laying claim to a sense.

This sense arising at the edge of signs, this imminence of the whole in the parts, is found throughout the history of culture. There is that moment at which Brunelleschi built the cupola of the cathedral in Florence in a definite relation to the configuration of the site. Should we say that he broke with the closed space of the Middle Ages and discovered the universal space of the Renaissance?[1] But *one* operation of arts is still a long way from being a deliberate use of space as the medium of a universe. Should we say then that this space is not yet there? But Brunelleschi did make for himself a strange device in which two views of the Battistero and the Palazzo della Signoria, with the streets and the squares which frame them, were reflected in a mirror, while a disc of polished metal projected the light of the sky upon the scene.[2] Thus he had done research and had raised a question of space. It is just as difficult to say when the generalized number begins in the history of mathematics. "In itself" (that is, as Hegel would say, for us who project it into history), it is already present in the fractional number which, before the algebraic number, inserts the whole number in a continuous series. But it is there as if it were unaware of its existence; it is not there "for itself." In the same way, one must give up trying to establish the moment at which Latin becomes French. Grammatical forms begin to be efficacious and outlined in a language before being systematically employed. A language sometimes remains a long time pregnant with transformations which are to come; and the enumeration of the means of expression in a language makes no sense, since those which fall into disuse continue to lead a diminished life in the language and since the place of those which are to replace them is sometimes already marked out—even if only in the form of a gap, a need, or a tendency.

Even when it is possible to date the emergence of a principle which exists "for itself," it is clear that the principle has been previously present in the culture as an obsession or anticipation, and, when it comes to consciousness and is posited as an explicit meaning, this merely completes its long incubation in the form of an operative sense. Now, the coming into consciousness never happens without leaving something left over. The space of the Renaissance will in turn be thought of later as a very particular case of possible pictorial space. Culture thus never gives us absolutely transparent meanings; the genesis of sense is never completed. What we rightly call our truth we never contemplate except in a symbolic context which dates our knowledge. We always have to do only with architectures of signs whose sense, being nothing other than the way in which the signs behave toward one another and are distinguished from one another, cannot be posited independently of them. We do not even have the morose consolation of a vague relativism, since each of these movements is indeed a truth and will be preserved in the more comprehensive truth of the future.

As far as language is concerned, it is the lateral relation of one sign to another which makes each of them significant, so that the sense appears only at the intersection of and as it were in the interval between words. This characteristic prevents us from forming the usual conception of the distinction and the union between language and its sense. Sense is usually thought to transcend signs in principle (just as thought is supposed to transcend the sounds or sights which indicate it), and to be immanent in the signs in the sense that each one of them, having *its* sense once and for all, could not conceivably slip any opacity between itself and us, or even give us food for thought. Signs would have only the role of monition; they would warn the hearer that he must consider such and such of *his* thoughts. But sense does not actually dwell in the verbal chain or distinguish itself from the chain in this way. If the sign means something only insofar as it is profiled against other signs, its sense is entirely involved in language. Speech always comes into play against a background of speech; it is always only a fold in the immense fabric of language. To understand it, we do not have to consult some inner lexicon which gives us, in regard to the words or the forms, the pure thoughts that they covered over; we have only to lend ourselves to its life, to its movement of differentiation and articulation, and to its eloquent gestures. There is thus an opacity of language. Nowhere does it stop and leave a place for pure sense; it is always limited only by more language, and the sense appears within it only set into the words. Like the charade, language is understood only through the interaction of signs, each of which, taken separately, is equivocal or banal, and makes sense only by being combined with others.

For the speakers no less than for the listener, language is definitely something other than a technique for ciphering or deciphering ready-made meanings. Before there can be such ready-made meanings, language must first make meanings exist as available entities by establishing them at the intersection of linguistic gestures as that which, by common consent, the gestures show. Our analyses of thought give us the impression that before it finds the words which express it, it is already a sort of ideal text that our sentences attempt to *translate*. But the author himself has no text to which he can compare what he has written and no language prior to language. If his speech satisfies him, it is through an equilibrium whose conditions his speech itself defines, through a perfection based on no model. More than a means, language is something like a being, and that is why it can so well make someone present: a friend's speech over the telephone gives us the friend himself, as if he existed entirely in this way of calling and saying goodbye to us, of beginning and ending his sentences, and of carrying on the conversation through things left unsaid. Because the sense is the total movement of speech, our thought crawls along in language. Yet for the same reason, our thought moves through language as a gesture goes beyond its points of passage. At the very moment language fills our minds up to the top without leaving the smallest place for thought not taken into its vibration, and exactly to the extent that we abandon ourselves to it, it passes beyond the "signs" toward their sense. And nothing separates us from that sense anymore. Language does not *presuppose* its table of correspondence; it unveils its secrets itself. It teaches them to every child who comes into the world. It is entirely a showing. Its opacity, its obstinate reference to itself and its turning and folding back upon itself are precisely what make it a spiritual power; for it in turn becomes something like a universe, in which it is capable of lodging the things themselves—after it has transformed them into their sense.

Now if we rid our minds of the idea that our language is the translation or cipher of an *original text,* we shall see that the idea of *complete* expression is nonsensical, and that all language is indirect or allusive—that it is, if you like, silence. The relation of sense to the spoken word can no longer be a point-for-point correspondence that we always have in view. Saussure notes that the English "the man I love" expresses just as completely as the French "l'homme *que* j'aime." We can say that the English does not express the relative pronoun. The truth is that instead of being expressed by a word, the relative pronoun passes into the language by means of a blank between the words. But we should not even say that it is implied. This notion of implication naively expresses our conviction that a language (generally our native tongue) has succeeded in capturing the things themselves in its forms; and that any other language, if it wants to reach things themselves too, must at least tacitly use the same kind of instruments. Now the reason French seems to us to go to the things themselves is certainly not that it has actually copied the articulations of being. French has a distinct word to express the relation, but it does not distinguish the function of being the object of a verb by means of a special flexional ending. It could be said that French implies the declension that German expresses (and the aspect that Russian expresses, and the optative that Greek expresses). The reason French seems to us to be traced upon things is not that it is, but that it gives us the illusion of being so by the internal relation of one sign to another. But "the man I love" does so just as well. The absence of a sign can be a sign, and expression is not the adjustment of an element of discourse to each element of the sense, but an operation of language upon language which suddenly decenters itself toward its sense. To speak is not to put a word under each thought; if it were, nothing would ever be said. We would not have the feeling of living in the language and we would remain silent, because the sign would be immediately obliterated by its own sense and because thought would never encounter anything but thought—the thought it wanted to express and the thought which it would form from a wholly explicit language. We sometimes have, on the contrary, the feeling that a thought had been *said*—not replaced by verbal counters but incorporated in words and made available in them. And finally, there is a power of words because, working against one another, they are attracted at a distance by thought like tides by the moon, and because they evoke their sense in this tumult much more imperiously than if each one of them brought back only a listless meaning of which it was the indifferent and predestined index.

Language speaks peremptorily when it gives up trying to say the thing itself. As algebra brings unknown magnitudes under consideration, speech differentiates meanings no one of which is known separately; and it is by treating them as known (and giving us an abstract picture of them and their interrelations) that language ends up imposing the most precise identification upon us in a flash. Language signifies when instead of copying thought it lets itself be taken apart and put together again by thought. Language bears the sense of thought as a footprint signifies the movement and effort of a body. The empirical use of already established language should be distinguished from its creative use. Empirical language can only be the result of creative language. Speech in the sense of empirical language—that is, the opportune recollection of a preestablished sign—is not speech in respect to an authentic language. It is, as Mallarmé said, the worn coin placed silently in my hand. True speech, on the contrary—speech which signifies, which finally renders "l'absente de tous bouquets" present and frees the sense captive in the thing—is only silence in respect to empirical usage, for it does not go so far as to become a common noun. Language is oblique and autonomous, and if it sometimes signifies a thought or a thing directly, that is only a secondary power derived from its inner life. Like the weaver, the writer works on the wrong side of his material. He has only to do with the language, and it is thus that he suddenly finds himself surrounded by sense.

If this account is true, the writer's operation is not very different from the painter's. We usually say that the painter reaches us across the silent world of lines and colors, and that he addresses himself to an unformulated power of deciphering within us that we control only after we have blindly used it—only after we have enjoyed the work. The writer is said, on the contrary, to dwell in already elaborated signs and in an already speaking world, and to require nothing more of us than the power to reorganize our meanings according to the indications of the signs which he proposes to us. But what if language expresses as much by what is between words as by the words themselves? By that which it does not "say" as by what it "says"? And what if, hidden in empirical language, there is a language raised to the second power in which signs once again lead the vague life of colors, and in which meanings never free themselves completely from the intercourse of signs?

There are two sides to the act of painting: the spot or line of color put on a point of the canvas, and its effect in the whole. The two are incommensurable, since the former is almost nothing yet suffices to change a portrait or a landscape. One who, with his nose against the painter's brush, observed the painter from too close would see only the wrong side of his work. The wrong side is a slight movement of the brush or pen of Poussin; the right side is the sunshine's breaking through, which that movement releases. A camera once recorded the work of Matisse in slow motion. The impression was prodigious, so much so that Matisse himself was moved, they say. That same brush that, seen with the naked eye, leaped from one act to another, was seen to meditate in a solemn, expanded time—in the imminence of a world's creation—to try ten possible movements, dance in front of the canvas, brush it lightly several times, and crash down finally like a lightning stroke upon the one line necessary. Of course, there is something artificial in this analysis. And Matisse would be wrong if, putting his faith in the film, he believed that he really chose between all possible lines that day and, like the God of Leibniz, solved an immense problem of maximum and minimum. He was not a demiurge; he was a human being. He did not have in his mind's eye all the gestures possible, and in making his choice he did not have to eliminate all but one. It is slow motion which enumerates the possibilities. Matisse, set within a human's time and vision, looked at the still-open whole of his work in progress and brought his brush toward the line which called for it in order that the painting might finally be that which it was in the process of becoming. By a simple gesture he resolved the problem which in retrospect seemed to imply an infinite number of data (as the hand in the iron filings, according to Bergson, achieves in a single stroke the arrangement which will make a place for it). Everything happened in the human world of perception and gesture; and the camera gives us a fascinating version of the event only by making us believe that the painter's hand operated in the physical world where an infinity of options is possible. And yet, Matisse's hand did hesitate. Consequently, there was a choice, and the chosen line was chosen in such a way as to observe, scattered out over the painting, a score of conditions which were unformulated and even unformulatable for anyone but Matisse, since they were only defined and imposed by the intention of executing *that particular painting which did not yet exist.*

The case is no different for the truly expressive word and thus for all language in the phase in which it is being established. The expressive word does not simply choose a sign for an already defined meaning, as one goes to look for a hammer in order to drive a nail or for a claw to pull it out. It gropes around a significative intention which is not guided by any text, and which is precisely in the process of writing the text. If we want to do justice to it, we must evoke some of the other words that might have taken its place and were rejected, and we must feel the way in which they might have touched and shaken the chain of language in another manner and the extent to which this particular word was really the only possible one if that meaning was to come into the world. In short, we must consider speech before it is pronounced, the background of silence which does not cease to surround it and without which it would say nothing. Or to put the matter another way, we must uncover the threads of silence with which speech is mixed. In already acquired expressions there is a direct sense which corresponds point for point to figures, forms, and instituted words. Apparently, there are no gaps or speaking silences here. But the sense of expressions which are in the process of being accomplished cannot be of that sort; it is a lateral or oblique sense which runs between words. It is another way of shaking the linguistic or narrative apparatus in order to tear a new sound from it. If we want to understand language as an originating operation, we must pretend never to have spoken, submit language to a reduction without which it would once more escape us by referring us to what it signifies for us, *gaze* at it as deaf people look at those who are speaking, compare the art of language to the other arts of expression, and try to see it as one of these mute arts. It is possible that the sense of language has a decisive privilege, but it is by trying out the parallel that we will perceive what may in the end make that parallel impossible. Let us begin by understanding that there is a tacit language, and that painting speaks in its own way.

* * *

Malraux says that painting and language are comparable only when they are detached from what they "represent" and are brought together under the category of creative expression. It is then that they are both recognized as two forms of the same endeavor. Painters and writers have worked for centuries without a suspicion of their relationship. But it is a fact that they have experienced the same adventure. At first, art and poetry are consecrated to the city, the gods, and the sacred, and it is only in the mirror of an external power that they can see the birth of their own miracle. Later, both know a classic age which is the secularization of the sacred age; art is then the representation of a Nature that it can at best embellish— but according to formulas taught to it by Nature herself. As La Bruyère would have it, speech has no other role than finding the exact expression assigned in advance to each thought by a language of the things themselves; and this double recourse to an art before art, to a speech before speech, prescribes to the work a certain point of perfection, completeness, or fullness which makes all human beings assent to it as they assent to the things which fall under their senses. Malraux has made a good analysis of this "objectivist" prejudice, which is challenged by modern art and literature. But perhaps he has not measured the depth at which the prejudice is rooted; perhaps he was too quick to concede that the domain of the visible world is "objective"; and perhaps it is this concession which led him, by contrast, to define modern painting as a return to subjectivity—to the "incomparable monster"—and to bury it in a secret life outside the world. His analysis needs to be reexamined.

Therefore, let us turn to the privilege given to oil painting. More than any other kind of painting, it permits us to attribute a distinct pictorial representative to each element of the object or of the human face and to look for signs which can give the illusion of depth or volume, of movement, of forms, of tactile qualities or of different kinds of material. (Think of the patient studies which brought the representation of velvet to perfection.) These processes, these secrets augmented by each generation, seem to be elements of a general technique of *representation* which ultimately should reach the thing itself (or the person himself), which cannot be imagined capable of containing any element of chance or vagueness, and whose sovereign function painting should try to equal. Along this road one takes steps that need not be retraced. The career of a painter, the productions of a school, and even the development of painting all go toward *masterpieces* in which what was sought after up until then is finally obtained; masterpieces which, at least provisionally, make the earlier attempts useless and stand out as landmarks in the progress of painting. Classical painting wants to be as convincing as things and does not think that it can reach us except as things do—by imposing an unimpeachable spectacle upon *our senses*. It relies in principle upon the perceptual apparatus, considered as a natural, given means of communication between human beings. Don't we all have eyes which function more or less in the same way? And if the painter has succeeded in discovering the sufficient signs of depth or velvet, won't we all, in looking at the painting, see the same spectacle, which will rival that of nature?

The fact remains that the classical painters were painters and that no valuable painting has ever consisted in simply representing. Malraux points out that the modern conception of painting as creative expression has been a novelty for the public much more than for the painters themselves, who have always practiced it, even if they did not construct the theory of it. That is why the works of the classical painters have a different sense and perhaps more sense than the painters themselves thought, why these painters frequently anticipate a kind of painting that is free from their canons, and why they are still necessary mediators in any initiation to painting. At the very moment when, their eyes fixed upon the world, they thought they were asking it for the secret of a sufficient representation, they were unknowingly bringing about that *metamorphosis* of which painting later became aware. Consequently, classical painting cannot be defined in terms of the representation of nature or in terms of a reference to "our senses," nor modern painting in terms of a reference to the subjective. The perception of classical painters already depended upon their culture, and our culture can still give form to our perception of the visible. We must not forsake the visible world to classical formulas or shut modern painting up in the recess of the individual. There is no choice to be made between the world and art, or between "our senses" and absolute painting, for they pass into one another.

Sometimes Malraux speaks as if "sense data" had never varied throughout the centuries, and as if the classical perspective had been imperative as long as painting referred to sense data. Yet it is clear that the classical perspective is only one of the ways humanity has invented for projecting the perceived world before itself, and not the copy of that world. The classical perspective is an optional interpretation of spontaneous vision, not because the perceived world contradicts the laws of classical perspective and imposes others, but rather because it does not require any particular one, and is not of the order of laws. In free perception, objects spread out in depth do not have any definite "apparent size." We must not even say that the perspective "deceives us" and that the faraway objects are "bigger" for the naked eye than their projection in a drawing or a photograph would lead us to believe—at least not according to that size which is supposed to be a common measure of backgrounds and foregrounds. The size of the moon on the horizon cannot be measured by a certain number of aliquot parts of the coin that I hold in my hand; it is a question of a "size-at-a-distance," and of a kind of quality which adheres to the moon as heat and cold adhere to other objects. Here we are in the order of the "ultra-things" which H. Wallon[3] speaks about and which do not arrange themselves according to a single graduated perspective in relation to nearby objects. Beyond a certain size and distance, we encounter the absolute of size in which all the "ultra-things" meet; and that is why children say that the sun is as "big as a house." If I want to come back from that way of seeing to perspective, I must stop perceiving the whole freely. I must circumscribe my vision, mark (on a standard of measurement I hold) what I call the "apparent size" of the moon and of the coin, and, finally, transfer these measurements onto paper. But during this time the perceived world has disappeared along with the true simultaneity of objects, which is not their peaceful coexistence in a single scale of sizes. When I was seeing the coin and the moon together, my glance had to be fixed on one of them. Then the other one appeared to me in marginal vision—"little-object-seen-up-close" or "big-object-seen-far-away"—incommensurable with the first. What I transfer to paper is not this coexistence of perceived things as rivals in my field of vision. I find the means of arbitrating their conflict, which makes depth. I decide to make them co-possible on the same plane, and I succeed by coagulating a series of local and monocular views, no one of which may be superimposed upon the elements of the living perceptual field. Once things competed for my gaze; and, anchored in one of them, I felt in it the solicitation of the others which made them coexist with the first—the demands of a horizon and its claim to exist. Now I construct a representation in which each thing no longer calls the whole of vision to itself, makes concessions to the other things, and no longer occupies on the paper any more than the space which they leave to it. Before, my gaze, running freely over depth, height, and width, was not subjected to any point of view, because it adopted them and rejected them in turn. Now I renounce that ubiquity and agree to let only that which could be seen from a certain reference point by an immobile eye fixed on a certain "vanishing point" of a certain "vanishing line" figure in my drawing. (A deceptive modesty, for I renounce the world itself by precipitating the narrow perspective upon the paper; I also stop seeing like a human being, who is open to the world because he is situated in it. I think of and dominate my vision as God can when he considers the *idea* that he has of me.) Before, I had the experience of a world of teeming, exclusive things which could be taken in only by means of a temporal cycle in which each gain was at the same time a loss. Now the inexhaustible being crystallizes into an ordered perspective within which backgrounds resign themselves to being only backgrounds (inaccessible and vague as is proper), and objects in the foreground abandon something of their aggressiveness, order their inner lines according to the common law of the spectacle, and already prepare themselves to become backgrounds as soon as it is necessary. A perspective, in short, within which nothing holds my gaze and takes the shape of a present. The whole scene is in the mode of the over and done with or of eternity. Everything takes on an air of propriety and discretion. Things no longer call upon me to answer, and I am no longer compromised by them. And if I add to this artifice that of aerial perspective, one senses at what point I who paint and they who gaze at my landscape dominate the situation. Perspective is much more than a secret technique for imitating a reality given as such to all humanity. It is the invention of a world dominated and possessed through and through by an instantaneous synthesis, which is at best roughed out by our gaze when it vainly tries to hold together all these things seeking individually to monopolize it. The faces of the classical portrait, always in the service of the subject's character, passion, or love—always signifying—or the babies and animals of the classical painting, so desirous to enter the human world, so unconcerned with rejecting it, manifest the same "adult" relation of human to the world, except when, giving in to his favorable daemon, the great painter adds a new dimension to this world too sure of itself by making contingency vibrate within it.

Now if "objective" painting is itself a creation, the fact that modern painting seeks to be a creation no longer provides any reasons for interpreting it as a movement toward the subjective and a ceremony glorifying the individual. And here Malraux's analysis seems to me to be on tenuous ground. There is only one subject in today's painting, he says—the painter himself.[4] Painters no longer look for the velvet of peaches, as Chardin did, but, like Braque, for the velvet of the painting. The classical painters were themselves classics without knowing it; the modern painter wants first of all to be original, and for him his power of expression is identical to his individual difference.[5] *Because* painting is no longer for faith or beauty, it is for the individual;[6] it is "the annexation of the world by the individual."[7] The artist is thus supposed to be "of the tribe of the ambitious and the drugged,"[8] and like them devoted to stubborn self-pleasure, to daemonic pleasure—that is, to the pleasure of all in humanity which destroys humanity. It is clear, however, that it would be hard to apply these definitions to Cézanne or Klee, for example. There are two possible interpretations of that tolerance for the incomplete shown by those moderns who present sketches as paintings, and whose every canvas, as the signature of a moment of life, demands to be seen on "show" in a series of successive canvases. It may be that they have given up the *work*, and no longer look for anything but the immediate, the sensed, the individual—"brute expression," as Malraux says. Or else, completion, the presentation that is objective and convincing for the *senses*, is no longer the means to or the sign of a work that is really *done*, because henceforth expression must go from person to person across the common world they *live*, without passing through the anonymous realm of the *senses* or of Nature. Baudelaire wrote—in an expression very opportunely recalled by Malraux—"that a work that is done was not necessarily finished, and a finished work not necessarily done."[9] The work that gets accomplished is thus not the work which exists in itself like a thing, but the work which reaches its viewer and invites him to take up the gesture which created it and, leaping over the intermediaries, to rejoin, without any guide other than a movement of the invented line (an almost incorporeal trace), the silent world of the painter, henceforth uttered and accessible. There is the improvisation of childlike painters who have not learned their own gesture and who believe, under the pretext that a painter is no more than a hand, that it suffices to have a hand in order to paint. They extract petty wonders from their body as a morose young man who observes his body with sufficient complacency can always find some little peculiarity in it to nourish his religion of himself. But there is also the improvisation of the artist who has turned toward the world that he wants to express and (each word calling for another) has finally composed for himself a learned voice which is more his than his original cry. There is the improvisation of automatic writing and there is that of the *Charterhouse of Parma.* Since perception itself is never finished, since our perspectives give us a world to express and think about that envelops and exceeds those perspectives, a world that announces itself in lightning signs as a spoken word or an arabesque, why should the expression of the world be subjected to the prose of the *senses* or of the concept? It must be poetry; that is, it must completely awaken and recall our pure power of expressing beyond things already said or seen. Modern painting presents a problem completely different from that of the return to the individual: the problem of knowing how one can communicate without the help of a preestablished Nature which all men's senses open upon, the problem of knowing how we are grafted to the universal by that which is most our own.

This is one of the philosophies toward which Malraux's analysis may be extended. It just has to be detached from the philosophy of the individual or of death which, with its nostalgic inclination toward civilizations of the sacred, is at the forefront of his thought. The painter does not put his immediate self—the very nuance of feeling—into his painting. He put his *style* there, and he has to win it as much from his own attempts as from the painting of others or from the world. How long it takes, Malraux says, before a writer learns to speak with his own voice. Similarly, how long it takes the painter—who does not, as we do, have his work spread out before him, but who creates it—to recognize in his first paintings the features of what will be the work that he has done, provided that he is not mistaken about himself. Even more: he is no more capable of *seeing* his paintings than the writer is capable of reading his work. It is in others that expression takes on its relief and really becomes signification. For the writer or painter, there is only the allusion of self to self, in the familiarity of one's personal hum, which is also called inner monologue. The painter works and leaves his wake; and except when he or she indulges in examining his earlier works to try to recognize what he has become, he does not like very much to gaze at his work. He has something better in his own possession; the language of his maturity eminently contains the feeble accent of his first works. Without going back to them, and by the sole fact that they have fulfilled certain expressive operations, he finds himself endowed with new organs; and experiencing the excess of what is to be said over and beyond their already verified power, he is capable (unless, as it has more than once occurred, a mysterious fatigue intervenes) of going "further" in the same direction. It is as if each step taken called for and made possible another step, or as if each successful expression prescribed another task to the spiritual automation or founded an institution whose efficacy it will have never finshed experiencing.

This "inner schema" which is more and more imperious with each new painting—to the point that the famous chair becomes, Malraux says, "a brutal ideogram of the very name of Van Gogh"—is legible *for Van Gogh* neither in his first works, nor even in his "inner life" (for in this case Van Gogh would not need painting in order to be reconciled with himself; he would stop painting). It *is* that very life, to the extent that it emerges from its inherence, ceases to be in possession of itself, and becomes a universal means of understanding and of making something understood, of seeing and of presenting something to see—and is thus not shut up in the depths of the mute individual but diffused throughout all he sees. Before the style became an object of predilection for others and an object of delectation for the artist himself (to the great detriment of his work), there must have been the fecund moment when the style germinated at the surface of the artist's experience, and when an operant and latent sense found the emblems which were going to disengage it and make it manageable for the artist and at the same time accessible to others. Even when the painter has already painted, and even if he has become in some respects master of himself, what is given to him with his style is not a manner, a certain number of procedures or tics that he can inventory, but a mode of formulation that is just as recognizable for others and just as little visible to him as his silhouette or his everyday gestures. Thus when Malraux writes that style is the "means of re-creating the world according to the values of the one who discovers it";[10] or that it is "the expression of a meaning lent to the world, a call for and not a consequence of a way of seeing";[11] or finally, that it is "the reduction to a fragile human perspective of the eternal world which draws us along according to a mysterious rhythm into a drift of stars";[12] he does not install himself in the very functioning of style. Like the public, he gazes at it from the outside. He indicates some of its consequences, which are truly sensational ones—the victory of humanity over the world—but ones the painter does not intend. The painter at work knows nothing of the antithesis of humanity and world, of meaning and the absurd, of style and "representation." He is far too busy expressing his communication with the world to become proud of a style which is born almost as if he were unaware of it. It is quite true that style for the moderns is much more than a means of representing. It does not have any external model; painting does not exist before painting. But we must not conclude from this, as Malraux does, that the representation of the world is only a *stylistic means*[13] for the painter, as if the style could be known and sought after outside all contact with the world, as if it were an *end*. We must see it developing in the hollows of the painter's perception as a painter; style is a demand that has issued from that perception. Malraux says as much in his best passages: perception already stylizes. A woman passing by is not first and foremost a corporeal contour for me, a colored mannequin, or a spectacle; she is "an individual, sentimental, sexual expression." She is a certain manner of being flesh which is given entirely in her walk or even in the simple click of her heel on the ground, just as that tension of the bow is present in each fiber of wood—a most remarkable variant of the norm of walking, gazing, touching, and speaking that I possess in my self-awareness because I am body. If I am also a painter, what will be transmitted to the canvas will no longer be only a vital or sensual value. There will be in the painting not just "a woman" or "an unhappy woman" or "a hatmaker." There will also be the emblem of a way of inhabiting the world, of treating it, and of interpreting it by her face, by clothing, the agility of the gesture and the inertia of the body—in short, the emblems of a certain relationship to being. But even though this truly pictorial style and sense are not in the woman seen—for in that case the painting would be already done—they are at least called for by her. "All style is a shaping of the elements of the world, allowing it to be oriented toward one of its essential parts." There is meaning when we submit the data of the world to a "coherent deformation."[14] That convergence of all the visible and intellectual vectors of the painting toward the same meaning, x, is already sketched out in the painter's perception. It begins as soon as he perceives—that is, as soon as he arranges certain gaps and fissures, figures and grounds, a top and a bottom, a norm and a deviation, in the inaccessible fullness of things. In other words, as soon as certain elements of the world take on the value of dimensions to which from then on we relate all the rest, and in whose *language* we express them. For each painter, style is the system of equivalences that he sets up for himself for that labor of manifestation. It is the universal index of the "coherent deformation" by which he concentrates the still-scattered sense of his perception and makes it exist expressly. The work is not made far from things and in some intimate laboratory to which the painter and the painter alone has the key. Whether he is gazing at real flowers or paper flowers, he always goes back to *his* world, as if the principle of the equivalences, by means of which he is going to manifest it, had been buried there since the beginning of time.

Writers must not underestimate the painter's labor and study, that effort which is so like an effort of thought and which allows us to speak of a language of painting. It is true that, scarcely having drawn his system of equivalences from the world, the painter invests it again in colors and a quasi-space on a canvas. The sense impregnates the picture, rather than the picture *expressing* it. "That yellow rent in the sky over Golgotha . . . is an anguish made thing, an anguish which has turned into a yellow rent in the sky, and which is immediately submerged and thickened by thing-like qualities."[15] Rather than being manifested by the painting, the sense sinks into it and trembles around it "like a wave of heat."[16] It is "like an immense and futile effort, always arrested halfway between heaven and earth," to express what the nature of painting prevents it from expressing. For professional users of language, the preceding impression is perhaps inevitable. The same thing happens to them that happens to us when we hear a foreign language which we speak poorly; we find it monotonous and marked with an excessively heavy accent and flavor, precisely because it is not our own and we have not made it the principal instrument of our relations with the world. The sense of the painting remains *captive* for those of us who do not communicate with the world through painting. But for the painter, and even for us if we set ourselves to living in painting, the sense is much more than a "wave of heat" at the surface of the canvas, since it is capable of demanding *that* color and *that* object in preference to all others, and since it commands the arrangement of a painting just as imperiously as a syntax or a logic. For not all the painting is in those little anguishes or local joys with which it is sown: they are only the components of a total sense which is less pathetic, more *legible*, and more enduring. Malraux is quite right to relate the anecdote of the innkeeper at Cassis who, seeing Renoir at work by the sea, comes up to him: "There were some naked women bathing in some other place. Goodness knows what he was looking at, and he changed only a little corner." Malraux comments: "The blue of the sea had become that of the brook in *The Bathers*. His vision was less a way of looking at the sea than the secret elaboration of a world to which that depth of blue whose immensity he was recapturing pertained."[17] Nevertheless, Renoir was gazing at the sea. And why did the blue of the sea pertain to the world of his painting? How was it able to teach him something about the brook in *The Bathers*? Because each fragment of the world—and in particular the sea, sometimes riddled with eddies and ripples and plumed with spray, sometimes massive and immobile in itself—contains all sorts of shapes of being and, by the way it has of responding to the attack of the gaze, evokes a series of possible variants and teaches, over and beyond itself, a general way of saying being. Renoir can paint women bathing and a freshwater brook while he is by the sea at Cassis because he asks the sea—which alone can teach what he asks— only for its way of interpreting the liquid element, of exhibiting it, and of making it interact with itself. In short, because he only asks for a typic of the manifestations of water. One can make paintings by gazing at the world because it seems to him that he finds the style which will define him in the eyes of others in the appearances themselves, and because he thinks he is spelling out nature at the moment he is re-creating it. "A certain peremptory equilibrium or disequilibrium of colors and lines overwhelms the person who discovers that the half-opened door over there is that of another world."[18] *Another world*—by this we mean the same world that the painter sees and that speaks his own language, only freed from the nameless weight which held it back and kept it equivocal. How would the painter or poet express anything other than his encounter with the world? What does abstract art itself speak of, if not a negation or refusal of the world? Now austerity and the obsession with geometrical surfaces and forms (or the obsession with infusorians and microbes; for the interdict put upon life, curiously enough, begins only with the metazoan) still have an odor of life, even if it is a shameful or despairing life. Thus the painting always says something. It is a new system of equivalences which demands precisely this particular upheaval, and it is in the name of a *truer* relation between things that their ordinary ties are broken. A vision or an action that is finally free decenters and regroups the objects of the world for the painter and the words for the poet. But breaking or burning up language does not suffice to write the *Illuminations,* and Malraux profoundly remarks of modern painters that "although no one of them spoke of truth, all, faced with the works of their adversaries, spoke of fraud."[19] They want nothing to do with a truth defined as the resemblance of painting and the world. They would accept the idea of a truth defined as a painting's cohesion with itself, the presence of a unique principle in it which affects each means of expression with a certain contextual value. Now when one stroke of the brush replaces the (in principle) complete reconstitution of the appearances in order to bring us into wool or flesh, what replaces the object is not the subject—it is the allusive logic of the perceived world. One always intends to signify something; there is always something to say, which one more or less approaches. It is just that Van Gogh's "going further" at the moment he paints *The Crows* no longer indicates some reality to be approached, but rather what still must be done in order to restore the encounter between his gaze and the things which solicit it, the encounter between the one who is to be and what is. And that relation is certainly not one of copying. "As always in art, one must lie to tell the truth," Sartre rightly says. It is said that the exact recording of a conversation which had seemed brilliant later gives the impression of poverty. The presence of those who were speaking, the gestures, the physiognomies, and the feeling of an event which is taking place and of a continuous improvisation, all are lacking in the recording. Henceforth the conversation no longer exists; it *is,* flattened out in the unique dimension of sound and all the more disappointing because this wholly auditory medium is that of a text read. In order to fill our mind as it does, the work of art—which often addresses itself to only one of our senses and never assails us from all sides as our lived experience does—must thus be something other than frozen existence. It must be, as Gaston Bachelard[20] says, "super-existence." But it is not arbitrary or, as we say, fictional. Modern painting, like modern thought generally, obliges us to admit a truth which does not resemble things, which is without any external model and without any predestined instruments of expression, and which is nevertheless truth.

If we put the painter back in contact with his world, as we are trying to, perhaps we will be better able to understand the metamorphosis which, through him, transforms the world into painting, changes him into himself from his beginnings to his maturity, and, finally, gives certain works of the past a sense in each generation that had not been perceived before. When a writer considers painting and painters, he is a little in the position of readers in relation to the writer, or the man in love who thinks of the absent woman. Our conception of the writer begins with his work; the man in love captures the essence of the absent woman in a few words and attitudes by which she expressed herself more purely. When he meets her again, he is tempted to repeat Stendhal's famous "What? Is this all?" When we make the writer's acquaintance, we feel foolishly disappointed at not finding, in each moment of his presence, that essence and impeccable speech that we have become accustomed to designating by his name. So that's what he does with his time? So that's the ugly house he lives in? And these are his friends, the woman with whom he shares his life? These, his mediocre concerns? But all this is only reverie—or even envy and secret hate. One admires as one should only after having understood that there are not any supermen, that there is no one who does not have a human's life to live, and that the secret of the woman loved, of the writer, or of the painter, does not lie in some realm beyond his empirical life, but is so mixed in with his mediocre experiences, so modestly confused with his perception of the world, that there can be no question of meeting it separately, face to face. In reading the *Psychology of Art*, we sometimes get the impression that Malraux, who certainly knows all this as a writer, forgets it where painters are concerned and dedicates the same kind of cult to them which we believe he would not accept from his readers. In short, he makes painters divine. "What genius is not fascinated by that extremity of painting, by that appeal before which time itself vacillates? It is the moment of possession of the world. Let painting go no further, and Hals the Elder becomes God."[21] This is perhaps the painter seen by others. The painter himself is a person at work who each morning finds in the shape of things the same questioning and the same call he never stops responding to. In his eyes, his work is never done; it is always in progress, so that no one can exalt it above the world. One day, life slips away; the body falls, cut off. In other cases, and more sadly, it is the question spread out through the world's spectacle which is no longer heard. Then the painter is no more, or he has become an honorary painter. But as long as he paints, his painting concerns visible things; or if he is or becomes blind, it concerns that unimpeachable world which he has access to through his other senses and which he speaks of in terms of one who sees. And that is why his labor, which is obscure for him, is nevertheless guided and oriented. It is always only a question of advancing the line of the already opened furrow and of recapturing and generalizing an accent which has already appeared in the corner of a previous painting or in some instant of his experience, without the painter himself ever being able to say (since the distinction makes no sense) what comes from him and what comes from things, what his new work adds to the previous ones, or what he has taken from others as opposed to what is his own. This triple reworking, which makes a sort of provisory eternity of the operation of expression, is not simply a metamorphosis in the fairy-tale sense of miracle, magic, and absolute creation in an aggressive solitude. It is also a response to what the world, the past, and the painter's own completed works demanded. It is accomplishment and fraternity. Husserl has used the fine word *Stiftung*—foundation or establishment—to designate first of all the unlimited fecundity of each present which, precisely because it is singular and passes, can never stop having been and thus being universally; but above all to designate that fecundity of the products of culture which continue to have value after their appearance and which open a field of investigations in which they perpetually come to life again. It is thus that the world as soon as he has seen it, his first attempts at painting, and the whole past of painting all deliver up a *tradition* to the painter—*that is,* Husserl remarks, *the power to forget origins* and to give to the past not a survival, which is the hypocritical form of forgetfulness, but a new life, which is the noble form of memory.

Malraux insists upon what is misleading and derisory in the comedy of the mind: those rival contemporaries, Delacroix and Ingres, whom posterity recognizes as twins, those painters who wanted to be classic and are only neoclassical, that is, the contrary, and those styles which escaped the view of their creators and become visible only when the museum gathered together works scattered about the earth, and photography enlarged miniatures, transformed a section of a painting by its way of framing it, changed rugs, coins, and stained glass windows into paintings, and brought to painting a consciousness of itself which is always retrospective.

But if expression re-creates and transforms, the same was already true of times preceding ours and even of our perception of the world before painting, since that perception already marked things with the trace of a human elaboration. The productions of the past, which are the data of our time, themselves once went beyond yet earlier productions toward a future which we are, and in this sense called for (among others) the metamorphosis which we impose upon them. One can no more inventory a painting (say what is there and what is not) than, according to the linguists, one can inventory a vocabulary—and for the same reason. In both cases it is not a question of a finite sum of signs, but of an open field or of a new organ of human culture. We cannot deny that in painting such and such a fragment of a painting, that classical painter had already invented the very gesture of this modern one. But we must not forget that he did not make it the principle of his painting and that in this sense he did not invent it, as Saint Augustine did not invent the cogito as a central thought but merely encountered it. And yet what Aron[22] called each age's dreamlike quest for ancestors is possible only because all ages pertain to the same universe. The classical and the modern pertain to the universe of painting conceived of as a single task, from the first sketches on the walls of caves to our "conscious" painting. No doubt one reason why our painting finds something to recapture in types of art which are linked to an experience very different from our own is that it transfigures them. But it also does so because they prefigure it, because they at least have something to say to it, and because their artists, believing that they were continuing primitive terrors, or those of Asia and Egypt, secretly inaugurated another history which is still ours and which makes them present to us, while the empires and beliefs to which they thought they *belonged* have disappeared long ago. The unity of painting does not exist in the museum alone; it exists in that single task which all painters are confronted with and which makes the situation such that one day they *will be* comparable in the museum, and such that these fires answer one another in the night. The first sketches on the walls of caves set forth the world as "to be painted" or "to be sketched" and called for an indefinite future of painting, so that they speak to us and we answer them by metamorphoses in which they collaborate with us. There are thus two historicities. One is ironic or even derisory, and made of misinterpretations, for each age struggles against the others as against aliens by imposing its concerns and perspectives upon them. This history is forgetfulness rather than memory; it is dismemberment, ignorance, externality. But the other history, without which the first would be impossible, is constituted and reconstituted step-by-step by the *interest* which bears us toward that which is not us and by that life which the past, in a continuous exchange, brings to us and finds in us, and which it continues to lead in each painter who revives, recaptures, and renews the entire undertaking of painting in each new work.

Malraux often subordinates this cumulative history, in which paintings join each other by what they affirm, to the cruel history in which paintings oppose each other because they deny. For him, reconciliation takes place only in death, and it is always in retrospect that one perceives the single problem to which rival paintings are responding and which makes them contemporaneous. But if the problem were really not already present and operative in the painters—if not at the center of their consciousness, at least at the horizon of their labors—what could the museum of the future derive it from? What Valéry said of the priest applies pretty well to the painter: he leads a double life, and half of his bread is consecrated. He is indeed that irascible and suffering person for whom all other painting is a rival. But his angers and hatreds are the waste product of a work. Wherever he goes, this poor wretch enslaved by his jealousy brings along an invisible double who is free from his obsessions—his self as he is defined by his painting—and he can easily recognize the filiations or kinships manifested by what Péguy called his "historical inscription" if only he consents not to take himself for God and not to venerate each gesture of his brush as unique. What makes "a Vermeer" for us—Malraux shows this perfectly—is not the fact that this canvas was one day painted by Vermeer the human being. It is the fact that the painting observes the system of equivalences according to which each of its elements, like a hundred pointers on a hundred dials, marks the same deviation—the fact that it speaks the language of Vermeer. And if the counterfeiter succeeded in recapturing not only the processes but the very style of the great Vermeers, he would no longer be a counterfeiter; he would be one of those painters who painted for the old masters in their studios. It is true that such counterfeiting is impossible: one cannot spontaneously paint like Vermeer after centuries of other painting have gone by and the sense of the problem of painting itself has changed. But the fact that a painting has been copied in secret by one of our contemporaries qualifies him as a counterfeiter only to the extent that it prevents him from truly reproducing the style of Vermeer. The fact is that the name of Vermeer and of each great painter comes to stand for something like an institution. And just as the business of history is to discover, behind "Parliament under the *ancien régime*" or "the French Revolution," what they really signify in the dynamics of human relations and what modulation of these relations they represent, and just as it must designate this as accessory and that as essential in order to accomplish its task—so a true history of painting must seek, beyond the immediate aspect of the canvases attributed to Vermeer, a structure, a style, and a sense against which the discordant details (if there are any) torn from his brush by fatigue, circumstance, or self-imitation cannot prevail. The history of painting can judge the authenticity of a canvas only by examining the painting, not simply because we lack information concerning origins, but also because the complete catalog of the work of a master does not suffice to tell us what is really *his*, because he himself is a certain word in the discourse of painting which awakens echoes from the past and future to the exact degree that it does not look for them, and because he is linked to all other attempts to the exact degree that he busies himself resolutely with his world. Retrospection may well be indispensable for this true history to emerge from empirical history, which is attentive only to events and remains blind to advents, but it is traced out to begin with in the total will of the painter. History looks toward the past only because the painter first looked toward the work to come; there is a fraternity of painters in death only because they live the same problem.

In this respect the museum's function, like the library's, is not entirely beneficent. It certainly enables us to see works of art scattered about the world and engulfed in cults or civilizations they sought to ornament as unified aspects of a single effort. In this sense our consciousness of painting as painting is based upon the museum. But painting exists first of all in each painter who works, and it is there in a pure state, whereas the museum compromises it with the somber pleasures of retrospection. One should go to the museum as the painters go there, in the sober joy of work; and not as we go there, with a somewhat spurious reverence. The museum gives us a thieves' conscience. We occasionally sense that these works were not after all intended to *end up* between these morose walls, for the pleasure of Sunday strollers or Monday "intellectuals." We are well aware that something has been lost and that this meditative necropolis is not the true milieu of art—that so many joys and sorrows, so much anger, and so many labors were not *destined* one day to reflect the museum's mournful light. By transforming attempts into "works," the museum makes a history of painting possible. But perhaps it is essential to men to attain greatness in their works only when they do not look for it too hard. Perhaps it is not bad that the painter and the writer do not clearly realize that they are founding humanity. Perhaps, finally, they have a truer and more vital feeling for the history of art when they carry it on in their work than when they made "art lovers" of themselves in order to contemplate it in the museum. The museum adds a false prestige to the true value of the works by detaching them from the chance circumstances they arose from and making us believe that the artist's hand was guided from the start by fate. Whereas style lived within each painter like his heartbeat, and was precisely what enabled him to recognize every effort which differed from his own, the museum converts this secret, modest, non-deliberated, involuntary, and, in short, living historicity into official and pompous history. The imminence of a regression gives our liking for such and such a painter a nuance of pathos which was quite foreign to him. He *labored* the whole lifetime of a human being; we see his work like flowers on the brink of a precipice. The museum makes the painters as mysterious for us as octopuses or lobsters. It transforms these works created in the fever of a life into marvels from another world, and in its pensive atmosphere and under its protective glass, the breath which sustained them is no more than a feeble flutter on their surface. The museum kills the vehemence of painting as the library, Sartre said, changes writings which were originally a man's gestures into "messages." It is the historicity of death. And there is a historicity of life of which the museum provides no more than a fallen image. This is the historicity which lives in the painter at work when with a single gesture he links the tradition that he carries on and the tradition that he founds. It is the historicity which in one stroke welds him to all which has ever been painted in the world, without his having to leave his place, his time, or his blessed or accursed labor. The historicity of life reconciles paintings by virtue of the fact that each one expresses the whole of existence—that they are all successful—instead of reconciling them in the sense that they are all finite and like so many futile gestures.

If we put painting back into the present, we shall see that it does not admit of the barriers between the painter and others, and between the painter and his own life, that our purism would like to impose. Even if the innkeeper at Cassis does not understand Renoir's transmutation of the blue of the Mediterranean into the water of *The Bathers,* it is still true that he wanted to see Renoir work. That *interests* him too—and after all, nothing stops him from discovering the path that the cave dwellers one day opened without tradition. Renoir would have been quite wrong to ask his advice and try to please him. In this sense, he was not painting for the innkeeper. By his painting, he himself defined the conditions under which he intended to be approved. But he did paint; he questioned the visible and made something visible. It was the world, the water of the sea, that he asked to reveal the secret of the water of *The Bathers;* and he opened the passage from one to the other for those who were caught up in the world with him. As Vuillemin[23] says, there was no question of speaking their language, but of expressing them by expressing himself. And the painter's relation to his own life is of the same order: his style is not the style of his life, but he draws his life also toward expression. It is understandable that Malraux does not like psychoanalytic *expressions* in painting. Even if Saint Anne's cloak is a vulture, even if one admitted that while da Vinci painted it as a cloak, a second da Vinci in da Vinci, head tilted to one side, deciphered it as a vulture like a reader of riddles (after all, it is not impossible: in the life of da Vinci there is a frightening taste for mystification which could very well have inspired him to enshrine his monsters in a work of art), no one would be discussing this vulture anymore if the painting did not have another sense. The explanation accounts for the details—at most for the materials. Admitting that the painter likes to handle colors (the sculptor, clay) because he is an "anal erotic," this still does not tell us what it is to paint or sculpt.[24] But the contrary attitude, the cult of the artist which forbids us to know anything about their lives and places their work beyond private or public history and outside the world like a miracle, hides their true greatness from us. The reason why Leonardo is something other than one of the innumerable victims of an unhappy childhood is not that he has one foot in the great beyond, but that he succeeded in making a means of interpreting the world out of everything he lived—it is not that he did not have a body or sight, but that he constituted his corporeal or vital situation in language. When one goes from the order of events to that of expression, one does not change worlds; the same circumstances which were previously submitted to now become a signifying system. Hollowed out, worked from within, and finally freed from the weight upon us which made them painful or wounding, they become transparent or even luminous, and capable of clarifying not only the aspects of the world which resemble them but the others too; yet transformed as they may be, they still do not cease to be there. The knowledge of them we may gain will never replace the experience of the work itself. But it helps measure the creation and it teaches us this passing over that stays in place, this passing over that is the only passing over which does not return. If we take the painter's point of view in order to be present at that decisive moment when what has been given to him to live by way of physical destiny, personal odyssey, or historical circumstances crystallizes into "the motif," we will recognize that his work, never an effect, is always a response to these givens, and that the body, life, landscapes, schools, mistresses, creditors, the police, and revolution which might suffocate painting, are also the bread his painting consecrates. To live in painting is still to breathe the air of this world—above all for the man who sees in the world something to paint. And there is a little of him in every human being.

Let us get to the heart of the problem. Malraux meditates upon miniatures and coins in which photographic enlargement miraculously reveals the very same style that is found in full-sized works; or upon works uncovered beyond the limits of Europe, far from all "influences"—works in which moderns are astonished to find the same style which a conscious painter has reinvented somewhere else. If one shuts art up in the most secret recess of the individual, he can explain the convergence of separate works only by invoking some destiny which rules over them.

> As if an imaginary spirit of art pushed forward from miniature to painting and from fresco to stained-glass window in a single conquest which it suddenly abandoned for another, parallel or suddenly opposed, as if a subterranean torrent of history unified all these scattered works by dragging them along with it, . . . a style known in its evolution and metamorphoses becomes less an idea than the illusion of a living fatality. Reproduction, and reproduction alone, has brought into art these imaginary super-artists of indistinct birth, possessed of a life, of conquests and concessions to the taste for wealth or seduction, of death and resurrection— known as styles.[25]

Thus Malraux encounters, at least as a metaphor, the idea of a history which unites the most disparate attempts, a painting that works behind the painter's back, and Reason in history of which he is the instrument. These Hegelian monstrosities are the antithesis and complement of Malraux's individualism. What do they become when the theory of perception puts the painter back into the visible world and retrieves the body as spontaneous expression?

Let us begin with the simplest fact (which we have already clarified in part). The magnifying glass reveals the very same style in a medallion or miniature as the one found in full-sized works because one's hand has its own ubiquitous style, which is undivided in one's gesture and does not need to lean heavily upon each point of the tracing in order to mark the material with its stripe. Our handwriting is recognized whether we trace letters on paper with three fingers of our hand or in chalk on the blackboard at arm's length; for it is not a purely mechanical movement of our body which is tied to certain muscles and destined to accomplish certain materially defined movements, but a general motor power of formulation capable of the transpositions which constitute the constancy of style. Or rather, there is not even any transposition; we simply do not write in space "in itself" with a thing-hand and a thing-body for which each new situation presents new problems. We write in perceived space, where results with the same form are immediately analogous—if we ignore differences of scale—just as the same melody played at different pitches is immediately identified. And the hand with which we write is a phenomenon-hand which possesses, in the formula of a movement, something like the effectual law of the particular cases in which the movement may have to be executed. The whole marvel of a style already present in the invisible elements of a work thus comes down to the fact that, working in the human world of perceived things, the artist comes to put his stamp upon even the inhuman world revealed by optical instruments—just as the swimmer unknowingly skims over a whole buried universe which would frighten him if he looked at it with undersea goggles; or as Achilles, in the simplicity of one step, effects an infinite summation of spaces and instants. There is no doubt that this marvel, whose strangeness the word "human" should not hide from us, is a very great one. But we can at least recognize that this miracle is natural to us, that it begins with our incarnate life, and that there is no reason to look for its explanation in some World Spirit which allegedly operates within us without our knowledge and perceives in our place, beyond the perceived world, on a microscopic scale. Here the spirit of the world is ourselves, as soon as we know how to *move* and *gaze*. These simple acts already enclose the secret of expressive action. As the artist makes his style radiate into the very fibers of the material he is working on, I move my body without even knowing which muscles and nerve paths should intervene, nor where I must look for the instruments of that action. I want to go over there, and here I am, without having entered into the inhuman secret of the bodily mechanism or having adjusted that mechanism to the givens of the problem. For example: without having adjusted the bodily mechanism to the position of a goal defined by its relation to some system of coordinates, I look at the goal, I am drawn by it, and the bodily apparatus does what must be done in order for me to be there. For me, everything happens in the human world of perception and gesture, but my "geographical" or "physical" body submits to the demands of this little drama which does not cease to bring about a thousand natural marvels in it. Just my gaze toward the goal already has its own miracles. It too installs itself in being with authority and conducts itself there as in a conquered country. It is not the object which obtains movements of accommodation and convergence from my eyes. It has been shown that on the contrary I would never see anything clearly, and there would be no object for me, if I did not use my eyes in such a way as to make a view of a single object possible. And it is not the mind which takes the place of the body and anticipates what we are going to see. No; it is my gazes themselves—their synergy, their exploration, and their prospecting—which bring the imminent object into focus; and our corrections would never be rapid and precise enough if they had to be based upon an actual calculation of effects. We must therefore recognize that what is designated by the terms "gaze," "hand," and in general "body" is a system of systems destined for the inspection of a world and capable of leaping over distances, piercing the perceptual future, and outlining hollows and reliefs, distances and deviations—a sense—in the inconceivable flatness of being. The movement of the artist tracing his arabesque in infinite matter amplifies, but also prolongs, the simple marvel of oriented locomotion or grasping movements. Already in its pointing gestures the body not only flows over into a world whose schema it bears in itself but possesses this world at a distance rather than being possessed by it. So much the more does the gesture of expression, which undertakes to delineate what it intends and make it appear "outside," retrieve the world. But already with our first oriented gesture, the infinite relationships of *someone* with his situation had invaded our mediocre planet and opened an inexhaustible field to our behavior. All perception, all action which presupposes it, and in short every human use of the body is already *primordial expression*. Not that derivative labor which substitutes for what is expressed signs which are given elsewhere with their sense and rule of usage, but the primary operation which first constitutes signs as signs, makes that which is expressed dwell in them through the eloquence of their arrangement and configuration alone, implants a sense in that which did not have one, and thus—far from exhausting itself in the instant at which it occurs—inaugurates an order and founds an institution or tradition.

Now, if the presence of style in miniatures which no one had ever seen (*and in a sense no one had ever made*) is one with the fact of our corporeality and does not call for any occult explanation, it seems to me that one can say as much of the singular convergences which, outside all influences, make works which *resemble one another* appear from one end of the world to another. We ask for a cause which explains these resemblances, and we speak of a Reason in history or of super-artists who guide artists. But to begin with, to speak of resemblances is to put the problem badly. Resemblances are, after all, of little importance in respect to the innumerable differences and varieties of cultures. The probability, no matter how slight, of a reinvention without guide or model suffices to account for these exceptional recurrences. The true problem is to understand why such different cultures become involved in the same search and have the same task in view (and when the opportunity arises, encounter the same modes of expression). We must understand why what one culture produces has a sense for another culture even if it is not its original sense; why we take the trouble to transform fetishes into art. In short, the true problem is to understand why there is *one* history or *one* universe of painting. But this is a problem only if we have begun by placing ourselves in the geographical or physical world, and by placing works of art there as so many separate events whose resemblance or mere connection then becomes improbable and calls for an explanatory principle. We propose on the contrary to consider the order of culture or meaning an original order of *advent*,[26] which should not be derived from the order, if it exists, of pure events, or treated as simply the effect of extraordinary encounters. If it is characteristic of the human gesture to signify beyond its simple existence in fact, to inaugurate a sense, it follows that every gesture is *comparable* to every other. They all arise from a single syntax. Each of them is both a beginning (and a continuation) which, insofar as it is not enclosed in its difference and finished once and for all like an event, points to a continuation or recommencement. It is valuable beyond its simple presence, and in this respect it is allied or implicated in advance with all the other efforts of expression. The difficult and essential point here is to understand that in positing a field distinct from the empirical order of events, we are not positioning a Spirit of Painting which is already in possession of itself on the other side of the world that it is gradually manifested in. There is not, above and beyond the causality of events, a second causality which makes the world of painting a "suprasensible world" with its own laws. Cultural creation is ineffectual if it does not find a vehicle in external circumstances. But if circumstances lend themselves in the least to creation, a preserved and transmitted painting develops a creative power in its inheritors which is without proportion to what it is—not only as a bit of painted canvas, but even as a work endowed by its creator with a definite meaning. This excess of the work over the deliberate intentions inserts it in a multitude of relationships with which the short history of painting and even the psychology of the painter bear only a few reflections, just as the body's gesture toward the world introduces it into an order of relations of which pure physiology and biology do not have the least idea. Despite the diversity of its parts, which makes it fragile and vulnerable, the body is capable of gathering itself up into a gesture which for a time dominates its dispersion and puts its stamp upon everything it does. In the same way, we may speak of a unity of human style which transcends spatial and temporal distances to gather up the gestures of all painters together into one sole expressive effort, and their works into a single cumulative history—into a single art. The enveloping movement which the unity of culture extends beyond the limits of the individual life is of the same type as that which unites all the moments of the individual life itself in advance at the moment of its institution or birth, when a consciousness (as they say) is sealed up in a body and a new being appears in the world. We know not what will happen in this new life, only that from now on something cannot fail to happen, be it but the end of what has just begun. Analytic thought breaks up the perceptual transition from moment to moment, from place to place, from one perspective to the next, and then seeks on the side of the mind the guarantee of a unity which is already there when we perceive. It also breaks the unity of culture and then tries to reconstruct it from without. After all, it says, there are only the works themselves—which in themselves are a dead letter—and individuals who freely give them a sense. How is it then that works resemble one another and that individuals understand one another? It is at this con-juncture that the Spirit of Painting is brought in. But just as we must rec-ognize the leaping over of diversity by existence, and in particular the bod-ily possession of space, as a fundamental fact; and just as our body, insofar as it *lives* and makes itself gesture, sustains itself only through its effort to be in the world, holds itself upright because its inclination is toward the top and because its perceptual fields draw it toward that risky position, and could not possibly receive this power from a separate spirit; so the history of painting, which runs from one work to another, rests upon itself and is borne only by the caryatid of our efforts, which converge by the sole fact that they are efforts to express. The intrinsic order of sense is not eternal. Although it does not follow each zigzag of empirical history, it sketches out, it calls for, a series of successive steps. For it is not defined simply (as we stated provisionally) by the kinship all of its moments bear to one an-other within a single task. Precisely because these moments are all those of painting, each one of them (if preserved and transmitted) modifies the situation of that overarching enterprise and requires precisely that those moments which come after it be different. Two cultural gestures can be identical only if they are unaware of one another. It is thus essential to art to develop: that is, both to change and, in Hegel's words, to "return to it-self," and thus to present itself in the form of history, and the sense of the expressive gesture upon which we have based the unity of painting is on principle a sense in genesis. The advent is a promise of events. The domi-nation of the one over the many in the history of painting, like that dom-ination which we have encountered in the functioning of the perceiving body, does not swallow up succession into an eternity. On the contrary, it requires succession; it needs it at the same time that it founds it in mean-ing. And there is more than just an analogy between the two problems: it is the expressive operation of the body, begun by the least perception, that develops into painting and art. The field of pictorial meanings has been open since one human appeared in the world. The first cave drawing founded a tradition only because it had received another one—that of perception. The quasi-eternity of art is of a piece with the quasi-eternity of incarnate existence; and in the use of our bodies and our senses, insofar as they involve us in the world, we have the means of understanding our cultural gesticulation insofar as it involves us in history. The linguists sometimes say that, since there is strictly no means of marking the date in history when, for example, Latin ends and French begins, there is only one sole language and nearly only one sole tongue at continuous work. Let us say more generally that the continued attempt at expression founds one sole history, as the hold our body has upon every possible object founds one sole space.

Thus understood, history would escape—here we can indicate this—the confused discussions it is the object of today and become once more what it should be for the philosopher: the center of his reflections. Not, certainly, as a "simple nature," absolutely clear in itself, but on the contrary as the place of all our questionings and wonderments. Whether it be to worship or to hate it, we conceive of history and the dialectic of history today as an external power. Consequently, we are forced to choose between this power and ourselves. To choose history means to devote ourselves body and soul to the advent of a future humanity not even outlined in our present life. For the sake of that future, we are asked to renounce all judgment upon the means of attaining it; and for the sake of efficaciousness, all judgment of value and all "self-consent to ourselves." This history idol secularizes a rudimentary conception of God, and it is not by accident that contemporary discussions return so willingly to a parallel between what is called the "horizontal transcendence" of history and the "vertical transcendence" of God.

Truly, this is to pose the problem badly two times. The finest encyclicals in the world are powerless against the fact that for at least twenty centuries Europe and a good part of the world renounced so-called vertical transcendence. And it is a little too much to forget that Christianity is, among other things, the recognition of a mystery in the relations of man and God, which stems precisely from the fact that the Christian God wants nothing to do with a vertical relation of subordination. He is not simply a principle of which we would be the consequence, a will whose instruments we are, or even a model of which human values are the only reflection. There is a sort of impotence of God without us, and Christ attests that God would not be fully God without becoming fully human. Claudel goes so far as to say that God is not above but beneath us—meaning that we do not find him as a suprasensible idea, but as another ourself, who dwells in and authenticates our darkness. Transcendence no longer hangs over humanity: we become, strangely, its privileged bearer.

Furthermore, no philosophy of history has ever transferred all the substance of the present into the future or *destroyed* the self to make room for the other. Such a neurotic attitude toward the future would be exactly non-philosophy, the deliberate refusal to know what one believes in. No philosophy has ever consisted in choosing between transcendences—for example, between that of God and that of a human future. They have all been concerned with mediating them (with understanding, for example, how God makes himself man or how man makes himself God) and with elucidating that strange envelopment which makes the choice of means already a choice of ends and the self become world, culture, history—but which makes the culture decline at the same time the self does. According to Hegel, as is endlessly repeated, all that is real is rational, and thus justified—but justified sometimes as a true acquisition, sometimes as a pause, and sometimes as an ebbing withdrawal for a new surge. In short, all is justified relatively as a moment in total history on condition that this history is done, and thus in the sense that our errors themselves are said to perform a positive task and that our progress is our mistakes understood—which does not erase the difference between growth and decline, birth and death, regression and progress.

It is true that in Hegel's works the theory of the state and the theory of war seem to reserve the judgment of historical works for the absolute knowledge of the philosopher, and take it away from all other humans. This is not a reason for forgetting that even in the *Philosophy of Right* Hegel rejects judging action by its results alone as well as by its intention alone. "The maxim: 'Ignore the consequences of actions' and the other: 'Judge actions by their consequences and make these the criterion of right and good' are both alike maxims of the abstract Understanding."[27] The twin abstractions Hegel wishes to avoid are lives so separated that one can limit the responsibilities of each to the deliberate and necessary consequences of what it has desired or conceived of, and a history that is one of equally unmerited failures and successes, and which consequently labels human beings glorious or infamous according to the external accidents which have come to deface or embellish what they have done. What he has in mind is the moment when the internal becomes external, that turning or veering by which we pass into others and the world as the world and others pass into us. In other words, action. By action, I make myself responsible for everything; I accept the aid of external accidents just as I accept their betrayals—"the transformation of necessity into contingence and vice versa."[28] I mean to be master not only of my intentions, but also of what events are going to make of them. I take the world and others as they are. I take myself as I am and I answer for all. "*To act is . . . to deliver oneself up to this law.*"[29] Action makes the event its own to such an extent that the botched crime is punished more lightly than the successful one, and Oedipus thinks of himself as a parricide and an incestuous person, even though he is so in fact only. Confronted with the folly of action, which assumes responsibility for the course of events, one may be tempted to conclude with equal justice that we are all guilty—since to act or even to live is already to accept the risk of infamy along with the chance for glory, and that we are all innocent—since nothing, not even crime, has been willed ex nihilo, no one having chosen to be born. But beyond these philosophies of the internal and the external before which all is equivalent, what Hegel suggests (since when all is said and done there is a difference between the valid and the invalid, and between what we accept and what we refuse) is a judgment of the attempt, of the undertaking, or of the *work*. Not a judgment of the intention or the consequences only, but of the use which we have made of our good will, and of the way in which we have evaluated the factual situation. What judges a human is not the intention and it is not the fact; it is that he or she has or has not made values pass into the facts. When this happens, the sense of the action does not exhaust itself in the situation which has occasioned it, or in some vague judgment of value; the action remains as an exemplary type and will survive in other situations in another appearance. It opens a field. Sometimes it even institutes a world. In any case it outlines a future. History according to Hegel is this maturation of a future in the present, not the sacrifice of the present to an unknown future; and the rule of action for him is not to be efficacious at any cost, but to be first of all fecund.

The polemics against "horizontal transcendence" in the name of "vertical transcendence" (admitted or simply regretted) are thus no less unjust toward Hegel than toward Christianity. And by throwing overboard along with history not only, as they think, a blood-smeared idol, but also the duty to make principles pass into things, they have the drawback of reintroducing a false simplicity which is no remedy for the abuses of the dialectic. Both the pessimism of the neo-Marxists and the laziness of non-Marxist thought, today as always one another's accomplice, present the dialectic—within and without us—as a power of lying and failure, a transformation of good into evil, and an inevitable disappointment. According to Hegel, this is only one side of the dialectic. It is also something like a grace in events which draws us away from evil toward the good, and which, for example, throws us toward the universal when we think we are pursuing only our own interest. The dialectic is, Hegel said approximately, *a movement which itself creates its course and returns to itself,* and thus a movement which has no other guide but its own initiative and which nevertheless does not escape outside itself but intersects itself and confirms itself across great distances. By another name, this was what we call the phenomenon of expression, which gathers itself up and launches itself again through a mystery of rationality. And we would undoubtedly recover the concept of history in the true sense of the term if we were to get used to modeling it after the example of the arts and language. For the fact of the intimacy of one expression to every expression, their belonging to one sole order, brings about the junction of the individual and the universal. The central fact to which the Hegelian dialectic returns in a hundred and one ways is that we do not have to choose between the *pour soi* and the *pour autrui,* between thought according to us and according to others, but that at the moment of expression the other to whom I address myself and I who express myself are linked together without concessions. The others such as they are (or will be) are not the sole judges of what I do. If I wanted to deny myself for their benefit, I would deny them too as "selves." They are worth exactly what I am worth, and all the powers I give them I give simultaneously to myself. I submit myself to the judgment of another *who is himself worthy of that which I have attempted,* that is to say, in the last analysis, to the judgment of a peer whom I myself have chosen. History is the judge—not history as the power of a moment or of a century, but history as the inscription and accumulation, beyond the limits of countries and epochs, of what, given the situation, we have done and said that is most true and valuable. Others will judge what I have done, because I painted in the realm of the visible and spoke for those who have ears—but neither art nor politics consists in pleasing or flattering them. What they expect of the artist or of the politician is that he draw them toward values in which they will only later recognize their values. The painter or the politician forms others much more often than he follows them. The public he aims at is not given; it is precisely the one which his work will elicit. The others he thinks of are not empirical "others," defined by what they expected of him at this moment. He thinks even less of *humanity* conceived of as a species which possesses "human dignity" or "the honor of being a human" as other species have a carapace or an air bladder. No, his concern is with others who have become such that he is able to live with them. The history that the writer participates in (and the less he thinks about "making history"—about making his mark in the history of letters—and honestly produces *his* work, the more he will participate) is not a power before which he must bend his knee. It is the perpetual conversation carried on between all spoken words and all valid actions, each in turn contesting and confirming the other, and each re-creating all the others. The appeal to the judgment of history is not an appeal to the complacency of the public (and even less, it must be said, an appeal to the lay public). It is inseparable from the inner certainty of having said what, in the things, waited to be said and what consequently could not fail to be understood by x. "I shall be read in one hundred years," Stendhal thinks. This means that he wants to be read, but also that he is willing to wait a century, and that his freedom invites a world as yet in limbo to become as free as he is by recognizing as acquired what he had to invent. This pure call to history is an invocation of truth, which is never created by what is inscribed in history, but which, insofar as it is truth, requires that inscription. It dwells not only in literature or art but also in every undertaking in life. Except perhaps in the case of some wretched souls who think only of winning or of being right, all action and all love are haunted by the hope for an account which will transform them into their truth—the coming of the day it will finally be known just what the situation was. Was it one person's reserve hiding under an apparent respect for others which one day definitively put the other off, who reflected that reserve back, magnified one hundredfold, or was the die cast from that moment on, and that impossible love . . . ? Perhaps this hope for a final, clear accounting will forever be in some way disappointed. People borrow from one another so constantly that each movement of our will and thought receives its impetus from contact with others, so that in this sense it is impossible to have more than a rough idea of what is due to each individual. It is nevertheless true that this desire for a total manifestation animates life as it does literature, and that beyond the petty motives it is this desire which makes the writer want to be read, sometimes prompts people to become writers, and in any case makes them speak, makes everyone want to account for him or herself in the eyes of *x*—which means that everyone thinks of his life and all lives as something that can recounted in all the senses of the word, as a story. The true history thus gets its life entirely from us. It is in our present that it gets the force to make everything else present. The other whom I respect gets his life from me as I get mine from him. A philosophy of history does not take away any of my rights or initiatives. It simply adds to my obligations as a solitary person the obligation to understand situations other than my own and to create a path between my life and that of others, that is, to express myself. Through the action of culture, I install myself in lives which are not mine. I confront them, I make one known to the other, I make them co-possible in an order of truth, I make myself responsible for all of them, and I create a universal life, just as by the thick and living presence of my body, in one fell swoop I install myself in space. And like the functioning of the body, that of words or paintings remains obscure to me. The words, lines, and colors which express me come out of me as gestures. They are torn from me by what I want to say as my gestures are by what I want to do. In this sense, there is in all expression a spontaneity which will not take orders, not even those which I would like to give to myself. Words, even in the art of prose, carry the speaker and the hearer into a common universe by drawing both toward a new meaning through their power to designate in excess of their accepted definition, through the muffled life they have led and continue to lead in us, and through what Ponge[30] appropriately called their "semantic thickness" and Sartre their "signifying soil." This spontaneity of language which unites us is not a command, and the history which it establishes is not an external idol: it is ourselves with our roots, our growth, and, as we say, the fruits of our toil.

Perception, history, expression—it is only by bringing together these three problems that we can rectify Malraux's analyses in keeping with their own direction. And, at the same time, we shall be able to see why it is legitimate to treat painting as a language. This way of dealing with the problem will emphasize a perceptual sense which is captured in the visible configuration of the painting and yet capable of gathering up a series of antecedent expressions into an eternity always to be redone. The comparison benefits not only our analysis of painting but also that of language. For it will perhaps lead us to detect beneath spoken language an operant or speaking language whose words live a little-known life and unite with and separate from one another as their lateral or indirect meaning demands, even though these relations seem *evident* to us once the expression is accomplished. The transparency of spoken language, that brave clarity of the word that is only sound and the sense that is only sense, the property it apparently has of extracting the sense from signs and isolating it in its pure state (which is perhaps simply the anticipation of several different formulations in which it would really remain *the same*), and its presumed power of recapitulating and enclosing a whole process of expression in one sole act—are these not simply the highest point of a tacit and implicit accumulation of the same sort as that of painting?

* * *

Like a painting, a novel expresses tacitly. Its subject matter, like that of a painting, can be recounted. But what counts is not so much Julien Sorel's trip to Verrières and his attempt to kill Mme de Rênal after he learns she has betrayed him; what counts is that silence, that dreamlike journey, that unthinking certitude, and that eternal resolution which follow the news. Now these things are nowhere *said*. There is no need of a "Julien thought" or a "Julien wished." In order to express them, Stendhal had only to slide himself into Julien and make objects, obstacles, means, and chance occurrences appear before our eyes with the swiftness of the journey. He had only to decide to recount in one page instead of five. That brevity, that unusual proportion of things omitted to things said, is not even the result of a *choice*. Consulting his own sensitivity to others, Stendhal suddenly found an imaginary body for Julien which was more agile than his own body. As if in a second life, he made the trip to Verrières according to a cadence of cold passion which chose for him the visible and the invisible, what was to be said and what was to remain unspoken. The desire to kill is thus not in the words at all. It is between them, in the hollows of space, time, and meanings they mark out, as movement at the cinema is between the immobile images which follow one another. The novelist speaks for his reader, and every person to every other, the language of the initiated—initiated into the world and into the universe of possibilities confined in a human body and a human life. What he has to say he presumes known. He installs himself in a character's behavior and gives the reader only a suggestion of it, its nervous and peremptory trace in the surroundings. If the author is a writer, that is, if he is capable of finding the elisions and caesuras which indicate the behavior, the reader responds to his call and joins him at the virtual center of the writing, *even if neither one of them is aware of it*. The novel as a report of events and a statement of ideas, theses, or conclusions (as manifest or prosaic meaning) and the novel as an expression of style (as oblique and latent meaning) are in a simple relationship of homonymy. Marx clearly understood this when he adopted Balzac. We can be sure that there was no question here of some return to liberalism. Marx meant that a certain way of *making visible* the world of money and the conflicts of modern society was worth more than Balzac's theses—even political—and that this vision, once acquired, would have its consequences, with or without Balzac's consent.

It is certainly right to condemn formalism, but it is ordinarily forgotten that its error is not that it esteems form too much, but that it esteems it so little that it detaches it from sense. In this respect formalism is no different than a literature of "subject matter," which also separates the sense of the work from its configuration. The true contrary of formalism is a good theory of style, or of speech, which puts both above "technique" or "device." Speech is not a means in the service of an external end. It contains its own rule of usage, ethics, and view of the world, as a gesture sometimes bears the whole truth about a human. This living use of language, ignored by both formalism and the literature of "subject matter," is literature itself as quest and acquisition. A language which only sought to reproduce reality itself would exhaust its instructive power in factual statements. On the contrary, a language which gives our perspectives on things and hollows out relief in them opens up a discussion that goes beyond the language and itself invites further investigation. What is irreplaceable in the work of art, what makes it, far more than a means of pleasure, a spiritual organ whose analogue is found in all productive philosophical or political thought, is the fact that it contains better than ideas, *matrices of ideas*—providing us with emblems whose sense we never stop developing. Precisely because it installs itself and installs us in a world we do not have the key to, the work of art teaches us to see and ultimately gives us something to think about as no analytical work can; for when we analyze an object, we find only what we have put into it. What is hazardous in literary communication, and ambiguous and irreducible to the theme in all the great works of art, is not a provisional weakness which we might hope to overcome. It is the price we must pay to have a literature, that is, a conquering language which introduces us to unfamiliar perspectives instead of confirming us in our own. We would not see anything if our eyes did not give us the means of catching, questioning, and giving form to an indefinite number of configurations of space and color. We would not do anything if our body did not enable us to leap over all the neural and muscular means of locomotion in order to move to the goal. Literary language fills the same kind of office. In the same imperious and brief way, the writer transports us without transitions or preparations from the world that is already said to something else. And as our body guides us among things only on condition that we stop analyzing it and make use of it, language is literary, that is, productive, only on condition that we stop asking justifications of it at each instant and follow it where it goes, letting the words and all the means of expression of the book be enveloped by that halo of meaning that they owe to their singular arrangement, and all that is written veer toward a second value where it almost rejoins the mute radiance of painting. The sense of a novel too is perceptible at first only as a *coherent deformation* imposed upon the visible. Nor will it ever be otherwise. Criticism may compare one novelist's mode of expression with another's and incorporate one type of narrative in a family of other possible ones. This work is legitimate only if it is preceded by a perception of the novel in which the particularities of "technique" merge with those of the overall project and sense, and if it is only intended to explain to us what we ourselves have already perceived. As the description of a face does not allow us to imagine it, though it may specify certain of its characteristics, the language of the critic, who claims to possess the object of his criticism, does not replace that of the novelist, who shows us what is true or makes it show through without touching it. It is essential to what is true to be presented first and forever in a movement which decenters our image of the world, distends it, and draws it toward fuller sense. It is thus that the auxiliary line introduced into a geometrical figure opens the road to new relations. It is thus that the work of art works and will always work upon us—as long as there are works of art.

But these remarks are far from exhausting the question. There are still the exact forms of language—and philosophy—to be considered. We may wonder whether their ambition to recover the slippery hold on our experience that literature gives us and gain actual possession of what is said does not express the essence of language much better than literature does. This problem would involve logical analyses which cannot be considered here. Without dealing with it completely, we can at least situate it and show that in any case no language ever wholly frees itself from the precariousness of the silent forms of expression, reabsorbs its own contingency, and melts away to make the things themselves appear; that in this sense the privilege language enjoys over painting or the practices of life remains relative; and, finally, that expression is not one of the curiosities that the mind may propose to examine but is its existence in act.

Certainly one who decides to write takes an attitude in respect to the past which is his alone. All culture continues the past. Today's parents see their childhood in their own children's and adopt toward them the behavior of their own parents. Or, through ill will, they go to the opposite extreme. If they have been subjected to an authoritarian upbringing, they practice a permissive one. And by this detour they often come back to tradition, for in twenty-five years the vertiginous heights of freedom will bring the child back to a system of security and make him an authoritarian father. The novelty of the arts of expression is that they bring tacit culture out of its mortal circle. Even the artist is not content to continue the past by veneration or revolt: he begins its attempt again on his or her own terms. One reason why the painter takes up his brush is that in a sense the art of painting still remains to be done. But the arts of language go much further toward true creation. Precisely because painting is always something to be done, the works which the new painter produces will be added to already created works. The new do not make the old useless, nor do they expressly contain them; they rival them. Today's painting denies the past too deliberately to be able truly to free itself from it. It can only forget it while exploiting it. The cost of its novelty is that in making what came before it seem an unsuccessful effort, it foreshadows a different painting tomorrow which will make it seem in turn another unsuccessful effort. Thus painting as a whole presents itself as an abortive effort to say something which still remains to be said. Although the writer is not content simply to extend existing language, he is no more anxious to replace it by an idiom which, like a painting, is sufficient unto itself and closed in upon its intimate signification. If you wish, he destroys ordinary language, but by realizing it. The given language, which penetrates him through and through and already offers a general representation of his most secret thoughts, does not stand before him as an enemy. It is entirely *ready* to convert everything new he stands for as a writer into an acquisition. It is as if it had been made for him, and he for it; as if the task of speaking to which he was destined in learning the language were more legitimately him than his heartbeat; and as if the established language called into existence, along with him, one of *his* possibilities. Painting fulfills a vow of the past. It has the power to act in the name of the past, but it does not contain it in its manifest state. It is memory for us, if we happen to know the history of painting, but it is not memory "for itself"—it does not claim to totalize what has made it possible. Speech, not content to push beyond the past, claims to recapitulate, retrieve, and contain it in substance. And since without repeating it textually speech could not give us the past in its presence, it makes the past undergo a preparation which is what defines language—it offers us the *truth* of it. It is not content to push the past aside in making a place for itself in the world: it wants to preserve it in its spirit or its sense. Thus speech twists back upon itself, takes itself up, and gets possession of itself once more. There is a critical, philosophical, universal use of language which claims to retrieve things as they are—whereas painting transforms them into painting—to retrieve everything, both language itself and the use other doctrines have made of it. From the moment he seeks the truth, the philosopher does not think that it had to wait for him in order to be true; he seeks it as what has always been true for everyone. It is essential to truth to be integral, whereas no painting has ever pretended to be. The Spirit of Painting appears only in the museum, because it is a Spirit external to itself. Speech, on the contrary, tries to gain possession of itself and conquer the secret of its own inventions. Man does not paint painting, but he speaks about speech, and the spirit of language wants to depend upon nothing but itself. A painting makes its charm dwell from the start in a dreaming eternity where we easily rejoin it many centuries later, even without knowing the history of the dress, furnishings, utensils, and civilization whose stamp it bears. Writing, on the contrary, relinquishes its most enduring sense to us only through a precise history which we must have some knowledge of. *The Provincial Letters* put the theological discussions of the seventeenth century back in the present; *The Red and the Black,* the gloom of the Restoration. But painting pays curiously for this immediate access to the enduring that it grants itself, for it is subject much more than writing to the passage of time. The pleasure of an anachronism is mixed with our contemplation of paintings, whereas Stendhal and Pascal are entirely in the present. To the exact extent that it renounces the hypocritical eternity of art and, boldly confronting time, displays it instead of vaguely evoking it, literature surges forth victorious and founds time on meaning. Although the statues of Olympia play a great part in attaching us to Greece, they also foster (in the state in which they have come down to us—bleached, broken, detached from the work as a whole) a fraudulent myth about Greece. They cannot resist time as a manuscript, even incomplete, torn, and almost illegible, does. Heraclitus's writing casts light for us as no broken statues can, because the meaning in it is deposited and concentrated in another way than theirs is in them, and because nothing equals the ductility of speech. In short, language speaks, and the voices of painting are the voices of silence.

This is because the statement claims to unveil the thing itself; language goes beyond itself toward what it signifies. It is of no avail that (as Saussure explains) each word draws its sense from all the others, the fact remains that at the moment it occurs the task of expressing is no longer deferred and referred to other words—it is accomplished, and we understand something. Saussure may show that each act of expression becomes significant only as a modulation of a general system of expression and only insofar as it is differentiated from other linguistic gestures. The marvel is that before Saussure we did not know anything about this, and that we forget it again each time we speak—as this very moment, as we speak of Saussure's ideas. This proves that each partial act of expression, as an act common to the whole of the given language, is not limited to expending an expressive power accumulated in the language, but re-creates both the power and the language by making us verify in the obviousness of the given and received sense the power that speaking subjects have of going beyond signs toward their sense. Signs do not simply evoke other signs for us and so on without end, and language is not like a prison we are locked into or a guide we must blindly follow; for at the crossroads of all these linguistic gestures, what they mean to say appears—to which we have been given such total access that it seems to us we no longer need the linguistic gestures to refer to it. Thus, when we compare language to the silent forms of expression such as gestures or painting, we must point out that unlike these forms language is not content to sketch out directions, vectors, a "coherent deformation," or a tacit sense on the surface of the world, exhausting itself as animal "intelligence" does in kaleidoscopically producing a new landscape for action. Language is not just the replacement of one sense by another, but the substitution of equivalent sense. The new structure is given as already present in the old, the latter subsists in it, and the past is now understood.

There is no doubt that language is the presumption to a total accumulation; and present speech confronts the philosopher with the problem of this provisional self-possession, which is provisional but which is not nothing. The fact remains that language could deliver up the thing itself only if it ceased to be in time and in situation. Hegel is the only one who thinks that his system contains the truth of all the others, and one who knew the others only through Hegel's synthesis would not know them at all. Even if Hegel were true from one end to the other, we cannot dispense with reading the "pre-Hegelians," for he can contain them only "in what they affirm." By what they deny they offer the reader another situation of thought which is not eminently contained in Hegel—which is not there at all—and in which Hegel is visible in a light which he is himself unaware of. Hegel is the only one to think that he has no existence "for others," and that he is in the eyes of others exactly what he knows himself to be. Even if it is admitted that there has been progress from them to him, there may be a passage of Descartes' *Meditations* or Plato's dialogues—and precisely because of the "naivetes" that held them back from Hegel's "truth"—a contact with things, a spark of meaning that we cannot recognize in Hegel unless we have already found it in the originals, to which we must always return, if only to understand Hegel. Hegel is the museum. He is, if you wish, all philosophies, but deprived of their finiteness and power of impact, embalmed, transformed, he believes, into themselves, but really transformed into Hegel. We only have to see how a truth wastes away when it is integrated into different ones (how the cogito, for example, in going from Descartes to the Cartesians, becomes almost a listlessly repeated ritual) to agree that the synthesis does not effectively contain all past systems of thought, that it is not all that they have been, that it is never a synthesis at once both "in and for itself"—that is, a synthesis which in the same movement is and knows, is what it knows, knows what it is, preserves and suppresses, realizes and destroys. If Hegel means that as the past becomes distant it changes into its sense, and that we can, after the fact, trace an intelligible history of thought, he is right; but on condition that in this synthesis each term remains the whole of the world at the date considered, and that in linking philosophies together we keep them all in their place like so many open meanings and let an exchange of anticipations and metamorphoses subsist between them. The sense of philosophy is the sense of a genesis. Consequently, it could not possibly be totalized outside of time, and it is still expression. More correctly, outside of philosophy, the writer can have the feeling of attaining the things themselves only through the use of language and not beyond language. Mallarmé himself was well aware that nothing would fall from his pen if he remained absolutely faithful to his vow to say everything without leaving anything unsaid, and that he was able to write minor books only by giving up the Book which would dispense with all the others. The meaning without any sign, the thing itself—the height of clarity—would be the disappearance of all clarity. And whatever clarity we can have is not at the beginning of language, like a golden age, but at the end of its efforts. Language and the system of truth do displace our life's center of gravity by suggesting that we cross-check and take up our operations in terms of one another, in such a way that each one shifts into all of them and they seem independent of the step-by-step formulations which we first gave them. They do thereby reduce the other expressive operations to the rank of "mute" and subordinate ones. Yet language and the system of truth are not themselves lacking in reticence, and sense is not so much designated by them as it is implied by their word structure.

We must therefore say the same thing about language in relation to sense that Simone de Beauvoir says about the body in relation to mind: it is neither first nor second. No one has ever made the body simply a means or an instrument, or maintained, for example, that one can love by principles. And since it is no more true that the body loves all by itself, we may say that it does everything and nothing, that it is and is not ourselves.

Neither end nor means, always involved in matters which go beyond it, always jealous nevertheless of its autonomy, it is powerful enough to oppose any end which is merely deliberate, but it has none to propose to us if we finally turn toward it and consult it. Sometimes—and then we have the feeling of being ourselves—it lets itself be animated and takes upon itself a life which is not simply its own. Then it is happy and spontaneous, and we with it. Similarly, language is not at the service of sense, and yet it does not govern sense. There is no subordination between them. Here no one commands and no one obeys. What we *mean* is not before us, outside all speech, as a pure meaning. It is only the excess of what we live over what has already been said. With our apparatus of expression we install ourselves in a situation to which the apparatus is sensitive, we confront it with the situation, and our statements are only the final balance of these exchanges. Political thought itself is of this order. It is always the elucidation of a historical perception in which all our knowledge, all our experiences, and all our values simultaneously come into play—and of which our theses are only the schematic formulation. All action and all knowledge which do not go through this elaboration, and which seek to set up values which have not been embodied in our individual or collective history (*or*—what comes down to the same thing—which seek to choose means by a calculus and a wholly technical process), fall short of the problems they are trying to solve. Personal life, expression, understanding, and history advance obliquely and not straight toward ends or concepts. What we strive for too reflectively eludes us, while values and ideas come forth abundantly to him who, in his meditative life, has learned to free their spontaneous source.

14

An Unpublished Text
by Maurice Merleau-Ponty

A Prospectus of His Work

The text given below was sent to me by Merleau-Ponty at the time of his candidacy to the Collège de France, when I was putting together a report of his qualifications for presentation to the assembly of professors.[1] In this report, Merleau-Ponty traces his past and future as a philosopher in a continuous line, and outlines the perspectives of his future studies from "The Origin of Truth" to "Transcendental Man." In reading these unpublished and highly interesting pages, one keenly regrets the death which brutally interrupted the élan of a profound thought in full possession of itself and about to fulfill itself in a series of original works which would have been landmarks in contemporary French philosophy.—Martial Guéroult

We never cease living in the world of perception, but we go beyond it in critical thought—almost to the point of forgetting the contribution of perception to our idea of truth. For critical thought encounters only *statements* which it discusses, accepts, or rejects. Critical thought has broken with the naive evidence of *things,* and when it affirms, it is because it no longer finds any means of denial. However necessary this activity of verification may be, specifying criteria and demanding from our experience its credentials of validity, it does not give an account of our contact with the perceived world which is simply before us, beneath the level of the verified true and of the false. Nor does critical thought even define the positive steps of thought or its most valid accomplishments. My first two works sought to restore the world of perception. My works in preparation would like to show how communication with others and thought take up and go beyond the perception which initiated us to the truth.

The perceiving mind is an incarnated mind. I have sought, first of all, to reestablish the roots of the mind in its body and in its world, going against doctrines which treat perception as a simple result of the action of external things on our body as well as against those which insist on the autonomy of becoming conscious. These philosophies have the following in common: they forget—in favor of pure exteriority or pure interiority— the corporeal insertion of the mind, the ambiguous relation which we entertain with our body and, correlatively, with perceived things. When one attempts, as I have in *The Structure of Behavior,* to trace out, on the basis of modern psychology and physiology, the relationships which obtain between the perceiving organism and its milieu, one clearly finds that they are not those of an automatic machine which needs an outside agent to set off its preestablished mechanisms. And it is equally clear that one does not account for this fact better by superimposing a pure, contemplative consciousness on the body, conceived as a thing. In the conditions of life—if not in the laboratory—the organism is less sensitive to certain isolated physical and chemical agents than to the "constellation" which they form and to the whole situation which they define. Behaviors reveal a sort of prospective activity in the organism, as if it were oriented toward the sense of certain elementary situations, as if it entertained familiar relations with them, as if there were an "a priori of the organism," privileged conducts and laws of internal equilibrium which predisposed the organism to certain relations with its milieu. At this level there is no question yet of a genuine becoming conscious or of an intentional activity. Moreover, the organism's prospective capability is exercised only within defined limits and depends on precise, local conditions. The functioning of the central nervous system presents us with the same kind of paradoxes. In its modern forms, the theory of cerebral localizations has profoundly changed the relation of function to substrate. It no longer assigns, for instance, a preestablished mechanism to each perceptual behavior. "Coordinating centers," of which the theory speaks, are no longer considered as storehouses of "cerebral traces," and their functioning is qualitatively different from one case to another, depending on the chromatic nuance to be evoked and the perceptual structure to be realized. Finally, this functioning reflects all the subtlety and all the variety of perceptual relationships. The perceiving organism seems to show us a Cartesian mixture of the soul with the body. Higher-order behaviors give a new sense to the life of the organism, but the mind here disposes of only a limited freedom; it needs simpler activities in order to stabilize itself in durable institutions and to realize itself truly in them. Perceptual behavior emerges from these relations to a situation and to a milieu which are not the workings of a pure, knowing subject.

In my work on the *Phenomenology of Perception* we are no longer present at the advent of perceptual behaviors; rather, we install ourselves in them in order to pursue the analysis of this exceptional relation between the subject, its body, and its world. For contemporary psychology and psychopathology the body is no longer merely *one of the objects in the world,* under the gaze of a separated mind. The body moves to the side of the subject; it is our *point of view on the world,* the place where the mind invests itself in a certain physical and historical situation. As Descartes once said profoundly, the soul is not merely in the body like a pilot in his ship; it is wholly intermingled with the body. The body, in turn, is wholly animated, and all its functions contribute to the perception of objects—an activity long considered by philosophy to be pure knowledge. We grasp external space through our bodily situation. A "corporeal or postural schema" gives us at every moment a global, practical, and implicit notion of the relation between our body and things, of our hold on them. A bundle of possible movements, or "motor projects," radiates from us to our surroundings. Our body is not in space like things; it inhabits or haunts space. It applies itself to space like a hand to an instrument, and this is why, when we want to move about, we do not move the body as we move an object. We transport it without instruments as if by a kind of magic, since it is ours and because through it we have access directly to space. For us the body is much more than an instrument or a means; it is our expression in the world, the visible form of our intentions. Even our most secret affective movements, those most deeply tied to the humoral infrastructure, help to shape our perception of things.

Now, if perception is thus the common act of all our motor and affective functions, no less than the sensory, we must rediscover the structure of the perceived world through a process similar to that of an archaeologist—for the structure of the perceived world is buried under the sedimentations of later knowledge. Then we would see that sensory qualities are not opaque, indivisible "givens" which are simply exhibited to a distant consciousness, about which classical conceptions spoke, and that colors (each surrounded by an affective atmosphere which psychologists have been able to study and define) are themselves different modalities of our coexistence with the world. We would see that spatial forms or distances are not so much relations between different points of objective space than relations between them and a perspectival center, which is our body—in short, that these relations are different ways for external stimuli to test, to solicit, and to vary our grasp on the world, our anchorage in the horizontal and vertical of the place, in a here-and-now. We would see that perceived things, unlike geometrical objects, are not bounded entities whose laws of construction our intelligence possesses a priori, but that they are open, inexhaustible wholes which we recognize through a certain style of development, although we are never able, in principle, to explore them entirely, and even though they never give us more than profiles and perspectival views of themselves. Finally, we see that the perceived world, in its turn, is not a pure object of thought without fissures or lacunae; it is, rather, like a universal style in which all perceptual beings participate. While the world no doubt coordinates these perceptual beings, we can never presume that its work is finished. Our world, as Malebranche said, is an "unfinished task."

If we now wish to define a subject capable of this perceptual experience, it obviously will not be a self-transparent thought, absolutely present to itself without the interference of its body and its history. The perceiving subject is not this absolute thinker; rather, it functions according to a natal pact between our body and the world, between ourselves and our body. The perceiving subject is like a continued birth, the subject to whom a physical and historical situation has been given to run, and it is this subject again at each instant. Each incarnate subject is like an open notebook in which we do not yet know what will be written. Or it is like a new language; we do not know what works it will produce but only that, once it has appeared, it cannot fail to say little or much, to have a history and a sense. The very productivity or freedom of human life, far from denying our situation, utilizes it and turns it into a means of expression.

This remark brings us to a series of further studies which I have undertaken since 1945 and which will definitively fix the philosophical direction of my earlier works while they, in turn, determine the route and the method of these later studies. I found in the experience of the perceived world a new type of relation between the mind and truth. The evidence of the perceived thing lies in its concrete aspect, in the very texture of its qualities, and in the equivalence among all its sensible properties—which caused Cézanne to say that one should be able to paint even odors. Before our undivided existence the world is true; it exists. The unity, the articulations of both are intermingled. And this is to say that we have a global notion of the world whose inventory is never complete, and that we experience in the world a truth which shows through and envelops us rather than being held and circumscribed by our mind. Now if we consider, above the perceived, the field of knowledge properly so called—i.e., the field in which the mind seeks to possess the truth, to define its objects itself, and thus to attain to a universal knowledge, not tied to the particularities of our situation—we must ask: Does not the order of the perceived take on the form of a simple appearance? Is not pure understanding a new source of knowledge, in comparison with which our perceptual familiarity with the world is only a rough, unformed sketch? We are obliged to answer these questions first with a theory of truth and then with a theory of intersubjectivity, both of which I have already touched upon in essays such as "Cézanne's Doubt," "The Novel and Metaphysics," and, on the philosophy of history, in *Humanism and Terror* [1947]. But the philosophical foundations of these essays are still to be rigorously elaborated. I am now working on two books dealing with a theory of truth.

It seems to me that knowledge and the communication with others which it presupposes not only are original formations with respect to the perceptual life, but they also preserve and continue our perceptual life even while transforming it. Knowledge and communication sublimate rather than suppress our incarnation, and the characteristic operation of the mind is in the movement by which we take up our corporeal existence and use it to symbolize instead of merely to coexist. This metamorphosis lies in the double function of our body. Through its "sensory fields" and its whole organization the body is, so to speak, predestined to model itself on the natural aspects of the world. But as an active body, active insofar as it is capable of gestures, of expression, and finally of language, it turns back on the world to signify it. As the observation of apraxics shows, there is in man, superimposed upon actual space with its self-identical points, a "virtual space" in which the spatial values that a point *would receive* (for any other position of our corporeal coordinates) are also recognized. A system of correspondence is established between our spatial situation and that of others, and each one comes to symbolize all the others. This "taking up," which inserts our factual situation as a particular case within the system of other possible situations, begins as soon as we *show* by pointing the finger at a point in space. For the gesture of designation, which the animals precisely do not understand, supposes that we are already installed in the virtual—at the end of the line prolonging our finger in a centrifugal and cultural space. This mimic usage of our body is not yet a conception, since it does not cut us off from our corporeal situation; on the contrary, it takes on all its sense. It leads us to a concrete theory of the mind which will show the mind in a relationship of reciprocal exchange with the instruments which it uses, but uses only while rendering to them what it has received from them and more.

In a general way, expressive gestures (in which the science of physiognomy sought in vain for the sufficient signs of emotional states) have a univocal sense only with respect to the situation which they underline and punctuate. But like phonemes, which have no sense by themselves, expressive gestures have a diacritical value: they indicate the constitution of a symbolical system capable of redesigning an infinite number of situations. They are a first language. And reciprocally, language can be treated as a gesticulation so varied, so precise, so systematic, and capable of so many intersections that the internal structure of the statement can ultimately agree only with the mental situation to which it responds and of which it becomes an unequivocal sign. The sense of language, like that of gestures, thus does not lie in the elements from which it is made. The sense is their common intention, and the spoken phrase is understood only if the hearer, following the "verbal chain," goes beyond each of its links in the direction that they all designate together. It follows that our thought, even when it is solitary, does not stop using the language which supports it, which rescues it from the transitory, and which throws it back again. Cassirer said that thought was the "shuttlecock" of language. And yet it follows that, taken piece by piece, language does not yet contain its sense, that all communication supposes in the listener a creative reenactment of what is heard. Therefore, language leads us to a thought which is no longer ours alone, to a thought which is presumptively universal, though this is never the universality of a pure concept which would be identical for every mind. It is rather the call which a situated thought addresses to other thoughts, equally situated, and each one responds to the call with its own resources. An examination of the domain of the algorithm would show there too, I believe, the same strange function which is at work in the so-called inexact forms of language. Especially when it is a question of conquering a new domain for exact thought, the most formal thought is always referred to some qualitatively defined mental situation from which it extracts the sense only by applying itself to the configuration of the problem. The transformation is never a simple analysis, and thought is never more than relatively formal.

Since I intend to treat this program more fully in my work "The Origin of Truth," I have approached it less directly in a partially written book dealing with literary language. In this area it is easier to show that language is never the mere clothing of a thought which otherwise possesses itself in full clarity. The sense of a book is given, in the first instance, not so much by its ideas as by a systematic and unexpected variation of the modes of language and of the narrative, or of the existing literary forms. This accent, this particular modulation of speech—if the expression is successful—is assimilated little by little by the reader, and it gives him access to a thought to which he was until then indifferent or even opposed. Communication in literature is not the simple appeal on the part of the writer to meanings which would be part of an a priori of the mind; rather, communication arouses these meanings in the mind through enticement and a kind of oblique action. In the writer, thought does not control language from the outside; the writer is himself a kind of new idiom, constructing itself, inventing ways of expression, and diversifying itself according to its own sense. Perhaps poetry is only that part of literature where this autonomy is ostentatiously displayed. All great prose is also a re-creation of the signifying instrument, henceforth manipulated according to a new syntax. Prosaic writing confines itself to using, through accepted signs, the meanings already installed in a given culture. Great prose is the art of capturing a sense which until then had never been objectified and of rendering it accessible to everyone who speaks the same language. When a writer is no longer capable of thus founding a new universality and of taking the risk of communicating, he has outlived his time. It seems to me that we could also say of other institutions that they have ceased to live when they show themselves incapable of carrying on a poetry of human relations—that is, the call of each individual freedom to all others. Hegel said that the Roman state was the prose of the world. I shall entitle my book "Introduction to the Prose of the World." In this work I shall elaborate the category of prose beyond the confines of literature to give it a sociological meaning.

These studies on expression and truth approach, from the epistemological side, the general problem of human interrelations—which will be the major topic of my later studies. The linguistic relations among men should help us understand the more general order of symbolic relations and of institutions, which assure the exchange not only of thoughts but of all types of values, the coexistence of men within a culture and, beyond its limits, within one sole history. Interpreted in terms of symbolism, the concept of history seems to escape the disputes always directed to it because one ordinarily means by this word—whether to accept it or to reject it— an external power in the name of which men would be dispossessed of consciousness. History is no more external to us than language. There is a history of thought: that is, the succession of the works of the spirit (no matter how many detours we see in it) is really a single experience which develops of itself and in whose development, so to speak, truth capitalizes itself. In an analogous sense we can say that there is a history of humanity or, more simply, *a* humanity. In other words, granting all the periods of stagnation and retreat, human relations are able to grow, to change their avatars into lessons, to pick out the truth of their past in the present, to eliminate certain mysteries which render them opaque and thereby make themselves more translucent. The idea of a single history or of a logic of history is, in a sense, implied in the least human exchange, in the least social perception. For example, anthropology supposes that civilizations very different from ours are comprehensible to us, that they can be situated in relation to ours and vice versa, that all civilizations belong to the same universe of thought, since the least use of language implies an idea of truth. Also, we can never pretend to dismiss the adventures of history as something foreign to our present action, since even the most independent search for the most abstract truth has been and is a factor of history (the only one, perhaps, that we are sure is not disappointing). All human acts and all human creations constitute a single drama, and in this sense we are all saved or lost together. Our life is essentially universal. But this methodological rationalism is not to be confused with a dogmatic rationalism which eliminates historical contingency in advance by supposing a "World Spirit" (Hegel) behind the course of events. If it is necessary to say that there is a total history, one sole tissue tying together all the enterprises of simultaneous and successive civilizations, all the results of thought and all the facts of economics, it must not be in the guise of a historical idealism or materialism—one handing over the government of history to thought; the other, to matter. Because cultures are just so many coherent systems of symbols and because in each culture the modes of work, of human relations, of language and thought, even if not parallel at every moment, do not long remain separated, cultures can be compared and placed under a common denominator. What makes this connection of sense between each aspect of a culture and all the rest, as between all the episodes of history, is the permanent, harmonious thought of this plurality of beings who recognize one another as "creatures," even when some seek to enslave others, and who are so commonly situated that adversaries are often in a kind of complicity.

Our investigations should lead us finally to a reflection on this *transcendental man,* or this "natural light" common to all, which appears through the movement of history—to a reflection on this Logos which gives us the task of vocalizing a hitherto mute world. Finally, they should lead us to a study of the Logos of the perceived world which we encountered in our earliest studies in the evidence of things. Here we rejoin the classical questions of metaphysics, but by following a route which removes them from their character as *problems*—that is, as difficulties which could be solved cheaply through the use of a few metaphysical entities constructed for this purpose. The notions of Nature and Reason, for instance, far from explaining the metamorphoses which we have observed from perception up to the more complex modes of human exchange, make them incomprehensible. For by relating them to separated principles, these notions mask a constantly experienced moment, the moment when an existence becomes aware of itself, grasps itself, and expresses its own sense. The study of perception could only teach us a "bad ambiguity," a mixture of finitude and universality, of interiority and exteriority. But there is a "good ambiguity" in the phenomenon of expression, a spontaneity which accomplishes what appeared to be impossible when we observed only the separate elements, a spontaneity which gathers together the plurality of monads, the past and the present, nature and culture, into a single whole. To establish this wonder would be metaphysics itself and would at the same time give us the principle of an ethics.

Part 3

The Collège de France Period (1952–1961)

Epilogue to *Adventures of the Dialectic*

On that day, everything was possible . . . the future was
present . . . that is to say, time was no more . . . a lightning flash
and eternity.
— Michelet, *History of the French Revolution*, IV, i[1]

The question today is less of revolutionizing than of establishing
the revolutionary government.
— Correspondence of the Committee of Public Safety

Dialectic is not the idea of a reciprocal action, or that of the solidarity of
opposites and of their sublation. Dialectic is not a development which
starts itself again, or the cross-growth of a quality that establishes as a new
order a change which until then had been quantitative—these are consequences or aspects of the dialectic. But taken in themselves or as properties of being, these relationships are marvels, curiosities, or paradoxes.
They enlighten only when one grasps them in our experience, at the junction of a subject, of being, and of other subjects; between *those* opposites,
in *that* reciprocal action, in *that* relationship between an inside and an
outside, between the elements of *that* constellation, in *that* becoming,
which not only becomes but becomes for itself, there is room, without
contradiction and without magic, for relationships with double meanings,
for reversals, for opposite and inseparable truths, for sublations, for a perpetual genesis, for a plurality of levels or orders. There is dialectic only in
that type of being in which a junction of subjects occurs, being which is
not only a spectacle that each subject presents to itself for its own benefit
but which is rather their common residence, the place of their exchange
and of their reciprocal interpretation. The dialectic does not, as Sartre
claims, provide finality, that is to say, the presence of the whole in that
which, by its nature, exists in separate parts; rather, it provides the global

and primordial cohesion of a field of experience wherein each element opens onto the others. It is always conceived as the expression or truth of an experience in which the commerce of subjects with one another and with being was previously instituted. It is a thought which does not constitute the whole but which is situated in it. It has a past and a future which are not its own simple negation; it is incomplete so long as it does not pass into other perspectives and into the perspectives of others. Nothing is more foreign to it than the Kantian conception of an ideality of the world which is the same in everyone, just as the number two or the triangle is the same in every mind, outside of meetings or exchanges: the natural and human world is unique, not because it is parallelly constituted in everyone or because the "I think" is indiscernible in myself and in the other, but because our difference opens onto that world, because we are imitatable and participatable through each other in this relationship with it.

The adventures of the dialectic, the most recent of which we have retraced here, are errors through which it must pass, since it is in principle a thought with several centers and several points of entry, and because it needs time to explore them all. With the name "culture," Max Weber identified the primary coherence of all histories. Lukács believes it possible to enclose them all in a cycle which is closed when all meanings are found in a present reality, the proletariat. But this historical fact salvages universal history only because it was first "prepared" by philosophical consciousness and because it is the emblem of negativity. Thence comes the reproach of idealism that is made against Lukács; and the proletariat and revolutionary society as he conceives them are indeed ideas without historical equivalents. But what remains of the dialectic if one must give up reading history and deciphering in it the becoming-true of society? Nothing of it is left in Sartre. He holds as utopian this continued intuition which was to be confirmed every day by the development of action and of revolutionary society and even by a true knowledge of past history. To dialectical philosophy, to the truth that is glimpsed behind irreconcilable choices, he opposes the demand of an intuitive philosophy which wants to see all meanings immediately and simultaneously. There is no longer any ordered passage from one perspective to another, no completion of others in me and of me in others, for this is possible only in time, and an intuitive philosophy poses everything in the instant: the Other thus can be present to the I only as its pure negation. And certainly one gives the Other his due, one even gives him the absolute right to affirm his perspective, the I consents to this in advance. But it only consents: how *could it accompany* the Other in his existence? In Sartre there is a plurality of subjects but no intersubjectivity. Looked at closely, the absolute right that the I accords to the other is rather a duty. They are not joined in action, in the relative and the probable, but only in principles and on condition that the other stick rigorously to them, that he does credit to his name and to the absolute negation that it promises. The world and history are no longer a system with several points of entry but a sheaf of irreconcilable perspectives which never coexist and which are held together only by the hopeless heroism of the I.

Is it then the conclusion of these adventures that the dialectic was a myth? The illusion was only to precipitate into a historical fact—the proletariat's birth and growth—history's total meaning, to believe that history itself organized its own recovery, that the proletariat's power would be its own suppression, the negation of the negation. It was to believe that the proletariat was in itself the dialectic and that the attempt to put the proletariat in power, temporarily exempted from any dialectical judgment, could put the dialectic in power. It was to play the double game of truth and authoritarian practice in which the will ultimately loses consciousness of its revolutionary task and truth ceases to control its realization. Today, as a hundred years ago and as thirty-eight years ago, it remains true that no one by himself is subject nor is he free, that freedoms interfere with and require one another, that history is the history of their dispute, which is inscribed and visible in institutions, in civilizations, and in the wake of important historical actions, and that there is a way to understand and situate them, if not in a system with an exact and definitive hierarchy and in the perspective of a *true,* homogeneous, ultimate society, then at least as different episodes of a single life, where each one is an experience of that life and can pass into those who follow. What then is obsolete is not the dialectic but the pretension of terminating it in an end of history, in a permanent revolution, or in a regime which, being the contestation of itself, would no longer need to be contested from the outside and, in fact, would no longer have anything outside it.

We have already said something about the concept of the end of history, which is not so much Marxist as Hegelian and—even if one construes it with A. Kojève[2] as the end of humanity and the return to the cyclical life of nature—is an idealization of death and could not possibly convey Hegel's core thought. If one completely eliminates the concept of the end of history, then the concept of revolution is relativized; such is the meaning of "permanent revolution." It means that there is no definitive regime, that revolution is the regime of creative imbalance,[3] that there will always be other oppositions to sublate, that there must therefore always be an opposition within revolution. But how can one be sure that an internal opposition is not an opposition to revolution? We thus see the birth of a very singular institution: official criticism, which is the caricature of permanent revolution. One would be wrong to think that it is only a

ruse, a mask, or an application of Machiavelli's famous prescription which
teaches that one rules better through persuasion than through force and
that the summit of tyranny is seduction. It is probable that true demands
and true changes pass through this door. But it is also certain that they only
serve to make the apparatus's grip stronger and that, when it has become
an element of power, criticism must stop at the moment at which it becomes interesting, when it would evaluate, judge, and virtually contest the
power in its totality. In principle, then, this power is unaware of its truth—
the picture that those who do not exercise the power have of it. The truth
that it claims is only that of its intentions, and thus its truth becomes a general license for coercion, while the regime's practical necessities become
an adequate basis for affirmation. Truth and action destroy each other,
while dialectic asks that they sustain each other. As we said, this is a caricature of permanent revolution; and one may perhaps propose a return to
the original. But the question is to know whether there is an original, other
than in the realm of the imaginary; whether the revolutionary enterprise,
a violent enterprise directed toward putting a class in power and spilling
blood to do so, is not obliged, as Trotsky said, to consider itself absolute;
whether it can make room in itself for a power of contestation and thereby
relativize itself; whether something of the belief in the end of history does
not always remain in it; whether the permanent revolution, a refined form
of that belief, does not strip itself, once in power, of its dialectical-
philosophical meaning; and finally, whether the revolution does not by
definition bring about the opposite of what it wants by establishing a new
elite, albeit in the name of permanent revolution. If one concentrates all
the negativity and all the meaning of history in an existing historical formation, the working class, then one has to give a free hand to those who
represent it in power, since *all that is other is an enemy*. Then there no
longer is an opposition, no longer a manifest dialectic. Truth and action
will never communicate if there are not, along with those who act, those
who observe them, who confront them with the truth of their action, and
who can aspire to replace them in power. There is no dialectic without opposition or freedom, and in a revolution opposition and freedom do not
last for long. It is no accident that all known revolutions have degenerated:
it is because as established regimes they can never be what they were as
movements; precisely because it succeeded and ended up as an institution,
the historical movement is no longer itself: it "betrays" and "disfigures" itself in accomplishing itself. Revolutions are true as movements and false
as regimes. Thus the question arises whether there is not more of a future
in a regime that does not intend to remake history from the ground up
but only to change it and whether this is not the regime that one must look
for, instead of once again entering the circle of revolution.

Inside revolutionary thought we find not dialectic but equivocalness. Let us try to lay bare its driving force while it is still in a state of purity. It always grants a double historical perspective. On the one hand, revolution is the "fruit" of history, it brings to light forces which existed before it; the course of things carries this apparent rupture in the course of things, and revolution is a particular case of historical development (Trotsky even said: an "incidental expense"[4] of historical development)— revolution puts the development back on tracks which are the tracks of history. Considered in such a way, revolution can happen only at a certain date when certain external conditions are united. It thus ripens in history, it is prepared in what precedes it through the constitution of a class which will eliminate the old ruling class and take its place; it is a fact or an effect, it imposes itself even on those who do not want to recognize it. This is what the Marxist term "objective conditions" so well expresses: for the objective conditions of revolution are the revolution insofar as it is in things and incontestable (if not for those who are not at all revolutionary, at least for theoreticians who are not immediately revolutionary); the "objective" conditions are, ultimately, the revolution seen from outside and by others. The elimination of a class by the one it oppressed or exploited is an advance that history itself accomplishes. Such is the foundation of revolutionary optimism. But it would not be revolutionary if it contented itself with recording an objective development. The objective conditions can indeed weigh heavily on the consciousness forming in the rising class, but in the end it is men who make their history. The historical advent of a class is not an effect or a result of the past; it is a struggle, and the consciousness that it gains of its strength on the occasion of its first victories itself modifies the "objective" relationship of the forces—victory calls for victory. There is an "internal mechanism" which makes the revolution exalt itself and, in meaning and power, go beyond the strict framework of the average objective conditions, the given historical surroundings. A little while ago revolution was a wave of history. Now, on the contrary, history reveals its revolutionary substance: it is continual revolution, and it is the phases of stagnation that are to be interpreted as particular cases and temporary modalities of an essential imbalance resident in all of history. In this new light, revolution as an objective fact, as the substitution of one ruling class for another, is far from being a completion. The establishment in power of a class, which was previously seen as progress, also appears as regression or reaction. Precisely because it rules, the new ruling class tends to make itself autonomous. The essence of revolution is to be found in that instant in which the fallen class no longer rules and the rising class does not yet rule. This is where one catches a glimpse, as Michelet put it, of "a revolution under the revolution."[5] He goes on to say: "The

French Revolution in its rapid appearance, in which it accomplished so little, saw, in the glimmers of lightning, unknown depths, abysses of the future."[6] To establish a class in power is, rather than revolution itself, to be robbed of the revolution; the open depths close themselves, the new ruling class turns against those who had helped it to triumph and who were already moving beyond it, reinstating over them its positive power, which is already being challenged. Revolution is progress when one compares it to the past, but it is deception and abortion when one compares it to the future that it allowed a glimpse of and smothered. Marxist thought attempts to unite and hold together these two concepts of revolution, revolution as an incidental expense of historical development and history as permanent revolution. Its equivocal character lies in the fact that it does not succeed in doing so. The synthesis is sought at that point of history's maturity in which historical and objective development will lend such support to the internal mechanism of history that the permanent revolution can establish itself in power. History as maturation and history as continued rupture would coincide: it would be the course of things which would produce as its most perfect fruit the negation of all historical inertia. In other words, history will secrete a class that will put an end to the mystifications of unsuccessful revolutions because it will not be a new positive power which, after dispossessing the fallen classes, would in turn assert its own particularity; rather, it will be the last of all classes, the suppression of all classes and of itself as a class. If one focuses history on this future, if one calls it the proletariat and the proletarian revolution, it becomes legitimate to attribute the equivocations of preceding revolutions to the "bourgeoisie": they were at once progress and failure, nothing in them was pure, nothing exemplary; they were contradictory because they put into power a class which was not universal. But *there is* a class which *is* universal and which therefore will accomplish what all the others have vainly begun. And in this certitude of an already present future, Marxism believes it has found the synthesis of its optimism and its pessimism. The whole Trotskyite analysis of permanent revolution, which allowed us to deeply penetrate revolution as the sublation of given conditions, as an interhuman drama, as a struggle and a trans-temporal creation, suddenly turns into the simple description of a state of historical maturity in which the subjective and objective conditions concur. Philosophical naturalism and realism, which remain the framework of Marxist thought at the very moment it plunges into the analysis of struggle and intersubjectivity, allow Trotsky, under the guise of an ineluctable future, to situate in the development of things, and to attribute to a class which objectively exists, this crossing of time and this permanent negativity and, finally, to give this philosophical investiture to proletarian power. But of course, once "naturalized," the revolutionary process is hardly recognizable; and once raised to the dignity of truth in action, proletarian power is autonomized, remaining revolution only for itself. It becomes extreme subjectivism, or, what amounts to the same thing, extreme objectivism, and cannot, in any case, bear the gaze of an opposition. The question is to know whether one can attribute to the *bourgeoisie* alone and can explain as the particularities of that same class (which would make them a surmountable historical fact) the equivocations, the betrayal, and the ebb of past revolutions; whether the proletarian revolution, as a revolution without equivocation, and the proletariat as the final class are something other than an arbitrary way of closing history or prehistory, an ingenuous meta-history into which we project all our disgust, taking the risk of assuring a new victory to the mystifications of history, which would be all the more serious since so much is expected.

These reflections arise when one reads the very beautiful book that Daniel Guérin has written on the French Revolution.[7] The double game of Marxist thought and the *coup de force* by which it finally escapes its equivocations are presented here in a light that is all the more convincing since, by virtue of knowledge, of revolutionary sympathy and honesty, the author has assembled rich historical material which contests his Marxist categories without his desiring or knowing it. In appearance everything is clear: the Mountain,[8] the revolutionary government, Robespierre's action, and indeed the French Revolution are progressive when one compares them to the past, regressive when one compares them to the Revolution of the Bras Nus.[9] Guérin shows very convincingly that we are witnessing the advent of the bourgeoisie, that it uses the support of the Bras Nus against the old ruling classes but then turns against them when they want to push on to direct democracy. When one speaks of the links between the Mountain and the bourgeoisie, it is not a matter of conjecture: the maneuver is conscious and clearly appears in the writings, action, speeches, and official correspondence of the members of the Committee of Public Safety,[10] particularly of the "specialists." Cambon[11] is a representative of the new bourgeoisie, not "objectively" and in spite of his intentions, but very deliberately, as his profitable operations on behalf of the national wealth show. And the evolution from the Gironde[12] to the Mountain takes place through the conversion of a part of the bourgeoisie, which until then had occupied itself with trade and shipping, to new forms of exploitation. No one can question, therefore, the equivocal character of the French Revolution or that it was the installation in power of a class which intended to stop the revolution the moment its own privileges were secured. There is no dispute about the fact, but there is reason to discuss its meaning. Can one be content with Guérin's analysis and say with him that the French Revolution and the revolutionary government's dictatorship are progress *and* reaction? Can one dissociate these two aspects or relations of the event? For Guérin stresses that the objective conditions of a total revolution were not present. At that time in France there was not a sufficient mass of conscious proletarians to pass beyond the bourgeoisie's interests and go on to the proletarian revolution. Thus, within the given conditions, only a bourgeois revolution was possible, and the revolution had to stop there. Yet, as Guérin says, borrowing a phrase from Vergniaud,[13] to stop is to recede. Thus the dictatorship of the revolutionary government had to be supplanted by Thermidor and Bonaparte. But with the same stroke, the whole is found to be justified and historically founded, true in relation to the circumstances of the time, and all the more reason to justify Robespierre's thought as an effort to reunite the two truths of the time, to stabilize the revolution. The Enragés and the Hébertists,[14] who were polemicizing against the revolutionary government and demanding application of the 1793 constitution, "forgot that the men of the Mountain were still a minority in the country and that new elections risked giving birth to an assembly even more reactionary than the Convention."[15] They "lost sight of the necessity of a dictatorship to subdue the counterrevolution."[16] "The persecutions of which the avant-garde had been the victim made it lose sight of the *relatively progressive* character of the revolutionary government, despite its reactionary aspects. With its thoughtless diatribes it played the game of counterrevolution."[17] If the proletarian revolution is not ripe, Robespierre is relatively progressive and the leftism of the Bras Nus relatively counterrevolutionary. Given the conditions of the time, the revolutionary government and Robespierre represent success. They were the ones who had a chance to make history advance, they are the ones who exist, if not humanly, at least politically and historically. Ultimately it was not the forced rate of the *assignats*,[18] the demonetization of money, the total taxation, the unlimited powers of the representatives in the field to suspend the laws, raise taxes, sentence to death, and contest the local powers or the agents of the central power; nor was it the subjection of hoarders to search without warrants or the expeditions of the "revolutionary armies" among the peasants which moved in the direction of the history of the moment. Rather, as was said in the correspondence of the Committee of Public Safety, ultra-revolution was counterrevolution; and Guérin cannot think differently, for he admits that at that date it could not pass into fact. "The question today is less of revolutionizing than of establishing the revolutionary government,"[19] wrote the Committee of Public Safety, and this means that the Bras Nus' action at the time in question was incompatible with any government. While imprisoned by the revolutionary government, Varlet[20] was to write that "for any reasoning being, gov-

ernment and revolution are incompatible."[21] This means that the government was counterrevolutionary but also that the revolution made government impossible and that, in a time when the direct democracy of the Bras
Nus could not lean upon a sufficiently numerous and solid avant-garde to
replace the government, Robespierre was right in his struggle against
them. The Bras Nus were impulse; together with the bourgeoisie, the revolutionary government was technique. Confronting each other here
through the existing classes were revolution as immediate will and instituted revolution, revolution as a fact of intersubjectivity and revolution as
a historical fact.

> The substitution of bourgeois technique for popular ardor is one of
> the essential phenomena of the last phase of the Revolution. We have
> already seen this take place in the domain of waging war. The mass
> movement that had conferred on the Revolution an irresistible impulse
> and had allowed it to face external danger and to crush the internal
> enemy found itself little by little driven back. The regime lost its
> dynamism. But this inconvenience also had corresponding advantages:
> the establishment of a strong power, administrative centralization, and
> the rational and methodical organization of requisitions, war manu-
> facturing, and military operations gave it a strength which no other
> European power possessed at that time. This skeleton of a totalitarian
> state, as one says today, assured it victory.[22]

Guérin adds that it was "a victory of the bourgeoisie, not of the people."
But at that time no other victory was possible but the bourgeoisie's, and
the choice was between that victory and the Restoration. Consequently, it
is paradoxical to look to the Bras Nus for *what really happened* and to recount the entire history of the French Revolution as merely an internal
quarrel of the bourgeoisie, as if the nuances of the bourgeoisie did not at
that time in history represent the gauge of human possibilities. When he
wants to find the 1793 proletariat, Guérin is, of course, obliged to put
aside the Gironde, but also the Mountain and, naturally, the "specialists"
and Robespierre and the Hébertists and even the "plebeians," who came
from the side of the Bras Nus but who were also thinking of holding office. In short, all the professional revolutionaries have to be listed on the
side of the bourgeoisie, and only those who had no part in the official
powers represent the proletariat. One cannot say of Robespierre that he
was a conscious bourgeois; unlike most of his colleagues, he did not take
advantage of the revolution to get rich. But he was a "petty bourgeois,"
that is to say, as Marx teaches, a living contradiction—capable of understanding the Bras Nus but still a man of order and of government. But if

this was the contradiction of the age, Robespierre, in his hour, was historical man; and one must say the same of his colleagues, even the corrupt ones and the bankers who "financed the revolution" or advised keeping the gold standard because the republic could not win the war without buying abroad. Focusing the whole revolution on the action of the Bras Nus which, one admits, could not succeed, leads us to underestimate the struggles between the Gironde and the Mountain, between Danton and Robespierre, between Robespierre and the Thermidorians, when indeed this is the history of the French Revolution, and to hold as true history a history which did not occur: that of the proletarian revolution, which emerged along with the action of the Bras Nus but which could not be a political fact. The history which was is replaced by the history which could have occurred in another time, and the French Revolution then completely disappears into a future that it hatched and smothered, the proletarian revolution. If we want to understand history—that which at a given moment was present and on which the contemporaries staked their lives—one must, on the contrary, admit that what exists historically is not the heroism of the Bras Nus, which could not, as we are told, inscribe itself in a politics and mark history, but rather it is what the others contrived to do in the juncture, according to the inspiration of the revolutionary spirit, but also keeping in mind the "ebb" and thus their prejudices, their idiosyncrasies, their manias, and also, on occasion, their role as "men of order." All this, summarily imputed to the "bourgeoisie," belongs to the history of the revolution—a bourgeois revolution, but at that time there was no other, and the "bourgeoisie" was history itself. The two historical perspectives that Marxist thought would like to assemble come apart: if history is maturation, objective development, then it is Robespierre who is right, and the Bras Nus are right only later on, which is to say that they are wrong for the moment. And if history is permanent revolution, time does not exist, there is no past, all of history is only the eve of a tomorrow which is always deferred, the privation of a being which will never be, it awaits a pure revolution in which it would sublate itself.

Guérin would undoubtedly say: *in which it will sublate itself*—and that is the whole question. For if we admit that in a given moment—let us say the French Revolution—it is impossible to distinguish between what is progressive and what is reactionary or to accept one as "proletarian" and to refuse the other as "bourgeois," if both must be accepted or refused together in the absolute of the moment as the objective aspect and the subjective aspect, the "outside" and the "inside" of the revolution, the question arises of knowing whether at every moment of every revolution the same kind of ambiguity will not be found again, whether revolution will not always have to take account of an inert "outside" in which it must nevertheless inscribe itself if it wants to pass into history and uncontested fact. Of course, stages will have been crossed, the proletariat will be more numerous and perhaps more homogeneous than it was in 1793, the constituted bourgeoisie will perhaps no longer be there to dispute the power. We do not at all want to say that history repeats itself and that everything amounts to the same thing; but the same typical situation will be reproduced, in the sense that we will always have to deal with something only "relatively progressive," that revolution, precisely if one calls it permanent, will always have to take inertia into account, that it will never break through history, that we will never see it face to face, that it will always be possible to treat the Robespierre of the epoch as a "petty bourgeois" and to condemn him in the perspective of the Bras Nus, as it will also always be possible to place in evidence the historical role of "specialists" and "technicians" at the expense of "popular ardor." For it to be otherwise, it would be necessary for the revolution to stop being a government, for the revolution itself to replace government. As Babeuf[23] said, "Those who govern make revolution only to continue governing. We want to make one to assure the people of an everlasting happiness through a true democracy."[24] This is exactly the question: is revolution an extreme case of government or the end of government? It is conceived in the second sense and practiced in the first. If it is the end of government, it is utopia; if it is a type of government, it always exists only in the relative and the probable, and nothing allows us to treat as the fact of a particular class and to group pell-mell under the designation of "bourgeoisie" the contradictions which break out between the exigencies of the government and those of the revolution, and even less to give ourselves, under the name of "proletarian power," a ready-made solution to this antinomy. Guérin wrote that "if the sansculottes[25] of this epoch had been able to elevate themselves to the notion of the dictatorship of the proletariat, they would have demanded *both* dictatorship against the enemies of the people and complete democracy for the people themselves."[26] This democracy for the people and dictatorship against the enemies of the people is not in the facts; it is in Guérin's mind. We recognize in it the classical notion of a proletarian power, and it is only by conceiving everything under this category that the emergence of the true revolution is divined in the action of the Bras Nus. But how can a power which is a dictatorship against the enemies of the people be completely democratic for the people themselves? Are the limits between the "inside" and the "outside" so clear? The people cannot be seduced by the bourgeoisie, and they do not have enemies among themselves? On the other hand, cannot some bourgeois, the "specialists," at least apparently rally to the people's cause? How is one to know when a sansculotte speaks as a sansculotte and when he speaks as a dupe of the bourgeoisie? How is one to know when a specialist speaks as a specialist and when he speaks as a bourgeois in disguise? Thus in the end the dialectical line that Guérin draws from the Bras Nus to the future is only the projection of a wish, the wish for a power that would be action, or violence *and* truth. Yet he will say, there were months when the Terror was that of the Bras Nus, when the dictatorship was "popular, democratic, decentralized, propelled from the bottom up."[27] "Danton proposed something completely different; he asked for a dictatorship from above. He proposed that the local administrators become agents of the central power, named by it and closely subordinated to it."[28] When the sansculottes demanded the Terror, they were asking for their own terror but were given another one, that of the revolutionary government, that is, one of them wrote, "the baleful spirit of vengeance and particular hatreds." Another terror? Is that certain? Is it not the same terror mediated, no longer only exercised but undergone, that is to say, become governmental, and consequently striking not only the counterrevolution, but also the ultrarevolution, which "plays its game"? Trotsky did indeed distinguish between them, but Guérin reproaches him for having believed "that in the end the two dictatorships merged, once the Convention got rid of the Girondins."[29] Guérin concedes that "it is true that immediately after May 31 the two tendencies appeared for an instant to mingle, but, as was proved by the following events, this merger was only ephemeral." Alas, Trotsky had governed, and one fears that he is right. Guérin proves very well that the revolutionary government turned against the immediate demands of the Bras Nus. But this does not prove that there were two opposing politics, and this is where the question lies. Guérin says that when Chaumette, the syndic prosecutor of the Paris Commune, had to take the title of national agent, he stopped being "the sansculottes' attorney" to become "the central power's domestic."[30] But Guérin also admits that this power is "the first since the beginning of the Revolution whose statute gives it the means of executing its will."[31] If the same man, as soon as he becomes "national agent," stops serving the true revolution, it is because the bourgeois spirit has spread well beyond the bourgeoisie, it is because it is then synonymous with official power, and because the proletarian spirit can arouse only an opposition. "Direct democracy," "dictatorship propelled from the bottom up"—Guérin's *true solution*, as different from government terror as from bourgeois democracy—is a pompous political concept with which one clothes the apocalypse. It is a dream of an "end of politics" out of which one wants to make a politics. Like "proletarian power," it is a problem that presents itself as a solution, a question which is given as an answer, the sublation of history in ideas.

It is true, one will say, that the Bras Nus's action in 1793 was not a political fact. But Guérin consciously takes an overview of the French Revolution. As he says, the proletarian revolution then was premature, and he himself introduces this idea in order to marshal the facts. But a more recent history would counterbalance ideas with experience. It is in relation to 1848, 1871, and 1917 that he is focusing. No one in 1793 could draw the future dialectical line, but we can see it retrospectively and throw light on 1793 by what followed. Yet could we ever, even in 1917, find realized, except episodically, a "dictatorship against the enemies of the people" which would be "completely democratic for the people themselves"? And if the episode did not last, if a truly soviet system is scarcely to be found in the history of the Russian Revolution, if it was especially before October 17 that it worked, it is perhaps because a revolution is proletarian only before it succeeds, in the movement which precedes the taking of power, in its "ardor," not in its technique. The fact is that today's soviet power reminds us more of the Committee of Public Safety than of the Bras Nus. And if one still wanted to attribute the "dictatorship from the top" to the bourgeoisie, to the "remnants" of the bourgeoisie in the Soviet Union or to the bourgeoisie pressing at its borders, this would be to admit that one does not want to look at the facts, that one masks as a historical process the idea of proletarian power as the resorption of the "outside" by the "inside," of the "objective" by the "internal mechanism," and that one is guided by the phantasm of a kind of final conflagration in which, at last, desire would immediately be reality. Guérin, a historian and a Marxist, knows better than we that the "dictatorship of the proletariat" was never more than the index of a problem, and he knows how difficult it is to find a path between social democracy and the dictatorship of the party. The idea of the dictatorship of the proletariat expresses in particular our desire to find ready-made in history a resolution of history's horrors, to think of history as an odyssey, to return to a solution already given in things, or at least to base our will on a movement of things. If one takes away this ideology, what remains? Only revolutionary movements which indeed avoid the alternatives of personal dictatorship and democratic consultation because they are a resistance, because they are not a recognized power, but which have no other reason for existing than to create one, which therefore do something other than what they want to do. The abortion of the French Revolution, and of all the others, is thus not an accident which breaks a logical development, which is to be attributed to the particularities of the rising class, and which will not take place when the rising class is the proletariat: the failure of the revolution is the revolution itself. Revolution and its failure are one and the same thing.

Guérin asks himself, incidentally, why the right wing of today's bourgeoisie hates the French Revolution, which put it in power. And he gives the profound reply that it considers the French Revolution "from the view-point of permanent revolution" and hates in it "revolution *itself.*"[32] These words bring a third dimension of the revolutionary dialectic out of the shadows: there is not only an objective development from the past which was to the present which is, and not only a subjective reconstruction of this development, starting with our present wills, but in addition there are, between the past and the present, vague links, contaminations, identifications, which cross the given or voluntary relationships of filiation, a kind of obliteration or deadening of the real past. Today's bourgeois is no longer the one who made the French Revolution or the one who was born from it. The bourgeoisie was, as the rising class, the revolution of the epoch, it was, for the epoch, revolution *itself;* and although it served particular interests, it was neither subjectively nor objectively reducible to these interests; its historical function was to precipitate and transform into institution, into acquisition, a new idea of social relations—and this is why, incidentally, it could sometimes rally the Bras Nus. But there is no definitive acquisition from which history can rise without losing an inch of the height it has attained: the bourgeoisie which was the revolution became the *ancien régime,* and, when reflecting on the French Revolution, it identifies itself with the old ruling class. At the same time that there is historical progress, there is, therefore, a consolidation, a destruction, a trampling of history; and at the same time as a permanent revolution, there is a permanent decadence which overtakes the ruling class in proportion as it rules and endures, for by ruling it abdicates what had made it "progressive,"[33] loses its rallying power, and is reduced to the protection of private interests. Throughout history, revolutions meet one another and institutions resemble one another; every revolution is the first revolution, and every institution, even a revolutionary institution, is *tempted* by historical precedents. This does not mean that everything is in vain and that nothing can be done: each time the struggle is different, the minimum of demandable justice rises, and besides, according to these very principles, conservatism is utopian. But this means that the revolution which would re-create history is infinitely distant, that there is a similarity among ruling classes insofar as they are ruling and among ruled classes insofar as they are ruled, and that, for this reason, historical advances cannot be added like steps in a staircase. The Marxists know this very well when they say that the dictatorship of the proletariat turns *the weapons of the bourgeoisie* against the bourgeoisie. But then a proletarian philosophy of history holds to the miracle that the dictatorship may use the bourgeoisie's weapons without becoming something like a bourgeoisie; that a class may rule without becoming decadent when in point of fact any class which rules the whole proves to be particular by that very action; that a historical formation, the proletariat, may be established as a ruling class without taking upon itself the liabilities of the historical role; that it may accumulate and keep intact in itself all the energy of all past revolution and unfailingly give life to its institutional apparatus and progressively annul its degeneration. It is to act as if everything that historically exists were not *at the same time* movement and inertia, it is to place in history, as *contents,* on the one hand the principle of resistance (called the bourgeoisie) and on the other the principle of movement (called the proletariat), when these are the very *structure* of history as a passage to generality and to the institution of relationships among persons. The Committee of Public Safety was progressive relative to 1793, that is to say, absolutely progressive in its time, regardless of the fact that it was a mixed historical reality and that one can already discern in it bourgeois interests becoming autonomous. In the same way, the dictatorship of the proletariat, even if one supposes its mission to be the implanting in history of the relationships among men as the proletariat discovers them, will accomplish this work only in ambiguity and with the loss of energy which is inseparable from power and social generality. To assume that the proletariat will be able to defend its dictatorship against entanglement is to assume in history itself a substantial and given principle which would drive ambiguity from it, sum it up, totalize it, and close it (even if only by opening to history a future of pure movement); whoever assumes this principle and attempts to put it in power thereby gives investiture to an impure power. If revolution is permanent in the sense that its "final" form is already anticipated in its initial outlines, it also must be permanent in the sense that it is never completed, always relative, and that in it victory and failure are one. For it is difficult to see how this excess of "internal mechanism" over "objective conditions" which makes for historical anticipations will be annulled when a stronger and more conscious proletariat is constituted: it is the excess of "ardor" over "technique," of immediate will over institutions, of the rising class over the class in power, of civil society over the state; and to say that these differences do not exist in a proletarian power is to give a nominal definition which teaches us nothing about things. To believe in proletarian revolution is to arbitrarily assert that history's sliding back on itself and the resurrection of past ghosts are bad dreams, that history carries within itself its own cure and will surprise us with it—and, precisely because one yields to this belief, a power is established which is all the more autonomous because it is thought to be founded on objective history. If one then wants to take back one's bet, if one protests that the proletarian society is, on the contrary, a society in permanent crisis, it is because one renounces revolution: for who would undertake to make a revolution without the conviction of creating another society, not only because it will contest itself and be able to correct itself, but also because it *is the good*? One does not kill for relative progress. The very nature of revolution is to believe itself absolute and to not be absolute precisely because it believes itself to be so. If it knows itself to be relative, if it admits that it is at each moment doing something merely "relatively progressive," then it is very close to admitting that revolution and non-revolution make a single history. On this basis a person can have sympathy for revolutions, judge them inevitable at certain times, ascertain their progress, and even associate himself with them: he still does not believe in them as they believe in themselves, he does not make them, he is not a revolutionary. There are undoubtedly many men of this sort in all revolutions: they work in the enterprise, they render it services, they do not put it in question, but precisely for this reason they are not revolutionaries. Revolutions allow for this astonishing division of roles: those who *are* the most revolutionary often go over to the opposition, and those who *make* the revolution are not always revolutionaries. Some few exceptional men top it all and succeed in governing while keeping their revolutionary consciousness; but whether they do so because they make the revolution or because their consciousness is satisfied with bird's-eye views, one cannot say. These men thus give the illusion of having achieved the synthesis, but the antinomy continues in them.

These remarks relatively justify Communism in what it is doing: it has renounced being a society of permanent crisis and continual imbalance, replacing government by revolution and making up for the objective conditions by their "internal mechanism." There would be something healthy in this disillusionment if it were lucid; but if it were lucid and acknowledged its condition, the U.S.S.R. would cease to be the fatherland of the revolution. The fiction of proletarian power, of direct democracy, and of the withering-away of the State must therefore be all the more energetically maintained as the reality becomes more and more distant, either because for some this fraud is consciously accepted as the heritage of a project which they do not want to betray or because, in the decadence of Marxist culture which results from it, the fraud ceases to be perceptible and is all the less conscious the more it is constantly lived. Perhaps no one is closer to the ideas we are defending here than an informed Soviet citizen: no one is more convinced that all revolution is relative and that there are only *progresses*. Today's Communism verges on *progressism*. If one sees more and more men who have never shared the "illusions" of Marxism gravitating around it, it is no accident; it is because Communism has indeed renounced these "illusions." But if it presented itself as the progressism that it is, it would lack the conviction, the vigilance, the authority, and the moral right to demand every sacrifice. This is why, as we have said, the progressist is never alone, he lives only in symbiosis: behind him he must have a solid Communist who works, who believes, or makes others believe, that the proletariat is in power. In itself the Soviet regime is a progressism, but it is important that in relation to capitalism it remains the absolute other. This is what remains in it of the revolutionary point of honor (the phrase, of course, being taken in the Marxist sense, for in other respects, from all the evidence, the regime transforms the countries it governs). It therefore amplifies, generalizes, makes irrevocable, and extends over the entire future the equivocalness essential to any revolutionary government, indeed to any institution. It eludes understanding in such a way that one cannot judge it. Of course, just as did the Committee of Public Safety, the U.S.S.R. works in the realm of the objective, makes history, wins wars. But one could more or less see what the Committee of Public Safety cost and what it yielded. When, on the contrary, the apparatus becomes so dense that there is no longer an "interior" of the revolution, no one can say what history it is making or at what price. It could be justifiable only relatively, and it refuses precisely this justification by presenting itself as absolute. The Marxist synthesis of the subjective and the objective comes apart, leaving two terminal formations: on the one hand, an extreme objectivism which no longer allows us to discern the system's meaning; on the other hand, a theory of permanent revolution which, on the contrary, overestimates the intersubjective factors but which ultimately challenges all instituted revolutions and therefore the very idea of revolution.

The revolutionary politics which, in the perspective of 1917, was historically to take the place of "liberal" politics—occupied with difficult organizational problems, with defense, and with improvements—has become more and more a politics for new countries, the means for semicolonial economies (or for civilizations long since paralyzed) to change to modern modes of production. The immense apparatus that it constructed, with its disciplines and its privileges, at the moment when it shows itself to be efficacious for building an industry or for putting a new proletariat to work, evacuates the terrain of the proletariat as ruling class and forfeits the mystery of civilization which, according to Marx, the Western proletariat carried. In the end, have the French, German, and Italian proletariats more to expect from a Communist-directed regime than from the one they now live under? Is the Czech proletariat happier today than before the war? The fact that the question is asked is enough to show that the great historical politics, which had for its motto the power of the workers of all countries, is itself in crisis. We will not speculate here about the "egoism" of the advanced proletariats. What we wonder is whether, even in the future and even deducting the sacrifices which the system will ask of them in order to help the backward proletariats, they can receive from it what the Communists expect. The so-called proletarian regimes frame their proletariat in an aggregate of powers whose output and social cost, and, finally, whose historical meaning, are as poorly known as the system of pre-capitalist societies and whose sociology is entirely left to be done. Thus, where there is a choice between famine and the Communist apparatus, the decision goes without saying; but, on the contrary, wherever modern modes of production exist and, with them, certain ways of doing things, the question is to know whether, for the proletariat, Communism is worth what it costs; then the enormous problem of its nature and of its real contours—a problem displaced elsewhere by the threat of death—again becomes primordial. Two rival and symmetrical maneuvers prevent us from considering Communism as an unknown to be understood: on the one side, the maneuver that presents it as the heir to Marxism, on the other, the maneuver that attempts to cover up the "free world's" problems under the pretext of anti-Communist defense; on the one side, the attempts to have Communism accepted under Marx's shadow, on the other, the attempt to eliminate Marx's problems in favor of the anti-Communist defense. Communism's nostalgia and the neurosis of anti-Communism join forces to promote the equivocation we mentioned earlier between the revolutionary ideology and the "progressist" reality of the U.S.S.R. and to forbid any direct and frank view of it even with our limited information. This situation can end only with the birth of a non-Communist left. The first article of this new left should be that the rivalry between the United States and the U.S.S.R. is not between "free enterprise" and Marxism. Under the cover of philosophies that date back a century or two, the established politics are building something entirely different. In the vices as in the virtues of the two systems there are so many geographical, historical, or political conditions which intervene that the philosophies they claim are clearly mere ornaments. If we want to abandon our daydreams, we must look at the *other thing* these ornaments are hiding and put ourselves in a state of methodical doubt in regard to them. We should give them the attention without reverence that is appropriate for large, confused undertakings whose analysis and balance sheet have not yet been made—and whose collision would be the greatest of catastrophes, since those who would die would not even know why they were dying. A non-Communist left therefore sets itself the constant task of evading the antagonists' hostility, of springing the traps that the one prepares for the other, of thwarting the complicity of their pessimisms. We are not dealing here with any opportunism of the golden mean or of pacifism. A-communism is a necessary condition for knowledge of the U.S.S.R. because it confronts what we know of Communist reality with

Communist ideology; and it is, at the same time and without paradox, the condition of a modern critique of capitalism because it alone poses Marx's problems again in modern terms. It alone is capable of a perpetual confrontation and comparison of the two systems. One glimpses a generalized economy of which they are particular cases. This awareness, and with it the action that it commands, is the task of a non-Communist left, which thus will not be a compromise between the given ideologies.

We see now in what sense one must speak of a new liberalism: it is not a question of returning to an optimistic and superficial philosophy which reduces the history of a society to speculative conflicts of opinion, political struggle to exchanges of views on clearly posed problems, and the coexistence of men to relationships of fellow citizens in the political empyrean. This kind of liberalism is no longer practiced anywhere. There is a class struggle and there must be one, since there are, and as long as there will be, classes. There is and there must be a means of exceptional action for the proletarian class, the strike, since its fate is also exceptional and since by definition it is in a minority. Moreover, this class has the right to be represented, if it so desires, by a party which refuses the rules of the democratic game, since this game places it at a disadvantage. The Communist Party is and must be legal. In addition, there have been and there will be revolutionary movements, and they are justified by their own existence, since they are proof that the society in which they arise does not allow the workers to live. If we speak of liberalism, it is in the sense that Communist action and other revolutionary movements are accepted only as a useful menace, as a continual call to order, that we do not believe in the solution of the social problem through the power of the proletarian class or its representatives, that we expect progress only from a conscious action which will confront itself with the judgment of an opposition. Like Weber's heroic liberalism, it lets even what contests it enter its universe, and it is justified in its own eyes only when it understands its opposition. For us a non-Communist left is this double position, posing social problems in terms of struggle and refusing the dictatorship of the proletariat. Someone will say: but since this struggle is the struggle for power, either you condemn a non-Communist left to exercise power only in a parliamentary or bourgeois sense, which is the socialist dream, or for it this power is only a transition on the way to dictatorship, and then your left is crypto-Communist. A non-Communist left exercises such a freedom of criticism in regard to the dictatorship of the proletariat that its action in itself distinguishes it from Communist action. To remove any equivocation, it is sufficient that the non-Communist left pose the problem of the nature of the Soviet state, which is not only to admit, with Sartre, that "the discussion is open," but to open it oneself or, in any case, to take part in it.

As for the limitations of parliamentary and democratic action, there are those which result from the institution, and they should be accepted, for Parliament is the only known institution that guarantees a minimum of opposition and of truth. There are other limitations which are the result of parliamentary usage and maneuvers; these deserve no respect at all, but they can be denounced in Parliament itself. Parliamentary mystification consists in not posing the true problems or in posing them only obliquely and too late. A non-Communist left could do much against these practices. We have somewhat lost the habit of parliamentary action, and the Communist Party has played its role in this decline of the system: committed to a strategy of defending the U.S.S.R. on a worldwide scale, it oscillates between agitation and opportunism. It foregoes a harassing action, which thus falls to the non-Communist left.

This is not "a solution," and we know it full well; what we are saying is that the social realm is only beginning to be known, and besides, a system of *conscious lives* will never admit of a solution the way a crossword puzzle does or an elementary problem of arithmetic. Our approach involves instead the resolution to keep a hand on both ends of the chain, on the social problem and on freedom. The only postulate of this attitude is that political freedom is not only, and not necessarily, a defense of capitalism. We said that there is no dialectic without freedom. But is there one with freedom? There is one if capitalism is no longer a rigid apparatus with *its* politics, *its* ideologies, and *its* imperious laws of functioning and if, under the cover of its contradictions, another politics than *its own* can pass. A non-Communist left is no more linked to free enterprise than to the dictatorship of the proletariat. It does not believe that capitalist institutions are the only mechanisms of exploitation, but it also does not judge them to be any more natural or sacred than the polished stone hatchet or the bicycle. Like our language, our tools, our customs, our clothes, they are instruments, invented for a definite purpose, which found themselves little by little burdened with an entirely different function. A complete analysis of this change in meanings has to be made, going beyond the famous analysis of surplus value, and a program of action established consequent upon it. What is sure is that nothing like this will take place without a system which proceeds, not only by plans, but also by balance sheets. Today revolutionary action is secret, unverifiable, and, just because it wants to re-create history, encumbered by burdens which have never been measured. At the same time, it has given up the philosophical guarantees of the dictatorship of the proletariat. This is why it appears to us to be less practicable now than ever before; but by this we in no way imply acceptance of the eternal laws of the capitalist order or any respect for this order. We are calling for an effort of enlightenment which appears to us impossible for reasons of principle under a Communist regime and possible in the non-Communist world. If we overestimate the freedom of this world, the "barometer of revolution" will say so.

* * *

It is always unbecoming to cite or to comment on oneself. But, on the other hand, anyone who has published his opinions on vital problems is obliged, if he changes them, to say so and to say why. In such matters, one cannot give an author the right to produce his ideas as a locomotive produces its smoke; he must relate what he thought yesterday to what he thinks today. Just as he would be wrong to look to his former writings for all the ideas he holds today—this would be to admit that he has not lived, that he has learned nothing in the interim—so he must explain the change. This is his main reason for being. That he thought one thing and now thinks another interests no one. But his path, his reasons, the way in which he himself understood what happened: this is what he owes to the reader, this is what he can say without any difficulty, if he has remained himself. One should not therefore be surprised that, in conclusion, we should like to connect these pages to a previous essay.[34]

Just after the war we tried to formulate a Marxist wait-and-see attitude. It seemed to us that the Soviet society was then very far from the revolutionary criteria defined by Lenin, that the very idea of a criterion of valid compromises had been abandoned, and that, consequently, the dialectic threatened to become once more the simple identity of opposites, that is to say, skepticism. A completely voluntaristic Communism became evident, based entirely on the consciousness of the leaders—a renewal of the Hegelian State and not the withering-away of the State. But however "grand" Soviet "politics" may have been, we observed that the struggle of Communist parties is in other countries the struggle of the proletariat as well, and it did not seem impossible that Soviet politics might thereby be brought back to the ways of Marxist politics. We said that the U.S.S.R. is not the power of the proletariat, but the Marxist dialectic continues to play its role throughout the world. It jammed when the revolution was limited to an underdeveloped country, but one feels its presence in the French and Italian labor movements. Even if the Marxist dialectic did not take possession of our history, even if we have nowhere seen the advent of the proletariat as ruling class, the dialectic continues to gnaw at capitalist society, it retains its full value as negation; it remains true, it will always be true, that a history in which the proletariat is nothing is not a human history. Since adherence to Communism was, we thought, impossible, it was all the more necessary to have a sympathetic attitude which would

protect the chances of a new revolutionary flow. We said that we do not
have to choose between Communism as it is and its adversary. Communism is strategically on the defensive. Let us take advantage of this pause,
let us watch for the signs of a renewal of proletarian politics, and let us do
what we can to help it. "If it happens tomorrow that the U.S.S.R. threatens
to invade Europe and to set up in every country a government of its
choice, a different question would arise and would have to be examined.
That question does not arise at the moment."[35]

The U.S.S.R. did not invade Europe, but the Korean War raised this
"different question," which was not posed in 1947; and it is with this question that we are now dealing. We know everything that one can say concerning the South Korean regime, and we do not claim that the U.S.S.R.
wanted or set off the Korean War. But since it ended it, it undoubtedly
could have prevented it; and since it did not prevent it, and military action
took place, our attitude of sympathy was obsolete, because its meaning
was changed. In a situation of force it became an adherence in disguise.
For it was very clear that any movement of the U.S.S.R. beyond its borders
would be based on the struggle of local proletariats; and, if one decided
to see in each affair only an episode of the class struggle, one brought to
its politics precisely the kind of support it wanted. Marxist wait and see
became Communist action. It remained itself only insofar as there was a
margin between Communism and non-Communism, and this margin was
reduced by the state of war. The Korean War has ended, and the Soviet
government seems to have become aware of the conditions for a true coexistence. But it remains the case that the United States has rearmed
and evolved toward fanaticism, that a politics of peace between it and the
Soviet Union has, because of this, become incomparably more difficult.
In this situation of force, any initiative from other countries is equivalent
to reversing alliances, and one must ask oneself whether this reversal would
not bring the U.S.S.R. back to a "hard" politics. In short, since the Korean
War, all questions have been considered on the level of relationships of
force and traditional diplomacy. The formula "Sympathy without adherence" had to be reexamined in a new situation. The Korean War obliged
us neither to desire the conquest of the whole country by one of the two
armies nor to set the Communist and non-Communist worlds face to face
like two blocs between which it was necessary to choose, reducing the
entire political problem to this choice; we thought, and we still think, that
Communism is ambiguous and anti-Communism even more so. We
thought, and we still think, that a politics founded on anti-Communism is
in the long run a politics of war and in the short run a politics of regression, that there are many ways of not being Communist, and that the problem has barely been taken up when one has said that one is not a Commu-

nist. But the critique of anti-Communism in a situation of force is distinct from adherence to Communism only if it places itself unequivocally outside Communism. The choice was never between "being Communist" and "being anti-Communist," but, *on the other hand, it was necessary to know whether one was Communist or not.* The polemic against anti-Communism remained independent only if it also attacked crypto-Communism. The struggle against these opposites, which live off each other, was a single struggle. Wait-and-see Marxism had been a position just after the war because it had objective conditions: those neutral zones throughout the world, in Czechoslovakia, in Korea, where the two actions had a pact. Since these zones were disappearing, wait-and-see Marxism was for us nothing more than a dream, and a dubious dream. It was necessary to emphasize that independence in itself situated us outside Communism. One could no longer be satisfied with not choosing: in the perspective of war, to put it clearly, the refusal to choose becomes the choice of a double refusal. Such are, it seems to us, the obligations of commitment.

But was it only a concession to practical realities? Could we keep on the level of thought the same favorable prejudice toward a Marxist philosophy of history? Or did the episode have the value of an experience from which, even on the theoretical level, one must draw the consequences? Could we continue thinking that, after all reservations had been made with respect to the Soviet solutions, the Marxist dialectic remained negatively valid and that history should be focused, if not on the proletariat's power, at least on its lack of it? We do not want to present as a syllogism what gradually became clear to us in contact with events. But the event was the occasion of a growing awareness and not at all one of those accidents that upsets without enlightening. The Korean War and its consequences confronted us with a condition of history from which the postwar years had only apparently freed us. It recalled to us the identity of practice and theory; it made us remember that even the refusal to choose must, to be considered a political position, become a thesis and form its own platform, and that the double truth ceases to be duplicity and complicity only when it is avowed and formulated unequivocally, even in its practical consequences. To say, as we did, that Marxism remains true as a critique or negation without being true as an action or positively was to place ourselves outside history, and particularly outside Marxism, was to justify it for reasons which are not its own, and, finally, was to organize equivocalness. In history, Marxist critique and Marxist action are a single movement. Not that the critique of the present derives as a corollary from perspectives of the future—Marxism is not a utopia—but because, on the contrary, Communist action is in principle only the critique continued, carried to its final consequences, and because, finally, revolution is the critique in power. If one verifies that it does not keep the promises of the critique, one cannot conclude from that: let us keep the critique and forget the action. There must be something in the critique itself that germinates the defects in the action. We found this ferment in the Marxist idea of a critique historically embodied, of a class which is the *suppression of itself*, which, in its representatives, results in the conviction of being the universal in action, in the right to assert oneself without restriction, and in unverifiable violence. It is the certitude of judging history in the name of history, of saying nothing that history itself does not say, of passing on the present a judgment which is inscribed in it, of expressing in words and ideas preexisting relationships such as they are in things; in short, it is materialism that, in the guise of modesty, makes the Marxist critique a dogma and prevents it from being self-criticism. It is therefore quite impossible to cut Communism in two, to say that it is right in what it negates and wrong in what it asserts: for its way of asserting is already concretely present in its way of negating; in its critique of capitalism there is already, as we have said, not a utopian representation of the future, but at least the absolute of a negation, or negation realized, the *classless* society called for by history. However things may appear from this perspective, the defects of capitalism remain defects; but the critique which denounces them must be freed from any compromise with an absolute of the negation which, in the long run, is germinating new oppressions. The Marxist critique must therefore be taken up again, reexposed completely, and generalized, and we were speaking abstractly when we said that Marxism "remains true as a negation." We said that perhaps no proletariat would come to play the role of ruling class that Marxism assigns it but that it is true that no other class can replace it in that role and that, in this sense, the failure of Marxism would be the failure of philosophy of history. This in itself shows well enough that we were not on the terrain of history (and of Marxism) but on that of the *a priori* and of morality. We meant to say that all societies which tolerate the existence of a proletariat are unjustifiable. This does not mean that they are all of equal worth and worth nothing or that there is no meaning in the history which produces them one after the other. This Marxism which remains true whatever it does, which does without proofs and verifications, is not a philosophy of history—it is Kant in disguise, and it is Kant again that we ultimately find in the concept of revolution as absolute action. The events which obliged us to consider from outside, "objectively," our wait-and-see Marxism estranged us in the end only from a Marxism of internal life.

"And so you renounce being a revolutionary, you accept the social distance which transforms into venial sins exploitation, poverty, famine. . . ."

"I accept it neither more nor less than you do. Yesterday a Communist wrote: 'There will be no more October 17s'. Today Sartre says that the dialectic is twaddle. One of my Marxist friends says that Bolshevism has already ruined the revolution and that it must be replaced with the masses' unpredictable ingenuity. To be revolutionary today is to accept a State of which one knows very little or to rely upon a historical grace of which one knows even less; and even that would not be without misery and tears. Is it then cheating to ask to inspect the dice?"

"*Objectively* you accept poverty and exploitation, since you do not join with those who reject it unconditionally."

"They say they reject it, they believe they reject it. But do they reject it *objectively*? And if they reply that the object is unknowable or formless, that truth is what the most miserable want, we must reply that no one has gotten rid of poverty by hailing the revolution. It does not require only our good will and our choice but our knowledge, our labor, our criticism, our preference, and our complete presence. Revolution today does not want any of this."

"Here it is, this terrible maturity which made Man, Mussolini, and so many others move from 'verbal international socialism' to 'lived national socialism.'"

"Those people wanted to rule, and, as is appropriate in that case, they appealed to darker passions. Nothing like this threatens us, and we would be happy if we could inspire a few—or many—to bear their freedom, not to exchange it at a loss; for it is not only their own thing, their secret, their pleasure, their salvation—it involves everyone else."

July 1953
April–December 1954

Preface to *Signs*

Between the philosophical attempts and the circumstantial proposals, nearly all political, in which this volume consists, what a difference there is, at first glance, what disparateness! The philosopher's path may be difficult, but we are sure that each step makes others possible. In politics, one has the oppressive sensation of a breakthrough that always has to be re-made. We are not even speaking of chance and the unforeseen; there are some errors of prognostication to be found in this volume, although frankly, fewer than were to be feared. The case is really more serious: it is as if some evil mechanism whisked events away at just the moment they appeared on the scene, as if history censored the dramas it is made up of; it is as if history loved to hide and half opened up to the truth only in brief moments of disarray, the rest of the time ingenuously working to block all the things "surpassed," working to bring back the stock formulas and roles, and to persuade us in short that nothing comes to pass. Maurras[1] used to say that he had found evident truth in politics, but never in pure philosophy. But that was because he gazed upon only the history that is over and done with, and dreamed of a philosophy that is established. If we take philosophy and history as they are being made, we shall see that philosophy finds its surest evidence at the instant it begins, and that history, when it is being born, is dream or nightmare. Whenever we reach the point of asking a question, whenever scattered anxieties and angers have ended up taking on an identifiable form in human space, we imagine that nothing thereafter can ever be as it was before. But if there are total interrogations, the answer, in its positivity, cannot be total. It is rather the question which is used up, a questionless state which happens, like a passion that one day stops, destroyed by its own duration. A country which lay bleeding from a war or revolution stands suddenly intact and whole. The dead are implicated in this abatement: only by living could they re-create the very lack and need of them which is being blotted out. Conservative historians record Dreyfus's innocence as a self-evident truth—and are no less conservative for it. Dreyfus is not avenged; he is not even rehabilitated. Having become a commonplace, his innocence is cheap at the price of his shame. It is not inscribed in history as he was robbed of it, or as it was demanded by his defenders. History takes still more from those who have lost everything, and gives yet more to those who have taken everything. For its sweeping judgments acquit the unjust and dismiss the pleas of their victims. History never *confesses*.

The familiarity of these truths in no way diminishes the force with which they strike us every time we meet them with the shock of recognition. The main concern of our time is going to be to reconcile the old world and the new. In the face of this problem, the U.S.S.R. and the recent adversaries are perhaps on the same side, the side of the old world. Be that as it may, the end of the Cold War is in sight. The West can scarcely show up well in peaceful competition if it does not invent a democratic way of managing its economy. At present, the development of industrial society here is marked by extraordinary disorder. Capitalism haphazardly extends its giant branches, puts the economies of nations at the mercy of dominant industries which choke their towns and highways, and destroys the classical forms of the human establishment. At all levels immense problems appear; not just techniques but political forms, motives, a spirit, reasons for living need to be found.

It is in these circumstances that an army which has long been isolated from the world in colonial wars, and which has learned about the social struggle there, falls back with its full weight upon the State it is supposed to be subordinate to, and floods the times once more with the Cold War ideology they were about to rid themselves of. Someone who twenty years ago knew how to judge "elites" (especially military elites) now thinks he can construct a lasting power by isolating himself at the summit of the State, and only frees it from the harassments of parties to expose it to factions. Someone who said that no man can take the place of the people (but no doubt this was only a formulation of despair and "useless service") now separates the nation's aspirations from what he calls its standard of living. As if any fully developed nation could accept such dilemmas. As if the economy in a real society could ever be subordinate like the commissary in the army's artificial society. As if bread and wine and labor were in themselves less grave and sacred things than history books.

Perhaps it will be said that this stationary, provincial history is France's alone. But is the world at large facing any more frankly the questions which confront it? Because these questions threaten to break down the frontiers between Communism and capitalism, the church does its best to silence them, revives forgotten interdicts, condemns anew all socialism which is not democratic, attempts to reoccupy the positions of a state religion, and suppresses on all sides—beginning in its own ranks—the spirit of inquiry and confidence in the truth.

As for Communist politics, we know how many filters the air of de-Stalinization had to pass through before it reached Paris or Rome. After so many denials of "revisionism," and above all after Budapest, we need sharp eyes to see that Soviet society is getting involved in another epoch and is liquidating the spirit of social warfare along with Stalinism and orienting itself toward new forms of power. This is called officially a transition to the highest stage of Communism. Does the prognostication of a spontaneous evolution toward world Communism hide unchanging schemes for domination, or is it simply a decent way of saying that the effort to force such a transition has been abandoned? Or is Soviet society taking a position between two lines, ready in case of danger to fall back to the old? The real question is not a question of aims, or of the face behind the mask. Perhaps these concerted schemes count less than the human reality and the movement of the whole. Perhaps the U.S.S.R. has many faces, and it is the events themselves which are equivocal. In that case the hot peace and somber humor which entered the international theater with Khrushchev ought to be greeted as a step toward clarity. If humor, as Freud said, is the mildness of the superego, perhaps this is the greatest degree of relaxation that history's superego will allow.

What good is there in having been right yesterday against Stalinism and today against the Algerian affair, what good in patiently untying the false knots of Communism and anti-Communism, and in setting down in black and white what both know better than we do, if these truths of tomorrow do not exempt a young man from the adventures of Fascism and Communism today? What good is it if these truths are sterile to the extent they are not said in a political way—in this language that speaks without saying, which touches the springs of hope and anger in every man—and which will never be the prose of what is true? Is it not an incredible misunderstanding that all, or almost all, philosophers have felt obliged to have a politics, whereas a politics arises from the "practice of life" and escapes understanding? The politics of philosophers is what no one *does*. Then is it a politics? Are there not many other things philosophers can talk about with greater assurance? And when philosophers map out wise perspectives about which the interested parties care nothing, are they not in fact confessing simply that they do not know what is at issue?

* * *

These reflections are latent a bit everywhere. We detect them in readers and writers who are or used to be Marxists and who, divided about everything else, seem to agree in *noting* the separation of philosophy and politics. More than anyone else these men have tried to unite the two in their lives. The question is dominated by their experience and must be reconsidered in the light of it.

One thing that is certain at the outset is that there has been a politi-

cal mania among philosophers which has not produced good politics or
good philosophy. Since politics, as we know, is the *modern tragedy*, we have
been waiting for its denouement. Under the pretext that all human questions are found in this drama, all political anger became holy wrath, and
reading the newspaper (as Hegel once said in his youth) the morning
prayer of philosophy. Marxism discovered all the abstract dramas of Being and Nothingness in history. It had put down an immense metaphysical burden there—and rightly so, since it was thinking of the inner framework, about the architectonic of history, about the insertion of matter and
spirit, of man and nature, and of existence and consciousness, of which
philosophy gives only the algebra or the schema. As the total reappropri-
ation of human origins in a new future, revolutionary politics passed
through this metaphysical center. But in the recent period, all forms of life
and spirit were linked to a purely tactical politics, a discontinuous series
of actions and episodes with no tomorrow. Instead of uniting their virtues,
philosophy and politics exchanged their vices: we had a disguised practice
and a superstitious thought. How many hours and arguments were wasted
over the vote of some parliamentary group or over a drawing by Picasso;
as if Universal History, Revolution, Dialectic, and Negativity were really
present in these thin communion wafers. In fact, these great historico-
philosophical concepts—deprived of all contact with knowledge, technics,
art, and changes in the economy—were bloodless. Except in the best, political strictness gave its hand to laziness, lack of curiosity, and improvisation. If this was the marriage of philosophy and politics, we are likely to
think we can only be pleased with the divorce. Some Marxist writers
have made their break with all this and are reconsidering their role. What
could be better? And yet there is a "bad" breakup between philosophy and
politics which preserves nothing and leaves both to their poverty.

Listening to these writers, we occasionally sense an uneasiness. They
say at times that they are still Marxists on the essential points (without
making it too clear which ones are essential or how one can be a Marxist
on certain points), perhaps smiling among themselves at the confusion in
which Marxists, Marxians, and Marxologists rub elbows. At other times,
on the contrary, they say that a new doctrine, almost a new system, is
needed; but they scarcely venture beyond a few borrowings from Heraclitus, Heidegger, or Sartre. The two timidities are understandable. These
men have philosophized for years inside Marxism. When they were discovering the young Marx, going back upstream to his Hegelian source,
and coming down again from there to Lenin, they often encountered the
abstract outlines of their future drama. They know that all the necessary
arms for one or several contrasting positions can be found in this tradition, and it is natural that they still think of themselves as Marxists. But

since it is also Marxism which, all things considered, has long provided them with their reasons for remaining Communists and renewing Communism's license as history's interpreter, it is understandable that, having "returned to the things themselves," they should want to put aside all intermediaries and demand a wholly new doctrine. To remain faithful to what one was; to begin everything again from the beginning—each of these two tasks is immense. In order to state the precise respects in which one is still a Marxist, it would be necessary to show just what is essential in Marx and when it was lost. One would have to point out the fork at which he stood on the genealogical tree if he wanted to be a new offshoot or main branch, or if he thought of rejoining the trunk's axis of growth, or if finally he was reintegrating Marx as a whole to an older and more recent way of thought, of which Marxism was only a transitory form. In short, one would have to redefine the relationships of the young Marx to Marx, of both to Hegel, of that whole tradition to Lenin, of Lenin to Stalin and even to Khrushchev, and finally, the relationships of Hegelo-Marxism to what had gone before and followed it. This Herculean task (of which all of Lukács' works together constitute a very guarded outline) tempted Marxists when they were in the Party because it was the only way at that time of philosophizing without seeming too evidently to do so. Now that they have left the Party, the task must seem crushing and derisory to them. And so they turn toward the sciences, art, and investigation free of Party commitments. But how upsetting it is to no longer be able to base one's calculations on the almost century-old background of Marxism, to have to *try things out* on one's own, naked, deprived of its machinery—and to do so, furthermore, in the annoying vicinity of those who have never done anything else yet were formerly dismissed rather than discussed.

They remain therefore undecided between their need to be faithful and their need to make a break, without fully accepting one or the other. Sometimes they write as if Marxism had never existed, treating history for example in terms of the formalism of the theory of games. But in other respects they keep Marxism in reserve, eluding all revision. As a matter of fact, revision is taking place; but they hide it from themselves, disguising it as a return to sources. For after all, they say, what has gone bankrupt in Marxist orthodoxy is its dogmatism, its philosophy. The true Marxism is not a philosophy, and that Marxism (which incidentally encompasses everything—Stalinism and anti-Stalinism, and the whole life of the world) is the one we hold to. Perhaps one day, after incredible detours, the proletariat will rediscover its role as the universal class, and will once more take over that universal Marxist criticism which for the moment has no historical impact or bearing. The Marxist identity of thought and action which the present calls into question is thus postponed till a later date. The appeal to an indefinite future preserves the doctrine as a way of thinking and a point of honor at the moment it is in difficulty as a way of living. According to Marx, this is precisely the vice of philosophy. But who would guess it, since at the same time it is philosophy which is made the scapegoat? Non-philosophy, which Marx taught for the profit of the revolutionary praxis, is now the refuge of uncertainty. These writers know better than anyone that the Marxist link between philosophy and politics is broken. But they act as if it were still *in principle* (and in a future—that is, an imaginary—world) what Marx said it was: philosophy simultaneously realized and destroyed in history, the negation that saves and the destruction that fulfills. This metaphysical operation has not taken place—and that is why these writers have abandoned Communism, which so incompletely realized the abstract values it destroyed in order to institute its own. These writers are not at all sure that it will ever take place. Whereupon, instead of examining its philosophical background, they transform its audacity and resolution into hopes and dreams. This consolation is not an innocent one, for it shuts the lid again on the debate which has begun within them and among them, and bottles up the questions which insist on being heard. To begin with, the question of knowing whether there is an operation of destruction-realization (particularly a realization of thought which makes its independent existence superfluous), or whether this schema does not presuppose an absolute positivity of nature and an absolute negativity of history (or antiphysis), which Marx thought were confirmed empirically but which are perhaps no more than philosophical assumptions that must be reexamined like any others. Next there is the question whether that "no" which is a "yes" (the philosophical formula of the revolution) does not justify an unlimited use of authority, and thereby raise the apparatus which has the historical role of the negative above any assignable criterion and any justifiable accusation of an inner "contradiction," even that of Budapest. It is this set of interrogations concerning Marxist ontology which is cleverly eliminated if Marxism is from the start declared valid as a truth for some later date. These questions have always constituted the pathos and profound life of Marxism, which was the trial or test of the creative negation, the realization-destruction. In forgetting them, we repudiate Marxism as revolution. In any case, if we grant without debate both Marxism's claim to be not a philosophy but the expression of a single great historical fact and its criticism of all philosophy as an alibi and sin against history, and if we confirm in another connection the present lack of any proletarian movement on a worldwide scale, we retire Marxism to inactive status and define ourselves as honorary Marxists. If philosophy alone is decreed at fault in the divorce between philosophy and politics, the divorce will be a failure. For divorces as well as marriages can fail.

We are not assuming any preestablished thesis in what we say here. Above all, we are not using the fact that Marxism and Communism alike reject philosophy as a pretext for lumping the two together before the tribunal of philosophy as absolute knowledge. There is a clear difference between the Marxist rule not to destroy philosophy without realizing it, and the Stalinist practice which simply destroys it. We are not even insinuating that this rule inevitably degenerates into that practice. What we are saying is that with the events of recent years Marxism has definitely entered a new phase of its history, in which it can inspire and orient analyses and retain a real heuristic value, but is certainly no longer true *in the sense it was believed to be true.* By placing Marxism in the order of the *second truth,* recent experience gives Marxists a new posture and almost a new method, which make it useless to call them into court. When they are asked—and ask themselves—if they are still Marxists, it is a bad question for which there are only bad answers. Not just because, as we said before, a precise answer would presuppose that an enormous labor of putting things in perspective had been accomplished, but because this task, even if it had been accomplished, could not arrive at any simple answer, since the question itself excludes a yes or a no as soon as it is asked. It would be senseless to picture recent events as one of those "crucial experiments" (which in spite of a tenacious legend do not exist even in physics) enabling us to conclude that a theory is "verified" or "refuted." It is incredible that the question should be put in these rudimentary terms, as if the "true" and the "false" were the only modes of intellectual existence. Even in the sciences, an outmoded theoretical framework can be reintegrated into the language of the one which replaced it; it remains significant, keeps *its* truth. When it is a question of reexamining the whole inner history of Marxism and its relationships to pre- and post-Marxist philosophy and history, we know from the outset that our conclusion can never be one of those platitudes heard all too often: that Marxism is "still valid" or that it is "contradicted by the facts." Behind Marxist statements, confirmed or disconfirmed, there is always Marxism as a matrix of intellectual and historical experiences, which can always be saved from total failure by means of some additional hypotheses, just as one can always maintain on the other hand that it is not validated in toto by success. For a century, the doctrine has inspired so many theoretical and practical endeavors, has been the laboratory for so many successful or unsuccessful experiments, and has been even for its opponents the stimulus of so many responses, obsessions, and profoundly meaningful counter-doctrines, that after all this it is simply as barbarous to speak of "refutation" as of "verification." Even though "errors" are to be found in the fundamental formulations or ontology of Marxism which we were just discussing, they are not of the type which one can simply strike out or forget. Even though there is no pure negation which is a yes or a yes which is an absolute negation of itself, the "error" here is not simply the contrary of the truth but rather a truth that failed. There is an internal relation of the positive and the negative, which Marx had in mind even though he mistakenly restricted it to the object-subject dichotomy. This relation is operative in whole segments of his works. Under his historical analysis, it opens new dimensions and enables them to stop being conclusive in Marx's sense of the term without ceasing to be sources of sense and open to reinterpretation. Marx's theses can remain true as the Pythagorean theorem is true: no longer in the sense it was true for the one who invented it—as an immutable truth and a property of space itself—but as a property of a certain model of space among other possible spaces. The history of thought does not summarily pronounce: this is true; that is false. Like all history, it has its veiled decisions. It dismantles or embalms certain doctrines, changing them into "messages" or museum pieces. There are others, on the contrary, which it keeps active. These do not endure because there is some miraculous adequation or correspondence between them and an invariable "reality"—such a punctual and fleshless truth is neither sufficient nor necessary in order for a doctrine to be great—but because they are still speaking beyond statements and propositions, they are intermediaries that we must use if we want to go further. These doctrines are the *classics*. They are recognizable by the fact that no one takes them literally, and yet new facts are never absolutely outside their province but call forth new echoes from them and reveal new reliefs in them. We are saying that a reexamination of Marx would be a meditation upon a classic, and that it could not possibly terminate in a *nihil obstat* or a listing on the Index. Are you or are you not a Cartesian? The question does not make much sense, since those who reject this or that in Descartes do so only in terms of reasons which owe a lot to Descartes. We say that Marx is in the process of passing into this second truth.

And we say it in the name of recent experience alone, especially that of Marxist writers. For in the last analysis, when as longtime Communists they came to leave the Party or let themselves be expelled from it, did they do so as "Marxists" or "non-Marxists"? By their actions they clearly showed that the dilemma was a verbal one, that it was necessary to move beyond it, that no doctrine could prevail against "the things themselves" or transform the suppression at Budapest into a victory for the proletariat. They did not break with orthodoxy in the name of freedom of conscience and philosophical idealism. They broke because that orthodoxy had made a proletariat decay to the point of rebellion and the harsh critique of arms, and with it the life of its unions and economy, and with its economy its inner truth and the life of art and science. Thus they made the break as Marxists. And yet in making the break they sinned against the equally Marxist rule which states that at each moment there is the camp of the proletariat and the camp of its adversaries, that every undertaking is to be evaluated in relation to this historical fissure, and that one should in no case "play the enemy's game." They were not fooling themselves then and are not fooling us now when they say that they are still Marxists, but with the added stipulation that their Marxism is no longer identified with any apparatus, that it is a view of history and not the actual movement of history—that it is, in short, a philosophy. At the moment when they made the break, they went out before or overtook, in anger or despair, one of history's silent promotions; and it is they after all who have made of Marx a classic or a philosopher.

They had been told that in the last analysis every undertaking and political or nonpolitical investigation is judged according to its political implications, the political line according to the interests of the Party, and the Party's interests according to its leaders' views. They rejected these assembly-line reductions of all proceedings and criteria to a single one. They declared that the course of history is made by different means and with a different rhythm on the level of political organization and in the proletariat, the unions, and the arts and sciences—that history has more than one focus, or more than one dimension, frame of reference, or source of meaning. Thereby they rejected a certain idea of Being as object, and of identity and difference. They have adopted the idea of a coherent Being of several foci or several dimensions. And they say they are not philosophers?

They retort: you talk about Marxism, but are you talking about it from within or without? The question no longer means much at the moment when Marxism is perhaps bursting apart and is in any case opening up. One talks about it from within when one can, and when there is no longer any way of doing so, from without. Who does any better? When one performs for Marxism the notorious "surpassing from within" which it recommended for all doctrines, is one outside or inside? One is already outside as soon as instead of re-saying things which have been said, one uses them to try to understand oneself and existing things. The question of knowing whether one is within or without arises only in respect to a historical movement or a doctrine at its birth. Marxism is less and more than that. It is an immense field of sedimented history and thought where one goes to practice and to learn to think. For the man who wanted to be the operation of history put into words, it is a grievous change. But this was precisely the height of philosophical arrogance.

There are certainly many situations of class struggle throughout the world. They exist in old countries—Yves Velan's Switzerland. They exist in countries newly come to independence. It is clear that their independence will be no more than a word if the poles of their development are defined in terms of the interests of advanced countries, and that the left wing of the new nationalisms is in conflict with the local middle classes. It is certain, on the other hand, that the new economic climates and the development of industrial society in Europe, which render the old way of parliamentary and political life decrepit, make the struggle for the control and management of the new economic apparatus the order of the day. One can of course start out from Marxism to invent the categories which orient analysis of the present, and "structural imperialism" would be one of them.[2] It is even correct to say that no *long-term* policy will be appropriate to our times if it ignores these problems and the Marxist frame of reference which discloses them. This is what we were saying before in calling Marx a classic. But is this kind of Marxism even the outline of a policy? Is the theoretical grasp of history it provides a practical one as well? In the Marxism of Marx the two went hand in hand. The answer was disclosed along with the question; the question was nothing but the beginning of the answer. Socialism was uneasiness—the course of capitalism itself. When we read that by uniting, the independent countries of North Africa will be in a position to control their development but "not to do without French capital, technicians, and trade outlets";[3] that in another connection the political and syndicalist Left in France is far from having even an imperfect grasp of the new problems; that the Communist Party in particular maintains a purely negative attitude toward neocapitalism; and finally that in the U.S.S.R., even after the Twentieth Congress, "structural imperialism" has not been abandoned; we would have to be colossal optimists to expect that "the most advanced wing of African nationalisms will soon find itself led to compare its concerns with those of the working classes of the economically dominant countries."[4] Even if this comparison took place, what policy could be drawn from it? Even if the proletariats recognized one another, what type of common action could they envisage? How could they return to the Leninist conception of the Party as such, and how could they return to it halfway? We are aware of the distance between Marxism as an instrument of theoretical analysis and the Marxism which defines theory as consciousness of practice. There are situations of class struggle, and we may if we wish formulate the world situation in terms of bourgeoisie and proletariat; but this is no longer anything but a way of speaking, and the proletariat but a name for a rationalistic politics.

What we are defending here under the name of philosophy is exactly the kind of thought which the Marxists have been driven to by events. A naive rationality can be deceived daily by our times. Discovering the fundamental through all its fissures, our age calls for a philosophical reading. Our times have not swallowed up philosophy; philosophy does not loom over our times. It is neither history's servant nor its master. Their relations are less simple than was believed. It is in a strict sense an *action at a distance,* each from the depths of its difference requiring mixture and promiscuity. We have yet to learn the good use of this encroachment. Above all, we have not yet learned a philosophy which is all the less tied down by political responsibilities to the extent it has its own, and all the more free to enter everywhere to the extent it does not take anyone's place (does not *play* at passions, politics, and life, or reconstruct them in imagination), but discloses exactly the Being in which we dwell.

* * *

The philosopher who maintains that the "historical process" passes through his study is laughed at. He gets his revenge by settling the accounts of history's absurdities. Such is his job in a vaudeville show which is now secular. Yet if we look farther back into the past, if we ask ourselves what philosophy can be today, we shall see that the philosophy that surveys was only one episode—and that it is over.

Now as before, philosophy begins with a "What is thinking?" and is absorbed in the question to begin with. No instruments or organs here. It is a pure "It appears to me that. . . ." The one before whom everything appears cannot be dissimulated from himself. He appears to himself first of all. He is this appearance of self to self. He springs forth from nothing; no thing and no one can stop him from being himself, or help him. He always was, he is everywhere, he is king on his desert island.

But the first truth can only be a half-truth. It opens upon something different. There would be nothing, if there were not that abyss of self. But an abyss is not nothing; it has its environs and edges. One always thinks of something, about, according to, after something, with regard to, in contact with something. Even the action of thinking is caught up in the upsurge of being. I cannot think identically of the same thing for more than an instant. The opening is in principle immediately filled, as if thought lived only in the nascent state. If thought maintains itself, it does so through and by means of the sliding movement which casts it into the inactual. For there is the in-actual of forgetfulness, but also the in-actual of the acquired. It is by time that my thoughts are dated. It is by time too that they make a date, open a future of thought, a cycle, a field, that the thoughts incorporate together, that they are one single thought, that they are me. Thought does not bore through time. It follows in the wake of previous thoughts, without even exercising the power (which it presumes) of retracing that wake as we could go look at the other slope of the hill again if we wished. But why do it, since the hill is there? Why assure myself that today's thought overlaps that of the day before? I know well that it does because today I see farther. It is not because I leap out of time into an intelligible world that I am able to think, or because each time I re-create significance from nothing, but because the arrow of time draws everything along with it and causes my successive thoughts to be simultaneous in a second sense, or at least to encroach legitimately upon one another. Thus I function by means of construction. I am installed on a pyramid of time which has been me. I take up a field and invent myself (but not without my temporal equipment), just as I move about in the world (but not without the unknown mass of my body). Time is that "body of the spirit" Valéry used to talk about. Time and thought are entangled in one another. In the dark night of thought dwells a glimmering of Being.

How could thought impose any necessity upon things? How could it reduce them to pure objects of its own construction? Along with time's secret link, I learn those of the perceived world, its incompatible and simultaneous "sides." I see it as it is before my eyes, but also as I would see it from another situation—and not possibly but actually, for from this moment forth it gleams *elsewhere* from many fires which are masked from me. When one says "simultaneity," do we mean time, do we mean space? That line from me to the horizon is a rail my gaze may move upon. The house on the horizon gleams solemnly like a thing past or hoped for. And inversely, my past has its space, its paths, its name-places, and its monuments. Beneath the crossed but distinct orders of succession and simultaneity, beneath the train of synchronizations added onto line by line, we find a nameless network—constellations of spatial hours, of point-events. Should we even say "thing," should we say "imaginary" or "idea," when each thing exists beyond itself, when each fact can be a dimension, when the ideas have their regions? The whole description of our landscape and the lines of our universe, and of our inner monologue, needs to be redone. Colors, sounds, and things—like Van Gogh's stars—are focal points and rays of being.

Take *others* at the moment they appear in the world's flesh. They would not exist for me, it is said, unless I recognized them, deciphering in them some sign of the presence to self whose sole model I hold within me. But though my thought is indeed only the other side of my time, of my passive and sensible being, whenever I try to grasp myself the whole fabric of the sensible world comes, and with it come the others who are caught in the fabric. Before others are or can be subjected to my conditions of possibility and reconstructed in my image, it is necessary that they be there as reliefs, divergences, and variants of one single Vision in which I too participate. For they are not fictions with which I might people my desert—offspring of my mind and forever unactualized possibilities—but my twins or the flesh of my flesh. Certainly I do not live their life; they are definitively absent from me and me from them. But that distance becomes a strange proximity as soon as we rediscover the being of the sensible, since the sensible is precisely that which can haunt more than one body without moving from its place. No one will see that table which now meets my eye: it would be necessary to be me to do that. And yet I know that at the same moment it presses upon every gaze in exactly the same way. For I see these other gazes too. Within the same field with things they sketch out a disposition of the table, linking its parts together for a new compresence. Over there, enveloped in the one I am now bringing into play, the articulation of a view of something visible is being renewed or propagated. My vision overlaps another one; or rather they function together and fall in principle upon the same Visible. Something visible to me is becoming a viewer. I am present at the metamorphosis. From now on it is no longer one thing among others; it is in circuit with them or interposes itself between them. When I look at it, my gaze no longer stops or terminates in it, as it stops or terminates in things. Through it, as through a relay, my gaze goes on toward things—the same things that I alone saw, that I alone shall ever see, but that it too, from now on, alone shall see in its way. I know that *it too* alone is itself. Everything is based upon the unsurpassable richness, the miraculous multiplication of the sensible, which gives the same things the power to be things for more than one, and makes some of the things—human and animal bodies—have not only hidden facets but have their "other side,"[5] another sentient being *taken into account on the basis of my sensible.* Everything depends upon the fact that this table over which my gaze now sweeps, probing its texture, does not belong to any "space of consciousness" and inserts itself equally well into the circuit of other bodies. Everything depends, that is, upon the fact that our gazes are not "acts of consciousness," each of which claims an indeclinable priority, but openings of our flesh which are immediately filled by the universal flesh of the world. All depends, in short, upon the fact that it is the lot of living bodies to close upon the world and become seeing bodies, touching bodies, and a fortiori sensible to themselves, since we would not be able to touch or see without being capable of being touched or of being seen. The whole enigma lies in the sensible, in that tele-vision which makes us simultaneous with others and the world in the most private aspects of our life.

What is it like when one of the others turns upon me, meets my gaze, and fastens his own upon my body and my face? Unless we have recourse to the cunning of speech, and put a common domain of thoughts between us as a third party, the experience is intolerable. There is nothing left to gaze upon but a gaze. Seer and seen are exactly interchangeable. The two gazes are immobilized upon one another. Nothing can distract them and distinguish them from one another, since things are abolished and each no longer has to do with anything but its duplicate. In terms of reflection, all we have here is "two points of view" with nothing in common—two "I think's," each of which can believe itself the winner of the trial (for after all, if I think the other is thinking of me, there is still nothing there but one of my thoughts). Vision produces what reflection will never understand—that the combat sometimes lacks a winner, and that thought henceforth lacks the one who has the right to possess it. I look at him. He sees that I look at him. I see that he sees it. He sees that I see that he sees it . . . The analysis is endless; and if that analysis were the measure of all things, gazes would slip from one another indefinitely—*there would never be but a single cogito at once.* Now, although reflections upon reflections go on, in principle, to infinity, vision is such that the obscure results of the two gazes adjust to each other, and there are no longer two consciousnesses with their own teleology but two gazes in one another, alone in the world. Vision sketches out what is accomplished by desire when it pushes two "thoughts" out toward that line of fire between them, that blazing surface where they seek a fulfillment which will be identically the same for the two of them, as the sensible world is for everyone.

Speech, as we were saying, would interrupt this fascination. It would not suppress it; it would defer it, carrying it on forward. For speech takes its impulse and is rolled in the wave of mute communication. It tears out or tears apart meanings in the undivided whole of the nameable, as our gestures do in that of the sensible. To make of language a means or a code for thought is to break it. When we do so we prohibit ourselves from understanding the depth to which words sound within us—from understanding that we have a need, a passion, for speaking and must (as soon as we think) speak to ourselves; the words have power to arouse thoughts and implant henceforth inalienable dimensions of thought; and that they put responses on our lips we did not know we were capable of, teaching us, Sartre says, our own thought. If language duplicated externally a thought which in its solitude legislates for every other possible thought, it would not be, in Freud's terms, a total "reinvestment" of our life. It would not be our element as water is the element of fish. A parallel thought and expression would each have to be complete in its own order; the irruption of one into the other, or the interception of one by the other, would be inconceivable. Now the very idea of a *complete* statement is inconsistent. We do not understand a statement because it is complete in itself; we say that it is complete or sufficient because we have understood. Nor is there any thought which is wholly thought and does not require of words the means of being present to itself. Thought and speech anticipate one another. They continually take one another's place. They are relays, stimuli for one another. All thought comes from spoken words and returns to them; every spoken word is born in thoughts and ends up in them. Between men and within each man there is an incredible vegetation of spoken words of which "thoughts" are the inner framework. But, someone will say, the reason why speech is more than noise or sound is that thought has deposited a quantity of sense in it—primarily its lexical or grammatical sense—so that there is never any contact except between thought and thought. Of course, sounds only speak for thought, but that does not mean that speech is derivative or second. Of course, the very system of language has its thinkable structure. But when we speak, we do not think about it as the linguist does; we do not even think about it—we think about *what we are saying*. It is not just that we cannot think of two things at once: they would say that, *in order to* have the signified before us (whether at emission or reception), we *must* stop representing to ourselves the code or even the message, and turn ourselves into pure operators of the spoken word. Operative language makes us think, and living thought magically finds its word. There is not *the* thought and *the* language; upon examination each of the two orders splits in two and puts out a branch into the other. There is speech that makes sense, which is called thought, and speech that lacks a sense, which is called language. It is when we do not understand that we say, "Those are words there," and, in contrast, that our own discourses are, for us, pure thought.[6] There is an inarticulate thought (the psychologists' *aha-Erlebnis*) and an accomplished thought, which suddenly and unaware discovers itself surrounded by words. Expressive operations take place between thinking language and speaking thought; not, as we thoughtlessly say, between thought and language. It is not because they are parallel that we speak; it is because we speak that they are parallel. The weakness of every "parallelism" is that it provides itself with correspondences between the two orders and conceals the operations which produced these correspondences by encroachment to begin with. The "thoughts" which weave speech and make a comprehensive system of it, the fields or dimensions of thought which the great authors and our own labor have installed in us, are open wholes of available meanings which we do not reactivate. They are the wake of thought which we do not retrace but follow along in. We have this acquisition as we have arms and legs. We make use of it without a thought, just as without thinking we "find" our arms and legs; and Valéry was right to call this speaking power in which expression premeditates itself the "animal of words." It cannot be understood as the union of two positive orders. But if the sign is only a certain deviation between signs, and the meaning a similar deviation between meanings, thought and speech overlap one another like two reliefs. As pure differences, they are indiscernible. Expression is a matter of reorganizing things-said, affecting them with a new index of curvature and folding them into a certain relief of the sense. There was that which is of itself comprehensible and sayable—notably that which more mysteriously summons all things from the depths of language beforehand as nameable. There is that which is to be said, and which is as yet no more than a precise uneasiness in the world of things-said. What is at issue is to make, somehow, the two overlap or cross one another. I would never take a step if my faraway view of the goal did not find in my body a natural art of transforming it into an approaching view. My thought could not advance one step if the horizon of sense it opens up did not become, through speech, what is called in the theater a *real décor* [*practicable*].

Language can vary and amplify inter-corporeal communication as much as we wish; it has the same source, even the same style, as inter-corporeal communication. In language too, what was secret must become public and almost *visible*. In inter-corporeal communication as in language, meanings come through in whole packages, scarcely sustained by a few peremptory gestures. In both cases I envision things and others together. Speaking to others (or to myself), I do not speak *of* my thoughts; I *speak them*, and what is between them—my afterthoughts and underthoughts. Someone will reply, "This is not *what* you say; it is what your interlocutor induces." Listen to Marivaux: "I do not dream of calling you coquettish. Those are things which are said before one dreams of saying them." Said by whom? Said to whom? Not by a mind to a mind, but by a being who has body and language to a being who has body and language, each drawing the other by invisible threads like those who hold the marionettes—*making* the other speak, *think*, and become what he is but never would have been by himself. Thus things *are said* and *are thought* by a Speech and by a Thought which we do not have but which has us. There is said to be a wall between us and others, but it is a wall we build together, each putting his stone in the niche left by the other. Even reason's labors presuppose such infinite conversations. All those we have loved, detested, known, or simply glimpsed speak through our voice. No more than space is made of points that are in themselves simultaneous, no more than our duration can sever its adherence to a space of durations, is the communicative world a bundle of parallel consciousnesses. The traces are confused and pass into one another; they make a single wake of "public durations."

We ought to think of the historical world according to this model. What good is it to wonder whether history is made by men or by things, since it is obvious that human initiatives do not cancel the weight of things, and since the "force of things" always acts through men? It is just this failure of analysis, when it tries to bring everything down to one level, which reveals history's true milieu. There is no "last analysis," because there is a flesh of history, because in it, as in our own body, everything counts and has a bearing—both the infrastructure and our idea of it, and above all the perpetual exchanges between the two in which the weight of things becomes a sign as well, thoughts become forces, and the balance of the two becomes events. It is asked, "*Where* is history made? Who makes it? What is this movement which traces out and leaves behind the figures of the wake?" It is of the same order as the movement of Thought and Speech, and, in short, of the sensible world's explosion between us. Everywhere there are senses, dimensions, and forms beyond what each "conscious-ness" could have produced, and yet it is men who speak and think and see. We are in the field of history as we are in the field of language and being.

These metamorphoses of private into public, of events into medita-tions, of thought into spoken words and spoken words into thought, this echo coming from everywhere makes it such that in speaking to others we also speak to ourselves, and speak of being. This swarming of words be-hind words, thoughts behind thoughts—this universal substitution is also a kind of stability. Joubert wrote to Chateaubriand that all he had to do was "shake his talisman." Although it is harder to live than to write books, it is a fact that, given our corporeal and linguistic equipment, everything we do ultimately has a sense and a name—even if we do not know at first which one. The ideas can no longer be considered a second positivity or second world which puts its riches on display beneath a second sun. In re-gaining the "vertical" world or being—the one which stands upright be-fore my upright body—and within it the others who are in it, we learn about a dimension in which ideas also obtain their true solidity. They are the secret axes or (as Stendhal said) the "pilings" of our spoken words, the centers of our gravitation, this very definite void around which the vault of language is constructed, and which exists actually only in the weight and counterweight of stones. But are the visible things and the world made any differently? They are always behind what I see of them, as hori-zons, and what we call visibility is this very transcendence. No thing, no side of a thing, shows itself except by actively hiding the others, denounc-ing them in the act of masking them. To see is, in principle, to see farther than one sees, to reach a being of latency. The invisible is the relief and the depth of the visible. The visible does not admit of pure positivity any more than the invisible does. As for the very source of thoughts, we now know that, in order to find it, we must seek beneath statements, and es-pecially the famous statement of Descartes. Its logical truth ("in order to think it is necessary to be") and its stated meaning betray it in principle, since they relate to an object of thought at the moment when it is necessary to find access to the one who thinks and to his native cohesion, for which the being of things and the being of the ideas are the replica. Descartes' spoken word is the gesture which shows in each of us that thinking thought to be discovered; it is the "open sesame" of fundamental thought. "Fundamental" because it is transported by nothing, but not fundamental as if with it one reached a ground upon which one ought to base oneself and stay. Fundamental thought is, in principle, bottomless, and, if you wish, an abyss. This means that it is never *with* itself, that we find it next to or setting out from things thought, that it is an opening—the other invisible extremity of the axis which affixes us to ideas and things. Must we say that this extremity is *nothing*? If it were "nothing," the differences between the near and the far (the relief of being) would be effaced before it. Dimensionality and opening would no longer make any sense. The absolutely open would be applied completely to an *unrestricted being;* and through the lack of another dimension from which it would have to be distinguished, what we call "verticality"—the present—would no longer mean anything. It would be better to speak of "the visible and the invisible," while repeating that they are not contradictory, than to speak of "being and nothingness." One says invisible as one says immobile—not in reference to what is foreign to movement, but in reference to what maintains itself there fixed. The invisible is the limit or degree zero of visibility, the opening of a dimension of the visible. There can be no question here of a zero in every respect or of an unrestricted being. When I speak of nothingness there is already being; thus this nothingness does not really annihilate, and this being is not self-identical and unquestioned. In a sense, the highest point of philosophy is perhaps no more than rediscovering these truisms: thought thinks, speech speaks, the gaze gazes. But between the two identical words there is, each time, the whole hiatus [*écart*] one straddles in order to think, in order to speak, and in order to see.

The philosophy which unveils this chiasma of the visible and the invisible is the exact opposite of a philosophy which surveys. It plunges into the perceptible, into time, into history, toward their jointures. It does not surpass them through the forces it has in its own right; it surpasses them only in their sense. Montaigne's saying that "every movement discovers us" was recently recalled and the conclusion rightly drawn from it that man exists only in movement.[7] Similarly the world holds, Being holds only in movement; it is only in this way that all things can be together. Philosophy is the recollection of this there-being [*être-là*][8] with which science is not concerned. Science is not concerned with it, because it conceives of the relationships of being and knowledge as those of the flat projections of the surveyor's plans [*géométral*]. Science forgets the being which surrounds and invests us, forgets what could be called the topology of being. But this philosophy which searches *beneath* science is not in turn "deeper" than the passions, politics, and life. There is nothing more profound than the experience which passes through the wall of being. Marivaux also wrote: "Our life is cheaper to us than ourselves, than our passions. Seeing at times what goes on in our instincts on this score, one would say that it is not necessary to live in order to be, that we live only by accident, but that it is by nature that we are." Those who go by way of passion and desire up to this being know all there is to know. Philosophy does not comprehend them better than they are comprehended; it is in their experience that it learns about being. Philosophy does not hold the world supine at its feet. It is not "a superior point of view" from which one embraces all local perspectives. It seeks contact with brute being, and instructs itself, as well, in the company of those who have never left that contact. It is just that, whereas literature, art, and the practice of life—making themselves with the things themselves, the sensible itself, beings themselves—can (except at their extreme limits) have and give the illusion of dwelling in the habitual and in the already constituted, philosophy—which paints without colors, in black and white, like copperplate engravings—does not allow us to ignore the strangeness of the world, which men confront as well as or better than it does, but as if in a half-silence.

* * *

Such in any case is the philosophy of which you will find here some attempts. It is not the philosophy, clearly, that it would be necessary to put in question, if one found that, in politics, we are speaking a bit loftily, a bit too wisely. Perhaps the truth is simply that one would need many lives to enter each realm of experience with the total abandon it demands.

But is this tone really so false? Does it have so little to recommend it? Everything we believed to be thought through, and thought through correctly—freedom and authority, the citizen against authority, the heroism of the citizen, liberal humanism, formal democracy and the real democracy which suppresses it and realizes it, revolutionary heroism and humanism—has all fallen into ruin. We are filled with scruples about these matters; we reproach ourselves for speaking about them too dispassionately. But we should be careful. What we call disorder and ruin, others who are younger live as though it were natural; and perhaps with ingenuity they are going to master it precisely because they no longer seek their bearings where we took ours. In the din of demolitions, many sullen passions, many hypocrisies or follies, and many false dilemmas also disappear. Who would have hoped it ten years ago? Perhaps we are at one of those moments when history moves on. We are stunned by French affairs or diplomacy's clamorous episodes. But underneath the noise a silence is being made, an expectation. Why could it not be a hope?

One hesitates to write these words at the moment when Sartre, in a fine recollection of our youth, has for the first time adopted the tone of despair and rebellion [in his preface to Paul Nizan's book *Aden, Arabie*].[9] But this rebellion is not a recrimination and an accusation brought against the world and others, nor is it a self-absolution. It does not revel in itself; it has a complete understanding of its own limits. It is like a rebellion of reflection. Exactly. It is the regret at not having begun by rebelling. It is an "I ought to have" which cannot be categorical, even in retrospect; for now as then Sartre knows perfectly well (and shows perfectly in his treatment of Nizan) that rebellion can neither remain rebellion nor be fulfilled in revolution. Thus he cherishes the idea of a rebellious youth, and it is a chimera, not just because there is no longer time, but because his precocious lucidity does not cut such a bad figure beside the violent delusions of others. One doubts that Sartre would have exchanged it (had he been at the age of illusions) for the illusions of wrath. It was not, as he insinuates, his natural indigence, but already the same acuteness, the same impatience with self-compromises and suspicious attitudes, the same modesty, and the same disinterestedness which have kept him from being shameless himself, and which are precisely the inspiration for the noble self-criticism we have just read. This preface to *Aden, Arabie*, is the mature Sartre lecturing the young Sartre, who like all young people pays no attention and persists there in our past; or more precisely, who is reborn at the turning of a page, forces his way into his judge, and speaks through his mouth; and speaks in such a decisive way that one finds it difficult to believe that he is so outmoded and blamable, and one comes to suspect what is after all likely, that there is only one Sartre. We do not advise young readers to believe too hastily that Sartre's life is a failure because he failed to rebel, and that they can thus expect forty or fifty irreproachable years if they are only sufficiently rebellious. Sartre offers us a debate carried on between Sartre and Sartre across the past, the present, and others. In order to make the truth manifest, he sternly confronts the Sartre of twenty and the Sartre of the Liberation and more recent years; these characters with the Nizan of twenty, Nizan the Communist, and the Nizan of September 1939; and all those people with today's "angry young men."[10] But we must not forget that the scenario is Sartre's. His continuing rule, since it is his freedom, is to refuse himself the excuses he gives so lavishly to others. His only fault, if it is one, is to set up this distinction between us and himself. In any case, it would be abusive of us to base our judgments upon it. Consequently, we must correct the perspective and recheck the balance sheet—on which, by the way, his cursed lucidity, in lighting up the labyrinths of rebellion and revolution, has recorded in spite of himself all we need to absolve him. This text is no mirror dawdled down Sartre's way; it is an act of today's Sartre. We who read and recall cannot so easily separate the guilty man from his judge; we find a family likeness in them. No, the Sartre of twenty was not so unworthy of the one who now disowns him, and today's judge still resembles him in the strictness of his sentence. As an effort of an experience to understand itself; as a self-interpretation and, through that self, an interpretation of all things; this text is not written to be read passively like a report or an inventory, but to be deciphered, meditated upon, and reread. It surely has—and this is the lot of all good literature—a richer and perhaps a different meaning than the one the author put into it.

If this were the place to do it, we would have to analyze this extraordinary rediscovery (after thirty years) of lost others. We would have to show what is fanciful in it. Not, certainly, that Nizan was not beneath his external appearance of elegance and the greatest talents the man whom Sartre describes—righteous, full of courage, and faithful to his endowments—but because the Sartre of those same days has no less reality or weight in our memory.

I kept telling him, Sartre says, that we are free, and the thin smile at the corner of his mouth which was his only answer said more about it than all my speeches. I did not want to feel the physical weight of my chains, or know the external causes which hid my true being from me and bound me as a point of honor to freedom. I saw nothing which could touch or threaten that freedom. Foolishly, I thought I was immortal. I found nothing worth thinking about in either death or anguish. I was aware of nothing in me which was in danger of being lost. I was saved, elected. In fact, I was a thinking or a writing subject; I was living externally; and the realm of Spirit, where I had my dwelling, was no more than my abstract condition as a student nourished at the Prytaneum. Being ignorant of the needs and bonds in my own self, I was unaware of them in others; that is, I was unacquainted with the travail of their lives. When I saw suffering and anguish, I imputed them to complacency or even to affectation. Squabbling, panic, horror of amours and friendships, decisions to displease—in a word, the negative—could not really last; they were chosen attitudes. I believed that Nizan had decided to be the perfect Communist. Because I was outside all struggles, particularly those of politics (and when I had engaged in politics it had been to bring my decency and my constructive, conciliatory humor to bear), I had no understanding of the effort Nizan had to make in order to emerge from childhood. Or of his loneliness. Or of his quest for salvation. His hatreds sprang from his life; they were solid gold. Mine came out of my head, counterfeit. . . .

On one point we admit that Sartre is right. It is indeed astounding that he did not see in Nizan what hit one squarely in the eye: the meditation upon death and the fragility beneath the irony and mastery. This means that there are two ways of being young, which do not easily understand one another. Some are fascinated by their childhood; it possesses them, holding them enchanted in a realm of privileged possibilities. Others, it casts out toward adult life; they believe that they have no past and are equally near to all possibilities. Sartre was one of the second type. Thus it was not easy to be his friend. The distance he put between himself and the conditions of his existence also separated him from what others have to live. No more than his own self did he allow other persons to "take hold"—to be their uneasiness or anxiety before his eyes as they were secretly and shamefully in themselves. In himself and in others, he had to learn that nothing is without roots, and that the decision not to have any roots is another way of admitting them.

But must we say that the others, those who prolonged their childhood or wanted to preserve it in going beyond it (and who thus were seeking recipes for salvation), were right and Sartre was wrong? They had to learn that one does not go beyond what one preserves, that nothing could give them the wholeness they were nostalgic for, and that if they stubbornly persisted they would soon have no choice but to be simpletons or liars. Sartre did not join them in their investigation. But could the investigation have been public? From compromise to compromise, did it not require a chiaroscuro? And they were well aware that it did. That is why the intimate and distant relations between them and Sartre were humorous. Sartre reproaches himself for them now, but would they have put up with any other sort? The most we can say is that reserve and irony are contagious. Sartre did not understand Nizan because Nizan transformed his suffering into dandyism. His books, the sequel to his life, and (for Sartre) twenty years of experience after his death were necessary before Nizan was finally understood. But did Nizan want to be understood? Is not the suffering which Sartre is now talking about the kind of admission one would rather make to a reader than to a friend? Would Nizan have ever tolerated this confidential tone between Sartre and himself? Sartre knows the answer better than we do. But let us bring up a few minor facts.

One day while we were preparing for the École Normale, we saw entering our classroom with the aura of the chosen few a former student visiting for some reason unknown to us. He was admirably dressed in dark blue, and wore the tricolor cockade of Valois. They told me it was Nizan. Nothing in his dress or carriage advertised the labors of the Khagne or of the École Normale. And when our professor (who on the contrary still felt their effect) smilingly suggested that Nizan take his place with us again, he said, "Why not?" in an icy voice and sat down quickly in an empty seat next to me, where he buried himself impassably in my Sophocles as if that had really been his only aim for the morning. When he came back from Aden, I found in my mail the card of Paul-Yves Nizan, who invited the conscript Merleau-Ponty, whose cousin he had known very well down there, to visit him one day soon in the pad he shared with Sartre. The meeting was according to protocol. Sartre's corner was empty and bare. Nizan in return had hung on the wall two foils crossed beneath a fencing mask, and it was against this background that the man whom I later knew had skirted suicide in Araby appeared to me. Much later, I ran into him on the back platform of bus S. He was married, a militant, and on this particular day loaded down with a heavy briefcase and untypically wearing a hat. He brought up Heidegger's name himself, and had a few words of praise for him in which I sensed a desire to show that he had not abandoned philosophy. But he spoke so coldly that I would not have dared to ask him openly. I like to recall these little facts. They prove nothing, but they are vital. They make us feel that if Sartre did not follow too closely the travail which was going on in Nizan, Nizan for his part—by virtue of humor, reserve, and politeness—entered more than halfway into the game. I have said that Sartre would understand him only after thirty years, because Sartre was Sartre, but also because Nizan was Nizan. And above all because they both were young; that is, peremptory and timid. And perhaps after all for one final, deeper reason.

Did the Nizan Sartre reproaches himself for having misunderstood exist entirely in 1928—before his family, his books, his life as a militant, his break with the Party, and above all his death at thirty-five? Because he perfected, enclosed, and immobilized himself in these thirty-five short years, they have slid twenty years behind us in a block, and now we would have it that everything he might have been is given at their inception and in each moment of them. Feverish like a beginning, his life is also solid like an ending. He is forever young. And because on the contrary we have been given time to be mistaken more than once, and to correct our mistakes, our comings and our goings cover up our tracks. Our own youth is worn out and insignificant for us, inaccessible to us as it really was. To another life which ends too soon, I apply the standard of hope. To mine, which is perpetuated, the severe rule of death. A young man has done a lot if he has been a "perhaps." It seems to us that a mature man who is still around has done nothing. As in the things of childhood, it is in the lost comrade that I find plenitude, *either because the faith which creates has dried up within me, or because reality takes shape only in memory.*[11] Another retrospective illusion, about which Bergson has not spoken: not that of preexistence, but that of the fall. Perhaps time does not flow from the future or the past. Perhaps it is the distance which makes for us the reality of the

other and especially the lost other. But that distance could also rehabili-
tate us if we could take it in relation to ourselves. As a balance to what
Sartre writes today about himself and Nizan at twenty, what the Nizan of
fifty could have said about their youth will be forever missing. For us, they
were two men starting out in life, and starting out opposite one another.

What makes Sartre's account melancholy is that in it one sees the two
friends slowly learning from experience what they could have learned
from one another at the outset. Nizan had been confiscated by his father's
image. He was possessed by the drama (older than he was) of a worker
who, having left his class, discovers that his life since then has been unreal
and a failure, and ends his days hating himself. Consequently, Nizan knew
from the start the weight of childhood, the body, and society, as well as the
interwoven ties that bind us to our parents and to history in one single
anxiety. He would not have put an end to this fascination with his father's
image, perhaps indeed he would have aggravated it, by simply choosing
marriage and the family, taking up the father's role for his own. If he
wanted to reenter the life cycle his father's life had turned him out of, he
had to purify its source, break with the society which had produced their
solitude, and undo what his father had done, setting out upon his road
again in the opposite direction. In proportion to the passing years, the
omens multiply, the evident truth approaches. The flight to Aden is the
last attempt at a solution through adventure. It would have been no more
than a diversion if Nizan had not found in the colonial regime (either by
chance or because confusedly he was looking for this particular lesson)
the clear image of our dependence in respect to the external world. So,
suffering has external causes; they are identifiable, have a name, can be
abolished. So, there is an external enemy, and we are helpless against him
if we stay by ourselves. So, life is war and social war. Nizan already knew
what Sartre said much later. In the beginning is not play but need. We do
not keep the world, or situations, or others at the length of our gaze like
a spectacle; we are intermingled with them, drinking them in through all
our pores. We are what is lacking in everything else; and within us, with
the nothingness which is the center of our being, a general principle of
alienation is given. Before Sartre, Nizan lived this pantragism, this flood
of anxiety which is also the flux of history.

But for this very reason, and because he was not living in the tragic,
Sartre understood much sooner the artifices of salvation and of the return
to the positive. He was not exactly an optimist; he never equated the Good
and Being. Nor was he saved, one of the elect. He was vigorous, gay, and
enterprising; all things which lay before him were new and interesting.
Precisely. He was *supralapsarian,* this side of tragedy and hope, and thus
well equipped to tease out their secret knots. His premonitions find their

factual demonstration in Nizan's experience during the ten years preceding the war; and when he tells about that experience today—when he takes it up again on his own account, profoundly and fraternally—he cannot help finding exactly what he has been telling us since then about conversions. One day a man declares himself a Christian or a Communist. Just what does he mean? We are not completely changed in an instant. What happens is simply that in recognizing an external cause of his destiny, man suddenly gets permission and even the mission (as I believe Maritain used to say) to *live in the bosom of the faith of his natural life*. It is neither necessary nor possible for his backslidings to stop; from then on they are "consecrated."[12] His torments are now stigmata whose stamp is an immense Truth. The sickness he was dying of helps him, and helps others, to live. He is not required to renounce his talents, if he has any. On the contrary, the loosening of the anxiety which had clutched his throat releases them. To live, to be happy, to write meant to give in to slumber; it was suspect and base. Now it means recovering from sin what sin presumptuously had claimed, or, as Lenin used to say, stealing from the bourgeoisie what the bourgeoisie had stolen. Looking ahead, Communism catches a glimpse of another man and another society. But for the time being, and for a whole long period which is called negative, what it turns against the bourgeois State is the machinery of the State. It turns the means of evil against the evil. From now on, each thing is divided in two, depending on whether it is considered according to its evil origin or in the perspective of the future it calls forth. The Marxist is the wretch he was; he is also that wretchedness restored to its place in the total scheme of things and known in terms of its causes. As a writer in a period of "demoralization," he prolongs bourgeois decadence; but in the very process of doing so he bears witness to it and surpasses it toward a different future. Nizan the Communist "saw the world and saw himself there."[13] He was subject and he was object. As object, lost along with his times; as subject, saved along with the future. Yet this divided life is one single life. Marxist man is a product of history, and he also participates from within in history as the production of a new society and a new man. How is this possible? He would have to be reintegrated as a finite being into the finite productivity. That is why many Marxists have been tempted by Spinozism, and Nizan was one of them. As Nizan did, Sartre liked Spinoza; but in opposition to the transcendent and the reconcilers, the equivalent of whose contrivances he was quick to find in Spinoza in the form of "the affirmative plentitude of the finite mode which at the same time bursts its bonds and returns to the infinite substance."[14] In the end, Spinoza does everything to hide the peculiar virtue and work of the negative; and Spinozist Marxism is simply a fraudulent way of assuring us in this life of the return of the positive. The adhesion to an infinite positivity is a pseudonym for naked anxiety—the pretense to have crossed the negative and reached the other shore; to have exhausted, totalized, internalized death. "We do not have even this, not even this unmediated communication with our nothingness."[15] Sartre found his philosophical formulation later. But he sensed at twenty-five that there is trickery and falsification when the savior counts himself out of the reckoning. Nizan wanted to stop thinking about himself and he succeeded; he had regard only for causal chains. But it was still he—the naysayer, the irreplaceable one—who annihilated himself in the things.[16] True negativity cannot be made of two positivities joined together, my being as a product of capitalism and the affirmation of a new future through me. For there is a rivalry between them, and one or the other must win. Having become a means of edification and a professional theme, rebellion may be no longer felt, no longer lived. Marxist man is saved by the doctrine and the movement. He sets himself up in his job. According to the old criteria, he is lost. Or (and this is what happens to the best) he does not forget or lie to himself—his wisdom is reborn from his continual suffering, and his incredulity is his faith—but he cannot say so, and in that case he must lie to others. Hence the impression we get from so many conversations with Communists: they possess the most objective thought there is, but the most anguished and, beneath its toughness, secretly slack and humid. Sartre has always known and said (and this is what has kept him from being a Communist) that the Communist negation, being positivity reversed, is not what it says it is, or that it double-talks like a ventriloquist.

Seeing the subterfuges of the "negative man" so well, it is astonishing that he should sometimes speak with such nostalgia of the phase that is quite critical prior to 1930, especially since the Revolution already had its counterfeit coin in its "constructive" period. The explanation is that Sartre has resigned himself to the inevitable, later and upon reflection, as to a lesser evil. He never simply reoccupied the positions Nizan held thirty years ago. He justifies them at one remove from them, for reasons which remain his own, in the name of any experience which led him to commitment without modifying what he has always thought of salvation. But this experience, which begins in 1939, we still have to trace again.

In 1939, Nizan is going to discover abruptly that one is not so quickly saved, that adherence to Communism does not free one from dilemmas and heart-rending anxiety, while Sartre, who knew it, begins that apprenticeship in history and the positive which was to lead him later on to a sort of Communism from without. Thus their paths cross. Nizan returns from Communist politics to rebellion, and the apolitical Sartre becomes acquainted with the social. This fine account must be read. It must be read over Sartre's shoulder, as his pen sets it forth—all mixed in with his reflections and mixing ours in too.

Nizan, he says, had admitted that the new man and the new society did not yet exist; that perhaps he would not see them himself; and that it was necessary to dedicate oneself to that unknown future without weighing the sacrifice or constantly haggling over and contesting the Revolution's means. He said nothing about the Purge Trials. Comes another, clearer, test for him. Responsible for the foreign affairs section of a Party journal, he has explained a hundred times that the Soviet alliance would avert both Fascism and war. He repeats it in July 1939, at Marseille, where Sartre accidentally runs into him.

Here I ask permission to add a word of my own: Nizan knew that perhaps we would not avoid both Fascism and war, and within himself he had accepted war if it was the only means of containing Fascism. It happens that I can bear witness to this. Maybe three weeks after his meeting with Sartre, I in turn saw Nizan. It was in Corsica, at Porto, at Casanova's,[17] if I am not mistaken. He was gay and smiling, as Sartre had seen him. But (whether his friends were getting him ready for a new line or whether they were themselves being worked on from higher up I do not know) he no longer said that Fascism would be brought to its knees by autumn. He says: "We will have war against Germany, but with the U.S.S.R. as an ally, and we shall win it in the end." He says it firmly, serenely (I can still hear his voice), as if he were released from himself at last.

Fifteen days later came the Nazi-Soviet Pact, and Nizan left the Communist Party. Not, he explained, because of the pact, which beat Hitler's Western friends at their own game. But the French Party should have saved its dignity, pretending indignation and giving the appearance of declaring its independence. Nizan realized that to be a Communist is not to play a role one has chosen but to be caught in a drama where without knowing it one receives a different role. It is a lifetime undertaking which one carries on in faith or ends up pulling out of, but which in any case exceeds agreed-upon limits and the promises of prudence. If it is like this, and if it is true that in the Communist life as in the other nothing is ever irrevocably accomplished—if years of labor and of action can be stricken in a twinkling with derision—in that case, Nizan thinks, I cannot do it, and the answer is no.

What is Sartre thinking at the same moment? He would like to believe that Nizan has deceived him. But no, Nizan resigns. He is the one who has been deceived. They are two children in the world of politics. A harsh world where the risks cannot be calculated and where peace is perhaps given only to those who do not fear war. One acts in a show of force only if one is determined to make use of it. If one shows it fearfully, one has war and defeat. "I discovered . . . the monumental error of a whole generation . . . : we were being pushed toward massacres across a fierce prelude to war, and we thought we were strolling on the lawns of peace."[18]

Thus Sartre and Nizan were deceived in different ways, and they learned a different lesson from their deception. Nizan had accepted force and war and death for a very clear cause; events made sport of his sacrifice, and he no longer had any sanctuary but himself. Sartre, who had believed in peace, discovered a nameless adversity which had to be clearly taken into account. A lesson he will not forget. It is the source of his pragmatism in politics. In a world bewitched, the question is not to know who is right, who follows the truest course, but who is the match for the Great Deceiver, and what action will be tough and supple enough to bring it to reason.

One can understand, then, the objections Sartre makes today to the Nizan of 1939, and why they are without weight against him. Nizan, he says, was angry. But is that anger a matter of mood? It is a mode of understanding which is not too inappropriate when the fundamental is at stake. For anyone who has become a Communist and has acted within the Party day after day, things said and done have a weight, because he has said and done them too. In order to take the change in line of 1939 as he should, Nizan would have to have been a puppet. He would have to have been broken, and he had not become a Communist to play the skeptic. Or, again, he would have to have been only a sympathizer. But the Party is not at issue, Sartre also says. Death does not come to Nizan through the Party. "The massacre was brought to birth by the Earth, and sprang forth on all sides."[19] All right. But this is justifying the Party relatively as a fact in the Earth's history. For Nizan, who is in it, it is all or nothing.

"An impulsive act," Sartre rejoins. "If he had lived, I tell myself that the Resistance would have brought him back into the ranks as it brought others."[20] Into the ranks, certainly. But into the ranks of the Party? That is another matter. It is almost the opposite: a function of authority, a mark of distinction. Even rallied to the cause, he would not have forgotten the episode. The Communism he had abandoned was the sagacious doctrine for which the Revolution is both family and fatherland. He would have found an adventurous Communism which played the role of the Revolution through the Resistance, after having played the role of defeatism, and in expecting to play, after the war, the role of reconstruction and compromise. Even if he had to, would Nizan have been able to follow this sequence—he who had believed in Marxism's truth? He would have been able to on the condition that he had not taken a position each time. It is one thing, from without or after the fact (which is the same thing), to justify with documents in hand the detours of Communism. It is another thing to organize the deception and to be the deceiver. I recall having written from Lorraine, in October 1939, some prophetic letters which divided the roles between us and the U.S.S.R. in a Machiavellian fashion. But I had not spent years preaching the Soviet alliance. Like Sartre, I had no party: a good position for serenely doing justice to the toughest of parties. We were not wrong, but Nizan was right. Communism from without has no lessons to teach Communists. Sometimes more cynical than they and sometimes less, rebellious where they consent, resigned where they reject, it is a natural lack of comprehension of Communist life. Nizan "unlearned," but that means learning, too. If his rebellion in 1939, which was based upon his reasons for being, and for being a Communist, was a strategic withdrawal, then so was the Budapest uprising.

One starting out from anxiety, the other from gaiety; one taking the road toward happiness, the other toward tragedy; both drawing near to Communism, one from its classical and the other from its shadowy side; and both finally rejected by events; Nizan and Sartre have perhaps never been closer to one another than today, at the hour when their experiences mutually clarify one another in these profound pages. In order to say now what conclusions all this tends toward, we must draw out some of the sparkling words which this meditation strikes from Sartre. What is unimpaired in Sartre is the sense of the new and freedom: "Lost freedom will not be found except by being invented. It is forbidden to look back, even in order to determine the dimensions of our 'authentic' needs."[21] But where in the present are the arms and emblems of this true negativity, which cannot be satisfied with giving different names to the same things? Should we look to the new course of events or to new peoples for what the Russia of the October generation has not given to the world? Can we displace our radicalism? History gives no pure and simple answers. Shall we say to the young: "Be Cubans, be Russian or Chinese, according to your taste, be Africans? They will answer that it is pretty late to change extraction."[22] What perhaps is clear in China is at least implicit and confused here; the two histories do not mesh. Who would dare maintain that China, even if she has the power some day, will *liberate*, let us say, Hungary or France? And where in the France of 1960 is the sense of wild freedom to be found? A few young people maintain it in their lives, a few Diogenes in their books. Where is it, let us not even say in public life, but in the masses? Freedom and invention are in the minority, of the opposition. Man is hidden, well hidden, and this time we must make no mistake about it: this does not mean that he is there beneath a mask, ready to appear. Alienation is not simply privation of what was our own by natural right; and to bring it to an end, it will not suffice to steal what has been stolen, to give us back our due. The situation is far more serious: there are no faces underneath the masks, historical man has never been human, and yet no man is alone.

Thus we see by what right and in what sense Sartre can take up the young Nizan's claim again and offer it to the rebellious young men of today. "Nizan used to speak bitterly of the old guys who laid our women and intended to castrate us."[23] Nizan wrote: "As long as men are not complete and free, they will dream at night."[24] Nizan said "that love was true and they kept us from loving; that life could be true, that it could give birth to a true death, but they made us die before we were even born."[25] Thus our brother love is there, our sister life, and even our sister bodily death, as promising as childbirth. Being is there within reach; we only have to free it from the reign of the old men and the rich. Desire, be insatiable: "Turn your rage upon those who have provoked it; do not try to escape your trouble; seek out its causes and smash them."[26] Alas! Nizan's story, which Sartre goes on to tell, shows clearly enough that it is not so easy to find the true causes—and *smash them* is precisely the language of a war in which the enemy cannot be grasped. The complete man, the man who does not dream, who can die well because he lives well, and who can love his life because he envisages his death is, like the myth of the Androgynes, the symbol of what we lack.

It is just that since this truth would be too harsh, Sartre retranslates it into the language of the young, the language of the young Nizan. "In a society which reserves its women for the old and the rich. . . ."[27] This is the language of sons. It is the Oedipal word one hears in each generation. Sartre quite properly says that each child in becoming a father simultaneously kills his father and regenerates him. Let us add that the good father is an accessory to the immemorial childishness; he offers himself up to the murder in which his childhood lives anew, and which confirms him as a father. Better to be guilty than to have been impotent. Noble dodge for hiding life from children. This bad world is the one "we have made for them."[28] These ruined lives are those "which have been made . . . which are being manufactured today for the young."[29] But that is not true. It is not true that we have at any moment been masters of things, nor that, having clear problems before us, we have botched everything by our futility. The young will learn precisely in reading Sartre's preface that their elders have not had such an easy life. Sartre is spoiling them. Or rather, exactly following the pattern he has always followed, he is hard on the children of his spirit, who are already in their forties, but grants everything to those who follow—and starts them out again in the eternal return of rivalry. It is Nizan who was right; there is your man; read him. . . .

I would like to add: read Sartre too. This little sentence, for example, which weighs so heavily: "The same reasons take happiness from us and render us forever incapable of possessing it."[30] Does he mean the same *causes,* and that it is not this humanity but another which will be happy? That would be, like Pascal, staking everything on a beyond. However, he says the same *reasons.* The fall is thus not an accident; its causes count us as accomplices. There is equal weakness in blaming ourselves alone and in believing only in external causes. In one way or another we will always *miss the mark* if we do. Evil is not *created* by us or by others; it is born in this web that we have spun between us—and that is suffocating us. What new men, and sufficiently tough, will be patient enough to remake it truly?

The conclusion is not rebellion, it is "virtù" [*la virtu*][31] without any resignation. A disappointment for whoever believed in salvation, and in a single means of salvation in all realms. Our history, where space reappears, where China, Africa, Russia, and the West are not advancing at the same pace, is a decline for whoever believed that history, like a fan, is going to fold in upon itself. But if this philosophy of time was still a reverie born of the old distress, why then should we judge the present from such a height in its name? There is no universal clock, but local histories take form beneath our eyes, and begin to regulate themselves, and haltingly are linked to one another and demand to live, and confirm the powerful in the wisdom which the immensity of the risks and the consciousness of their own disorder had given them. The world is more present to itself in all its parts than it ever was. In world capitalism and in world Communism and between the two, more truth circulates today than twenty years ago. History never confesses, not even its lost illusions, but it does not begin them again.

February and September 1960

Eye and Mind

What I am trying to translate for you is more mysterious; it is en-
twined in the very roots of being, in the impalpable source of
sensations.

    —J. Gasquet, *Cézanne*

I

Science manipulates things and gives up dwelling in them. It gives itself
internal models of the things, and, operating on the basis of these indices
or variables, the transformations that are permitted by their definition,
science confronts the actual world only from greater and greater distances. It is, and always has been, that admirably active, ingenious, and
bold way of thinking, that one-sided thought that treats every being as an
"object in general," that is, at once as if all being were nothing to us and,
however, is discovered predestined for our artifices.

    But classical science held onto the feeling of the opaqueness of the
world, and through its constructions it intended to join back up with the
world. This is why it believed that it had to look for a transcendent or transcendental foundation for its operations. There is today—not in science
but in a widely prevalent philosophy of the sciences—something entirely
new: the constructive practice takes itself to be and gives itself off as autonomous. Thought is deliberately reduced to the set of collecting and
capturing techniques that thought invents. To think is thus to try out, to
operate, to transform—the only restriction being that this activity is regulated by an experimental control that admits only the most "worked-up"
phenomena, phenomena produced by our machines rather than recorded
by them. Whence all sorts of vagabond endeavors. Today more than ever,
science is sensitive to intellectual fashions. When a model has succeeded
in one order of problems, it is tried out everywhere else. Currently, our
embryology and biology are full of *gradients*. Just how these differ from
what the classical tradition called "order" or "totality" is not at all clear.

This question, however, is not and must not be asked. The gradient is a net we throw out to sea, without knowing what it will haul in. Or yet, it is the slender branch upon which unforeseeable crystallizations will form. No doubt this freedom of operation will serve well to overcome many a pointless dilemma—provided only that from time to time we bring it into focus, and we ask ourselves why the apparatus works in one place and fails in others. In short, this flowing science must understand itself. It must see itself as a construction based on a brute or existent world and not claim for its blind operations the constitutive value that the "concepts of nature" were able to have in an idealist philosophy. To say that the world *is*, by nominal definition, the object x of our operations is to adjust the scientist's epistemic situation to the absolute, as if everything that was and is has never existed save in order to enter the laboratory. Thinking "operationally" becomes a sort of absolute artificialism, such as we see in the ideology of cybernetics, where human creations are derived from a natural information process, but which is itself conceived on the model of human machines. If this kind of thinking takes over humanity and history, and if, pretending to be ignorant of what we know about humanity and history through contact and through location, it sets out to construct them on the basis of a few abstract indices as a decadent psychoanalysis and culturalism have done in the United States, since man truly becomes the *manipulandum* he thinks he is, then we enter into a cultural regimen in which there is neither truth nor falsehood concerning humanity and history, then we enter into a sleep or nightmare from which nothing would be able to awaken us.

It is necessary that the thought of science—surveying thought, thought of the object in general, be placed back in the "there is" which precedes it, back in the site, back upon the soil of the sensible world and the soil of the worked-upon world such as they are in our lives and for our bodies, not that possible body which we may legitimately think of as an information machine, but this actual body I call mine, this sentinel standing silently under my words and my acts. It is necessary that *associated bodies* be awakened along with my body, "others," who are not my congeners, as the zoologist says, but others who haunt me and whom I haunt; "others" along with whom I haunt a single, present, and actual Being as no animal has ever haunted the others of his own species, territory, or habitat. In this primordial historicity, the agile and improvisatory thought of science will learn to ground itself upon the things themselves and upon itself, and will once more become philosophy. . . .

Now art and especially painting draw from this pool of brute sense, about which activism wants to know nothing. Art and painting alone do this in full innocence. From the writer and the philosopher, we want opinions and advice. We will not allow them to hold the world suspended. We want them to take a stand; they cannot waive the responsibilities of man who speaks. Music, at the other extreme, is too far on the hither side of the world and of the designatable to depict anything but certain sketches of Being—its ebb and flow, its growth, its upheavals, its turbulence. Only the painter is entitled to gaze upon everything without being obliged to appraise what he sees. For the painter, we might say, the watchwords of knowledge and action lose their meaning and force. Political regimes which denounce "degenerate" painting rarely destroy the pictures. They hide them, and one senses here an element of "one never knows" amounting almost to an acknowledgment. The reproach of escapism is seldom aimed at the painter; we do not hold it against Cézanne that he lived hidden away at L'Estaque during the Franco-Prussian War. Everyone recalls with respect his "Life is frightening," although the most insignificant student, after Nietzsche, would flatly reject philosophy if it was said that philosophy does not teach us how to live life to the fullest. It is as if in the painter's calling there were an urgency that passed beyond every other urgency. The painter is there, strong or frail in life, but sovereign incontestably in his rumination on the world, sovereign without any other "technique" than the one that his eyes and hands are given by means of seeing, by means of painting; he is there relentless to pull from this world, in which the scandals and achievements of history resound, *canvases* which will hardly add to the angers or the hopes of humanity; and no one mutters. What, then, is the secret science which he has or which he seeks? That dimension by means of which Van Gogh wants to go "further"? What is this fundamental of painting, perhaps of all culture?

II

The painter "takes his body with him," says Valéry. And indeed, we cannot see how a Mind could paint. It is by lending his body to the world that the artist changes the world into paintings. To understand these transubstantiations we must go back to the working, actual body—not the body as a chunk of space or a bundle of functions but that body which is an intertwining of vision and movement.

It is enough to see something in order to know how to reach it and deal with it, even if I do not know how that is done in the machine made of nerves. My moving body counts in the visible world, participates in it; that is why I can direct my body in the visible. Moreover, it is also true that vision depends on movement. We see only what we gaze upon. What would vision be without any eye movement, and how would the movement of the eyes not blur things if movement were itself a reflex or blind, if it did not have its antennae, its clairvoyance, if vision were not prefigured in it? All my changes of place figure in principle in an area of my landscape; they are carried over onto the map of the visible. Everything I see is in principle within my reach, at least within the reach of my sight, and is marked upon the map of the "I can." Each of the two maps is complete. The visible world and the world of my motor projects are both total parts of the same Being.

This extraordinary overlapping, which we never give enough thought to, forbids us to conceive of vision as an operation of thought that would set up before the mind a picture or a representation of the world, a world of immanence and of ideality. Immersed in the visible by his body, itself visible, the seer does not appropriate what he sees; he merely approaches it by means of the gaze, he opens onto the world. And for its part, that world in which he participates is not in-itself or matter. My movement is not a decision made by the mind, an absolute doing which would decree, from the depths of a subjective retreat, some change of place miraculously executed in extended space. It is the natural sequel to and the maturation of vision. I say of a thing that it is moved, but my body moves *itself;* my movement unfolds *itself.* It is not in ignorance of itself, blind to itself; it radiates from a self. . . .

The enigma derives from the fact that my body is simultaneously seeing and visible. The one who gazes upon all things can also be gazed upon and can recognize, in what he sees then, the "other side" of his seeing power. He sees himself seeing; he touches himself touching; he is visible and sensitive for himself. He is a self, not by transparency, like thought, which never thinks anything except by assimilating it, constituting it, transforming it into thought—but a self by confusion, narcissism, inherence of the one who sees in what he sees, of the one who touches in what he touches, of the sensing in the sensed—a self, therefore, that is caught up in things, having a front and a back, a past and a future. . . .

This initial paradox cannot but produce others. Visible and mobile, my body is a thing among things; it is one of them. It is caught in the fabric of the world, and its cohesion is that of a thing. But because it sees and moves itself, it holds things in a circle around itself. Things are an annex or prolongation of my body; they are incrusted in its flesh, they are part of its full definition; the world is made of the very stuff of the body. These reversals, these antinomies, are different ways of saying that vision is caught or is made in the middle of things, where something visible undertakes to see, becomes visible for itself and through the vision of all things, where the indivision of the sensing and the sensed persists, like the original fluid within the crystal.

This interiority does not precede the material arrangement of the human body, and it no more results from it. If our eyes were made in such a way as to prevent our seeing any part of our body, or if some diabolical contraption were to let us move our hands over things while preventing us from touching our own body—or if, like certain animals, we had lateral eyes with no intersection of visual fields, this body, which would not reflect itself, would not sense itself, this nearly adamantine body, which would not be entirely flesh, would not be a human body, and there would be no humanity. But humanity is not produced as an effect through our articulations or through the way our eyes are implanted in us (still less by the existence of mirrors, though they alone can make our entire bodies visible to us). These contingencies and others like them, without which there would be no man, do not by simple summation bring it about that there is one sole man. The body's animation is not the assemblage or juxtaposition of its parts. Nor is it a question of a mind coming down from somewhere else into an automaton—which would still imply that the body itself is without an inside and without a "self." A human body is present when, between seeing and visible, between touching and touched, between one eye and the other, between the hand and the hand a kind of crossover is made, when the spark of the sensing-sensible is lit, when the fire starts to burn that will not stop burning until some accident of the body unmakes what no accident would have sufficed to make. . . .

Now, as soon as this strange system of exchanges is given, all the problems of painting are there. These problems illustrate the enigma of the body and the enigma justifies the problems. Since things and my body are made of the same stuff, it is necessary that my body's vision be made somehow in the things, or yet that their manifest visibility doubles itself in my body with a secret visibility. "Nature is on the inside," says Cézanne. Quality, light, color, depth, which are over there before us, are there only because they awaken an echo in our bodies and because the body welcomes them. Why would this internal equivalence, this carnal formula of their presence that the things arouse in me not arouse an outline that is again visible, in which every other gaze would find again the motifs that support their inspection of the world? Thus there appears a visible to the second power, a carnal essence or icon of the first. It is not a faded copy, a trompe l'oeil, or another *thing*. The animals painted on the walls of Lascaux are not there in the same way as are the fissures and limestone formations. Nor are they *elsewhere*. Pushed forward here, held back there, supported by the wall's mass they use so adroitly, they radiate about the wall without ever breaking their elusive moorings. I would be hard-pressed to say *where* the picture is that I am gazing at. For I do not gaze at it as one gazes at a thing, I do not fix it in its place. My gaze wanders within it as in the halos of Being. Rather than seeing it, I see according to, or with it.

The word "image" is in bad repute because we have thoughtlessly believed that a drawing was a tracing, a copy, a second thing, and that the mental image was such a drawing, belonging among our private bric-a-brac. But if in fact it is nothing of the kind, then neither the drawing nor the picture belongs to the in-itself any more than the image does. They are the inside of the outside and the outside of the inside, which the duplicity of sensing [le sentir] makes possible and without which we would never understand the quasi-presence and imminent visibility which make up the whole problem of the imaginary. The picture, the actor's mimicry—these are not extras that I borrow from the real world in order to aim across them at prosaic things in their absence. The imaginary is much nearer to and much farther away from the actual. It is nearer because it is the diagram of the life of the actual in my body, its pulp and carnal obverse exposed to view for the first time. In this sense, Giacometti says energetically, "What interests me in all paintings is resemblance—that is, what resemblance is for me: something that makes me uncover the external world a little."[1] And the imaginary is much further away from the actual because the picture is an analogue only according to the body; because it does not offer to the mind an occasion to rethink the constitutive relations of things, but rather it offers to the gaze traces of the vision of the inside, in order that the gaze may espouse them; it offers to vision that which clothes vision internally, the imaginary texture of the real.

Shall we say, then, that there is a gaze from the inside, a third eye that sees the pictures and even the mental images, as we used to speak of a third ear which grasps messages from the outside through the noises they caused inside us? But what's the use of saying this, when the whole point is to understand that our fleshly eyes are already much more than receptors for beams of light, colors, and lines? They are computers of the world, which have the gift for the visible as we say of the inspired man that he has the gift of tongues. Of course this gift is earned by exercise; it is not in a few months, or in solitude, that a painter comes into full possession of his vision. That is not the question: precocious or belated, spontaneous or cultivated in museums, his vision in any event learns only by seeing and learns only from itself. The eye sees the world, and it sees what the world lacks in order to be a painting, and what the picture lacks in order to be itself, and, on the palette, the colors for which the picture is waiting; and it sees, once it is done, the picture that responds to all these lacks, and it sees the paintings of others, the other responses to other lacks. It is no more possible to make a restrictive inventory of the visible than it is to catalog the possible usages of a language or even its vocabulary and turns of phrase. The eye is an instrument that moves itself, a means which invents its own ends; it is that which has been moved by some impact of the world, which it then restores to the visible through the traces of a hand. In whatever civilization it is born, from whatever beliefs, motives, or thoughts, no matter what ceremonies surround it—and even when it appears devoted to something else—from Lascaux to our time, pure or impure, figurative or not, painting celebrates no other enigma but that of visibility.

What we have just said amounts to a truism. The painter's world is a visible world, nothing but visible: a world almost mad, because it is complete though only partial. Painting awakens and carries to its highest power a delirium which is vision itself, since to see is *to have at a distance;* painting extends this strange possession to all aspects of Being, aspects which must somehow be made visible in order to enter into painting. When, apropos of Italian painting, the young Berenson spoke of an evocation of tactile values, he could hardly have been more mistaken; painting evokes nothing, least of all the tactile. What it does is entirely different, almost the inverse. Painting gives visible existence to what profane vision believes to be invisible; thanks to painting we do not need a "muscular sense" in order to possess the voluminosity of the world. This voracious vision, reaching beyond the "visual givens," opens upon a texture of Being of which the discrete sensorial messages are only the punctuations or the caesurae. The eye dwells in this texture as man dwells in his house.

Let us remain within the visible in the narrow and prosaic sense. The painter, any painter, *while he is painting,* practices a magical theory of vision. He has to admit really that the things pass into him or that, according to Malebranche's sarcastic dilemma, the mind goes out through the eyes to wander among the things, since he never stops adjusting his seeing upon their basis. (It makes no difference if he does not paint from "nature"; he paints, in any case, because he has seen, because the world has at least once engraved in him the ciphers of the visible.) He must affirm, as one philosopher has said, that vision is a mirror or concentration of the universe or that, in another's words, the *idios kosmos* opens by virtue of vision upon a *koinos kosmos,* finally that the same thing is both out there in the heart of the world and here in the heart of vision—the same or, if you will, a *similar* thing, but according to an efficacious similarity which is the parent, the genesis, the metamorphosis of being into his vision. It is the mountain itself which from over there makes itself seen by the painter; it is the mountain that he interrogates with his gaze.

What exactly does he ask of it? To unveil the means, which are nothing but visible, by which the mountain makes itself into a mountain before our eyes. Light, lighting, shadows, reflections, color, all these objects of his investigation are not altogether real beings; like ghosts, they have only visual existence. In fact they exist only at the threshold of profane vision; they are not commonly seen. The painter's gaze asks them how they make something suddenly be there, and how they compose this talisman of a world, this thing, how they make us see the visible. The hand pointing toward us in *The Night Watch* is truly there when its shadow on the captain's body presents the hand to us simultaneously in profile. The spatiality of the captain lies at the crossing of the two perspectives which are incompossible and yet together. Everyone with eyes has at some time or other witnessed this play of shadows, or something like it, and has been made by it to see things and a space. But it worked in them without them; it dissimulated itself in order to show the thing. In order to see the thing, it was not necessary to see the play of shadows and light around it. The visible in the profane sense forgets its premises; it rests upon a total visibility which is to be re-created and which liberates the phantoms captive in profane vision. The moderns, as we know, have liberated many others; they have added many a muted tone to the official gamut of our means of seeing. But the interrogation of painting in any case aims at this secret and feverish genesis of things in our body.

The interrogation, therefore, is not the question of someone who knows to someone who does not know; it is not the schoolmaster's question. It is the question of someone who does not know to a vision that knows everything, a vision that we do not make but that is made in us. Max Ernst (and surrealism) is right to say, "Just as the role of the poet since [Rimbaud's] famous *Lettre du voyant* consists in writing under the dictation of what is being thought, of what articulates itself in him, the painter's role is to circumscribe and project what is making itself seen within himself."[2] The painter lives in fascination. The actions most proper to him—those gestures, those outlines of which he alone is capable and which will be revelations to others because they do not have the same lacks as he does— they seem to emanate from the things themselves, like figures emanating from constellations. Inevitably the roles between the painter and the visible switch. That is why so many painters have said that things look at them. As André Marchand says, following Klee: "In a forest, I have felt many times over that it was not I who looked at the forest. Some days I felt that the trees were looking at me, were speaking to me. . . . I was there, listening. . . . I think that the painter must be penetrated by the universe and not want to penetrate it. . . . I expect to be inwardly submerged, buried. Perhaps I paint to break out."[3] What we call "inspiration" should be taken literally. There really is inspiration and expiration of Being, respiration in Being, action and passion so slightly discernible that we no longer know who sees and who is seen, who paints and what is painted. We say that a human being is born the moment when something that was only virtually visible within the mother's body becomes at once visible for us and for itself. The painter's vision is an ongoing birth.

> the fact that one is 'seeing' and is visible in painting testifies to the act of looking, being a 'bringing into reach' of one's bodily space. One sees' oneself in the fact that one sees at all. Vision is for [of] my body / my world (XI)

In the pictures themselves we could seek a figured philosophy of vision—its iconography, perhaps. It is no accident, for example, that frequently in Dutch paintings (as in many others) an interior in which no one is present is "digested" by the "round eye of the mirror."[4] This prehuman gaze is the emblem of the painter's gaze. More completely than lights, shadows, and reflections, the specular image sketches, within things, the work of vision. Like all other technical objects, such as tools and signs, the mirror has sprung up along the open circuit running from the seeing body to the visible body. Every technique is a "technique of the body." The technique figures and amplifies the metaphysical structure of our flesh. The mirror emerges because I am both seeing and visible, because there is a reflexivity of the sensible; the mirror translates and reproduces that reflexivity. Through it, my outside becomes complete. Everything that is most secret about me passes into that *face,* that flat, closed being of which I was already dimly aware, from having seen my reflection mirrored in water. Schilder observes that, smoking a pipe before a mirror, I feel the sleek, burning surface of the wood not only where my fingers are but also in those glorious fingers, those merely visible ones inside the mirror.[5] The mirror's phantom draws my flesh outside, and at the same time the invisible of my body can invest the other bodies that I see. Hence my body can include segments drawn from the body of others, just as my substance passes into them; man is a mirror for man. Mirrors are instruments of a universal magic that changes things into spectacles and spectacles into things, me into another and another into me. Painters have often dreamed about mirrors because beneath this "mechanical trick" they recognized, as they did in the case of the "trick" of perspective,[6] the metamorphosis of seeing and the visible that defines both our flesh and the painter's vocation. This also explains why they have so often loved to draw themselves in the act of painting (they still do—witness Matisse's drawings), adding to what *they* could see of things at that moment, what *things* could see of them—as if to attest to there being a total or absolute vision, outside of which nothing remains, and which closes itself back up upon them. How can we name, where are we to place in the world of the understanding these occult operations, together with the portions and idols they concoct? Consider, as Sartre did in *Nausea,* the smile of a long-dead monarch which keeps producing and reproducing itself on the surface of a canvas. It is too little to say that it is there as an image or as an essence; it is there itself, as that which was always most alive about it, the moment I gaze upon the picture. The "world's instant" that Cézanne wanted to paint, an instant long since passed away, is still hurled toward us by his canvases. His *Mont. Sainte-Victoire* is made and remade differently from one end of the world to the other but no less energetically than in the hard rock above Aix.

The self-portrait as a "being seen"—a "total vision" (a fundamental ontology of seeing?)

Essence and existence, imaginary and real, visible and invisible—painting blurs all our categories, spreading out before us its oneiric universe of carnal essences, efficacious resemblances, muted meanings.

III

How crystal clear everything would be in our philosophy if only we would exorcise these spectres, make illusions or objectless perceptions out of them, brush them to one side of an unequivocal world! Descartes' *Optics* is an attempt to do just that. It is the breviary of a thought that wants no longer to haunt the visible and decides to reconstruct it according to the model of the visible that this thought has provided for itself. It is worthwhile to remember this attempt and its failure.

Here there is no concern to cling to vision. The problem is to know "how it is done," but only enough to invent, whenever the need arises, certain "artificial organs" which correct it.[7] We are to reason not so much upon the light we see as upon the light which, from the outside, enters our eyes and regulates our vision. And for that we are to rely upon "two or three comparisons which help us to conceive it [light]" in such a way as to explain its known properties and deduce others.[8] The question being so formulated, it is best to think of light as an action by contact—not unlike the action of things upon the blind man's cane. The blind, says Descartes, "see with their hands."[9] The Cartesian model of vision is modeled after the sense of touch.

At one swoop, then, Descartes eliminates action at a distance and relieves us of that ubiquity which is the whole problem of vision (as well as its peculiar virtue). Why should we henceforth puzzle over reflections and mirrors? These unreal duplications are a class of things; they are real effects like a ball bouncing back. If the reflection resembles the thing itself, it is because this reflection acts upon the eyes more or less as a thing would. It deceives the eye by engendering a perception which has no object, yet this perception does not affect our idea of the world. In the world there is the thing itself, and outside this thing itself there is that other thing which is only reflected light rays and which happens to have an ordered correspondence with the real thing; there are two individuals, then, connected by causality from the outside. As far as the thing and its mirror image are concerned, their resemblance is only an external denomination; the resemblance belongs to thought. The disturbing relationship of resemblance is a clear relationship of projection into the things. A Cartesian does not see *himself* in the mirror; he sees a puppet, an "outside," which, he has every reason to believe, other people see in the very same way, but which is no more for himself than for others a flesh. His "image" in the mirror is an effect of the mechanics of things. If he recognizes himself in it, if he thinks it "looks like him," it is his thought that weaves this connection. The specular image is in no sense *a part of* him.

There is no longer any power of icons. However vividly an etching may "represent to us" forests, towns, men, battles, storms, it does not resemble them. It is only a bit of ink put down here and there on paper. A figure flattened down onto a plane surface scarcely retains the forms of things; it is a deformed figure that *must* be deformed—the square becomes a lozenge, the circle an oval—*in order to* represent the object. It is an image of the object only on the condition of "not resembling it."[10] If not through resemblance, how, then, does it work? It "excites our thought" to "conceive," as do signs and words "which in no way resemble the things they signify."[11] The etching gives us sufficient indices, unequivocal "means" for forming an idea of the thing that does not come from the icon itself; rather, it arises in us, as "occasioned" by the icon. The magic of intentional species—the old idea of efficacious resemblance so strongly suggested to us by mirrors and paintings—loses its final argument if the entire power of the picture is that of a text to be read, a text totally free of promiscuity between the seeing and the visible. We need no longer try to understand how a painting of things in the body could make them felt in the soul— an impossible task, since the resemblance between this painting and those things would have to be seen in turn, since we would "have to have other eyes in our brain with which to apperceive it,"[12] and since the problem of vision remains intact even after we have introduced these simulacra, wandering between things and us. What the light casts upon our eyes, and thence upon our brain, does not resemble the visible world any more than etchings do. Nothing goes from things to the eyes, and from the eyes to vision, no more than from things to a blind man's hands, and from his hands to his thoughts. Vision is not the metamorphosis of the things themselves into the vision of them; it is not the double belonging of the things to the big world and to a little private world. It is a thinking that strictly deciphers the signs given within the body. Resemblance is the result of perception, not its basis. Thus, the mental image, the visualization [*la voyance*] which renders present to us what is absent, is a fortiori nothing like a breakthrough to the heart of Being. It is still a thought relying upon bodily indices—this time insufficient ones—which are made to say more than they mean. Nothing is left of the oneiric world of analogy. . . .

What interests us in these famous analyses is that they make us aware of the fact that every theory of painting is a metaphysics. Descartes does not say much about painting, and one might think it unfair on our part to make so much of a few pages on engravings. Yet the very fact that he speaks of painting only in passing is itself significant. Painting for him is not a central operation contributing to the definition of our access to being; it is a mode or a variant of thinking, where thinking is canonically defined as intellectual possession and self-evidence. His very brevity is the indication of a choice; a closer study of painting would draw a different philosophy. It is significant, too, that when he speaks of "pictures" [*tableaux*] he takes the drawing as typical. We shall see that the whole of painting is present in each of its modes of expression; there is a drawing, a line that embraces all of painting's boldness. But what Descartes likes about engravings is that they preserve the form of objects, or at least they give us sufficient signs of their forms. They present the object by its outside, or its envelope. If he had examined that other, deeper opening upon things given us by the secondary qualities, especially color, then—since there is no rule-governed or projective relationship between them and the true properties of things, and we understand their message all the same—he would have found himself faced with the problem of a conceptless universality and opening upon things. He would have been obliged to find out how the uncertain murmur of colors can present us with things, forests, storms—in short the world. He would have been obliged, perhaps, to integrate perspective, as a particular case, into a broader ontological power. But for him it goes without saying that color is an ornament, mere coloring, and that the entire power of painting lies in that of drawing, and the power of drawing rests upon the ordered relationship between it and objective space established by perspectival projection. Pascal's famous saying that painting is frivolous because it attaches us to images whose originals would not move us is a Cartesian saying. For Descartes it is self-evident that one can paint only existing things, that their existence consists in being extended, and line drawing makes painting possible by making possible the representation of extension. Thus painting is only an artifice that puts before our eyes a projection similar to the one things themselves would (and do, according to the commonsense view) inscribe in them. Painting causes us to see, in absence of the true object, just as we see the true object in life; and in particular it makes us see space where there is none.[13] The picture is a flat thing that gives to us artificially what we would see in the presence of "diversely positioned" things, by offering sufficient diacritical signs, through height and width, of the dimension that it lacks. Depth is a *third dimension* derived from the other two.

It will be worth our while to dwell for a moment upon this third dimension. There is, at first glance, something paradoxical about it. I see objects that hide each other and that consequently I do not see since they are

one behind the other. I see depth and yet it is not visible, since it is reckoned from our bodies to things, and since we are glued to our bodies.
This mystery is a false mystery. I do not truly see depth or, if I do, it
is only another *width*. On the line from my eyes to the horizon, the foreground forever hides all the other planes, and if on either side I think I see
things staggered at intervals, it is because they do not completely hide
each other. Thus I see each thing outside the others, according to a width
measured differently.[14] We are always on the hither side of depth, or
beyond it. Never *are* the things one behind the other. The encroachment
and latency of the things do not enter into their definition. They express
only my incomprehensible solidarity with one of them—my body; and by
their positivity they are thoughts that I form and not attributes of things.
I know that at this very moment another man, situated elsewhere—or
better, God, who is everywhere—could penetrate their hiding place and
see them openly deployed. What I call depth is either nothing, or else it is
my participation in a Being without restriction, first and foremost a participation in the being of space beyond every particular point of view.
Things encroach upon one another *because they are outside one another.* The
proof of this is that I can see depth by looking at a picture which everyone
agrees has none and which organizes for me an illusion of an illusion. . . .
This two-dimensional being, which makes me see a third, is a being that
is pierced [*troué*]—as people said during the Renaissance, a window. . . .
But in the final analysis the window opens only upon *partes extra partes,*
upon height and width merely seen from another angle—upon the absolute positivity of Being.

It is this space without hiding places which in each of its points is
only what it is, neither more nor less, this identity of Being that underlies
the analysis of engravings. Space is in itself; or rather, it is the in-itself par
excellence. Its definition is *to be* in itself. Every point of space is, and is
thought as being, right where it is—one here, another there; space is the
self-evidence of the "where." Orientation, polarity, envelopment are, in
space, derived phenomena connected to my presence. Space remains absolutely in itself, everywhere equal to itself, homogeneous; its dimensions,
for example, are by definition interchangeable.

Like all classical ontologies, this one elevates certain properties of
beings into a structure of Being, and in so doing it is both true and false.
Reversing Leibniz's remark, we might say that it is true in what it denies
and false in what it affirms. Descartes' space is true, when contrasted with
a thought too empirically dominated, which dares not construct. It was
necessary first to idealize space, to conceive of that being—perfect of its
kind, clear, manageable, and homogeneous—which thought surveys [*la
pensée survole*] without a viewpoint: a being which thought transcribes in

Poussin's foreground would fit this

its entirety onto three right-angled axes. This had to be done so that we could one day experience the limitations of that construction and understand that space does not have three, neither more nor less, dimensions, as an animal has either four or two legs, that dimensions are taken by different systems of measurement from a single dimensionality, a polymorphous Being, which justifies all of them without being fully expressed by any. Descartes was right in liberating space. His mistake was to erect it into a positive being, beyond all points of view, all latency and depth, devoid of any real thickness.

He was also right in taking his inspiration from the perspectival techniques of the Renaissance; they encouraged painting to produce freely experiences of depth and in general presentations of Being. These techniques were false only in that they claimed to close the investigation and history of painting, in that they claimed to found once and for all an exact and infallible art of painting. As Panofsky has shown concerning the Renaissance, this enthusiasm was not without bad faith.[15] The theoreticians tried to forget the spherical visual field of the ancients, their angular perspective which connects the apparent size not to distance but to the angle from which we see the object. They wanted to forget what they disdainfully called *perspectiva naturalis,* or *communis,* in favor of a *perspectiva artificialis* capable in principle of founding an exact construction. To accredit this myth, they went so far as to expurgate Euclid, omitting from their translations the eighth theorem, which bothered them. But the painters knew from experience that no technique of perspective is an exact solution and that there is no projection of the existing world which respects it in all aspects and which deserves to become the fundamental law of painting. They knew that linear perspective was far from being an ultimate breakthrough; on the contrary, it opened several pathways for painting. For example, the Italians took the way of representing the object, but the Northern painters discovered and worked out the formal technique of *Hochraum, Nahraum,* and *Schrägraum.* Thus plane projection does not always stimulate our thought to rediscover the true form of things, as Descartes believed. Beyond a certain degree of deformation, it refers us back, on the contrary, to our own vantage point; as for the things, they flee into a remoteness that no thought traverses. Something about space evades our attempts to survey it from above. The truth is that no acquired means of expression resolves the problems of painting or transforms it into a technique. For no symbolic form ever functions as a stimulus. Symbolic form works and acts only in conjunction with the entire context of the work, and not at all by means of trompe l'oeil. The *Stilmoment* never dispenses with the *Wermoment.*[16] The language of painting is never "instituted by nature"; it must be made and remade. The perspective of the Renaissance is no infallible "gimmick." It is only one particular case, a moment in a poetic information of the world which continues after it.

Yet Descartes would not have been Descartes if he had thought to *eliminate* the enigma of vision. There is no vision without thought, but it is not enough to think in order to see. Vision is a conditioned thought; it is born "as occasioned" by what happens in the body; it is "incited" to think by the body. It does not *choose* either to be or not to be or to think this thing or that. It must carry in its heart that heaviness, that dependence which cannot come to it by some intrusion from outside. Such bodily events are "instituted by nature" in order to bring us to see this thing or that. The thinking that belongs to vision functions according to a program and a law which it has not given itself. It does not possess its own premises; it is not a thought altogether present and actual; there is in its center a mystery of passivity. Thus the situation is as follows. Everything we say and think of vision turns vision into a *thought*. When, for example, we wish to understand how we see the situation of objects, we have no other recourse than to suppose the soul to be capable, knowing where the parts of its body are, of "transferring its attention from there" to all the points of space that lie along the prolongation of its bodily members.[17] But this is still only a "model" of the event. For how does the soul know that space of its body which it extends toward things, that primary *here* from which all the *theres* will come? This space is not, like them, just another mode or specimen of extension; it is the place of the body that the soul calls "mine," a place the soul inhabits. The body it animates is not, for it, one object among objects, and it does not deduce from its body all the rest of space as an implied premise. The soul thinks according to the body, not according to itself, and space, or exterior distance, is also stipulated within the natural pact that unites them. If, at a certain degree of accommodation and convergence of the eye, the soul sees a certain distance, the thought which draws the second relationship from the first is like an immemorial thought inscribed in our inner workings. "Usually this comes about without our reflecting upon it—just as, when we clasp a body with our hand, we conform the hand to the size and shape of the body and thereby sense the body, without having need to think of those movements of the hand."[18] The body is both the soul's native space, and the matrix of every other existing space. Thus vision is double. There is the vision upon which I reflect; I cannot think it except *as* thought, the mind's inspection, judgment, a reading of signs. And then there is the vision that actually occurs, an honorary or instituted thought, collapsed into a body—its own body, of which we can have no idea except in the exercise of it, and which introduces, between space and thought, the autonomous order of the composite of soul and body. The enigma of vision is not eliminated; it is shifted from the "thought of seeing" to vision in act.

Still, this de facto vision and the "there is" which it contains do not upset Descartes' philosophy. Since it is thought united with a body, it cannot, by definition, truly be conceived. One can practice it, exercise it, and, so to speak, exist it; yet one can draw nothing from it which deserves to be called true. If, like Queen Elizabeth,[19] we want at all costs to think something about it, all we can do is go back to Aristotle and scholasticism, and conceive thought as corporeal, which does not conceive itself, but which is the only way to formulate, for the understanding, the union of soul and body. The truth is that it is absurd to submit to pure understanding the mixture of understanding and body. These would-be thoughts are the emblems of "the practice of everyday life," the verbal blazons of the union, legitimate on the condition that we do not take them to be thoughts. They are indices of an order of existence—of humanity and world as existing—that we are not burdened to think. This order marks out no terra incognita on our map of Being. It does not confine the scope of our thoughts, because the order as well as the scope of our thoughts is sustained by a Truth which grounds its obscurity as well as our own lights. We have to go to these lengths to find in Descartes something like a metaphysics of depth. For we are not present at the birth of this Truth; God's being is for us an abyss. An anxious trembling quickly mastered; for Descartes it is just as futile to plumb that abyss as it is to think the space of the soul and the depth of the visible. Our position disqualifies us from looking into such things. That is the secret of Cartesian equilibrium: a metaphysics which gives us definitive reasons to do metaphysics no longer, which validates our self-evidence while limiting it, which opens up our thinking without rending it.

The secret has been lost, and lost for good, it seems. If we are ever again to find an equilibrium between science and philosophy, between our models and the obscurity of the "there is," it must be a new equilibrium. Our science has rejected the justifications as well as the restrictions which Descartes assigned to its domain. It no longer claims to deduce its invented models from the attributes of God. The depth of the existing world and that of an unfathomable God no longer double the flatness of "technicized" thought. Science manages without the detour into metaphysics that Descartes had to make at least once in his life; it begins from the point he ultimately reached. Operational thought claims for itself, in the name of psychology, that domain of contact with oneself and with the world which Descartes reserved for a blind but irreducible experience. Operational thought is fundamentally hostile to philosophy as thought in contact, and if it rediscovers the sense of that philosophy, it will be through the very excess of its daring; it will rediscover this sense when, having introduced all sorts of notions that Descartes would have held to arise from confused thought—quality, scalar structures, solidarity of observer and observed—it suddenly realizes that one cannot summarily speak of all these beings as *constructa*. Meanwhile, philosophy maintains itself against such operationalist thinking, plunging itself into that dimension of the composite of soul and body, of the existent world, of the abyssal Being that Descartes opened up and so quickly closed again. Our science and our philosophy are two faithful and unfaithful offshoots of Cartesianism, two monsters born of its dismemberment.

Nothing is left for our philosophy but to set out to prospect the actual world. We *are* the compound of soul and body, and so there must be a thought of it. It is to this knowledge by position or situation that Descartes owes what he himself says of it, or what he sometimes says of the presence of the body "against the soul," or of the exterior world "at the tip" of our hands. Here the body is no longer the means of vision and touch, but their depository. Our organs are not instruments; on the contrary, our instruments are added-on organs. Space is not what it was in the *Optics*, a network of relations between objects such as would be seen by a third party witnessing my vision, or by a geometer who reconstructs my vision and surveys it. It is, rather, a space to be reckoned starting from me as the null point or degree zero of spatiality. I do not see it according to its exterior envelope; I live it from the inside; I am immersed in it. After all, the world is around me, not in front of me. Light is found once more to be action at a distance. It is no longer reduced to the action of contact or, in other words, conceived as it might be by those who cannot see. Vision reassumes its fundamental power of manifestation, of showing more than itself. And since we are told that a bit of ink suffices to make us see forests and storms, light must have its own power to generate *its* imaginary. Its transcendence is not delegated to a reading mind which deciphers the impacts of the light qua thing upon the brain and which could do this quite as well if it had never inhabited a body. No longer is it a matter of speaking about space and light, but of making the space and the light that are there speak. There is no end to this questioning, since the vision to which it is addressed is itself a question. All the investigations we believed closed have been reopened. What is depth, what is light, τί τo ὄv? What are they—not for the mind that cuts itself off from the body but for the mind Descartes says is suffused throughout the body? And what are they, finally, not only for the mind but for themselves, since they pass through us and around us?

This philosophy, which is still to be made, is what animates the painter—not when he expresses opinions about the world but in that instant when his vision becomes gesture, when, in Cézanne's words, he "thinks in painting."[20]

IV

The entire history of painting in the modern period, with its efforts to detach itself from illusionism and acquire its own dimensions, has a metaphysical significance. There can be no question of demonstrating this claim. Not because of the limits of objectivity in history and the inevitable plurality of interpretations, which would forbid linking a philosophy and an event, for the metaphysics we have in mind is not a separate body of ideas for which inductive justifications could then be sought in the experiential realm—and there are, in the flesh of contingency, a structure of the event and a virtue peculiar to the scenario that do not prevent the plurality of interpretations but in fact are the deepest reason for it. They make the event a durable theme of historical life, and have a right to philosophical status. In a sense everything that may have been said and will be said about the French Revolution has always been and will henceforth be within it, in that wave arising from a roil of discrete facts, with its froth of the past and its crest of the future. And it is always by looking better at *how it was made* that we provide and will go on providing new representations of it. As for the history of works of art, in any case, if they are great, the sense we give to them after the fact has issued from them. It is the work itself that has opened the field from which it appears in another light. It metamorphoses *itself* and *becomes* what follows; the interminable reinterpretations to which it is *legitimately* susceptible change it only into itself. And if the historian unearths beneath its manifest content a surplus and thickness of sense, the texture which was preparing a long future, then this active manner of being, this possibility he unveils in the work, this monograph he finds there—all are grounds for a philosophical meditation. But such a labor demands a long familiarity with history. We lack everything for its execution, both the competence and the location. But since the power or the generativity of works of art exceeds every positive causal or filial relation, it is not illegitimate for a layman, speaking from his memory of a few pictures and books, to say how painting enters into his reflections, and to register the feeling of a profound discordance, a mutation in the relationship between man and Being, when he brings a universe of classical thought into confrontation with the investigations of modern painting. A sort of history by contact that perhaps does not go beyond the limits of one person, though it owes everything to the frequentation of others. . . .

Giacometti says, "I believe Cézanne was seeking depth all his life."[21] Robert Delaunay says, "Depth is the new inspiration."[22] Four centuries after the "solutions" of the Renaissance and three centuries after Descartes, depth is still new, and it insists on being sought, not "once in his life" but all throughout a life. It is not possible that what is at issue is an interval without any mystery, an interval as seen from an airplane, between these trees nearby and those farther away. Nor is it a matter of the sleight of hand by means of which one thing is replaced by another, as a perspective drawing represents to me so vividly. These two views are very explicit and raise no question. What brings about the enigma is their connection; the enigma is what is between them. I see things, each one in its place, precisely because they eclipse one another; they are rivals before my gaze precisely because each one is in its own place. The enigma is their known exteriority in their envelopment and their mutual dependence in their autonomy. Once depth is understood in this way, we can no longer call it a third dimension. In the first place, if it were a dimension, it would be the first one; there are forms and definite planes only if it is stipulated how far from me their different parts are. But a first dimension and one that contains all the others is no longer a dimension, at least in the ordinary sense of a *certain relationship* according to which we make measurements. Depth thus understood is, rather, the experience of the reversibility of dimensions, of a global "locality" in which everything is at the same time, a locality from which height, width, and distance are abstracted, the experience of a voluminosity we express in a word when we say that a thing is there. In pursuing depth, what Cézanne is seeking is this deflagration of Being, and it is all in the modes of space, and in the form as well. Cézanne already knew what cubism would restate: that the external form, the envelope, is secondary and derived, that it is not what makes a thing take form, that that shell of space must be shattered—the fruit bowl must be broken. But then what should be painted instead? Cubes, spheres, and cones—as he said once? Pure forms having the solidity of what could be defined by an internal law of construction, forms which taken together, as traces or cross-sections of the thing, let it appear between them like a face in the reeds? This would be to put Being's solidity on one side and its variety on the other. Cézanne had already made an experiment of this kind in his middle period. He went directly to the solid, to space—and came to find that inside this space—this box or container too large for them—the things begin to move, color against color, they begin to modulate in the instability.[23] Thus we must seek space and its content together. The problem becomes generalized; it is no longer solely that of distance, line, and form; it is as well the problem of color.

Color is the "place where our brain and the universe meet," he says in that admirable idiom of the artisan of Being which Klee liked to quote.[24] It is for the sake of color that we must break up the form qua spectacle. Thus the question is not of colors, "simulacra of the colors of nature."[25] The question, rather, concerns the dimension of color, that dimension which creates—from itself to itself—identities, differences, a texture, a materiality, a something. . . . However, decidedly, there is no recipe for the visible, and color alone is no closer to being such a recipe than space is. The return to color has the virtue of getting somewhat nearer to "the heart of things,"[26] but this heart is beyond the color envelope just as it is beyond the space envelope. The *Portrait of Vallier* sets white spaces between the colors which take on the function of giving shape to, and setting off, a being more general than yellow-being or green-being or blue-being. Similarly, in the watercolors of Cézanne's last years, space (which had been taken to be self-evidence itself and of which it was believed that the question of *where* was not to be asked) radiates around planes that cannot be assigned to any place at all: "a superimposing of transparent surfaces," "a flowing movement of planes of color which overlap, advance and retreat."[27]

As we can see, it is no longer a matter of adding one dimension to the two of the canvas, of organizing an illusion or an objectless perception whose perfection consists in resembling as much as possible empirical vision. Pictorial depth (as well as painted height and width) comes "I know not whence" to germinate upon the support. The painter's vision is no longer a view upon an *outside*, a merely "physical-optical"[28] relation with the world. The world no longer stands before him through representation; rather, it is the painter who is born in the things as by the concentration and the coming-to-itself of the visible. And, ultimately, the picture relates to anything at all among experienced things only on the condition of being first of all "auto-figurative." It is a spectacle of something only by being a "spectacle of nothing,"[29] by breaking the "skin of things"[30] to show how the things are made into things, how the world made world. Apollinaire said that in a poem there are phrases which do not appear to have been *created*, which seem to have *formed themselves*. And Henri Michaux said that sometimes Klee's colors seem to have been born slowly upon the canvas, to have emanated from some primordial ground, "exhaled at the right spot"[31] like a patina or a mold. Art is not skillful construction, skillful artifice, the skillful relation, from the outside, to a space and a world. It is truly the "inarticulate cry," as Hermes Trismegistus said, "which seemed to be the voice of the light." And once art is present it awakens powers that are asleep in ordinary vision, a secret of preexistence. When through the water's thickness I see the tiled bottom of the pool, I do not see it *despite* the water and the reflections; I see it through them and because of them. If there were no distortions, no ripples of sunlight, if I saw, without this flesh, the geometry of the tiles, then I would stop seeing the tiled bottom as it is, where it is, namely, farther away than any identical place. I cannot say that the water itself—the aqueous power, the syrupy and shimmering element—is *in* space; all this is not somewhere else either, but it is not in the pool. It dwells in it, is materialized there, yet it is not contained there; and if I lift my eyes toward the screen of cypresses where the web of reflections plays, I must recognize that the water visits it as well, or at least sends out to it its active and living essence. This inner animation, this radiation of the visible, is what the painter seeks beneath the names of depth, space, and color.

Anyone who thinks about the matter finds it astonishing that very often a good painter can also produce good drawings or good sculpture. Since neither the means of expression nor the creative gestures are comparable, this is proof that there is a system of equivalences, a Logos of lines, of lighting, of colors, of reliefs, of masses—a non-conceptual presentation of universal Being. The effort of modern painting has been directed not so much toward choosing between line and color, or even between figurative depiction and the creation of signs, as it has been toward multiplying the system of equivalences, toward severing their adherence to the envelope of things. This effort may require the creation of new materials or new means of expression, but it may well be realized at times by the reexamination and reuse of those already at hand. There has been, for example, a prosaic conception of the line as a positive attribute and property of the object in itself. Thus, it is the contour of the apple or the border between the plowed field and the meadow, considered as present in the world, such that, guided by points taken from the real world, the pencil or brush would only have to pass over them. But this line has been contested by all modern painting, and probably by all painting, as we are led to think by da Vinci's comment in his *Treatise on Painting:* "The secret of the art of drawing is to discover in each object the particular way in which a certain flexuous line, which is, so to speak, its generating axis, is directed through its whole extent."[32] Both Ravaisson and Bergson sensed something important in this, without daring to decipher the oracle all the way. Bergson scarcely looked for the "sinuous individual [*serpentement individuel*]" anywhere else than in living beings, and he rather timidly advanced the idea that the undulating line "could be no one of the visible lines of the figure," that is "no more here than there," and yet "gives the key to the whole."[33] He was on the threshold of that gripping discovery, already familiar to the painters, that there are no lines visible in themselves, that neither the contour of the apple nor the border between field and meadow is in this place or that, that they are always on the near or the far side of the point we look at. They are always between or behind whatever we fix our eyes upon; they are indicated, implicated, and even very imperiously demanded by the things, but they themselves are not things. They were supposed to circumscribe the apple or the meadow, but the apple and the meadow "form themselves" from themselves, and come into the visible as if they had come from a pre-spatial world behind the scenes. Now the contestation of the prosaic line does not rule out all lines in painting, as perhaps the impressionists have believed. It is simply a matter of freeing the line, of revivifying its constituting power; and we are not faced with a contradiction when we see it reappear and triumph in painters like Klee or Matisse, who more than anyone believed in color. For henceforth, as Klee said, the line no longer imitates the visible, it "renders visible," it is the sketch of a genesis of things. Perhaps no one before Klee had "let a line dream."[34] The beginning of the line's path establishes or installs a certain level or mode of the linear, a certain manner for the line to be and to make itself a line, "d'aller ligne."[35] Relative to it, every subsequent inflection will have a diacritical value, will be another aspect of the line's relationship to itself, will form an adventure, a history, a sense of the line, insofar as the line slants more or less, more or less rapidly, more or less subtly.

Making its way in space, it nevertheless eats away at prosaic space and its *partes extra partes;* it develops a way of extending itself actively into that space which subtends the spatiality of a thing quite as well as that of an apple tree or a man. It is just that, as Klee said, in order to give the generating axis of a man, the painter "would have to have a network of lines so entangled that it could no longer be a question of a truly elementary representation."[36] It makes little difference whether the painter decides, like Klee, to hold rigorously to the principle of the genesis of the visible, the principle of fundamental, indirect, or—as Klee used to say—absolute painting, and then leave it up to the *title* to designate by its prosaic name the being thus constituted, in order to leave the painting free to function more purely as a painting; or alternatively, like Matisse in his drawings, the painter decides to put into a single line both the prosaic, identifying characteristics of the being and the hidden operation that composes in the being the indolence or inertia and the force in order to constitute it as *nude,* as *face,* or as *flower.* There are the two holly leaves that Klee has painted in the most figurative way. These two holly leaves are rigorously indecipherable at first, and they remain to the end monstrous, unbelievable, phantasmic, *because of exactness.* And Matisse's women (let us keep in mind his contemporaries' sarcasm) were not immediately women; they became women. It is Matisse who taught us to see his shapes not in a "physical-optical" way but rather as structural filaments [*des nervures*], as the axes of a corporeal system of activity and passivity. Whether it be figurative or not, the line is no longer a thing or an imitation of a thing. It is a certain disequilibrium contrived within the indifference of the white paper; it is a certain drilling operation practiced within the in-itself, a certain constitutive emptiness—an emptiness which, as Moore's statues show decisively, sustains the supposed positivity of things. The line is no longer, as in classical geometry, the appearance of a being against the emptiness of a background. It is, as in the modern geometries, the restriction, segregation, or modulation of a pre-given spatiality.

Just as painting has created the latent line, it has made for itself a movement without a change of place, a movement by vibration or radiation. And well it should, since, as they say, painting is an art of space, is made upon a canvas or sheet of paper and so lacks the wherewithal to devise things that actually move. But an immobile canvas could suggest a change of place, just as a shooting star's track on my retina suggests to me a transition, a motion not contained in it. The picture itself would then offer to my eyes almost the same thing offered them by real movements: a series of appropriately blurred, instantaneous views along with, if it is a matter of a living thing, attitudes unstably suspended between a before and an after—in short, the outsides of a change of place which the spectator would read in its trace. Here Rodin's well-known remark reveals its full weight: instantaneous views, unstable attitudes petrify movement, as is shown by so many photographs in which an athlete in motion is forever frozen. We could not thaw him out by multiplying the glimpses. Marey's photographs, the cubists' analyses, Duchamp's *Bride* do not move; they give a Zenonian reverie on movement. We see a rigid body as if it were a piece of armor going through its motions; it is here and it is there, magically, but it does not *go* from here to there. Cinema portrays movement, *but how?* Is it, as we are inclined to believe, by copying more closely the changes of place? We may presume not, since slow motion shows a body floating between objects like seaweed, but not *moving itself*. Movement is given, says Rodin, by an image in which the arms, the legs [*les jambes*], the trunk, and the head are each taken at a different instant, an image which therefore portrays the body in an attitude which it never at any instant really held and which imposes fictive linkages between the parts, as if this mutual confrontation of incompossibles could—and alone could—make transition and duration to well up in bronze and on canvas.[37] The only successful instantaneous views of movement are those which approach this paradoxical arrangement—when, for example, a walking man or woman is taken at the moment when both feet are touching the ground; for then we almost have the temporal ubiquity of the body which brings it about that the person *bestrides* [*enjambe*] space. The picture makes movement visible by its internal discordance. Each member's position, precisely by virtue of its incompatibility with that of the others (according to the body's logic), is dated differently, and since all of them remain visibly within the unity of one body, it is the body which comes to bestride duration. Its movement is something conspired between legs, trunk, arms, and head in some virtual focal point, and it breaks forth only subsequently by change of place. When a horse is photographed at that instant when he is completely off the ground, with his legs almost folded under him—an instant, therefore, when he must be moving—why does he look as if he were leaping in place? And why, by contrast, do Géricault's horses run on canvas, in a posture impossible for a real horse at a gallop? It is because the horses in *Epsom Derby* bring me to see the body's grip upon the ground and, according to a logic of body and of the world that I know well, these grips upon space are also grips upon duration. Rodin said profoundly, "It is the artist who is truthful, while the photograph lies; for, in reality, time never stops."[38] The photograph keeps open the instant which the onrush of time closes up forthwith; it destroys the overtaking, the overlapping, the "metamorphosis" of time. This is what painting, in contrast, makes visible, because the horses have in them that "leaving here, going there,"[39] because they have a foot in each instant. Painting searches not for the outside of the movement but for its secret ciphers. There are some still more subtle than those of which Rodin spoke: all flesh, and even that of the world, radiates beyond itself. But whether, depending on the epochs and the "schools," one is attached more to manifest movement or to the monumental, painting is never altogether outside time, because it is always within the carnal.

Now perhaps we have a better sense of how much is contained in that little word "see." Vision is not a certain mode of thought or presence to self; it is the means given me for being absent from myself, for being present from the inside at the fission of Being only at the end of which do I close up into myself.

Painters have always known this. Da Vinci invoked a "pictorial science" which does not speak in words (and still less in numbers) but in works that exist in the visible just as natural things do—and which yet communicates itself through them "to all the generations of the universe."[40] It is this silent science, says Rilke (apropos of Rodin), that brings into the work the forms of things "whose seal has not yet been broken"; it comes from the eye and addresses itself to the eye.[41] We must understand the eye as the "window of the soul." "The eye . . . through which the beauty of the universe is revealed to our contemplation is of such excellence that whoever should resign himself to losing it would deprive himself of the knowledge of all the works of nature, the sight of which makes the soul live happily in its body's prison, thanks to the eyes which show him the infinite variety of creation: whoever loses them abandons his soul in a dark prison where all hope of once more seeing the sun, the light of the universe, must vanish." The eye accomplishes the prodigious work of opening the soul to what is not soul—the joyous realm of things and their god, the sun. A Cartesian can believe that the existing world is not visible, that the only light is of the mind, and that all vision takes place in God. A painter cannot agree that our openness to the world is illusory or indirect, that what we see is not the world itself, or that the mind has to do only with its thoughts or another mind. He accepts, with all its difficulties, the myth of the windows of the soul; what is without place must be subjected to a body—or, what is even more: what is without place must be initiated by the body to all the others and to nature. We must take literally what vision teaches us: that through it we touch the sun and the stars, that we are everywhere at once, and that even our powers to imagine ourselves elsewhere—"I am in Petersburg in my bed, in Paris, my eyes see the sun"[42]— or freely to aim at real beings, wherever they are, borrows from vision and employs again means we owe to it. Vision alone teaches us that beings that are different, "exterior," foreign to one another, are yet absolutely *together,* are "simultaneity"; which is a mystery psychologists handle the way a child handles explosives. Robert Delaunay says succinctly, "The railroad track is the image of succession which comes closest to the parallel: the parity of the rails."[43] The rails converge and do not converge; they converge *in order* to remain equidistant farther away. The world is in accordance with my perspective *in order to be* independent of me, is for me in *order* to be without me, to be a world. The "visual quale" gives me, and is alone in doing so, the presence of what is not me, of what is simply and fully.[44] It does so because, as a texture, it is the concretion of a universal visibility, of one sole Space that separates and reunites, that sustains every cohesion (and even that of past and future, since there would be no such cohesion if they were not essentially parts of the same Space). Every visual something, as individual as it is, functions also as a dimension, because it is given as the result of a dehiscence of Being. What this ultimately means is that what defines the visible is to have a lining of invisibility in the strict sense, which it makes present as a certain absence. "In their time, our erstwhile-opposites, the Impressionists, were perfectly right in electing domicile among the scrub and stubble of the daily spectacle. As for us, our heart throbs to get closer to the depths. . . . These oddities will become . . . realities . . . because instead of being limited to the diversely intense restoration of the visible, they also annex the occultly perceived portion of the invisible."[45] There is that which reaches the eye head on, the frontal properties of the visible; but there is also that which reaches it from below—the deep postural latency whereby the body raises itself to see—and that which reaches vision from above like the phenomena of flight, of swimming, of movement, where it participates no longer in the heaviness of origins but in free accomplishments.[46] Through vision, then, the painter touches both extremities. In the immemorial depth of the visible, something has moved, caught fire, which engulfs his body; everything he paints is in answer to this incitement, and his hand is "nothing but the instrument of a distant will." Vision is the encounter, as at a crossroads, of all the aspects of Being. "A certain fire wills to live; it wakes. Working its way along the hand's conductor, it reaches the canvas and invades it; then, a leaping spark, it arcs the gap in the circle it was to trace: the return to the eye, and beyond."[47] There is no break at all in this circuit; it is impossible to say that here nature ends and the human being or expression begins. It is, then, silent Being that itself comes to show forth its own sense. Herein lies the reason why the dilemma between figurative and nonfigurative art is badly posed; it is at once true and uncontradictory that no grape was ever what it is in the most figurative painting and that no painting, no matter how abstract, can get away from Being, that even Caravaggio's grape is the grape itself.[48] This precession of what is upon what one sees and makes seen, of what one sees and makes seen upon what is—this is vision itself. And to give the ontological formula of painting we hardly need to force the painter's own words, Klee's words written at the age of thirty-seven and ultimately inscribed on his tomb: "I cannot be grasped in immanence."[49]

V

Because depth, color, form, line, movement, contour, physiognomy are all branches of Being and because each entwines the tufts of all the rest, there are no separated, distinct "problems" in painting, no really opposed paths, no partial "solutions," no cumulative progress, no options that cannot return. There is nothing to prevent the painter from going back to one of the emblems he has shied away from—making it, of course, speak differently. Rouault's contours are not those of Ingres. Light is the "old sultana," says Georges Limbour, "whose charms withered away at the beginning of this century."[50] Expelled at first by the painters of matter, it reappears finally in Dubuffet as a certain texture of matter. One is never sheltered from these returns or from the least expected convergences; there are fragments of Rodin which are statues by Germaine Richier *because they were sculptors*—that is, connected back to one single, identical network of Being. For the same reason, nothing is ever an acquisition. By "working over" a favorite problem, even if it is just the problem of velvet or wool, the true painter unknowingly upsets the givens of all the other problems. His investigation is total even when it looks partial. At the moment when he comes to acquire a certain "savoir-faire," he sees that he has reopened another field where everything he has been able to express must be said again in a different way. Thus what he has found he does not yet have. It remains to be sought out; the discovery itself calls for other investigations. The idea of universal painting, of a totalization of painting, of painting's being fully and definitively realized is an idea that makes no sense. For painters, if any remain, the world will always be yet to be painted; even if it lasts millions of years . . . it will all end without having been completed. Panofsky shows that the "problems" of painting that animate its history are often solved obliquely, not in the course of investigations that had first posed them, but, on the contrary, when painters, having reached an impasse, look like they have forgotten those problems and allow themselves to be attracted somewhere else. Then suddenly, their attention elsewhere, they happen upon the old problems and surmount the obstacle. This hidden historicity, advancing through the labyrinth by detours, transgressions, slow encroachments and sudden drives, does not mean that the painter does not know what he wants, but that what he wants is on the hither side of means and goals, commanding from above all our *useful* activity.

We are so fascinated by the classical idea of intellectual adequation that painting's mute "thought" sometimes leaves us with the impression of a vain swirl of meanings, a paralyzed or miscarried speech. And if one answers that no thought ever detaches itself completely from a support; that the sole privilege of speaking thought is to have rendered its own support manipulable, that no more than those of painting, the figurations of literature and philosophy are not truly acquisitions and do not accumulate themselves into a stable treasure, that even science learns to recognize a zone of the "fundamental," peopled with dense, open, rent beings of which an exhaustive treatment is out of the question—like the cyberneticians' "aesthetic information" or mathematico-physical "groups of operations," and that, finally, we are never in a position to take stock of everything objectively or to think of progress in itself; and that the whole of human history is, in a certain sense, stationary—then the understanding says, like [Stendhal's] Lamiel, *what, is that all there is to it?* Is this the highest point of reason, to realize that the soil beneath our feet is shifting, to pompously call "interrogation" what is only a persistent state of stupor, to call "research" what is only trudging in a circle, to call "Being" that which never fully is?

But this disappointment issues from a false imaginary, which claims for itself a positivity that fills in its own emptiness. It is the regret of not being everything, a regret that is not even entirely grounded. For if we cannot establish a hierarchy of civilizations or speak of progress—either in painting or even elsewhere—it is not because some fate impedes us; it is, rather, that in a sense the very first painting went to the furthest reach of the future. If no painting completes painting, if no work even is itself absolutely completed, each creation changes, alters, clarifies, deepens, confirms, exalts, re-creates, or creates in advance all the others. If creations are not acquisitions, it is not just that, like all things, they pass away; it is also that they have almost their entire lives before them.

Merleau-Ponty in Person

An Interview with Madeleine Chapsal,
February 17, 1958

CHAPSAL: Finding oneself face to face with a philosopher is a rather unsettling privilege. What is the status of the philosopher? Is the philosopher entirely a member of the same species as other people? In your inaugural lecture at the Collège de France, didn't you yourself speak of what you called the "philosophical life"?

MERLEAU-PONTY: I never said, or meant to say, that the philosophical life was another life and the philosopher another species. Nietzsche thought that a married philosopher is a vaudeville character. He thought it was impossible to be a philosopher and also participate in secular life. This is certainly not what I meant.

Let's consider an example. What I said in 1952 is that political commitment never consists, for the philosopher, in accepting the dilemmas of the time as they are, and in choosing by keeping his reservations to himself. Obviously, from the moment one voices one's reservations, there is no question of acting as directly or as immediately as the political individual does. The action of the philosopher is much more long-term, but it is action all the same.

Hegel said the truth cannot by expressed by one single proposition, and this sentence could serve as a motto for all philosophers. There are moments for the "yes" and the "no": these are moments of crisis. Beyond these moments, "yes" and "no" are the politics of an amateur. Let me emphasize this point: by refusing to abide by the *yes* and the *no* the philosopher does not stand outside politics, but is confined to doing what everyone, and especially the professional politician, *does.* For I do not believe that great politicians are ever as Manichean as is purported. Marx, who had his philosophical side, was not Manichean. He thought that capitalism was in decline, *but* that it had been a great thing, that it is necessary to destroy philosophy, *but* that it is also necessary to realize it, that the revolution is a rupture with the past, *but* that it is also its accomplishment. Lenin may have been Manichean or, more precisely, forced himself to be so. It is said that after listening to a Beethoven sonata, he declared that one should not listen to this kind of music since it tended to promote forgiveness, and that on the contrary one must continue to be ruthless.

But precisely the great lesson of these last years is perhaps that, in being Manichean and ruthless, Communism has become distorted. This means that, even when you have chosen, you must say why and under what conditions. You continue to think beyond what you *do*. Or rather, political action is not the confounding thunderbolt Hitler believed it to be. It is an action upon humans, which therefore seeks to persuade or seduce. The "yes" and the "no" are interesting only in order to punctuate a cycle of action. For my part, I wanted to react against a sort of purism of action which would oblige us to choose between action and truth, but that is ultimately a caricature of action.

CHAPSAL: Thus the philosopher not only has duties toward himself and his truth? His function, for you, commits him vis-à-vis other humans?

MERLEAU-PONTY: These are inseparable, and this is the difficulty of being a philosopher, and even, more generally, a writer. . . . One does not write solely for oneself, or solely for truth, but not simply for others either. One writes. That is all, and in doing so one aims at all of that at once. Those who write imply that all of this can happen in the same movement.

The specificity of the philosopher here is only to practice the same principle more strictly, because, unlike the writer, the philosopher does not have the right to take up residence in the inner life. The philosopher claims to think the world of everyone. Very few philosophers have been anarchists. Nearly all of them admit that a State and a power are necessary. They do not wash their hands of it, and yet they do not consent to the myth. Or, when they do, they nonetheless give warning that it is a myth. This is the source of their uneasiness. It is not an anomaly or an aristocratic malady.

CHAPSAL: Accepting the existence of a state power, isn't this something of a novelty for the philosopher, a submission imposed by the modern shape of society?

MERLEAU-PONTY: The case of Socrates is a good example.

CHAPSAL: With the difference that Socrates could rise against the powers that be, which he did openly and publicly whenever he judged it appropriate to do so.

MERLEAU-PONTY: He did so only by risking his life.

CHAPSAL: In a modern society, if you find yourself in disagreement with a tax collector or the justice of the peace, philosopher though you might be, you find yourself compelled to comply. . . .

MERLEAU-PONTY: Socrates complied when he saw fit. He had been a soldier and behaved honorably. He thought that where it is necessary for there to be an army, the soldier must obey when the general commands.

He also thought that the soldier could question the generals either before battle or once back home. This raises a further issue: how far must one obey and how far should one contest? The Communists simplified it. They thought that one should obey certain generals and disobey certain others. Things are not so simple. Should a Russian revolutionary in Budapest (if there are any) obey the general or not? It is not so easy to know where the revolution is, and Socrates' question remains crucial: when must one obey and when must one criticize?

CHAPSAL: If, in every case where individuals find themselves in conflict with society, you, as a philosopher, decide to abide by your principles and comply only with that which goes in the direction of freedom, you will come quickly and directly to martyrdom.

MERLEAU-PONTY: No more than the non-philosophers. People would be very unhappy if they were to look closely at what lies beneath the words they use so readily. This is why they prefer, for the most part, not to do so. But sooner or later, events put them in a state of philosophical uneasiness.

CHAPSAL: How did you enter into the philosophical life? Suddenly? For intellectual reasons?

MERLEAU-PONTY: To the biographical question, I would say that the day I entered a philosophy class, I knew that what I wanted to do was philosophy. Neither then, nor since, have I ever had the slightest doubt about this.

CHAPSAL: Does being a philosopher imply separating oneself from the society in which one lives? Have you experienced a crisis comparable to the one of which Lévi-Strauss speaks? He claims that the ethnologist who studies other societies comes to feel like a stranger in his or her own society.

MERLEAU-PONTY: When Lévi-Strauss left Europe for South America in search of societies which he appreciated, he sought immediate beauty, innocence, and nature; he proceeded like a poet or a rebel. With this adventure, as with all things, one can produce philosophy. Someone different from Lévi-Strauss would not have extracted a philosophy from it. The poet and philosopher are, in this case, united in the same individual. This is not to say that the philosophical rupture is always as sensational as the poetic one. The ethnologist, having returned from South America, sees the West with new eyes, if you like, with the eyes of the primitives. But Husserl, who hardly ever left Germany, became interested at the end of his life in the primitives.

The philosopher's break with the society that surrounds him may be silent and may not even involve travel. This is not a matter of uncertainty rather than certainty, emptiness rather than fullness. Instead, it is a question of distancing the world, but only in order to see it and understand it.

CHAPSAL: The philosopher, then, would constantly leave what surrounds him. Do they break with their own ideas in order to serve them better?

MERLEAU-PONTY: The philosopher does not have ideas in the way that one has a table and a chair; other people talk about the philosopher's ideas. The philosopher, like the writer or the scholar, has an attentive yet very simple gaze.

CHAPSAL: But isn't there a contradiction in what you say? How can one experience oneself like a gaze over all things, therefore free and detached, and at the same time feel that one is in the service of others?

MERLEAU-PONTY: I see that I still haven't succeeded in making you see what it is to be a philosopher! When he works, a philosopher does not think about the service of others, and even less about his work. Philosophical work, like any other work, has its evidence in itself. The philosopher has no more devotion or ambition than the peasant who tills the soil or the worker who produces things. Is it inconceivable to you that one could at once be there and be distant? And yet this is the very definition of the philosopher and perhaps even of human existence.

CHAPSAL: The philosopher may very well be a human just like the farmer and the worker. However, isn't the philosopher's work elevated above that of the farmer and the worker? Hasn't philosophy been accused precisely of being a gaze which scans all fields of work or investigation without having one of its own?

MERLEAU-PONTY: Philosophy does not have a proper field in the sense that the sciences have a field. But this is because in another sense it has all of them. Scientific thought seeks *holds* in the sector of the real that it *manipulates*. It allows itself to be guided initially by a substratum of pre-scientific ideas which help it to formulate hypotheses and to consider facts. Later, scientific thought realizes that the conceptions it has developed by successive corrections are hardly compatible with its original philosophy: it therefore seeks to find another philosophy. Thus, scientists come to discuss space, time, causality, the object, being. Their science does not define entirely the philosophy which their science would need, and this philosophy is not obtained by calculation or experimentation. Were this the case scientists would agree sooner or later. Now, in fact, they are as divided over the philosophy of their science as the professional philosophers are over philosophy in general. This is where we are today.

People often quote Laplace's famous comment in which he defines his ideal of physicalistic knowledge: the entire world as one single great fact whose state at one instant strictly determines the state at every later instant. Today most physicists no longer accept this image of the world. Some say that physical being is made up of "behaviors" and others say "operational groups," without being able to say what is the subject of this behavior or of these operations, without having even assumed a subject for them. Others still remain Cartesians. You say that philosophy is expelled from physics, when in fact it is physics that is overrun by philosophy.

CHAPSAL: But aren't you talking about the philosophy of physicists and not the philosophy of philosophers?

MERLEAU-PONTY: When physicists depart from their own language, mathematics, and offer an interpretation of their science in meaningful language, they are no longer the sole judges of what they propose, because their science does not hold the key to the notions which they invoke ("observer," "object," "existence," "truth," etc.). Philosophers cannot ignore the critique of commonsense ideas to which science devotes itself. They also cannot find in science the complete elucidation of the notions of which I just spoke and which stem from total human experience and not simply from scientific experience. What is true of the natural sciences is even truer of the so-called human sciences, which you mentioned earlier.

CHAPSAL: You mean that psychoanalysis and ethnology require a philosophical elaboration that extends them? Fine. But is this also the case with respect to Marxism?

MERLEAU-PONTY: I find that the situation is the same everywhere. Does psychoanalysis render the human individual transparent? Does it allow us to dispense with philosophy? On the contrary, the questions that psychoanalysis now asks, even more energetically than ever before, are questions that one cannot begin to answer without philosophy: how can the human being be at once wholly spiritual and wholly corporeal? The psychoanalyst's techniques contribute in conjunction with many other investigations in resolving this question, and philosophy is again at their crossroads. The ethnology of which you spoke cannot decipher culture without wondering what a culture is, what a symbol is, how it is that we are able to comprehend cultures, and whether it is possible for us to compare and classify them. The ethnologist is then at home with the philosophical problem of our knowledge of others, and there is indeed something of the philosopher in every ethnologist.

As for Marxism, to say whether it is ultimately philosophy or not is an enormous question. The classical Marxists thought that philosophy was an indirect manner of expressing the contradictions of class society and that in a society where an equilibrium of people with people and humans with nature had been realized, there would be no place for philosophy. Without arguing over the fundamental issues and without being polemical, let us say that today the Soviets emphasize that even a society which has experienced the Marxist revolution must live with contradictions. They add only that contradictions are not antagonisms. In terms of the question with which we are concerned, it suffices to say that the existing society is not transparent even for Marxists, and, to that extent, philosophical expression remains necessary. Precisely from their point of view, the "suppression" of philosophy would be historically false. Philosophy would be overcome only if the individual had become, as they say, the total human, without enigmas and free of problems. But this total human does not exist: to act as if it did is to throw away the arms of critical thought. To affirm that it *will be* is, precisely in the Marxist sense of the word, utopian. Thus, philosophy has never had more to do than today.

CHAPSAL: Then how do you explain the impression that philosophy is in a state of crisis?

MERLEAU-PONTY: I do not share this impression at all.

CHAPSAL: In a small book called *Why Philosophers?* J.-F. Revel echoes an opinion that seemed rather general.[1]

MERLEAU-PONTY: On the contrary, I think that it is a particular case. One gets the feeling in reading the book that the author does not like anything at all. He tips his hat to the so-called human sciences, but one is not sure which ones he supports, since he derides their best practitioners. He tips his hat to great philosophy, but which great philosophy, since he does not recognize it in the investigations where it comes back to life? Whether or not one likes Husserl or Heidegger, it must be admitted that with all the shortcomings of contemporary philosophy (which is the price of their radicalism), they meditate upon the same issues as Descartes and the great philosophy, namely, being, time, the object, the body. This book is the work of a jaded consumer, one who is quick to ridicule with anecdotes those whose only sin lies in attempting to do something, without proposing anything definite of his own.

This book brings to mind the exposés written at the height of Stalinism, which, in the name of a philosophy that was never made, were used to smash all human effort. At least the Communists had their hidden god and believed that they were serving a great cause. Anyone fair-minded would take this into account. In Revel's book, this sort of attitude is nowhere to be found. It offers nothing. Moreover, when I see Jean Paulhan crowning Revel with his right hand and slipping a rather difficult Heidegger text into the *N. R. F.* with his left,[2] I tell myself that there really is love beneath this hatred, and that philosophers might be wrong to be so concerned.

CHAPSAL: Does one not find in the public spirit today, as well as in academe, a distinct preference for scientific culture, a kind of priority of the sciences over philosophy?

MERLEAU-PONTY: I do not believe that what one gives to the sciences is taken from philosophy. There are not enough engineers or statisticians in France; we will need many more. I do not object to efforts to attract young people to these fields. What I regret is the often-implied polemic against philosophy. There is a bad mood toward philosophy, because in the period following the war, the bad mood often appeared in the students as a nostalgic meditation about Communism, and, as you know, the wind does not blow in that direction anymore. But in fact, if we need more statisticians and engineers, we also need (and will need more than ever) sociologists, psychoanalysts, psychiatrists, ethnologists, and even psychologists and economists to think about the "artificial mechanisms" necessary for regulating capitalism.

However, I do not believe that these questions can actually be considered without philosophical preparation. If our problems did not concern the principles of our thought and our societal system, officials and business leaders would not need philosophy. But if, on the contrary, as I believe, our problems call into question contemporary mental, political, and economic systems, then we will need many people who can see beyond the surface into the depth of such things. We will not be able to rely solely on common sense in matters of social and political philosophy. We will need, as Balzac said, "profound people," and not merely those who calculate; radical minds and not merely technicians. Thus, we will need people trained through doubt and examination. The havoc caused by routine politics and political improvisation is clear enough today.

The practices of the science that is done could provide these profound qualities. But the science that is done is not the science that is taught, and a teaching that would be only scientific would leave young people without any critical resources to confront the chaos.

CHAPSAL: But is the philosophy on which you count so heavily alive today? Is there a philosophical life—encounters, debates, and exchanges?

MERLEAU-PONTY: There are congresses, conferences, and journals. There is a philosophical life just as there is a medical or scientific one, and it suffers from the same perpetual malaise: one never sees Heidegger or Sartre at a conference.

There are some informal meetings: Heidegger came to Cerisy, the English to Royaumont.

Yet Western philosophy is not only divided, which would be natural, but partitioned. Logical positivism reigns in Anglo-American countries and Scandinavia; there is, in Freiburg, the Heidegger circle; in France and Italy, investigations inspired by phenomenology and Marxism. Clearly, these tendencies are not looking for confrontation, each proceeding with its own monologue.

Why? One might wonder whether it has not always been so in philosophy, as in any other discipline. The rifts were profound between Einstein and the particle physicists. It is an American idea—and an extreme one—to believe that clarity comes from a conference. One might wonder if truly productive and creative work can be accommodated by confrontations between people and by improvised exchanges. However, having said that, perhaps the society of philosophers has never been dispersed as at present. Of course, the problem is not only in the West. In July 1957, the International Institute of Philosophy organized an East-West meeting at Warsaw. Judging from all accounts, no active philosophizing took place and no real problems were addressed. The East also has its formalisms, which are even more imperious than our own.

On the whole, philosophical life remains provincial, almost clandestine, the sacred fire passing from individual to individual. One could say that there is an occultation of philosophy.

However, this does not mean that philosophy has nothing more to say or that philosophy is destined to disappear. On the contrary, what paralyzes or renders philosophy mute is that it cannot, by traditional means, express what the world is now living through. Anglo-American analytic philosophy is a deliberate retreat into a universe of thought where contingency, ambiguity, and the concrete have no place.

Marxism should have been a philosophy of the concrete, but it assumed all too quickly that it had discovered the key—the proletarian philosophy of history. It turned away from all the problems to which this key could not give immediate access, whether it be the sophisticated literature of the moderns, the study of painting, the analysis of sexuality, the neo-capitalist experience, or social demography. Official Marxism did not inspire the progress that we have been able to make in economic and social knowledge; rather, it has paralyzed these developments. This is where we stand and will remain as long as both analytic philosophy and Marxism refuse to desist or to recognize the weaknesses of their position.

CHAPSAL: What you have just said, why do you not write about it?

MERLEAU-PONTY: Refutations are not very interesting. It is better to attempt to do what one reproaches others for not bringing forth.

CHAPSAL: For instance?

MERLEAU-PONTY: A philosophy. Far from everything being done, in philosophy everything remains to be done or redone. We can catch only a glimpse of what is on the horizon by studying Husserl, Heidegger, and Sartre, and in some intuitions of biologists, ethnologists, and psychoanalysts.

CHAPSAL: Do you think, then, that Heidegger and Sartre prefigure the philosophy of tomorrow? And what place would you give to Marxism in this philosophy?

MERLEAU-PONTY: Both Heidegger and Sartre have long maintained, and quite rightly, that philosophy must redefine being. In particular, it must redefine the connections between what is a thing and what is not a thing, between being and nothingness, and between the positive and the negative. It must reformulate what the traditional correlation between the object and the subject, preponderant even in Hegel, does not adequately express.

Whatever the accomplishments of Marxism, it suffers because it has not raised this issue. In principle, it has relied on the Hegelian categories of subject and object, and limited itself to reversing the relation. This inverted, and yet conserved, Hegelianism was profoundly obscure. One could show that the origins of all the surprises that Marxism has left for those who follow it through history can be found in this initial obscurity. The ontological problem posed by Heidegger and Sartre is now more than ever the order of the day.

Nature, animals, bodies, humans, words, thought, social bodies, institutions, events—knowledge of the properties of all of them is divided up among the sciences. After all, this extremely rich landscape is drawn like an etching in black and white. Ontology is concerned with this black and white. It investigates the areas that are thick and the areas that are empty as well as the thin line in between. And because of that, at once it is in contact with all the sciences, with all human endeavor, and it is something different.

Ontology is everywhere—in the painter's articulation of the world, in the scientist's flashes of insight drawn from things, in the passions, in the modes of labor and sociality. There is an ontological history, a deployment of our relation with being, or a modulation of the relation of being to nothingness. This ontological history is not outside "history"; it might even be the most rigorous formula of "history"; it is the truth of dialectical materialism.

Marx's error is not that he attempted a philosophical reading of history; it is to have believed or to let be believed that the philosophy of philosophers was a lie. His error is not that he thought that history is undivided, body and mind, but to have believed or to let be believed that the mixture was headed toward noncontradiction or identity. His error is not that he believed that every civilization is an ontological complex, but to have believed that a civilization was being prepared that would take the place of ontology. There is no "destruction" of philosophy which could be its "realization." To postulate such a state of history is precisely to do bad philosophy, to make an ontology without depth or a "flat" ontology, as Hegel said.

CHAPSAL: Could you offer an idea of ontological investigation as you understand it?

MERLEAU-PONTY: One of the important ontologies of the West treats the visible world as the only possible manifestation of an infinite productivity. If something had to be, it could be only this world. Being is thus conceived as full being [*être plein*]. There is not a trace in it of the least hesitation; it is, with the indubitability of what could not be otherwise. It has the solidity of the object.

This ontology is not the only one the West has known. In any one of its philosophers, for instance in Descartes, one could find along with this ontology a sketch of many others. But this suffices by way of example. Consider the idea of an absolutely transparent world where all visible properties result from the properties of an infinity that supports the world and where the reasons for what appears to us at first as a simple fact are clearly developed.

It is certain that an ontology of this sort has been very favorable to the development of an "enlightenment" science as well as to the development of an "enlightenment" politics. In short, we owe much of what has engendered Western historical progress to it. But it is also clear that this ontology is no longer clear either in our knowledge or in our life. Today, this ontology no longer finds its justification, and if one maintains it forcibly, one cannot save what it once protected. It no longer encourages research as it has in the past, but rather obstructs it. It no longer inspires us; it persists only on the margins of our life.

We have seen that science itself has been led to surrender, on many points, its conception of being as a pure object. The crisis running through the politics and the wisdom which accompany this ontology need not be emphasized. It has outlived itself for a long time. Even scientists such as Laplace, who proclaimed that it is useless to hypothesize an infinity at the origin of the world, reintroduced it under other guises. The mind of the scientist, supposed to be all-powerful in principle, or simply the world itself, taken as a single fact, coherent and homogenous in all its parts, maintained the ontology of the object. Yet today, science itself has stopped looking for inspiration in this secularized god, namely, Laplace's ideal physicist.

CHAPSAL: Do you mean the new ontology would be atheistic?

MERLEAU-PONTY: I would prefer not to *define* it that way, not out of a false spirit of reconciliation or in order to equivocate, but because it is unworthy of philosophy to begin with a denial [*dénégation*]. Yet, having said this, it is nonetheless true that Catholicism, for example, is closely tied to the ontology of the object. Frankly, I do not believe that another ontology could be compatible with traditional forms of theology. But what good is it to defend these traditional forms when one knows that all of what works actively in Christian philosophy is in fact rather alien to an ontology of *ens realissimum*? Sooner or later, official relations between Catholicism and non-

Catholicism—like those between Communism and non-Communism—
must begin to resemble their relations such as they are, for example, in the
minds of the best of our students. Catholic or not, atheist or not, and even,
for certain, Communist or not, they really know that neither the philosophy of the Enlightenment, nor Marxism, nor the philosophy of *ens realissimum* is *the truth*. This intimate certainty shines forth in their conversations. However, in them, this is still only good will and intelligence. If they
succeed in understanding one another beyond their borders, it is at the
price of a genuine inner rending. Philosophy would have to reunite what
is disjointed in them, what they gather up only by the strength of their
courage. For the time being, all of this is lost when they enter "the real
world," that is, the adult world where each pursues his or her own whims.

Eugen Fink, a contemporary German philosopher, writes that we
live in the "ruins of thought." In these ruins, or because of them, there is
the approaching possibility of a great and healthy skepticism which is indispensable for the rediscovery of the fundamental. The idea that in
France today some people are divided as to whether Thomas Aquinas and
Friedrich Engels are right or wrong in what they said about Nature—this
idea looks dismaying to me when one considers all there is to know and
understand.

A philosophy cannot be sketched out in a few words. Let us only say
that it must necessarily be a philosophy of *brute being* and not one of docile
being which would have us believe the world can be fully explained. It
must also be an attentive study of *sense,* a sense wholly other than the sense
of ideas, a volatile and allusive sense which lacks any direct power over
things—even though it may appear and proliferate in things, once certain
obstacles have been cleared away.

CHAPSAL: And politics?

MERLEAU-PONTY: Like every philosophy, the one to seek is the one
that will inspire a politics. First, negatively, it would have to reveal the illusions of classical politics. Nothing authorizes us to believe that the
human world is a cluster of rational wills, that it could, like a learned society, be governed by an immutable rule based on a law derived from timeless principles, or make its decisions through academic debates in which
the most rational end up convincing all the others.

As both life and animality have invented and scattered forms,
mechanisms, organisms, and even some kinds of institutions across the
surface of the earth, the human world—except for fortunate periods during which it lives off its former accomplishments—must also create forms
and mechanisms of culture; and superior values, in which it takes such
great pride, are sustained within these historical matrices.

Marx's error is not to have said that, but to have believed that there was a matrix of the *true human society,* that the matrix was a class that already existed, and that when this class seized power a true society would be born. This was all too geometrical.

The chaos of our politics may be based precisely in the fact that there is no longer a ruling class. There is a bourgeoisie, but it no longer leads and no longer has a body of ideas which empowers it to run the State. There is a proletariat, but the principal party that represents it no longer has a class politics and is tripped up by its own machinations.

There are interests, rivalries, pressure groups, and antagonisms, but there is no longer a line of action and a line of history. This situation is undoubtedly tied to France's position in the world, I mean to the fact that it is involved in a game in which it does not hold the high cards, even though its stakes are nonetheless considerable.

Even taking the two superpowers into consideration, I do not think that the historical direction of their rivalry is clear: neither American capitalism nor Russian "socialism" can be defined by an essence. Everywhere the struggle is confused, unaware of its proper goals, if it has any. The remedy? The question is precisely whether a single unambiguous force remains. Perhaps the exhaustion of the classes will bind us to a *pure politics,* founded above all on the propagation of information and knowledge. I do not have such a high opinion of our capacities for abstraction, but given the classes' current state of decadence, I do not see what will make us *wise and profound in spite of ourselves* as the classes once did. There is no "Poujadist"[3] or military civilization. Unfortunately, the same causes which would make the renewal of information and the enlightened urgent make it unlikely.

CHAPSAL: You have written several books on politics. Will you write more?

MERLEAU-PONTY: The political philosophy will come with all the rest. As for practical conclusions, I have already indicated them. What good is it to begin again? The war in Algeria has revived passions that had just begun to die out, setting France back many years. We had begun to understand that the question of questions was not whether one was Communist or not. The war in Algeria has dimmed the dawn of this understanding. It has installed in France a feeble, torn, and hesitant regime which is no more capable of governing than the one preceding it. This regime has thus far been able to restrain an insurrection in the south only by continuing the war. Everything will have to begin again, in politics as well as in philosophy. This will become clearer as soon as the French hypnosis or (depending on the case) euphoria comes to an end along with the Algerian War. Under the pressure of an increase in population, the problems of modern society—from those of urbanism (including the question of traffic), employment, the new peasantry, and planning, to those of the motives, movement, and vitality of the nation—will have to be confronted. Suddenly it will become obvious that "national ambition," "counter-subversion," and the financing of private schools do not make a nation live and breathe. This *abyss* of modern society—one that certain writers and philosophers have sensed or suspected on the horizon for the past fifty or a hundred years—will become evident in everyday life. Our time is now experiencing this abyss as its misery and its greatness.

19

The Intertwining—The Chiasm

If it is true that as soon as philosophy declares itself to be reflection or co-incidence it prejudges what it will find, then once again it must recommence everything, reject the instruments reflection and intuition had provided themselves, and install itself in a place where they have not yet been distinguished, in experiences that have not yet been "worked over," that offer us all at once, pell-mell, both "subject" and "object," both existence and essence, and hence give philosophy resources to redefine them. Seeing, speaking, even thinking (with certain reservations, for as soon as we distinguish thought from speaking absolutely we are already in the order of reflection), are experiences of this kind, both irrecusable and enigmatic. They have a name in all languages, but a name which in all of them also conveys meanings in tufts, thickets of proper senses and figurative senses, so that, unlike those of science, not one of these names clarifies by attributing to what is named a circumscribed meaning. Rather, they are the repeated index, the insistent reminder of a mystery as familiar as it is unexplained, of a light which, illuminating the rest, remains at its source in obscurity. If we could rediscover within the exercise of seeing and speaking some of the living references that assign them such a destiny in a language, perhaps they would teach us how to form our new instruments, and first of all to understand our research, our interrogation, themselves.

The visible about us seems to rest in itself. It is as though our vision were formed in the heart of the visible, or as though there were between it and us an intimacy as close as between the sea and the strand. And yet it is not possible that we blend into it, or that it pass into us, for then the vision would vanish at the moment of formation, by disappearance of the seer or of the visible. What there is then are not things first identical with themselves, which would then offer themselves to the seer, nor is there a seer who is first empty and who, afterward, would open himself to them—but something to which we could not be closer than by palpating it with our look, things we could not dream of seeing "all naked" because the gaze itself envelops them, clothes them with its own flesh. Whence does it happen that in so doing it leaves them in their place, that the vision we acquire of them seems to us to come from them, and that to be seen is for them but a degradation of their eminent being? What is this talisman of color, this singular virtue of the visible that makes it, held at the end of the gaze, nonetheless much more than a correlative of my vision, such that it imposes my vision upon me as a continuation of its own sovereign existence? How does it happen that my look, enveloping them, does not hide them, and, finally, that veiling them, it unveils them?[1]

We must first understand that this red under my eyes is not, as is always said, a quale, a pellicle of being without thickness, a message at the same time indecipherable and evident, which one has or has not received, but of which, if one has received it, one knows all there is to know, and of which in the end there is nothing to say. It requires a focusing, however brief; it emerges from a less precise, more general redness, in which my gaze was caught, into which it sank, before—as we put it so aptly—*fixing* it. And now that I have fixed it, if my eyes penetrate into it, into its fixed structure, or if they start to wander round about again, the quale resumes its atmospheric existence. Its precise form is bound up with a certain woolly, metallic, or porous [?][2] configuration or texture, and the quale itself counts for very little compared with these participations. Claudel has a phrase saying that a certain blue of the sea is so blue that only blood would be more red. The color is yet a variant in another dimension of variation, that of its relations with the surroundings: this red is what it is only by connecting up from its place with other reds about it, with which it forms a constellation, or with other colors it dominates or that dominate it, that it attracts or that attract it, that it repels or that repel it. In short, it is a certain node in the woof of the simultaneous and the successive. It is a concretion of visibility, it is not an atom. The red dress a fortiori holds with all its fibers onto the fabric of the visible, and thereby onto a fabric of invisible being. A punctuation in the field of red things, which includes the tiles of rooftops, the flags of gatekeepers and of the revolution, certain terrains near Aix or in Madagascar, it is also a punctuation in the field of red garments, which includes, along with the dresses of women, robes of professors, bishops, and advocate generals, and also in the field of adornments and that of uniforms. And its red literally is not the same as it appears in one constellation or in the other, as the pure essence of the Revolution of 1917 precipitates in it, or that of the eternal feminine, or that of the public prosecutor, or that of the gypsies dressed like hussars who reigned twenty-five years ago over an inn on the Champs-Elysées. A certain red is also a fossil drawn up from the depths of imaginary worlds. If we took all these participations into account, we would recognize that a naked color, and in general a visible, is not a chunk of absolutely hard, indivisible being, offered all naked to a vision which could be only total or null, but is rather a sort of strait between exterior horizons and interior horizons ever gaping open, something that comes to touch lightly and makes diverse regions of the colored or visible world resound at the distances, a certain differentiation, an ephemeral modulation of this world—less a color or a thing, therefore, than a difference between things and colors, a momentary crystallization of colored being or of visibility. Between the alleged colors and visibles, we would find anew the tissue that lines them, sustains them, nourishes them, and which for its part is not a thing, but a possibility, a latency, and a *flesh* of things.

If we turn now to the seer, we will find that this is no analogy or vague comparison and must be taken literally. The look, we said, envelops, palpates, espouses the visible things. As though it were in a relation of pre-established harmony with them, as though it knew them before knowing them, it moves in its own way with its abrupt and imperious style, and yet the views taken are not desultory—I do not look at a chaos, but at things—so that finally one cannot say if it is the look or if it is the things that command. What is this prepossession of the visible, this art of interrogating it according to its own wishes, this inspired exegesis? We would perhaps find the answer in the tactile palpation where the questioner and the questioned are closer, and of which, after all, the palpation of the eye is a remarkable variant. How does it happen that I give to my hands, in particular, that degree, that rate, and that direction of movement that are capable of making me feel the textures of the sleek and the rough? Between the exploration and what it will teach me, between my movements and what I touch, there must exist some relationship by principle, some kinship, according to which they are not only, like the pseudopods of the amoeba, vague and ephemeral deformations of the corporeal space, but the initiation to and the opening upon a tactile world. This can happen only if my hand, while it is felt from within, is also accessible from without, itself tangible, for my other hand, for example, if it takes its place among the things it touches, is in a sense one of them, opens finally upon a tangible being of which it is also a part. Through this crisscrossing within it of the touching and the tangible, its own movements incorporate themselves into the universe they interrogate, are recorded on the same map as it; the two systems are applied upon one another, as the two halves of an orange. It is not different for vision—except, it is said, that here the exploration and the information it gathers do not belong "to the same sense." But this delimitation of the senses is crude. Already in the "touch" we have just found three distinct experiences which subtend one another, three dimensions which overlap but are distinct: a touching of the sleek and of the rough, a touching of the things—a passive sentiment of the body and of its space—and finally a genuine touching of the touching, when my right hand touches my left hand while it is palpating the things, where the "touching subject" passes over to the rank of the touched, descends into the things, such that the touch is formed in the midst of the world and as it were in the things. Between the massive sentiment I have of the sack in which I am enclosed, and the control from without that my hand exercises over my hand, there is as much difference as between the movements of my eyes and the changes they produce in the visible. And as, conversely, every experience of the visible has always been given to me within the context of the movements of the look, the visible spectacle belongs to the touch neither more nor less than do the "tactile qualities." We must habituate ourselves to think that every visible is cut out in the tangible, every tactile being in some manner promised to visibility, and that there is encroachment, infringement, not only between the touched and the touching, but also between the tangible and the visible, which is encrusted in it, as, conversely, the tangible itself is not a nothingness of visibility, is not without visual existence. Since the same body sees and touches, visible and tangible belong to the same world. It is a marvel too little noticed that every movement of my eyes—even more, every displacement of my body—has its place in the same visible universe that I itemize and explore with them, as, conversely, every vision takes place somewhere in the tactile space. There is double and crossed sublation of the visible in the tangible and of the tangible in the visible; the two maps are complete, and yet they do not merge into one. The two parts are total parts and yet are not superposable.

Hence, without even entering into the implications proper to the seer and the visible, we know that, since vision is a palpation by means of the gaze, it must also be inscribed in the order of being that it discloses to us; he who looks must not himself be foreign to the world that he looks at. As soon as I see, it is necessary that the vision (as is so well indicated by the double sense of the word) be doubled with a complementary vision or with another vision: myself seen from without, such as another would see me, installed in the midst of the visible, occupied by considering it from a certain place. For the moment we shall not examine how far this identity of the seer and the visible goes, if we have a complete experience of it, or if there is something missing, and what it is. It suffices for us for the moment to note that he who sees cannot possess the visible unless he is possessed by it, unless he *is of it*,[3] unless, in principle, according to what is required by the articulation of the look with the things, he is one of the visibles, capable, by a singular reversal, of seeing them—he who is one of them.[4]

We understand then why we see the things themselves, in their places, where they are, according to their being which is indeed more than their being-perceived—and why at the same time we are separated from them by all the thickness of the look and of the body; it is that this distance is not the contrary of this proximity, it is deeply consonant with it, it is synonymous with it. It is that the thickness of flesh between the seer and the thing is constitutive for the thing of its visibility as for the seer of his corporeity; it is not an obstacle between them, it is their means of communication. It is for the same reason that I am at the heart of the visible and that I am far from it: because it has thickness and is thereby naturally destined to be seen by a body. What is indefinable in the quale, in the color, is nothing else than a brief, peremptory manner of giving in one sole something, in one sole tone of being, visions past, visions to come, by whole clusters. I who see have my own depth also, being backed up by this same visible which I see and which, I know very well, closes in behind me. The thickness of the body, far from rivaling that of the world, is on the contrary the sole means I have to go unto the heart of things, by making myself a world and by making them flesh.

The body interposed is not itself a thing, an interstitial matter, a connective tissue, but a *sensible for itself,* which means, not that absurdity: color that sees itself, surface that touches itself—but this paradox [?]: a set of colors and surfaces inhabited by a touch, a vision, hence an *exemplar sensible,* which offers to him who inhabits it and senses it the wherewithal to sense everything that resembles himself on the outside, such that, caught up in the tissue of the things, it draws it entirely to itself, incorporates it, and, with the same movement, communicates to the things upon which it closes over that identity without superposition, that difference without contradiction, that divergence between the within and the without that constitutes its natal secret.[5] The body unites us directly with the things through its own ontogenesis, by welding to one another the two outlines of which it is made, its two lips: the sensible mass it is and the mass of the sensible wherein it is born by segregation and upon which, as seer, it remains open. It is the body and it alone, because it is a two-dimensional being that can bring us to the things themselves, which are themselves not flat beings but beings in depth, inaccessible to a subject that would survey them from above, open to him alone that, if it be possible, would coexist with them in the same world. When we speak of the flesh of the visible, we do not mean to do anthropology, to describe a world covered over with all our own projections, leaving aside what it can be under the human mask. Rather, we mean that carnal being, as a being of depths, of several leaves or several faces, a being in latency, and a presentation of a certain absence, is a prototype of Being, of which our body, the sensible sentient, is a very remarkable variant, but whose constitutive paradox already lies in every visible. For already the cube gathers up within itself incompossible *visibilia,* just as my body is at once phenomenal body and objective body, and if finally it is, it, like my body, is by a tour de force. What we call a visible is, we said, a quality pregnant with a texture, the surface of a depth, a cross-section upon a massive being, a grain or corpuscle borne by a wave of Being. Since the total visible is always behind, or after, or between the aspects we see of it, there is access to it only through an experience which, like it, is wholly outside of itself. It is thus, and not as the bearer of a knowing subject, that our body commands the visible for us, but it does not explain it, does not clarify it, it only concentrates the mystery of its scattered visibility; and it is indeed a paradox of Being, not a paradox of man, that we are dealing with here. To be sure, one can reply that, between the two "sides" of our body, the body as sensible and the body as sentient (what in the past we called objective body and phenomenal body), rather than a divergence, there is the abyss that separates the In Itself from the For Itself. It is a problem—and we will not avoid it—to determine how the sensible sentient can also be thought. But here, seeking to form our first concepts in such a way as to avoid the classical impasses, we do not have to honor the difficulties that they may present when confronted with a cogito, which itself has to be reexamined. Yes or no: do we have a body—that is, not a permanent object of thought, but a flesh that suffers when it is wounded, hands that touch? We know: hands do not suffice for touch—but to decide for this reason alone that our hands do not touch, and to relegate them to the world of objects or of instruments, would be, in acquiescing to the bifurcation of subject and object, to forego in advance the understanding of the sensible and to deprive ourselves of its lights. We propose on the contrary to take it literally to begin with. We say therefore that our body is a being of two leaves [*feuillet*: "leaves of a page"], from one side a thing among things, and otherwise what sees them and touches them; we say, because it is evident, that it unites these two properties within itself, and its double belongingness to the order of the "object" and to the order of the "subject" reveals to us quite unexpected relations between the two orders. It cannot be by incomprehensible accident that the body has this double reference; it teaches us that each calls for the other. For if the body is a thing among things, it is so in a stronger and deeper sense than they: in the sense that, we said it *is of them,* and this means that it detaches itself upon them, and, accordingly, detaches itself from them. It is not simply a thing *seen* in fact (I do not see my back), it is visible in principle, it falls under a vision that is both ineluctable and deferred. Conversely, if it touches and sees, this is not because it would have the visibles before itself as objects: they are about it, they even enter into its enclosure, they are within it, they line its looks and its hands inside and outside. If it touches them and sees them, this is only because, being of their family, itself visible and tangible, it uses its own being as a means to participate in theirs, because each of the two beings is an archetype for the other, because the body belongs to the order of the things as the world is universal flesh. One should not even say, as we did a moment ago, that the body is made up of two leaves, of which the one, that of the "sensible," is bound up with the rest of the world. There are not in it two leaves or two layers; fundamentally it is neither thing seen only nor seer only, it is Visibility sometimes wandering and sometimes gathered back up. And as such it is not in the world, it does not detain its view of the world as within a private enclosure: the body sees the world itself, the world of everybody, and without having to leave "itself," because it is wholly—because its hands, its eyes, are nothing else than— this reference of a visible, this reference of a tangible standard to all those with which it bears the resemblance and whose evidence it collects by a magic that is vision and touch themselves. To speak of leaves or of layers is still to flatten and to juxtapose, under the reflective gaze, what coexists in the living and upright body. If one wants metaphors, it would be better to say that the body sensed and the body sentient are as the obverse and the reverse, or again, as two segments of one sole circular course which goes above them from left to right and below from right to left, but which is but one sole movement in its two phases. And everything said about the sensed body pertains to the whole of the sensible of which it is a part, and to the world. If the body is one sole body in its two phases, it incorporates into itself the whole of the sensible and with the same movement incorporates itself into a "sensible in itself." We have to reject the age-old assumptions that put the body in the world and the seer in the body, or, conversely, the world and the body in the seer as in a box. Where are we to put the limit between the body and the world, since the world is flesh? Where within [dans] the body are we to put the seer, since evidently there is in the body only "shadows stuffed with organs," that is, more of the visible? The world seen is not "within" [dans] my body, and my body is not "in" the visible world ultimately: as flesh applied to a flesh, the world neither surrounds it nor is surrounded by it. A participation in and kinship with the visible, the vision neither envelops it nor is enveloped by it definitively. The superficial pellicle of the visible is only for my vision and for my body. But the depth beneath this surface contains my body and hence contains my vision. My body as a visible thing is contained within [dans] the full spectacle. But my seeing body subtends this visible body, and all the visibles with it. There is reciprocal insertion and intertwining of one in the other. Or rather, if, as once again we must, we renounce the thinking by planes and perspectives, there are two circles, or two vortexes, or two spheres, concentric when I live naively, and as soon as I question myself, the one slightly decentered with respect to the other. . . .

We have to ask ourselves what exactly we have found with this strange adhesion of the seer and the visible. There is vision, touch, when a certain visible, a certain tangible, turns back upon the whole of the visible, the whole of the tangible, of which it is a part, or when suddenly it finds itself *surrounded* by them, or when between it and them, and through their commerce, is formed a Visibility, a Tangible in itself, which belongs properly neither to the body qua fact nor to the world qua fact—as upon two mirrors facing one another where two indefinite series of images set in one another arise which belong really to neither of the two surfaces, since each is only the rejoinder of the other, and which therefore form a couple, a couple more real than either of them. Thus since the seer is caught up in what he sees, it is still himself he sees: there is a fundamental narcissism of all vision. And thus, for the same reason, the vision he exercises, he also undergoes from the things, such that, as many painters have said, I feel myself looked at by the things, my activity is identically passivity—which is the second and more profound sense of the narcissism: not to see within [*dans*] the outside, as the others see it, the contour of a body one inhabits, but especially to be seen by the outside, to exist in [*en*] it, to emigrate into it, to be seduced, captivated, alienated by the phantom, so that the seer and the visible reciprocate one another and we no longer know which sees and which is seen. It is this Visibility, this generality of the Sensible in itself, this anonymity innate to Myself that we have previously called flesh, and one knows there is no name in traditional philosophy to designate it. The flesh is not matter, in the sense of corpuscles of being which would add up or continue on one another to form beings. Nor is the visible (the things as well as my own body) some "psychic" material that would be—God knows how—brought into being by the things factually existing and acting on my factual body. In general, it is not a fact or a sum of facts "material" or "spiritual." Nor is it a representation for a mind: a mind could not be captured by its own representations; it would rebel against this insertion into the visible which is essential to the seer. The flesh is not matter, is not mind, is not substance. To designate it, we should need the old term "element," in the sense it was used to speak of water, air, earth, and fire, that is, in the sense of a *general thing*, midway between the spatiotemporal individual and the idea, a sort of incarnate principle that brings a style of being wherever there is a fragment of being. The flesh is in this sense an "element" of Being. Not a fact or a sum of facts, and yet adherent to *location* and to the *now*. Much more: the inauguration of the *where* and the *when*, the possibility and exigency for the fact; in a word: facticity, what makes the fact be a fact. And, at the same time, what makes the facts make sense, makes the fragmentary facts dispose themselves about "something." For there is flesh, that is, if the hidden fact of the cube radiates forth somewhere as well as does the fact I have under my eyes, and coexists with it, and if I who see the cube also belong to the visible, I am visible from elsewhere, and if I and the cube are together caught up in one same "element" (should we say of the seer, or of the visible?), this cohesion, this visibility in principle, prevails over every momentary discordance. In advance every vision or every partial visible that would here definitively come to naught is not nullified (which would leave a gap in its place), but, what is better, it is replaced by a more exact vision and a more exact visible, according to the principle of visibility, which, as though through a sort of abhorrence of a vacuum, already invokes the true vision and the true visible, not only as substitutes for their errors, but also as their explanation, their relative justification, so that they are, as Husserl says so aptly, not erased, but "crossed out." . . . Such are the extravagant consequences to which we are led when we take seriously, when we question, vision. And it is, to be sure, possible to refrain from doing so and to move on, but we would simply find again confused, indistinct, non-clarified scraps of this ontology of the visible mixed up with all our theories of knowledge, and in particular with those that serve, desultorily, as vehicles of science. We are, to be sure, not finished ruminating over them. Our concern in this preliminary outline was only to catch sight of this strange domain to which interrogation, properly so-called, gives access. . . .

But this domain, one rapidly realizes, is unlimited. If we can show that the flesh is an ultimate notion, that it is not the union or compound of two substances, but thinkable by itself, if there is a relation of the visible with itself that traverses me and constitutes me as a seer, this circle which I do not form, which forms me, this coiling over of the visible upon the visible, can traverse, animate other bodies as well as my own. And if I was able to understand how this wave arises within me, how the visible which is yonder is simultaneously my landscape, I can understand a fortiori that elsewhere it also closes over upon itself and that there are other landscapes besides my own. If it lets itself be captivated by one of its fragments, the principle of captation is established, the field open for another Narcissus, for an "intercorporeity." If my left hand can touch my right hand while it palpates the tangibles, can touch it touching, can turn its palpation back upon it, why, when touching the hand of another, would I not touch in it the same power to espouse the things that I have touched in my own? It is true that "the things" in question are my own, that the whole operation takes place (as they say) "in me," within my landscape, whereas the problem is to institute another landscape. When one of my hands touches the other, the world of each opens upon that of the other because the operation is reversible at will, because they both belong (as they say) to one sole space of consciousness, because one sole man touches one sole thing through both hands. But for my two hands to open upon one sole world, it does not suffice that they be given to one sole *conscious-*

ness—or if that were the case the difficulty before us would disappear:
since other bodies would be known by me in the same way as would be my
own, they and I would still be dealing with the same world. No, my two
hands touch the same things because they are the hands of one same
body. And yet each of them has its own tactile experience. If nonetheless
they have to do with one sole tangible, it is because there exists a very peculiar relation from one to the other, across the corporeal space—like
that holding between my two eyes—making of my hands one sole organ
of experience, as it makes my two eyes the channels of one sole cyclopean
vision. A difficult relation to conceive—since one eye, one hand, are capable of vision, of touch, and since what has to be comprehended is that
these visions, these touches, these little subjectivities, these "consciousnesses of . . . ," could be arranged like flowers into a bouquet, when each
being "consciousness of," being For Itself, reduces the others into objects.
We will get out of the difficulty only by renouncing the bifurcation of the
"consciousness of" and the object, by admitting that my synergic body is
not an object, that it gathers up into a cluster the "consciousnesses" adherent to its hands, to its eyes, by an operation that is in relation to them
lateral, transverse; that "my consciousness" is not the synthetic, uncreated,
centrifugal unity of a multitude of "consciousnesses of . . ." which would
be centrifugal like it is, that it is sustained, subtended, by the pre-reflective
and pre-objective unity of my body. This means that while each monocular vision, each touching with one sole hand has its own visible, its tactile,
each is bound to every other vision, to every other touch; it is bound in
such a way as to make up with them the experience of one sole body before one sole world, through a possibility for reversion, reconversion of its
language into theirs, transfer, and reversal, according to which the little
private world of each is not juxtaposed to the world of all others, but surrounded by it, levied off from it, and all together are a Sentient in general
before a Sensible in general. Now why would this generality, which constitutes the unity of my body, not open it to other bodies? The handshake
too is reversible; I can feel myself touched as well and at the same time as
touching, and surely there does not exist some huge animal whose organs
our bodies would be, as, for each of our bodies, our hands, our eyes are
the organs. Why would not the synergy exist among different organisms,
if it is possible within each? Their landscapes interweave, their actions and
their passions fit together exactly: this is possible as soon as we no longer
make belongingness to one same "consciousness" the primordial definition of sensibility, and as soon as we rather understand it as the return of
the visible upon itself, a carnal adherence of the sentient to the sensed
and of the sensed to the sentient. For, as overlapping and fission, identity
and difference, it brings to birth a ray of natural light that illuminates all

flesh and not only my own. It is said that the colors, the tactile reliefs given to the other, are for me an absolute mystery, forever inaccessible. This is not completely true; for me to have not an idea, an image, or a representation, but as it were the imminent experience of them, it suffices that I look at a landscape, that I speak of it with someone. Then, through the concordant operation of his body and my own, what I see passes into him, this individual green of the meadow under my eyes invades his vision without quitting my own, I recognize in my green his green, as the customs officer recognizes suddenly in a traveler the man whose description he had been given. There is here no problem of the alter ego because it is not *I* who sees, not *he* who sees, because an anonymous visibility inhabits both of us, a vision in general, by virtue of that primordial property that belongs to the flesh, being here and now, of radiating everywhere and forever, being an individual, of being also a dimension and a universal.

What is open to us, therefore, with the reversibility of the visible and the tangible, is—if not yet the incorporeal—at least the inter-corporeal being, a presumptive domain of the visible and the tangible, which extends further than the things I touch and see at present.

There is a circle of the touched and the touching, the touched takes hold of the touching; there is a circle of the visible and the seeing, the seeing is not without visible existence;[6] there is even an inscription of the touching in the visible, of the seeing in the tangible—and the converse; there is finally a propagation of these exchanges to all the bodies of the same type and of the same style which I see and touch—and this by virtue of the fundamental fission or segregation of the sentient and the sensible which, laterally, makes the organs of my body communicate and founds transitivity from one body to another.

As soon as we see other seers, we no longer have before us only the look without a pupil, the plate glass of the things with that feeble reflection, that phantom of ourselves they evoke by designating a place among themselves whence we see them: henceforth, through other eyes we are for ourselves fully visible; that lacuna where our eyes, our back, lie is filled, filled still by the visible, of which we are not the titulars. To believe that, to bring a vision that is not our own into account, it is to be sure inevitably, it is always from the unique treasury of our own vision that we draw, and experience therefore can teach us nothing that would not be outlined in our own vision. But what is proper to the visible is, we said, to be the surface of an inexhaustible depth: this is what makes it able to be open to visions other than our own. In being realized, they therefore bring out the limits of our factual vision, they betray the solipsist illusion that consists in thinking that every going beyond is a surpassing accomplished by oneself. For the first time, the seeing that I am is for me really visible; for the first time I appear to myself completely turned inside out under my own eyes. For the first time also, my movements no longer proceed unto the things to be seen, to be touched, or unto my own body occupied in seeing and touching them, but they address themselves to the body in general and for itself (whether it be my own or that of another), because for the first time, through the other body, I see that, in its coupling with the flesh of the world, the body contributes more than it receives, adding to the world that I see the treasure necessary for what the other body sees. For the first time, the body no longer couples itself up with the world, it clasps another body, applying [itself to it][7] carefully with its whole extension, forming tirelessly with its hands the strange statue which in its turn gives everything it receives; the body is lost outside of the world and its goals, fascinated by the unique occupation of floating in Being with another life, of making itself the outside of its inside and the inside of its outside. And henceforth movement, touch, vision, applying themselves to the other and to themselves, return toward their source and, in the patient and silent labor of desire, begin the paradox of expression.

Yet this flesh that one sees and touches is not all there is to flesh, nor this massive corporeity all there is to the body. The reversibility that defines the flesh exists in other fields; it is even incomparably more agile there and capable of weaving relations between bodies that this time will not only enlarge, but will pass definitively beyond the circle of the visible. Among my movements, there are some that go nowhere—that do not even go find in the other body their resemblance or their archetype: these are the facial movements, many gestures, and especially those strange movements of the throat and mouth that form the cry and the voice. Those movements end in sounds and I hear them. Like crystal, like metal and many other substances, I am a sonorous being, but I hear my own vibration from within; as Malraux said, I hear myself with my throat. In this, as he also has said, I am incomparable; my voice is bound to the mass of my own life as is the voice of no one else. But if I am close enough to the other who speaks to hear his breath and feel his effervescence and his fatigue, I almost witness, in him as in myself, the awesome birth of vociferation. As there is a reflexivity of the touch, of sight, and of the touch-vision system, there is a reflexivity of the movements of phonation and of hearing; they have their sonorous inscription, the vociferations have in me their motor echo. This new reversibility and the emergence of the flesh as expression are the point of insertion of speaking and thinking in the world of silence.[8]

At the frontier of the mute or solipsist world where, in the presence of other seers, my visible is confirmed as an exemplar of a universal visibility, we reach a second or figurative sense of vision, which will be the *intuitus mentis,* or idea, a sublimation of the flesh, which will be mind or thought. But the factual presence of other bodies could not produce thought or the idea if its seed were not in my own body. Thought is a relationship with oneself and with the world as well as a relationship with the other; hence it is established in the three dimensions at the same time. And it must be brought to appear directly in the infrastructure of vision. Brought to appear, we say, and not brought to birth: for we are leaving in suspense for the moment the question whether it would not be already implicated there. Manifest as it is that feeling is dispersed in my body, that for example my hand touches, and that consequently we may not in advance ascribe feeling to a thought of which it would be but a mode—it yet would be absurd to conceive the touch as a colony of assembled tactile experiences. We are not here proposing any empiricist genesis of thought: we are asking precisely what is that central vision that joins the scattered visions, that unique touch that governs the whole tactile life of my body as a unit, that "I think" that must be able to accompany all experiences. We are proceeding toward the center, we are seeking to comprehend how there is a center, what the unity consists of, we are not saying that it is a sum or a result; and if we make the thought appear upon an infrastructure of vision, this is only by virtue of the uncontested evidence that one must see or feel in some way in order to think, that every thought known to us occurs to a flesh.

Once again, the flesh we are speaking of is not matter. It is the coiling over of the visible upon the seeing body, of the tangible upon the touching body, which is attested in particular when the body sees itself, touches itself seeing and touching the things, such that, simultaneously, *as* tangible it descends among them, *as* touching it dominates them all and draws this relationship and even this double relationship from itself, by dehiscence or fission of its own mass. This concentration of the visibles about one of them, or this bursting forth of the mass of the body toward the things, which makes a vibration of my skin become the sleek and the rough, makes me *follow with my eyes* the movements and the contours of the things themselves, this magical relation, this pact between them and me according to which I lend them my body in order that they inscribe upon it and give me their resemblance, this fold, this central cavity of the visible which is my vision, these two mirror arrangements of the seeing and the visible, the touching and the touched, form a close-bound system that I count on, define a vision in general and a constant style of visibility from which I cannot detach myself, even when a particular vision turns out to be illusory, for I remain certain in that case that in looking closer I would have had the true vision, and that in any case, whether it be this one or another, *there is a true vision.* The flesh (of the world or my own) is not contingency, chaos, but a texture that returns to itself and conforms to itself. I will never see my own retinas, but if one thing is certain for me it is that *one* would find at the bottom of my eyeballs those dull and secret membranes. And finally, I believe it—I believe that I have a man's senses, a human body—because the spectacle of the world that is my own, and which, to judge by our confrontations, does not notably differ from that of the others, with me as with them refers with evidence to typical dimensions of visibility, and finally to a virtual focus of vision, to a detector also typical, so that at the joints of the opaque body and the opaque world there is a ray of generality and of light. Conversely, when, starting from the body, I ask how it makes itself a seer, when I examine the critical region of the aesthesiological body, everything comes to pass (as we have shown in an earlier work)[9] as though the visible body remained incomplete, gaping open; as though the physiology of vision did not succeed in closing the nervous functioning in upon itself, since the movements of fixation and convergence are suspended upon the advent, for the body, of a visible world, for which the movements were supposed to furnish the explanation; as though, therefore, the vision came suddenly to give to the material means and instruments left here and there in the working area a convergence which they were waiting for; as though, through all these channels, all these prepared but unemployed circuits, the current that will traverse them was rendered probable, in the long run inevitable: the current making of an embryo a newborn infant, of a visible a seer, and of a body a mind, or at least a flesh. In spite of all our substantialist ideas, the seer is being premeditated in counterpoint in the embryonic development; through a labor upon itself the visible body provides for the hollow whence a vision will come, inaugurates the long maturation at whose term suddenly it will see, that is, will be visible for itself, will institute the interminable gravitation, the indefatigable metamorphosis of the seeing and the visible whose principle is posed and which gets underway with the first vision. What we are calling flesh, this interiorly worked-over mass, has no name in any philosophy. As the formative medium of the object and the subject, it is not the atom of being, the hard in-itself that resides in a unique place and moment: one can indeed say of my body that it is not *elsewhere,* but one cannot say that it is *here* or *now* in the sense that objects are; and yet my vision does not survey them, it is not the being that is wholly knowing, for it has its own inertia, its ties. We must not think the flesh starting from substances, from body and spirit—for then it would be the union of contradictories—but we must think it, as we said, as an element, as the concrete emblem of a general manner of being. To begin with, we spoke summarily of a reversibility of the seeing and the visible, of the touching and the touched. It is time to emphasize that it is a reversibility always imminent and never realized in fact. My left hand is always on the verge of touching my right hand touching the things, but I never reach coincidence; the coincidence eclipses at the moment of realization, and one of two things always occurs: either my right hand really passes over to the rank of touched, but then its hold on the world is interrupted; or it retains its hold on the world, but then I do not really touch it—my right hand touching, I palpate with my left hand only its outer covering. Likewise, I do not hear myself as I hear the others, the sonorous existence of my voice is for me as it were poorly exhibited; I have rather an echo of its articulated existence, it vibrates through my head rather than outside. I am always on the same side of my body; it presents itself to me in one invariable perspective. But this incessant escaping, this impotence to superpose exactly upon one another the touching of the things by my right hand and the touching of this same right hand by my left hand, or to superpose, in the exploratory movements of the hand, the tactile experience of a point and that of the "same" point a moment later, or the auditory experience of my own voice and that of other voices—this is not a failure. For if these experiences never exactly overlap, if they slip away at the very moment they are about to rejoin, if there is always a "shift," a "divergence," between them, this is precisely because my two hands are part of the same body, because it moves itself in the world, because I hear myself both from within and from without. I experience—and as often as I wish—the transition and the metamorphosis of the one experience into the other, and it is only as though the hinge between them, solid, unshakeable, remained irremediably hidden from me. But this hiatus between my right hand touched and my right hand touching, between my voice heard and my voice uttered, between one moment of my tactile life and the following one, is not an ontological void, a nonbeing: it is spanned by the total being of my body, and by that of the world; it is the zero of pressure between two solids that makes them adhere to one another. My flesh and that of the world therefore involve clear zones, clearings, about which pivot their opaque zones, and the primary visibility, that of the quale and of the things, does not come without a second visibility, that of the lines of force and dimensions, the massive flesh without a rarefied flesh, the momentary body without a glorified body. When Husserl spoke of the horizon of the things—of their exterior horizon, which everybody knows, and of their "interior horizon," that darkness stuffed with visibility of which their surface is but the limit—it is necessary to take the term seriously. No more than are the sky or the earth is the horizon a collection of things held together, or a class name, or a logical possibility of conception, or a system of "potentiality of consciousness"; it is a new type of being, a being by porosity, pregnancy, or generality, and he before whom the horizon

Heidegger

opens is caught up, included within it. His body and the distances participate in one same corporeity or visibility in general, which reigns between
them and it, and even beyond the horizon, beneath his skin, unto the
depths of being.

We touch here the most difficult point, that is, the bond between the
flesh and the idea, between the visible and the interior armature which it
manifests and which it conceals. No one has gone further than Proust in
fixing the relations between the visible and the invisible, in describing an
idea that is not the contrary of the sensible, that is its lining and its depth.
For what he says of musical ideas he says of all cultural beings, such as *The
Princess of Clèves* and *René*, and also of the essence of love which "the little
phrase" not only makes present to Swann, but communicable to all who
hear it, even though it is unbeknown to themselves, and even though later
they do not know how to recognize it in the loves they only witness. He says
it in general of many other notions which are, like music itself, "without
equivalents": "the notions of light, of sound, of relief, of physical volup-
tuousness, which are the rich possessions with which our inward domain
is diversified and adorned."[10] Literature, music, the passions, but also the
experience of the visible world are—no less than is the science of Lavoisier
and Ampère—the exploration of an invisible and the disclosure of a universe of ideas.[11] The difference is simply that this invisible, these ideas, unlike those of that science, cannot be detached from the sensible appearances and be erected into a second positivity. The musical idea, the literary
idea, the dialectic of love, and also the articulations of light, the modes of
exhibition of sound and of touch speak to us, have their logic, their coherence, their points of intersection, their concordances, and here also
the appearances are the disguise of unknown "forces" and "laws." But it is
as though the secrecy wherein they lie and whence the literary expression
draws them were their proper mode of existence. For these truths are not
only hidden like a physical reality which we have not been able to discover,
invisible in fact but which we will one day be able to see facing us, which
others, better situated, could already see, provided that the screen that
masks it is lifted. Here, on the contrary, there is no vision without the
screen: the ideas we are speaking of would not be better known to us if we
had no body and no sensibility; it is then that they would be inaccessible
to us. The "little phrase," the notion of the light, are not exhausted by
their manifestations, any more than is an "idea of the intelligence"; they
could not be given to us *as ideas* except in a carnal experience. It is not only
that we would find in that carnal experience the *occasion* to think them; it
is that they owe their authority, their fascinating, indestructible power,
precisely to the fact that they are in transparency behind the sensible, or
in its heart. Each time we want to get at it[12] immediately, or lay hands on

it, or circumscribe it, or see it unveiled, we do in fact feel that the attempt is misconceived, that it retreats in the measure that we approach. The explicitation does not give us the idea itself; it is but a second version of it, a more manageable derivative. Swann can of course close in the "little phrase" between the marks of musical notation, ascribe the "withdrawn and chilly tenderness" that makes up its essence or its sense to the narrow range of the five notes that compose it and to the constant recurrence of two of them: while he is thinking of these signs and this sense, he no longer has the "little phrase" itself, he has only "bare values substituted for the mysterious entity he had perceived, for the convenience of his understanding."[13] Thus it is essential to this sort of ideas that they be "veiled with shadows," appear "under a disguise." They give us the assurance that the "great unpenetrated and discouraging night of our soul" is not empty, is not "nothingness"; but these entities, these domains, these worlds that line it, people it, and whose presence it feels like the presence of someone in the dark, have been acquired only through its commerce with the visible, to which they remain attached. As the secret blackness of milk, of which Valéry spoke, is accessible only through its whiteness, the idea of light or the musical idea doubles up the sights and sounds from beneath, is their other side or their depth. Their carnal texture presents to us what is absent from all flesh; it is a furrow that traces itself out magically under our eyes without a tracer, a certain hollow, a certain interior, a certain absence, a negativity that is not nothing, being limited very precisely to *these* five notes between which it is instituted, to that family of sensibles we call lights. We do not see, do not hear the ideas, and not even with the mind's eye or with the third ear: and yet they are, behind the sounds or between them, behind the lights or between them, recognizable through their always special, always unique manner of entrenching themselves behind them, "perfectly distinct from one another, unequal among themselves in value and in significance."[14]

With the first vision, the first contact, the first pleasure, there is initiation, that is, not the positing of a content, but the opening of a dimension that can never again be closed, the establishment of a level in terms of which every other experience will henceforth be situated. The idea is this level, this dimension. It is therefore not a de facto invisible, like an object hidden behind another, and not an absolute invisible, which would have nothing to do with the visible. Rather it is the visible *of* this world, that which inhabits this world, sustains it, and renders it visible, its own and interior possibility, the Being of this being. At the moment one says "light," at the moment that the musicians reach the "little phrase," there is no lacuna in me; what I live is as "substantial," as "explicit," as a positive thought could be—even more so: a positive thought is what it is, but, precisely, is only what it is and accordingly cannot hold us. Already the mind's volubility takes it elsewhere. We do not possess the musical or sensible ideas, precisely because they are negativity or absence circumscribed; they possess us. The performer is no longer producing or reproducing the sonata: he feels himself, and the others feel him to be, at the service of the sonata; the sonata sings through him or cries out so suddenly that he must "dash on his bow" to follow it. And these open vortexes in the sonorous world finally form one sole vortex in which the ideas fit in with one another. "Never was the spoken language so inflexibly necessitated, never did it know to such an extent the pertinence of the questions, the evidence of the responses."[15] The invisible and, as it were, weak being is alone capable of having this close texture. There is a strict ideality in experiences that are experiences of the flesh: the moments of the sonata, the fragments of the luminous field, adhere to one another with a cohesion without concept, which is of the same type as the cohesion of the parts of my body, or the cohesion of my body with the world. Is my body a thing, is it an idea? It is neither, being the *measurant* of the things. We will therefore have to recognize an ideality that is not alien to the flesh, that gives it its axes, its depth, its dimensions.

But once we have entered into this strange domain, one does not see how there could be any question of *leaving* it. If there is an animation of the body; if the vision and the body are tangled up in one another; if, correlatively, the thin pellicle of the quale, the surface of the visible, is doubled up over its whole extension with an invisible reserve; and if finally, in our flesh as in the flesh of things, the actual, empirical, ontic visible, by a sort of folding back, invagination, or padding, exhibits a visibility, a possibility that is not the shadow of the actual but is its principle, that is not the proper contribution of a "thought" but is its condition, a style, allusive and elliptical like every style, but like every style inimitable, inalienable, an interior horizon and an exterior horizon between which the actual visible is a provisional partitioning and which, nonetheless, opens indefinitely only upon other visibles—then (the immediate and dualist distinction between the visible and the invisible, between extension and thought, being impugned, not that extension be thought or thought extension, but because they are the obverse and the reverse of one another, and the one forever behind the other) there is to be sure a question as to how the "ideas of the intelligence" are initiated over and beyond, how from the ideality of the horizon one passes to the "pure" ideality, and in particular by what miracle a created generality, a culture, a knowledge come to add to and recapture and rectify the natural generality of my body and of the world. But, however we finally have to understand it, the "pure" ideality already streams forth along the articulations of the aes-

thesiological body, along the contours of the sensible things, and, however new it is, it slips through ways it has not traced, transfigures horizons
it did not open, it derives from the fundamental mystery of those notions
"without equivalent," as Proust calls them, that lead their shadowy life in
the night of the mind only because they have been divined at the junc-
tures of the visible world. It is too soon now to clarify this type of surpassing that does not leave its field of origin. Let us only say that the pure
ideality is itself not without flesh or freed from horizon structures: it
lives from them, though they be another flesh and other horizons. It is as
though the visibility that animates the sensible world were to emigrate,
not outside of every body, but into another less heavy, more transparent
body, as though it were to change flesh, abandoning the flesh of the body
for that of language, and thereby would be emancipated but not freed
from every condition. Why not admit—as Proust knew very well and said
in another place—that language as well as music can sustain a sense by
virtue of its own arrangement, catch a sense in its own mesh, that it does
so without exception each time it is conquering, active, creative language,
each time something is, in the strong sense, said? Why not admit that, just
as the musical notation is a *facsimile* made after the event, an abstract portrait of the musical entity, language as a system of explicit relations between signs and signified, sounds and sense, is a result and a product of
the operative language in which sense and sound are in the same relationship as the "little phrase" and the five notes found in it afterward?
This does not mean that musical notation and grammar and linguistics
and the "ideas of the intelligence"—which are acquired, available, honorary ideas—are useless, or that, as Leibniz said, the donkey that goes
straight to the fodder knows as much about the properties of the straight
line as we do; it means that the system of objective relations, the acquired
ideas, are themselves caught up in something like a second life and perception, which make the mathematician go straight to entities no one has
yet seen, make the *operative* language and algorithm make use of a second
visibility, and make ideas be the other side of language and calculus. When
I think they animate my interior speech, they haunt it as the "little phrase"
possesses the violinist, and they remain beyond the words as it remains
beyond the notes—not in the sense that under the light of another sun
hidden from us they would shine forth, but because they are that certain
divergence, that never-finished differentiation, that openness ever to be
reopened between the sign and the sign, as the flesh is, we said, the dehiscence of the seeing into the visible and of the visible into the seeing.
And just as my body sees only because it is a part of the visible in which it
opens forth, the sense upon which the arrangement of the sounds opens
reflects back upon that arrangement. For the linguist language is an ideal

system, a fragment of the intelligible world. But, just as for me to see it is not enough that my look be visible for *x,* it is necessary that it be visible for itself, through a sort of torsion, reversal, or specular phenomenon, which is given from the sole fact that I am born; so also, if my words have a sense, it is not *because* they present the systematic organization the linguist will disclose, it is because that organization, like the look, refers back to itself: operative Speech is the obscure region whence comes the instituted light, as the muted reflection of the body upon itself is what we call natural light. As there is a reversibility of the seeing and the visible, and as at the point where the two metamorphoses cross what we call perception is born, so also there is a reversibility of speech and what it signifies; the meaning is what comes to seal, to close, to gather up the multiplicity of the physical, physiological, linguistic means of elocution, to contract them into one sole act, as the vision comes to complete the aesthesiological body. And, as the visible takes hold of the look which has unveiled it and which forms a part of it, the meaning rebounds upon its own means, it annexes to itself the speech that becomes an object of science, it antedates itself by a retrograde movement which is never completely disappointed—because already, in opening the horizon of the nameable and of the sayable, the speech acknowledged that it has its place in that horizon; because no locutor speaks without making himself in advance allocutary, *be it only for himself;* because with one sole gesture he closes the circuit of his relation to himself and that of his relation to the others and, with the same stroke, also sets himself up as *delocutary,* speech of which one speaks: he offers himself and offers every speech to a universal Speech. We shall have to follow more closely this transition from the mute world to the speaking world. For the moment we want only to suggest that one can speak neither of a destruction nor of a conservation of silence (and still less of a destruction that conserves or of a realization that destroys—which is not to solve but to pose the problem).When the silent vision falls into speech, and when speech in turn, opening up a field of the nameable and the sayable, inscribes itself in that field, in its place, according to its truth— in short, when it metamorphoses the structures of the visible world and makes itself a gaze of the mind, *intuitus mentis*—this is always by virtue of the same fundamental phenomenon of reversibility which sustains both the mute perception and the speech and which manifests itself by an almost carnal existence of the idea, as well as by a sublimation of the flesh. In a sense, if we were to make completely explicit the architectonics of the human body, its ontological framework, and how it sees itself and hears itself, we would see that the structure of its mute world is such that all the possibilities of language are already given in it. Already our existence as seers (that is, we said, as beings who turn the world back upon itself and

[handwritten marginal note, left side] Compare to Althusser on interpellation / "hailing" (which concedes no such reversibility / interfacing — as is un-ethical for the sake of the politics" of the Enlightenment subject)

who pass over to the other side, and who catch sight of one another, who see one another with eyes) and especially our existence as sonorous beings for others and for ourselves contain everything required for there to be speech from the one to the other, speech about the world. And, in a sense, to understand a phrase is nothing else than to fully welcome it in its sonorous being, or, as we put it so well, to *hear what it says* [*l'entendre*]. The sense is not on the phrase like the butter on the bread, like a second layer of "psychic reality" spread over the sound: it is the totality of what is said, the integral of all the differentiations of the verbal chain; it is given with the words for those who have ears to hear. And conversely, the whole landscape is overrun with words as with an invasion; the landscape is no longer anything but a variant of speech for our eyes, and to speak of its "style" is to make a metaphor for our eyes. In a sense, all philosophy, as Husserl says, consists in restoring a power to signify, a birth of sense, or a wild sense, an expression of experience by experience, which in particular clarifies the special domain of language. And in a sense, as Valéry said, language is everything, since it is the voice of no one, since it is the very voice of the things, the waves, and the forests. And what we have to understand is that there is no dialectical reversal from one of these views to the other; we do not have to gather them up into a synthesis: they are two aspects of the reversibility which is the ultimate truth.

New Working Notes from the Period of
The Visible and the Invisible

Labyrinthe de l'ontologie. 17 septembre 1958

Contre l'idée que ce monde est le seul possible, *cet* être synonyme de *l'*être, qu'il n'y a le choix qu'entre rien et cela, que ceci est la figure in-évitable [?][1] d'un être illimité mais je ne veux pas dire: un autre monde a été possible (une "bonté"), une "finalité," a réalisé celui-ci. De quelque manière qu'on le conçoive, ce principe finalement devra exprimer une exigence d'existence intérieure aux possibles (Leibniz) un mécanisme métaphysique qui fait prédominer *ce qui a le plus d'être*. C'est donc encore *l'ontologie de l'objet*—ou si ce n'est pas l'ontologie de l'objet, si le choix est "immotivé," l'existence de ce monde-ci est un fait brut [ou pur]—ce qui est mon idée.

Mais l'idée d'un monde comme fait brut ne sous-entend-t-elle pas toujours le contraste de ce monde avec d'autres possibles? *L'évocation de ces autres possibles n'est-elle pas indispensable pour que ce monde-ci garde le relief du fait?* La contingence de l'existant peut-elle être pensée autrement que comme un résidu, une opacité qui demeure après qu'on a examiné l'essence et reconnu qu'elle n'était pas impossible, pas contradictoire?

Justement, c'est cette idée qu'il faut chasser. Comprendre que le réel, l'effectif en tant que tel diffère *tota caelo* de tout possible (et du même réel, considéré en idée ou dans son essence)—qu'il n'y a pas à [maintenir?] le porte à faux des vérité de raison et des vérités de fait, du possible logique et du réel, de l'événement et de l'objet, fut-ce pour [imputer?] le réel à un autre ordre que le possible. Or le réel n'a pas à être pensé à partir du pos-sible, mais au contraire le possible à partir du réel et comme vaiante du réel (sens de la [?] bergsonienne du possible)—le possible est encore une forme de l'idéologie nécessitaire, de l'idéologie de l'intrinsèque: le néces-saire n'est qu'un possible pleinement possible, et le possible n'est qu'une nécessité qui inexplicablement, s'arrête sur son propre chemin.

Ce possible là est second par rapport au réel—il se définit par la noncontradiction, ou l'identité, par l'essence, il semble à ce titre renfermer comme une sphère plus vaste le cas particulier de ce monde-ci qui n'est plus que le plus possible parmi les possibles. C'est toute cette idéologie qu'il faut rejeter: car [. . .] ou elle ramène la nécessité—ou elle ne permet [. . . .] la contingence que comme irrationnel, comme opacité, comme résidu. Montrer que tous nos concepts, toutes nos essences, (l'essence "monde," ou bien l'essence "objet" ou l'essence "être," le monde, l'objet, l'être comme significations) loin de nous fournir le point de départ d'où, par addition d'un principe obscur, on passerait à l'actuel, sont *au contraire des idéalisations du contact primordial avec l'être, le monde, l'objet.*

Ce contact primordial n'est pas "choc" sans signification. [5 lignes]

Il n'y a pas des essences et des existences, des possibles non-contradictoires et des réalités qui ne seraient que le plus haut point de la non-contradiction *plus* un facteur [?] de l'actualité pure. L'univers des significations est une reprise de l'universe des structures.

Cette subordination du possible logique (subordination qui n'est pas sa négation, qui n'est pas [. . . .] puisque c'est par un processus fondé que l'on passe à l'univers des significations et du langage) n'est *en aucun cas un "actualisme": l'actualisme est tributaire, comme le possibilisme de Leibniz, de la dichotomie essence-existence, c'est un cas majeur d'ontologie de l'objet, d'idéologie de l'eccéité.* Il est permis de dire que notre point de vue est *une réhabilitation du possible tout autant qu'une subordination du possible logique.* Ce que je appelle ici possible, c'est non plus le non-contradictoire, (notion qui *se donne* une tendance de l'être à persévérer dans l'être *sauf s'il* comporte des éléments [?] incompossibles) mais la totalité implicite, ce qui prépare l'amblystome à nager avant même que les organes de la natation soient en place. Et cette possibilité là (le possible organique) elle existe même dans l'être physique, puisque lui non plus n'est pas par définition, puisque le quelque chose physique n'est pas lui non plus pur objet de pensée.

Mon effort pour introduire une [démonologie?] (une téléologie husserlienne, qui n'est pas finalité leibnizienne) entre la pensée finaliste et la pensée mécaniste (qui sont des pensées artificialistes) correspond à une réhabilitation d'un nouveau possible, ingrédient comme tel de l'être, contre l'*actualisme* et le *possibilisme.*

Labyrinth of ontology. September 17, 1958

Against the idea that this world is the only one possible, *this* being synonymous with *the* being, that there is a choice only between nothing and that, that this is the inevitable [or genuine] figure of an unlimited being, but I do not want to say: another world has been possible and another principle (a "goodness"), a "finality," has realized the other world. No matter how we conceive it, this principle finally will have to express a requirement of the interior existence to the possibles (Leibniz) a metaphysical mechanism which makes *what has the most being* predominate. This is therefore still the ontology of the object—or if this is not the ontology of the object, if the choice is "unmotivated," the existence of this world is a brute [or pure] fact—which is my idea.

But does not the idea of a world as a brute fact imply always the contrast of this world with other possible ones? *Is not the evocation of these other possible worlds indispensable so that this world holds onto the relief of being a fact?* Can the contingency of existing be thought in a way other than as a residue, an opacity which remains after we have examined the essence and recognized that it was not impossible, not contradictory?

Precisely, it is this idea that we must chase away. To understand that the real, the effective as such differs *tota caelo* from every possible (and from the same real, considered as an idea or in its essence)—that it does not have to [maintain] there the truths of reason and the truths of fact, the logically possible and the real, the event and the object out of kilter, perhaps in order to [impute?] the real to an order other than the possible. Now, the real is not to be thought on the basis of the possible, but on the contrary the possible on the basis of the real and as a variant of the real (the meaning of Bergson's [?] of the possible)—the possible is still a form of the ideology of the necessary, of the ideology of the intrinsic: the necessary is only a possible that is fully possible, and the possible is only a necessity which inexplicably stops on its own path.

That possible is second in relation to the real—it is defined by noncontradiction, or identity, by essence, it seems thereby to close back up as a sphere that is vaster than the particular case of this world which is no more than the most possible among the possible ones. It is this whole ideology that we must reject: for [. . .] or it brings necessity back—or it allows contingency only as something irrational, as opacity, as residue. Show that all of our concepts, all of our essences (the essence "world" or the essence "object" or the essence "being," the world, the object, being as meanings), far from providing us with the starting point from which, through the addition of an obscure principle, we would pass to the actual, are *on the contrary idealizations of the primordial contact with being, the world, and the object.*

This primordial contact is not a "shock" without meaning. [5 lines indecipherable]

There are no essences and existences, noncontradictory possibles and realities which would be only the highest point of noncontradiction, plus a [?] factor of pure actuality. The universe of meanings is a repetition of the universe of structures.

This subordination of the logically possible (a subordination which is not its negation, which is not [. . . .] since it is by means of a founded process that we pass to the universe of meanings and language) is *in no way an "actualism": actualism is dependent, like Leibniz's possibilism, on the essence-existence dichotomy, it's a major case of the ontology of the object, of the ontology of the haeceity.* We're allowed to say that our viewpoint is a rehabilitation of the possible as much as a subordination of the logically possible. What I am here calling possible is as well not the noncontradictory (a notion which gives itself a tendency of being to persevere in being unless it involves [?] imcompossible elements), but the implicit totality, which prepares the salamander to swim even before the organs of swimming are in place. And this possibility (the organically possible), it exists even in physical being, since it as well is not by definition, since the physical something is not as well a pure object of thought.

My effort in order to introduce a [demonology?] (a Husserlian teleology, which is not a Leibnizian finality) between finalistic thought and mechanistic thought (which are artificialist thoughts) corresponds to a rehabilitation of a new possible, an ingredient as such of being, against *actualism* and *possibilism.*

* * *

11 octobre 1958

Il s'agit d'un plan. Je propose d'examiner les tentatives de Husserl Sartre Heidegger.

Ce qui les bloque: chez Husserl l'idéologie de la "conscience"
chez Sartre une positivité seconde du Néant (le néant n'est pas)
→ la philosophie terminée
chez Heidegger, qui veut [vraiment?] penser le néant (et par suite le pense comme Être) l'approche des limites de l'expression (cf. Lettre sur l'humanisme) → quasi silence

[. . .] "Insister sur le fait que les philosophies classiques sont *toutes vraies.* . ."
[. . .] "Montrer dans introduction qu'il faut absolument dépasser la bifurcation essence-existence: *Wesen* (verbal). Le montrer à partir de la "*Gestalt.*"

October 11, 1958

What's in question is a plan. I propose to examine the attempts of Husserl, Sartre, Heidegger.

What stops them: in Husserl the ideology of "consciousness"
in Sartre a second positivity of Nothingness (nothingness is not)
→ philosophy over and done with
in Heidegger, who wants [truly?] to think nothingness (and then think it as Being) the approach of the limits of expression (cf. The Letter on Humanism) → quasi silence

[. . .] "Insist on the fact that the classical philosophies are *all true*. . ."
[. . .] "Show in the introduction that it is necessary to overcome absolutely the essence-existence bifurcation: (verbal) *Wesen*. Show it on the basis of the "*Gestalt.*"

* * *

L'évidence en musique [1958]

En écoutant une musique belle: impressions que ce mouvement qui commence est déjà à son terme, qu'il va avoir été, ou s'enfoncer dans l'avenir que l'on tient aussi bien que le passé—quoiqu'on ne puisse dire exactement ce qu'il sera. Rétrospection anticipée—Mouvement rétrograde *in futuro:* il descend vers moi tout fait.

The evidence found in music [1958]

While listening to a piece of beautiful music: impressions that this movement which is beginning is already at its end, that it is going to have been, or sinking into the future that we hold as well as the past—though we cannot say exactly what it will be. Anticipated Retrospection—retrograde Movement *in futuro:* it is descending toward me already made.

* * *

[1958]

Tout ce que Goethe dit de la Nature comme principe barbare de Bien et du Mal, il faut bien le dire à partir du moment où la Nature n'est ni chose pure, ni Dieu, ni simple "collection des objets des sens"—où il y a un lien interne dans le multiple qui n'est pas celui de l'entendement divin.

On dira: vous n'expliquez rien, vous constatez. Mais expliquer, c'est toujours: ramener la Nature à Dieu ou la ramener au spectacle de l'homme—ne pas voir la nature. En réalité, ce qu'il faut *apprendre, c'est que l'être est cela,* c'est précisément *à ne pas expliquer.*

[1958]

All of what Goethe says about nature as the barbarous principle of Good and Evil, we really have to say that on the basis of the moment when Nature is neither pure thing nor God nor the simple "collection of the objects of the senses"—when there is an internal connection in the multiple which is not that of the divine understanding.

Someone will say: you explain nothing, you observe. But to explain is always: to bring Nature back to God or to bring it back to the spectacle of man—not to see nature. In reality, what one has *to learn is that being is that,* it is precisely *not to explain.*

* * *

Projet de cours de 1959. *Cours* (Simondon) (Sur régulation, individuation etc.)—*Fin*

Le point de vue de Simondon est [transperceptif]: la perception est pour lui de l'ordre de l'interindividuel, incapable de rendre compte du collectif vrai. Il y a là quelque chose de vrai: poser tous les problèmes en termes de perception, c'est encore l'attitude phénoménologique au sens où Fink le critique. Nous ne percevons pas constamment, la perception n'est pas coextensive à notre vie. Néanmoins, on ne sait plus de quoi l'on parle si l'on installe dans le [méta-perceptif]. Il faut philosophie à plusieurs entrées mais il y a *des entrées.* Pour moi, la philosophie de l'être brut (ou perceptif) nous fait sortir du [sujet] cartésian, de l'intersubjectivité sartrienne, nous fait voir que le langage *nous a,* qu'il y a un mystère de l'histoire, nous dévoile des institutions par-delà le flux des *Erlebnisse,* et des fulgurations de la décision—mais pour elle, le foyer reste le champ perceptif, en tant qu'il contient tout: nature et histoire.

Simplement, au lieu de dire: être perçu et perception, je ferais mieux de dire être brut ou sauvage et "fondation" (*Stiftung*).

1959 Course Project. Course (Simondon) (Concerning regulation, individuation, etc.)—*End*

Simondon's viewpoint is [transperceptual]: perception is for him of the order of the inter-individual, incapable of giving an account of the true collective. There is something true there: posing the problem in terms of perception is still the phenomenological attitude in the sense that Fink criticizes it. We do not perceive constantly, perception is not coextensive with our life. Nevertheless, one no longer knows that of which one is speaking if one sets oneself up in the [meta-perceptual]. We need a philosophy with several entrances but there are *entrances*. For me, the philosophy of brute (or perceptual) being makes us emerge from the Cartesian [subject], from Sartrian intersubjectivity, makes us see that language *has us*. That there is a mystery to history, unveils for us institutions beyond the flux of *Erlebnisse,* and the fulgurations of decision—but for this philosophy the focal point remains the perceptual field, insofar as it contains everything: nature and history.

Simply, instead of saying: perceived being and perception, I would do better to say brute or wild being and "foundation" (*Stiftung*).

* * *

Projet de cours de 1959. 28 septembre 1955

Reprendre la question de la *cosmogonie du monde perçu.*

J'admets que le corps est conditionnant par rapport au spectacle perçu, que l'installation de ce spectacle se fait *grâce à* l'apparition, dans le monde perçu, de cet appareil à vivre qu'on appelle mon corps vivant. J'admets dans cette mesure l'antériorité de l'en-soi sur le pour-soi. Mais, par ailleurs, cet *en-soi,* je me refuse à le concevoir comme le fait le réalisme des savants, je dis que dans sa texture même, il renvoie à mon (un) centre de perspective, qui est à concevoir en termes de spectacle perçu.

J'admets donc une dialectique, un double point de vue. Mais que signifie cette dualité, à moins que ce ne soit passage d'un point de vue dans l'autre? Et que signifie passage? Car il ne faut pas que ce soit "enveloppement." Il faut que ce soit contact à distance, contact indirect, obtenu justement parce qu'il n'est pas chosifié, et qui, sous le regard de la réflexion, devient *l'impossible*.

Surgissement *dans* mon champ d'un au-délà de mon champ (mes prédécesseurs, mes consorts),—non pas seulement l'X qui m'objective ou me [. . .], mais un alter ego qui est "de mon côté," comme on dit qu'un enfant est "du côté" de son père [avec qui j'entretiens un rapport (d'ailleurs réversible) de générativité (et si je suis son père, il est mon père—ubiquité de la situation, totalité à l'intérieur de la partialité)].[2]

La "nature" n'est pas seulement *en-soi* d'où nous nous . . . , mais elle comporte cette couche de socialité: ce milieu "général" des consorts, leur apparition comme rameaux d'une même souche.

Et cependant, ce qui est rendu *possible* par ces [préparations] "naturelles" les rejette à distance, au passé, ou dépassé quand il passe à l'actuel. Suscitation d'une liberté par une liberté, l'une est entée sur l'autre comme un corps sur un corps. Et nous sommes entés sur l'animalité, et l'animalité sur la nature. L'homme ne peut pas devenir homme, sinon en présence d'un adulte (les enfants "sauvages"). Ceci est l'attestation de l'irréalité de l'individu.

Reelement, un enfant n'est *rien* si ne s'offre à lui cet instrument, dont il apprend à jouer, avec lequel il apprend à devenir homme, et qui est un alter ego. Projection et introjection, non "conscience."

Et cependant, tout ceci est pour lui appel à être soi, individu de classe. La généralité "naturelle" est donc conservée et transformée. La culture est, dans son contenu, tout autre que la nature, et cependant elle est enracinée dans la *Fortpflanzung*, la *Fortpflanzung* apparaît comme une préparation du rapport alter ego, comme faite pour lui et lui, fait pour elle.

Donc on ne rattache pas le pour-soi à un en-soi comme à une condition par rapport à laquelle il serait *ultérieur*. Le corps lui-même ne peut être perçu qu'intérieur au champ phénoménal. Mais pas davantage il ne faut enfermer le corps et le monde "réel" qui traîne après lui dans "ma représentation." Car celle-ci se donne à moi-même comme [continuant] une histoire et une nature, qui ne sont pas pour . . . la suite. [Inutile] d'espérer *enfermer* tout ce déploiement extérieur dans un absolu qui soit sujet: comme il ne serait pas le sujet au sens où nous le sommes, il serait pour nous objet pur. N'étant pas *né* comme nous, fils de la terre, il ne serait pas un toi pour nous: il n'y a de toi que celui qui peut me répondre, à qui je suis aussi nécessaire qu'il m'est nécessaire.

Ce qu'il y a, c'est donc des perspectives dont chacune s'éprouve comme différente par rapport aux autres, manque des autres et les éprouve comme différences par rapport à soi (= X)—dont chacune sont des [parois épaisses] parce qu'elles sont tous les autre sédimentés: mon corps est les autres corps, ma "psyché" les autres psychés, moi comme sujet transcendental n'importe quel autre . . . et cela non en vertu d'une universalité solipsiste, mais parce que je pose le pied là où quelque chose est prêt à le recevoir, j'enjambe les "conditions," je les implique dans mon geste, chacun de mes gestes prend l'inconnu pour *connu*.

1959 Course Project. September 28, 1955

Take up the question of the *cosmogony of the perceived world*.

I admit that the body is conditioning in relation to the perceived spectacle, that the installation of this spectacle is made *thanks to* the appearing, in the perceived world, of this apparatus for living that we call my living body. I admit in this regard the priority of the in-itself over the for-itself. But, moreover, this *in-itself*, I reject conceiving it as the realism of the scientists conceives it, I say that in its very texture, it refers to my (one) center of perspective, which is to be conceived in terms of the perceived spectacle.

I admit therefore a dialectic, a double viewpoint. But what does this duality mean, unless it means a passage from one of the viewpoints into the other? And what does passage mean? For this must not be "envelopment." It is necessary that this is contact at a distance, indirect contact, obtained precisely because it is not reified, and which, under the gaze of reflection, becomes something *impossible*.

Arising *in* my field (my predecessors, my consorts)—not merely the X who objectifies me [. . .], but an alter ego who "has my look," as we say that a child "has the look" of his father [with whom I carry on a relation (that is moreover reversible) of generativity (and if I am his father, he is my father—ubiquity of the situation, totality within partiality)].[2]

"Nature" is not only *in-itself* whence we . . . , but it involves this layer of sociality: this "general" milieu of consorts, their appearing as a branch of one identical trunk.

And yet, what is made *possible* by these "natural" [preparations] throws them out at a distance, to the past, or beyond when it passes to the actual. Instigation of a freedom by a freedom, the one is grafted on the other as a body is grafted on a body. And we are grafted on animality, and animality on nature. A human cannot become human, except in the presence of an adult (the "wild" children). This is the attestation of the irreality of the individual.

THE MERLEAU-PONTY READER

Really, a child is *nothing* if this instrument is not offered to him, this instrument with which he learns to play, with which he learns to become human, and which is an alter ego. Projection and introjection, not "consciousness."

And yet, all of this is for him a call to be a self, individual of a class. "Natural" generality is therefore conserved and transformed. Culture is, in its content, entirely different from nature, and yet it is rooted in the *Fortpflanzung* [propagation], the *Fortpflanzung* appears as a preparation of the alter ego relation, as made for him and him, made for her.

Therefore we are not reattaching the for-itself to an in-itself as to a condition in relation to which it would be *subsequent*. The body itself cannot be perceived except as internal to the phenomenal field. But as well we must not enclose the body and the "real" world which trails after it in "my representation." For my representation gives itself to me as [continuing] a history and a nature, which are not for . . . the consequence. [It's not necessary] to hope to *enclose* all of this external development in an absolute which would be a subject: as it would not be the subject as we are subjects, it would be for us pure object. Not being *born* as we are, sons of the earth, it would not be a you for us: there is no you but the one who can respond to me, to whom I am as necessary as he is necessary to me.

What there is, is therefore perspectives, each of which experiences itself as different in relation to the others, lack of others and experiences them as differences in relation to the self (= X)—each of which are its [thick linings] because they are all the sedimented others: my body is their bodies, my "psyche" the other psyches, me as transcendental subject like any other . . . and that is the case not because of a solipsistic universality, but because I place my foot where something is ready to receive it, I straddle the "conditions," I imply them in my gesture, each of my gestures takes the unknown *for known*.

* * *

Dimanche 20 septembre 1959. Musée
d'Art moderne. Portrait de Franz [Hallens]
par Modigliani

Comment peut-on peindre un visage?—c'est qu'il aussi une chose—mais son expression? Il faut bien qu'elle soit aussi quelque chose comme une *propriété* de cette chose singulière, puisqu'on *voit les autres*. Le regard se peint comme la lumière.

On a appris à figurer le regard comme la lumière—oui, mais cette figuration par un point de blanc dans l'oeil n'est qu'un cas particulier.

Modigliani figure le regard par une infime variation de noir dans l'oeil tout noir. Donc le visage peut se peindre à condition que sa peinture, même figurative, ne soit pas langage des choses, mais auto-manifestation. Soit, mais le cas du visage n'est pas particulier: on peut en dire autant de toutes les choses qui se peignent—oui, mais cela montre justement qu'entre les choses et les visages, qu'entre la "Nature" and la "Culture," il n'y a aucune limite nette. On peut peindre un visage (comme une chose) parce qu'il n'y a ni "intérieur," ni "extérieur."

Sunday, September 20, 1959. Museum
of Modern Art. Portrait of Franz [Hallens]
by Modigliani

How can anyone paint a face? It's also a thing—but its expression? The expression also really has to be something like a *property* of this singular thing, since we *see the others*. The gaze is depicted like light.

We have learned to draw the gaze like light—yes, but this figuration by means of a spot of white in the eye is only one particular case. Modigliani draws the gaze by means of a miniscule variation of black in the eye that is entirely black. Therefore the face can be depicted on the condition that its painting, even if it is figurative, is not the language of things, but auto-manifestation. Okay, but the case of the face is not particular: we can say just as much about it as about everything which is depicted—yes, but that shows precisely that between the things and the faces, between "Nature" and "Culture," there is no clear limit. We can paint a face (like a thing) because there is neither "interior" nor "exterior."

* * *

22 octobre 1959. Personne

La subjectivité, c'est vraiment *personne*. C'est vraiment le désert. Ce qui est constitutif du sujet, c'est d'être intégralement aux choses, au monde, de n'avoir pas d'intérieur positivement assignable, d'être *généralité*. La subjectivité, c'est cette brume à l'entrée du monde, que le monde ne dissipe jamais. C'est là la vérité de ce que Sartre dit sur le néant.

Mais ce qu'on dit ainsi de la subjectivité comme néant doit aussitôt être traduit: donc il n'y a pas à parler de *cela*, cela n'est pas, ce néant n'est pas, et la négation de ce néant, la négintuition de ce néant n'est pas un commencement en une partie de la philosophie, à laquelle on pourrait ensuite ajouter une contrepartie ou un complément de facticité. Le désert de la subjectivité, cette notion est solidaire de celle de l'Être-objet. Et les deux notions sont rejetées ensemble précisément par la reconnaissance du néant comme *nichtiges Nichts*. Ce dont il y a lieu de parler, ce qui est, c'est le monde vertical, non-projectif, et c'est le sujet voyant, parlant— pensant seulement *à partir de ces opérations*. Ce sujet n'est pas conscience, ni *Ichheit*, pas même comme négativités "pures." Il est Parole et Expérience, et corrélativement l'Être est non un lointain que *j'*éloigne, mais un lointain de transgression, d'empiétement et de dépassement, et cet être *m'entoure*, et à la limite toutes mes pensées en font partie. Le vrai néant, le néant qui est vrai, c'est l'Être comme distant et comme *non caché* (c'est-à-dire aussi caché).

October 22, 1959. No one

Subjectivity is truly *no one*. It is truly the desert. What is constitutive of the subject is to be integrally with the things, with the world, to have no positively assignable interior, to be *generality*. Subjectivity is this foam at the mouth of the world, that the world never dissipates. This is where we find the truth of what Sartre says about nothingness.

But what we thus say about subjectivity as nothingness must be immediately translated: therefore there is nothing to say about *that,* that is not, this nothingness is not, and the negation of this nothingness, the negintuition of this nothingness is not a beginning in one part of philosophy, to which we could then add a counterpart or a complement of facticity. The desert of subjectivity, this notion is one with that of object-Being. And the two notions are both thrown back precisely through the acknowledgment of nothingness as *nichtiges Nichts*. That of which it is suitable to speak, that which is, is the vertical, non-projective world, and it is the seeing, speaking subject—thinking only *on the basis of these operations*. This subject is not consciousness, nor *Ichheit*, not even as "pure" negativities, it is Speech and Experience, and correlatively, Being is not a distance that *I* extend, but a distance of transgression, of encroachment and overcoming, and this being *surrounds me,* and at the limit all my thoughts participate in it. The true nothingness, the nothingness that is true, is Being as distant and as *non-hidden* (that is, also hidden).

* * *

Novembre 1959. Concert. Domaine
musical. Sartre

Ce qui est intéressant c'est l'idée: l'équivalence universelle de toutes les
stuctures musicales—mais cette idée ni lui ni moi ne la rejoignons par expérience des oeuvres.

Il pourrait se faire que le principe soit bon et vrai comme le sont les
concepts, c'est-à-dire négativement, et que, transformé en règle imméd-
ate et positive des oeuvres d'à présent, il ne suscite que des oeuvres man-
quées. Négativement, il est vrai que hauteur, intensité, rythme, etc., ne
sont *pas* des moments indépendants, qu'ils n'ont que dans le cas très particulier de la tonalité, existence positive et distincte, que l'oeuvre taille
dans le bloc indivis d'un Être musical et que toute la musique classique est
à réinterpreter dans le cadre généralisé d'un Être musical polymorphe.
Mais cette indivision de l'oeuvre musicale peut-elle être prise pour fin im-
médiate? Ne repose-t-elle pas comme sur un socle sur les articulations
de l'oeuvre tonale? N'est-ce pas illusion majeure de vouloir l'obtenir di-
rectement, de la viser comme si elle était donnée? Pour avoir une existence *musicale*, n'a-t-elle pas à se donner une pluralité de moments? Pour
se réaliser dans des oeuvres où elle soit reconnaissable, et qui ne soient
pas *informes*, n'a-t-elle pas à s'inventer des appareils diacritiques? N'est-ce
pas une folie de chercher à se procurer le *Gestalthaft* sans aucune configuration?

November 1959. Concert. Musical
domain. Sartre

What is interesting is the idea: the universal equivalence of all musical
structures—but this idea, neither him nor me, do we join back up with by
means of the experiences of the works.

It could turn out that the principle is good and true just as the concepts are, that is, negatively, and that, transformed into an immediate and
positive rule of current works, it brings forth only failed works. Negatively,
it is true that volume, intensity, rhythm, etc., are *not* independent moments,
that they have positive and distinct existence only in the very particular
case of tonality, that the work carves into the undivided block of a musical Being and that all classical music is to be reinterpreted in the generalized framework of a polymorphous, musical Being. But can this indivision
of the musical work be taken for the immediate purpose? Does it not rest
on a base on the articulations of the tonal work? Is it not a major illusion

to want to obtain it directly, to aim at it as if this indivision was given? Is it not the case that, in order to have a *musical* existence, a plurality of moments has to be given? Is it not the case that some diacritical apparatuses have to be invented in order for the indivision to realize itself in works where it is recognizable and which are not *formless*? Is it not madness to seek to procure the *Gestalthaft* without any configuration?

* * *

Décembre 1959. Parole et *Gestalt*

La nature même de l'expression: le fait qu'on ne peut y dénombrer ce qui est dit et ce qui est "sous-entendu"—pas même y dénombrer les *moyens* d'expression, ceux qui sont employés et ceux qui ne le sont pas (vocabulaire d'une langue)—montre que l'expression tout entière est présente à chaque note d'expression, que le langage tout entier double chaque parole comme une sous-parole—ou *plutôt* que chaque parole n'est qu'un pli dans la parole, qu'elle est de sa nature *figure sur fond* (de silence actif ou *Gestalt*), qu'elle est, plutôt que "proposition" au sens de la logique, proposition au sens de Claudel, un *Etwas*, une *Gestalt* qui se vide intérieurement de sa chair pour laisser transparaître une structure, une masse travaillée de l'intérieur par une sorte d'ébullition, un creux dans l'Être, un écart par rapport à la non-différence ou à l'in-différence—lui-même venant d'où? Certainement pas des actes du "sujet" ou de son "faire."

Science et *mode*. La science est opinions communes—n'est pas rationalité. Est méthodiquement pensée selon le mode (ou art) parce qu'elle est pensée d'un [. . .], qui travaille selon lignes de moindre résistance du *réel*.

December 1959. Speech and *Gestalt*

The very nature of expression: the fact that we cannot enumerate in expression what is said and what is implied—not even enumerate in expression the *means* of expression, those which are employed and those which are not (the vocabulary of a language)—show that the entire expression is present in each note of expression, that the entire language doubles each word as an implied word—or *rather* that each word is only a fold in speech, that it is its nature to be a *figure on a ground* (to be active silence or *Gestalt*), that it is, rather than a "proposition" in the logical sense, a proposition in Claudel's sense, an *Etwas,* a *Gestalt* which empties itself internally of its flesh in order to allow a structure to show through, a worked-over mass of the interior through a sort of boiling, a hollow in Being, a divergence in relation to non-difference or to in-difference—itself coming whence? Certainly not from acts of the "subject" or from its "doing."

Science and *fashion.* Science is common opinions—is not rationality. Is methodically thought according to fashion (or art) because it is the thought of a [. . .], which works according to the lines of least resistance of the *real.*

* * *

Décember 1959. Catalogue de Giorgo de [Gisgi?]. [20 lignes de citations]

Cette idée des "éléments,"—non seulement des éléments de la nature, mais des éléments de notre vie: la sculpture 58–59 est l'*élément* route de Carpentras à Aix avec maman : lignes solennelles bordées d'ombres verticals comme des cyprès ou horizontales comme les plans du Lubéron— cette idée à appliquer à analyse nouvelle de la subjectivité: erreur immense de la considérer comme flux des *Erlebnisse.* Elle est avant tout *champ,* et même sa temporalité a cette structure. Absurdité de la concevoir comme un présent ponctuel et la série indéfinie des *Erlebnisse* ponctuels-individuels qui seraient *le passé.* Par exemple, ces sculptures me rappellent de beaux minerais,—un jour où quelqu'un me montrait, avec une sorte de ferveur qui me surprenait, des minerais, et m'en donnait quelques uns, non sans hésitation. Je n'arrive pas à préciser le souvenir ni le lieu et reste dans le doute: *il me semble* (mais plutôt par raisonnement, que c'était au Congo belge, à E. . .-ville. Ce ne peut être que là. Mais qui? Je sais seulement que c'était une femme). Or ce "*souvenir*" n'est pas un *Erlebnis* individuel rejoint par rétention de rétention dans sa singularité. Ni par "association." Il est:

1. une catégorie, un existential [lié], il est vraiment *déposé* dans cette sculpture que je vois, comme est déposé dans les trois arbres de Martinville un *certain* appel.
2. Un *élément* donc au sens de l'eau, de l'air etc., c'est-à-dire non pas un objet, ni un individu, mais un mode de sentir. Le souvenir comme référence à un *Zeitpunkt,* est à comprendre comme cas limite de ces *matrices.* Il n'y a pas de *Zeitpunkt,* pas plus que de point spatial. Il n'y a que des taches, temporelles comme spatiales, i.e. des êtres de transcendance. Et celui qui comprend ces êtres de transcendance est champ et non pas du tout "représentation."

December 1959. Catalogue for Giorgo
de [Gisgi?]. [20 lines of quotations from
the catalogue]

This idea of "elements"—not only elements of nature, but elements of our
life: the 58–59 sculpture is the *element* road from Carpentras to Aix with
mom: solemn lines edged with vertical shadows like cypresses or horizon-
tals like the planes of Lubéron—apply this idea to the new analysis of subjectivity: immense mistake to consider it as flux of *Erlebnisse.* Subjectivity is
first of all a *field,* and even its temporality has this structure. Absurdity to
conceive it as a punctual present and the indefinite series of punctual-
individual *Erlebnisse* which would be the *past.* For example, these sculptures remind me of beautiful rocks—one day when someone was showing
me, with a sort of fervor which surprised me, some rocks, and gave me
some of them, not without some hesitation. I don't specify the memory or
the place and it remains in doubt: *it seems to me* (but rather through reasoning, that it was in the Belgian Congo, at E. . .-ville. It must be there. But
who? I know merely that it was a woman). Now this "memory" is not an individual *Erlebnis* joined back through retention of retention in its singu-
larity. Nor by "association." It is:

1. a category, an existential [connected], it is truly *deposited* in this sculpture that I am seeing, as a *certain* call is deposited in the three trees of
   Martinville.
2. An *element* therefore in the sense of water, of air, etc., that is, not an object or an individual, but a mode of sensing. The memory as a reference to a *Zeitpunkt* is to be understood as a limit case of these *matrixes.*
   There is no *Zeitpunkt,* no more than there is a spatial point. There are
   only spots, temporal as well as spatial, i.e., beings of transcendence.
   And the one who understands these beings of transcendence is a field
   and not "representation" at all.

* * *

Janvier 1960

La perception de la distance et de la taille n'est pensable que par la transcendance charnelle.

Quand j'essaie de comprendre pourquoi post-image vue sur le plan
d'un écran éloigné paraît plus grande, ou pourquoi lune à l'horizon
paraît plus grande, je me dis: pour une "grandeur apparente" donnée
(c'est en réalité grandeur de l'image rétinienne) plus l'espace recouvert

sur le plan de référence est grand dans le cas de la post-image,—ou plus (dans le cas de la lune) la distance supposée est grande (ou vivement représentée) plus il faut que la "chose vue" le soit elle-même pour couvrir tant d'objets en largeur ou pour garder taille si importante en dépit de la distance. Reconstitution de phénomène qui est bâtarde et n'est satisfaisante ni du point de vue objectif, ni du point de vue phénoménal: phénoménalement, il n'y a pas [de réajustement] de la grandeur de l'image rétinienne (c'est ce qu' on est en train de constater),—objectivement, la quantité d'espace couverte sur le plan de la projection ou l'épaisseur d'espace traversé par les rayons lumineux ne sont pas des stimuli: elles n'ont d'existence que phénoménale. Cette analyse se place à la fois dans l'en soi et dans le pour-nous. Au fond elle suppose une machine corporelle sensible aux *phénomèmes* et un phénomène calqué sur l'en soi du corps. C'est seulement ainsi qu'on peut avoir l'impression d'expliquer le phénomène (que ce soit d'ailleurs comme "interprétation," jugement des signes,—ou que ce soit comme conditions commandant une *Gestaltung*). L'explication est profondément obscure dans les deux cas.

Que faudrait-il donc dire? Ne pas considérer la grandeur [. . .] vue comme un *produit* (de conditions objectives, ou de la connaissance de ces conditions opérant comme signes). La considérer comme *synonyme* phénoménalement de la vision d'objets interposés ou d'un certain recouvrement, *synonyme* de la distance, une autre manière de dire et de voir cette distance; la grandeur vue n'est pas un certain "tableau visuel" dont il faudrait expliquer la genèse par des conditions ou des opérations intellectuelles. C'est l'insertion même de mon regard dans le champ. Le renforcement de la distance n'est pas un *fait* qui explique un *autre fait,* [. . .] d'un "tableau visuel." Le renforcement de la distance est *accentuation* de *transcendance* qui se confond avec *Il y a* de grandeur plus massif.

Finalement, dans théorie de la perception, grandeur et distance renvoient l'une à l'autre: on juge de grandeur réelle par distance (pour un objet inconnu). Mais cette distance, comment la connaître sinon par grandeur réelle et son écart par rapport à grandeur apparente? Finalement, l'une signifie l'autre et toutes deux ne signifient rien. Pour nous, inversement elles sont deux perceptions convergentes dont l'une peut suppléer l'autre parce qu'elles sont deux modalisations du *Il y a,* de la transcendance, qui leur donne sens à toutes deux. C'est ce Il y a, normé par prise corporelle, qui contient tout.

Considérer la dimensionnalité physiognomique-vitale (Michotte) comme dimensionnalité spatiale aussi bien, d'un espace topologique ou d'enveloppement, qui n'est pas l'espace sans centre, purement relationnel, d'Euclide,—et qui en réalité le soutient.

Quand Descartes dit: institution de la nature pour nous faire avoir tels et tels jugements naturels il essaie de recomposer l'Être charnel avec l'Être de jugement + l'Être de l'espace objectif. Le corps comme moyen de contact d'un En soi et d'un Pour soi—ce qui est inintelligible. Personne ne comprendra jamais qu'un jugement (même naturel) soit porté en un lieu du corps. Cette synthèse primitive d'une pensée et d'un en soi est tout à fait impensable, verbale. Il faut inverser le problème, partir de l'expérience charnelle du sensible (avec ses implications entières, sa référence aux choses, sa référence au *Leib*) et considérer et l'espace objectif et la pensée comme creux dans cette expérience charnelle, rayons issus d'elle, objectivations ou idealisations de cette "profondeur" sensible.

Transcendance ne veut rien dire en dehors de la notion de "chair."

Avec la notion de chair, veut dire: il y a éclatement: il y a éclatement vers monde ou être. Je participe à cet éclatement comme les autres corps humains. Cet éclatement ne se fait pas "en moi," mais *devant moi*. C'est comme une ligne de feu tendue devant mon corps objectif, qu'il déclenche lui-même, mais qui n'est pas une de ses propriétés: je ne suis avec mon corps que le déclencheur de cet embrasement.

January 1960

The perception of distance and size can be thought only by means of carnal transcendence.

When I try to understand why an afterimage seen upon the plane of a distant screen looks larger, or why the moon at the horizon looks larger, I say to myself: in the case of the afterimage, the more the space overlaps with the plane of reference a given "apparent height" (this is in reality the size of the retinal image) is large—or still (in the case of the moon) the supposed distance is large (or really represented) the more it is necessary that the "thing seen" be large in order to cover over so many objects in width or in order to keep the so-important size despite the distance. The reconstitution of the phenomenon is a bastard one and is satisfying neither from an objective viewpoint nor from a phenomenal viewpoint: phenomenally, there is no [readjustment] of the height of the retinal image (it is what we are in the process of observing)—objectively, the quantity of space covered on the plane of projection and the thickness of space traversed by the light rays are not stimuli: they have only phenomenal existence. This analysis is placed at once in the "in-itself" and in the "for us." Fundamentally, it assumes a corporeal sensible machine in the phenomena and a phenomenon copied off the in-itself of the body. It is however in this way that we can have the impression of explaining the phenomenon (either moreover as an "interpretation," a judgment of signs—or as conditions commanding a *Gestalt*). The explanation is profoundly obscure in the two cases.

What therefore must we say? Don't consider the height [. . .] seen as a *product* (of objective conditions or the knowledge of these conditions functioning as signs). Consider it as synonymous phenomenally with the vision of interposed objects or of a certain overlapping, synonymous with the distance, another way of saying and of seeing this distance; the height seen is not a certain "visual picture" whose genesis we would have to explain by means of intellectual conditions and workings. It is the very insertion of my gaze in the field. The reinforcement of the distance is not a *fact* that explains *another fact*, [. . .] of a "visual picture." The reinforcement of the distance is the *accentuation* of *transcendence* which is mixed with the "there is" of a more massive size.

Finally, in the theory of perception, size and distance refer to one another: we judge real height by distance (for an unknown object). But this distance, how can we know it except by real height and its divergence in relation to apparent height? Finally, the one means the other and both mean nothing. For us, conversely, they are two convergent perceptions of which the one supplants the other because they are two modalizations of the "there is," of transcendence, which gives them both meaning. It is this "there is," formed into a vector by means of the corporal grasp, which contains everything.

Consider physiognomic-vital dimensionality (Michotte) as spatial dimensionality as well, of a topological space or of envelopment, which is not Euclid's purely rational, centerless space—and which in reality supports it.

When Descartes says: the institution of nature in order to make us have such and such natural judgments, he is trying to recompose carnal Being with the Being of judgment + the Being of objective space. The body as a means of contact with an In-itself and a For-itself—which is unintelligible. No one will ever understand that a judgment (even a natural one) is carried in a connection of bodies. This primitive synthesis of a thought and an in-itself is entirely unthinkable, verbal. We have to reverse the problem, starting from the carnal experience of the sensible (with its entire implications, its references to things, its reference to *Leib*) and consider objective space and thought as a hollow in this carnal experience, rays coming from the experience, objectifications or idealizations of this "deep" sensible.

Transcendence means nothing outside of the notion of the "flesh."

With the notion of the flesh, mean: there is an explosion toward the world or being. I participate in this explosion like other human bodies.

This explosion is not made "in me," but *in front of me*. It is like a fuse held in front of my objective body, which the body lights itself, but which is not one of its properties: I am, along with my body, only the one who lights this conflagration.

* * *

Janvier 1960. *Sich bewegen*. Sa *dimension propre* (voir F. Meyer: l'organisme comme *organisateur de fluctuations*)

Le *Sich bewegen*, abstraction faite de toute conscience: le fait que la fluctu- ation dans le corps qui *sich bewegt* est *multipliée;* c'est l'instauration d'une instabilité telle qu'aucun [fonctionnement] avec ce qu'il comporte d'in- variance ne peut être concevable que comme *invariance dans la variation;* la variation est établie comme dimension propre, assumée—ce qui veut dire que ce corps ne se déplace plus dans un En-soi, mais dans un milieu où dimension dont [de?] variation sont aussi dimensions de stabilité, ou il n'y a plus d'en-soi que les vecteurs, dans un *"Umwelt"* ou Être d'infra- structure, intérieurement accordé aux charpentes de l'Être extérieur. Le rapport d'*Umwelt* à *Welt* n'est pas apparence à réalité mais le schéma dy- namique à pleine réalisation.

On peut ainsi *déduire* la *perception* et l'esthésiologie du fait même que l'organisme est un édifice d'instabilités compensées (cf. marche, chute, rattrapée).

Sich bewegen = organizer soi-même l'instabilité, et *par là* la dominer (le *Sich* défini sans "conscience").

January 1960. *Sich bewegen*. Its *own dimension* (see F. Meyer: the organism as *organizer of fluctuations*)

The *Sich bewegen*, an abstraction made from all consciousness: the fact that the fluctuation in the body which *sich bewegt* is *multiplied;* it's the estab- lishment of an instability such that any [functioning] with what it involves that is invariant can be conceivable only as *invariance in the variation;* the variation is established as dimension proper, taken up—which means that this body no longer moves itself in an In-itself, but in a milieu where the dimension of which [of?] the variation are also dimensions of stability, or there is no in-itself but the vectors, in an *"Umwelt"* or infrastructural Be- ing, internally in agreement with the build of exterior Being. The relation of the *Umwelt* to *Welt* is not that of appearance to reality but the dynamic schema to its full realization.

Thus we can *deduce perception* and aesthesiology from the very fact that the organism is an edifice of compensated instabilities (cf. walk, lose one's balance, catch oneself).

Sich bewegen = to organize the instability oneself, and *thereby* dominate it (the *Sich* defined without "consciousness").

* * *

Avril 1960. *Chair*

L'explication par le génital, ou même par le sexuel, ne termine pas les problèmes: car les états de plaisir renvoient au désir, et le désir n'est pas la prévision ou recherche d'un état de plaisir, il est intentionnalité i.e. récognition aveugle, i.e. transcendance (par exemple, l'*Erfüllung unique* qui est, dit Husserl, cherchée par les deux corps, ne peut être unique qu'en étant, non pas semblable ici et là, mais *dasselbe*), i.e. à condition de n'être pas identique idéalement, mais *le même à distance* (comme la route est *la même à distance* à travers le ratatinement perceptif). Cela veut dire que l'*Erfüllung* n'est pas plein objectif, mais *plein du vide* (définition du sensible,—qui fait qu'il est aussi imperception), c'est-à-dire finalement *écart* par rapport à lieu absolu, à ici absolu en filigrane. Les perspectives, ni l'*Erfüllung* ("perspective possible") ne sont du *positif.*

"L'explication" n'explique rien: l'expliquant nous met en présence de l'énigme, qui est toujours la même: comment et pourquoi y a-t-il Eros, c'est-à-dire rapport de quelque chose qui est à quelque chose qui a à être, "écart." Le "génital" et même le "sexuel" sont tout parce qu'ils sont la *chair* (c'est-à-dire non pas un "phénomène" ou un "corps phénomènal," mais un *être à deux faces,* qui est ce qu'il est et aussi ce qu'il n'est pas et a à être, une ouverture, une "lumière" au sens où l'on parle de "lumière" dans les bouches à feu. Si l'on veut un "pour soi" (*eine Art der Reflexion*) mais qui est aussi un pour-autrui, un regard mais qui est aussi regardé et donc rapport à un être de proximité.

April 1960. *Flesh*

The explanation by the genital, or even by the sexual, does not finish off the problems: for the pleasure states refer to the desire, and the desire is not the prevision or search of a pleasure state, it is intentionality, i.e., blind recognition, i.e., transcendence (for example, the unique *Erfüllung* which is, Husserl says, sought for by the two bodies, can be unique only by being, not similar here and there, but *dasselbe*), i.e., on the condition of not being ideally identical, but *the same at a distance* (as the road is *the same at a distance* by means of the perceptual shriveling up). That means that the *Erfüllung* is not fully objective, but *fraught with emptiness* (definition of the sensible—which makes that it is also imperception), that is, finally, divergence in relation to the absolute place, to the absolute "here" between the lines. The perspectives, but also the *Erfüllung* ("possible perspective") are not *positive*.

The "explanation" explains nothing: what explains put us in the presence of the enigma, which is always the same: how and why is there Eros, that is, a relation of something which is to something which has to be, "divergence." The "genital" and even the "sexual" exist because they are the *flesh* (that is, not a "phenomenon" or a "phenomenal body," but a *being with two facets*, which is what it is and also what it is not and has to be, an openness, a "light" in the sense that we speak of "lighting" the canon. If you like a "for itself" (*eine Art der Reflexion*) but which is also a for others, a gaze but which is also gazed upon and therefore relation to a being in proximity.

* * *

Avril 1960. *Parole verticale*

Dans l'ordre "vertical": il n'y a pas de différence entre parole à soi et parole à autrui—pas plus qu'il n'y a de différence entre soi et autrui, entre l'*Abschattung* (inconnue) et l'*Abgeschattet*.

La parole verticale à retrouver—c'est l'expérience muette exprimant son propre sens. C'est las parole du silence. C'est la parole parlante et non parlée.

Qu'elle est indispensable pour comprendre la parole constituée.

Le recours au vertical, au présent, n'est pas recours à présent *empirique*, présent de fait (il n'y a pas plus de présent de simple fait qu'il n'y a de sensible définissable par identité à soi). C'est recours à dimension de présent, i.e. à l'Être.

Le recours au présent n'est pas recours au sensible comme fait: c'est aussi bien recours à l'*Erzeugung*. Dans l'ordre du vertical il n'y a pas plus de difficulté à comprendre l'*Erzeugung* qu'à comprendre la perception: le culturel est *par définition* ce qui se donne à des actes d'*Erzeugung*. Comme le passé est par définition ce qui se donne à des actes de remémoration, i.e. de re-vivre.

Comment restituer par la philosophie (i.e. dans l'ordre des significations) la parole verticale (qui est avant les significations)? Mais les significations que propose la philosophie sont rébus à déchiffrer par l'expérience propre.

April 1960. *Vertical Speech*

In the "vertical" order: there is no difference between speech to oneself and speech to the other—any more than there is a difference between self and other, between (unknown) *Abschattung* and the *Abgeschattet.*

Vertical speech to be rediscovered—it is the mute experience expressing its own sense. It is the speech of silence. It is speaking speech and not spoken speech.

Which is indispensable for understanding constituted speech.

The recourse to the vertical, to the present, is not the recourse to the *empirical* present, the factual present (there is no more a simple factual present than there is a sensible that can be defined by self-identity). It is recourse to the present dimension, i.e., to Being.

The recourse to the present is not a recourse to the sensible as a fact: it is as well recourse to *Erzeugung.* In the order of the vertical there is no more difficulty in understanding *Erzeugung* than in understanding perception: the cultural is *by definition* what is given in acts of *Erzeugung.* As the past is by definition what is given to acts of memory, i.e., to be relived.

How to restore by philosophy (i.e., in the order of meanings) vertical speech (which is prior to meanings)? But the meanings which philosophy proposes are the rebus which is to be deciphered by experience proper.

* * *

Mai 1960. Être sensible

Être.

Montrer que le "sensible" comme tel est transcendance i.e. accessibilité de l'inaccessible.

Le "*Logos* du monde esthétique": cet "envers" du *quale,* de la pellicule projective, le sens tacite et de téléologie. Ce sens est inséparable de l'apparence, du corps. Il fait que le monde est "chair." Et qu'il est cumulatif.

C'est ce *Logos* qu'on dévoile en remontant de "mes perceptions," douteuses une à une, au monde comme lieu d'inscription et de sédimentation, instance de vérité. C'est le lieu du *Wesen* (verbal). Rayonnement d'ester. Ici "perception" et "perçu" sont *esemble inscrits. On* de la perception (celui qui perçoit est "personne," et c'est aussi bien "un autre"). Différenciation avec des horizons d'indifférenciation. C'est la masse de l'Être sensible.

C'est ce *Logos* qui est et restera toujours source de sens (*Sinnsquelle*). Non sans doute dans son *contenu* (il varie avec les cultures, la "Nature" de chacune est "subjective")—mais dans sa *structure charnelle,*—i.e. un type d'*Erfüllung* qui n'est pas l'adéquation spinoziste, qui est emboîtement des ek-stases, jusqu'au *Il y a* fondamental (*Weltthesis*).

Le ressort de toute la connaissance, de toute *pensée* (*Erzeugung* de l'invisible) se trouve dans ce *Logos* du monde visible: [traditionalité], sédimentation, appuyées sur la Présence sensible, en tant qu'elle a un double fond ontologique—(voir c'est avoir de l'invisible puisque c'est avoir une *Urstiftung*).

A ce niveau la distinction sujet-objet, noèse-noème, n'a pas de sens puisque nous n'avons pas encore des *actes* et des *Erlebnisse.* Passé primordial, intemporel, indestructible. C'est le ça, c'est l'in-conscient. De même qu'ici il n'y a pas noèse et noème, mais corps et chose (la chair qui "connaît" la chair, le réseau de transcendance anonyme corps-choses),—de même en passant à l'Ego et à ses *Erzeugungen,* il n'y a pas noèse et noème, il y a genèse simultanée de Parole et Signification (sans rapport de priorité) comme *contrôle* de flux muet. La Parole (qui est, verticalement, fondement de tous mes actes empiriques de parole, comme la *Welt* de toute mes perceptions aussi bien que des Perçus) n'est pas plus que l'espace ou le temps, un concept, c'est un Figuratif.

May 1960. Sensible Being

Being.
Show that the "sensible" as such is transcendence, i.e., accessibility of the inaccessible.

The "*Logos* of the aesthetic world": this "reverse side" of the quale, of the projective pellicule, the tacit sense and teleology. This sense is inseparable from the appearance, from the body. It makes the world be "flesh." And that it is cumulative.

It is this Logos that we unveil by reascending from "my perceptions," which are doubtful one by one, to the world as the place of inscription and sedimentation, agency of truth. It is the place of the (verbal) *Wesen.* Rays of *ester.*[3] Here "perception" and "perceived" are *inscribed together.* The "someone" of perception (the one who perceives is "no one," and it is as well an "other"). Differentiation with the horizons of indifferentiation. It is the mass of sensible Being.

It is this *Logos* that exists and will always remain the source of sense

(*Sinnsquelle*). Not without doubt in its content (it varies with cultures, the "Nature" of each is "subjective")—but in its carnal structure—i.e., a kind of *Erfüllung* which is not Spinozist adequation, which is the encasement of *ek-stases*, going as far as the fundamental "there is" (*Welthesis*).

The capacity for all knowledge, of all *thought* (*Erzeugung* of the invisible), is found in this *Logos* of the visible world: [traditionality], sedimentation, taking support upon sensible Presence, insofar as it has a double ontological ground—(to see is to have the invisible since it is to have an *Urstiftung*).

At this level the subject-object distinction, noesis-noema, makes no sense since we do not yet have *acts* and *Erlebnisse*. Primordial past, intemporal, indestructible. It is the id, it is the unconscious. Just as here there is no noesis and noema, but body and thing (the flesh which "knows" flesh, the network of anonymous body-things transcendence)—by passing to the Ego and to its *Erzeugungen*, there is no noesis and noema, there is the simultaneous genesis of Speech and Meaning (without a relation of priority) as the *control* of mute flux. Speech (which is, vertically, the foundation of all my empirical acts and words, as the *Welt* of all of my perceptions as well as of the Perceiveds) is not, any more than space or time, a concept, it is the Figurative.

* * *

13 Mai 1960. Peinture ([Chastel])

Les aquarelles de Cézanne. Qu'est-ce qu'un *Bild*? Il est manifeste ici que le *Bild* ne se regarde pas comme on regarde un *objet*. On regarde *selon le Bild*, on ne *le* regarde que pour expliciter (croit-on) ses moyens d'expression. Il opère non en nous offrant un en soi à observer, mais en agissant latéralement sur le regard, en esquissant une signification que le regard valide. Et cette ségrégation *ouvre* . . . Quoi? Non pas des "*significations*" (et encore moins des *choses* comme les choses visibles), mais des *être* tels que l'ombre du fil de fer tordu de Metzger, êtres régionaux, *Wesen* verbaux. Que la peinture ici suscite elle-même la reprise corporelle-existentielle qui pourtant lui donnera seule un sens, qui sera la *Sinngebung* par le corps, qu'elle donne ce qu'elle n'a pas, qu'elle s'accroisse de ses dons, c'est l'*Einfühlung* perceptive, c'est là ce que Sartre appelait l'analogon—mais cet un analogon *qui lui-même suscite l'analogie* dont, après-coup, il apparaît comme le porteur.

Si cela est, si le *Bild* est cela, s'il réside dans un espace de chair entre nous et les *choses même*, il ne peut être question de lui imposer une règle de ressemblance aux choses-même et de "figuration." Les "figures" naturelles elles-mêmes ne sont telles que par fond non figural. A plus forte raison le *Bild* n'a-t-il pas à avoir avec elles une ressemblance "projective." A la vérité, quand on examine rigoureusement ce que c'est que *voir,* et quand on voit que toute vision est aussi latence, il n'y a plus de [frontière] définie par le projectif-visible et que la peinture devrait observer. Figuratif et non-figuratif sont équivoques. Le point est imperceptible où le figuratif devient non-figuratif: l'aquarelle de Cézanne vue à la Galerie Monte-Carlo et qui est non-figurative.

Il faut comparer perception de *Bild* et perception de la chose, mais en prenant celle-ci non dans son résultat (tableau visuel, en soi) mais dans son *ontogenèse.* On voit alors que déjà un sentir comporte la transcendance et que la perception du tableau, c'est le sentir étendu au-delà de sa zone "naturelle,"—c'est le devenir-visible de l'invisible.

May 13, 1960. Painting ([Chastel])

Cézanne's watercolors. What is a *Bild?* It is obvious that the *Bild* is not gazed upon as we gaze upon an *object.* We gaze *according to the Bild,* we gaze at *it* only in order to explain (so we think) the means of expression. It works not by offering us an in itself to be observed, but by acting laterally upon the gaze, by sketching a meaning that the gaze validates. And this segregation *opens* . . . What? Not "*meanings*" (and still less *things* as visible things), but *beings* such as the shadow of Metzger's twisted iron wire, regional beings, verbal *Wesens.* That the painting here itself brings about the corporeal-existential appropriation which however alone gives to it a sense, which will be the *Sinngebung* by means of the body, that it gives what it does not have, that it grows from its gifts, is the perceptual *Einfühlung,* this is what Sartre called the *analogon*—but this one *analogon that itself brings about the analogy* of which, after the fact, it appears as the bearer.

If that is, if the *Bild* is that, if it resides in a carnal space between us and the *things themselves,* there can be no question of imposing upon it a rule of resemblance to the things themselves and "figuration." The natural "figures" themselves are such only by means of a non-figural ground. All the more reason that the *Bild* does not have to do with a "projective" resemblance. Truly, when we examine rigorously what it is to see, and we see that all vision is also latency, there is no longer a [frontier] defined by the projective-visual and that the painting should observe. Figurative and non-figurative are equivocal. The point where the figurative becomes non-figurative is imperceptible: Cézanne's watercolor seen at the Monte Carlo Gallery and which is non-figurative.

It is necessary to compare the perception of the *Bild* and the perception of the thing, but by taking the latter not in its result (visual picture, in itself) but in its *ontogenesis*. We see that already a sensing involves transcendence and that the perception of the picture is sensing extended beyond its "natural" zone—this is the becoming-visible of the invisible.

* * *

Mai 1960. Le sommeil

La "conscience" comporte, est, présence au monde "vertical," esthésiologie assumée. On ne peut *penser* si l'on n'a le champ de l'Être sensible. Sentir n'est pas penser, mais la pensée ne s'établit que sur le socle du *sentir*. Par ailleurs on ne peut penser si l'on sent trop (Pascal). Il y a un dénominateur commun à penser et sentir qui fait que l'un soutient l'autre et que l'un empêche l'autre. Même rapport que de langage à pensée.

Le sommeil est à la fois [absence] du monde *vertical* et fin de la pensée (pas de *négation*). C'est ce qu'il reste de l'être-au-monde quand on en soustrait le visible au sens strict. Ce n'est donc nullement la *conscience* (même "livrée à elle-même," néantisant sans condition et faisant valoir le rien comme quelque chose). C'est le champ qui reste *vide*, qui n'est plus champ temporel au sens plein.

[Suit une citation de Valéry sur le sommeil.]

Pourtant il y a une ressemblance du sommeil, non avec le visible, mais avec le fond invisible du visible qui est onirique,—et avec cette [frange] onirique de la vie éveillée qui est le rayonnement d'autrui autour de son corps et le rayonnement d'une réunion autour de moi. Mais si l'on veut parler de rayonnement onirique du visible, il reste que ce rayonnement dans le sommeil est extrêmement imprécis, lacunaire, que les autres du rêve et les fantasmes sont plutôt inconscience de ne pas voir que vision. En quoi d'ailleurs ils marquent encore rapport au monde (l'imaginaire des sens reste une activité, sinon les sens).

Le réveil par exemple par un bruit. Le bruit apporte non pas exactement un contenu, mais la dimensionnalité du *Es Selbst*, la pierre de touche. En quel sens les sens restent "ouverts": par leur imaginaire.

May 1960. Sleep

"Consciousness" involves, is, presence to the "vertical" world, an aesthesiology that is taken up. We cannot *think* if we have no field of sensible Being. To sense is not to think, but thought is established only upon the base of *sensing*. Moreover, we cannot think if we sense too much (Pascal). There is a common denominator to thinking and sensing which makes the one support the other and the one stop the other. Same relation that language has to thought.

Sleep is at once [absence] of the *vertical* world and the end of thought (no *negation*). It is what remains of being-in-the-world when we subtract from it the visible in the strict sense. This is therefore in no way *consciousness* (even "delivered to itself," nihilating unconditionally and valuing the nothing as something). It is the field that remains *empty*, which is no longer a temporal field in the complete sense.

[Here there is a quotation from Valéry concerning sleep.]

However there is a resemblance of sleep, not with the visible, but with the invisible ground of the visible which is oneiric—and with this oneiric [fringe] of wakeful life which is the ray of the other around his body and the ray of the reunion around me. But if we speak of the oneiric fringe of the visible, it is still the case that this ray in sleep is extremely imprecise, lacunary, that the others of the dream and the phantasm are unconscious from not seeing rather than vision. In what moreover they still mark a relation to the world (the imaginary of the senses is still an activity, if not the senses).

Being awoken, for example, by a noise. The noise brings not exactly a content, but the dimensionality of the *Es Selbst*, the touchstone. In what sense do the senses remain "open": through their imaginary.

* * *

Novembre 1960. Négativité. Chiasme

Rapports du négatif et de l'image en miroir. Le négatif n'est que sur un fond d'identité (identité de la chose et de son reflect). Négatif: *envers* de l'identité.

L'espace,—et aussi le temps—: les deux moitiés de l'orange.

Le chiasme chose-image spéculaire, ou chose-"image mentale": imagination inhérente à chaque sous-champ de ce sens. C'est dans ce champ que se déploie l'imaginaire—qui est donc charnel.

L'imaginaire: *décentration* du sensible.

Le concept: *décentration* de l'imaginaire.

Chiasme moi-monde: les choses me regardent. Je me regarde (par les yeux des choses).

Le chiasme c'est l'idée de l'Être comme élévation du relatif à l'Absolu par le diaphragme et le Il y a.

November 1960. Negativity. Chiasm

Relations of the negative and of the mirror image. The negative exists only upon a ground of identity (identity of the thing and of its reflection). Negative: *the reverse side* of identity.

Space—and also time—the two halves of the orange.

The specular thing-image, or thing-"mental image" chiasm: imagination inherent to each subfield of this sense. The imaginary deploys itself in this field—which is therefore carnal.

The imaginary: *decentering* of the sensible.

The concept: *decentering* of the imaginary.

Me-world Chiasm: the things gaze upon me. I gaze upon myself (through the eyes of the things).

The chiasm is the idea of Being as the elevation of the relative to the Absolute by means of the diaphragm and the "there is."

* * *

Note non datées

La *Verflechtung* (entrelacement, enchevêtrement avec autrui).

Signifie finalement:

Nous ne sommes pas *d'un côté du mur* mais des deux.

Et finalement:

Nous ne sommes pas des perspectives sur un géométral (car alors on ne comprendrait pas substitution). Nous sommes deux dans *un Être*.

Faire dans mon livre un chapitre: *Être et Mémoire* (la mémoire comme cas particulier *d'inter-être*).

Non-dated note

Verflechtung (interweaving, entanglement with others).

Means finally:

We are not *one side of the wall* but two.

And finally:

We are not perspectives upon a surveyor's plan (for then one would not understand substitution). We are two in *one Being*.

Make a chapter in my book: *Being and Memory* (memory as a particular case of *inter-being*).

* * *

Quelques notes, adjointes au brouillon de plan et de rédaction de *Être et Monde*

Juin 1959. Transcendance et cogito. L'idée. L'*eidos*

Il ne s'agit pas tant de nier l'*eidos* que de le comprendre bien: L'*eidos* (et la variation par fantaisie donnant l'in-variant) à comprendre non comme essence positive, mais comme articulations ou charnières de l'Être.[4] Elle est comme ces jointures des phénomènes que la peinture non figurative représente par une croix ou un "trait flexueux." Non tant archétype que *membrure* de l'Être, non pas enveloppant l'Être mais enveloppé par lui. C'est ce qui se voit dans le terme même d'in-variant—qui indique qu'il ne s'agit pas d'un *résidu* inductif, du type de l'Être *statique,* mais d'un *non-variant* c'est-à-dire d'un terme de référence qui est sur un autre *plan* que les phénomènes, qui est en profondeur, en épaisseur. L'invariant, puisqu'il n'est saisi que *par la variation,* est aux variants (= aux "écarts") ce qu'est le "mobile" au "movement" c'est-à-dire non pas un terme positif dont le mouvement serait "propriété," mais *l'intégration des mouvements naissants.*

Le "il y a" du mouvement, l'*Etwas* qui est tout entier dans son [ou une?] *opération.* Le passage à l'*eidos* doit se comprendre comme intégration qualitative.

Mais quelle est la chair, le corps propre de l'*eidos,* cette gangue à travers laquelle il apparaît? Ce milieu ontologique, ce champ dont il présuppose toujours la présence? Certes, c'est le charnel sensible (cf. Wertheimer: conception structurale de la vérité). Mais c'est le charnel *devenu capable d'abriter,* de cerner, de figurer ses propres invariants, sa propre membrure: et ses systèmes diacritiques qui formulent, au-delà de ceux du sensible, l'operation de ceux du sensible, qui suivent l'impulsion donnée par eux, qui les déborde par l'élan même qu'ils reçoivent d'eux comme volants et comme *Urstiftung,*—ce sont les systèmes diacritiques de la parole. Ne pas les penser à partir du *Je pense,* au contraire, penser le *Je pense* à partir d'eux, i.e. penser le Je pense d'autrui en même temps que le mien, comme jumelage du mien, comme excès de moi-même sur moi-même (de moi comme institution sur moi comme constitution). Penser le Je pense (et même le mien) non pas comme système de penser, mais comme institution de l'Être à . . . Me saisir (aussi bien qu'autrui) avant nos pensées particulières, comme "champ," tels que nous sommes l'un pour l'autre dans le dialogue où *nous comprenons non pas des pensées,* mais des variations de l'existence,—où nous répondons, non par des "pensées," mais pas des variations de la [chaîne] d'existence.

Some notes attached to the draft of the plan and revision of *Being and World*

June 1959. Transcendence and cogito. Idea. *Eidos*

What is at issue is not so much as to deny the *eidos* as to understand it well: the *eidos* (and the variation by means of fantasy giving the invariant) is to be understood not as a positive essence, but as articulations or hinges of Being.[4] It is like the jointures of phenomena that the non-figurative painting represents by a cross or a "flexuous line." Not so much archetype as *inner framework* of Being, not enveloping Being but enveloped by it. It is what is seen in the term itself "invariant"—which indicates that what is at issue is not an inductive *residue,* the type of *static* Being, but a *non-variant,* that is, a term of reference which is upon another *plane* than the phenomena, which is in depth, in thickness. The invariant, since it is grasped only *through the variation,* is in the variants (= in the "divergences") which is the "mobile" in the "movement," that is, not a positive term whose movement would be a "property," but *the integration of nascent movements.*

The "there is" of the movement, the *Etwas* which is entirely in its [or one?] operation. The passage to the *eidos* must be understood as qualitative integration.

But what is the flesh, the body proper of the *eidos,* this gangue across which it appears? This ontological milieu, this field whose presence it always presupposes? Certainly, it is the sensible carnal (cf. Wertheimer: structural concept of the truth). But it is the carnal *having become capable of sheltering,* of encircling, of figuring its own invariants, its own inner framework: and its diacritical systems which formulate, beyond those of the sensible, the operation of those of the sensible, which follow upon the impulsion given by them, which overflows them by the very impulse that they receive from them as flywheels and as *Urstiftung*—these are the diacritical systems of speech. Don't conceive them on the basis of the "I think," on the contrary, conceive the "I think" on the basis of them, i.e., conceive the "I think" of the other at the same time as mine, as the twin of mine, as the excess of myself over myself (of me as institution over me as constitution). Conceive the "I think" (and even mine) not as a system of thought, but as the institution of Being in . . . Grasp me (as well as the other) prior to our particular thoughts, as "field," such that we are together in dialogue in which *we understand not thoughts,* but variations of existence—in which we respond, not by "thoughts," but by variations of the [chain] of existence.

Biography of Maurice Merleau-Ponty

Maurice Merleau-Ponty was born on March 14, 1908, in Rochefort-sur-Mer, a town on the west coast of France, in the province of Charente-Maritime.[1] In Paris he was an excellent student at the famous Lycée Louis-le-Grand. From 1926 to 1930 Merleau-Ponty was a student at the École Normale Supérieure, "rue d'Ulm," as people say. He attended Husserl's lectures at the Sorbonne in 1929, and also followed Georges Gurvitch's courses on German philosophy from 1928 to 1930. Merleau-Ponty belonged to the generation of university students that included Jean-Paul Sartre, Simone de Beauvoir, Georges Politzer, Emmanuel Mounier, Raymond Aron, and Jean Hyppolite. As is well known, he became friends with both Sartre and Beauvoir. "Merleau," as they called him, passed the *aggrégation* (the licensing exam to teach at the lycée level) in philosophy in 1930. He served in the military for one year, and then taught philosophy at the lycée level in Beauvais and Chartres from 1931 to 1935. In 1933, while at Beauvais, Merleau-Ponty received a subvention from the Caisse National des Sciences to pursue research on the nature of perception.[2] When the request for a renewal was denied, he returned to teaching at Chartres. From 1935 to 1939 he was a lecturer at the École Normale Supérieure in Paris, and during this period he attended Alexandre Kojève's famous lectures on Hegel's *Phenomenology of Spirit*. He completed his thesis, *The Structure of Behavior,* in 1938. In 1939 Merleau-Ponty traveled to Louvain, Belgium, to see the newly opened Husserl Archives; he read some manuscripts and was authorized to take copies of certain manuscripts back to Paris in order to found the Husserl Archives in Paris, which is still housed at the École Normale Supérieure.[3] As World War II started, during 1939–40, he was mobilized as an infantry officer. From 1940 to 1944, Merleau-Ponty was again a professor of philosophy at the lycée level in Paris. During this time when he was finishing his main thesis, he was active in the French Resistance. His main thesis was the *Phenomenology of Perception,* for which, along with *The Structure of Behavior,* he was awarded "very remarkable" in 1945.

After the war, Merleau-Ponty founded with Sartre and Beauvoir the journal *Les Temps Modernes* and published his first political work, *Human-*

ism and Terror (1947), an examination of the justifications for violence within Communism in the wake of the Moscow trials. In the following year he published his first collection of essays, *Sense and Non-Sense* (1948), devoted to the arts, philosophy, and politics. Also in 1948, after having been the equivalent of an assistant professor, Merleau-Ponty achieved the rank of professor of philosophy at the University of Lyon. Here he taught a course on the union of the body and soul in Malebranche, Maine de Biran, and Bergson; apparently Michel Foucault was in the audience for these lectures.[4] In 1949 Merleau-Ponty returned to Paris and occupied the chair in child psychology and pedagogy at the Sorbonne. Then toward the end of 1952, he was elected to the Collège de France in the chair in "Modern Philosophy," the youngest person, at the age of forty-four, to have held this position. On January 15, 1953, Merleau-Ponty presented his inaugural address, "In Praise of Philosophy." During the early 1950s his friendship with Sartre and Beauvoir became quite chilly, in particular over their support of Stalin and the Soviet Union, leading to Merleau-Ponty's withdrawal from the editorial board of *Les Temps Modernes* in 1952. This dispute exploded publicly in 1955 with the publication of *Adventures of the Dialectic,* to which Beauvoir responded in a vicious review.[5] In 1956 Merleau-Ponty edited a large and handsome volume dedicated to the "famous philosophers," *Les philosophes célèbres,* which included contributions from over forty of his contemporaries, including Gaston Bachelard, Jean Beaufret, Gilles Deleuze, Gilbert Ryle, Alfred Schutz, and Jean Starobinski. On May 3, 1961, "Merleau" died suddenly of a heart attack at his desk in Paris; Descartes' *Dioptics* was open on his desk. His last two publications were a collection of his essays, *Signs,* in 1960 and "Eye and Mind" in spring 1961. He was in the process of writing a major new work when he died, *The Visible and the Invisible* (1964), the incomplete manuscript of which was published by his student and friend Claude Lefort. Lefort also published an earlier unfinished manuscript, perhaps abandoned by the author, entitled *The Prose of the World* (1968). Merleau-Ponty's wife, Suzanne, and daughter are still alive in Paris.

Notes

English translations and other explanatory materials added by the editors or translators to Merleau-Ponty's notes are enclosed in brackets. Separate notes added by them are credited to either the editors or the translator of a particular chapter.

Editors' Introduction

1. See the "Chronological Bibliography of Merleau-Ponty's Works" for a complete list of recent publications and translations.

2. Key secondary sources in these and other areas are collected in *Merleau-Ponty: Critical Assessments of Leading Philosophers,* 4 vols., ed. Ted Toadvine (London: Routledge, 2006).

3. Levinas's essay, "Reality and Its Shadow," appears in English translation by Alphonso Lingis in *Collected Philosophical Papers* (Dordrecht: Martinus Nijhoff, 1987), 1–13.

Chapter 1

The text for this chapter is taken from "The Relations of the Soul and the Body and the Problem of Perceptual Consciousness," from *The Structure of Behavior,* trans. Alden Fisher (Pittsburgh: Duquesne University Press, 1983), 185–224. Original French: "Les relations de l'âme et du corps et le problème de la conscience perceptive," in *La structure du comportement* (Paris: Presses Universitaires de France, 1990 [1942]), 200–241.

1. This distinction between direct perception and verbal account remains valuable even if linguistic consciousness is primary (see the preceding chapter [of *The Structure of Behavior*]) and even in regard to the latter.

2. *Abschattungen.* See E. Husserl, "Ideen zu einer reinen Phänomenologie und phänomenologischen Philosophie," in *Jahrbuch für Philosophie und phänomenologische Forschung* (Halle: M. Niemeyer, 1913), passim [E. Husserl, *Ideen zu einer reinen Phänomenologie und phänomenologischen Philosophie, Erstes Buch,* ed. Karl Schuhmann, Husserliana, vol. 3.1 (The Hague: Martinus Nijhoff, 1976); *Ideas Pertaining to a Pure Phenomenology and to a Phenomenological Philosophy, First Book,* trans. Fred Kersten (The Hague: Martinus Nijhoff, 1982)].

3. See P. Guillaume, "Le problème de la perception de l'espace et la psychologie de l'enfant," *Journal de Psychologie* 21 (1924).

4. We are trying to translate the German "Erscheinung."

5. J. Piaget, *La représentation du monde chez l'enfant* (Paris: F. Alcan, 1926) [J. Piaget, *The Child's Conception of the World,* trans. Joan Tomlinson and Andrew Tomlinson (London: Routledge and Kegan Paul, 1929)].

6. Descartes, *La dioptrique,* "Discours quatrième," in *Oeuvres de Descartes,* ed. Victor Cousin, vol. 5 (Paris: F. G. Levrault, 1824), 39–40 [Descartes, *La dioptrique,* in *Oeuvres de Descartes,* ed. Charles Adam and Paul Tannery, rev. ed., vol. 6 (Paris: Vrin, 1996), 113–14 (cited hereafter as AT6); *Optics,* in *The Philosophical Writings of Descartes,* vol. 1, trans. John Cottingham, Robert Stoothoff, and Dugald Murdoch (Cambridge: Cambridge University Press, 1985), 165–66].

7. Ibid., "Discours premier," 7–8 [AT6, 85; *Optics,* 153–54].

8. Ibid., "Discours sixième," 54 [AT6, 130; *Optics,* 167].

9. "This is what occasions his soul to have sensory perception of just as many different qualities in these bodies as there are differences in the movements caused by them in his brain" (ibid., "Discours quatrième," 40) [AT6, 114; *Optics,* 166].

10. Descartes, *Traité des passions,* art. 32 and 35 [Descartes, *Les passions de l'ame,* in *Oeuvres de Descartes,* ed. Charles Adam and Paul Tannery, rev. ed., vol. 11 (Paris: Vrin, 1996), 352–53, 355–56 (cited hereafter as AT11); *The Passions of the Soul,* in *The Philosophical Writings of Descartes,* 1:340, 341–42]; *Dioptrique,* "Discours cinquième" [correcting Merleau-Ponty's "quartième"], 53 [AT6, 129].

11. *Traité des passions,* art. 34 [AT11, 354–55; *The Passions of the Soul,* 341].

12. *La dioptrique,* "Discours sixième," 64 [AT6, 141; *Optics,* 172].

13. Ibid. [AT6, 141; *Optics,* 172].

14. Bergson still uses this language.

15. Descartes, "Réponses aux Cinquièmes objections," in *Oeuvres et lettres,* ed. André Bridoux (Paris: Bibliothèque de Pléiade, N.R.F., Gallimard, 1949), 376 [Descartes, "Author's Replies to the Fifth Set of Objections," in *The Philosophical Writings of Descartes,* vol. 2, trans. John Cottingham, Robert Stoothoff, and Dugald Murdoch (Cambridge: Cambridge University Press, 1984), 249].

16. "I was not here dealing with sight and touch, which occur by means of bodily organs, but was concerned solely with the thought of seeing and touching, which, as we experience every day in our dreams, does not require these organs" ("Réponses aux Cinquièmes objections," 376) ["Author's Replies to the Fifth Set of Objections," 249].

17. Descartes, "Sixième méditation," *Méditations touchant la philosophie première,* in *Oeuvres de Descartes,* ed. Charles Adam and Paul Tannery, rev. ed., vol. 9 (Paris: Vrin, 1996), 57–58 [Descartes, "Sixth Meditation," *Meditations on First Philosophy,* in *The Philosophical Writings of Descartes,* 2:50–51].

18. Ibid., 59 [*Meditations,* 2:52].

19. Ibid., 58 [*Meditations,* 2:51].

20. Ibid., 63 [*Meditations,* 2:55].

21. *Traité des passions,* pt. 1 [AT11, 327–70; *The Passions of the Soul,* pt. 1, pp. 328–48].

22. Ibid., art. 30 [AT11, 351; *The Passions of the Soul,* art. 30, pp. 339–40].

23. "I know very well that a cubic foot is of the same nature as every other extension, but it is distinguished from every other by its existence" (Malebranche, *Correspondance avec Mairan,* new ed., ed. J. Moreau [Paris: Vrin, 1947], 139).

24. *Traité des passions,* art. 31 [AT11, 351–52; *The Passions of the Soul,* art. 31, pp. 340].

25. "The body which by some special right I called 'mine'" ("Sixième méditation," 60) [*Meditations,* 2:52].

26. Ibid., 64 [*Meditations,* 2:56].

27. "À Élizabeth, 21 mai 1643," in *Oeuvres de Descartes,* ed. Charles Adam and Paul Tannery, vol. 3 (Paris: Cerf, 1904; rev. ed., Vrin, 1996), 666 ["To Princess Elizabeth, 21 May 1643," in *The Philosophical Writings of Descartes,* vol. 3, trans. John Cottingham et al. (Cambridge: Cambridge University Press, 1991), 218].

28. "One may wish to conceive of the soul as material (which is, strictly speaking, to conceive of its union with the body)" ("À Élizabeth, 28 juin 1643," ibid., 3:691) ["To Princess Elizabeth, 28 June 1643," in *The Philosophical Writings of Descartes,* 3:226)].

29. The "Replies to the Sixth Set of Objections" speaks, concerning the perception of size, distance, and shape, of explicit reasoning in childhood and refers in this connection to the *Optics.* But though it is true that the *Optics* describes, with respect to the situation of objects, a "mental act which, though only a very simple act of the imagination, involves a kind of reasoning" ("Discours sixième," 62 [AT6, 138; *Optics,* 170]), Descartes accepts the fact that the soul knows directly the situation of objects without passing through that of the members, and this by an "institution of nature" ("instituée de la nature," "Discours sixième," 61 [AT6, 134–35; "ordained by nature," *Optics,* 169]) which brings it about that such and such a situation is "seen" (ibid., 63 [AT6, 138–40; *Optics,* 170–72]) when this or that disposition of the parts of the brain is realized. It is only when Descartes analyzes perception from within, as happens in the *Meditations,* that the "natural geometry" (*Traité de l'homme,* in *Oeuvres de Descartes,* ed. Victor Cousin, vol. 4 [Paris: F. G. Levrault, 1824], 380; *Treatise of Man,* trans. Thomas Steele Hall [Cambridge, Mass.: Harvard University Press, 1972], 62) of perception becomes a reasoning of the soul itself and perception an inspection of the mind (see Sixième méditation," 66 [*Meditations,* 2:57–58]). The *Optics* enunciates the "natural judgments," that is, the "naturized" thought of Malebranche ("The soul does not perform all the judgments that I attribute to it—these natural judgments are only sensations," *Recherche de la vérité,* 1, chapter 9 [Malebranche, *The Search after Truth,* trans. Thomas M. Lennon and Paul J. Olscamp (Cambridge: Cambridge University Press, 1997), 41, note A]; "God fashions them in and for us in such a way that we could form them ourselves if we knew optics and geometry as God does" (ibid. [*The Search after Truth,* 46]). The implicit reasonings of perception arise from God, not as world and place of ideas, but as creative will and legislator of occasional causes. On the other hand, the *Meditations* enunciate the "naturizing" thought of Spinoza.

30. P. Claudel, "Traité de la co-naissance au monde et de soi-même," in *Art poétique* (Paris: Mercure de France, 1907) [Claudel, "Discourse on the Affinity with the World and on Oneself," in *Poetic Art,* trans. Renee Spodheim (New York: Philosophical Library, 1948), 39–125].

31. E. Husserl, "Vorlesungen zur Phänomenologie des inneren Zeitbewusstseins," in *Jahrbuch für Phänomenologie und phänomenologische Philosophie* 9 (1928), 5 [E. Husserl, "Vorlesungen zur Phänomenologie des inneren Zeitbewusstseins," in *Zur Phänomenologie des inneren Zeitbewusstseins (1893–1917)*, ed. Rudolf Boehm, Husserliana, vol. 10 (The Hague: Martinus Nijhoff, 1966), 6; *On the Phenomenology of the Consciousness of Internal Time (1893–1917)*, trans. John Brough (Dordrecht: Kluwer Academic, 1991), 6–7].

32. M. Wahl seems to find in it a discovery of contemporary philosophy (preface to *Vers le concret* [Paris: Vrin, 1932]).

33. Kant, *Esthétique transcendental* (trans. Barni, 1, pp. 64, 68, 70, 80) [Kant, "The Transcendental Aesthetic," in *Critique of Pure Reason*, trans. N. K. Smith (London: Macmillan, 1933), 65–91] goes so far as to relate, besides the empirical contents, the form of space itself to the contingencies of the human constitution.

34. It is known how the second edition of the *Critique of Pure Reason* withdraws "formal intuition" from the sensibility—the "Transcendental Aesthetic" spoke of the "manner in which we are affected"—and gives it to the understanding, how it abandons the three syntheses of transcendental imagination—which, even if each one presupposed the following one, gave the appearance of a structure of the mind—in order to manifest better the presence of the "I think" at all the levels of consciousness which an abstract analysis could distinguish.

35. Brunschvicg, *L'expérience humaine et la causalité physique* (Paris: Alcan, 1922), 466.

36. Ibid., 73.

37. J. Cassou, *Le Greco* (Paris: Rieder, 1931), 35.

38. R. Mourgue, *Neurobiologie de l'hallucination* (Brussels: Lamerin, 1932).

39. M. Scheler, *Die Wissenformen und die Gesellschaft* (Leipzig: Der Neue Geist, 1926), 394.

40. "Without leaving the natural attitude one could show how the problems of totality (*Ganzheitsprobleme*) of the natural world, pursued to their root, end up instigating the passage to the transcendental attitude." E. Fink, "Vergenwärtigung un Bild," *Jahrbuch für Philosophie und phänomenologische Forschung* 11 (1930), 279.

41. We are thinking of a philosophy like that of L. Brunschvicg and not of Kantian philosophy, which, particularly in the *Critique of Judgment*, contains essential indications concerning the problems of which it is a question here.

42. See *The Structure of Behavior*, chap. 1.

43. See *The Structure of Behavior*, chap. 1, p. 227, n.31 (*La structure du comportement*, p. 16, n. 3), and chap. 2.

44. See above.

45. Hegel, *Vorlesungen über die Philosophie der Geschichte*, in *Hegels Sammtliche Werke kritische Ausgabe*, ed. G. Lasson (Leipzig: Meiner, 1905) [Hegel, *The Philosophy of History*, trans. J. Sibree, rev. ed. (New York: Wiley, 1944)].

46. "I do not accept your statement that the mind grows and becomes weak along with the body. You do not prove this by any argument. It is true that the mind does not work so perfectly when it is in the body of an infant as it does when in an adult's body, and that its actions can often be slowed down by wine and other corporeal things. But all that follows from this is that the mind, so long as it is joined

to the body, uses it like an instrument to perform the operations which take up most of its time. It does not follow that it is made more or less perfect by the body. Your inference here is no more valid than if you were to infer from the fact that a craftsman works badly whenever he uses a faulty tool that the good condition of his tools is the source of his knowledge of his craft" ("Réponses aux Cinquièmes objections," *Oeuvres et lettres*, 371) ["Author's Replies to the Fifth Set of Objections," 245]. It is not a question of approving Gassendi, who attributed to the biological body what belongs to the phenomenal body—but this is not a reason for speaking of a perfection of the mind in itself. If the body plays a role in preventing the actualization of the mind, it is because the body is involved with the mind when this actualization is achieved.

47. See chap. 2, section 3, of *The Structure of Behavior.*

48. "The soul is the sense of the body and the body is the manifestation of the soul; neither of the two acts on the other because neither of the two belongs to the world of things. . . . The soul is inherent in the body as the concept is inherent in speech: the former is the sense of the word, the latter is the sense of the body; the word is the clothing of thought and the body the manifestation of the soul. And there are no souls without manifestations any more than there are concepts without speech" (L. Klages, *Vom Wesen des Bewusztsein* [Leipzig: Barth, 1921]).

49. "The hand that kept thrusting the blankets aside with a gesture which formerly would have meant that those blankets were oppressing her, but now meant nothing" (Proust, *Le côté des Guermantes*, 2 [Paris: Nouvelle Revue Française, 1921], 27) [Proust, *À la recherche du temps perdu*, vol. 2 (Paris: Gallimard, 1988), 632; *The Guermantes Way*, vol. 2, in *Remembrance of Things Past*, trans. C. K. Scott-Moncrieff and Terence Kilmartin (New York: Random House, 1981), 348]. "Released by the twofold action of the oxygen and the morphine, my grandmother's breath no longer laboured, no longer whined, but, swift and light, glided like a skater toward the delicious fluid. Perhaps the breath, imperceptible as that of the wind in the hollow stem of a reed, was mingled in this song with some of those more human sighs which, released at the approach of death, suggest intimations of pain or happiness in those who have already ceased to feel, and came now to add a more melodious accent, but without changing its rhythm, to that long phrase which rose, soared still higher, then subsided, to spring up once more, from the alleviated chest, in pursuit of oxygen" (ibid., 31) [*À la recherche du temps perdu*, 2:636; *The Guermantes Way*, 2:352].

50. Nevertheless, there would be a place for investigating more thoroughly the distinction of our "natural body," which is always already there, already constituted for consciousness, and our "cultural body," which is the sedimentation of its spontaneous acts. The problem is posed by Husserl when he distinguishes "originary passivity" and "secondary passivity." See in particular "Formal und transzendental Logik," in *Jahrbuch für Philosophie und phänomenologische Forschung* 10 (1929), 287 [Husserl, *Formale und transzendentale Logik*, ed. Paul Janssen, Husserliana, vol. 17 (The Hague: Martinus Nijhoff, 1974), 324–25; *Formal and Transcendental Logic*, trans. Dorion Cairns (The Hague: Martinus Nijhoff, 1978), 327].

51. See *The Structure of Behavior*, 162 (*La structure du comportement*, 175).

52. See *The Structure of Behavior*, 136 (*La structure du comportement*, 147).

53. See *The Structure of Behavior*, 144 (*La structure du comportement*, 156).

54. We reserve the question of whether there is not, as Heidegger suggests, a perception of the *world*, that is, a manner of acceding to an indefinite field of objects which gives them in their reality. What is certain is that the perceived is not limited to that which strikes my eyes. When I am sitting at my desk, the space is closed behind me not only in idea but also in reality. Even if the horizon of the perceived can be expanded to the limits of the world, the perceptual consciousness of the world as existing remains distinct from the intellectual consciousness of the world as the object of an infinity of true judgments.

55. Husserl, "Ideen zu einer reinen Phänomenologie und phänomenologischen Philosophie," *Jahrbuch*, 89. [*Ideen 1*, Husserliana, vol. 3.1, p. 101; *Ideas 1*, 107].

56. We are defining here the "phenomenological reduction" in the sense which is given to it in Husserl's final philosophy.

57. The notion of intentionality will be of help in this regard.

58. J.-P. Sartre, "La transcendence de l'ego," *Recherche philosophique*, 1936–37 [J.-P. Sartre, *The Transcendence of the Ego*, trans. Forrest Williams and Robert Kirkpatrick (New York: Farrar, Straus, and Giroux, 1957)].

59. See *The Structure of Behavior*, 184 (*La structure du comportement*, 199).

60. This is the thesis of J.-P. Sartre in *The Transcendence of the Ego*.

61. See *The Structure of Behavior*, 126 (*La structure du comportement*, 137).

Chapter 2

The text for this chapter is taken from "The War Has Taken Place," from *Sense and Non-Sense*, trans. Hubert L. Dreyfus and Patricia Allen Dreyfus (Evanston, Ill.: Northwestern University Press, 1964), 139–52. Original French: "La guerre a eu lieu," in *Sens et non-sens* (Paris: Nagel, 1948; reprinted Paris: Gallimard, 1996), 169–85. Originally published in *Les Temps Modernes*, no. 1 (October 1945): 48–66.

Chapter 3

The text for this chapter is taken from "What Is Phenomenology?" preface to *Phenomenology of Perception*, trans. Colin Smith (London: Routledge and Kegan Paul, 1962; reprinted, 2002), vii–xxiv. Original French: "Avant-Propos," in *Phénoménologie de la perception* (Paris: Gallimard, 1945), i–xvi.

1. E. Husserl, *Méditations Cartésiennes* (Paris: Colin, 1931), 120ff. [E. Husserl, *Cartesian Meditations*, trans. Dorion Cairns (The Hague: Martinus Nijhoff, 1960), 139ff.].

2. See Eugen Fink's *Sixth Cartesian Meditation*, unpublished manuscript, to which Gaston Berger has kindly referred us. [Unpublished in Merleau-Ponty's time, this manuscript is now available: *VI Cartesianische Meditation: Teil 1* (Dordrecht: Kluwer Academic, 1988); *Sixth Cartesian Meditation*, trans. Ronald Bruzina (Bloomington: Indiana University Press, 1995).]

3. E. Husserl, *Logische Untersuchungen: Prolegomena zur reinen Logik*, 4th ed.

(Halle: Niemeyer, 1928), 93, n. 3 [E. Husserl, *Logical Investigations*, vol. 1, trans. J. N. Findlay (London: Routledge and Kegan Paul, 1977), 122, n. 1].

4. "In te redi; in interiore homine habitat veritas"—Saint Augustine. [The quote comes from *De vera religione*, 39, n. 72. The full quote is "Noli foras ire, in te redi, in interiore homine habitat veritas," which in English is: "Do not wish to go out; go back into yourself. Truth dwells in the inner man." This quote is also the final sentence of Husserl's *Cartesian Meditations*.]

5. E. Husserl, *Die Krisis der europäischen Wissenschaft und die transzenentale Phänomenologie*, pt. 3 (unpublished). [Unpublished in 1945, *The Crisis* has been available since 1954: *Die Krisis der europäischen Wissenschaft und die transzendentale Phänomenologie: Eine Einleitung in die phänomenologische Philosophie* (The Hague: Martinus Nijhoff, 1954); *The Crisis of European Sciences and Transcendental Phenomenology: An Introduction to Phenomenological Philosophy*, trans. David Carr (Evanston, Ill.: Northwestern University Press, 1970). Part 3 is called "The Clarification of the Transcendental Problem and the Related Function of Psychology."]

6. E. Fink, *Die Phänomenologische Philosophie Edmund Husserl in der gegenwärtigen Kritik*, 331ff. [Merleau-Ponty is referring to the original *Kantstudien* publication of the essay: *Kantstudien*, Band 38, 3/4 (Berlin, 1933). Collected in Eugen Fink, *Studien zur Phänomenologie* (The Hague: Martinus Nijhoff, 1966). English translation as "The Phenomenological Philosophy of Edmund Husserl and Contemporary Criticism," in *The Phenomenology of Husserl*, ed. R. O. Elveton (Chicago: Quadrangle Books, 1970), 109ff.]

7. *Méditations Cartésiennes*, 33 [*Cartesian Meditations*, 38–39].

8. Jean Wahl, *Réalisme, dialectique et mystère* (L'Arbalète, 1942), unpaginated.

9. *Das Erlebnis der Wahrheit* (Husserl, *Logische Untersuchungen: Prolegomena zur reinen Logik*, 190) [*Logical Investigations*, 1:194].

10. See chap. 1 (from *The Structure of Behavior*) in the present volume for the idea of a "naturizing thought" (*pensée naturante*), p. 215 in the French. The idea apparently comes from Brunschvicg.—Eds.

11. E. Husserl, *Formale und transzendentale Logik*, 142, says in substance that there is no apodictic evidence. [E. Husserl, *Formal and Transcendental Logic*, trans. Dorion Cairns (The Hague: Martinus Nijhoff, 1978), 158–59.]

12. We find this term a lot in the unpublished manuscripts. The idea can be found already in *Formale und transzendentale Logik*, 184ff. [*Formal and Transcendental Logic*, 208ff.].

13. *Sixth Cartesian Meditation* (unpublished). [See note 2 above.]

14. *Sixth Cartesian Meditation* (unpublished). [See note 2 above.]

15. The unpublished manuscripts say: "Rückbeziehung der Phänomenologie auf sich selbst" [in English: "Connection of phenomenology back to itself"].

16. We owe this last expression to G. Gusdorf (actually a prisoner in Germany), who, moreover, used it perhaps in a different sense.

Chapter 4

The text for this chapter is taken from "Cézanne's Doubt," from *The Merleau-Ponty Aesthetics Reader*, ed. Galen Johnson and Michael Smith (Evanston, Ill.: Northwestern University Press, 1993), 59–75. Original English translation: *Sense and Non-Sense*, trans. Hubert L. Dreyfus and Patricia Allen Dreyfus (Evanston, Ill.: Northwestern University Press, 1964), 9–25. Original French: "Le doute de Cézanne," *Fontaine* 8, no. 47 (December 1945): 80–100; reprinted in *Sens et non-sens* (Paris: Nagel, 1948; reprinted Paris: Gallimard, 1996), 13–33.

1. Cézanne's conversations with Bernard are recorded in *Souvenirs sur Paul Cézanne* (Paris: R. G. Michel, 1912).—Trans.

2. P. Valéry, "Introduction à la méthode de Léonard de Vinci," in *Variété*, 185 [P. Valéry, *Introduction to the Method of Leonardo da Vinci*, trans. Thomas McGreevey (London: J. Rodker, 1929)].

3. Sigmund Freud, *Un souvenir d'enfance de Léonard de Vinci*, 65 [*Leonardo da Vinci: A Study in Psychosexuality*, trans. A. A. Brill (New York: Random House, 1947)].

4. Ibid., 189.

5. Merleau-Ponty's expression, "restes d'une fête inconnue," referring to Cézanne's canvases, appears to echo Marcel Proust's "la fête inconnue et colorée" (see *À la recherche du temps perdu*, vol. 3 [Paris: Gallimard, 1954], 375), describing Vinteuil's music.—Trans.

Chapter 5

The text for this chapter was taken from "The Contemporary Philosophical Movement," original translation of "Le mouvement philosophique moderne" by David Gougelet, in Merleau-Ponty, *Parcours, 1935–1951* (Lagrasse: Éditions Verdier, 1997), 65–68. Originally published in *Carrefour*, no. 92 (May 23, 1946): 6.

1. The italic text in this chapter was written by Maurice Fleurent.

2. This word appears both in French, *comportement*, and in English in the original.—Trans.

Chapter 6

"The Primacy of Perception and Its Philosophical Consequences," in *The Primacy of Perception*, trans. James Edie (Evanston, Ill.: Northwestern University Press, 1964), 12–42. Original French: "Le primat de la perception et ses conséquences philosophiques," *Bulletin de la Société Française de Philosophie* 49 (December 1947): 119–53.

1. This address to the French Philosophical Society (Société Française de Philosophie) was given shortly after the publication of Merleau-Ponty's major work, the *Phenomenology of Perception*, and it represents his attempt to summarize and defend the central thesis of that work. The following translation gives the complete text of Merleau-Ponty's address and the discussion which followed it, with the exception of a few incidental remarks unrelated to the substance of the discussion. These minimal omissions are indicated by the insertion of ellipses in the text. The discussion took place on November 23, 1946, and was published in the *Bulletin de la Société Française de Philosophie* 49 (December 1947): 119–53.—Eds.

2. Merleau-Ponty is apparently referring to terminology found in Husserl's

Experience andJudgment (trans. James S. Churchill and Karl Ameriks [Evanston, Ill.: Northwestern University Press, 1973]), section 19, pp. 82–83, in particular.—Eds.

3. Émile Bréhier (1876–1952), historian of philosophy, mainly ancient Greek philosophy.—Trans.

4. Jean Hyppolite (1907–1968), historian of philosophy, especially Hegel. —Eds.

5. Jean Beaufret (1907–1982), the main disseminator of Heidegger's thought in France.—Eds.

Chapter 7

The text for this chapter was taken from "Reality and Its Shadow," original translation of "La réalité et son ombre" by David Gougelet, in Merleau-Ponty, *Parcours, 1935–1951* (Lagrasse: Éditions Verdier, 1997), 122–24. Originally published in *Les Temps Modernes*, no. 38 (November 1948): 769–70.

1. An English translation of Levinas's article, "Reality and Its Shadow," can be found in E. Levinas, *Collected Philosophical Papers,* trans. Alphonso Lingis (Dordrecht: Martinus Nijhoff, 1987), 1–13.—Eds.

2. Jean-Paul Sartre, *L'imaginaire* (Paris: Gallimard, 1940) [Jean-Paul Sartre, *The Psychology of Imagination,* trans. Bernard Frechtman (New York: Washington Square, 1966)].

Chapter 8

The text for this chapter was taken from "A Note on Machiavelli," in *Signs,* trans. Richard McCleary (Evanston, Ill.: Northwestern University Press, 1964), 211–23. Original French: "Note sur Machiavel," in *Signes* (Paris: Gallimard, 1960), 267–83. Originally published as "Machiavelisme et Humanisme," *Les Temps Modernes*, no. 48 (October 1949): 577–93.

"A Note on Machiavelli" was originally a paper delivered to the Umanesimo e Scienza Politica Congress (Humanism and Political Science Congress), Rome-Florence, September 1949.

1. N. Machiavelli, *The Prince,* chap. 25.

2. N. Machiavelli, *Discourses,* 2.23, quoted by A. Renaudet, *Machiavel,* 305.4; *The Prince,* chap. 14.

3. *The Prince,* chap. 14.

4. Ibid., chap. 17.

5. Ibid., chap. 18.

6. Ibid.

7. Ibid., chap. 3.

8. Ibid., chap. 16.

9. Ibid., chap. 17.

10. Ibid., chap. 14.

11. Ibid., chap. 5.

12. Ibid., chap. 15.

13. Ibid., chap. 5.

14. Ibid., chap. 3.

15. Ibid., chap. 17.

16. Ibid., chap. 9. We are not far from the definition of the State in Thomas More's *Utopia:* "quaedam conspiratio divitum de suis commodis reipublicae nomine titulogue tractantium."

17. Ibid., chap. 23.

18. Ibid., chap. 5.

19. Ibid., chap. 15.

20. By failing to wipe out the families which divided the Pistoia into factions.

21. Ibid., chap. 17.

22. "I think that one must be a prince to know the people's nature well, and a man of the people to know that of the prince" (dedication to *The Prince*).

23. Ibid., chap. 18.

24. Ibid. (my italics).

25. Ibid.

26. Ibid., chap. 7.

27. Ibid., chap. 25.

28. *Discourses*, 2.29, quoted by Renaudet, *Machiavel*, 132.

29. *The Prince*, chap. 25.

30. Ibid.

31. Ibid.

32. Ibid., chap. 26.

33. *Discourses*, 1.26, quoted by Renaudet, *Machiavel*, 231.

34. Renaudet, *Machiavel*, 301.

35. James, *Les Jacobins noirs*, 127.

36. Ibid., 49.

37. Ibid., 295.

38. *Discourses* 1, quoted by Renaudet, *Machiavel*, 75.

39. Letter to Francesco Vettori, quoted by Renaudet, *Machiavel*, 72.

Chapter 9

The text for this chapter is taken from "The Adversary Is Complicit," original translation of "L'adversaire est complice" by David Gougelet, in Merleau-Ponty, *Parcours, 1935–1951* (Lagrasse: Éditions Verdier, 1997), 134–45. Originally published in *Les Temps Modernes*, no. 57 (July 1950): 1–11.

1. David Julievitch Dallin and Boris Ivanovic Nicolaevsky, *Forced Labor in Russia* (1947).

2. *Receuil chronologique des lois et décrets de Présidium du Soviet Suprême et ordonnances du gouvernement de la RFSSR au 1ᵉʳ mars 1940*, vol. 9, O.G.I.Z (Union des Maisons d'Édition d'État Gospolitizdat, 1941).

3. Parenthetically, your position on this point seems to me different from that of the other collaborators at the *Révolution Prolétarienne*—from that of R. Louzon, for instance, who asks for arms for Mao Tse-tung and therefore does not a priori hold Mao Tse-tung's victory to be a Stalinist victory.

Chapter 10

The text for this chapter is taken from "The Child's Relations with Others," extract, from *The Primacy of Perception*, trans. William Cobb (Evanston, Ill.: Northwestern University Press, 1964), 113–55. Original French: *Les relations avec autrui chez l'enfant* (Paris: Centre de Documentation Universitaire, 1951), 25–81. Reprinted in *Parcours, 1935–1951* (Lagrasse: Éditions Verdier, 1997), 147–229.

1. Paul Guillaume, *L'imitation chez l'enfant* (Paris: Alcan, 1925).—Eds.

2. Jacques Jean Lhermitte, *L'image de notre corps* (Paris: Éditions de la Nouvelle Revue Critique, 1939).—Eds.

3. Henri Wallon, *Les origines du caractère chez l'enfant: Les préludes du sentiment de personnalité* (Paris: Presses Universitaires de France, 1949).—Eds.

4. Wolfgang Köhler, *The Mentality of Apes* (New York: Harcourt Brace, 1927). —Eds.

5. Daniel Lagache, *Les hallucinations verbales et la parole* (Paris: Alcan, 1934). —Eds.

6. Wallon, *Les origines du caractère chez l'enfant*, 177.—Eds.

7. See Jacques Lacan, "Le stade du miroir comme formateur de la fonction du Je," *Revue française de Psychanalyse* 4 (October-December 1949): 449–55; translated by Alan Sheridan as "The Mirror Stage as Formative of the Function of the I," in *Écrits: A Selection* (New York: W. W. Norton, 1977), 1–7. See also "Les effets psychiques du mode imaginaire," *L'Évolution Psychiatrique* (January-March 1947). —Eds.

8. Charlotte Buhler, Hildegard Hetzer, and Beatrix Tudor-Hart, eds., *Soziologische und psychologische Studien über das erste Lebensjahr* (Jena: Gustav Fisher, 1927).—Eds.

9. Elsa Köhler, *Die Personlichkeit des dreijahrigen Kindes* (Leipzig: Hirzel, 1926).

10. See Wallon, "La maladresse," *Journal de Psychologie* (1928): 61–78.—Eds.

Chapter 11

The text for this chapter is taken from "Human Engineering: The New 'Human' Techniques of American Big Business," original translation of "Human engineering: Les nouvelles techniques 'humaines' du big business américain" by David Gougelet, in Merleau-Ponty, *Parcours, 1935–1951* (Lagrasse: Éditions Verdier, 1997), 230–34. Originally published in *Les Temps Modernes*, no. 69 (July 1951): 44–48.

The terms "human engineering" and "big business" are in English in the original text.—Eds.

Chapter 12

The text for this chapter is taken from "Man and Adversity," followed by discussion, essay in *Signs*, trans. Richard McCleary (Evanston, Ill.: Northwestern University Press, 1964), 224–43. Original French: "L'homme et l'adversité," in *Signes* (Paris: Gallimard, 1960), 284–308. English translation of discussion by Ted Toadvine, from *La connaissance de l'homme au XXᵉ siècle: Texte des conférences et des entretiens organisés par les Rencontres Internationales de Geneva, 1951* (Neuchatel: Éditions de la Baconnière, 1952), 215–52. The discussion can also be found in *Parcours deux, 1951–1961* (Lagrasse: Éditions Verdier, 2000), 321–76.

"Man and Adversity" is a conference paper delivered on September 10, 1951, at the Rencontres Internationales at Geneva.—Eds.

1. The full citation for *Essais de psychanalyse* is Sigmund Freud, *Essais de psychanalyse*, trans. from the German with the author's authorization by S. Jankélévitch (Paris: Payot, 1927).—Eds.

2. Merleau-Ponty cites Valéry's *Mauvaises Pensées*, p. 200. See Paul Valéry, *Œuvres, II,* edited and annotated by Jean Hatier, Bibliothèque de la Pléiade (Paris: Gallimard NRF, 1960), 895–96; "Bad Thoughts and Not So Bad," in *Analects*, trans. Stuart Gilbert, in *The Collected Works of Paul Valéry,* ed. Jackson Mathews, vol. 14 (Princeton: Princeton University Press, 1970), 508.—Eds.

3. Merleau-Ponty cites Valéry's *Tel Quel*, p. 42. See Paul Valéry, *Œuvres, II,* 490–91; "Odds and Ends," in *Analects,* 26.—Eds.

4. Merleau-Ponty cites Breton's *Point du jour, le langage automatique.* The intended reference is surely "Le Message automatique," in *Point du jour.* See André Breton, *Œuvres completes, II,* ed. Marguerite Bonnet, Bibliothèque de la Pléiade (Paris: Gallimard NRF, 1992), 375–92; "The Automatic Message," in *Break of Day,* trans. Mark Polizzotti and Mary Ann Caws (Lincoln: University of Nebraska Press, 1999), 125–43.—Eds.

5. Merleau-Ponty is referring to a journal, *Littérature,* that Breton started with Louis Aragon and Philippe Soupault in March 1919. In November 1919, the journal invited responses to the question *pourquoi écrivez-vous?* (why do we write?).—Eds.

6. Merleau-Ponty cites Breton's *Légitime défense.* See "Légitime defense," in *Point du jour, Œuvres completes, II,* pp. 282–96; "In Self-Defense," in *Break of Day,* pp. 22–39.—Eds.

7. Merleau-Ponty cites Malraux's *Psychologie de l'art.* This quotation is probably a paraphrase from *Psychologie de l'art: La création artistique* (Geneva: Albert Skira, 1948), 114: "combine de jours faut-il à un écrivain pour écrire avec le son de sa proper voix?"; *The Voices of Silence,* trans. Stuart Gilbert (Princeton: Princeton University Press, 1978), 280: "how long it takes a writer to learn to write with the sound of his own voice!"—Eds.

8. Merleau-Ponty cites Valéry's *Mon Faust*, p. 157. See Paul Valéry, *Œuvres, II,* 354; "My Faust" in *Plays,* trans. David Paul and Robert Fitzgerald, in *The Collected Works of Paul Valéry,* ed. Jackson Mathews, vol. 3 (Princeton: Princeton University Press, 1960), 107–8.—Eds.

9. This discussion originally appeared in Marcel Giaule et al., *La Connaissance de l'homme au XXᵉ siècle* (Neuchatel: Éditions de la Baconnière, 1952), 215–52. The original editors of the discussion summarized comments made by certain speakers; the summaries appear in italics.—Eds.

10. Herman Melville, *Pierre ou les Ambiguïtes* (Paris: Gallimard, 1939; rev. 1967); Herman Melville, *Pierre; or The Ambiguities* (New York: Alfred Knopf, 1930). —Eds.

11. Edmund Husserl, *Ideen zu einer reinen Phänomenologie und phänomenolo-*

gischen Philosophie, Erstes Buch, ed. Karl Schuhmann, Husserliana, vol. 3.1 (The Hague: Martinus Nijhoff, 1976); *Ideas Pertaining to a Pure Phenomenology and to a Phenomenological Philosophy, First Book,* trans. Fred Kersten (The Hague: Martinus Nijhoff, 1982).—Eds.

12. Jean Prévost, *La création chez Stendhal* (Marseille: Sagittaire, 1942; Paris: Mercure de France, 1971; Paris: Gallimard, 1996). See p. 199 of this volume.—Eds.

13. The phrase "matter of fact" appears in English in the original.—Eds.

14. Ferdinand de Saussure, *Cours de linguistique générale,* ed. Charles Bally and Albert Sechehaye (Paris: Payot, 1916; new ed., ed. Tullio de Mauro, 1972); Ferdinand de Saussure, *Course in General Linguistics,* trans. Wade Baskin (New York: Philosophical Library, 1959).—Eds.

15. See p. 202 of this volume.—Eds.

Chapter 13

The text for this chapter is taken from "Indirect Language and the Voices of Silence," from *The Merleau-Ponty Aesthetics Reader,* ed. Galen Johnson and Michael Smith (Evanston, Ill.: Northwestern University Press, 1993), 76–120. Original English translation: "Indirect Language and the Voices of Silence," in *Signs,* trans. Richard C. McCleary (Evanston, Ill.: Northwestern University Press, 1964), 39–83. Original French: "Le langage indirect et les voix du silence," in *Signes* (Paris: Gallimard, 1960), 49–103. Originally published in *Les Temps Modernes,* no. 80 (June 1952): 2113–44, and *Les Temps Modernes,* no. 81 (July 1952): 70–94.

1. Pierre Francastel, *Peinture et société,* 17ff.

2. Ibid.

3. Henri Wallon, French professor of child psychology, at the Collége de France until his retirement.—Trans.

4. André Malraux, *Le musée imaginaire,* 59. These pages were already written when the definitive edition of the *Psychologie de l'art* (*The Voices of Silence,* published by Gallimard) appeared. We quote from Albert Skira's edition.

5. Ibid., 79.

6. Ibid., 83.

7. André Malraux, *La monnaie de l'absolu,* 118.

8. André Malraux, *La création esthétique,* 144.

9. *Le musée imaginaire,* 63.

10. *La création esthétique,* 51.

11. Ibid., 154.

12. Ibid.

13. Ibid., 158.

14. Ibid., 152.

15. Jean-Paul Sartre, *Situations,* 2, p. 61.

16. Ibid., 60.

17. *La création esthétique,* 113.

18. Ibid., 142.

19. *La monnaie de l'absolu,* 125.

20. Gaston Bachelard, French philosopher, whose several works on the "psychoanalysis of the elements" had some influence on Merleau-Ponty and Sartre in the 1940s.—Trans.

21. *La création esthétique,* 150.

22. Raymond Aron, French political philosopher, perhaps best known in the United States for his *The Century of Total War,* but also one of the first to make German phenomenology known in France.—Trans.

23. Jules Vuillemin, French philosopher of science, successor to Merleau-Ponty in the chair of philosophy at the Collège de France.—Trans.

24. Besides, Freud never said that he explained da Vinci by the vulture; he said in effect that analysis stops where painting begins.

25. *Le musée imaginaire,* 52.

26. The expression is that of Paul Ricoeur.

27. Merleau-Ponty cites *Principes de la philosophie du droit,* para. 118. The English translation provided here comes from Georg Hegel, *Hegel's Philosophy of Right,* trans. T. M. Knox (London: Oxford University Press, 1952), section 118, p. 80.—Eds.

28. Ibid.

29. Ibid.

30. Francis Ponge, contemporary French poet and essayist.—Trans.

Chapter 14

The text for this chapter is taken from "An Unpublished Text by Maurice Merleau-Ponty: A Prospectus of His Work," in *The Primacy of Perception,* trans. Arleen Dallery (Evanston, Ill.: Northwestern University Press, 1964), 3–11. Original French: "Un inédit de Maurice Merleau-Ponty," *Revue de métaphysique et de morale,* no. 4 (1962): 401–9. Reprinted in *Parcours deux, 1951–1961* (Lagrasse: Éditions Verdier, 2000), 36–48.

1. "Un inédit de Maurice Merleau-Ponty" was first published in *Revue de Métaphysique et de Morale,* no. 4 (October 1962): 401–9. Martial Guéroult, who was in charge of the report that Merleau-Ponty had to present for his candidacy to the Collège de France in 1951, arranged for this first publication and wrote the above introductory note for it.

Chapter 15

The text for this chapter is taken from "Epilogue" to *Adventures of the Dialectic,* trans. Joseph Bien (Evanston, Ill.: Northwestern University Press, 1973), 203–33. Original French: "Épilogue," in *Les aventures de la dialectique* (Paris: Gallimard, Folio-Essais, 1955), 281–322.

1. For Michelet's *History of the French Revolution,* Merleau-Ponty cites IV, i. He does not indicate a particular edition. One can find the passage in Jules Michelet, *Histoire de la revolution Française I,* edited and annotated by Gérard Walter, Biblio-

thèque de la Pléiade (Paris: Gallimard NRF, 1952), book 4, chap. 1, p. 430: "C'est-à-dire, plus de temps . . . Un éclair et l'éternité." No complete English translation of Michelet's *Histoire* is available.—Eds.

2. Alexandre Kojève, the author of several noted philosophical works, including the *Introduction à la lecture de Hegel* (Paris: Gallimard, 1947). Selections from this work have been translated into English by James Nichols in *Introduction to the Reading of Hegel* (New York: Basic Books, 1969). Merleau-Ponty and Sartre were influenced by his lectures at the École des Hautes Études during the latter part of the 1930s.—Trans.

3. "For an indefinitely long time and in constant internal struggle, all social relations undergo transformation. Society keeps on changing its skin. . . . Revolutions in economy, technique, sciences, the family, morals, and everyday life develop in complex reciprocal action and do not allow society to achieve equilibrium" (Leon Trotsky, *The Permanent Revolution and Results and Prospects*, trans. J. Wright and B. Pearce [New York: Merit, 1969], 132).

4. "We do not want to negate or underrate revolutionary cruelties and horrors; . . . they are inseparable from the whole historical development. . . . These tragic hazards enter into the inevitable incidental expenses of a revolution *which is itself an incidental expense in the historical development*" (italics added; Leon Trotsky, *Histoire de la Révolution russe*, 3:177, 63 [Leon Trotsky, *History of the Russian Revolution*, trans. Max Eastman (London: V. Gollancz, 1932–33)]). Cited by Daniel Guérin, *La lutte des classes sous la Première république*, 2 vols. (Paris: Gallimard, 1946), 2:50.

5. Jules Michelet, *Histoire de la Révolution française* (Paris: Nouvelle Revue Française, 1939), 19; English translation by Charles Cocks, *History of the French Revolution* (Chicago: University of Chicago Press, 1967). [The reference is to the 1868 second preface, which is not found in the English edition. Michelet (1798–1874) was known for his liberal views and exactitude in historical study.—Trans.]

6. *Histoire de la Révolution française*, 21 [*History of the French Revolution*, 13, translation modified].

7. Guérin, *La lutte des classes*.

8. The Mountain or Montagne: a group in the Convention which occupied the highest benches, from which comes their name. They voted the most violent measures in the Convention. Danton, also one of the founders of the Committee of Public Safety, was one of its members. He was executed by Robespierre in 1794.—Trans.

9. Guérin takes the term "Bras Nus" from Michelet's *History of the French Revolution*, where it originally referred to the workers doing difficult physical labor. Guérin uses it to distinguish, insofar as was possible at the time, the workers from the petty bourgeoisie.—Trans.

10. The Committee of Public Safety, consisting of twelve members and headed by Robespierre, was organized in 1793 to concentrate the executive powers of the Convention. Robespierre was its leading member until he was overthrown on the ninth of Thermidor, Year II (July 27, 1794).—Trans.

11. Joseph Cambon, member of the Convention, who in 1793 drew up the Grand Livre of the public debt.—Trans.

12. The Gironde: a group of revolutionary delegates whose original leaders

came from the department of the Gironde. They sat on the right side of the Convention and were opposed to the "Mountain" group, seated on the left. The Girondists were ousted by the men of the Mountain in 1793 and many of their members were guillotined, among them Brissot.—Trans.

13. Pierre-Victurnien Vergniaud, member of the Convention.—Trans.

14. Jacques Rene Hébert, editor of *Père Duchesne,* one of the violent revolutionary newspapers, which approved the September massacres. Arrested by Robespierre, he was executed together with a large number of his followers, who were called Hébertists or Enragés.—Trans.

15. Guérin, *La lutte des classes,* 2:60.

16. Ibid., 2:332, footnote.

17. Ibid., 2:351.

18. *Assignats* was the name for French paper money from 1789 to 1797. —Trans.

19. Guérin, *La lutte des classes,* 2:7.

20. Jean Varlet, a young postal clerk, who became famous in 1791. A champion of the industrial workers, he was referred to as an Enragé and was a member of the Hébertist party.—Trans.

21. Guérin, *La lutte des classes,* 2:59.

22. Ibid., 2:22.

23. François-Noël Babeuf, French revolutionary who espoused a sort of communism.—Trans.

24. Guérin, *La lutte des classes,* 2:347.

25. Sansculottes: the name given by the aristocrats to the revolutionaries, who wore long pants rather than knee breeches.—Trans.

26. Guérin, *La lutte des classes,* 2:232.

27. Ibid., 2:4–5.

28. Ibid., 2:9.

29. Ibid., 2:6, footnote.

30. Ibid., 2:12.

31. Sainte-Claire Deville, cited by Guérin, ibid.

32. Ibid., 2:368.

33. Ibid.

34. Merleau-Ponty, *Humanisme et terreur* (Paris: Gallimard, 1947); [Merleau-Ponty, *Humanism and Terror,* trans. John O'Neill (Boston: Beacon Press, 1969)].

35. *Humanisme et terreur,* 202 [*Humanism and Terror,* 184–85].

Chapter 16

The text for this chapter is taken from "Introduction" to *Signs,* trans. Richard McCleary (Evanston, Ill.: Northwestern University Press, 1964), 3–35. Original French: "Préface," in *Signes* (Paris: Gallimard, 1960), 7–48.

1. Charles Maurras, French writer and editor of the proto-Fascist *Action Française.*—Eds.

2. Serge Mallet, "Gaullisme et néo-capitalisme," *Esprit* (February 1960): 205–28.

3. Ibid., 211.

4. Ibid., 214.

5. Merleau-Ponty cites only the name Husserl, but he is referring to Husserl's descriptions of *Abschattungen* in *Ideas I*. See Edmund Husserl, *Ideen zu einer reinen Phänomenologie und phänomenologischen Philosophie*, Husserliana, 3.1, ed. Karl Schuhmann (The Hague: Martinus Nijhoff, 1976); *Ideas Pertaining to a Pure Phenomenology and to a Phenomenological Philosophy, First Book*, trans. Fred Kersten (The Hague: Martinus Nijhoff, 1982). For Merleau-Ponty's definition of phenomenology, see also chapter 3 of this book.—Eds.

6. Merleau-Ponty cites only the name Jean Paulhan.—Eds.

7. Jean Starobinski, "Montaigne en mouvement," *La Nouvelle Revue Française* (February 1960).

8. "Etre-là" is Merleau-Ponty's translation of Heidegger's German term, "Dasein."—Eds.

9. Merleau-Ponty cites only the preface to *Aden Arabie*, ed. F. Maspéro. The English translation is by Joan Pinkham as *Aden, Arabie* (New York: Columbia University Press, 1987).—Eds.

10. In English in the original.—Eds.

11. Merleau-Ponty cites only *Swann*, I, 265. See Marcel Proust, *Du côté de chez Swann*, pt. 1: Combray, p. 265; English translation by C. K. Scott-Moncrieff and Terence Kilmartin, vol. 1 of *Remembrance of Things Past* (New York: Random House, 1981), 201.—Eds.

12. Preface to *Aden Arabie*, 51 [*Aden, Arabie*, 46].

13. Ibid., 48 [ibid., 44].

14. Ibid., 55 [ibid., 50].

15. Ibid., 41 [ibid., 37].

16. Ibid., 55 [ibid., 50].

17. Laurent Casanova, French Resistance leader and (until he lost out to the Stalinist element) high-ranking Communist official and deputy. His wife Danielle, killed by the Nazis, became one of the most popular martyrs of the Resistance.—Eds.

18. Preface to *Aden Arabie*, 57 [*Aden, Arabie*, 51–52].

19. Ibid., 60 [ibid., 54].

20. Ibid., 58 [ibid., 52].

21. Ibid., 44–45 [ibid., 40].

22. Ibid., 17 [ibid., 16].

23. Ibid., 29 [ibid., 27].

24. Ibid., 30 [ibid., 27].

25. Ibid., 45 [ibid., 40].

26. Ibid., 18 [ibid., 17].

27. Ibid., 29 [ibid., 27].

28. Ibid., 18 [ibid., 17].

29. Ibid., 61 [ibid., 55–56].

30. Ibid., 51 [ibid., 46].

31. Here we are following the original English translation, which rendered Merleau-Ponty's neologism "la virtu"—the normal French term is "la vertu"—with the Italian "virtù." This introduction of an Italian term makes sense since Merleau-Ponty is probably referring to his essay "A Note on Machiavelli," in which he discusses political virtue, and one time uses the Italian "virtù" (see *Signs,* 217; *Signes,* 275; and p. 128 of this volume). By using "la virtu," it is possible that Merleau-Ponty is suggesting the literal sense of "la vertu," from the Latin, "virtus," which means masculine strength, as in "virile." But his usage also suggests potential, as in "virtuality."—Eds.

Chapter 17

The text for this chapter is taken from "Eye and Mind," from *The Merleau-Ponty Aesthetics Reader,* ed. Galen Johnson and Michael Smith (Evanston, Ill.: Northwestern University Press, 1993), 121–49. Original English translation: "Eye and Mind," trans. Carleton Dallery, in *The Primacy of Perception,* ed. James M. Edie (Evanston, Ill.: Northwestern University Press, 1964), 159–92. Original French: *L'œil et l'esprit* (Paris: Gallimard, Folio Essais, 1964). Originally published in *Art de France* 1, no. 1 (January 1961): 187–208; reprinted in *Les Temps Modernes,* no. 184–85 (October 1961): 193–227.

1. Georges Charbonnier, *Le monologue du peintre* (Paris: R. Julliard, 1959), 172.

2. Ibid., 34.

3. Ibid., 143–45.

4. Paul Claudel, *Introduction à la peinture hollandaise* (Paris: Gallimard, 1935, 1946).

5. P. Schilder, *The Image and Appearance of the Human Body* (New York: International Universities Press, 1935, 1950).

6. Robert Delaunay, *Du cubisme à l'art abstrait,* cahiers publiés par Pierre Francastel (Paris: Pierre Francastel, 1957).

7. Descartes, *La dioptrique,* "Discours 7" [conclusion], in *Oeuvres de Descartes,* Adam and Tannery edition, 6:165.

8. Descartes, "Discours 1," op. cit. p. 83. [*Oeuvres et lettres de Descartes,* ed. André Bridoux, Edition Pléade, 181. Page references from the Bridoux selections have been added in the belief that this volume is more widely accessible today than the Adam and Tannery complete edition. English translation as "Optics," in *The Philosophical Writings of Descartes,* vol. 1, trans. J. Cottingham, R. Stoothoff, and D. Murdoch (Cambridge: Cambridge University Press, 1985), 152.]

9. Descartes, "Discours 1," Adam and Tannery edition, 84 [Bridoux, 182; "Optics," 153].

10. "Discours 4," Adam and Tannery edition, 112–14 [Bridoux, 203–4; "Optics," 165–66].

11. "Discours 4," Adam and Tannery edition, 112–14 [Bridoux, 203–4; "Optics," 165–66].

12. "Discours 6," Adam and Tannery edition, 130 [Bridoux, 217; "Optics," 167].

13. The system of means by which painting makes us see is a scientific matter. Why, then, do we not methodically produce perfect images of the world, arriving at a universal painting purged of personal art, just as the universal language would free us of all the confused relationships that lurk in existent languages?

14. "Discourse 5" of the *Dioptriques,* especially Descartes' diagrams, helps considerably to clarify this compressed passage.—Michael Smith and Galen Johnson's comment.

15. E. Panofsky, *Die Perspecktive als symbolische Form,* in *Vorträge der Bibliotek Warburg,* 4 (1924–25).

16. Ibid.

17. Descartes, "Discours 6," Adam and Tannery edition, 135 [Bridoux, 220; "Optics," 169].

18. "Discours 6," Adam and Tannery edition, 137 [Bridoux, 222; "Optics," 170.].

19. No doubt Merleau-Ponty is speaking of Princess Elizabeth.—Comment by Johnson and Smith.

20. B. Dorival, *Paul Cézanne* (Paris: P. Tisné, 1948), 103ff. [B. Dorival, *Paul Cézanne,* trans. H. H. A. Thackthwaite (London: House of Beric, 1948), 101–3].

21. Charbonnier, *Le monologue,* 176.

22. Delaunay, *Du cubisme,* 109.

23. F. Novotny, *Cézanne und das Ende der wissenschaftichen Perspective* (Vienna: Phaidon Press, 1938).

24. W. Grohmann, *Paul Klee* (Paris: Flinker, 1954), 141 [W. Grohmann, *Paul Klee* (New York: H. N. Abrams, 1956)].

25. Delaunay, *Du cubisme,* 118.

26. P. Klee, *Journal,* French trans. P. Klossowski (Paris: Grasset, 1959).

27. George Schmidt, *Les aquarelles de Cézanne,* 21 [George Schmidt, *The Water-colours of Cézanne* (New York: British Book Centre, 1953)].

28. Klee, *Journal.*

29. C. P. Bru, *Esthétique de l'abstraction* (Paris: Presses Universitaires de France, 1955), 86, 99.

30. Henri Michaux, *Aventures de lignes.*

31. Michaux, *Aventures de lignes.*

32. Ravaisson, cited by Bergson, "La vie et l'oeuvre de Ravaisson," in *La pensée et le mouvant* (Paris: Alcan, 1934), 264–65. [The passage quoted here is from M. L. Andison's translation of that work, *The Creative Mind* (New York: Philosophical Library, 1946), 229. It remains moot whether these are Ravaisson's or da Vinci's words.—Comment by Galen Johnson and Michael Smith.]

33. Bergson, ibid.

34. Michaux, *Aventures de lignes.*

35. Ibid. ["to go in the direction of being a line"].

36. Grohmann, *Klee,* 192.

37. Rodin, *L'art.* Interviews collected by Paul Gsell (Paris: Grasset, 1911).

38. Ibid., 86. Rodin uses the word "metamorphose" quoted below.

39. Michaux, *Aventures de lignes.*

40. Cited by Delaunay, *Du cubisme,* 175.

41. Rilke, *Auguste Rodin,* French trans. Maurice Betz (Paris: Emile-Paul Frères, 1928), 150 [English translation by Jessie Lemont and Hans Trausil (New York: Sunwise, 1919; republished, United Book Guild, 1948)].

42. Delaunay, *Du cubisme,* 115, 110.

43. Ibid.

44. Ibid.

45. Klee, *Conférence d'Iena* (1924), according to Grohmann, *Paul Klee,* 365.

46. Klee, *Wege des Naturstudiums* (1923), as found in G. di San Lazzaro, *Klee.*

47. Klee, cited by Grohmann, *Paul Klee,* 99.

48. A. Berne-Joffroy, *Le dossier Caravage* (Paris: Éditions de Minuit, 1959); and Michel Butor, "La corbeille de l'Ambrosienne," *Nouvelle Revue Française* (1959): 969–89.

49. Klee, *Journal* ["Je suis insaisissable dans l'immanence"].

50. G. Limbour, *Tableau bon levain à vous de cuire la pâte: L'art brut de Jean Dubuffet* (Paris: R. Drovin, 1953), 54–55.

Chapter 18

The text for this chapter is taken from "Merleau-Ponty in Person," from *Texts and Dialogues,* trans. James Barry, Jr. (Atlantic Highlands, N.J.: Humanities, 1992), 2–13. Original French: "L'écrivans en personne," in *Parcours deux, 1951–1961* (Lagrasse: Éditions Verdier, 2000), 285–301. From an interview on February 17, 1958, originally published in Madeleine Chapsal, *Les écrivains en personne* (Paris: Julliard, 1960), 145–63.

1. *Pourquoi des philosophes?* (Paris: Julliard, 1957; Jean-Jacques Pauvert, 1958). See the presentation made by Sartre on December 5, 1959, at Neuchâtel, Switzerland. "Pourquoi des Philosophes?" published in *Le Débat* (March 29, 1984): 29–42. —Eds.

2. The reference is to *La Nouvelle Revue Française,* which was revived in 1953 and became one of the major outlets of intellectual expression in France in the 1950s and 1960s. Merleau-Ponty is apparently referring to Heidegger's piece, translated into French as "Le Sentier" ("The Path") by Jacques Gérard, which appeared in the *La Nouvelle Revue Française* in early 1954. It is a translation of Heidegger's "Der Feldweg," which is included in *Aus der Erfahrung des Denkens,* vol. 13 of Heidegger's *Gesammtausgabe* (Frankfurt: Klostermann, 1983). See *La Nouvelle Revue Française* 3 (January-June 1954): 41–45.—Trans.

3. The political movement "Poujadism" maintains that nothing is more important politically than the immediate desires of "the people." Named after Pierre Poujade, Merleau-Ponty's contemporary, who founded l'Union de défense des commerçant et des artisans (in English, the Organization for the Protection of Shopkeepers and Artisans). He was a self-proclaimed "man of the people" and an outspoken opponent of government controls, taxation, etc. He tended to blame intellectuals for many of France's problems. See Merleau-Ponty's column, "Le Forum," in the March 19, 1955, issue of *L'Express,* "M. Poujade, a-t-il un petit cerveau?"—Trans.

Chapter 19

The text for this chapter is taken from "The Intertwining—The Chiasm," from *The Visible and the Invisible*, trans. Alphonso Lingis (Evanston, Ill.: Northwestern University Press, 1968), 130–55. Original French: "L'entrelacs—le chiasme," in *Le visible et l'invisible* (Paris: Gallimard, Tel, 1964), 172–204.

1. Here in the course of the text, these lines are inserted: "It is that the look is itself incorporation of the seer into the visible, quest for itself, which *is of it,* within the visible—it is that the visible of the world is not an envelope of quale, but what is between the qualia, a connective tissue of exterior and interior horizons—it is as flesh offered to flesh that the visible has its aseity, and that it is mine.—The flesh as *Sichtigkeit* and generality. → when vision is question and response. . . . The openness through flesh: the two leaves of my body and the leaves of the visible world. . . . It is between these intercalated leaves that there is visibility. . . . My body model of the things and the things model of my body: the body bound to the world through all its parts, up against it → all this means: the world, the flesh not as fact or sum of facts, but as the place of an inscription of truth: the false crossed out, not nullified."—Ed. (Lefort)

2. Lefort inserted the question mark to indicate an illegible word in Merleau-Ponty's original text.—Eds.

3. The *Urpräsentierbarkeit* is the flesh.

4. The visible is not a tangible zero, the tangible is not a zero of visibility (relation of encroachment).

5. Here, in the course of the text itself, between brackets, these lines are inserted: "One can say that we perceive the things themselves, that we are the world that thinks itself—or that the world is at the heart of our flesh. In any case, once a body-world relationship is recognized, there is a ramification of my body and a ramification of the world, and a correspondence between its inside and my outside, between my inside and its outside."—Ed. (Lefort)

6. Here is inserted between brackets, in the course of the text itself, the note: "What are these adhesions compared to those of the voice and the hearing?"—Ed. (Lefort)

7. These words, which we reintroduce into the text, had been erased apparently by error.—Ed. (Lefort)

8. Inserted here between brackets: "In what sense we have not yet introduced thinking: to be sure, we are not in the in-itself. From the moment we said seeing, visible, and described the dehiscence of the sensible, we were, if one likes, in the order of thought. We were not in it in the sense that the thinking we have introduced was *there is,* and not *it appears to me that* . . . (appearing that would make up the whole of being, self-appearing). Our thesis is that this *there is* by inherence is necessary, and our problem is to show that thought, in the restrictive sense (pure meaning, thought of seeing and of sensing), is comprehensible only as the accomplishment by other means of the wish of the *there is,* by sublimation of the *there is* and realization of an invisible that is exactly the reverse of the visible, the power of the visible. Thus between sound and sense, speech and what it means to say, there is still the relation of reversibility, and no question of priority, since the ex-

change of words is exactly the differentiation of which the thought is the integral."—Ed. (Lefort)

9. Maurice Merleau-Ponty, *The Structure of Behavior* [trans. Alden L. Fisher (Boston: Beacon Press, 1963)].

10. M. Proust, *Du côté de chez Swann*, pt. 2 (Paris: Gallimard, 1926), 190 [M. Proust, *Swann's Way*, trans. C. K. Scott-Moncrieff (New York: Modern Library, 1928), 503].

11. *Du côté de chez Swann*, pt. 2, 192 [*Swann's Way*, 505].

12. It: that is, the idea.—Ed. (Lefort)

13. *Du côté de chez Swann*, pt. 2, 189 [*Swann's Way*, 503].

14. Ibid.

15. *Du côté de chez Swann*, pt. 2, 192 [*Swann's Way*, 505].

Chapter 20

The text for this chapter has been transcribed by Renaud Barbaras and translated by Leonard Lawlor. These notes are published and translated here for the first time with the kind permission of Madame Merleau-Ponty. We are particularly grateful to Renaud Barbaras for his transcription.

1. Barbaras has indicated illegible words with a question mark in square brackets: [?]. Words of which he was uncertain are placed in square brackets and followed by a question mark: [example?].—Eds.

2. Merleau-Ponty's square brackets.

3. Apparently, Merleau-Ponty was using the 1958 French translation of Heidegger's *Einführung in die Metaphysik* by Gilbert Kahn, who translated "Seyn" as "ester" and "Wesen" by "estance." In Kahn's glossary for the translation (p. 225 [Paris: Gallimard, 1980]), he says, "wesen: ester, se réaliser historialement comme essence, sans donc que celle-ci soit donnée hors du temps comme modèle pour cette réalisation." "Ester," it seems, is a neologism manufactured on the basis of the Latin "stare," which is the infinitive "to be," in the active sense of realization. It would be used to say the being of a contingent, spatiotemporal property such as tiredness. Although clumsy, in English one would say "I am being tired," in order to indicate that this condition is an ongoing event. See also *Le visible et l'invisible*, 256n; *The Visible and the Invisible*, 203n44.—Eds.

4. Next to the heading of this piece, Merleau-Ponty wrote the following in the margin: "bon" ("good").—Eds.

Biography of Maurice Merleau-Ponty

1. The biography is based on those found in two texts: Xavier Tillette's *Merleau-Ponty ou la mesure de l'homme* (Paris: Seghers, 1970) and Alan Schrift's *Twentieth-Century French Philosophy* (Malden, Mass.: Blackwell, 2005).

2. See Forrest Williams, "Merleau-Ponty's Early Project Concerning Perception," Appendix 1 in *Texts and Dialogues,* ed. Hugh J. Silverman and James Barry,

Jr. (Atlantic Highlands, N.J.: Humanities, 1992), 146–49; and Maurice Merleau-Ponty, "The Nature of Perception: Two Proposals," in *Texts and Dialogues*, 74–84.

3. For an account of Merleau-Ponty's visit and subsequent efforts to establish the Husserl Archives in Paris, see H. L. Van Breda, "Merleau-Ponty and the Husserl Archives at Louvain," Appendix 2 in *Texts and Dialogues*, 150–61.

4. See Jacques Taminiaux's "Preface to the English Translation," in *The Incarnate Subject: Malebranche, Biran, and Bergson on the Union of Body and Soul*, trans. Paul B. Milan, ed. Andrew G. Bjelland, Jr., and Patrick Burke (Amherst, N.Y.: Humanity Books, 2001).

5. The documents relating to this quarrel, including letters exchanged between Sartre and Merleau-Ponty, may be found in *The Debate Between Sartre and Merleau-Ponty*, ed. Jon Stewart (Evanston, Ill.: Northwestern University Press, 1998).

Chronological Bibliography of Merleau-Ponty's Works

This bibliography includes all of Merleau-Ponty's works that are available in English translation, and all of his book-length works published in French. For a more complete listing of Merleau-Ponty's works and of secondary sources, see François Lapointe and Clara Lapointe, *Maurice Merleau-Ponty and His Critics: An International Bibliography* (New York and London: Garland, 1976); and Kerry Whiteside, "The Merleau-Ponty Bibliography: Additions and Corrections," *Journal of the History of Philosophy* 21 (1983): 195–201.

La structure du comportement. Paris: Presses Universitaires de France, 1942. Translated by Alden Fisher as *The Structure of Behavior* (Boston: Beacon, 1963; London: Methuen, 1965).

Phénoménologie de la perception. Paris: Gallimard, 1945. Translated by Colin Smith as *Phenomenology of Perception* (New York: Humanities, 1962; London: Routledge and Kegan Paul, 1962; translation revised by Forrest Williams, 1981; reprinted, Routledge, 2002).

Humanisme et terreur: Essai sur le problème communiste. Paris: Gallimard, 1947. Translated by John O'Neill as *Humanism and Terror: An Essay on the Communist Problem* (Boston: Beacon, 1969).

Sens et non-sens. Paris: Nagel, 1948; reprinted, Paris: Gallimard, 1996. Translated by Herbert L. Dreyfus and Patricia Allen Dreyfus as *Sense and Non-Sense* (Evanston, Ill.: Northwestern University Press, 1964).

Les relations avec autrui chez l'enfant. Paris: Centre de Documentation Universitaire, 1951; reprinted, 1975.

Éloge de la philosophie: Leçon inaugurale faite au Collège de France, le jeudi 15 janvier 1953. Paris: Gallimard, 1953. Translated by John Wild and James M. Edie as *In Praise of Philosophy* (Evanston, Ill.: Northwestern University Press, 1963).

Les aventures de la dialectique. Paris: Gallimard, 1955. Translated by Joseph Bien as *Adventures of the Dialectic* (Evanston, Ill.: Northwestern University Press, 1973; London: Heinemann, 1974).

Les philosophes célèbres (editor). Paris: Mazenod, 1956.

Les sciences de l'homme et la phénoménologie. Paris: Centre de Documentation Universitaire, 1958; reprinted, 1975.

Éloge de la philosophie et autres essais. Paris: Gallimard, 1960.

"Préface" to *L'oeuvre de Freud,* by A. Hesnard. Paris: Payot, 1960. Translated by Alden L. Fisher as "Phenomenology and Psychoanalysis: Preface to Hesnard's *L'oeuvre de Freud.*" In *Review of Existential Psychology and Psychiatry* 18

(1982); reprinted as *Merleau-Ponty and Psychology,* edited by Keith Hoeller (Atlantic Highlands, N.J.: Humanities, 1993).

Signes. Paris: Gallimard, 1960. Translated by Richard C. McCleary as *Signs* (Evanston, Ill.: Northwestern University Press, 1964).

Merleau-Ponty à la Sorbonne: Résumés de ses cours établi par des étudiants et approuvé par lui-même. Special issue of *Bulletin de Psychologie,* 18, no. 236 (November 1964). Reprinted as *Merleau-Ponty à la Sorbonne: Résumés de cours 1949–1952.* Paris: Cynara, 1988; and as *Psychologie et pedagogie de l'enfant: Cours de Sorbonne 1949–1952.* Lagrasse: Éditions Verdier, 2001.

L'oeil et l'esprit. Paris: Gallimard, 1964.

The Primary of Perception and Other Essays on Phenomenological Psychology, the Philosophy of Art, History and Politics. Edited by James M. Edie. Evanston, Ill.: Northwestern University Press, 1964.

Le visible et l'invisible, suivi de notes de travail. Paris: Gallimard, 1964. Translated by Alphonso Lingis as *The Visible and the Invisible, Followed by Working Notes* (Evanston, Ill.: Northwestern University Press, 1968).

Résumés de cours: Collège de France 1952–1960. Paris: Gallimard, 1968. Translated by John O'Neill as *Themes from the Lectures at the Collège de France, 1952–1960* (Evanston, Ill.: Northwestern University Press, 1970).

L'union de l'âme et du corps chez Malebranche Biran, et Bergson: Notes prises au cours de Maurice Merleau-Ponty. Paris: J. Vrin, 1968. Translated by Paul B. Milan as *The Incarnate Subject: Malebranche, Biran, and Bergson on the Union of Body and Soul,* edited by Andrew G. Bjelland, Jr., and Patrick Burke (New York: Humanity Books, 2001).

The Essential Writings of Merleau-Ponty. Edited by Alden L. Fisher. New York: Harcourt, Brace and World, 1969.

La prose du monde. Paris: Gallimard, 1969. Translated by John O'Neill as *The Prose of the World* (Evanston, Ill.: Northwestern University Press, 1973).

Existence et dialectique. Paris: Presses Universitaires de France, 1971.

"La nature de la perception." Appendix to *Vers une nouvelle philosophie transcendantale: La genèse de la philosophie de Maurice Merleau-Ponty jusqu'à la "Phénoménologie de la perception,"* by Theodore F. Geraets (The Hague: Martinus Nijhoff, 1971). Translated by Forrest Williams as "Study Project on the Nature of Perception (1933)" and "The Nature of Perception (1934)." *Research in Phenomenology* 10 (1980); reprinted as *Merleau-Ponty: Perception, Structure, Language,* edited by John Sallis (Atlantic Highlands, N.J.: Humanities, 1981).

Consciousness and the Acquisition of Language. Translated by Hugh J. Silverman. Evanston, Ill.: Northwestern University Press, 1973.

Phenomenology, Language, and Sociology: Selected Essays of Merleau-Ponty. Edited by John O'Neill. London: Heinemann, 1974.

"Philosophie et non-philosophie depuis Hegel: Notes de cours." *Textures,* nos. 8–9 (1974) and 10–11 (1975). Translated by Hugh J. Silverman as "Philosophy and Non-Philosophy Since Hegel." In *Philosophy and Non-Philosophy Since*

Merleau-Ponty (New York: Routledge, 1988; reprinted, Evanston, Ill.: Northwestern University Press, 1997).

"Table of Contents of *Phenomenology of Perception:* Translation and Pagination." Translated by Daniel Guerrière. *Journal of the British Society for Phenomenology* 10, no. 1 (January 1979).

Approches phénoménologiques. Paris: Hachette, 1981.

"The Experience of Others." Translated by Fred Evans and Hugh J. Silverman. *Review of Existential Psychology and Psychiatry* 18 (1982). Reprinted as *Merleau-Ponty and Psychology,* edited by Keith Hoeller (Atlantic Highlands, N.J.: Humanities, 1993).

In Praise of Philosophy and Other Essays. Evanston, Ill.: Northwestern University Press, 1988.

Le primat de la perception et ses conséquences philosophiques: Précédé de Projet de travail sur la nature de la perception (1933) et La nature de la perception (1934). Grenoble: Cynara, 1989; reprinted, Lagrasse: Éditions Verdier, 1996.

Texts and Dialogues. Edited by Hugh J. Silverman and James Barry, Jr. Atlantic Highlands, N.J.: Humanities, 1991.

The Merleau-Ponty Aesthetics Reader: Philosophy and Painting. Edited by Galen Johnson. Evanston, Ill.: Northwestern University Press, 1993.

"Sartre, Merleau-Ponty: Les lettres d'une rupture." *Magazine Littéraire,* no. 320 (April 1994). Translated by Jon Stewart as "Philosophy and Political Engagement: Letters from the Quarrel Between Sartre and Merleau-Ponty." In *The Debate Between Sartre and Merleau-Ponty,* edited by Jon Stewart (Evanston, Ill.: Northwestern University Press, 1998).

La nature, notes, cours du Collège de France. Paris: Seuil, 1995. Translated by Robert Vallier as *Nature: Course Notes from the Collège de France* (Evanston, Ill.: Northwestern University Press, 2003).

Notes de cours, 1959–1961. Paris: Gallimard, 1996.

"Notes de lecture et commentaires sur *Théorie du champ de la conscience* de Aron Gurwitsch." *Revue de Métaphysique et de Morale,* no. 3 (1997). Translated by Elizabeth Locey and Ted Toadvine as "Reading Notes and Comments on Aron Gurwitsch's *The Field of Consciousness.*" *Husserl Studies* 17, no. 3 (2000).

Parcours, 1935–1951. Paris: Éditions Verdier, 1997.

Notes de cours sur L'origine de la géométrie de Husserl. Paris: Presses Universitaires de France, 1998. Translated by Leonard Lawlor as *Husserl at the Limits of Phenomenology, Including Texts by Edmund Husserl* (Evanston, Ill.: Northwestern University Press, 2002).

Parcours deux, 1951–1961. Paris: Éditions Verdier, 2000.

"Deux notes inédites sur la musique." *Chiasmi International* 3 (2001). Translated by Leonard Lawlor as "Two Unpublished Notes on Music," *Chiasmi International* 3 (2001).

Causeries 1948. Paris: Seuil, 2002. Translated by Oliver Davis as *The World of Perception* (London: Routledge, 2005).

L'institution dans l'histoire personnelle et publique: Le problème de la passivité, le sommeil, l'inconscient, la mémoire: Notes de cours au Collège de France, 1954–1955. Paris: Belin, 2003.

Merleau-Ponty: Basic Writings. Edited by Thomas Baldwin. New York: Routledge, 2004.

"Notes de travail inédites sur Gilbert Simondon (1959)." *Chiasmi International* 7 (2005). Translated by Leonard Lawlor as "Unpublished Working Notes on Gilbert Simondon (1959)," *Chiasmi International* 7 (2005).

Bibliography of Works on Merleau-Ponty

Books

Ballard, Edward. *The Philosophy of Merleau-Ponty*. New Orleans: Tulane University Press, 1960.

Bannan, John F. *The Philosophy of Merleau-Ponty*. New York: Harcourt, Brace and World, 1967.

Barbaras, Renaud. *The Being of the Phenomenon: Merleau-Ponty's Ontology*. Translated by Ted Toadvine and Leonard Lawlor. Bloomington: Indiana University Press, 2004.

Barral, Mary Rose. *Merleau-Ponty: The Role of the Body-Subject in Interpersonal Relations*. Pittsburgh: Duquesne University Press, 1965.

Bayer, Raymond. *Merleau-Ponty's Existentialism*. Buffalo: University of Buffalo Press, 1951.

Carbone, Mauro. *The Thinking of the Sensible: Merleau-Ponty's A-Philosophy*. Evanston: Northwestern University Press, 2004.

Cataldi, Sue. *Emotion, Depth, and Flesh: A Study of Sensitive Space*. Albany: SUNY Press, 1993.

Cooper, Barry. *Merleau-Ponty and Marxism: From Terror to Reform*. Toronto: University of Toronto Press, 1979.

Crossley, Nick. *The Politics of Subjectivity: Between Foucault and Merleau-Ponty*. Aldershot: Avebury, 1994.

Descombes, Vincent. *Modern French Philosophy*. Cambridge: Cambridge University Press, 1980.

Dillon, Martin C. *Merleau-Ponty's Ontology*. Bloomington: Indiana University Press, 1988; second edition, Evanston, Ill.: Northwestern University Press, 1997.

Diprose, Rosalyn. *Corporeal Generosity: On Giving with Nietzsche, Merleau-Ponty, and Levinas*. Albany: SUNY Press, 2002.

Dwyer, Philip. *Sense and Subjectivity: A Study of Wittgenstein and Merleau-Ponty*. Leiden: Brill Academic, 1997.

Edie, James. *Merleau-Ponty's Philosophy of Language: Structuralism and Dialectics*. Washington, D.C.: Center for Advanced Research in Phenomenology and University Press of America, 1987.

Froman, Wayne. *Merleau-Ponty: Language and the Act of Speech*. Lewisburg, Pa.: Bucknell University Press, 1982.

Gier, Nicholas. *Wittgenstein and Phenomenology: A Comparative Study of the Later Wittgenstein, Husserl, Heidegger, and Merleau-Ponty*. Albany: SUNY Press, 1981.

Gill, Jerry H. *Merleau-Ponty and Metaphor.* Atlantic Highlands, N.J.: Humanities Press, 1991.

Gutting, Gary. *French Philosophy in the Twentieth Century.* Cambridge: Cambridge University Press, 2001.

Hadreas, Peter J. *In Place of the Flawed Diamond: An Investigation of Merleau-Ponty's Philosophy.* New York: Peter Lang, 1986.

Hamington, Maurice. *Embodied Care: Jane Addams, Maurice Merleau-Ponty, and Feminist Ethics.* Champaign, Ill.: University of Illinois Press, 2004.

Hamrick, William S. *An Existential Phenomenology of Law: Maurice Merleau-Ponty.* Dordrecht: Martinus Nijhoff, 1987.

Heinämaa, Sara. *Toward a Phenomenology of Sexual Difference: Husserl, Merleau-Ponty, Beauvoir.* Lanham, Md.: Rowman and Littlefield, 2003.

Johnson, Galen. *Earth and Sky, History and Philosophy: Island Images Inspired by Husserl and Merleau-Ponty.* New York: Peter Lang, 1989.

Kaelin, Eugene F. *An Existentialist Aesthetic: The Theories of Sartre and Merleau-Ponty.* Madison: University of Wisconsin Press, 1966.

Kruks, Sonia. *The Political Philosophy of Merleau-Ponty.* Atlantic Highlands, N.J.: Humanities, 1981.

Kwant, Remy C. *From Phenomenology to Metaphysics: An Inquiry into the Last Period of Merleau-Ponty's Philosophical Life.* Pittsburgh: Duquesne University Press, 1966.

———. *The Phenomenological Philosophy of Merleau-Ponty.* Pittsburgh: Duquesne University Press, 1963.

Langan, Thomas. *Merleau-Ponty's Critique of Reason.* New Haven, Conn.: Yale University Press, 1966.

Langer, Monika. *Merleau-Ponty's "Phenomenology of Perception": A Guide and Commentary.* Tallahassee: Florida State University Press, 1989.

Lanigan, Richard L. *Phenomenology of Communication: Merleau-Ponty's Thematics in Communicology and Semiology.* Pittsburgh: Duquesne University Press, 1988.

Lawlor, Leonard. *Thinking Through French Philosophy: The Being of the Question.* Bloomington: Indiana University Press, 2003.

Low, Douglas. *The Existential Dialectic of Marx and Merleau-Ponty.* New York: Peter Lang, 1987.

———. *Merleau-Ponty's Last Vision: A Proposal for the Completion of "The Visible and the Invisible."* Evanston, Ill.: Northwestern University Press, 2000.

MacAnn, Christopher. *Four Phenomenological Philosophers: Husserl, Heidegger, Sartre, Merleau-Ponty.* London: Routledge, 1993.

Madison, Gary. *The Phenomenology of Merleau-Ponty.* Athens: Ohio University Press, 1981.

Mallin, Samuel B. *Merleau-Ponty's Philosophy.* New Haven, Conn.: Yale University Press, 1979.

Matthews, Eric. *The Philosophy of Merleau-Ponty.* Montreal: McGill-Queen's University Press, 2002.

———. *Twentieth-Century French Philosophy.* Oxford: Oxford University Press, 1996.

McCurdy, John. *Visionary Appropriation*. New York: Philosophical Library, 1978.

Miller, James. *History and Human Existence: From Marx to Merleau-Ponty*. Berkeley: University of California Press, 1979.

O'Neill, John. *The Communicative Body: Studies in Communicative Philosophy, Politics, and Sociology*. Evanston: Northwestern University Press, 1989.

———. *Perception, Expression and History: The Social Phenomenology of Maurice Merleau-Ponty*. Evanston, Ill.: Northwestern University Press, 1970.

Priest, Stephen. *Merleau-Ponty*. London: Routledge, 1998.

Primozic, Daniel T. *On Merleau-Ponty*. Belmont, Calif.: Wadsworth, 2000.

Rabil, Albert, Jr. *Merleau-Ponty: Existentialist of the Social World*. New York: Columbia University Press, 1967.

Reynolds, Jack. *Merleau-Ponty and Derrida: Intertwining Embodiment and Alterity*. Athens: Ohio University Press, 2004.

Rosenthal, Sandra B., and Patrick L. Bourgeois. *Mead and Merleau-Ponty: Toward a Common Vision*. Albany: SUNY Press, 1991.

Sallis, John. *Phenomenology and the Return to Beginnings*. Pittsburgh: Duquesne University Press, 1973; reprinted, 2003.

Schmidt, James. *Maurice Merleau-Ponty: Between Phenomenology and Structuralism*. New York: St. Martin's, 1985.

Schrift, Alan. *Twentieth-Century French Philosophy*. Malden, Mass.: Blackwell, 2005.

Sobchack, Vivian. *The Address of the Eye: A Phenomenology of Film Experience*. Princeton, N.J.: Princeton University Press, 1992.

Spurling, Laurie. *Phenomenology and the Social World: The Philosophy of Merleau-Ponty and Its Relation to the Social Sciences*. London: Routledge and Kegan Paul, 1978.

Taminiaux, Jacques. *Dialectic and Difference: Modern Thought and the Sense of Human Limits*. Atlantic Highlands, N.J.: Humanities, 1985.

Vasseleu, Cathryn. *Textures of Light: Vision and Touch in Irigaray, Levinas, and Merleau-Ponty*. London: Routledge, 1998.

Whiteside, Kerry H. *Merleau-Ponty and the Foundation of an Existential Politics*. Princeton, N.J.: Princeton University Press, 1988.

Zaner, Richard. *The Problem of Embodiment: Some Contributions to a Phenomenology of the Body*. The Hague: Martinus Nijhoff, 1964.

Collections

Burke, Patrick, and Jan Van Der Veken, eds. *Merleau-Ponty in Contemporary Perspective*. Dordrecht: Kluwer, 1993.

Busch, Thomas W., and Shaun Gallagher, eds. *Merleau-Ponty: Hermeneutics and Postmodernism*. Albany: SUNY Press, 1992.

Carman, Taylor, and Mark B. N. Hansen, eds. *The Cambridge Companion to Merleau-Ponty*. Cambridge: Cambridge University Press, 2005.

Davis, Duane H. *Merleau-Ponty's Later Works and Their Practical Implications: The Dehiscence of Responsibility*. Atlantic Highlands, N.J.: Humanity Books, 2001.

Dillon, Martin C., ed. *Ecart and Différance: Merleau-Ponty and Derrida on Seeing and Writing*. Atlantic Highlands, N.J.: Humanities, 1997.

———, ed. *Merleau-Ponty Vivant*. Albany: SUNY Press, 1991.

Evans, Fred, and Leonard Lawlor, eds. *Chiasms: Merleau-Ponty's Notion of the Flesh*. Albany: SUNY Press, 2000.

Fóti, Veronique, ed. *Merleau-Ponty: Difference, Materiality, Painting*. Atlantic Highlands, N.J.: Humanities, 1996.

Gillan, Garth, ed. *The Horizons of the Flesh: Critical Perspectives on the Thought of Merleau-Ponty*. Carbondale: Southern Illinois University Press, 1973.

Hass, Lawrence, and Dorothea Olkowski, eds. *Rereading Merleau-Ponty: Essays Beyond the Continental-Analytic Divide*. Atlantic Highlands, N.J.: Humanities, 2000.

Hatley, James, Janice McLane, and Christian Diehm, eds. *Interrogating Ethics: Embodying the Good in Merleau-Ponty*. Pittsburgh: Duquesne University Press, 2006.

Hoeller, Keith, ed. *Merleau-Ponty and Psychology*. Atlantic Highlands, N.J.: Humanities, 1993.

Johnson, Galen, and Michael Smith, eds. *Ontology and Alterity in Merleau-Ponty*. Evanston, Ill.: Northwestern University Press, 1990.

Olkowski, Dorothea, and James Morley, eds. *Merrleau-Ponty, Interiority and Exteriority, Psychic Life and the World*. Albany: SUNY Press, 1999.

Pietersma, Henry, ed. *Merleau-Ponty: Critical Essays*. Washington, D.C.: Center for Advanced Research in Phenomenology and University Press of America, 1989.

Sallis, John, ed. *Merleau-Ponty: Perception, Structure, Language*. Atlantic Highlands, N.J.: Humanities, 1981.

Silverman, Hugh J., ed. *The Horizons of Continental Philosophy: Essays on Husserl, Heidegger, and Merleau-Ponty*. Dordrecht: Kluwer, 1988.

Silverman, Hugh J., John Sallis, and Thomas Seebohm, eds. *Continental Philosophy in America*. Pittsburgh: Duquesne University Press, 1983.

Stewart, Jon, ed. *The Debate Between Sartre and Merleau-Ponty*. Evanston, Ill.: Northwestern University Press, 1998.

Toadvine, Ted, ed. *Merleau-Ponty: Critical Assessments of Leading Philosophers*. 4 vols. London: Routledge, 2006.

Toadvine, Ted, and Lester Embree, eds. *Merleau-Ponty's Reading of Husserl*. Dordrecht: Kluwer, 2002.

Tymieniecka, Anna-Teresa, and S. Matsuba, eds. *Immersing in the Concrete: Maurice Merleau-Ponty in the Japanese Perspective*. Dordrecht: Springer, 1998.

Journal

Chiasmi International: Trilingual Studies Concerning the Thought of Merleau-Ponty. Published by Vrin, Mimesis, and the University of Memphis. Annual, founded 1999.

Volume 1 (1999): "Merleau-Ponty: The Contemporary Heritage"
Volume 2 (2000): "Merleau-Ponty: From Nature to Ontology"
Volume 3 (2001): "Merleau-Ponty: Non-Philosophy and Philosophy"
Volume 4 (2002): "Merleau-Ponty: Figures and Grounds of the Flesh"
Volume 5 (2003): "Merleau-Ponty: The Real and the Imaginary"
Volume 6 (2004): "Merleau-Ponty: Between Aesthetics and Psychoanalysis"
Volume 7 (2005): "Merleau-Ponty: Life and Individuation"

Index

advent, 267, 269, 270, 297, 299, 313, 406
Alain (Émile-Auguste Chartier), 182
Algeria, 321, 390
alienation, 148, 165, 166, 342, 347
ambiguity, 117, 208–17, 221–28, 290; and
  consciousness, 210–12; and history,
  227, 228, 302, 307, 314; and language,
  217, 219, 220, 223, 224; of perception,
  194; and politics, 228–33; and skepticism, 211. *See also* being: and ambiguity
  of; body: and ambiguity
America, 137, 139, 140, 232–33, 390
animals: behavior of, 100, 101, 124, 155,
  160, 174; bodies of, 177, 331; and humans, 204, 280; perception of, 116, 163,
  355
anonymity, 149, 194, 400, 403. *See also*
  body: generality of
anti-Semitism, 44, 45, 54. *See also* Jews;
  Nazism
aphasia, 159, 228
Apollinaire, Guillaume, 370
apraxia, 159, 287
Aristotle, 15, 208–12, 214, 366
Aron, Raymond, 260, 447, 462n22
art, 67, 78, 119, 120, 178, 252–58, 276, 277,
  352, 353, 370; and audience, 262, 273;
  history of, 368; and nature, 72, 73, 76;
  and science, 112, 352. *See also* artist; culture: and art; impressionism; painting;
  surrealism
artist, 78, 258, 259, 263, 264. *See also* art
Asia, 202, 230–32. *See also* China
attitude: natural, 55, 61; phenomenological, 114; transcendental, 19, 24
Augustine of Hippo, Saint, 58, 260, 455n4

Babeuf, François-Noël, 303, 464n23
Bachelard, Gaston, 113, 258, 448, 462n20

Balzac, Honoré de, 68, 75, 77–78, 276,
  385
Baudelaire, Charles-Pierre, 197, 252
Beaufret, Jean, 117, 448, 457n5
Beauvoir, Simone de, 281, 447, 448
behavior: and American thought, 86, 186;
  and body, 20, 148; and Freudianism,
  193; localization of, 24; of others, 37,
  94; perceptual, 22, 284; and social development, 169, 170, 180; and specular
  image, 159
being: ambiguity of, 420; brute, 337, 389,
  415, 417, 420, 421; carnal, 397, 430, 432,
  433; and Cartesianism, 366, 367; and
  chiasm, 442, 443; dehiscence of, 375,
  405, 411, 469n8; and dialectic, 293, 294;
  expression of, 255, 256, 353–55, 358,
  371; and flesh as "element," 400, 401,
  406, 429, 430; foundation of, 67; intersubjective, 93, 94; -in-the-world, 61, 62;
  musical, 427; and nothingness, 336,
  342, 425, 426, 429; politics of, 327–29,
  348; and possibility, 415–17; psycho-
  physical, 33; relations of, 165, 434; of
  sense, 115, 116; sensible, 396–400, 403,
  404, 406, 409, 437–39, 441, 442, 444,
  445; style of, 400; unity of, 103, 352–54,
  368, 377, 434, 443–46; and visibility,
  354, 355, 357, 358, 361, 363, 364, 369,
  371, 374–77, 397, 398
Being and Nothingness (Sartre), 87
Being and Time (Heidegger), 55
Bergson, Henri, 17, 29, 100, 108, 114, 247,
  341, 371, 415, 417, 448
Berkeley, George, 92
Bernard, Émile, 70–73, 75, 76, 78
Bild, 439, 440
biology, 21, 26, 268, 351
Blanchot, Maurice, 120, 198

486

INDEX

Giraudoux, Jean, 206
Gironde, 299, 301, 302, 304, 463n12
God, 103, 116, 117, 206, 233–40. *See also*
Catholicism; Christianity
Goethe, Johann Wolfgang von, 130, 176,
420
Gogh, Vincent van, 254, 257, 330, 353
Goldstein, Kurt, 36
government: English, 47, 130, 131;
French, 42, 48, 131, 390; German, 42–
45, 47–50, 52, 53, 200; and power, 123–
28, 133, 201; and revolution, 303, 304;
role of, 123, 201; Soviet, 135; Vichy, 49,
52. *See also* America; Fascism; politics;
U.S.S.R.
Guérin, Daniel, 299–304
Guéroult, Martial, 283
Guillaume, Paul, 146, 149, 153, 156, 159,
160, 171, 174, 178
Gurvitch, Georges, 447

hallucination, 23, 35, 108, 163, 181
Head, Henry, 147
Hébertists, 300, 301, 464n14
Hegel, Georg Wilhelm Friedrich, 56, 65,
86, 112, 170, 243, 269, 271, 272, 280,
281, 322, 323; and dialectic, 295, 379
Heidegger, Martin, 81, 117, 386, 387;
Being and Time, 55; and "being-in-the-
world," 62; phenomenology of, 55, 56,
86, 418, 419
Heraclitus, 279, 322
history: and art, 259–65, 267–70, 273,
278; and chance, 129; and class
struggle, 49, 297–99, 311, 327, 328; and
concept of human, 189–91; and development of consciousness, 23, 25, 289,
290; dialectic of, 271–73, 280, 293–317;
dimensions of, 65, 66, 101, 282; and
intersubjectivity, 101, 289, 290; ontological, 387; and philosophy, 113, 270, 273,
319–21, 324–29, 349; political, 41–54,
200–203, 295–317; and revolution, 297,
298, 302–12; social, 185–88; and
struggle, 130, 131
Hitler, Adolf, 136, 140, 232, 345
human: condition, 86, 117, 190, 191; engineering, 185–88; nature, 191; unity of,
8, 115
humanism: contingency and, 190, 203–6;

meaning of, 134, 191, 204; and politics,
42, 43, 46, 53, 125, 130–34, 202
Humanism and Terror (Merleau-Ponty),
287, 447–48
Hume, David, 95, 105
Husserl, Edmund, 66, 68, 92, 105, 117,
148, 259, 381, 401, 407, 413; *Ideas,* 212;
and Kant, 57, 65; and passivity, 453n50;
phenomenology of, 55, 56, 59, 61, 62,
86, 418, 419
Hyppolite, Jean, 115–17, 457n4

idealism, 17, 59, 63, 64, 85, 117
Ideas (Husserl), 212
impressionism, 71, 74
Ingres, Jean-Auguste-Dominique, 259,
376
intersubjectivity: and consciousness, 60;
and perception, 28, 93, 286; and society, 187, 301; and world, 67, 286, 420,
421. *See also* Sartre, Jean-Paul: intersubjectivity in
introceptivity, 144–46, 151–53, 155, 158,
162, 163, 167, 168

jealousy, 171–73
Jews, 41, 43–45, 47, 49. *See also* anti-
Semitism
judgment: and perception, 7, 19, 58, 431,
433; and political action, 49, 138; and
value, 270–73

Kant, Immanuel, 93, 95, 99, 102, 110, 316;
Critique of Judgment, 64, 65; *Critique of
Pure Reason,* 18, 64–65, 452n34; and
subjectivity, 57; and "Transcendental
Aesthetic," 18, 452n34; transcendental
idealism of, 14, 15, 17, 61
Khrushchev, Nikita, 321, 323
Kierkegaard, Søren, 235–37
Klee, Paul, 252, 358, 370, 372, 376
Klein, Melanie, 217
Köhler, Elsa, 175, 179
Köhler, Wolfgang, 100, 155–56
Kojève, Alexandre, 295, 447, 463n2

Lacan, Jacques, 164–65
Lagache, Daniel, 163
Lagneau, Jules, 98–99
language, 62, 241–48, 275–82; and body,

Maurice Merleau-Ponty (1908–61) is the author of *In Praise of Philosophy; The Primacy of Perception; Sense and Non-Sense; Signs; Themes from the Lectures at the Collège de France, 1952–1960; The Prose of the World; Adventures of the Dialectic; Consciousness and the Acquisition of Language;* and *Husserl at the Limits of Phenomenology,* all published by Northwestern University Press.

Ted Toadvine is an assistant professor of philosophy and environmental studies at the University of Oregon and is the coeditor of *Merleau-Ponty's Reading of Husserl* and *Eco-Phenomenology: Back to the Earth Itself.* He and Leonard Lawlor translated Renaud Barbaras's *The Being of the Phenomenon.*

Leonard Lawlor is the Faudree-Hardin Professor of Philosophy at the University of Memphis and the author of *The Challenge of Bergsonism: Phenomenology, Ontology, Ethics* and *Thinking Through French Philosophy: The Being of the Question.* He is also the editor of Merleau-Ponty's *Husserl at the Limits of Phenomenology,* which he translated with Bettina Bergo.